INVESTIGATION OF
THE ASSASSINATION OF PRESIDENT JOHN F. KENNEDY

HEARINGS

Before the President's Commission

on the Assassination

of President Kennedy

PURSUANT TO EXECUTIVE ORDER 11130, an Executive order creating a Commission to ascertain, evaluate, and report upon the facts relating to the assassination of the late President John F. Kennedy and the subsequent violent death of the man charged with the assassination and S.J. RES. 137, 88TH CONGRESS, a concurrent resolution conferring upon the Commission the power to administer oaths and affirmations, examine witnesses, receive evidence, and issue subpenas

Volume
III

UNITED STATES GOVERNMENT PRINTING OFFICE
WASHINGTON, D.C.

Reprinted by Michigan Legal Publishing Ltd.
www.michlp.com
ISBN: 978-1-942842-23-1

PRESIDENT'S COMMISSION
ON THE
ASSASSINATION OF PRESIDENT KENNEDY

CHIEF JUSTICE EARL WARREN, *Chairman*

SENATOR RICHARD B. RUSSELL   REPRESENTATIVE GERALD R. FORD
SENATOR JOHN SHERMAN COOPER   MR. ALLEN W. DULLES
REPRESENTATIVE HALE BOGGS   MR. JOHN J. McCLOY

J. LEE RANKIN, *General Counsel*

Assistant Counsel

FRANCIS W. H. ADAMS   ALBERT E. JENNER, Jr.
JOSEPH A. BALL   WESLEY J. LIEBELER
DAVID W. BELIN   NORMAN REDLICH
WILLIAM T. COLEMAN, Jr.   W. DAVID SLAWSON
MELVIN ARON EISENBERG   ARLEN SPECTER
BURT W. GRIFFIN   SAMUEL A. STERN
LEON D. HUBERT, Jr.   HOWARD P. WILLENS*

Staff Members

PHILLIP BARSON
EDWARD A. CONROY
JOHN HART ELY
ALFRED GOLDBERG
MURRAY J. LAULICHT
ARTHUR MARMOR
RICHARD M. MOSK
JOHN J. O'BRIEN
STUART POLLAK
ALFREDDA SCOBEY
CHARLES N. SHAFFER, Jr.

Biographical information on the Commissioners and the staff can be found in the Commission's *Report*.

---

*Mr. Willens also acted as liaison between the Commission and the Department of Justice.

Preface

The testimony of the following witnesses is contained in volume III: Ruth Hyde Paine, an acquaintance of Lee Harvey Oswald and his wife; Howard Leslie Brennan, who was present at the assassination scene; Bonnie Ray Williams, Harold Norman, James Jarman, Jr., and Roy Sansom Truly, Texas School Book Depository employees; Marrion L. Baker, a Dallas motorcycle officer who was present at the assassination scene; Mrs. Robert A. Reid, who was in the Texas School Book Depository Building at the time of the assassination; Luke Mooney and Eugene Boone, Dallas law enforcement officers who took part in the investigative effort in the Texas School Book Depository Building immediately following the assassination; Patrolman M. N. McDonald, who apprehended Lee Harvey Oswald in the Texas Theatre; Helen Markham, William W. Scoggins, Barbara Jeanette Davis, and Ted Callaway, who were in the vicinity of the Tippit crime scene; Drs. Charles James Carrico and Malcolm Perry, who attended President Kennedy at Parkland Hospital; Robert A. Frazier, a firearms identification expert with the Federal Bureau of Investigation; Ronald Simmons, an expert in weapons evaluation with the U.S. Army Weapons Systems Division; Cortlandt Cunningham, a firearms identification expert with the Federal Bureau of Investigation; and Joseph D. Nicol, a firearms identification expert with the Bureau of Criminal Identification and Investigation of the Illinois Department of Public Safety.

Contents

COMMISSION EXHIBITS INTRODUCED

Hearings Before the President's Commission

on the

Assassination of President Kennedy

Thursday, March 19, 1964—Afternoon Session

TESTIMONY OF RUTH HYDE PAINE RESUMED

The President's Commission reconvened at 2:05 p.m.

Mr. JENNER. May we proceed, Mr. Chairman?

Mr. McCLOY. Yes; we are all ready whenever you are. You are still under affirmation.

Mr. JENNER. I was at the point of describing the driver's license application, but before I do that, Mrs. Paine, may I hand you the document again?

Mrs. PAINE. Yes.

Mr. JENNER. It has been marked Commission Exhibit 426. You were making a comparison with the block printing on that document with like block printing that you testified yesterday had been written in your address book. I have forgotten the exhibit number, but in your address book which you have before you——

Mrs. PAINE. Yes.

Mr. JENNER. And the printing in your address book to which you were addressing yourself was what?

Mrs. PAINE. His printing of the place where he worked in April of 1963.

Mr. JENNER. And that is Jaggars-Chiles-Stovall?

Mrs. PAINE. Right.

Mr. JENNER. You were comparing that printing which you saw him put in your address book with what?

Mrs. PAINE. The printing on this application for Texas driver's license.

Mr. JENNER. And any particular printing on that application?

Mrs. PAINE. Was put in in pen. I do observe that the printing here uses a mixture of upper case and lower case letters, as does the printing in my phone book, most of it being block upper case.

Mr. JENNER. The form and shape of the printing in both of the documents is——

Mrs. PAINE. Is similar.

Mr. JENNER. Similar. All right, thank you.

Mr. Chairman, because of the point raised by Representative Ford with particular reference to the word "photographer" which, by the way, is misspelled, it is spelled "f-o-t-o-g-r-a-p-e-r," and things of that sort do occur as you have already noted in many of his writings, very bad misspellings.

Mr. McCLOY. Yes, his grammar seems to be better than this spelling.

Mr. JENNER. Yes. This form is an official form printed of the Texas State License Bureau entitled "Application for Texas driver's license," on the line provided for "name" there appears over "first name", "Lee"; over "middle name", "Harvey"; and "last name", "Oswald."

The second set of spaces, provisions for address, birth, and occupation. He gives as his address, 2545 West Fifth Street, Irving, Tex. Was that the address of their home when you first became acquainted with them?

Mrs. PAINE. No.

Mr. JENNER. Is the address 2545 Irving Street familiar to you?

Mrs. PAINE. I think it is 2515.

Mr. JENNER. Perhaps we will have to have it interpreted by someone else. It looks like a "4" to me, but it may be a "1." This birthday, October 18, 1939. The age last birthday 24, and then under "occupation" appears the word I have already related. Sex, male; color of eyes, gray; weight, 146 pounds; race, the letter "C"; color of hair, brown; height, 5 foot 9 inches.

Mr. McCLOY. Were you about to comment?

Mrs. PAINE. I was interested in his comment on his race.

Mr. JENNER. I assume C means Caucasian. There are a series of questions, printed questions on the form, and he answered them, they are from 1 to 12, as follows:

"Question No. 1" he answers in the negative, "Have you ever held a Texas license?"

Question No. 2. All these are in the negative.

"Have you ever been examined for a Texas license?

"Have you ever held a license in any other State?

"Have you ever been denied a license?

"Has your license and driving privilege ever been suspended, revoked, or canceled?

"Have you ever been convicted of driving while intoxicated, failure to stop and render aid, aggravated assault with a motor vehicle, negligent homicide with a motor vehicle or murder with a motor vehicle?"

All answered in the negative.

"Have you ever been convicted of any other moving traffic violation?

"Have you ever been involved as a driver in a motor vehicle accident?

"Have you ever been subject to losses of consciousness or muscular control?

"Have you ever been addicted to the use of intoxicating liquor or narcotic drugs?

"Do you have any physical or mental defects?"

And, lastly: "Have you ever been a patient in a hospital for mental illness?"

The side as to the driving record, that is the reverse side, nothing appears thereon, and nothing in any portion of the form which deals with the record of his examination.

I am a little at a loss, Mr. Chairman, as to whether I should offer this in evidence at the present moment, because it is a document found among his effects in his room, and my statement of fact would be pure hearsay.

Mr. McCLOY. How did we get in possession of it?

Mr. JENNER. It was supplied to us by the FBI.

The document was turned over to the FBI. May I withhold offering the document in evidence? We may have another witness who will be able to qualify it.

Mr. McCLOY. Who can identify it?

Mr. JENNER. I am sure we will have a witness. We do want the document in evidence. [Commission Exhibit No. 426 is also Commission Exhibit No. 112, vol. I, p. 113.]

Identifying as Commission Exhibit 427 a form of employee identification questionnaire of the Jaggars-Chiles-Stovall Co. Please examine Exhibit 427. I direct your attention to the signature in the lower left-hand corner. Are you familiar with that signature?

Mrs. PAINE. I can't say I am familiar with it.

Mr. JENNER. Did you ever have any discussion with Lee Oswald relating to his obtaining of a position with Jaggars-Chiles-Stovall?

Mrs. PAINE. Yes.

Mr. JENNER. And when did that discussion occur?

Mrs. PAINE. In New Orleans on the second trip, the end of September, when we talked about the possibility of Marina's coming back to have the baby in Texas where they could qualify as one year residents, he equipped me to show that he had been in Texas, and in Dallas for a year by giving me a receipt or part of a paycheck, I don't know just what it was, with the Jaggars-Chiles-Stovall name on it, in October.

Mr. JENNER. What was the purpose——

Mrs. PAINE. He was supplying me with documents that would admit her to Parkland Hospital as a patient. He gave me his——

Mr. JENNER. To show the necessary——

Mrs. PAINE. That he had worked with Stovall.

Mr. JENNER. And the necessary residential period of time in Texas?

Mrs. PAINE. And the necessary residence.

Mr. JENNER. I see.

Did you take that document with you?

Mrs. PAINE. Yes; I did.

Mr. JENNER. And what did you do with it?

Mrs. PAINE. Took it to Parkland Hospital. And subsequently returned it to him.

Mr. JENNER. For what purpose had you gone to Parkland Hospital?

Mrs. PAINE. For prenatal care and care at the time of the birth of Marina Oswald's second child.

Mr. JENNER. And is Parkland Hospital a public institution in Dallas?

Mrs. PAINE. Yes.

Mr. JENNER. With the necessary residential period of time, Marina, if she had qualified in that respect, or did qualify then she could receive treatment with respect to the birth of her child either at no cost to her or at reduced cost, is that correct?

Mrs. PAINE. I understood it to be cost fitted to their ability to pay.

Mr. JENNER. And so you did, yourself, affirmatively arrange that?

Mrs. PAINE. That is right. What arrangement?

Mr. JENNER. Affirmatively. You did it yourself?

Mrs. PAINE. Oh, yes.

Mr. JENNER. We have now reached the summer period of 1963, and covered some of it in part. My recollection of your testimony is that you vacationed in the summer of 1963.

Mrs. PAINE. That is right.

Mr. JENNER. You visited various members of your family up north?

Mrs. PAINE. Yes.

Mr. JENNER. You departed Irving, Tex., some time in July, is that correct?

Mrs. PAINE. I believe it was the 27th of July.

Mr. JENNER. And just tell us whom of your family you visited and where you visited, without telling us what you did.

Mrs. PAINE. I visited my mother-in-law and stepfather-in-law.

Mr. JENNER. That is Mr. and Mrs. Young, Arthur Young?

Mrs. PAINE. That is right.

Mr. JENNER. In Paoli, Pa.?

Mrs. PAINE. I first went to Naushon Island off the coast of Massachusetts.

Mr. JENNER. Were you driving in the station wagon?

Mrs. PAINE. Yes; I was.

Mr. JENNER. With your children?

Mrs. PAINE. Yes.

Mr. JENNER. And you went from there to where? Whom did you visit next?

Mrs. PAINE. How detailed do you want to be?

Mr. JENNER. Just tell us whom you visited is all.

Mrs. PAINE. I stopped and saw Miss Mary Forman, in Connecticut, one night.

Mr. JENNER. She is an old friend of yours?

Mrs. PAINE. She is an old friend of mine from Columbus, Ohio, and went on then to Paoli the next day, and stayed there, again with the Youngs, until the early part of September.

Mr. McCLOY. Is that Paoli, Pa.?

Mrs. PAINE. That is right.

Mr. JENNER. Did you visit your mother and your father or either of them?

Mrs. PAINE. My father came to Paoli and visited me there.

Mr. JENNER. Did I ask you yesterday, Mrs. Paine, and please forgive me if this is a repetition, the occupation of your father.

Mrs. PAINE. He is an insurance underwriter; he composes the fine print.

Mr. JENNER. Was he at one time an actuary?

Mrs. PAINE. What does actuary mean?

Mr. JENNER. A man who computes the probabilities and works in connection with——

Mrs. PAINE. He may be. I am not certain exactly what his position is.

3

Mr. JENNER. For what company, please?

Mrs. PAINE. The Nationwide Insurance Company.

Mr. JENNER. Where is there main office?

Mrs. PAINE. In Columbus, Ohio.

Mr. JENNER. Your father visited you at Paoli. Did you see your mother during that summer period?

Mrs. PAINE. Yes; I did. I saw her briefly on the way to Naushon Island, and then again I saw her on my way back to the south and west, in Columbus, Ohio.

Mr. JENNER. At Columbus, she was living there then?

Mrs. PAINE. Yes.

Mr. JENNER. Did you see your sister on that trip?

Mrs. PAINE. Yes; I did.

Mr. JENNER. And where did you see her?

Mrs. PAINE. She lives in suburban Washington, and I saw here there at her home. I also saw Michael's brother, and his wife, who live in Baltimore.

Mr. JENNER. Would you identify Michael's brother, please?

Mrs. PAINE. His name is Cameron Paine, C-a-m-e-r-o-n.

Mr. JENNER. What is his occupation or business?

Mrs. PAINE. He works with Social Security.

Mr. JENNER. For the State or the United States Government?

Mrs. PAINE. For the United States Government.

Mr. JENNER. That covers generally the people you visited that summer?

Mrs. PAINE. No. I also visited by brother, in Yellow Springs, Ohio.

Mr. JENNER. That is your brother, the physician?

Mrs. PAINE. That is right. I visited with friends in the Philadelphia area, while I was at Paoli.

Mr. JENNER. Do you mean by the term "friends" there to mean in the sense I would mean friends?

Mrs. PAINE. Yes.

Mr. JENNER. Or members of the Friends Society?

Mrs. PAINE. Some were both, but I meant it as personal friends. And then I saw also friends, also both, capital F and small, in Richmond, Ind., and then from there I headed directly south to New Orleans.

(Discussion off the record.)

Mrs. PAINE. Shall I go on to arrival at New Orleans?

Mr. JENNER. This spanned a period of a little over 2 months, did it not?

Mrs. PAINE. It was just short of 2 months total that I was away from my home in Irving.

Mr. JENNER. And in the meantime you had had the correspondence with Marina that you had related this morning, during the course of your going along, had you?

Mrs. PAINE. During that vacation she and I exchanged one letter each.

Mr. JENNER. Yes. Had you advised her that you were coming to New Orleans?

Mrs. PAINE. Yes.

Mr. JENNER. For what purpose?

Mrs. PAINE. To visit. And to talk.

Mr. JENNER. About what?

Mrs. PAINE. To see if it was appropriate for her to come to my house for the birth of the baby.

Mr. JENNER. At that moment, at that time, when you were about to return or about to go to New Orleans, this concept was limited to her coming to be with you for the birth of the child?

Mrs. PAINE. That is correct.

Mr. JENNER. At least temporarily she abandoned the notion of joining you on a semipermanent basis?

Mrs. PAINE. It was abandoned. It was not taken up again.

Mr. JENNER. You arrived in New Orleans?

Mrs. PAINE. That is right.

Mr. JENNER. The 20th of September.

Mr. McCLOY. Maybe you are going to get to this. Maybe I am anticipating your case, so to speak, but during these visits that you paid to your friends on this trip, did you talk about your association with Marina?

Mrs. PAINE. Yes; I did.

Mr. McCLOY. You did?

Mrs. PAINE. Quite a lot. It was rather an important thing to me.

Mr. JENNER. I have some questions to put to Mrs. Paine on that subject, but they are in the area of the collateral that I spoke of this morning, so I did not go into them at the moment.

Now, starting with your arrival in New Orleans, you got there in the morning or afternoon?

Mrs. PAINE. I arrived midafternoon, as I remember.

Mr. JENNER. And you went directly to their home, did you?

Mrs. PAINE. Yes.

Mr. JENNER. What did you find when you reached the home?

Mrs. PAINE. I was expected. They had groceries bought.

Mr. JENNER. Who was home?

Mrs. PAINE. Marina and Lee, and the baby June.

Mr. JENNER. I don't have a calendar before me. The 20th of September is what day of the week?

Mrs. PAINE. Is a Friday.

Mr. JENNER. 1963?

Mrs. PAINE. I spent the night there that night and the succeeding 2 nights.

Lee who bought the groceries while I was there, was host. At one point Mrs. Ruth Kloepfer, who has been previously mentioned, came and visited with her sister—excuse me, with her two daughters. This was after I had made a telephone call to her.

Mr. JENNER. These daughters were adults or were they children?

Mrs. PAINE. The daughters were grown daughters.

Mr. JENNER. Grown?

Mrs. PAINE. In college, college-age daughters, and one had been studying Russian, didn't know very much. I was impressed with the role that Lee took of the general host, talking with them, looking over some slides that one of the daughters had brought of her trip, recent trip to Russia, showing sights that they recognized, I guess, in Moscow.

Mr. JENNER. That the girls recognized?

Mrs. PAINE. No; that Lee and Marina recognized of Moscow, or Lee did, at least. And he was very outgoing and warm and friendly. He seemed in good spirits that weekend. I found him—he made a much better impression on me, I will say, that weekend than the last weekend I had seen him, which was in May.

I could see, and it was the first time that I felt that he was concerned about his wife's physical welfare and about where she could go to have the baby, and he seemed distinctly relieved to consider the possibility of her going to Dallas County and getting care through Parkland Hospital, and clearly pleased that I wanted to offer this, and pleased to have her go, which relieved my mind a good deal.

I hadn't wanted to have such an arrangement come about without his being interested in having it that way.

Mr. JENNER. During the course of this, did you say you were there 3 days?

Mrs. PAINE. Three nights, two days.

Mr. JENNER. Two days and three nights; there was then a discussion between yourself and Marina, yourself on the one hand, Marina and Lee on the other, in which it was determined that Marina would return with you to Irving, Tex., for the purpose of having the birth of her child in Irving?

Mrs. PAINE. That is right.

Mr. JENNER. And Lee did participate in those discussions?

Mrs. PAINE. Yes.

Mr. JENNER. Now, during the course of the time you were there, was there any discussion of the fact that Lee was at that time jobless and would be seeking a position?

Mrs. PAINE. I knew from Marina's letters that he was out of work.

Mr. JENNER. Yes.

Mrs. PAINE. We did have one short conversation and this was in English. I began it. He was willing to proceed in English.

Mr. JENNER. This is one of the few occasions in which he permitted himself to speak with you in English?

Mrs. PAINE. That is correct. I asked him if he thought his application was any impediment to his getting and keeping a job. He said he didn't know, and went on to say that he had already lost his job when he was arrested for passing out pro-Cuba literature here in New Orleans. And he said he spent the night in jail, and I said, "Did Marina know that?"

"Yes, she knew it."

Mr. JENNER. I want you to finish the conversation.

Mrs. PAINE. This was as much of a revelation, accurate revelation of what he had done as I ever got from him.

Mr. JENNER. Excuse me, Mrs. Paine. I am going to get into that with you. I would like to have you finish the conversation first before you give your reaction.

Mrs. PAINE. That was the end of it.

Mr. JENNER. That was the end?

Mrs. PAINE. Yes.

Mr. JENNER. Now, with respect to the Fair Play for Cuba Committee activity, had you up to this moment heard of Lee Harvey Oswald's activities, if any, of any character and to any extent, with respect to the Fair Play for Cuba Committee?

Mrs. PAINE. I had not heard of any such activities.

The name of the committee was not mentioned. I did not know the name of the committee until it appeared in the newspapers after the assassination.

Mr. JENNER. Now, how did Lee Harvey Oswald describe that? What did he say?

Mrs. PAINE. He said that he was passing out pro-Castro or pro-Cuba literature, and that there were some anti-Castro people who also caused some disturbance, and that he had spent the night in jail.

Mr. JENNER. And did I understand you correctly to say that he assigned that as a possible——

Mrs. PAINE. No, on the contrary.

Mr. JENNER. As possibly having had some effect on his loss of position?

Mrs. PAINE. On the contrary, he made the point that he had already lost his job before this happened.

Mr. JENNER. That he had lost his position before the Fair Play for Cuba incident?

Mrs. PAINE. So that he did not know, he could not cite an instance where his application had made it difficult for him in his work.

Mr. JENNER. Had you had conversation with Marina prior to this time in which she might have suggested or did suggest that his application and his history of having gone to Russia and then returned to the United States as having an adverse effect on his efforts to obtain employment?

Mrs. PAINE. No; nothing of that nature was said.

Mr. JENNER. That was never discussed in your presence?

Mrs. PAINE. No.

Mr. JENNER. Was it ever discussed in your presence or raised in your presence by anybody other than Lee Harvey Oswald or Marina?

Mrs. PAINE. Not to my recollection.

Mr. JENNER. Was it ever discussed with you by anybody even though they weren't present? By "they" I mean Lee and Marina. You recall none? This is the first instance of any discussion of that character, and you raised it, did you?

Mrs. PAINE. That is right.

Mr. JENNER. And you have exhausted your recollection of this particular conversation, have you?

Mrs. PAINE. Yes.

Mr. JENNER. I gather from your testimony that you found the relations between Marina and Lee improved on this occasion?

Mrs. PAINE. They certainly appeared to be improved. The weekend time was certainly much more comfortable than the weekend in early May had been when I first was in New Orleans.

Mr. JENNER. You described yesterday an irritability as between Marina and Lee when you were there in the spring?

Mrs. PAINE. Yes.

Mr. JENNER. And that that had continued during all the time you were in New Orleans. You found the situation different?

Mrs. PAINE. Yes.

Mr. JENNER. On your return in the fall?

Mrs. PAINE. Yes.

Mr. JENNER. Now, you have already related the incident about touring Bourbon Street, and that occurred on this occasion, did it?

Mrs. PAINE. During that weekend, yes; those days.

Mr. JENNER. And Lee Harvey Oswald stayed home that evening or that day. It was late in the day, was it, rather than the evening?

Mrs. PAINE. It was early evening.

Mr. JENNER. Early evening. What did he do at home, do you know?

Mrs. PAINE. When we got back Marina noticed that the dishes had been cleaned up and put away. I take it back, they had been washed, not put away. And I believe he did some packing.

Mr. JENNER. In anticipation of your returning to Irving, Tex., with Marina?

Mrs. PAINE. That is right.

I was impressed during these 2 days with his willingness to help with the packing. He did virtually all the packing and all the loading of the things into the car. I simply thought that gentlemanly of him at the time. I have wondered since whether he wasn't doing it by preference to having me handle it.

Mr. JENNER. I was about to ask you your impression in that direction. Did he seem eager to do the packing?

Mrs. PAINE. He did, distinctly.

Mr. JENNER. Distinctly eager?

Mrs. PAINE. I recall he began as early, you see, as Saturday night and we left Tuesday morning.

Mr. JENNER. And you are aware of the fact he did some packing while you and Marina were on tour?

Mrs. PAINE. It couldn't have been Saturday night, because I only arrived on Saturday. More likely it was Sunday. Is Bourbon Street open on Sunday?

Mr. JENNER. Bourbon Street is open all the time.

Mrs. PAINE. Then it would have to be——

(Discussion off the record.)

Mr. JENNER. Did you have the feeling at the time that he was quite eager to do the packing?

Mrs. PAINE. Yes.

Mr. JENNER. And did you have the feeling it was just a touch out of the ordinary?

Mrs. PAINE. It didn't occur to me that it was.

Mr. JENNER. But on reflection now, you think it was out of the ordinary?

Mrs. PAINE. On reflection now I think it wasn't simply a gesture of the gentleman.

Mr. JENNER. But at the time it didn't arouse enough interest on your part to have a question in your mind?

Mrs. PAINE. No; I would have expected it of other men, but this was the first I saw him taking that much interest.

Mr. JENNER. It did arrest your attention on that score, in any event?

Mrs. PAINE. Yes.

Mr. JENNER. Now, you were there for 2 full days and 3 evenings. Would you tell us, conserving your description in your words, what did you do during these 2 days and 3 nights. When I say "you", I am including all three of you.

Mrs. PAINE. Of course, afternoons we usually spent in rest for the children, having all small children, all of us having small children.

Mr. JENNER. Whenever this doesn't include Lee Harvey Oswald would you be good enough to tell us?

Mrs. PAINE. When he was not present?

Mr. JENNER. That is right.

Mrs. PAINE. My recollection is that he was present most of the weekend. He went out to buy groceries, came in with a cheery call to his two girls, saying, "Yabutchski," which means girls, the Russian word for girls, as he came in the door. It was more like Harvey than I had seen him before. He remembered this time. I saw him reading a pocketbook.

Mr. JENNER. The Commission is interested in his readings. To the best of your ability to recall, tell us. You noticed it now, of course.

Mrs. PAINE. Yes. I don't recall the title of it. I do recall that I loaned him a pocketbook at one point. I can't even recall what it was about. But I might if I saw it.

Mr. JENNER. Was it a book on any political subject?

Mrs. PAINE. No.

Representative FORD. Was it an English book?

Mrs. PAINE. But it was in English, unless it was a parallel text of Russian-English short stories, something like that, I can't remember. It might have been Reid's Ten Days That Shook the World, or something like that, but I am not at all certain. I would have thought he would have read that, anyway.

Representative FORD. Was it a book that you recall having had with you that summer? Ten Days——

Mrs. PAINE. It is a book I should still own, and I don't recall for sure whether I have that one.

Representative FORD. Ten Days That Shook the World?

Mrs. PAINE. I am very shaky in my memory. I had prepared a collection of books for the course in Russian at Saint Marks School, and they included history and literature and English.

Representative FORD. But you were still anticipating teaching Russian at Saint Marks School in Irving?

Mrs. PAINE. That is right, and this was just part of a bibliography of things of interest that included some of the more historical texts from many points of view regarding Soviet life.

Representative FORD. I interrupted you.

Mr. JENNER. I was asking you to tell us in general what was done during those 2 days and 3 nights.

Mrs. PAINE. We went out to wash diapers at the local washiteria, and stayed while they were done and went back.

Mr. JENNER. You and Lee?

Mrs. PAINE. I don't think that he went. My recollection is that Marina and I went.

Mr. JENNER. He remained home?

Mrs. PAINE. Yes.

Mr. JENNER. Did you visit with any of their in-laws?

Mrs. PAINE. No.

Mr. JENNER. Did they visit while you were there?

Mrs. PAINE. No.

Mr. JENNER. Did they come there?

Mrs. PAINE. No. I have already referred to a visit from Mrs. Kloepfer, with her two girls which must have been the day before we left or Monday.

No, Sunday, it must have been Sunday. It wasn't much time altogether, because Sunday was the day before we left.

Mr. JENNER. Is Mrs. Kloepfer a native American?

Mrs. PAINE. I have no idea. She speaks natively.

Mr. JENNER. But she does have a command of the Russian language?

Mrs. PAINE. Oh, no, no. Her daughter has had 1 year of Russian in college, and was much too shy to begin to say anything, thoroughly overwhelmed by meeting someone who really spoke.

Mr. JENNER. I must have misinterpreted your testimony this morning.

Mrs. PAINE. Her daughter had visited in the Soviet Union just recently and had slides that she had taken that summer.

Mr. JENNER. But Mrs. Kloepfer, as far as you are informed, had no command of the Russian language?

Mrs. PAINE. Absolutely none. She was the only person I knew to try to contact to ask if she knew or could find anyone in New Orleans who knew Russian, and she said she didn't know anyone, over the phone.

Mr. JENNER. I see.

Mrs. PAINE. And I, therefore, also tried to get Mrs. Blanchard to seek out someone who could talk to Marina.

Mr. JENNER. Mrs. Blanchard had no command of the Russian language, as far as you knew?

Mrs. PAINE. I would be certain she didn't.

Mr. JENNER. Have you described for us generally the course of events in the 2 days and 3 nights you were there?

Mrs. PAINE. Well, much of the last portion, some of the last portion of Sunday was spent packing up. It was a very well loaded automobile by then, because I already had a great many of my own, including a boat on the top of the car to which we attached the playpen, stroller, and other things on top. I should describe in detail the packing, which was another thing that made me feel that he did care for his wife.

We left on Monday morning, yes, Monday morning early, the 23d, and it seemed to me he was very sorry to see her go. They kissed goodbye and we got in the car and I started down intending really to go no farther than the first gas station because I had a soft rear tire and I wasn't going to have a flat with this great pile of goods on top of not only my car but my spare, so I went down to the first gas station that was open a couple blocks down, and prepared to buy a tire.

Lee having watched us, walked down to the gas station and talked and visited while I arranged to have the tire changed, bought a new one and had it changed. I felt he wished or thought he should be offering something toward the cost of the tire. He said, "That sure is going to cost a lot, isn't it?" And I said, "Yes; but car owners have to expect that." This is as close as he came to offering financial help. But it was at least a gesture.

Mr. JENNER. Then there was no financial help given you?

Mrs. PAINE. There was no financial help.

Mr. JENNER. Given you by Lee Harvey Oswald?

Mrs. PAINE. No.

Mr. JENNER. In connection with the return of Marina to Irving, Tex.?

Mrs. PAINE. And he did not at this time give her, so far as I know, any small change or petty cash to take with her, whereas when he left her in late April to go to my house, she to go to my house, and he to go to New Orleans, he left $10 or so with her. She spent that on incidentals.

Mr. JENNER. Mrs. Paine, did he ever, during all of the period of your acquaintance with the Oswalds, ever offer any reimbursement financially or anything at all to you?

Mrs. PAINE. No; he never offered anything to me.

Mr. JENNER. Was there any discussion between you and him on the subject?

Mrs. PAINE. No. As close as we came to such discussion was saying that when they had enough money and perhaps after Christmas they would get an apartment again, and I judged, felt that he was saving money towards renting a furnished apartment for his family.

Mr. JENNER. Now, I used the term "offer." Did he ever offer? Did he in fact ever give you any money?

Mrs. PAINE. He in fact never gave me any money, either. He did give Marina.

Mr. JENNER. The one incident of which you are speaking or on other occasions?

Mrs. PAINE. There was that one incident in April.

Mr. JENNER. Yes.

Mrs. PAINE. He did give her, I think, $10, just prior, or some time close to the time of the assassination, because she planned to buy some shoes.

Mr. JENNER. Shoes for herself, or her children?

Mrs. PAINE. For herself, flats. But when he gave that to her I am not certain. I do know that we definitely planned to go out on Friday afternoon, the 22d of November, to buy those shoes. We did not go.

Mr. JENNER. That is you girls planned to do that?

Mrs. PAINE. She and I did; yes.

Representative FORD. Mr. Jenner, do you plan to ask questions about the process of packing of the car?

Mr. JENNER. Yes; I do. Now, this improvement in the attitude of Lee Harvey Oswald, arrested your deliberate attention—didn't it?

Mrs. PAINE. Yes; it did. It was really the first I had felt any sympathy for him at all.

Mr. JENNER. Did you have any feeling that he, in turn, felt that he might not be seeing Marina any more?

Mrs. PAINE. I had no feeling of that whatever.

Mr. JENNER. None whatsoever.

Mrs. PAINE. He told me that he was going to try to look for work in Houston, and possibly in Philadelphia; these were the two names he mentioned.

Mr. JENNER. We are interested in that, in this particular phase of the investigation. Did he make that statement in your presence, in the presence of Marina?

Mrs. PAINE. I don't recall.

Mr. JENNER. I take it that this was elicited by a discussion of the subject of his going to look for work after you girls had left, is that correct?

Mrs. PAINE. About what he would do after we left?

Mr. JENNER. Yes.

Mrs. PAINE. Yes.

Mr. JENNER. Now, would you repeat just what he said on that subject?

Mrs. PAINE. He told me that he was going to go to Houston to look for work, or possibly to Philadelphia.

Mr. JENNER. Did he say anything about having any acquaintances or friends in either of those towns?

Mrs. PAINE. He did. You recalled to my mind he said he had a friend in Houston.

Mr. JENNER. Did he mention other towns he might undertake to visit?

Mrs. PAINE. No; he didn't. Or any other friends.

Mr. JENNER. Was there any inference or did you infer from anything he said or which might have been said in your presence that after you girls left he intended to leave New Orleans? To look——

Mrs. PAINE. He was definitely planning to leave New Orleans after we left.

Mr. JENNER. Promptly?

Mrs. PAINE. Yes.

Mr. JENNER. You had that definite impression?

Mrs. PAINE. Yes.

Mr. JENNER. And he put it in terms of leaving New Orleans to go to Houston, or what was the other town?

Mrs. PAINE. Possibly Philadelphia.

Mr. JENNER. Possibly Philadelphia. Now, during all that weekend, was there any discussion of anybody going to Mexico?

Mrs. PAINE. No.

Mr. JENNER. Was the subject of Mexico discussed at any time and in any respect?

Mrs. PAINE. Not at any time nor any respect.

Mr. JENNER. On the trip back to Irving, Tex., did Marina say anything on the subject of Mexico?

Mrs. PAINE. No.

Mr. JENNER. Did you girls discuss what Lee was going to do during this interim period?

Mrs. PAINE. Only to the extent that he was looking for a job, but I think that discussion, my memory of it comes from a discussion with Lee rather than a discussion with her. I may say that we never talked about any particular time, he would see Marina again.

Mr. JENNER. You did not?

Mrs. PAINE. He kissed her a very fond goodbye, both at home and then again at the gas station, and I felt he cared and he would certainly see her. And this I recalled the other night. It should be put in here. As he was giving me this material, I have already mentioned, that indicated his claim to 1 year residence in Texas, I can't remember just what I said that elicited it from him, but some reference to, shall I say that you have gone, or how can I—what shall I say about the husband, where is the husband?

Mr. JENNER. Do the best in your own words.

Mrs. PAINE. Shall I say that you have gone away or away looking for work or something? What shall I say about you?

Mr. JENNER. This is Marina?

Mrs. PAINE. This is in English now, this one English conversation.

Mr. JENNER. By you?

Mrs. PAINE. Apropos of being prepared to admit her to Parkland. I asked, what shall I say about him, that he is gone or what?

He said, "Oh, no, that might appear that I had abandoned her."

And I was glad to hear him say that he didn't at all want it to appear or to feel of himself that he had abandoned her.

Mr. JENNER. Did he say anything as to what representations you might make to Parkland Hospital and other State authorities in that respect?

Mrs. PAINE. No; I don't recall.

Mr. JENNER. On the trip back to—may I defer the packing until Representative Ford returns—on the trip back to Irving, Tex., did you and Marina discuss the subject matter of Lee's going to Houston, Tex., or to Philadelphia to look for a job?

Mrs. PAINE. No; we didn't.

Mr. JENNER. At any time during the weekend you were in New Orleans or driving from New Orleans to Irving, Tex., was the friend identified, the supposed friend?

Mrs. PAINE. No.

Mr. JENNER. In Houston, identified?

Mrs. PAINE. No; I remember wondering if there was one.

Mr. JENNER. You wondered at the time?

Mrs. PAINE. I wondered to myself if there was one.

Mr. JENNER. What made you wonder?

Mrs. PAINE. I may say, also, I wondered, as I have already indicated for the Commission, I had wondered, from time to time, whether this was a man who was working as a spy or in any way a threat to the Nation, and I thought, "This is the first I have heard anything about a contact. I am interested to know if this is a real thing or something unreal." And waited to see really whether I would learn any more about it. But this thought crossed my mind.

Mr. JENNER. It did? Now, many of my questions are directed towards trying to find out what this man did with his time. When he went job hunting, according to some of the records here, he appeared to return home rather promptly. That is, he would leave in the morning but he would be home before noontime.

Mrs. PAINE. Oh?

Mr. JENNER. Did you notice anything of that nature?

Mrs. PAINE. I never saw him when he was job hunting. The times in New Orleans, of course, I wasn't there. The times in April he was job hunting from a base of 214 Neely Street, and in October he was operating from the base of the room on Beckley Street. So I never saw him.

Mr. JENNER. So that as far as—this I would like to bring out, Mr. Chairman—as far as your contact with Lee Harvey Oswald as such, Mrs. Paine, your opportunities for knowing what he did with his time were limited, were they not?

Mrs. PAINE. They were limited.

Mr. JENNER. That is in the spring, there was this New Orleans period when he was absent in New Orleans altogether during the 2 weeks that Marina was with you?

Mrs. PAINE. Right.

Mr. JENNER. It is the period preceding the trip to New Orleans that they lived a little distance from you, and that was in a period of your really becoming more acquainted with them. Were you aware of what Mr. Oswald was doing during the daytime, or evening along in that period of time?

Mrs. PAINE. No.

Mr. JENNER. In the fall when you saw him then for 2 days and 3 nights in the early fall of 1963, he was out of work. He was at the home substantially all of that time?

Mrs. PAINE. Yes.

Mr. JENNER. You returned to Irving, then, and you didn't see him until he appeared as you testified this morning, on October 4, 1963?

Mrs. PAINE. That is right.

Mr. JENNER. Now, he was in your home from October 4, 1963, until what was it—the 15th of October? Is that correct?

Mrs. PAINE. No.

Mr. JENNER. He was not?

Mrs. PAINE. Not at all. He was in the home for the weekend of October 4. I then took him to the bus around noon on the 7th, that is a Monday, to the Intercity Bus between Irving and Dallas. You can't walk to it from my house. There is no way to get anywhere from my house unless you use a car.

Mr. JENNER. We are interested in that, also, Mrs. Paine, about his ability to get to your home from whatever means of public transportation there was. Would you be good enough to describe the problems in that connection?

Mrs. PAINE. He called on the afternoon of the 4th.

Mr. JENNER. Would you give us the problems first, the physical problems? Where was the bus located? What was the bus terminal? How far was it from your home?

Mrs. PAINE. The bus terminal in Irving where you could get a bus going to Dallas was several miles away, 2 to 3 miles away from my home, a 10 minute car ride.

Mr. JENNER. And what means of transportation was there from the bus terminal to your home?

Mrs. PAINE. Walking?

Mr. JENNER. Any public transportation.

Mrs. PAINE. There was nothing public.

Mr. JENNER. You would have to hitchhike or walk or be driven?

Mrs. PAINE. That is correct.

Mr. JENNER. I take it, then, there were occasions when you would have to go and pick him up at the bus terminal?

Mrs. PAINE. I recall at least one such occasion, and that was on the 12th of October, a Saturday, which was the next time he came out.

Mr. JENNER. That was the next time following the October 4 weekend?

Mrs. PAINE. Yes.

Mr. JENNER. When was the first time that you heard, or had any notice of the fact that this man had been in Mexico, or possibly may have been in Mexico?

Mrs. PAINE. They are two different questions. I will answer the first one. I heard that he had been in Mexico after the assassination in one of the papers.

Mr. JENNER. Was that the first time?

Mrs. PAINE. Yes; that was the first time. Looking back then, with that knowledge, I could see that I might have guessed this from two other things, that had happened.

Mr. JENNER. All right, give us them in sequence, please.

Mrs. PAINE. One was, I can describe by an incident that took place at our home, I am not certain which weekend, one of the times that Lee was out. He wanted to drill a hole in a silver coin for Marina so she could wear it around her neck, and presumed to use my husband's drill press, which is one of the many things in the garage, and I complained. But he convinced me that he knew how to operate it and knew just what he was doing.

So I said, all right, and he proceeded to drill a hole in this coin, and then Marina showed it to me later. I didn't look closely at it. It wasn't until— although I could have perfectly well in this situation. I did see that it was a foreign coin.

Mr. JENNER. It was a what?

Mrs. PAINE. It was a foreign coin. It was not a coin I recognized. It was about the size of a silver dollar, but not as thick, as I remember it. And it was not then until perhaps a week or something less after the assassination when an FBI agent asked me was there anything left in the house that would be pertinent, and he and I went together and looked in the drawer in the room where Marina had been staying, and found there this drilled coin, looked at it closely, and it was a peso, the Republic of Mexico. This is the first I had looked at it closely. Also, with this peso was a Spanish-English Dictionary.

My tendency to be very hesitant to look into other people's things was rather put aside at this point, and I was very curious to see what this book was, and I observed that the price of it, or what I took to be the price was in a corner at the front was not in English money, and at the back in his hand or somebody's hand in small scribble was the notation, "Buy tickets for bull fight, get silver bracelet for Marina" and there in the drawer also was a silver bracelet with the name Marina on it, which I took to be associated with this notation.

Mr. JENNER. Was it inscribed on the bracelet?

Mrs. PAINE. It was inscribed, the name Marina. And some picture post-cards with no message, just a picture of Mexico City in this dictionary, and these I gave to the——

Mr. JENNER. Had you seen any of these items in your home at anytime prior to this occasion that you have now described?

Mrs. PAINE. None of these items except the peso which I had not noticed to be that, seen it, of course.

Mr. JENNER. Now, that is one incident.

Mrs. PAINE. That is one incident. Another refers to a rough draft of a letter that Lee wrote and left this rough draft on my secretary desk.

Mr. JENNER. Would you describe the incident? In the meantime, I will obtain the rough draft here among my notes.

Mrs. PAINE. All right. This was on the morning of November 9, Saturday. He asked to use my typewriter, and I said he might.

Mr. JENNER. Excuse me. Would you please state to the Commission why you are reasonably firm that it was the morning of November 9? What arrests your attention to that particular date?

Mrs. PAINE. Because I remember the weekend that this note or rough draft remained on my secretary desk. He spent the weekend on it. And the weekend was close and its residence on that desk was stopped also on the evening of Sunday, the 10th, when I moved everything in the living room around; the whole arrangement of the furniture was changed, so that I am very clear in my mind as to what weekend this was.

Mr. JENNER. All right, go ahead.

Mrs. PAINE. He was using the typewriter. I came and put June in her high-chair near him at the table where he was typing, and he moved something over what he was typing from, which aroused my curiosity.

Mr. JENNER. Why did that arouse your curiosity?

Mrs. PAINE. It appeared he didn't want me to see what he was writing or to whom he was writing. I didn't know why he had covered it. If I had peered around him, I could have looked at the typewriter and the page in it, but I didn't.

Mr. JENNER. It did make you curious?

Mrs. PAINE. It did make me curious. Then, later that day, I noticed a scrawling handwriting on a piece of paper on the corner at the top of my secretary desk in the living room. It remained there.

Sunday morning I was the first one up. I took a closer look at this, a folded sheet of paper folded at the middle. The first sentence arrested me because I knew it to be false. And for this reason I then proceeded——

Mr. JENNER. Would you just hold it at that moment. This is for purposes of identification, Mr. Chairman, rather than admission of the document in evidence. I have marked pages 321 and 322 of Commission Document No. 385 generally referred to by the staff as the Gemberling Report. He is an FBI agent. I have now placed that before the witness. You examined that yesterday with me, did you not, Mrs. Paine?

Mrs. PAINE. Yes.

Mr. JENNER. The document I am now showing you?

Mrs. PAINE. Yes.

Mr. JENNER. Is that a transcript, a literal transcript of the document you saw?

Mrs. PAINE. Of course the document was in English, transcribing of what was said; yes.

13

Mr. JENNER. By transcript I meant that it has been retyped, that it is literal.

Mrs. PAINE. That is the document; yes.

Mr. JENNER. That is interesting. You noticed that the document was in English.

Mrs. PAINE. Oh, yes.

Mr. JENNER. You saw it. And it was folded at what point, now that you have the transcript of it before you?

Mrs. PAINE. At the top of what I could see of the paper. In other words, it was just below the fold. It said, "The FBI is not now interested in my activities."

Mr. JENNER. Is that what arrested your attention?

Mrs. PAINE. Yes.

Mr. JENNER. What did you do?

Mrs. PAINE. I then proceeded to read the whole note, wondering, knowing this to be false, wondering why he was saying it. I was irritated to have him writing a falsehood on my typewriter, I may say, too. I felt I had some cause to look at it.

Mr. JENNER. May I have your permission, Mr. Chairman. The document is short. It is relevant to the witness' testimony, and might I read it aloud in the record to draw your attention to it?

Mr. MCCLOY. Without objection.

Mr. JENNER. Mrs. Paine, would you help me by reading it, since you have it there.

Mrs. PAINE. Do you want me to leave out all the crossed out——

Mr. JENNER. No; I wish you would indicate that too.

Mrs. PAINE. "Dear Sirs:

"This is to inform you of events since my interview with comrade Kostine in the Embassy of the Soviet Union, Mexico City, Mexico."

(Discussion off the record.)

Mrs. PAINE. He typed it early in the morning of that day because after he typed it we went to the place where you get the test for drivers. It was that same day.

Mr. JENNER. It was election day and the driver's license place was closed, is that correct?

Mrs. PAINE. Yes.

Mr. JENNER. And that was November 9?

Mrs. PAINE. Yes.

Mr. JENNER. Now you have reached the point where you are reading the letter on the morning of November 10.

Mrs. PAINE. That is right; after I had noticed that it lay on my desk the previous evening.

"I was unable to remain in Mexico City (because I considered useless—)"—because—it is crossed out.

Mr. JENNER. Excuse me, Mr. Chairman. In this transcript wherever there are words stricken out, the transcriber has placed those words in parenthesis and transcribed the words, but then has written the words "crossed out" to indicate in the original the words crossed out.

Proceed, Mrs. Paine.

Mrs. PAINE. "Indefinitely because of my (visa—crossed out) Mexican visa restrictions which was for 15 days only.

"(I had a—crossed out) I could not take a chance on applying for an extension unless I used my real name so I returned to the U.S.

"I and Marina Nicholyeva are now living in Dallas, Texas. (You all ready ha—crossed out).

"The FBI is not now interested in my activities in the progressive organization FPCC of which I was secretary in (New Orleans, La.—crossed out) New Orleans, Louisiana since I (am—crossed out) no longer (connected with—crossed out) live in that state.

"(November the November—crossed out) the FBI has visited us here in Texas on November 1st. Agent of the FBI James P. Hasty warned me that if I attempt to engage in FPCC activities in Texas the FBI will again take an 'interest' in me. The agent also 'suggested' that my wife could 'remain in the U.S. under

FBI protection', that is, she could (refuse to return to the—crossed out) defect from the Soviet Union. Of course I and my wife strongly protested these tactics by the notorious FBI.

"(It was unfortun that the Soviet Embassy was unable to aid me in Mexico City but—crossed out) I had not planned to contact the Mexico City Embassy at all so of course they were unprepared for me. Had I been able to reach Havana as planned (I could have contacted—crossed out) the Soviet Embassy there (for the completion of would have been able to help me get the necessary documents I required assist me—crossed out) would have had time to assist me, but of course the stuip Cuban consule was at fault here. I am glad he has since been replaced by another."

Mr. JENNER. Now I would like to ask you a few questions about your reaction to that. You had read that in the quiet of your living room on Sunday morning, the 10th of November.

Mrs. PAINE. That is correct.

Mr. JENNER. And there were a number of things in that that you thought were untrue.

Mrs. PAINE. Several things I knew to be untrue.

Mr. JENNER. You knew to be untrue. Were there things in there that alarmed you?

Mrs. PAINE. Yes; I would say so.

Mr. JENNER. What were they?

Mrs. PAINE. To me this—well, I read it and decided to make a copy.

Mr. JENNER. Would having the document back before you help you?

Mrs. PAINE. No, no. I was just trying to think what to say first. And decided that I should have such a copy to give to an FBI agent coming again, or to call. I was undecided what to do. Meantime I made a copy.

Mr. JENNER. But you did have the instinct to report this to the FBI?

Mrs. PAINE. Yes.

Mr. JENNER. And you made a copy of the document?

Mrs. PAINE. And I made a copy of the document which should be among your papers, because they have that too. And after having made it, while the shower was running, I am not used to subterfuge in any way, but then I put it back where it had been and it lay the rest of Sunday on my desk top, and of course I observed this too.

Mr. JENNER. That is that Lee didn't put it away, just left it out in the room?

Mrs. PAINE. That he didn't put it away or didn't seem to care or notice or didn't recall that he had a rough draft lying around. I observed it was untrue that the FBI was no longer interested in him. I observed it was untrue that the FBI came——

Mr. JENNER. Why did you observe that that was untrue?

Mrs. PAINE. Well, the FBI came and they asked me, they said——

Mr. JENNER. Had the FBI been making inquiries of you prior to that time?

Mrs. PAINE. They had been twice.

Mr. JENNER. November 1 and——

Mrs. PAINE. November 1, and they told me the 5. I made no record of it whatever.

Mr. JENNER. But it was a few days later?

Mrs. PAINE. Yes; a few days later. And the first visit I understood to be a visit to convey to Marina that if any blackmail pressure was being put upon her, because of relatives back home, that she was invited, if she wished, to talk about this to the FBI. This is a far cry from being told she could defect from the Soviet Union, very strong words, and false both.

Mr. JENNER. Did you ever hear anything at all insofar as the FBI is concerned reported to you by Marina or Lee Harvey Oswald during all of your acquaintance with either of them of any suggestion by the FBI or anybody else that Marina defect in that context to the United States?

Mrs. PAINE. No, absolutely not.

Mr. JENNER. Or anything of similar import?

Mrs. PAINE. Nothing of similar import.

Mr. JENNER. I limited it to the FBI. Any agency of the Government of the United States?

15

Mrs. PAINE. Nothing of that sort.

Mr. JENNER. And did you see or observe anything during all of that period of your acquaintance, which stimulated you to think at all or have any notion that any agency of the Government of the United States was seeking to induce her to defect?

Mrs. PAINE. To the United States?

Mr. JENNER. To the United States.

Mrs. PAINE. No, and her terminology in view of it was so completely different from such stereotyped and loaded words that I was seeing as I read this. What I was most struck with was what kind of man is this.

Mr. JENNER. Is who?

Mrs. PAINE. Why is Lee Oswald writing this? What kind of man? Here is a false statement that she was invited to defect, false statement that the FBI is no longer interested, false statement that he was present, "they visited I and my wife."

Mr. JENNER. Was he present?

Mrs. PAINE. He was not present. False statement that "I and my wife protested vigorously." Having not been present he could not protest.

Mr. JENNER. He was not present when the FBI interviewed you on November 1. Was Marina present then?

Mrs. PAINE. She was present.

Mr. JENNER. And was Marina present when the FBI came later on November 5?

Mrs. PAINE. She came into the room just after basically the very short visit was concluded.

Mr. JENNER. The second interview was a rather short one?

Mrs. PAINE. The second interview was conducted standing up. He simply asked me did I know the address. My memory had been refreshed by him since.

Mr. JENNER. The first interview, however, was a rather lengthly one?

Mrs. PAINE. But it was not strictly speaking an interview.

Mr. JENNER. What was it?

Mrs. PAINE. It was, as Mr. Hosty has described to me later, and I think this was my impression too of it at the time, an informal opening for confidence. He presented himself. He talked. We conversed about the weather, about Texas, about the end of the last World War and changes in Germany at the time.

He mentioned that the FBI is very careful in their investigations not to bring anyone they suspect in public light until they have evidence to convict him in a proper court of law, that they did not convict by hearsay or public accusation.

He asked me, and here I am answering why I thought it was false to say the FBI is no longer interested in Lee Oswald; he asked first of all if I knew did Lee live there, and I said "No." Did I know where he lived? No, I didn't, but that it was in Dallas.

Did I know where he worked? Yes, I did.

And I said I thought Lee was very worried about losing this job, and the agent said that well, it wasn't their custom to approach the employer directly. I said that Lee would be there on the weekend, so far as I knew, that he could be seen then, if he was interested in talking to Lee.

I want to return now to the fact that I had seen these gross falsehoods and strong words, concluding with "notorious FBI" in this letter, and gone to say I wondered whether any of it was true, including the reference to going to Mexico, including the reference to using a false name, and I still wonder if that was true or false that he used an assumed name, though I no longer wonder whether he had actually gone.

Mr. JENNER. There was a subsequent incident in which you did learn that he used an assumed name, was there not?

Mrs. PAINE. Yes, a week later.

Mr. JENNER. We will get to that in a moment. But was this——

Mrs. PAINE. But this was the first indication I had that this man was a good deal queerer than I thought, and it didn't tell me, perhaps it should have but it didn't tell me just what sort of a queer he was. He addressed it "Dear Sirs."

It looked to me like someone trying to make an impression, and choosing the words he thought were best to make that impression, even including assumed name as a possible attempt to make an impression on someone who was able to do espionage, but not to my mind necessarily a picture of someone who was doing espionage, though I left that open as a possibility, and thought I'd give it to the FBI and let them conclude or add it to what they knew.

I regret, and I would like to put this on the record, particularly two things in my own actions prior to the time of the assassination.

One, that I didn't make the connection between this phone number that I had of where he lived and that of course this would produce for the FBI agent who was asking the address of where he lived.

Mr. JENNER. I will get to that, Mrs. Paine.

Mrs. PAINE. Well, that is regret 1.

Mr. JENNER. I don't want to cover too many subjects at the moment.

Mrs. PAINE. But then of course you see in light of the events that followed it is a pity that I didn't go directly instead of waiting for the next visit, because the next visit was the 23d of November.

Mr. JENNER. Now I am going to get to that. What did you do with your copy of the letter?

Mrs. PAINE. I put my copy of the letter away in an envelope in my desk. I then, Sunday evening, also took the original. I decided to do that Sunday evening.

Mr. JENNER. He had left?

Mrs. PAINE. No, he had not left.

Mr. JENNER. He had not left?

Mrs. PAINE. I asked the gentlemen present, it included Michael, to come in and help me move the furniture around. I walked in and saw the letter was still there and plunked it into my desk. We then moved all the furniture. I then took it out of the desk and placed it.

Mr. JENNER. When did you take it out of the desk?

Mrs. PAINE. I don't think he knew that I took it. Oh, that evening or the next morning, I don't recall.

Mr. JENNER. And this was the 10th of November?

Mrs. PAINE. Yes.

Mr. JENNER. Did you ever have any conversation with him about that?

Mrs. PAINE. No. I came close to it. I was disturbed about it. I didn't go to sleep right away. He was sitting up watching the late spy story, if you will, on the TV, and I got up and sat there on the sofa with him saying, "I can't speak," wanting to confront him with this and say, "What is this?" But on the other hand I was somewhat fearful, and I didn't know what to do.

Representative FORD. Fearful in what way?

Mrs. PAINE. Well, if he was an agent, I would rather just give it to the FBI, not to say "Look, I am watching you" by saying "What is this I find on my desk."

Mr. JENNER. Were you fearful of any physical harm?

Mrs. PAINE. No; I was not.

Representative FORD. That is what I was concerned about.

Mrs. PAINE. No; I was not, though I don't think I defined my fears. I sat down and said I couldn't sleep and he said, "I guess you are real upset about going to the lawyer tomorrow."

He knew I had an appointment with my lawyer to discuss the possibility of a divorce the next day, and that didn't happen to be what was keeping me up that night, but I was indeed upset about the idea, and it was thoughtful for him to think of it. But I let it rest there, and we watched the story which he was interested in watching. And then I excused myself and went to bed.

Mr. JENNER. What did you do ultimately with your draft of the letter and the original?

Mrs. PAINE. The first appearance of an FBI person on the 23d of November, I gave the original to them. The next day it probably was I said I also had a copy and gave them that. I wanted to be shut of it.

Mr. JENNER. So I take it, Mrs. Paine, you did not deliver either the original or the copy or call attention to the original or the copy with respect to the FBI.

Mrs. PAINE. Prior.

Mr. JENNER. Prior to the 23d did you say?

Mrs. PAINE. That is right.

Mr. JENNER. And what led you to hold onto this rather provocative document?

Mrs. PAINE. It is a rather provocative document. It provoked my doubts about this fellow's normalcy more than it provoked thoughts that this was the talk of an agent reporting in. But I wasn't sure.

I of course made no—I didn't know him to be a violent person, had no thought that he had this trait, possibility in him, absolutely no connection with the President's coming. If I had, hindsight is so much better, I would certainly have called the FBI's attention to it. Supposing that I had?

Mr. JENNER. If the FBI had returned, Mrs. Paine, as you indicated during the course of your meeting with the FBI November 1, would you have disclosed this document to the FBI?

Mrs. PAINE. Oh, I certainly think so. This was not something I was at all comfortable in having even.

Mr. JENNER. Were you expecting the FBI to return?

Mrs. PAINE. I did expect them to come back. As I say, I had said that Lee was here on weekends and so forth. It might have been a good time to give them this document. But as far as I knew, and I know now certainly, they had not seen him and they were still interested in seeing him.

Representative FORD. How did you copy the note?

Mrs. PAINE. Handwritten.

Representative FORD. Handwritten?

Mrs. PAINE. I perhaps should put in here that Lee told me, and I only reconstructed this a few weeks ago, that he went, after I gave him—from the first visit of the FBI agent I took down the agent's name and the number that is in the telephone book to call the FBI, and I gave this to Lee the weekend he came.

Mr. JENNER. You gave it to Lee?

Mrs. PAINE. I gave it to Lee.

Mr. JENNER. What weekend was that?

Mrs. PAINE. I am told that came out on the 1st of November, so that would have been the weekend of the 2d, the next day.

Mr. JENNER. You have your calendar there. The 1st of November is what day of the week?

Mrs. PAINE. It is a Friday. Then he told me, it must have been the following weekend, that same weekend of the 9th.

Mr. JENNER. Did he say anything when you gave him Agent Hosty's name on the telephone?

Mrs. PAINE. No.

Mr. JENNER. Nothing at all?

Mrs. PAINE. I don't recall anything Lee said. I will go on as to the recollections that came later. He told me that he had stopped at the downtown office of the FBI and tried to see the agents and left a note. And my impression of it is that this notice irritated.

Mr. JENNER. Irritating?

Mrs. PAINE. Irritated, that he left the note saying what he thought. This is reconstructing my impression of the fellows bothering him and his family, and this is my impression then. I couldn't say this was specifically said to him later.

Mr. JENNER. You mean he was irritated?

Mrs. PAINE. He was irritated and he said, "They are trying to inhibit my activities," and I said, "You passed your pamphlets," and could well have gone on to say what I thought, but I don't believe I did go on to say, that he could and should expect the FBI to be interested in him.

He had gone to the Soviet Union, intended to become a citizen there, and come back. He had just better adjust himself to being of interest to them for years to come.

Mr. JENNER. What did he say to that?

Mrs. PAINE. Now as I say, this I didn't go on to say. This was my feeling. I didn't actually go on to say this. I did say, "Don't be inhibited, do what you think you should." But I was thinking in terms of passing pamphlets or expressing a belief in Fidel Castro, if that is why he had, I defend his right to express such a belief. I felt the FBI would too and that he had no reason to be irritated. But then that was my interpretation.

Mr. JENNER. Have you given all of what he said and what you said, however, on that occasion?

Mrs. PAINE. Yes. I will just go on to say that I learned only a few weeks ago that he never did go into the FBI office. Of course knowing, thinking that he had gone in, I thought that was sensible on his part. But it appears to have been another lie.

Mr. JENNER. I will return to that FBI visit in a moment. I want to cover that as a separate subject.

Representative Ford is interested in another subject. I would like to return to the day or the period that your station wagon was being parked just before you took off. You have already testified to the fact, either earlier this afternoon or late this morning, that Lee Harvey Oswald appeared to be quite active in doing packing.

Mrs. PAINE. Right.

Mr. JENNER. Of household wares or goods that were being taken back to Irving, Tex. Were you present when the station wagon was loaded with the various materials?

Mrs. PAINE. Yes, I was present for most if not all of that.

Mr. JENNER. Who did that?

Mrs. PAINE. He put the things in. I knew that we would spend one night on the road, that there were certain things we would have to get too, and I knew where these were, and he didn't, so that I talked about where these things should be placed, and helped with some of the binding, tying things to the boat on the car rack.

Mr. JENNER. The boat on top of the station wagon?

Mrs. PAINE. Yes.

Mr. JENNER. Now would you please tell us what there was in the way of luggage placed in the station wagon?

Mrs. PAINE. There again the two large duffels which were heavier than I could move, he put those in.

Mr. JENNER. Describe their appearance, please.

Mrs. PAINE. Again stuffed full, a rumply outside.

Mr. JENNER. With what?

Mrs. PAINE. Rumply.

Mr. JENNER. Rumply? No appearance of any hard object pushing outwards?

Mrs. PAINE. No.

Mr. JENNER. Against the sides or ends of the duffel bags?

Mrs. PAINE. No.

Mr. JENNER. You saw nothing with respect to those duffel bags which might have led you to believe——

Mrs. PAINE. A board in it, no.

Mr. JENNER. A tent pole, a long object, hard?

Mrs. PAINE. No.

Mr. JENNER. Nothing at all?

Mrs. PAINE. No.

Mr. JENNER. And how many pieces of luggage?

Mrs. PAINE. Again these same suitcases, 2 or 3, I think 3 including quite a small one, and the little radio.

Mr. JENNER. What about the zipper bag?

Mrs. PAINE. That was there. I think so. Oh no, it probably wasn't. I don't recall the zipper bag as being part of that.

Mr. JENNER. I wish you would reflect a little on this because it is important, Mrs. Paine, if you can remember it as accurately as possible.

Mrs. PAINE. I don't recall the zipper bag among those things.

Mr. JENNER. Do you recall the zipper bag when you arrived in Irving?

Mrs. PAINE. I think I saw him arrive with it himself, but I am not certain. No, wait, that may not be because I didn't see him when he first arrived.

Mr. JENNER. When you arrived in Irving, Mrs. Paine, not when he arrived.

Mrs. PAINE. I don't recall that. I distinctly recall the duffels because it was all I could do to get them off of the car and set them on the grass until Michael could come and put them into the garage.

Mr. JENNER. Do you distinctly recall the hard-sided luggage you described yesterday?

Mrs. PAINE. Yes.

Mr. JENNER. All of the pieces that you saw?

Mrs. PAINE. Well, I don't recall that it was all. I couldn't even recall too well how many went down to New Orleans originally.

Mr. JENNER. Was there more than one?

Mrs. PAINE. There was certainly more than one.

Mr. JENNER. Do you think there were more than two?

Mrs. PAINE. I don't recall specifically.

Mr. JENNER. Do you have a recollection as to whether there was a piece of luggage still apart from the zipper bag, still in the apartment at 4907 Magazine Street when you girls pulled out to go back to Irving?

Mrs. PAINE. I have no specific recollection.

Mr. JENNER. Is it fair to say it is your best recollection at the moment that the zipper bag you have described earlier, you described yesterday, was not placed in the station wagon, and did not return with you to Irving?

Mrs. PAINE. I do not recall it being in the station wagon.

Mr. JENNER. Now, was there a separate long package of any kind?

Mrs. PAINE. I do not recall such a package.

Mr. JENNER. Was there a separate package of any character wrapped in a blanket?

Mrs. PAINE. No. There was a basket such as you use for hanging your clothes. It carried exactly that, clothes and diapers, and they weren't as neat as being in suitcases and duffels would imply. There was leftovers stuffed in the corner, clothes and things, but rather open.

Mr. JENNER. So you saw no long rectangular package of any kind or character loaded in or placed in your station wagon?

Mrs. PAINE. No, it doesn't mean it wasn't there, but I saw nothing of that nature.

Mr. JENNER. You saw nothing?

Mrs. PAINE. I saw nothing.

Mr. JENNER. When you arrived in Irving, Tex., were you present when your station wagon was unpacked?

Mrs. PAINE. Marina and I did that with the exception of the duffels.

Mr. JENNER. You did it all yourself and you took out of the station wagon everything in it other than the two duffel bags?

Mrs. PAINE. Yes.

Mr. JENNER. Now, in the process of removing everything other than the two duffel bags on the occasion on the 24th of September 1963 when you reached Irving, Tex., did you find or see any long rectangular package?

Mrs. PAINE. I recall no such package.

Mr. JENNER. Did you see any kind of a package wrapped in the blanket?

Mrs. PAINE. Not to my recollection.

Mr. JENNER. Did you see any package——

Mrs. PAINE. I don't recall seeing the blanket either.

Mr. JENNER. On that occasion?

Mrs. PAINE. On that occasion, not until later.

Mr. JENNER. Not until later.

Representative FORD. Did you see the blanket in New Orleans?

Mrs. PAINE. On the bed or something. I am asking myself. I don't recall it specifically.

Mr. JENNER. Of course we all know the blanket to which we are referring, which I will ask you about in a moment. I might show it to you at the moment, or at least ask you if it is the blanket. I am exhibiting to the witness Commission Exhibit No. 140. Is this blanket familiar to you?

Mrs. PAINE. Yes, it is.

Mr. JENNER. And give us the best recollection you have when you first saw it.

Mrs. PAINE. My best recollection is that I saw it on the floor of my garage sometime in late October.

Mr. JENNER. 1963?

Mrs. PAINE. Right.

Mr. JENNER. Do you have a recollection of ever having seen it before that time?

Mrs. PAINE. No. I might say also now that I know certainly I have never seen this binding until last night.

Mr. JENNER. When you say "this binding," you are pointing to what appears to be some black binding?

Mrs. PAINE. Some hemstitching, it is sewn.

Mr. JENNER. On the edge of the blanket.

Mrs. PAINE. Yes. This binding was not apparent, did not show.

Mr. JENNER. You never noticed the binding before, if the binding had always been on it, is that what you mean to say?

Mrs. PAINE. When I saw the blanket the binding was not showing.

Representative FORD. How carefully did you analyze the blanket on the previous occasions?

Mrs. PAINE. I stepped over it. I didn't pick it up or look at it closely.

Representative FORD. Didn't turn it over?

Mrs. PAINE. No.

Representative FORD. Didn't move it?

Mrs. PAINE. No, I didn't.

Representative FORD. So you only saw one surface more or less?

Mrs. PAINE. Yes, only one surface, except I saw that it had been moved.

Representative FORD. But you didn't move it yourself?

Mrs. PAINE. No.

Mr. JENNER. In what shape, that is form, was the blanket when you first saw it? And I take it you first saw it in your garage.

Mrs. PAINE. That is my recollection.

Mr. JENNER. And it was subsequent to the time that you and Marina had returned to Irving?

Mrs. PAINE. Yes.

Mr. JENNER. And you are certain that you did not see the blanket in your station wagon when you arrived in Irving?

Mrs. PAINE. I do not recall seeing the blanket in my station wagon.

Mr. JENNER. And you didn't see it in their apartment at 4907 Magazine Street when you were there?

Mrs. PAINE. I don't recall seeing it there.

Mr. JENNER. Either in the spring or in the fall, is that true?

Mrs. PAINE. That is true.

Mr. JENNER. Now tell us—I take it from your testimony that the blanket, when you first saw it in a garage, was in a configuration in the form of a package?

Mrs. PAINE. It was a long rectangle shape with the ends tucked in.

Mr. JENNER. Would you be good enough to re-form that blanket so that it is in the shape and the dimension when you first saw it?

Mrs. PAINE. About like so.

Mr. JENNER. For the record if you please, Mr. Chairman, the length of the form is just exactly 45 inches, and it is across exactly 12 inches.

Representative FORD. That is across lying flat.

Mr. JENNER. Across lying flat, thank you.

Now, what else about the form of the blanket did you notice on the occasion when you first saw it on your garage floor? Anything else?

Mrs. PAINE. I recall from either that occasion or another that there were parallel strings around it.

Mr. JENNER. Tied?

Mrs. PAINE. Into a bundle, yes, 3 or 4.

Mr. JENNER. How many were there?

Mrs. PAINE. 3 or 4, I don't recall.

Mr. JENNER. 3 or 4?

Mrs. PAINE. Yes. I suppose it would be four. It would be very well spaced if it was only three, and I think they were closer than that.

Mr. JENNER. Your best recollection now.

Mrs. PAINE. Is four.

Mr. JENNER. Rather than rationalization.

Mrs. PAINE. Yes, there were four.

Mr. JENNER. There were four string ties across the 12-inch side of the blanket. Were those string ties pulled so they seemed to hold something inside the blanket?

Mrs. PAINE. They didn't seem particularly tight, but then I don't have a strong recollection of them prior to the 22d.

Mr. JENNER. Did you ever pick up that package?

Mrs. PAINE. No, I never did.

Mr. JENNER. That was wrapped in the blanket. Did you ever have any discussion with Marina Oswald about the package in your garage?

Mrs. PAINE. Not until the afternoon of the 22d.

Mr. JENNER. Did you see anybody move it about your garage at any time?

Mrs. PAINE. No, I did not see anyone move it.

Mr. JENNER. And how long after you returned to Texas did you notice that package in your garage?

Mrs. PAINE. I said I thought it was late October perhaps. I wouldn't be at all certain about when I first noticed it.

Mr. JENNER. And did you notice from time to time that it was in a different position or places in your garage?

Mrs. PAINE. I recall two places I saw it.

Mr. JENNER. And the first was where?

Mrs. PAINE. Over near—the radial saw, what do you call it, buzz saw?

Mr. JENNER. Bandsaw.

Mrs. PAINE. No, buzz saw.

Mr. JENNER. Oh yes, a disc type, a buzz saw, near the buzz saw. Then on the second occasion when you saw it, where was it?

Mrs. PAINE. Over near the work bench in front of part of the work bench, one end extending toward the bandsaw.

Mr. JENNER. And on both of those occasions was the package lying flat on the floor or was it upended?

Mrs. PAINE. Flat on the floor.

Mr. JENNER. And you never had any curiosity with respect to it to lead you to step on it or feel it in any respect?

Mrs. PAINE. No, I didn't.

Mr. JENNER. Did you have a lot of debris or articles in the garage?

Mrs. PAINE. Indeed, and do yet. Our things and most of the Oswald things were stored there. I have mentioned several pieces of machine tools.

Mr. JENNER. We identified the garage picture at the tail end of yesterday, and I think the Chairman is seeking it.

Mr. McCLOY. I am trying to find it now.

Mrs. PAINE. That of course was taken more recently, but it is reasonably typical of its condition at that time too.

(Discussion off the record.)

Mr. JENNER. This is a photograph numbered eight, entitled garage interior, which I have marked with Commission number 429, and I now exhibit that to Mrs. Paine.

Are you familiar with what is depicted in that photograph?

Mrs. PAINE. Very.

Mr. JENNER. Do you know when that photograph was taken?

Mrs. PAINE. It was taken about 2 weeks ago.

Mr. JENNER. Were you present?

Mrs. PAINE. Yes.

Mr. JENNER. And does it accurately depict everything that was there and in its relative position at the time the picture was taken?

Mrs. PAINE. Yes.

Mr. JENNER. And it is your garage?

Mrs. PAINE. It is.

Mr. JENNER. Would you locate on that, and I would like to have you place an X at the point in that picture that you first saw the package?

Mrs. PAINE. Underneath that box.

Mr. JENNER. All right. You have written an arrow or X next to "on floor" and it is underneath the box that is on the floor.

Mrs. PAINE. It was in front as I recall it; this was the buzz saw I was talking about, right here.

Mr. JENNER. Right here the witness is pointing to the right hand upper middle section of the photograph.

Mr. DULLES. Is this the first location of the package?

Mrs. PAINE. It was over on that side of the garage, towards the door or——

Mr. DULLES. The first location of it?

Mrs. PAINE. Yes.

Mr. JENNER. Toward what door, Mrs. Paine?

Mrs. PAINE. Toward the front of the garage.

Mr. JENNER. Where did you see it on the second occasion?

Mrs. PAINE. Part of it in front of this work bench, one right under this box here.

Mr. JENNER. Put a double X here, between this workbench and this bandsaw.

Mrs. PAINE. On the floor.

Mr. JENNER. The workbench and the bandsaw to which the witness is pointing are on the left hand side of the photograph, the bandsaw being about the upper middle. Is that correct?

Mrs. PAINE. Yes. The package was farther to the interior from the bench.

Mr. JENNER. It was toward the back rather than toward the door?

Mrs. PAINE. It was the other side of the bandsaw so it was farther to the interior than its first location.

Mr. JENNER. I offer in evidence as Commission Exhibit No. 429 the document which the witness has identified which in turn was identified as Commission Exhibit 429.

Mr. McCLOY. It will be admitted.

(The photograph referred to, previously identified as Commission Exhibit No. 429, was received in evidence.)

Mr. JENNER. For the record, I am placing the rifle in the folded blanket as Mrs. Paine folded it. This is being done without the rifle being dismantled.

May the record show, Mr. Chairman, that the rifle fits well in the package from end to end, and it does not——

Mrs. PAINE. Can you make it flatter?

Mr. JENNER. No; because the rifle is now in there.

Mrs. PAINE. I just mean that——

Mr. JENNER. Was that about the appearance of the blanket wrapped package that you saw on your garage floor?

Mrs. PAINE. Yes; although I recall it as quite flat.

Mr. JENNER. Flatter than it now appears to be?

Mrs. PAINE. Yes. But it is not a clear recollection.

Mr. JENNER. You have a firm recollection that the package you saw was of the length?

Mrs. PAINE. Yes, definitely.

Mr. JENNER. That is 45 inches, approximately. You had no occasion when you stepped on the package——

Mrs. PAINE. I stepped over it.

Mr. JENNER. You always stepped over it?

Mrs. PAINE. Yes; until the afternoon of the 22d.

Mr. JENNER. By accident or otherwise, did you happen to come in contact with it?

Mrs. PAINE. No.

Mr. JENNER. You don't know whether there was anything solid or hard in it?

Mrs. PAINE. No.

Mr. DULLES. Did it look about the way this package looks?

Mrs. PAINE. Yes.

Mr. McCLOY. Except for the fact it had some cord around it?

Mrs. PAINE. Yes.

Representative FORD. When it had some cord around it, did the way it was tied pull it in or distort the shape?

Mrs. PAINE. No; it didn't distort the shape.

Representative FORD. About the same shape even with the cord?

Mrs. PAINE. Yes.

Mr. DULLES. The cords weren't pulled tight?

Mrs. PAINE. Yes.

Mr. JENNER. They were relatively loosley tied?

Mrs. PAINE. I recall this definite shape.

Mr. JENNER. To hold the blanket in that form rather than to hold the contents of the package firm, is that your impression?

Mrs. PAINE. Yes.

Mr. McCLOY. Are you going to ask about the husband's testimony in connection with the moving of the package?

Mr. JENNER. I did not intend to.

Mr. McCLOY. I was not present but your husband testified he had moved the blanket from time to time but had not opened it. Did he ever refer to it? Did he ever speak to you about having had to move it while he was——

Mrs. PAINE. Not until after the assassination.

Mr. McCLOY. Not until after the assassination but before the assassination he had not complained about its being there or any difficulty in moving it?

Mrs. PAINE. No; he did not mention it, and I was not present when he moved it.

Representative FORD. Was he the person who used these various woodworking pieces of equipment?

Mrs. PAINE. Yes.

Representative FORD. Did he work in the garage?

Mrs. PAINE. Well, he had—he made the workbench, and he had worked in the garage when he lived at the home and it has since been somewhat filled up.

Representative FORD. But during the time that you and Marina came back he didn't work in the garage?

Mrs. PAINE. He did still cut occasionally something on the saws. Indeed, I did, too. I like to make children's blocks. I am trying to think when I last, if it is pertinent, when I used the saw.

Mr. McCLOY. Did you use the saw while the blanket was on floor?

Mrs. PAINE. Yes; I believe so.

Mr. McCLOY. You had to step over the blanket to do that?

Mrs. PAINE. Or around it.

Mr. McCLOY. Or around it. But in the course of your use of the saw you never had the necessity or the occasion to readjust the blanket or move it in any way?

Mrs. PAINE. No.

Mr. DULLES. Did we get the three locations here? I only see two.

Mr. JENNER. There were only two?

Mrs. PAINE. Two that I recall.

Mr. DULLES. Only two.

Representative FORD. She made a mistake in the first drawing of the second one.

Mrs. PAINE. I touched it by mistake.

Representative FORD. I think that ought to be clarified on the record.

Mr. JENNER. On the right-hand side of Commission Exhibit 429 there is an X or an arrow above which is written the words "on floor". That is the first location point at which you saw the package?

Mrs. PAINE. Yes.

Mr. JENNER. On the left-hand side, the lower half of the photograph there is a double X.

Mrs. PAINE. Which I could not put in enough to give the proportion.

Mr. JENNER. You mean in the photograph?

Mrs. PAINE. Yes.

Mr. JENNER. Is that where you saw the package for the second time?

Mrs. PAINE. Yes; as I have described it. The position I have described is more accurate than the XX.

Mr. JENNER. There is a red strip above the table with the tablecloth on it.

Mrs. PAINE. That is an accident with my hand.

Mr. JENNER. That was an accident on your part?

Mrs. PAINE. Yes.

Mr. JENNER. So there are only two locations?

Mrs. PAINE. Right.

Mr. JENNER. Now, Mr. Chairman, may I reinsert the rifle in the package, on the opposite side from what it was before, and have the witness look at it?

Mr. McCLOY. You may.

We are back on the record.

Mr. JENNER. Yes.

Mr. Chairman, I have now placed the opposite side of the rifle to the floor, and may the record show that the package is much flatter. The rifle when inserted firstly was turned on the side of the bolt which operates the rifle which forced it up higher.

Now does the package look more familiar to you, Mrs. Paine?

Mrs. PAINE. I recall it as being more like this, not as lumpy as the other had been.

Mr. JENNER. More in the form it is now?

Mrs. PAINE. Yes.

Mr. JENNER. Now directing your attention to the rifle itself, which is Commission Exhibit 139, when did you first see that rifle, if you have ever seen it?

Mrs. PAINE. I saw a rifle I judge to have been the same one at the police station on the afternoon of November 22, I don't recall the strap.

Mr. JENNER. You don't recall at the time you saw it on the 22d of November in the police station that it had a strap?

Mrs. PAINE. It may well have had one but I don't specifically recall it. I was interested in the sight.

Mr. JENNER. Had you ever seen this rifle prior to the afternoon of November 22?

Mrs. PAINE. No.

(At this point, Senator Cooper entered the hearing room.)

Mr. JENNER. Now, we do have some particular interest, Mrs. Paine, in the rifle strap. Had you ever had around your house a luggage strap or a guitar strap similar to the strap that appears on Commission Exhibit 139?

Mrs. PAINE. No; in fact, I don't recall ever seeing a strap of that nature.

Mr. JENNER. Whether in your home or anywhere else?

Mrs. PAINE. Precisely.

Mr. JENNER. And you are unable to identify or suggest its source?

Mrs. PAINE. That is right.

Mr. JENNER. What do you have in your home, Mrs. Paine, by way of heavy wrapping paper?

Mrs. PAINE. I have the sort of paper you buy at the dime store to wrap packages, about 36 inches long, coming in a roll.

Mr. JENNER. Exhibiting to you Commission Exhibit No. 364, is the wrapping paper that you have in your home as heavy as that?

Mrs. PAINE. I don't believe it is quite that heavy and it certainly isn't quite that long. Well, it could have been cut the otherway, couldn't it, possibly?

Mr. JENNER. What about its shade, color?

Mrs. PAINE. It would be similar to that.

Mr. JENNER. Similar in shade.

Do you have the broad banded sticky tape or sticky tape of this nature?

Mrs. PAINE. There is no tape this wide in my home nor to my recollection has there ever been.

Mr. JENNER. You have whole rolls of this tape, of the paper in your home?

Mrs. PAINE. A whole roll.

Mr. JENNER. A whole roll?

Mrs. PAINE. Which I use for wrapping packages, mailing.

Mr. JENNER. Do you have string in your home that you use in attaching to this wrapping?

25

Mrs. PAINE. Yes.

Mr. JENNER. Did you by any chance know the weight of the string that wrapped the blanket package as against the strength or weight of the string that you normally used in your home for packages?

Mrs. PAINE. It was similar in weight, rather thin.

Representative FORD. Color was the same?

Mrs. PAINE. I think it was a whitish color on the blanket and one of the rolls I have is that.

Representative FORD. Yes.

Mr. JENNER. Would you say it was a relatively light package string?

Mrs. PAINE. Yes.

Mr. JENNER. Not a rope type?

Mrs. PAINE. Oh, no.

Mr. JENNER. And the string you saw on the blanket package was of the lighter weight type and not——

Mrs. PAINE. And of the lighter color too. I think.

Mr. JENNER. And the lighter color.

Now, you and Marina arrived home on the 24th of September, with the packages and contents of the station wagon, and, save the duffelbags, they were moved into your home, and everybody settled down?

Mrs. PAINE. Yes.

Mr. JENNER. When next was there—did you hear from Lee Harvey Oswald at any time thereafter?

Mrs. PAINE. Not until the afternoon of the 4th, which I have already referred to.

Mr. JENNER. No word whatsoever from him from the 24th of September?

Mrs. PAINE. 23d we left him in New Orleans.

Mr. JENNER. 23d of September, until the 4th of October?

Mrs. PAINE. That is correct; no word.

Mr. JENNER. By letter, telephone?

Mrs. PAINE. Or pigeon.

Mr. JENNER. Or otherwise, anything whatsoever?

Mrs. PAINE. No word.

Mr. JENNER. Did you and Marina have discussions in that 10-day period about where Lee was or might be?

Mrs. PAINE. No.

Mr. JENNER. None whatsoever? Did you have any discussion about the fact that you hadn't heard from Lee Harvey Oswald in 14 days or 10 days?

Mrs. PAINE. No; we didn't.

Mr. JENNER. No discussion on that at all. What did you and Marina discuss during that 10-day period?

Mrs. PAINE. I can't recall which was during that period or which was after; general conversation.

Mr. JENNER. Was it generally small talk, ladies talk about the house?

Mrs. PAINE. It was generally what my vocabulary permitted and then she would reminisce, her vocabulary being much larger, about her life in Russia, about the movies she had seen. We talked about the children and their health. We talked about washing, about cooking.

Mr. JENNER. Did you have ladies visit. Did ladies in the neighborhood come and visit?

Mrs. PAINE. Yes.

Mr. JENNER. Did you go to neighbors homes?

Mrs. PAINE. Yes.

Mr. JENNER. With Marina?

Mrs. PAINE. Again, I can't recall which was before October 4th and which was after, but there was the normal flow nonetheless——

Mr. JENNER. And interested people?

Mrs. PAINE. Of my visiting at other people's homes and particularly Mrs. Roberts or Mrs. Craig.

Mr. JENNER. Mrs. Roberts was your next door neighbor and Mrs. Craig was how many doors down or across the street?

Mrs. PAINE. She is, you have to drive. You have to drive to her home. She is the young German woman to whom I referred.

Mr. JENNER. Yes. Was there any discussion during this 10-day period of Marina's relations with her husband, Lee?

Mrs. PAINE. Not that I recall.

Mr. JENNER. She expressed no concern during this 10-day period, that no word had been heard from Lee?

Mrs. PAINE. No.

Mr. JENNER. Did he evidence any—did she do or say anything during that period to indicate she did not expect to hear from him during that 10 days period?

Mrs. PAINE. No; she did not.

Mr. JENNER. There was nothing?

Mrs. PAINE. There was nothing.

Mr. JENNER. Did it come to your mind that it was curious you hadn't heard from Lee Harvey Oswald for 10 whole days?

Mrs. PAINE. No; it didn't seem curious. I know he had spent at least 2 weeks looking for work on previous occasions in different cities and I thought he wanted to find something before he communicated.

Mr. JENNER. But in view of the affection that had been evidenced on the day of departure on the 23d, you were not bothered by the fact that not even a telephone call had been received in 10 days?

Mrs. PAINE. If he was not in town I wouldn't have at all expected a telephone call because that would have cost him dearly.

Mr. JENNER. He might have made it collect.

Mrs. PAINE. I didn't expect that either.

Mr. JENNER. But there was no telephone call, there was no postcard, there was no letter?

Mrs. PAINE. No.

Mr. JENNER. There was nothing?

Mrs. PAINE. There could well have been a letter but there was none.

Mr. DULLES. Where did you think he was at this time?

Mrs. PAINE. Houston.

Mr. DULLES. Houston, looking for a job? Houston?

Mrs. PAINE. Houston, possibly.

Mr. JENNER. Because of the conversation on the morning of the 23d, because of the possibility of his going to Houston or Philadelphia, your frame of mind was that he was either in Houston or Philadelphia?

Mrs. PAINE. I thought he probably was in Houston. The Philadelphia reference was very slight.

Mr. JENNER. Was there any reference or discussion between you and Marina during that period of the possibility that he was off in Houston looking for work?

Mrs. PAINE. No, there was not.

Mr. JENNER. You are sure there was just no discussion of the subject at all during that whole 10 days period with Marina?

Mrs. PAINE. I don't recall any discussion of it.

Mr. JENNER. She expressed no concern and you none?

Mrs. PAINE. That is right.

Mr. JENNER. That nobody had heard from Lee.

All right.

You heard from him on the 4th of October?

Mrs. PAINE. Yes.

Mr. JENNER. Would you give the Commission the circumstances, the time of day and how it came about?

Mrs. PAINE. He telephoned in early afternoon, something after lunchtime.

Mr. JENNER. The phone rang. Did you answer it?

Mrs. PAINE. Yes.

Mr. JENNER. And did you recognize the voice?

Mrs. PAINE. He asked to speak to Marina.

Mr. JENNER. Whose voice was it?

Mrs. PAINE. Well, after he asked to speak to Marina, I was certain it was Lee's.

Mr. JENNER. What did you say?

Mrs. PAINE. I said "here" and gave her the phone.

Mr. JENNER. You didn't say "where are you", or "I am glad to hear from you, where have you been?"

Mrs. PAINE. No. I thought that was her's to ask. He wished to speak to her and I gave her the phone and, of course, that is what was then asked. I heard her say to him——

Mr. JENNER. You heard her side of the conversation, did you?

Mrs. PAINE. Yes.

Mr. JENNER. All right.

What did you hear her say?

Mrs. PAINE. I heard her say, "No, Mrs. Paine, she can't come and pick you up."

Mr. JENNER. Was she speaking in Russian?

Mrs. PAINE. Yes.

Mr. JENNER. Throughout?

Mrs. PAINE. Yes.

Mr. JENNER. When Lee asked for Marina, did he speak in English or Russian?

Mrs. PAINE. I don't recall. And Marina went on to say that Mrs. Paine, "Ruth has just been to Parkland Hospital this morning to donate blood, she shouldn't be going driving now to pick you up."

Mr. JENNER. Did she refer to you as Mrs. Paine or Ruth?

Mrs. PAINE. No; I am trying to make it clear who is being talked about.

Mr. JENNER. I see. You might give your testimony the wrong cast.

Mrs. PAINE. No; of course. She referred to me as "Ruth" or "she".

To Junie, she called me Aunt Ruth. To Junie, speaking of me to her little girl, she referred to me as Aunt Ruth.

Mr. JENNER. You are giving the conversation now, the end of it that you heard?

Mrs. PAINE. Yes. Then I heard Marina say "Why didn't you call?"

Mr. JENNER. You did hear her say that?

Mrs. PAINE. I believe so. I certainly remember her saying it afterward. She hung up and she explained the conversation to me.

Mr. JENNER. What did she say to you?

Mrs. PAINE. That he had asked for me to come in to downtown Dallas to pick him up and she said no; he should find his own way.

Mr. JENNER. To come to downtown Dallas?

Mrs. PAINE. To come to downtown Dallas to pick him up, and she never asked me whether I wanted to or would have, told him, no; it was an imposition, that I had just given blood at Parkland Hospital.

Mr. JENNER. And you had in fact given blood?

Mrs. PAINE. Oh, yes; indeed.

Mr. JENNER. That morning?

Mrs. PAINE. Yes. I have a card or the FBI does to that effect. Then she said that he had said that he was at the Y, staying at the Y, and had been in town a couple of days, to which she said, "Why didn't you call right away?", in other words, "why didn't you call right away upon getting to town?"

Then he also asked whether he could come out; this was, of course, during the conversation, and she referred the question to me, could he come out for the weekend, and I said, yes, he could.

Mr. JENNER. This was while she was still talking on the telephone?

Mrs. PAINE. Yes. Prior to his asking for a ride.

So then they hung up and I went grocery shopping, and when——

Mr. JENNER. You left the home?

Mrs. PAINE. I left the home.

Mr. JENNER. You have now exhausted your recollection as to everything that was said to you by Marina after she hung up and was relating to you, at least a summary of the conversation with her husband?

Mrs. PAINE. I believe it was also said that he wanted to look for work in Dallas. He was here, staying at the Y. Could he come out for the weekend. He planned to look for work in Dallas.

Mr. JENNER. I see.

Did you say anything about—were you stimulated to say anything to Marina about any of the subject matters of that conversation as she reported it to you?

Mrs. PAINE. No.

Mr. JENNER. You expressed no response, made no response to her having made a statement to her husband that—of her surprise as to why he hadn't called and if he were just over in Dallas and staying at the Y?

Mrs. PAINE. I thought that but I didn't try to put it in Russian.

Mr. JENNER. There was no discussion is all I am getting at.

What did she say as to his coming out by whatever means he could get there? Was there any discussion of that?

Mrs. PAINE. It implied whatever means, that he shouldn't ask me to——

Mr. JENNER. He was coming?

Mrs. PAINE. Yes.

Mr. JENNER. But that you were not going to go to get him?

Mrs. PAINE. Yes.

Mr. JENNER. And you left and went to the grocery store or market?

Mrs. PAINE. Yes.

Mr. JENNER. When you returned, was Lee at your home?

Mrs. PAINE. He was already there, which surprised me greatly.

Mr. JENNER. Why did it surprise you?

Mrs. PAINE. Because I thought he would have to take a public bus to Irving, they run very rarely if at all during the afternoon, and I thought he would have considerable difficulty getting out. I thought it would be at least supper time before he got there.

Mr. JENNER. How much time elapsed between the time you left and the time you returned?

Mrs. PAINE. Shopping? Oh, I don't know, perhaps an hour, perhaps a little less.

Representative FORD. Where did you go shopping?

Mrs. PAINE. The grocery store in the same parking lot where we practiced.

Mr. JENNER. That was three blocks away?

Mrs. PAINE. It is a little more than that. These would be long blocks.

Mr. JENNER. Did any conversation ensue as to how he had, by what means he had come from Dallas to Irving?

Mrs. PAINE. Yes. He then said that he had hitchhiked out, caught a ride with someone who brought him straight to the door, a Negro man.

Mr. JENNER. To your door?

Mrs. PAINE. Yes. To whom he said that he had been away from his wife and child and he was just now getting home, and the man kindly brought him directly to the door.

Mr. JENNER. Where did this conversation take place?

Mrs. PAINE. In the home that afternoon.

Mr. JENNER. When you returned to your home, that was in the afternoon, wasn't it?

Mrs. PAINE. Yes.

Mr. JENNER. Where was Lee Harvey Oswald?

Mrs. PAINE. I don't recall.

Mr. JENNER. Was he inside the home or outside?

Mrs. PAINE. Inside, I believe.

Mr. JENNER. Did any conversation ensue as to where he had been in that 10-day interim?

Mrs. PAINE. Where he had been?

Mr. JENNER. Where he had been in the intervening 10 days?

Mrs. PAINE. Yes; he said to me that he had been in Houston and that he hadn't been able to find work there and was now going to try in Dallas.

Mr. JENNER. Did he say anything about Philadelphia?

Mrs. PAINE. Nothing.

Mr. JENNER. From your testimony I gather he did not say anything about Mexico?

Mrs. PAINE. No; he did not.

Mr. JENNER. Was Marina present when he stated to you that he had been in Houston looking for work?

29

Mrs. PAINE. That is my recollection of it; yes.

Mr. JENNER. You never had any conversation with her up to the 23d or 22d of November on the subject of whether Lee had or had not been in Mexico?

Mrs. PAINE. We never had such a conversation.

Mr. JENNER. Despite your having read that letter on the 10th of November in which he stated that he had been?

Mrs. PAINE. Yes. Now there was no occasion in that letter that she may have known that he went any more than there was certain indication to my mind that this was true and not false. Had I looked at the peso, this would have been the only occasion that she knew.

Mr. JENNER. But the fact is, apart from your rationalization now there was no conversation on that subject?

Mrs. PAINE. That is right.

Mr. JENNER. How long did he remain in your home?

Mrs. PAINE. Monday morning——

The CHAIRMAN. Before you get to that, I want to ask a question about giving the blood that day. Did you give it for a particular person or for a blood bank?

Mrs. PAINE. It was for Marina. For each of the persons who come in under county care they ask you to donate two pints of blood, one at a time.

The CHAIRMAN. I see. And you donated one pint for her?

Mrs. PAINE. Yes.

The CHAIRMAN. Thank you.

Mr. JENNER. How long did he remain in your home on this visit?

Mrs. PAINE. Until Monday morning, the 7th of October, almost noon, in fact, when I took him to an Intercity bus at the Irving bus station.

Mr. JENNER. This is that bus terminal approximately 3 miles from your home?

Mrs. PAINE. That same day I gave him a map to assist him in job hunting.

Mr. JENNER. All right. I would like to get to that.

I show you what is in evidence, I don't know whether it is received or not; it is a Commission Exhibit No. 128, and ask you if you have ever seen that before?

Mrs. PAINE. Yes; I have.

Mr. JENNER. Is that the map to which you now have reference?

Mrs. PAINE. I would say it is.

Mr. JENNER. What did you do with the map with respect to Lee Harvey Oswald on this occasion?

Mrs. PAINE. I don't recall who asked, who mentioned a map first, but, of course, I knew, and he did, that it would be a useful thing to have job hunting. I think he asked if I had a map of the city of Dallas and I said, yes, I did, and I can easily get another at the gas station, one of these.

Mr. JENNER. Mrs. Paine, it is your clear recollection that this document, Commission Exhibit No. 128, a map, is the map that you gave Lee Harvey Oswald, this was October 7th?

Mrs. PAINE. It was certainly this kind of map, whether it is the identical map, I couldn't say for sure, but I much prefer the ENCO map of the city and this is the kind I always get to use. So this is the kind I had in mind.

Mr. JENNER. So, to the best of your recollection, the coloring has been changed a little bit because of attempts to draw fingerprints from it?

Mrs. PAINE. Yes.

Mr. JENNER. But your best recollection now, observing it, is that this is the document?

Mrs. PAINE. Yes.

Mr. JENNER. Would you examine it carefully and see that there might be something on it that would arrest your attention as your having placed thereon or Lee?

Mrs. PAINE. I have examined this carefully and a copy of it.

Mr. JENNER. On other occasions?

Mrs. PAINE. On other occasions, and I could not at any time find a marking that I had made.

Mr. JENNER. Do you recall having made markings?

Mrs. PAINE. I do not recall having made any markings on this particular map. Sometime on some maps I knew I had made remarks where I was going.

Mr. JENNER. Just for the purpose of the record, may I reverse it, and you see no markings on the reverse side, I take it?

Mrs. PAINE. No; which is Fort Worth, not Dallas, isn't it?

Mr. JENNER. Yes; it is.

All right, now tell us about that incident?

Mrs. PAINE. The map?

Mr. JENNER. Yes.

Mrs. PAINE. I have.

Mr. JENNER. That is all there was to it?

Mrs. PAINE. Yes.

Mr. JENNER. Did you suggest, was there any discussion of, particular places of employment?

Mrs. PAINE. There was no such discussion.

Mr. JENNER. As to which he might inquire?

Mrs. PAINE. No.

Mr. JENNER. What did he—did you hand him the map?

Mrs. PAINE. Yes.

Mr. JENNER. And was it opened before you and Lee in your discussions?

Mrs. PAINE. No, no; we didn't discuss. He said, do I have a map, and I said, yes, I do, you may have it.

Mr. JENNER. You handed it to him, and that was all that occurred?

Mrs. PAINE. Yes.

Mr. JENNER. And did he place it in his pocket or did he go into his room or his and Marina's room and place it there?

Mrs. PAINE. He may have already been on his way to the bus station when this conversation occurred and took it with him.

Mr. JENNER. All right.

I notice what appears to be a notation that the document has not as yet been offered in evidence, Mr. Chairman, and I offer in evidence, therefore, as Commission Exhibit No. 128, the document heretofore identified by that exhibit number.

Mr. McCLOY. It may be admitted.

(The document referred to, heretofore marked as Commission Exhibit No. 128 for identification, was received in evidence.)

Mr. JENNER. Was Marina present during this discussion of his job hunting?

Mrs. PAINE. I don't recall. I seem to think we were on our way out already to go in our car to the bus station.

Mr. JENNER. Did Marina accompany you?

Mrs. PAINE. No; she did not.

Mr. JENNER. She did not?

Mrs. PAINE. She stayed home with the baby. My children probably went with me, I don't recall specifically.

Mr. JENNER. That is the baby, you mean June?

Mrs. PAINE. June.

Mr. JENNER. You drove into the bus terminal approximately 3 miles from your home. Did you remain until the bus came along?

Mrs. PAINE. I think so.

Mr. JENNER. You saw him depart?

Mrs. PAINE. Yes.

Mr. JENNER. Was anything said about where he would reside in Dallas before he left?

Mrs. PAINE. I am not certain, but I think he said the Y was rather expensive. He was going to look for a room.

Mr. McCLOY. What was the date you took him into the bus station?

Mrs. PAINE. That is the 7th of October.

Mr. McCLOY. The 7th of October?

Mrs. PAINE. Yes.

Mr. JENNER. Was there an occasion in this early period that you drove him all the way into Dallas?

Mrs. PAINE. I can't recall ever driving him all the way into Dallas.

Mr. JENNER. At any time?

Mrs. PAINE. We drove, except to the Oak Cliff Station for this driver training test.

Mr. JENNER. That is the only occasion?

Mrs. PAINE. Yes; that is the only one I recall. Can you refresh my memory. I can't think of any other.

Mr. JENNER. You are clear that you drove him from your home to the bus terminal in Irving?

Mrs. PAINE. Yes.

Mr. JENNER. And either you left immediately or waited to see him board the bus, but it is your definite recollection you did not drive him to the Dallas downtown area on that occasion?

Mrs. PAINE. Oh, I did once drive him to the Dallas downtown area, because I recall where he got out. Now why I was going—yes, I think I may know why I was going.

Mr. JENNER. Fix the time first.

Mrs. PAINE. I do recall now driving him into downtown Dallas because I was already going and it was probably Monday, the 14th of October.

Mr. JENNER. This is the day before his employment began with the Texas School Book Depository?

Mrs. PAINE. It would have been 2 days before, the day before he applied. I have several recollections but which day they attach to is not quite as clear.

I recall taking him to the bus. I recall picking him up at the bus. I recall going in and dropping him off at a corner of Ross Avenue and something else, which was near the employment office.

Mr. JENNER. In downtown Dallas?

Mrs. PAINE. Near the employment office station. I was on my way to get a key fixed on my Russian typewriter which is what was taking me downtown. I hadn't been thinking—I at no time made a purposeful trip just to take him to downtown Dallas, but I was going and he went along and I am pretty sure that was a Monday and he got out at that corner and Marina was with me and we went on to get this typewriter fixed either to pick it up or to leave it. I am quite certain it was the 12th, Saturday, that I picked him up at the station.

Mr. JENNER. At the bus terminal?

Mrs. PAINE. Yes. And I am pretty certain that it was the 7th I took him to the bus station. I recall it being already noon, and I thought he might well have started looking for a job earlier that day.

Mr. JENNER. When next did you hear from Mr. Oswald?

Mrs. PAINE. After the 7th. Probably on the 12th when he called again to ask if he could come out for the weekend.

Mr. JENNER. The 12th is what day of the week?

Mrs. PAINE. The 12th is a Saturday.

Mr. JENNER. Do you recall that he did call?

Mrs. PAINE. Pardon?

Mr. JENNER. Did you recall that he did telephone and ask permission to come?

Mrs. PAINE. Oh, indeed he did.

Mr. JENNER. Did he always do that?

Mrs. PAINE. He always did that with the exception of the 21st of November.

Mr. JENNER. We will get to that in a very few moments.

Mr. McCLOY. Before you get to that you said you went all the way into Dallas with this errand, that Marina was with you.

Mrs. PAINE. That is my recollection.

Mr. McCLOY. What did you do with the children?

Mrs. PAINE. We always take them.

Mr. McCLOY. Took them all, put them all in the station wagon?

Mrs. PAINE. Yes; big station wagon.

Mr. JENNER. By the way, I would like to go back a little. When you picked him up at the bus station on the afternoon of the 4th of October, what did he have——

Mrs. PAINE. On the afternoon of the 12th, around noon of the 12th.

Mr. JENNER. Please, when he first returned to Irving after——

Mrs. PAINE. He hitchhiked out.

Mr. JENNER. On the occasion that he told you he had been in Houston looking for a job?

Mrs. PAINE. The 4th, he hitchhiked out.

Mr. JENNER. Yes.

It is that occasion that I have in mind.

What did he have with him in the way of luggage?

Mrs. PAINE. I don't recall certainly. It does seem to me that I remember he took the zipper bag on Monday, the following Monday, with him to town, along with some clothes over his arm, ironed shirts, things that are hung on hangers.

Mr. JENNER. With respect to that trip——

Mrs. PAINE. You must remember I was shopping when he arrived on the afternoon of the 4th.

Mr. JENNER. Yes.

Mrs. PAINE. So I didn't see him when he arrived that moment.

Mr. JENNER. But you do have a recollection of having seen the zipper bag on Monday?

Mrs. PAINE. The 7th.

Mr. JENNER. When you took him to the bus terminal for the purpose of his returning to downtown Dallas?

Mrs. PAINE. To find a room and live there, and have sufficient clothing there. That is my best recollection.

Mr. JENNER. Is that the first time you had seen the zipper bag?

Mrs. PAINE. No.

Mr. JENNER. From the time you had left New Orleans on the 23d?

Mrs. PAINE. So far as I recall.

Mr. JENNER. Did you notice anything else in the way of pieces of luggage in your home after you came back from the shopping center that afternoon of October 4th that hadn't been there prior to his arrival?

Mrs. PAINE. No.

Mr. JENNER. The only piece of luggage of which you have any recollection then is the zipper bag which you saw him take with him when he left on Monday morning, the 7th?

Mrs. PAINE. And that is, I would not say a certain recollection. But that is the best I have.

Mr. JENNER. It is your best recollection anyhow?

Mrs PAINE. Yes.

Mr. JENNER. Now, when you returned to your home did you have any discussion with Marina about Lee's departure and his future plans and her understanding of them?

Mrs. PAINE. No; nothing I recall specifically.

Mr. JENNER. None at all.

What discussion went on between you and Marina, that is the subject matter with respect to his weekend visits?

Mrs. PAINE. She wanted to be certain it was all right for him to come out, you know that it wasn't too much of an imposition on me. We got into discussing his efforts to find a job. Then Monday, the 14th as best as I recall, was the first time we talked about him, more than to say it was too bad he didn't find something. This is the——

Mr. JENNER. During the course of the week was there discussion between you and Marina respecting Lee Oswald's attempt at employment?

Mrs. PAINE. No.

Mr. JENNER. Now, there came an occasion, did there not, that weekend or the following weekend at which there was a discussion at least by you with some neighbors with respect to efforts to obtain employment for Lee Harvey Oswald?

Mrs. PAINE. As best I can reconstruct it this was, while having coffee at my immediate neighbors, Mrs. Ed Roberts, and also present was Mrs. Bill Randle, and Lee had said over the weekend that he had gotten the last of the unemployment compensation checks that were due him, and that it had been smaller than the others had been, and disappointing in its smallness and he looked very discouraged when he went to look for work.

Mr. JENNER. Did he say anything about amount?

Mrs. PAINE. I didn't hear the question.

Mr. JENNER. Did he say anything about amount?

Mrs. PAINE. No; he didn't, just less.

Mr. JENNER. All right.

Mrs. PAINE. And the subject of his looking for work and that he hadn't found work for a week, came up while we were having coffee, the four young mothers at Mrs. Roberts' house, and Mrs. Randle mentioned that her younger brother, Wesley Frazier thought they needed another person at the Texas School Book Depository where Wesley worked.

Marina then asked me, after we had gone home, asked me if I would call——

Mr. JENNER. Was Marina present during this discussion?

Mrs. PAINE. Yes; Marina was present, yes, indeed.

Mr. JENNER. Did she understand the conversation?

Mrs. PAINE. It was a running translation, running, faulty translation going on.

Mr. JENNER. You were translating for her?

Mrs. PAINE. I was acting as her translator. And then after we came home she asked me if I would call the School Book Depository to see if indeed there was the possibility of an opening, and at her request, I did telephone——

Mr. JENNER. Excuse me, please.

Mrs. PAINE. Yes.

Mr. JENNER. While you were still in the Roberts' home was there any discussion at all of the subject mentioned by you or by Mrs. Randle or Mrs. Roberts or anyone else, of calls to be made, or that might be made, to the Texas School Book Depository in this connection?

Mrs. PAINE. I don't recall this discussion. As I recall it was a suggestion made by Marina to me after we got home, but I may be wrong.

Mr. JENNER. But that is your best recollection that you are now testifying to?

Mrs. PAINE. Yes.

Mr. JENNER. Is that correct?

Mrs. PAINE. Yes.

Mr. JENNER. You reached home and Marina suggested that "Would you please call the Texas School Depository?"

Mrs. PAINE. Yes.

Mr. JENNER. What did you do?

Mrs. PAINE. I looked up the number in the book, and dialed it, was told I would need to speak to Mr. Truly, who was at the warehouse. The phone was taken to Mr. Truly, and I talked with him and said——

Mr. JENNER. You mean the call was transferred by the operator?

Mrs. PAINE. To Mr. Truly, and I said I know of a young man whose wife was staying in my house, the wife was expecting a child, they already had a little girl and he had been out of work for a while and was very interested in getting any employment and his name, and was there a possibility of an opening there, and Mr. Truly said he didn't know whether he had an opening, that the young man should apply himself in person.

Mr. JENNER. Which made sense.

Mrs. PAINE. Made very good sense for a personnel man to say.

Mr. JENNER. Did you make more than one call to this Texas School Book Depository?

Mrs. PAINE. No.

Mr. JENNER. Only the one?

Mrs. PAINE. Only the one.

Mr. JENNER. What was the date of this call?

Mrs. PAINE. Reconstructing it, I believe it was October 14.

Mr. JENNER. What day of the week is October 14?

Mrs. PAINE. It is a Monday.

Mr. JENNER. Following that call and your talking with Mr. Truly, what did you do?

Mrs. PAINE. Began to get dinner. Then Lee call the house.

Mr. JENNER. In the evening?

Mrs. PAINE. In the early evening.

Mr. JENNER. Did you talk with him?

Mrs. PAINE. Marina talked with him, then asked—then Marina asked me to tell Lee in English what had transpired regarding the possible job opening, and then I did say that there might be an opening in the School Book Depository, that Mr. Truly was the man to apply to. Shall I go on?

Mr. JENNER. Yes.

Mrs. PAINE. The next day——

Mr. JENNER. Excuse me, I meant go on as far as the conversation was concerned.

Mrs. PAINE. That is all there was.

Mr. JENNER. Mrs. Paine, I would like to return just for a moment to the conversation in the Roberts' home.

Was any possible place of employment in addition to the Texas School Depository mentioned?

Mrs. PAINE. No.

Mr. JENNER. You have no recollection of any other suggestion as to possible places of employment?

Mrs. PAINE. I have no recollection of that.

Mr. JENNER. You have no recollection of any other, at least two other places being suggested, and you, in turn, stating that they would be unsatisfactory, one because an automobile had to be used, or it would be necessary for Lee to have an automobile, and the other that he was lacking in the possible qualifications needed? None of that refreshes your recollection?

Mrs. PAINE. None of that refreshes my recollection. I certainly know that I thought, for instance, he couldn't have applied to Bell Helicopter or to any place apart from the city area.

Mr. JENNER. But Bell Helicopter was not mentioned?

Mrs. PAINE. I don't recall it being mentioned.

Mr. JENNER. Your husband is employed by Bell Helicopter, is he not?

Mrs. PAINE. Yes.

Mr. JENNER. Had you made an inquiry of your husband as to the possibility of employment by Lee Harvey Oswald with Bell Helicopter?

Mrs. PAINE. No; I hadn't, especially knowing that he had no way of getting there.

Mr. JENNER. Unless he knew how to drive a car?

Mrs. PAINE. Unless he knew how to drive a car.

Mr. JENNER. You didn't believe he was proficient enough at this moment to operate it?

Mrs. PAINE. We have got on record here that I gave him the first lesson on the 13th of October.

Mr. JENNER. And in any event were you aware he had no driver's license?

Mrs. PAINE. I certainly was.

Mr. JENNER. Especially that week?

Mrs. PAINE. Yes.

Mr. JENNER. Did you give him the telephone number and the address of the Texas School Book Depository on the occasion when you talked to him, this is the 14th?

Mrs. PAINE. The address, I don't think so. I probably gave the phone number. I don't recall that I gave him an address.

Mr. JENNER. Directing your attention to your address book, you have an entry in your address book of the Texas School Depository, do you not? Would you turn to that page?

Mrs. PAINE. Yes; I have it here.

Mr. JENNER. Is there an entry of address of the Texas School Depository on that page?

Mrs. PAINE. Yes; which I believe I made after he gained employment there.

Mr. JENNER. Rather than at the time that you advised him of this possibility?

Mrs. PAINE. Indeed.

Mr. JENNER. Have you made an entry of the telephone number of the Texas School Book Depository on that date?

Mrs. PAINE. Yes; I have and of the address.

Mr. JENNER. And that is the telephone number and the address of the Texas School Depository Building where——

Mrs. PAINE. On Elm Street.

Mr. JENNER. I heard you mention the Texas School Depository warehouse. Did you think the warehouse was at 411 Elm?

Mrs. PAINE. No. I had seen a sign on a building as I went along one of the limited access highways that leads into Dallas, saying "Texas School Book Depository Warehouse" and there was the only building that had registered on my consciousness as being Texas School Book Depository.

I was not aware, hadn't taken in the idea of there being two buildings and that there was one on Elm, though, I copied the address from the telephone book, and could well have made that notation in my mind but I didn't.

The first I realized that there was a building on Elm was when I heard on the television on the morning of the 22d of November that a shot had been fired from such a building.

Mr. JENNER. For the purpose of this record then I would like to emphasize you were under the impression then, were you, that Lee Harvey Oswald was employed?

Mrs. PAINE. At the warehouse.

Mr. JENNER. Other than at 411, a place at 411 Elm?

Mrs. PAINE. I thought he worked at the warehouse. I had in fact, pointed out the building to my children going into Dallas later after he had gained employment.

Mr. JENNER. Did you ever discuss with Lee Harvey Oswald where he actually was employed, that is the location of the building?

Mrs. PAINE. No; I didn't.

Mr. JENNER. Did he ever mention it?

Mrs. PAINE. No.

Mr. JENNER. There never was any discussion between you and, say, young Mr. Frazier or Mrs. Randle or anyone in the neighborhood as to where the place of employment is located?

Mrs. PAINE. No. It may be significant here to say, my letter to which I have already referred——

Mr. JENNER. Commission Exhibit No.——

Mrs. PAINE. 425, which says, "Lee Oswald is looking for work in Dallas," does not give a time of day.

Mr. JENNER. What is the date of that letter?

Mrs. PAINE. October 14, Monday.

Mr. JENNER. This is the letter to your mother?

Mrs. PAINE. But I don't normally write letters any time except when the children are asleep, they sometimes nap but usually this is in the evening.

If it were in the evening it means that he had gotten the suggestion as to a place to apply, but I didn't mention that. I only mentioned that he was looking and was discouraged.

I bring this out simply to say that I had no real hopes that he would get a job at the School Book Depository.

I didn't think it too likely that he would, but it was worth a try.

Mr. JENNER. Did you hear from him then either on the 14th or 15th in respect to his effort to obtaining employment at the Texas School Depository?

Mrs. PAINE. He called immediately on Tuesday, the 15th, after he had been accepted and said he would start work the next day.

Mr. JENNER. When you say immediately, what time of day was that?

Mrs. PAINE. Midmorning I would say, which was contrary to his usual practice of calling in the early evening.

Mr. JENNER. By the way, is the call from Dallas, Tex., to Irving a toll call?

Mrs. PAINE. No.

Mr. JENNER. What is its cost, 10 cents?

Mrs. PAINE. I expect so.

Mr. JENNER. Did you answer the phone on the occasion he called?

Mrs. PAINE. Yes.

Mr. JENNER. What happened?

Mrs. PAINE. He asked for Marina.

Mr. JENNER. He said nothing to you about his success?

Mrs. PAINE. No.

Mr. JENNER. As soon as you answered he asked for Marina?

Mrs. PAINE. Yes.

Mr. JENNER. Did he identify himself?

Mrs. PAINE. No; but I am certain he knew that I knew who he was.

Mr. JENNER. You recognized his voice, did you?

Mrs. PAINE. Yes.

Mr. JENNER. You called her to the phone.

Did you hear her end of the conversation?

Mrs. PAINE. Yes.

Mr. JENNER. What took place by way of of conversation?

Mrs. PAINE. She said, "Hurray, he has got a job." Immediately telling me as she still talked to the telephone that he had been accepted for work at the school book depository and thanks to me and she said, "We must thank Mrs. Randle."

Mr. JENNER. Did you return to the telephone and speak with him?

Mrs. PAINE. No.

Mr. JENNER. You did not. Where was he residing then, did you know?

Mrs. PAINE. No; I did not know.

Mr. JENNER. Had you had any information that he was not residing at the YMCA?

Mrs. PAINE. Yes.

Mr. JENNER. How did you come by that information?

Mrs. PAINE. He gave me a telephone number, possibly this same weekend.

Mr. JENNER. That is of importance, Mrs. Paine. Would you give us the circumstances, please?

Mrs. PAINE. He said that he was at a——

Mr. JENNER. Excuse me, where was he when he said this?

Mrs. PAINE. He was at the home so far as I remember. It might have been during one of his telephone calls to the house, but I don't think so. He rarely talked with me when he was out.

Mr. JENNER. This would be the weekend of what?

Mrs. PAINE. So this must have been the weekend of the 12th of October, the same weekend.

Mr. JENNER. That was the weekend following his return to Dallas on the 7th of October?

Mrs. PAINE. Fourth of October.

Mr. JENNER. He departed on the 7th.

Mrs. PAINE. His return to Dallas, I am sorry.

Mr. JENNER. Yes; now, give it as chronologically as you can; how you came by that telephone number, the circumstances under which it was given to you.

Mrs. PAINE. He said this is the telephone number.

Mr. JENNER. Was Marina present?

Mrs. PAINE. Yes. He said of the room where he was staying, renting a room, and I could reach him here if she went into labor.

Mr. JENNER. I see, the coming of the baby was imminent?

Mrs. PAINE. Yes.

Mr. JENNER. When was the baby expected?

Mrs. PAINE. Any time after the first week in October. Any time, in other words.

Mr. JENNER. The obstetrician predicted the birth of the child as when?

Mrs. PAINE. As due on the 22d.

Mr. JENNER. Did Marina have a different notion?

Mrs. PAINE. She thought it might be due around the 8th.

Mr. JENNER. So there was a considerable variance in the expectation between the date and when the baby actually did arrive? When did the baby actually arrive?

Mrs. PAINE. On the 20th of October, a Sunday.

Mr. JENNER. Did he give you more than one telephone number?

Mrs. PAINE. Yes.

Mr JENNER. At this occasion did he give you more than one telephone number?

Mrs. PAINE. No.

Mr. JENNER. Just stick to this particular occasion. What telephone number— did you record it?

Mrs. PAINE. Yes.

Mr. JENNER. In what?

Mrs. PAINE. In ink in my telephone book.

Mr. JENNER. Your telephone and address book?

Mrs. PAINE. Yes.

Mr. JENNER. Have you opened that telephone address book to the page in which you have made that recording?

Mrs. PAINE. Yes; I have.

Mr. JENNER. Is that the page you identified yesterday?

Mrs. PAINE. Yes.

Mr. JENNER. Excuse me, Mr. Chairman, may I examine it for a moment here. Now, relate for the record the telephone number that Mr. Oswald gave you, the first one he gave you on this particular occasion?

Mrs. PAINE. The number was WH 2–1985.

Mr. JENNER. And that is at the bottom of the page written in ink.

Mrs. PAINE. Yes.

Mr. JENNER. Is that in your handwriting?

Mrs. PAINE. Yes; it is.

Mr. JENNER. What exchange is "WH" in Dallas?

Mrs. PAINE. I don't know. I did not know. I know now, maybe I know, Whitehall, something. I know now what it is, but I didn't know then.

Mr. JENNER. Did he on that occasion say anything about where the apartment or room was?

Mrs. PAINE. No; he did not.

Mr. JENNER. He did not give you an address?

Mrs. PAINE. No.

Mr. JENNER. Didn't locate it in any area in Dallas?

Mrs. PAINE. No.

Mr. JENNER. All he gave you was the telephone number?

Mrs. PAINE. Yes.

Mr. JENNER. Did he say anything that would indicate to you that you are other than free to call him and ask for him by his surname you knew him by?

Mrs. PAINE. No; he did not make such a limitation.

Mr. JENNER. I take it from your testimony that the number was given to you, at least the discussion was, so that you could call him in connection with the oncoming event of the birth of his child?

Mrs. PAINE. Yes.

Mr. JENNER. Am I correct about this?

Mrs. PAINE. That is correct.

Mr. JENNER. Now, you have mentioned a second number that Mr. Oswald, Lee Harvey Oswald, gave you. Did you receive that second number subsequent to the birth of Rachel or prior to that time?

Mrs. PAINE. Also prior to the birth of Rachel.

Mr. JENNER. Now, relate for the Commission the circumstances under which you received a second number?

Mrs. PAINE. He gave me a second number, I suppose by phone, but I don't recall.

Mr. JENNER. When?

Mrs. PAINE. It was certainly before the birth of the baby because again it was so that I could reach him if she went to the hospital.

Mr. JENNER. He called you or related this to you in your home?

Mrs. PAINE. What?

Mr. JENNER. He either called you by telephone or he was present in your home and gave you the second number?

Mrs. PAINE. Yes.

Mr. JENNER. Which recollection serves you best, that he called or that he gave it to you in your home?

Mrs. PAINE. I don't recall.

Mr. JENNER. What did he say?

Mrs. PAINE. He said he moved to different rooms, was paying a dollar a week more, $8 instead of $7; incidentally, I needed to know how much he was paying in order to put this on the form of Parkland Hospital, but that it was a little more comfortable and he had television privileges and privileges to use the refrigerator. And he gave me this number.

Mr. JENNER. This was after he obtained employment with the Texas School Book Depository, was it?

Mrs. PAINE. I would rationalize that I have judged so.

Mr. JENNER. Is it your best recollection?

Mrs. PAINE. Yes.

Mr. JENNER. On the second occasion did he give you the location or even the area in Dallas where his second room was located?

Mrs. PAINE. No.

Mr. JENNER. Did you inquire of him?

Mrs. PAINE. No.

Mr. JENNER. No address?

Mrs. PAINE. No.

Mr. JENNER. Was the telephone number given you with any reservation as to when you might call him?

Mrs. PAINE. No such reservation.

Mr. JENNER. Any indication that you should ask him, asking for him by other than his surname by which you knew him?

Mrs. PAINE. No such indication.

Mr. JENNER. Now, the baby was born on the——

Mrs. PAINE. Twentieth.

Mr. JENNER. Twentieth of October. Was Lee present, in town, I mean?

Mrs. PAINE. He was at the house in Irving when labor began, and stayed at the house to take care of June and my two children who were sleeping while I took Marina to the hospital since I was the one who could drive.

Mr. JENNER. All right. The 20th is—when did you take her to the hospital?

Mrs. PAINE. Around 9 o'clock in the evening.

Mr. JENNER. What day?

Mrs. PAINE. Sunday, the 20th of October.

Mr. JENNER. And Lee Harvey Oswald was out there on that weekend on one of his regular visits?

Mrs. PAINE. Yes. The first one since he had employment.

Representative FORD. Did you ever call either one of those numbers?

Mrs. PAINE. Yes. We will get to it.

Mr. JENNER. You will forgive me because I would like to bring out the particular circumstances of the call.

Representative FORD. Yes.

Mr. JENNER. Did Lee go back into town on Monday to go to work?

Mrs. PAINE. Yes; he did. I informed him in the morning that he had a baby girl. He was already asleep when I got back—no; that is not right. He was not asleep when I got back from the hospital, but he had gone to bed, and I stayed up and waited to call the hospital to hear what word there was. So, that I knew after he was already asleep that he had a baby girl. I told him in the morning before he went to work.

Mr. JENNER. You called him in Dallas?

Mrs. PAINE. No.

Mr. JENNER. I am a little confused.

Mrs. PAINE. No; I am sorry, I will begin again. I took her to the hospital and then I returned. I didn't feel I could stay. I thought I should get back to my children.

Mr. JENNER. This was Sunday night?

Mrs. PAINE. Sunday night.

He went to bed, put Junie to bed. I stayed up and waited until what I considered a proper time and then called the hospital to hear what news there was. They had implied I could come and visit, too, but that would have been incorrect, and learned that he had a baby girl. I then went to bed and told him in the morning.

Mr. JENNER. You did not awaken him then?

Mrs. PAINE. I did not awaken him. I thought about it and I decided if he was not interested in being awake I would tell him in the morning.

Mr. JENNER. And the morning was Monday?

Mrs. PAINE. Yes.

Mr. JENNER. Having learned that he was the father of a baby girl, I assume you told him that?

Mrs. PAINE. Yes.

Mr. JENNER. Did he go to work that day?

Mrs. PAINE. Yes.

Mr. JENNER. Did he return to Irving that evening?

Mrs. PAINE. Yes. It was agreed when he left that he would return that evening.

Mr. JENNER. How did he—was he brought back to Irving that evening?

Mrs. PAINE. I imagine Wesley brought him.

Mr. JENNER. At least you did not?

Mrs. PAINE. I did not.

Mr. JENNER. Did he visit with Marina at the hospital that evening?

Mrs. PAINE. When he arrived it was not decided whether he would go to the hospital or not. He thought not, and I thought he should, and encouraged him to go.

Mr. JENNER. Why did he think he ought not to go?

Mrs. PAINE. I am uncertain about this. This thought crossed my mind that perhaps he thought they would find out he was working, but I had already told them he was working since I had been asked at the hospital when she was admitted and I mentioned this and it may have changed his mind about going, but this is conjecture on my part.

Mr. JENNER. In any event he did go?

Mrs. PAINE. He did go. It was a good thing as he was the only one admitted, I was not either a father or grandmother so I was not permitted to get in.

Mr. JENNER. I see, and you waited until his visit was over and returned home with him?

Mrs. PAINE. That is right.

Mr. JENNER. Did he return to work the next morning?

Mrs. PAINE. Yes; he did.

Mr. JENNER. When next did you hear from him?

Mrs. PAINE. The following Friday he came out again.

Mr. JENNER. Do you know how he returned to Dallas that following morning, that is the 22d?

Mrs. PAINE. Probably went with Wesley also.

Mr. JENNER. And he came out the following weekend, did he?

Mrs. PAINE. Yes. That was his birthday.

Mr. JENNER. The 18th of October is his birthday. Did you have a party for him?

Mrs. PAINE. We had a cake; yes, sir.

Mr. JENNER. Was that weekend uneventful?

Mrs. PAINE. Well, Marina was already home.

Mr. JENNER. The baby was now home. She came home very quickly?

Mrs. PAINE. Very quickly, a day and a half. She was home on Tuesday, the 16th, is that right—skipped a day, the 22d. So that his party was the week before, too. I was wrong then.

Mr. JENNER. When did he return, on Friday of that week?

Mrs. PAINE. Yes, which was the 25th. I was mistaken.

Mr. JENNER. Did he call in each day in the interim?

Mrs. PAINE. Yes.

Mr. JENNER. And talk to Marina and to you?

Mrs. PAINE. Well, to Marina.

Mr. JENNER. Inquire about the baby?

Mrs. PAINE. Yes.

Mr. JENNER. You overheard some of the conversation?

Mrs. PAINE. Yes.

Mr. JENNER. Was anything said about the nature of his reaction to his position at the Texas School Book Depository on the second weekend when he came home?

Mrs. PAINE. You are talking about the weekend of the 26th?

Mr. JENNER. That is right.

Mrs. PAINE. No; I don't recall anything being said.

Mr. JENNER. Now, the next weekend was November 1st to 3d, which is Friday to Sunday, is that correct?

Mrs. PAINE. Right.

Mr. JENNER. Was he home on that weekend?

Mrs. PAINE. Yes; he was.

Mr. JENNER. And did anything eventful occur on that weekend?

Mrs. PAINE. Just a minute. What I was looking for, I wanted to find out whether I had taught a Russian lesson to my single student whom I saw some Saturday afternoon on that weekend, and I recall that I did not. So, the answer is no. I was there that Saturday. May I say if there was a weekend other than October 12 when he came on Saturday instead of Friday night, it was to have been that weekend?

Mr. JENNER. Which weekend?

Mrs. PAINE. The weekend of the 1st to the 3d. That is my best recollection anyway.

Mr. JENNER. All right. But other than that possibility, there was nothing— it was a normal weekend at your home?

Mrs. PAINE. Yes.

Mr. JENNER. Now, following that weekend, which was the weekend of November 8 through 10, I think you have already described that weekend. That was the one on which you went to the Texas driver's application bureau, is it not?

Mrs. PAINE. Yes. I recall him writing something on the early morning of Saturday—this "Dear Sirs" letter.

Mr. JENNER. Yes; this is the letter or draft of letter dealing with his reporting his visit to Mexico.

Mrs. PAINE. Or stating that he had done such a thing, which I did not fully credit.

Mr. JENNER. Did he come the following weekend, that is the weekend of November 15 through 17?

Mrs. PAINE. No; he did not.

Mr. JENNER. Why?

Mrs. PAINE. Marina asked him not to.

Mr. JENNER. This was the weekend preceding the ill-fated assassination day?

Mrs. PAINE. That is correct.

Mr. JENNER. Why did she ask him not to?

Mrs. PAINE. She felt he had overstayed his welcome the previous weekend which had been 3 days, 9th, 10th, and 11th because he was off Veterans Day, the 11th of November, and she felt it would be simpler and more comfortable if he didn't come out.

Mr. JENNER. Had you had a discussion with her prior to that time on that subject?

Mrs. PAINE. I had not suggested that to her.

Mr. JENNER. Did you overhear her tell him that?

Mrs. PAINE. I did tell her I was planning a birthday party for my little girl, and I heard her tell Lee not to come out because I was having a birthday party. At some point in this same telephone conversation likely I told him he did not need to have a car but to go himself to the driver training station.

Mr. JENNER. You have described that event for us heretofore this afternoon.

Mrs. PAINE. Yes.

Mr. JENNER. Or this morning, I have forgotten which.

Mr. MoCLOY. May I interrupt here. I wonder whether or not you would want to take a rest now. We have been pretty arduous and let's take a little recess now.

(Short recess.)

Mr. JENNER. Mr. Reporter, would you read the last interchange or question and answer?

41

(The reporter read the question and answer.)

Mr. JENNER. Would you fix as best you can for us, the date or time that you first saw the wrapped blanket after you had returned to Irving? How long after that event did you see it to the best of your recollection?

Mrs. PAINE. I have said it was the latter part of October. I don't think I can fix it more exactly.

Mr. JENNER. That would be almost or would be over a month afterwards? You returned on September 24?

Mrs. PAINE. I don't recall thinking, that is, that anything like that marks it as being particular noticeable. So that I am judging that I recall seeing it in October, somewhere towards the end.

Mr. JENNER. Had anything occurred at that time that now leads you to fix it at the latter part of October?

Mrs. PAINE. No; there is no way that I have to fix it.

Mr. JENNER. Did you stumble over it or something?

Mr. McCLOY. Could it have been as early as October 4 or the 7th when you first got the call from him when he first returned to Dallas?

Mrs. PAINE. Conceivably, but I don't remember.

Mr. DULLES. Then you saw it on another occasion, how many days later was that?

Mrs. PAINE. I can't fix it that near.

Mr. DULLES. It was several days later, was it, the time when it seemed to have been moved from position "X" to position "XX"?

Mrs. PAINE. Oh, yes; that was later.

Mr. McCLOY. Can you place it at all, can you place your recollection at all as having seen it in relation to the assassination? The date of the assassination? Was it 2 weeks before, 3 weeks before?

Mrs. PAINE. I have inquired of myself for some weeks, was such a package in my station wagon when I arrived from New Orleans, and I cannot recall it, but I cannot be at all certain that there wasn't. I certainly didn't unload it. I never lifted such a package.

Mr. JENNER. Only you and Marina took things out of your station wagon at that time?

Mrs. PAINE. That is correct.

Mr. JENNER. And you did not——

Mrs. PAINE. So I think I would have seen it.

Mr. DULLES. In your earlier testimony I think in reply to a question, you indicated that you and Marina had only talked about this after the assassination that afternoon.

Mrs. PAINE. That is right.

Mr. DULLES. If it is not out of order, I would like to get that into the testimony maybe at this date what took place between them at that time.

Mr. JENNER. On the 22d?

Mr. DULLES. Yes.

Mr. McCLOY. I think it is best to leave it at the 22d.

Mr. JENNER. I was going to take her chronologically.

Mr. DULLES. Just so you recall that.

Mr. McCLOY. But you can't recall having gone into the garage for any purpose and having stepped over this thing or around it at any time that you would associate with his return from New Orleans and Houston, if he went to Houston?

Mrs. PAINE. My best recollection is that it was after, it was in October, therefore.

Mr. McCLOY. But later than the 7th of October, you think?

Mrs. PAINE. Later than that, yes. That is the best I can do.

Mr. McCLOY. But well before the day of November 22?

Mrs. PAINE. Yes.

Mr. JENNER. I think I have oriented myself without having the reporter read and may I proceed, Mr. Chairman?

Mr. McCLOY. Surely.

Mr. JENNER. We have now reached the weekend of the 15th, 16th, and 17th, which is the weekend that Lee Harvey Oswald did not return to your home.

Mrs. PAINE. Yes.

Mr. JENNER. You had just finished relating that Marina had told him not to come that particular weekend?

Mrs. PAINE. Yes.

Mr. JENNER. Now, was there an occasion during the course of that weekend when a phone call was made to Lee Harvey Oswald. I direct your attention particularly to Sunday evening, the 17th of November.

Mrs. PAINE. Looking back on it, I thought that there was a call made to him by me on Monday the 18th, but I may be wrong about when it was made.

Mr. JENNER. Did Marina call him this Sunday evening, November 17?

Mrs. PAINE. No. There was only one call made at any one time to him, to my knowledge.

Mr. JENNER. Do you recall an occasion when a call was made to him and you girls were unable to reach him when that call was made?

Mrs. PAINE. Yes. I will describe the call, and there is a dispute over what night it was.

Mr. JENNER. I would like your best recollection, first as to when it occurred. Was it during the weekend that he did not return to your home, the weekend immediately preceding the assassination day? Do you recall that Marina was lonesome and she wished you to make a call to Lee and you did so at her request?

Mrs. PAINE. I recall certainly we had talked with Lee, on the telephone already that weekend because he called to say that he had been to attempt to get a driver's license permit.

Mr. JENNER. Yes.

Mrs. PAINE. Whether he called that Saturday or whether he had called Sunday, I am not certain. Indeed, I am not certain but what he had called the very day, had already called and talked with Marina the very day that I then, at her request, tried to reach him at the number he had given me, with his number in my telephone book.

Junie was fooling with the telephone dial, and Marina said, "Let's call papa" and asked me——

Mr. JENNER. Was this at night?

Mrs. PAINE. It was early evening, still light.

Mr. JENNER. Was it on a weekend?

Mrs. PAINE. I would have said it was Monday but I am not certain of that.

Mr. JENNER. Was it——

Mrs. PAINE. That is my best recollection, is that it was Monday.

Mr. JENNER. All we want is your best recollection. If it was a Monday, was it the Monday following the weekend that he did not come?

Mrs. PAINE. Yes, certainly it was.

Mr. JENNER. I see. That is if it was a Monday, it was the Monday preceding November 22?

Mrs. PAINE. Yes.

Mr. JENNER. All right.

Mr. DULLES. Could I ask one question?

Mr. JENNER. Yes.

Mr. DULLES. Was there any evidence that the hint you gave, or that was given, to Lee Harvey not to come over this weekend caused him any annoyance? Was he put out by this, and did he indicate it?

Mrs. PAINE. I made no such request of him. Marina talked with him on the phone.

Mr. DULLES. I realize that.

Mrs. PAINE. And she made no mention of any irritation. Of course, I didn't hear what he said in response to her asking him not to come.

Mr. DULLES. And it didn't come out in any of these subsequent telephone messages which we are now discussing?

Mrs. PAINE. No; I think I probably talked with him during that same telephone conversation to say that he could go without a car, and there was no irritation I noticed.

Mr. DULLES. Thank you.

Mr. JENNER. But it is your definite recollection that his failure to come on the weekend preceding the assassination was not at his doing but at the request of Marina, under the circumstances you have related?

Mrs. PAINE. I am absolutely clear about that.

Mr. JENNER. You are absolutely clear about that. All right. Now, state, you began to state the circumstances of the telephone call. Would you in your own words and your own chronology proceed with that, please?

Mrs. PAINE. Marina had said, "Let's call papa," in Russian and asked me to dial the number for her, knowing that I had a number that he had given us. I then dialed the number——

Mr. JENNER. Excuse me, did you dial the first or the second number?

Mrs. PAINE. The second number.

Mr. JENNER. And that number is?

Mrs. PAINE. WH 3–8993.

Mr. JENNER. When you dialed the number did someone answer?

Mrs. PAINE. Someone answered and I said, "Is Lee Oswald there?" And the person replied, "There is no Lee Oswald here," or something to that effect.

Mr. JENNER. Would it refresh your recollection if he said, "There is nobody by that name here"?

Mrs. PAINE. Or it may have been "nobody by that name" or "I don't know Lee Oswald." It could have been any of these.

Mr. JENNER. We want your best recollection.

Mrs. PAINE. My best recollection is that he repeated the name.

Mr. JENNER. He repeated the name?

Mrs. PAINE. But that is not a certain recollection.

Mr. JENNER. I take it then from the use of the pronoun that the person who answered was a man?

Mrs. PAINE. Was a man.

Mr. JENNER. And if you will just sit back and relax a little. I would like to have you restate, if you now will, in your own words, what occurred?

You dialed the telephone, someone answered, a male voice?

Mrs. PAINE. Yes.

Mr. JENNER. What did he say and what did you say?

Mrs. PAINE. I said, "Is Lee Oswald there." He said, "There is no Lee Oswald living here." As best as I can recall. This is the substance of what he said. I said, "Is this a rooming house." He said "Yes." I said, "Is this WH 3–8993?" And he said "Yes." I thanked him and hung up.

Mr. JENNER. When you hung up then what did you next do or say?

Mrs. PAINE. I said to Marina, "They don't know of a Lee Oswald at that number."

Mr. JENNER. What did she say?

Mrs. PAINE. She didn't say anything.

Mr. JENNER. Just said nothing?

Mrs. PAINE. She looked surprised.

Mr. JENNER. Did she evidence any surprise?

Mrs. PAINE. Yes; she did, she looked surprised.

Mr. DULLES. You are quite sure you used the first name "Lee," did you, you did not say just "Mr. Oswald," or something of that kind?

Mrs. PAINE. I would not say "Mr. Oswald." It is contrary to Quaker practice, and I don't normally do it that way.

Mr. JENNER. Contrary to Quaker practice?

Mrs. PAINE. They seldom use "Mister."

Mr. JENNER. I see.

Mr. DULLES. And you wouldn't have said "Harvey Oswald," would you?

Mrs. PAINE. I knew he had a middle name but only because I filled out forms in Parkland Hospital. It was never used with him.

Mr. JENNER. You do recall definitely that you asked for Lee Oswald?

Mrs. PAINE. I cannot be that definite. But I believe I asked for him. Oh, yes; I recall definitely what I asked. I cannot be definite about the man's reply, whether he included the full name in his reply.

Mr. JENNER. But you did?

Mrs. PAINE. I asked for the full name, "Is Lee Oswald there."

Mr. JENNER. Did you report this incident to the FBI?

Mrs. PAINE. I had no occasion to see them, and I did not think it important enough to call them after that until the 23d of November.

Mr. JENNER. Perhaps I may well have deferred that question until after I asked ou the next.

Mrs. PAINE. Yes.

Mr. JENNER. Did any event occur the following day with respect to this telephone call?

Mrs. PAINE. Yes; Lee called——

Mr. JENNER. What was it?

Mrs. PAINE. Lee called at the house and asked for Marina. I was in the itchen where the phone is while Marina talked with him, she clearly was upset, nd angry, and when she hung up——

Mr. JENNER. Excuse me, did you overhear this conversation?

Mrs. PAINE. I overheard the conversation but I can't tell you specific content.

Mr. JENNER. Please, Mrs. Paine, would you do your very best to recall what vas said?

Mrs. PAINE. I can tell you what she said to me which was immediately after, vhich is what I definitely recall.

Mr. JENNER. Thank you.

Mrs. PAINE. She said immediately he didn't like her trying to reach him at he phone in his room at Dallas yesterday. That he was angry with her for aaving tried to reach him. That he said he was using a different name, and he said, "This isn't the first time I felt 22 fires," a Russian expression.

Mr. JENNER. This is something she said?

Mrs. PAINE. She said this. This is not the first time, but it was the first time she had mentioned it to me.

Mr. JENNER. Give her exact words to me again.

Mrs. PAINE. When she felt 22 fires.

Mr. JENNER. That is the expression she used?

Mrs. PAINE. Yes.

Mr. JENNER. Did you understand what she meant or, if not, did you ask for an explanation?

Mrs. PAINE. I did not ask for an explanation. I judged she meant, she disagreed with his using a different name, but didn't feel like, empowered to make nim do otherwise or even perhaps ask to as a wife.

Mr. DULLES. How long a conversation was this. Was it——

Mrs. PAINE. Fairly short.

Mr. DULLES. Fairly short.

Mrs. PAINE. That is my recollection.

Representative FORD. What day of the month and what day of the week was this?

Mrs. PAINE. Well, reconstructing it, I thought they succeeded each other, the original call to the WH number on Monday and his call back on Tuesday.

Representative FORD. When he called back it was late in the afternoon or early evening?

Mrs. PAINE. It was the normal time for him to call back, early evening, around 5:30.

Mr. JENNER. You have a definite impression she was angry when she hung up?

Mrs. PAINE. Yes.

Mr. JENNER. Was she abrupt in her hanging up. Did she hang up on him?

Mrs. PAINE. No; she was angry, she was upset.

Mr. JENNER. And her explanation of her being upset was that he used the assumed name?

Mrs. PAINE. Well, she didn't explain it as such, but she said he had used it.

Mr. JENNER. He was angry with her because you had made the call?

Mrs. PAINE. Yes.

Mr. JENNER. Or she had made it through you?

Mrs. PAINE. Yes.

Mr. JENNER. Did any further discussion take place between you and Marina on that subject?

Mrs. PAINE. Yes. The following day he did not call at the usual time.

Mr. JENNER. That would be the following day, the 20th?

Mrs. PAINE. I believe that was a Wednesday and that is how I slipped a day.

Mr. JENNER. He didn't call at all on the succeeding day?

Mrs. PAINE. He didn't call at all, and she said to me as the time for normally calling passed, "He thinks he is punishing me."

Mr. JENNER. For what?

Mrs. PAINE. For having been a bad wife, I would judge, for having done something he didn't want her to do, the objection.

Mr. JENNER. To wit, the telephone call about which you have told us?

Mrs. PAINE. Yes.

Mr. JENNER. Did you and Marina go through a normal day that day, or was there any other subject of discussion with respect to Lee Oswald on that day?

Mrs. PAINE. Nothing I would specifically recall; no.

Mr. JENNER. This was the 20th of November, a Wednesday?

Mrs. PAINE. To the best of my recollection.

Mr. JENNER. Let's proceed with the 21st. Did anything occur on the 21st with respect to Lee Harvey Oswald, that is a Thursday?

Mrs. PAINE. I arrived home from grocery shopping around 5:30, and he was on the front lawn. I was surprised to see him.

Mr. JENNER. You had no advance notice?

Mrs. PAINE. I had no advance notice and he had never before come without asking whether he could.

Mr. JENNER. Never before had he come to your home in that form without asking your permission to come?

Mrs. PAINE. Without asking permission; that is right.

Mr. JENNER. And he was out on the lawn as you drove up, on your lawn?

Mrs. PAINE. That is right. Playing with June and talking with Marina, who was also out on the lawn.

Mr. JENNER. And you were, of course, surprised to see him?

Mrs. PAINE. Yes.

Mr. JENNER. Did you park your car in the driveway as usual?

Mrs. PAINE. Yes.

Mr. JENNER. Did you walk over to speak with him?

Mrs. PAINE. Yes, got out, very likely picked some groceries out of the car and he very likely picked some up too, and this is I judge what may have happened.

Mr. JENNER. Tell the Commission what was said between you and Lee Oswald?

Mrs. PAINE. Between me and Lee Oswald?

Mr. JENNER. Yes; on that occasion.

Mrs. PAINE. That is not what I recall. I recall talking with Marina on the side.

Mr. JENNER. First. Didn't you greet him?

Mrs. PAINE. Yes; I greeted him.

Mr. JENNER. And then what did you do, walk in the house?

Mrs. PAINE. As we were walking in the house, and he must have preceded because Marina and I spoke in private to one another, she apologized.

Mr. JENNER. Was Marina out on the lawn also?

Mrs. PAINE. Yes, sir. She apologized for his having come without permission and I said that was all right, and we said either then or later—I recall exchanging our opinion that this was a way of making up the quarrel or as close as he could come to an apology for the fight on the telephone, that his coming related to that, rather than anything else.

Mr. JENNER. That was her reaction to his showing up uninvited and unexpectedly on that particular afternoon, was it?

Mrs. PAINE. Well, it was rather my own, too.

Mr. JENNER. And it was your own?

Mrs. PAINE. Yes.

Mr. JENNER. And because of this incident of the telephone call and your not being able to reach him, and the subsequent talk between Lee and Marina in which there had been some anger expressed, you girls reached the conclusion the afternoon of November 21 that he was home just to see if he could make up with Marina?

Mrs. PAINE. Yes.

Mr. JENNER. Do I fairly state it?

Mrs. PAINE. Yes.

Mr. JENNER. What did you do that evening? Did you have occasion to note what he did?

Mrs. PAINE. We had dinner as usual, and then I sort of bathed my children, putting them to bed and reading them a story, which put me in one part of the house. When that was done I realized he had already gone to bed, this being now about 9 o'clock. I went out to the garage to paint some children's blocks, and worked in the garage for half an hour or so. I noticed when I went out that the light was on.

Mr. JENNER. The light was on in the garage?

Mrs. PAINE. The light was on in the garage.

Mr. JENNER. Was this unusual?

Mrs. PAINE. Oh, it was unusual for it to be on; yes. I realized that I felt Lee, since Marina had also been busy with her children, had gone out to the garage, perhaps worked out there or gotten something. Most of their clothing was still out there, all of their winter things. They were getting things out from time to time, warmer things for the cold weather, so it was not at all remarkable that he went to the garage, but I thought it careless of him to have left the light on. I finished my work and then turned off the light and left the garage.

Mr. JENNER. Have you completed that now?

Mrs. PAINE. Yes.

Mr. JENNER. You stated that he was in the garage, how did you know he was in the garage?

Mr. McCLOY. She didn't state that.

Mrs. PAINE. I didn't state it absolutely. I guessed it was he rather than she. She was busy with the children and the light had been on and I know I didn't leave the light on.

Mr. JENNER. Then, I would ask you directly, did you see him in the garage at anytime from the time you first saw him on the lawn until he retired for the night?

Mrs. PAINE. No.

Mr. JENNER. Until you retired for the night?

Mrs. PAINE. No.

Mr. JENNER. Was he out on the lawn after dinner or supper?

Mrs. PAINE. I don't believe so.

Mr. JENNER. Did you hear any activity out in the garage on that evening?

Mrs. PAINE. No; I did not.

Mr. JENNER. Any persons moving about?

Mrs. PAINE. No.

Mr. JENNER. The only thing that arrested your attention was the fact that you discovered the light on in the garage?

Mrs. PAINE. That is right.

Mr. JENNER. Before you retired?

Representative FORD. You discovered that when you went out to work there?

Mrs. PAINE. When I went out to work there.

Mr. McCLOY. When you went out there, did you notice the blanket?

Mrs. PAINE. I don't recall specifically seeing the blanket. I certainly recall on the afternoon of the 22d where it had been.

Mr. DULLES. Was there any evidence of any quarreling or any harsh words between Lee Harvey and Marina that evening that you know of?

Mrs. PAINE. No.

Mr. JENNER. Was there a coolness between them?

Mrs. PAINE. He went to bed very early, she stayed up and talked with me some, but there was no coolness that I noticed. He was quite friendly on the lawn as we——

Mr. JENNER. I mean coolness between himself and—between Lee and Marina.

Mrs. PAINE. I didn't notice any such coolness. Rather, they seemed warm, like a couple making up a small spat, I should interject one thing here, too, that I recall as I entered the house and Lee had just come in, I said to him, "Our President is coming to town."

And he said, "Ah, yes," and walked on into the kitchen, which was a common reply from him on anything. I was just excited about this happening, and there was his response. Nothing more was said about it.

Mr. DULLES. I didn't quite catch his answer.

Mrs. PAINE. "Ah, yes," a very common answer.

Mr. JENNER. He gave no more than that laconic answer?

Mrs. PAINE. That is right.

Mr. JENNER. Had there been any discussion between you and Marina that the President was coming into town the next day?

Mrs. PAINE. Yes.

Mr. JENNER. Did she say anything on that subject in the presence of Lee that evening?

Mrs. PAINE. I don't recall anything of that sort.

Mr. JENNER. What time did you have dinner that evening?

Mrs. PAINE. 6 or 6:30, I would guess.

Mr. JENNER. And calling on your recollection, Mrs. Paine, following dinner do you remember any occasion that evening when Lee was out of the house and you didn't see him around the house, and you were conscious of the fact he was not in the house?

Mrs. PAINE. I was not at anytime of the opinion that he was out of the house, conscious of it.

Mr. JENNER. You have no recollection of his being out of the house anytime that evening?

Mrs. PAINE. No.

Mr. DULLES. Did he do any reading that evening—books, papers, anything?

Mrs. PAINE. Not to my recollection.

Mr. JENNER. What were you doing that evening?

Mrs. PAINE. I have tried already to describe that after dinner, and probably after some dishes were done.

Mr. JENNER. Who did the dishes?

Mrs. PAINE. Very likely Marina, it depended on who made the meal. I normally cooked the meal and then she did the dishes or we reversed occasionally. But I have tried to say I was very likely involved in the back bedroom and in the bathroom giving the children a bath, getting them in their pajamas and reading a story for as much as an hour.

Mr. JENNER. That would take as much as an hour?

Mrs. PAINE. That takes as much as an hour.

Mr. JENNER. By this time we are up to approximately 7:30 or 8 o'clock, are we?

Mrs. PAINE. Oh no; we are up to nearly 9 o'clock by now. We eat from 6:30 to after 7, do some dishes, brings it up toward 8, and then put the children to bed.

Mr. JENNER. When you had had your children put to bed and came out of their room, was Lee, had he then by that time retired?

Mrs. PAINE. That is my recollection.

Mr. DULLES. Did you have any words with Marina about the light in the garage? Was that a subject of conversation between you?

Mrs. PAINE. No; we didn't discuss it.

Mr. DULLES. You didn't mention it to her?

Mrs. PAINE. No; I didn't discuss it.

Representative FORD. Did he ever help in the kitchen at all, in any way whatsoever?

Mrs. PAINE. Well, I have said he once did dishes in New Orleans, but that is about all I recall that he did.

Representative FORD. But in Dallas, in your home, he never volunteered?

Mrs. PAINE. No.

Mr. McCLOY. Marina did help around the house?

Mrs. PAINE. She helped a great deal.

Mr. McCLOY. She was a good helper?

Mrs. PAINE. She is a hard worker.

Mr. JENNER. Tell us, the time you came out of the bedroom and put your children to bed when you noticed the light in the garage; fix as well as you can the time of evening.

Mrs. PAINE. I think it was about 9 o'clock.

Mr. JENNER. That is when you noticed the light in the garage, around 9 o'clock after you put your children to bed, and at that time Lee was already retired?

Mrs. PAINE. Yes.

Mr. JENNER. Marina was still up?

Mrs. PAINE. Yes.

Mr. JENNER. How long did she remain up?

Mrs. PAINE. I don't recall that evening from that point on much like any others, with the two of us up, we probably folded some diapers, laundry. Some evening close to that time, either that evening or the one before, we discussed plans for Christmas.

Mr. JENNER. You and Marina?

Mrs. PAINE. Yes. But it was probably the evening before. I was thinking about making a playhouse for the children.

Mr. JENNER. Would you describe Lee's attire when you first saw him on the lawn when you returned that evening?

Mrs. PAINE. I don't recall it.

Mr. JENNER. You have no recollection of that? Did he bring—do you know whether he brought anything with him in the way of paper or wrapper or baggage or this sticky tape, anything of that nature?

Mrs. PAINE. I don't recall seeing anything of that nature.

Mr. JENNER. Did you see any paper, wrapping paper, of the character that you have identified around your home that evening?

Mrs. PAINE. No.

Mr. McCLOY. Can't you recall a little more clearly how he generally was dressed? Did he have a coat on such as I have got on now, or did he have——

Mrs. PAINE. I never saw him in a suit jacket.

Mr. McCLOY. Suit jacket? What was his normal outer wear apparel?

Mrs. PAINE. His normal attire was T-shirt, cotton slacks, sometimes the T-shirt covered by a shirt, flannel or cotton shirt.

Mr. McCLOY. Do you recall whether he had that type of shirt over his T-shirt that night?

Mrs. PAINE. I don't recall.

Mr. McCLOY. You don't recall?

Mr. JENNER. Did he have any kind of a shirt other than a T-shirt on him when you saw him?

Mrs. PAINE. I don't really remember.

Mr. JENNER. I wonder, Mr. Chairman, if despite the fact I haven't reached the next day, if we might excuse Mrs. Paine? She did tell me she had an appointment at 5:30 this evening, and I would like to have her think over more so she can be refreshed in the morning as to this particular evening. And, Mrs. Paine, I would have you trace the first thing in the morning as best as you can recall Lee Harvey Oswald's movements that evening and where he was, to the best that you are able to recall. Would you try to do that for us?

Mrs. PAINE. I think I probably have done the best I can, but I will do it again if you like.

Mr. JENNER. May we have permission to adjourn, Mr. Chairman?

Mr. McCLOY. Very well.

Mr. DULLES. Could I ask just one question? With regard to this sketch of the house, I was interested to know where you would see the light in the garage. Was it from out here?

Mrs. PAINE. This is a doorway into the garage from the kitchen area.

Mr. DULLES. And you saw that light from the kitchen area?

Mrs. PAINE. I think I was probably on my way to the garage anyway, opened the door, there was the light on.

Mr. DULLES. I see. There are no windows or anything. The door was closed and the light would not be visible if you hadn't gone into it?

Mrs. PAINE. It would be visible if it was dark in here.

Mr. DULLES. I understand. Through the door.

Representative FORD. And you spent about a half hour in the garage painting some blocks?

Mrs. PAINE. Yes.

Representative FORD. What part of the garage——

Mrs. PAINE. Close to the doorway here, the entrance, this entrance.

Representative FORD. The entrance going into the——

Mrs. PAINE. The doorway between the garage and the kitchen-dining area. Right here.

Representative FORD. You didn't move around the garage?

Mrs. PAINE. I moved around enough to get some shellac and brush and make a place, a block is this big, to paint.

Representative FORD. Where do you recollect, if you do, the blanket was at this time?

Mrs. PAINE. I don't recollect. It was the next day——

Representative FORD. It was the forepart of the garage on the left-hand side?

Mrs. PAINE. Beyond.

Mr. McCLOY. Does anyone have any further questions?

Mr. JENNER. No questions, Mr. Chairman.

Representative Ford has directed the attention of the witness to the document which is now Exhibit No. 430, and when we reconvene in the morning I will qualify the exhibit.

Mr. McCLOY. Is that all?

We will reconvene at 9 a.m., tomorrow.

(Whereupon, at 5:30 p.m., the President's Commission recessed.)

Friday, March 20, 1964

TESTIMONY OF RUTH HYDE PAINE RESUMED

The President's Commission met at 9:05 a.m. on Friday, March 20, 1964, at 200 Maryland Avenue NE., Washington, D.C.

Present were Chief Justice Earl Warren, Chairman; Senator John Sherman Cooper, Representative Gerald R. Ford, and John J. McCloy, members.

Also present were J. Lee Rankin, general counsel; Albert E. Jenner, Jr., assistant counsel; and Wesley J. Liebeler, assistant counsel.

Senator COOPER. Mrs. Paine, you, I think, yesterday affirmed, made affirmation as to the truthfulness of your testimony?

Mrs. PAINE. Yes, I did.

Senator COOPER. You are still under that affirmation?

Mrs. PAINE. I understand that I am under that affirmation.

Mr. JENNER. May I proceed?

Thank you. Mrs. Paine, just to put you at ease this morning, Mr. Chairman, may I qualify some documents?

The CHAIRMAN. Good morning, gentlemen and ladies. How are you, Mrs. Paine? I am glad to see you this morning.

Mr. JENNER. Mrs. Paine, I show you Commission Exhibit No. 425 which you produced and which you testified was the original of a letter of October 14, 1963, to your mother, part of which you read at large in the record. Is that document in your handwriting entirely?

Mrs. PAINE. Yes; it is.

Mr. JENNER. You testified it is a letter from you to your mother?

Mrs. PAINE. That is right.

Mr. JENNER. Did you dispatch the letter?

Mrs. PAINE. I did.

Mr. JENNER. In view of that fact would you explain for the record how you came into possession of the letter since you sent it to your mother?

Mrs. PAINE. She gave it to me a few days ago.

Mr. JENNER. Is the document now in the same condition it was when you mailed it to your mother?

Mrs. PAINE. Yes; it is. You have the first page of two. The other page not being relative to this case.

Mr. JENNER. In other words, that there be no question about it, do you have the other page?

Mrs. PAINE. I have the other page.

Mr. JENNER. May I have it?

Mrs. PAINE. The other page, of course, contains my signature.

Mr. JENNER. Yes. May the record be amended to show that Commission Exhibit No. ——.

Mrs. PAINE. I'd rather not have that part of it——

Mr. JENNER. It is not going into the record, Mrs. Paine. Just be patient. Commission Exhibit 425 consists of two pages, that is two sheets. The pages are numbered from one through four. Would you look at the page numbered 4? There is a signature appearing at the bottom of it. Is that your signature?

Mrs. PAINE. Yes; it is.

Mr. JENNER. Mr. Chairman, may I postpone the offer of this document in evidence until I do read the second page, which the witness has now produced. You see, Mrs. Paine, that it may be important to the Commission to have the entire letter which would indicate the context in which the statements that are relevant were made.

You testified yesterday with regard to the draft of what appeared to be a letter that Mr. Oswald, Lee Harvey Oswald, was to send. It was thought he might send it to someone. I hand you a picture of a letter in longhand which has been identified as Commission Exhibit 103. Would you look at that please? Do you recognize that handwriting?

Mrs. PAINE. No. This is the only time I saw—this is the only handwriting of his I have seen.

Mr. JENNER. You can't identify the document as such, that is, are you familiar enough with his handwriting——

Mrs. PAINE. To know that this is his handwriting?

Mr. JENNER. To identify whether that is or is not his handwriting.

Mrs. PAINE. No.

Mr. JENNER. Have you ever seen that Document before?

Mrs. PAINE. Yes; I have.

Mr. JENNER. When did you first see it?

Mrs. PAINE. I first saw that on Saturday, the 9th of November. I don't believe I looked to see what it said until the morning of the 10th.

Mr. JENNER. I see. Now, do you recognize it, however, as a picture of the document that you did see on the 9th of November, or did you say 10th?

Mrs. PAINE. I'll say 10th, yes; it is that document.

Senator COOPER. What is the answer?

Mrs. PAINE. It is that document.

Mr. JENNER. And I take it from your testimony that after you had seen the original of this document, this document happens to be a photo, you saw a typed transcript of this document or substantially this document?

Mrs. PAINE. I never saw a typed transcript.

Mr. JENNER. You did not?

Mrs. PAINE. No.

Mr. JENNER. Mrs. Paine, you testified yesterday that Lee Harvey Oswald asked you if he could use your typewriter?

Mrs. PAINE. That is right.

Mr. JENNER. And he did proceed to use the typewriter to type a letter or at least some document?

Mrs. PAINE. Yes.

Mr. JENNER. And that you saw a document folded in half and one portion of it arrested your attention?

Mrs. PAINE. Yes; that is correct.

Mr. JENNER. Was the document that arrested your attention the typed document or was it the document that is before you?

Mrs. PAINE. I never saw the typed document. It was the document that is before me, which I take to be a rough draft of what he typed.

Mr. JENNER. And you said you made a duplicate of the document. Did you make a duplicate in longhand or on your typewriter?

Mrs. PAINE. I made a duplicate in longhand.

Mr. JENNER. But you do have a present recollection that this, Commission Exhibit No. 103 for identification, is the document which you saw in your home on your desk secretary?

Mrs. PAINE. That is right.

Mr. JENNER. Mr. Chairman, I offer in evidence as Commission Exhibit No. 103 the document—oh, it is already in evidence. I withdraw that offer.

Senator COOPER. It is in evidence.

Mr. JENNER. Mr. Redlich informs me, Mr. Chairman, that the document has already been admitted in evidence.

Now, would you follow me as I go through these? There has been marked as Commission's Exhibit 430, which is the mark at the moment for identification, what purports to be a floor plan outline of the Paine home at 2515 Fifth Street, Irving, Tex., and the witness made reference to that yesterday close to the close of her testimony yesterday afternoon. Directing your attention to that exhibit, is that an accurate floor plan outline of your home at 2515 Fifth Street, Irving, Tex.?

Mrs. PAINE. It is an approximately accurate floor plan.

Mr. JENNER. And is it properly entitled, that is, are the rooms and sections of the home properly entitled?

Mrs. PAINE. Yes; they are.

Mr. JENNER. And does it accurately reflect the door openings, the hallways in your home and the garage?

Mrs. PAINE. Yes; it is perfectly accurate.

Mr. JENNER. I think one thing only needs some explanation. In the upper left-hand corner of the floor plan outline, there is a square space which has no lettering to identify that space. It is the area immediately to the left of the—of what is designated as kitchen-dining area.

Mrs. PAINE. Yes. That space is all one room with that which is designated kitchen-dining area. That is one large room.

Mr. JENNER. I see. So that even though on the floor plan outline the words "kitchen-dining area" appear in the right half of that space, that lettering and wording is to apply to all the space?

Mrs. PAINE. That is right.

Mr. JENNER. And the driveway about which you testified is that portion of the ground outline which has the circle with the figure "8" and an arrow, is that right?

Mrs. PAINE. That is the driveway.

Mr. JENNER. And the driveway is where the car was parked because the garage always had too many things in it to get your car in?

Mrs. PAINE. That is right.

Mr. JENNER. Referring to Commission Exhibit No. 431 for identification, is that a front view of your home?

Mrs. PAINE. Yes; it is.

Mr. JENNER. Were you present when the picture was taken?

Mrs. PAINE. Yes; I was.

Mr. JENNER. Commission Exhibit 432, is that a rear view of your home?

Mrs. PAINE. Yes; it is.

Mr. JENNER. Were you present when that was taken?

Mrs. PAINE. Probably. I don't recall.

Mr. JENNER. But that is an accurate depiction?

Mrs. PAINE. Yes.

Mr. JENNER. Of the rear of your home?

Mrs. PAINE. It is certainly accurate.

Mr. JENNER. And showing some of your yard. The next Exhibit 433, is that a view of the east side of your home?

Mrs. PAINE. East and north; yes.

Mr. JENNER. And were you present when that was taken?

Mrs. PAINE. I wouldn't know.

Mr. JENNER. But it is an accurate depiction of that area of your home?

Mrs. PAINE. Yes.

Mr. JENNER. Commission Exhibit 434, is that a view of the west side of your home?

Mrs. PAINE. West and north.

Mr. JENNER. Were you present when that was taken?

Mrs. PAINE. I don't recall.

Mr. JENNER. Despite that, is it accurate?

Mrs. PAINE. It is perfectly accurate.

Mr. JENNER. Now, is Commission Exhibit 435 a view inside your home looking through the door leading to the garage from your kitchen?

Mrs. PAINE. Yes; it is.

Mr. JENNER. And were you present when that was taken?

Mrs. PAINE. Yes; I was

Mr. JENNER. And is it accurate?

Mrs. PAINE. Yes; it is.

Mr. JENNER. Commission Exhibit 436, is that a picture of the doorway area leading to the backyard of your home?

Mrs. PAINE. Yes; it is.

Mr. JENNER. Were you present when that was taken?

Mrs. PAINE. Yes; I was.

Mr. JENNER. Is it accurate?

Mrs. PAINE. Yes.

Mr. JENNER. Commission Exhibit 437, is that the kitchen area in your home?

Mrs. PAINE. Yes; it is.

Mr. JENNER. Now, were you present when that was taken?

Mrs. PAINE. Yes; I was.

Mr. JENNER. And is it accurate?

Mrs. PAINE. Yes.

Mr. JENNER. Returning now to the floor plan exhibit, Commission Exhibit 430, is Commission Exhibit 437, which is the kitchen area in your home, that portion of Commission Exhibit 430 which is lettered "kitchen-dining area."

Mrs. PAINE. It is a picture of that portion.

Mr. JENNER. Of that portion, rather than the portion to the left which is unlettered?

Mrs. PAINE. That is right.

Mr. JENNER. The garage interior we identified yesterday. By the way, have you ever been in the Randle home?

Mrs. PAINE. Yes; I have.

Mr. JENNER. Have you been there often enough to identify a floor plan and pictures of the Randle home?

Mrs. PAINE. Yes. I have been there perhaps once or twice.

Mr. McCLOY. Do you intend to call Mrs. Randle?

Mr. JENNER. Unfortunately Mrs. Randle has already testified and Mr. Ball when he questioned her did not have this exhibit. It wasn't in existence.

I show you a page marked Commission Exhibit No. 441 entitled "Randle Home, 2439 West Fifth Street, Irving, Tex.," purporting to be a floor plan outline of the Randle home. You have been in the Randle home?

Mrs. PAINE. Yes; I have.

Mr. JENNER. On several occasions?

Mrs. PAINE. Two or three; yes.

Mr. JENNER. And are you familiar with the general area of the Randle home?

Mrs. PAINE. Yes.

Mr. JENNER. Surrounding the Randle home?

Mrs. PAINE. Indeed; I am.

Mr. JENNER. And looking at Commission Exhibit 441, is that an accurate floor plan outline and general community outline of the Randle home?

Mrs. PAINE. Yes; I would say it is.

Mr. JENNER. I show you Commission Exhibit 442. Is that an accurate and true and correct photograph showing the corner view of the Randle home?

Mrs. PAINE. Yes; it is.

Mr. JENNER. Exhibit 443, is that an accurate photograph of a portion of the kitchen portion, the front of the kitchen window of the Randle home?

Mrs. PAINE. I believe so.

Mr. JENNER. Does your recollection serve you——

Mrs. PAINE. I am trying to see if I know which is west and north there and I am not certain.

Mr. JENNER. Let us return to the floor plan.

Mrs. PAINE. This would be, yes, that is what I thought. This is looking then west.

Mr. JENNER. You have now oriented yourself. And is it an accurate picture of the front of the kitchen?

Mrs. PAINE. Yes.

Senator COOPER. Which exhibit are you referring to now?

Mr. JENNER. The front of the Randle home No. 443. The next number, 444, is that an accurate photograph of the area of the Randle home showing a veiw from the field from the Randle's kitchen window?

Mrs. PAINE. That is accurate.

Mr. JENNER. Across the street?

Mrs. PAINE. Correct.

Mr. JENNER. Commission Exhibit 445, is that an accurate photograph of the kitchen of the Randle home looking at the direction of the carport from the Randle home?

Mrs. PAINE. That is an accurate picture showing the door opening to the carport; yes.

Mr. JENNER. And the kitchen portion of the Randle home facing on the carport?

Mrs. PAINE. Correct.

Mr. JENNER. Have you ever been in the carport area of the Randle home?

Mrs. PAINE. Yes; I have.

Mr. JENNER. And is Commission Exhibit 446 a view of a portion of the carport area of the Randle home?

Mrs. PAINE. It looks like it.

Mr. JENNER. Now 447 is a photograph taken from the street looking toward the Randle home, is that right?

Mrs. PAINE. Yes.

Mr. JENNER. And it is the west side of the Randle house?

Mrs. PAINE. Yes.

Mr. JENNER. Showing that carport area?

Mrs. PAINE. Yes.

Mr. JENNER. And it is accurate, isn't it?

Mrs. PAINE. It is accurate.

Mr. JENNER. Commission Exhibit 438, is that an accurate photograph of the area of Irving Street showing not only the Randle house but also your home?

Mrs. PAINE. Yes; that is accurate.

Mr. JENNER. And is Commission Exhibit 448——

Senator COOPER. What was the number of the photograph which you just referred to?

Mr. JENNER. 438. 438 is view looking northeast showing the Paine home at the left and the Randle home at the far right. Directing your attention to Commission Exhibit 448, is that an accurate photograph showing a view of the Randle home looking West Fifth Street?

Mrs. PAINE. Yes.

Mr. JENNER. Is Commission Exhibit 438 an accurate photograph showing a view looking west along Fifth Street to your home?

Mrs. PAINE. Yes; it is.

Mr. JENNER. And is the arrow that appears on that photograph—does that point to your home?

Mrs. PAINE. Yes.

Mr. JENNER. Is Commission Exhibit No. 450, which I now show you, an accurate photograph of the intersection of Westbrook Drive and West Fifth Street viewed from immediately outside the Randle kitchen window?

Mrs. PAINE. It looks to be exactly that.

Mr. JENNER. I now show you Commission Exhibit No. 440 entitled "Paine and Randle homes, Irving, Tex." which purports to be, and I believe is, a scale drawing of the area in Irving, Tex., along West Fifth Street and Westbrook Drive, in which your home at 2515 West Fifth Street is shown in outline, and the location and form of the Randle home down the street and on the corner is likewise shown.

Mrs. PAINE. Yes.

Mr. JENNER. Is that accurate?

Mrs. PAINE. That is accurate.

Senator COOPER. Are you going to make part of the record these exhibits which she has identified?

Mr. JENNER. Yes; I am about to offer these and I would ask Mr. Redlich if he would assemble the exhibit numbers so I can make the offer, please.

Mrs. Paine, now that you have had a rest over night, we would like to return to the late afternoon and the evening of November 21. Did Lee Harvey Oswald come to Irving, Tex., at anytime that day?

Mrs. PAINE. He came some time shortly before 5:30 in the evening on the 21st.

Mr. JENNER. Had either you or Marina, I limit it to you first, had you had any notice or intimation whatsoever that Lee Harvey Oswald would appear on that day?

Mrs. PAINE. Absolutely none.

Mr. JENNER. And his appearance was a complete surprise to you?

Mrs. PAINE. That is correct.

Mr. JENNER. Did anything occur during the day or during that week up to the time that you saw Lee Harvey Oswald that afternoon that impressed you or led you to believe that Marina had any notion whatsoever that her husband would or might appear at your home on that day?

Mrs. PAINE. Nothing. I rather had the contrary impressions.

Mr. JENNER. Now, what was your first notice, what was the circumstances that brought your attention to the fact that Lee Harvey Oswald was in Irving, Tex., that afternoon.

Mrs. PAINE. I arrived home from the grocery store in my car and saw he was on the front lawn at my house.

Mr. JENNER. You had had no word whatsoever from anybody prior to that moment?

Mrs. PAINE. No word whatsoever.

Mr. JENNER. Now where was he? And we may use the exhibits we have just identified. Mr. Chairman, I offer in evidence the photographs and the floor plans and the area outlines the witness has just identified and testified about as they are Commission Exhibit Nos. 429 through 448 both inclusive, and 450 and 452.

Senator COOPER. The exhibits offered will be received in evidence.

(Commission Exhibits Nos. 429 through 448 both inclusive, and 450 and 452 were received in evidence.)

The CHAIRMAN. Senator Cooper, at this time I am obliged to leave for our all-day conference on Friday at the Supreme Court, and I may be back later in the day, but if I don't, you continue, of course.

Senator COOPER. I will this morning. If I can't be here this afternoon, whom do you want to preside?

The CHAIRMAN. Congressman Ford, would you be here this afternoon at all?

Representative FORD. Unfortunately Mr. McCloy and I have to go to a conference out of town.

The CHAIRMAN. You are both going out of town, aren't you?

Senator COOPER. I can go and come back if it is necessary.

The CHAIRMAN. I will try to be here myself. Will Mr. Dulles be here?

Mr. McCLOY. He is out of town.

The CHAIRMAN. If you should not finish, Mr. Jenner, will you phone me at the Court and I will try to suspend my own conference over there and come over.

Senator COOPER. I will be here anyway all morning and will try to come back this afternoon.

The CHAIRMAN. Thank you very much. Mrs. Paine, I want to thank you for coming and for being so patient with our long questioning.

Mrs. PAINE. I am glad to do what I can.

The CHAIRMAN. You know that it is necessary.

Mrs. PAINE. Indeed.

The CHAIRMAN. Thank you very much.

Mr. JENNER. You might use the ruler, and I have set the floor plan and the area plan of your home, Mrs. Paine, Exhibit 430, on the blackboard. As you testify, it might be helpful to point to those areas. Now in which direction were you coming?

Mrs. PAINE. I was coming from the east.

Mr. JENNER. From the east?

Mrs. PAINE. Along West Fifth.

Mr. JENNER. You were going west. Your home is on the right-hand side.

Mrs. PAINE. That is right.

Mr. JENNER. When did you first sight, where were you when you first saw Lee in your courtyard?

Mrs. PAINE. Just past the corner of Westbrook and Fifth.

Mr. JENNER. That area is open from that point to your home; is it?

Mrs. PAINE. The area of the front yard; yes.

Mr. JENNER. Your home is well set back from the street or sidewalk?

Mrs. PAINE. Moderately set back.

Mr. JENNER. What would you judge that distance to be?

Mrs. PAINE. Two car lengths from the opening of the garage to the sidewalk.

Mr. JENNER. Now where was Lee Oswald when you first saw him?

Mrs. PAINE. He was on the grass just to the east of the driveway.

Mr. JENNER. Near the driveway just to the east, but he was out in front of your home?

Mrs. PAINE. That is correct.

Mr. JENNER. What did you do then? You proceeded down the street?

Mrs. PAINE. I parked my car, yes; parked my car in its usual position in the driveway.

Mr. JENNER. In your driveway?

Mrs. PAINE. Yes.

Mr. JENNER. Up close to the garage opening?

Mrs. PAINE. Yes.

Mr. JENNER. And that left you then, you were on the left side or the driving side of your automobile. You got out, did you?

Mrs. PAINE. Yes.

Mr. JENNER. Which way? Did you get out to your left or did you swing across the seat and get out at the right hand door?

Mrs. PAINE. I got out on the driver's side, on the left.

Mr. JENNER. Then what did you do? First tell us what you did. Did you go into your home directly? Did you walk around?

Mrs. PAINE. No. I greeted Lee and Marina, who were both on the front lawn.

Mr. JENNER. Was their daughter June out in front as well?

Mrs. PAINE. Their daughter June was out in front. It was warm. Lee was playing with June.

Mr. JENNER. How was he attired?

Mrs. PAINE. I don't recall specifically.

Mr. JENNER. You said that he normally wore a T-shirt.

Mrs. PAINE. Yes.

Mr. JENNER. Was he in a T-shirt or shirt?

Mrs. PAINE. I'd be fairly certain he didn't have a jacket on, but that whatever it was was tucked in.

Mr. JENNER. Do you remember the color of his trousers?

Mrs. PAINE. No.

Mr. JENNER. Now at that point you were surprised to see him?

Mrs. PAINE. I was.

Mr. JENNER. What did you say to him?

Mrs. PAINE. I don't recall.

Mr. JENNER. But you do recall greeting him?

Mrs. PAINE. Yes.

Mr. JENNER. You don't recall that you evidenced any surprise that he was there?

Mrs. PAINE. Oh, I think I did.

Mr. JENNER. Had there ever been an occasion prior thereto that he had appeared at your home without prior notice to you and permission from you for him to appear?

Mrs. PAINE. There had been no such occasion. He had always asked permission prior to coming.

Mr. JENNER. And there never had been an exception to that up to this moment?

Mrs. PAINE. No exception.

Mr. JENNER. May we have the time again? You say it was late in the afternoon, but can you fix the time a little more?

Mrs. PAINE. It was getting on toward 5:30.

Mr. JENNER. Did you tarry and talk with Lee and Marina?

Mrs. PAINE. I remember only that Marina and I were still on the grass at the entryway to the house when she spoke of her embarrassment to me in an aside, that is to say, not in Lee's hearing, that she was sorry he hadn't called ahead and asked if that was all right. And I said "Why, that is all right."

Mr. JENNER. Nothing was said by her as to why he had come out?

Mrs. PAINE. Nothing.

Mr. JENNER. And nothing was——

Mrs. PAINE. She was clearly surprised also.

Mr. JENNER. Yes. You made no inquiry of her I take it then of any explanation made by Lee Oswald as to why he had come out unannounced and unexpectedly?

Mrs. PAINE. No.

Mr. JENNER. At least not as of that moment.

Mrs. PAINE. No.

Mr. JENNER. Now when you had your aside with Marina, where was Lee Oswald?

Mrs. PAINE. On the grass near the tree playing with June as closely as I can remember.

Mr. JENNER. How long did you and Marina remain in conversation at that place, position?

Mrs. PAINE. Less than a minute.

Mr. JENNER. Then what did you do?

Mrs. PAINE. I can only reconstruct it.

Mr. JENNER. That is all I am asking you to do.

Mrs. PAINE. I must have gotten groceries from the car.

Mr. JENNER. You mean reconstruct in the sense of rationalizing?

Mrs. PAINE. Yes.

Mr. JENNER. I wish you would give me first your recollection.

Mrs. PAINE. I am certain of going into the house, and I recall standing just inside the doorway.

Mr. JENNER. Of your home?

Mrs. PAINE. Of my home.

Mr. JENNER. But inside the home?

Mrs. PAINE. But inside now.

Mr. JENNER. Which way were you facing when you were standing inside the doorway?

Mrs. PAINE. I was facing partly toward the door, toward the loud speaker. I was facing this way.

Mr. JENNER. Why were you facing outwardly?

Mrs. PAINE. I believe I turned. I was coming in. I believe I turned to speak to Lee as he came in.

Mr. JENNER. Lee followed you in the house?

Mrs. PAINE. Yes.

Mr. JENNER. And did Marina come in?

Mrs. PAINE. I don't recall whether she was already in or still out.

Mr. JENNER. But you do have a recollection that Lee followed you into your home.

Mrs. PAINE. And I recall very clearly the position I was in in the room and the position he was in.

Mr. JENNER. Tell us.

Mrs. PAINE. I was turned part way toward the door. He was coming in, having just entered the door and in front of this loud speaker to which I refer.

Mr. JENNER. What was the loud speaker?

Mrs. PAINE. The loud speaker is part of the Hi-Fi set. It stands—it is a big thing.

Mr. JENNER. Did something occur at that moment?

Mrs. PAINE. And it was at that time that I said to him "Our President is coming to town." I believe I said it in Russian, our President is coming to town in Russian.

Mr. JENNER. And you gave us his response yesterday but you might do it again.

Mrs. PAINE. He said "Uh, yeah" and brushed on by me, walked on past.

Mr. JENNER. Did he have an attitude of indifference?

Mrs. PAINE. It was clearly both indifference and not wanting to go on and talk, because he moved away from me on into the kitchen.

Mr. JENNER. He went into your kitchen. What did you do?

Mrs. PAINE. I don't recall specifically.

Mr. JENNER. We are anxious to follow minute by minute, to the extent possible, all the movements of which you had any knowledge of Lee Oswald on this late afternoon and throughout the evening. Did Lee Oswald remain in your presence right at this time when you entered the house? If so, how long? You had this short conversation. Did he leave your presence then and go to some other part of your home?

Mrs. PAINE. He might have gone to some other part of the home. He didn't leave the house to my recollection.

Mr. JENNER. I didn't mean to imply that, only whether he remained in the general area in which you were in your home?

Mrs. PAINE. I don't recall.

Mr. JENNER. Did he pass from your sight?

Mrs. PAINE. Probably.

Mr. JENNER. Before you guess about it, give us your best recollection.

Senator COOPER. Tell what you remember.

Mr. MCCLOY. Yes; just in your own words tell us what your best recollection of this afternoon was without second to second sequence.

Mrs. PAINE. Clearly just having come from the grocery store I put the bags down in the kitchen and unpacked them, put them away, started supper.

Mr. JENNER. Did you have any sense that Lee Oswald was in and about the inside of the house while you were doing this?

Mrs. PAINE. Yes.

Mr. JENNER. Do you have a recollection that he did not go out into the yard during this period?

Mrs. PAINE. I don't recall. If he did, it would have been the back. It would have been unusual for him to go in the front yard.

Mr. JENNER. Now you were preparing your dinner in your kitchen, were you not?

Mrs. PAINE. Yes.

Mr. JENNER. And does the entrance to your garage—is there an entrance to your garage opening from your kitchen into the garage?

Mrs. PAINE. There is an entrance to the garage from the kitchen; yes.

Mr. JENNER. And one of the exhibits we qualified this morning is a picture of that area of your home, is it not?

Mrs. PAINE. Yes.

Mr. JENNER. Your answer was yes?

Mrs. PAINE. That is right.

Mr. JENNER. At anytime while you were preparing dinner was Lee Oswald in the garage?

Mrs. PAINE. No.

Mr. JENNER. And you were aware of that fact, were you?

Mrs. PAINE. That is my best recollection that he was not in the garage while I was preparing dinner.

Mr. JENNER. Do you know where he was while you were preparing dinner?

Mrs. PAINE. I don't recall specifically.

Mr. JENNER. Did you have occasion to look into your garage area at anytime during the period you were preparing dinner?

Mrs. PAINE. Not that I recall.

Mr. JENNER. Where was Marina during the period you were preparing dinner?

Mrs. PAINE. I'd have to guess.

Senator COOPER. Just tell what you know.

Mr. JENNER. Tell what you know first.

Mrs. PAINE. I don't recall specifically.

Mr. JENNER. Do you have a recollection with respect to whether she was inside the house or outside the house?

Mrs. PAINE. I recall that she was inside the house.

Mr. JENNER. And where was the child June with respect to whether she was inside or outside the house?

Mrs. PAINE. She was inside.

Mr. JENNER. Having located Marina and the Oswald daughter inside your home, does that refresh your recollection as to whether Lee was also inside the house?

Mrs. PAINE. As far as I remember, he was also inside the house.

Mr. JENNER. Was he playing with his daughter?

Mrs. PAINE. I don't recall.

Mr. JENNER. How long did it take you to prepare dinner?

Mrs. PAINE. Probably half an hour.

Mr. JENNER. I am unaware of the shades of evening and night in Texas. By the time you had completed dinner had night fallen or was it still light?

Mrs. PAINE. I don't recall.

Mr. JENNER. What time does nightfall come in Texas in November, late November?

Mrs. PAINE. I would say between 7 and 7:30.

Mr. JENNER. I shouldn't have been as broad as I was. I meant to locate it in Irving, Tex., rather than Texas generally. About 7:30?

Mrs. PAINE. Between 7 and 7:30. I don't know exactly.

Mr. JENNER. When did you sit down for dinner?

Mrs. PAINE. I suppose around 6:30.

Mr. JENNER. Is that your best recollection?

Mrs. PAINE. I don't recall specifically.

Mr. JENNER. Was it still light outside, natural light?

Mrs. PAINE. Yes.

Mr. JENNER. Did Lee Oswald join you for dinner?

Mrs. PAINE. Yes; he did.

Mr. JENNER. And how long did dinner take?

Mrs. PAINE. Perhaps half an hour.

Mr. JENNER. Did he remain in your presence during all of the dinner period?

Mrs. PAINE. Either there or in the living room.

Mr. JENNER. At anytime during the dinner period, did Lee Oswald leave your home?

Mrs. PAINE. No.

Mr. JENNER. You have a firm recollection of that?

Mrs. PAINE. Yes.

Mr. JENNER. Did Marina?

Mrs. PAINE. No.

Mr. JENNER. At anytime during that period did Lee Oswald enter the garage area?

Mrs. PAINE. No.

Mr. JENNER. Did Marina?

Mrs. PAINE. Not to my recollection.

Mr. JENNER. Did you?

Mrs. PAINE. The deepfreeze is in the garage. I don't recall having gone, but I go all the time for goods for the baby, for my little boy.

Mr. JENNER. And did you use anything from the deepfreeze normally, in connection with the preparation of an evening meal?

Mrs. PAINE. I could have gone out then too.

Mr. JENNER. Though you don't recall it specifically, it is possible that you went into the garage.

Mrs. PAINE. It is possible.

Mr. JENNER. Garage area.

Senator COOPER. But you don't remember?

Mrs. PAINE. I don't remember. This is something I do as habit.

Mr. JENNER. It is so much habit that you don't single it out?

Mrs. PAINE. No.

Mr. JENNER. In any event, if you entered the garage, it was pursuant to a normal practice of preparing dinner and not because you were seeking to look for something out of the ordinary?

Mrs. PAINE. That is right.

Mr. JENNER. Or that your attention was arrested by something out of the ordinary?

Mrs. PAINE. That is right.

Mr. JENNER. After the dinner hour or half hour, whatever it took, what did you do? Let's take say the 1-hour period following your dinner?

Mrs. PAINE. I was busy putting my children to bed.

Mr. JENNER. Where were you located during that period of time?

Mrs. PAINE. I normally read them a story in the bedroom which is the back bedroom on the north side.

Senator COOPER. Did you do it that evening?

Mrs. PAINE. Yes.

Senator COOPER. Not normally but do you remember that you did it?

Mrs. PAINE. I am certain I read them a story.

Senator COOPER. What?

Mrs. PAINE. I am certain I read them a story. Whether they also had a bath that night I can't remember.

Mr. JENNER. Now being in your children's bedroom, which I take it was also your bedroom——

Mrs. PAINE. Yes.

Mr. JENNER. That would be the rear portion of your home at the corner?

Mrs. PAINE. Yes.

Mr. JENNER. When you were in that room, what can you see with respect to other portions of your home?

Mrs. PAINE. The view from the bedroom door.

Mr. JENNER. Looking into what?

Mrs. PAINE. Looking west looks into the kitchen-dining area right past the doorway entrance to the garage.

Mr. JENNER. Can you see into the living room area of your home?

Mrs. PAINE. From that doorway you can; yes.

Mr. JENNER. If you stand in the doorway, I take it you can do so.

Mrs. PAINE. But sitting on the bed reading a story; no.

Mr. JENNER. But if you stood in the middle of the room and looked out that doorway from your bedroom, you would look into the kitchen area, not into the living room area?

Mrs. PAINE. Yes.

Mr. JENNER. How long did you remain in your bedroom putting your children to bed?

Mrs. PAINE. That process can take as much as an hour and often does.

Mr. JENNER. Give us your very best recollection of how long it took this evening?

Mrs. PAINE. I don't recall specifically how long.

Mr. JENNER. Is it your recollection that you pursued your normal course in getting them to bed. You read a story, I take it, did you?

Mrs. PAINE. Yes.

Mr. JENNER. And you undressed the children and placed them in the crib or bed and you say that normally takes approximately an hour?

Mrs. PAINE. Yes.

Mr. JENNER. And you remained in the bedroom during all of that 1 hour period?

Mrs. PAINE. Well, I wouldn't be certain of that; no. I also prepare a bottle which involves going to the kitchen, and heating milk. I also chase my children. They don't always just stay in the bedroom.

Mr. JENNER. Did you see Lee Harvey Oswald either in or about your home from time to time during this hour period that you were preparing your children for sleep that evening?

Mrs. PAINE. I don't recall specifically except that I was aware he was in the home.

Senator COOPER. How would you be aware he was in the home?

Mrs. PAINE. I would have noticed it if he had gone out the door it seems to me, out the front door. One can easily hear, and that would be an unusual thing.

Mr. JENNER. Why would it be unusual?

Mrs. PAINE. Well, he never did go out the front door in the evening.

Mr. JENNER. Once he entered your home his normal practice was to stay inside?

Mrs. PAINE. Was to turn on the television set and sit.

Mr. JENNER. Did he turn on the television set?

Mrs. PAINE. I don't believe he watched television that evening.

Mr. JENNER. Could you tell us of any awareness on your part of his presence in the home, that is you were definitely conscious that he remained inside the house?

Mrs. PAINE. Yes.

Mr. JENNER. And was not out in the yard?

Senator COOPER. How would you know that?

Mrs. PAINE. It is a small house. You can hear if the front door or the back door opens. But I can't be absolutely certain.

Senator COOPER. Is what you are saying that you don't remember, or rather that you don't remember that the front door or the back door did open?

Mrs. PAINE. That is right. I am also saying there is very little about that evening that stood out as unusual. I have tried to say what I could think of that did stand out as unusual. I think the rest melds together with other evenings which were similar.

Senator COOPER. I don't want to interrupt you but I think she has got to tell what she remembers that evening.

Mr. McCLOY. Yes. I think without the meticulous minute by minute, just say what it is.

Senator COOPER. If you don't remember, you don't remember.

Mrs. PAINE. I am sorry.

Mr. McCLOY. You can't break it down into sequence that far back?

Senator COOPER. Just tell what you remember.

Mr. JENNER. Go ahead and tell us, Mrs. Paine, the course of events that evening, with particular reference to what we are interested in, what Lee Oswald did and where he was during the course of that evening.

Mrs. PAINE. I have already said that after I had my children in bed, I went to the garage to work.

Mr. JENNER. Was it now nighttime?

Mrs. PAINE. It was now dark, I recall about 9 o'clock. I noticed that the light was on.

Mr. JENNER. Was the door to the garage open?

Mrs. PAINE. No; it was closed.

Mr. JENNER. It was closed. And you noticed the light on when you opened the door.

Mrs. PAINE. Yes.

Mr. JENNER. Had the light been on at anytime to your knowledge prior to that?

Mrs. PAINE. Not that evening; no.

Mr. JENNER. When entering and leaving the garage during the course of your preparing dinner, to your recollection, was there any light on at that time?

Mrs. PAINE. No.

Mr. JENNER. You didn't turn the light on at anytime up to this moment of which you speak?

Mrs. PAINE. No.

Senator COOPER. Had you been in the garage that evening before the time that you found the light on?

Mrs. PAINE. If I had only in this course of habit which also included if it was dark, flipping the switch on and flipping it off.

Senator COOPER. You don't remember if you did that or not before.

Mrs. PAINE. Specifically, no.

Mr. McCLOY. She said she might have been.

Mr. JENNER. Is that a hand switch?

Mrs. PAINE. Yes.

Mr. JENNER. You must trip it. Where is the switch located, in the kitchen or in the garage?

Mrs. PAINE. The switch is in the garage.

Mr. JENNER. Mr. Chairman, the witness has before her Commission Exhibit 435, which is a picture of her home, looking through the door leading to the garage from the kitchen. Is the light switch shown in that picture?

Mrs. PAINE. No; it is not.

Mr. JENNER. And why is it not shown?

Mrs. PAINE. The light switch that turns on the light in the garage is on the interior of the garage approximately through the wall from the switch you see in the picture, which lights the kitchen, or the dining area overhead light.

Mr. JENNER. And the switch that is shown in the picture, is it to the right of the doorjamb?

Mrs. PAINE. That is right.

Mr. JENNER. And rather high?

Mrs. PAINE. Yes.

Mr. JENNER. Placed high, and on the picture it is shown as having, oh, is that a white plastic plate?

Mrs. PAINE. It is exactly.

Mr. JENNER. And the switch that lights the garage light, is directly opposite on the other side of the wall inside the garage?

Mrs. PAINE. That is my recollection; yes.

Mr. JENNER. Now directing your attention to Commission Exhibit 429, that is a picture, is it not, of the garage interior of your home taken from the outlet door of the garage and looking back toward the kitchen?

Mrs. PAINE. Yes.

Mr. JENNER. Is that correct? And does that show the doorway from the garage into your kitchen?

Mrs. PAINE. Yes.

Mr. JENNER. In other words, the opposite side of the wall, which is shown in Commission Exhibit 435?

Mrs. PAINE. Yes.

Mr. JENNER. And are you able to locate the light switch on Commission Exhibit 429 which is the garage interior exhibit? That is, can you see the switch?

Mrs. PAINE. No; I am not certain I can. This is something else.

Mr. JENNER. I point out to you the configuration which is halfway down the garage doorjamb outline.

Mrs. PAINE. Right next to the top surface of the deepfreeze.

Mr. JENNER. Yes. Is that the light switch?

Mrs. PAINE. I thought it was higher.

Senator COOPER. You know there is a light switch there, don't you?

Mr. McCLOY. There is a light switch there.

Mrs. PAINE. I know I don't pull the string which is there clearly in the picture.

Mr. JENNER. You step down into the garage do you, or is it at the kitchen floor level?

Mrs. PAINE. Are you still asking?

Mr. JENNER. Yes.

Mrs. PAINE. No; you don't step down, perhaps 3 inches all together.

Mr. JENNER. The floor of the garage and the floor of the kitchen are at a level?

Mrs. PAINE. Approximately at a level.

Mr. JENNER. Why did you enter the garage on that occasion?

Mrs. PAINE. I was about to lacquer some children's large blocks, playing blocks.

Mr. JENNER. These are blocks that you had cut at some other time?

Mrs. PAINE. I had cut them on the saw in the garage; yes; previously.

Mr. JENNER. Proceed.

Representative FORD. Mr. Jenner, may I ask a question there?

Mr. JENNER. Yes.

Representative FORD. Some people have a habit of turning lights on and off again regularly. Others are a little careless about it. Would you describe your attitude in this regard?

Mrs. PAINE. I am definitely a person with the habit of turning them off.

Representative FORD. This is a trait that you have?

Mrs. PAINE. Yes.

Representative FORD. Now, if you were to go out from the kitchen to the garage, is it easy for you as you go out the door to turn the light on?

Mrs. PAINE. And off; yes.

Representative FORD. It is very simple for you to do so?

Mrs. PAINE. Yes.

Representative FORD. Both going out and coming in?

Mrs. PAINE. Yes.

Representative FORD. And as you go out on your right or left?

Mrs. PAINE. It is on my left as I go out of the garage.

Representative FORD. And as you come in from the garage to the kitchen it is on your right.

Mrs. PAINE. As you come into the garage from the kitchen——

Mr. McCLOY. When you are going out to the garage, on which side is it?

Mrs. PAINE. It is on my right.

Mr. McCLOY. On your right. Coming out from the garage to the kitchen it is on your left?

Mrs. PAINE. That is what he said.

Mr. McCLOY. You said it just the opposite, I think.

Representative FORD. I thought I asked the question and she responded in the reverse.

Mr. McCLOY. Maybe.

Representative FORD. And it surprised me a little bit. The record may show two different responses there.

Mr. JENNER. Could we recover that now?

Mrs. PAINE. The switch is on the west doorjamb of that door between the two rooms.

Mr. JENNER. Perhaps that may help, Mrs. Paine. When you are in the kitchen about to enter the garage, the doorway from the kitchen to the garage, and you are going to enter from the kitchen into the garage, where is the switch with respect to whether it is on your right side or your left side?

Mrs. PAINE. Just coming into the garage it is on my right side.

Mr. JENNER. That is leaving your kitchen entering the garage it is on your right side. Now when you are in the garage and you are about to enter the kitchen, the switch then is on your left? Is that correct?

Mrs. PAINE. Yes.

Representative FORD. That clarifies it. May I now ask in your observations of either Marina or Lee, were they the type that were conscious of turning light switches on or off? Was this an automatic reaction? Were they careless about it? What was their trait if you have any observation?

Mrs. PAINE. I don't recall any other time that the garage light had been left on, and I would say certainly I saw enough of Marina to be able to state what I thought would be a trait, and she would normally turn off a light when she was done, in the room.

Representative FORD. She had the normal reaction of turning a light off if she left a room?

Mrs. PAINE. Her own room. Now you see most of the rooms—if she was the last one in the room she would turn it off; yes; going to bed or something like that she certainly would turn it off.

Mr. JENNER. Of course if she was going to bed she would turn the light off. But when she was leaving the room, was it her tendency to turn off the light?

Mrs. PAINE. Well, the garage light is the only room in my house you leave not to come back to right away. The whole house is active all the time until bedtime. It is hard to answer.

Mr. JENNER. So the lights are on?

Mrs. PAINE. Yes.

Representative FORD. Would you make any observation about Lee's tendencies or traits in this regard?

Mrs. PAINE. I can't say I have observation as to his tendencies.

Mr. JENNER. It was your habit, however, as far as you are concerned with respect to the light in the garage to turn it off when you left the garage?

Mrs. PAINE. Yes.

Mr. JENNER. What were your habits with respect to closing the main garage door, that is the door opening onto the street?

Mrs. PAINE. That was always closed except to open just to take out the trash can.

Mr. JENNER. And though it is shown in one of the photographs as open.

Mrs. PAINE. That was done for the purpose of the photograph by the FBI.

Mr. JENNER. So that normally your garage door is down?

Mrs. PAINE. That is right.

Mr. JENNER. Was it down when you arrived?

Mrs. PAINE. Yes; it was.

Mr. JENNER. At your home when you were surprised to see Lee Oswald?

Mrs. PAINE. Yes; it certainly was.

Mr. JENNER. Do you have recollection whether anytime that evening of hearing the garage door being raised or seeing the garage door up?

Mrs. PAINE. I have no such recollection.

Mr. JENNER. Do you have a recollection that it was down at all times?

Mrs. PAINE. I wasn't in the garage.

Mr. JENNER. Well, you entered the garage did you not that evening?

Mrs. PAINE. Except then; yes, at 9 or so. It was certainly down.

Mr. JENNER. It was down then?

Mrs. PAINE. Yes.

Mr. JENNER. You say your home is small and you can hear even the front door opening. Does the raising of the garage door cause some clatter?

Mrs. PAINE. Yes; it does.

Mr. JENNER. And had the garage door been raised, even though you were giving attention to your children, would you have heard it?

Mrs. PAINE. If it was raised slow and carefully; no, I would not have heard it.

Mr. JENNER. But if it were raised normally?

Mrs. PAINE. Yes.

Mr. JENNER. You would have heard it. And it is your recollection that at no time that evening were you conscious of that garage door having been raised.

Mrs. PAINE. That is correct.

Mr. JENNER. You had reached the point at which you said you entered the garage to, did you say, lacquer some blocks which you had prepared?

Mrs. PAINE. That is right.

Mr. JENNER. What did you notice in the garage when you entered it to lacquer those blocks?

Mrs. PAINE. The garage was as I always found it, and I went and got the lacquer from the workbench on the west side of the garage and painted the blocks on top of the deepfreeze. My motions were in the interior portion.

Mr. JENNER. That is in the area of the garage near the kitchen entrance?

Mrs. PAINE. Right.

Mr. JENNER. How long were you in the garage on that occasion?

Mrs. PAINE. About a half an hour.

Mr. JENNER. Did you leave the garage light on while you worked in the garage?

Mrs. PAINE. Yes.

Mr. JENNER. You are definitely conscious, however, of the fact that when you entered the garage the light was on?

Mrs. PAINE. I am certain of that. I thought it quite sloppy to have left it on.

Mr. JENNER. Did you make any inquiry of Marina or of Lee Oswald as to the light having been left on?

Mrs. PAINE. No.

Mr. JENNER. No comment at all?

Mrs. PAINE. It is my recollection that by the time I was ready to go to the garage to work, say 9 o'clock, Lee had already retired.

Mr. JENNER. Now we would like to know, tell us how you were definitely conscious that he had retired by that time?

Mrs. PAINE. He was in the bedroom. Traffic between the bedroom where he was and the bathroom crosses in front of the doorway, the front of the room where I was.

Senator COOPER. Did you see him in the bedroom?

Mrs. PAINE. In the bedroom?

Senator COOPER. Yes.

Mrs. PAINE. No; but I'd be——

Senator COOPER. What?

Mrs. PAINE. No; but I'd be fairly certain I saw him go to it.

Senator COOPER. You saw him go to it?

Mrs. PAINE. Yes.

Mr. JENNER. You saw him passing back and forth from the bedroom to the bathroom and he had his ablutions and then returned to the bedroom to retire, is that correct?

Mrs. PAINE. That is my best recollection.

Mr. JENNER. That is your definite consciousness?

Mrs. PAINE. All of this was so common that I made no specific note of it.

Senator COOPER. I think you have got to tell what you remember that night. If you can't remember it, you can't remember it.

Mrs. PAINE. Yes.

Mr. JENNER. But you do remember him passing back and forth from the bedroom that he and Marina normally occupied when he was there, and she occupied when she was there, to the bathroom, and then back to the bedroom. You do have that recollection?

Mrs. PAINE. I recall specifically the feeling that he was in the room, and this grounded no doubt in his having been back and forth as you have described.

Mr. JENNER. You remained in the garage about a half hour lacquering your children's blocks.

Mrs. PAINE. Yes.

Mr. JENNER. You left the garage then, did you?

Mrs. PAINE. Yes; I did.

Mr. JENNER. And where did you go when you left the garage?

Mrs. PAINE. To the kitchen or living room.

Mr. JENNER. Did you see anybody when you entered the kitchen or living room?

Mrs. PAINE. Yes; Marina was still up.

Mr. JENNER. Did you see Lee Oswald?

Mrs. PAINE. No.

Mr. JENNER. Did you see Lee Oswald anytime from that moment forward until you retired for the evening?

Mrs. PAINE. I saw Lee Oswald at no time from that moment forward.

Mr. JENNER. The answer to my question is no?

Mrs. PAINE. No.

Mr. JENNER. Did you speak with him or he with you at anytime from that moment forward until you retired?

Mrs. PAINE. No.

Mr. JENNER. Were you conscious that he spoke to Marina at anytime from that moment forward until you retired that evening?

Mrs. PAINE. I was not conscious that he spoke to Marina; no.

Mr. JENNER. Or she with him?

Mrs. PAINE. Or she with him.

Mr. JENNER. What time that evening did you retire?

Mrs. PAINE. I would guess around 11 or 11:30.

Mr. JENNER. Did Marina remain up and retire at anytime or had she retired earlier?

Mrs. PAINE. It seems to me we remained up and retired at about the same time, having folded laundry on the sofa before we retired, and talked.

Mr. JENNER. Were you looking at the television while you were doing the folding?

Mrs. PAINE. I don't recall. I don't think so.

Mr. JENNER. Now let us return to the garage for a moment. When you were in the garage for the half hour, did you notice the blanket wrapped package you testified about yesterday?

Mrs. PAINE. I don't specifically recall seeing it; no.

Mr. JENNER. You first weren't conscious of it?

Mrs. PAINE. That is correct.

Mr. JENNER. You didn't stumble over it.

Mrs. PAINE. No.

Mr. JENNER. It wasn't drawn to your attention in any fashion. Is that correct?

Mrs. PAINE. That is correct.

Mr. JENNER. Now, as you and Marina sat that evening, folding the ironing, what did you discuss?

Mrs. PAINE. I don't recall specifically.

Mr. JENNER. Was there any discussion that might serve to refresh your recollection, any discussion of the fact that Lee Oswald had come home or come to Irving in the first place on a Thursday afternoon, which is unusual, or that he had come home unannounced and without invitation, which also as you have testified was unusual? Wasn't there any discussion between you and Marina, speculation at least on your part as to why he was home?

Mrs. PAINE. Yes, there was discussion. I can't recall exactly what time in the evening it took place but I recall the content of the discussion.

Mr. JENNER. You tell us about it.

Mrs. PAINE. She suggested that he was making up the quarrel that they had had because of her attempt to reach him by telephone, and I agreed, concurred with that judgment of it.

Mr. JENNER. What was the attitude that evening?

Mrs. PAINE. He was very warm and friendly.

Mr. JENNER. Was there anything unusual about his attitude and conduct that evening?

Mrs. PAINE. Nothing except he went to bed a little earlier than he normally would have on a Sunday evening before work.

Mr. JENNER. Were you conscious of the fact that he was retiring a little earlier than he normally would?

Mrs. PAINE. Yes.

Mr. JENNER. And did you speculate in your mind as to why that might be?

Mrs. PAINE. No. I knew that he would go to bed as early as 10 o'clock say on the Sunday evening before going to work the next day. This was just, still early.

Mr. JENNER. What was Marina's attitude toward him that evening? Was she reserved because of this quarrel?

Mrs. PAINE. No. I think she felt the best thing was to pass it by and not discuss it.

Mr. JENNER. That was your impression of her?

Mrs. PAINE. Yes.

Mr. JENNER. Of her conduct.

Senator COOPER. That is just your idea about it, isn't it?

Mrs. PAINE. Well, and that I saw her do exactly, that too.

Mr. JENNER. Do exactly what?

Mrs. PAINE. She didn't ask him why he had come.

Mr. JENNER. Excuse me. You were present when Marina put a question to——

Mrs. PAINE. She did not ask him.

Mr. JENNER. Oh, she did not.

Mr. McCLOY. She did not.

Mr. JENNER. Oh, I am sorry.

Mrs. PAINE. Certainly not in my presence.

Mr. JENNER. Do you have any impression as to how long he had been at your home prior to your driving down the street and first seeing him?

Mrs. PAINE. He usually arrived from his ride with Wesley Frazier somewhere around a quarter of 5, so I guess it was a few minutes to 10 minutes.

Mr. JENNER. You arrived at your home in the neighborhood of 5:25 or 5:30. So it is your impression that he had been at your home from 10 to 15 minutes?

Mrs. PAINE. No; I say from a few minutes to 10 minutes.

Mr. JENNER. A few minutes to 10 minutes. Did Marina say anything that evening of his having a package with him when he came to your home?

Mrs. PAINE. No; she didn't.

Mr. JENNER. No discussion of that nature occurred?

Mrs. PAINE. No.

Mr. JENNER. I am going to put a general question to you. Do you have any recollection at all of Lee Oswald actually being in the garage of your home that evening?

Mrs. PAINE. I have said that I had the feeling from traffic that had preceded it that he was in the bedroom when I saw he was no longer in the rest of the house. When I saw the light was on, my distinct thought was that he had left it on. I think that was founded upon an awareness of what Marina had been doing and I suppose what he was doing.

Mr. JENNER. You say doing. You mean an awareness——

Mrs. PAINE. In other words, it was common for both Marina and Lee to go to the garage, but when I saw the light was on I was certain it was Lee that had left it on.

Mr. JENNER. Rather than Marina?

Mrs. PAINE. Rather than Marina.

Mr. JENNER. Because of her habit of turning off lights?

Mrs. PAINE. Not only that. I feel that I—memory of what she had been doing during the time that I was also putting the children to bed. She was involved with the children.

Mr. JENNER. May we possibly do this. Did you see Marina in the garage at anytime?

Mrs. PAINE. That evening?

Mr. JENNER. That evening.

Mrs. PAINE. No.

Mr. JENNER. You did not see Lee Oswald in the garage at anytime that evening?

Mrs. PAINE. Did not see him in the garage; no.

Mr. JENNER. Mr. Chairman, I intend at this moment to proceed to the next day. I wondered if members of the Commission have any further questions of Mrs. Paine with respect to the afternoon or evening of November 21?

Mr. McCLOY. I don't have any. I think she has covered it all. I would remind you that we have got to be leaving, Mr. Ford and I, and Senator Cooper around noon. We would like to make as much progress as we can before we go.

Mr. JENNER. That is fine. I will have completed this phase.

Senator COOPER. If you can get through the events of the 22d.

Mr. JENNER. You retired along about 11:30?

Mrs. PAINE. That is my recollection.

Mr. JENNER. The evening of the 21st. Did you sleep through the night?

Mrs. PAINE. Yes. I woke at 7:30.

Mr. JENNER. The children did not awaken you at anytime during the night and nothing else awakened you?

Mrs. PAINE. I don't recall that anything woke me; no.

Mr. JENNER. Is your recollection sufficient that you were not awakened during the night, that is your definite impression at the moment?

Mrs. PAINE. I get up often in the night to change a diaper or cover a child, but this is a matter of habit and I don't recall whether this night contained such a getting up or not.

Mr. JENNER. You sleep with your children, do you not?

Mrs. PAINE. We are in the same bedroom.

Mr. JENNER. You awakened when in the morning?

Mrs. PAINE. At 7:30.

Mr. JENNER. And when you awakened, immediately after you awakened what did you do?

Mrs. PAINE. When I awoke I felt the house was extremely quiet and the thought occurred to me that Lee might have overslept. I wondered if he had gotten up in time to get off around 7 o'clock because I knew he had to go to meet Wesley Frazier to catch his ride. I looked about and found a plastic coffee cup in the sink that had clearly been used and judged he had had a cup of coffee and left.

Mr. JENNER. Did you see any other evidence of his having had breakfast?

Mrs. PAINE. That was all he normally had for breakfast.

Mr. JENNER. A plastic coffee cup with some remains in it of coffee?

Mrs. PAINE. Instant coffee; yes.

Mr. JENNER. What was his habit with respect to his breakfast when he made his visits?

Mrs. PAINE. It was very normal for him to take coffee.

Mr. JENNER. Was Marina up and about when you arose at 7:30?

Mrs. PAINE. No; she was not.

Mr. JENNER. Do you have a recollection of the garage area? Was the door to the garage, the entrance to the garage from the kitchen, closed or open?

Mrs. PAINE. It was closed. Would it help if I tried to narrate what happened?

Mr. JENNER. Yes.

Mr. McCLOY. Go ahead and narrate.

Mrs. PAINE. I fixed breakfast for myself and my children, turned on the television set to hear President Kennedy speak in Fort Worth, and had breakfast there. I left the house about 9 with my little girl and boy, because she had a dentist appointment, the little girl. I left the television set on, feeling that Marina might not think to turn it on, but I knew that she would be interested to see President Kennedy.

I then was gone until nearly noon, 11:30 or so, both to the dentist and on some errands following that, came back and there was coverage of the fact of the motorcade in Dallas, but there was no television cameras showing it, as you know, and Marina thanked me for having left the television set on. She said she woke up in kind of a bad mood, but she had seen the arrival of President Kennedy and Mrs. Kennedy at the airport in Dallas, and had been thrilled with this occasion and with the greeting he had received, and it had lifted her spirits.

Very shortly after this time, I had only just begun to prepare the lunch, the announcement was made that the President had been shot, and I translated this to Marina. She had not caught it from the television statement. And I was crying as I did the translation. And then we sat down and waited at the television set, no longer interested in the preparing of lunch, and waited to hear further word.

I got out some candles and lit them, and my little girl also lighted a candle, and Marina said to me, "Is that a way of praying?", and I said "Yes, it is, just my own way." And it was well over an hour before we heard definitely that the President was dead.

Mr. JENNER. How did that come to your attention?

Mrs. PAINE. It was announced on the television. I think it was even still in the intervening time. It was announced on the television that the shot which was supposed to have killed the President was fired from the Texas School Book Depository Building on Elm.

Mr. JENNER. Did you communicate that to her?

Mrs. PAINE. Marina at this time was in the yard hanging some clothes. I recall going out to her and telling her this.

Mr. JENNER. What did she say?

Mrs. PAINE. I don't believe she said anything. I then also——

Mr. JENNER. Excuse me. You say "I don't believe she said anything." Is it your recollection?

Mrs. PAINE. I don't recall anything at all that she said.

Mr. JENNER. Would you——

Mr. McCLOY. You told her that you had heard over the television?

Mrs. PAINE. I heard that the shot had been made——

Mr. McCLOY. Coming from the Texas School Book Depository?

Mrs. PAINE. Schoolbook depository, and I believe I also said I didn't know there was a building on Elm.

Senator COOPER. Why did you go out to tell her, this fact?

Mrs. PAINE. I felt this was terribly close, somebody working in that building had been there. I thought Lee might be able to say somewhat about what happened, had been close to the event. This was my thought, that we would know somebody who would be able to give or possibly give a first-hand——

Senator COOPER. Did you have any thought at all that Lee Oswald might have been the man who fired the shot?

Mrs. PAINE. Absolutely none; no.

Mr. JENNER. Why was that, Mrs. Paine?

Mrs. PAINE. I had never thought of him as a violent man. He had never said anything against President Kennedy, nor anything about President Kennedy. I had no idea that he had a gun. There was nothing that I had seen about him that indicated a man with that kind of grudge or hostility.

Mr. McCLOY. But you told this to Marina because of the association of Lee Oswald with the schoolbook depository?

Mrs. PAINE. Yes. I then proceeded to hang some clothes.

Mr. JENNER. She did not comment.

Mrs. PAINE. She did not comment.

Mr. JENNER. Made no comment?

Mrs. PAINE. That is my recollection, that she made no comment. I then helped hang the clothes. My recollection skips then to being again in front of the television listening, and it was then that we heard that the President was dead. We were both sitting on the sofa.

Mr. JENNER. Marina had come in from the yard?

Mrs. PAINE. Yes.

Mr. JENNER. From the hanging of the clothes?

Mrs. PAINE. I don't recall whether we came in together or whether she preceded me into the house while I finished hanging up the clothes. But I do recall then next sitting on the sofa when the announcement was definitely made that the President was dead. And she said to me "What a terrible thing this was for Mrs. Kennedy and for the two children." I remember her words were, "Now the two children will have to grow up without the father." It was very shortly after this we were still sitting on the sofa.

Mr. McCLOY. Just take a little time and compose yourself.

Mrs. PAINE. My neighbor, Mrs. Roberts, came in, really I think to see if we had heard, and——

Senator COOPER. Why don't you rest a few minutes?

Mrs. PAINE. I can proceed. I recall my feeling of anger with her for not being more upset, or she didn't appear to me to be, any more than reporting a remarkable news item. Then it was shortly after that that the bell rang and I went to the door and met some six officers from the sheriff's office and police station.

Mr. JENNER. Was this approximately 3:30 p.m.?

Mrs. PAINE. Oh, I think it was earlier, but I wouldn't be certain. I know that we had put our children to bed. They were all taking a nap, though I am not certain. Yes, my little girl was asleep also. I cried after I had heard that the President was dead, and my little girl was upset, too, always taking it from me more than from any understanding of the situation. And she cried herself to sleep on the sofa, and I moved her to her bed, and Christopher was already asleep in his crib. June was in bed asleep.

Mr. JENNER. Was Marina emotional at all? Did she cry?

Mrs. PAINE. No. She said to me, "I feel very badly also, but we seem to show that we are upset in different ways." She did not actually cry.

Mr. McCLOY. May I go back a moment there, if I may. You said you were sitting on the sofa—that she and you were sitting on the sofa. While you were listening or looking at the television, was there any announcement over the television of a suspicion being cast at Lee?

Mrs. PAINE. It had just been announced that they had caught someone in a theatre, but there was no name given.

Mr. McCLOY. So up to this point there was no suggestion that Lee was involved?

Mrs. PAINE. No; not until the time the officers came to the door.

Mr. McCLOY. Not until the officers came?

Mrs. PAINE. Do you want to ask me about that?

Mr. JENNER. Yes. Now, the officers came to the door——

Mr. McCLOY. Pardon me. Were you asking a question?

Mr. JENNER. I was waiting for you.

Mr. McCLOY. Senator Cooper reminded me that there were comments, apparently to the effect that somebody from that building had fired the shots. Did you hear that when you were sitting on the sofa with Marina? Did you hear that comment on the television?

Mrs. PAINE. No; that was earlier.

Mr. McCLOY. That was even earlier?

Mrs. PAINE. Yes; before it was announced that he was dead.

Senator COOPER. But when you were all sitting there——

Mrs. PAINE. It was at that point that I went out to the yard to tell her.

Senator COOPER. To tell her?

Mrs. PAINE. Yes.

Senator COOPER. After that when you went back in and you all were sitting on the sofa and she was there, were there any other comments over the television that someone from this building had fired the shot or that any suspects from——

Mrs. PAINE. You mean, someone associated with the building?

Senator COOPER. Yes.

Mrs. PAINE. No; that was not said.

Senator COOPER. There was nothing else said about that?

Mrs. PAINE. No; just that the shot came from the building.

Mr. McCLOY. Nothing else that you heard?

Mrs. PAINE. Nothing else about it.

Mr. JENNER. Mrs. Paine, you do have a definite recollection that you communicated to Marina out in the yard that the shot had come from the Texas School Book Depository?

Mrs. PAINE. Yes.

Mr. JENNER. And what did she do when you communicated that to her, apart from what she said? You told us what she said. What did she do? Did she come in the house?

Mrs. PAINE. I don't recall.

Mr. JENNER. Did she enter the garage?

Mrs. PAINE. I don't know. I never saw her enter the garage, but my recollection is that I was outside hanging clothes after I told her this, but what I can't recall is whether she remained with me hanging the clothes or whether she went in the house.

Mr. JENNER. She might have gone into the house?

Mrs. PAINE. She might have gone into the house.

Mr. JENNER. But, in any event, you do not recall her entering the garage following your advising her of the announcement that the shot had come, or was thought to have come from the Texas School Book Depository?

Mrs. PAINE. I do not recall.

Senator COOPER. When you went out to tell her, was she hanging clothes?

Mrs. PAINE. She was hanging clothes.

Senator COOPER. Then did you go help her, and then both of you were hanging clothes?

Mrs. PAINE. I then helped her. What I can't remember is whether she remained and finished the job with me. I remember I finished, remained until they were all hung.

70

Senator COOPER. Do you remember at anytime after that whether or not you were hanging clothes alone?

Mrs. PAINE. That is what I am not certain about. I could well have been.

Mr. JENNER. At anytime that afternoon, in any event, up to the time that the policeman rang your doorbell, did you observe or were you aware that Marina had entered the garage?

Mrs. PAINE. I wasn't aware that she had entered, if she did.

Mr. JENNER. I take it from your testimony it is possible that Marina, after you advised her that the shot was thought to have come from this Texas School Book Depository, that she might have been inside your home while you were still out in the yard?

Mrs. PAINE. That is right.

Mr. JENNER. And, of course, if that is so, then she could have entered the garage while she was inside your home, and you were out in the yard hanging clothes?

Mrs. PAINE. And I would not have seen her; that is right.

Mr. JENNER. Now, this clothes-hanging occurred in the rear, the yard portion in the rear of your home; is that correct?

Mrs. PAINE. Yes.

Mr. JENNER. Is it possible—is there a window in the garage opening on the rear of your home on to that yard area, or is the wall blank?

Mrs. PAINE. The window one can look into from the area where one hangs clothes goes to the dining area. From where I stood, I could not have seen the door entering the garage, which would be just beyond——

Mr. JENNER. You are talking about the inside door?

Mrs. PAINE. Yes.

Mr. JENNER. First I would like to know this——

Mrs. PAINE. The answer to your question is clear if you see the plan of the interior of the house. No part of the garage shows, no wall or window or any part of the garage shows from the back——

Mr. JENNER. There is no opening from the rear of the garage, is there?

Mrs. PAINE. No.

Mr. JENNER. So you can't see into the garage, at least from——

Mrs. PAINE. From the back of my house you can't; no.

Mr. JENNER. There are windows opening from your kitchen into the back part, into the yard, are there not?

Mrs. PAINE. Yes.

Mr. JENNER. And being in the yard, could you see when somebody passed across that window, let us say, headed for the garage area?

Mrs. PAINE. No. Heading for the garage area, you would not pass across that window.

Mr. JENNER. You would not. In any event, you had no consciousness at anytime that day or afternoon of Marina having entered the garage up to the time the police came?

Mrs. PAINE. That is right.

Mr. JENNER. Is that true of the time in the morning that you have been describing?

Mrs. PAINE. Yes.

Mr. JENNER. At anytime from 7:30 in the morning, from the time you awakened until the time the police came, you have no consciousness that Marina was in the garage?

Mrs. PAINE. No consciousness of that.

Mr. JENNER. Did you enter the garage during this period of time?

Mrs. PAINE. I have no specific recollection of having done so.

Mr. JENNER. And you have given us Marina's total exclamation or response to your advising her that the shot had come from the Texas School Book Depository?

Mrs. PAINE. That is right.

Mr. JENNER. You have recounted that your next-door neighbor, Mrs. Robert— or is it Roberts?

Mrs. PAINE. Yes.

Mr. JENNER. Came over. Was Marina present——

Mrs. PAINE. Yes.

Mr. JENNER. When she arrived at your home? Were you girls in the living room?

Mrs. PAINE. Yes.

Mr. JENNER. Did you sit down and talk?

Mrs. PAINE. No. She just came to the door to see if we had heard the news.

Mr. JENNER. She was there just a bit of the time?

Mrs. PAINE. Yes. She did not come, actually, into the house.

Mr. JENNER. She did not. She stood in the doorway?

Mrs. PAINE. Yes.

Mr. JENNER. Is that correct?

Mrs. PAINE. Yes.

Mr. JENNER. And did she speak to you and to Marina?

Mrs. PAINE. Well, she spoke in English, and I doubt she said much more than, "Have you heard?".

Mr. JENNER. Did Marina say anything to you for translation of Mrs. Reynolds?

Mrs. PAINE. No. Roberts.

Mr. JENNER. Mrs. Roberts; while Mrs. Roberts was there?

Mrs. PAINE. No.

Mr. JENNER. Learning that you girls were aware of the events up to that moment, she left and, as far as you know, returned to her home?

Mrs. PAINE. Yes.

Mr. JENNER. Now, that morning—if I may, Mr. Chairman, because of the entry of the police, that is a good cutoff point, I would like to go back to the morning for the moment, or the evening before. Mrs. Paine, did you then have what might be called some curtain rods in your garage?

Mrs. PAINE. I believe there were.

Mr. JENNER. Do you have a recollection?

Mrs. PAINE. Yes; they were stored in the garage, wrapped in loose brown paper.

Mr. JENNER. Is it the brown paper of the nature and character you described yesterday that you get at the market and have in a roll?

Mrs. PAINE. Yes.

Mr. JENNER. Had you wrapped that package yourself?

Mrs. PAINE. Yes.

Mr. JENNER. Now, curtain rods can be of various types. One type of curtain rod, as I remember, is a solid brass rod. Others are hollow. Some are shaped. Would you describe these curtain rods, please?

Mrs. PAINE. They were a light weight.

Mr. JENNER. Excuse me; do you still have them?

Mrs. PAINE. I still have them.

Mr. JENNER. All right.

Mrs. PAINE. Metal rods that you slip the curtain over, not with a ring but just with the cloth itself, and they are expansion rods.

Mr. JENNER. Are they flat on one side?

Mrs. PAINE. They are flat on one side; about an inch wide and about a quarter of an inch thick.

Mr. JENNER. And assume we are holding the rod horizontally, do the edges of the rod slip over?

Mrs. PAINE. Yes.

Senator COOPER. Did you wrap these rods in the paper? Had you wrapped them?

Mrs. PAINE. Sometime previously I had.

Senator COOPER. How long before?

Mrs. PAINE. Oh, possibly a year.

Senator COOPER. What?

Mrs. PAINE. Possibly a year.

Senator COOPER. As far as you know, they had never been changed?

Mrs. PAINE. Moved about, but not changed.

Senator COOPER. Can you just describe the length?

Mrs. PAINE. Yes.

Senator COOPER. The length of the rods, at the time you wrapped them.

Mrs. PAINE. They would be 36 inches when pushed together.

Senator COOPER. What?

Mrs. PAINE. They would be about maybe 36 inches when pushed together.

Senator COOPER. You remember wrapping them. Do you remember what the size, the length of the rods were at the time you wrapped them?

Mrs. PAINE. Yes.

Senator COOPER. How long?

Mrs. PAINE. Didn't I answer about 36 inches?

Mr. JENNER. In other words, you pushed them together so that then, they were then their minimum length, unexpanded?

Mrs. PAINE. Yes.

Mr. JENNER. They were not extended, and in that condition they were 36 inches long?

Mrs. PAINE. Something like that.

Mr. JENNER. Now, how many of them were there?

Mrs. PAINE. Two.

Mr. JENNER. These were lightweight metal?

Mrs. PAINE. Very. Now, there was another item that was both heavier and longer.

Mr. JENNER. In that same package?

Mrs. PAINE. No; I don't think so. In another similar package wrapped up just to keep the dust off were two venetian blinds. I guess they were not longer, more like 36 inches also, that had come from the two windows in my bedroom. I took them down to change, and put up pull blinds in their place.

Mr. JENNER. And had you wrapped them?

Mrs. PAINE. Yes.

Mr. JENNER. How many were there?

Mrs. PAINE. Two.

Mr. JENNER. And what was their length?

Mrs. PAINE. I think around 36 inches. The width of these windows in the back bedroom.

Mr. JENNER. Let us return to the curtain rods first. Do you still have those curtain rods?

Mrs. PAINE. I believe so.

Mr. JENNER. You believe so, or you know; which?

Mrs. PAINE. I think Michael went to look after the assassination, whether these were still in the garage.

Mr. JENNER. Did you have a conversation with Michael as to whether he did or didn't look?

Mrs. PAINE. Yes.

Mr. JENNER. Why was he looking to see if the curtain rod package was there?

Mrs. PAINE. He was particularly interested in the wrapping, was the wrapping still there, the brown paper.

Mr. JENNER. When did this take place?

Mrs. PAINE. After the assassination, perhaps a week or so later, perhaps when one of the FBI people were out; I don't really recall.

Mr. JENNER. And was the package with the curtain rods found on that occasion?

Mrs. PAINE. It is my recollection it was.

Mr. JENNER. What about the venetian blind package?

Mrs. PAINE. Still there, still wrapped.

Mr. JENNER. You are fully conscious of the fact that that package is still there?

Mrs. PAINE. Yes.

Mr. JENNER. And to the best of your knowledge, information, and belief the other package, likewise, is there?

Mrs. PAINE. Yes.

Senator COOPER. Let me ask a question there. After the assassination, at anytime did you go into the garage and look to see if both of these packages were there?

Mrs. PAINE. A week and a half, or a week later.

Senator COOPER. At any time?

Mrs. PAINE. Did I, personally?

Senator COOPER. Have you seen these packages since the assassination?

Mrs. PAINE. It seems to me I recall seeing a package.

Senator COOPER. What?

Mrs. PAINE. I don't recall opening it up and looking in carefully. I seem to recall seeing the package.

Senator COOPER. Both of them?

Mrs. PAINE. Yes.

Senator COOPER. Or just one?

Mrs. PAINE. Both.

Senator COOPER. Did you feel them to see if the rods were in there?

Mrs. PAINE. No. I think Michael did, but I am not certain.

Senator COOPER. But you never did, yourself?

Mrs. PAINE. It was not my most pressing——

Senator COOPER. What?

Mrs. PAINE. It was not the most pressing thing I had to do at that time.

Senator COOPER. I know that. But you must have read after the assassination the story about Lee Oswald saying, he told Mr. Frazier, I think, that he was carrying some curtain rods in the car?

Mrs. PAINE. Yes.

Senator COOPER. Do you remember reading that?

Mrs. PAINE. Yes; I remember reading that.

Senator COOPER. Didn't that lead you—Did it lead you then to go in and see if the curtain rods were there?

Mrs. PAINE. It was all I could do at that point to answer my door, answer my telephone, and take care of my children.

Senator COOPER. I understand you had many things to do.

Mrs. PAINE. So I did not.

Senator COOPER. You never did do it?

Mrs. PAINE. I am not certain whether I specifically went in and checked on that. I recall a conversation with Michael about it and, to the best of my recollection, things looked as I expected to find them looking out there. This package with brown paper was still there.

Mr. JENNER. By any chance, does that package appear in the photograph that you have identified of the interior of your garage?

Mrs. PAINE. I think it is this that is on a shelf almost to the ceiling.

Mr. JENNER. May I get over here, Mr. Chairman?

Mrs. PAINE. Along the west edge of the garage, up here.

Mr. JENNER. In view of this, I think it is of some importance that you mark on Commission Exhibit 429 what appears to you to be the package in which the curtain rods were.

Mrs. PAINE. To the best of my recollection.

Mr. JENNER. Now the witness has by an arrow indicated a shelf very close to the ceiling in the rear of the garage, and an arrow pointing to what appears to be a long package on that shelf, underneath which she has written "Wrapping paper around venetian blinds"——

Mrs. PAINE. "And thin."

Mr. JENNER. What is the next word?

Mrs. PAINE. "Curtain rods."

Mr. JENNER. There were two packages, Mrs. Paine, one with the rods and one with the venetian blinds?

Mrs. PAINE. I can't recall. The rods were so thin they hardly warranted a package of their own, but that is rationalization, as you call it.

Mr. JENNER. You do have a recollection that those rods were a very lightweight metal?

Mrs. PAINE. Yes.

Mr. JENNER. Do you?

Mrs. PAINE. Yes. They were not round.

Mr. JENNER. They were flat and slender?

Mrs. PAINE. Yes.

Mr. JENNER. They were not at all heavy?

Mrs. PAINE. That is right.

Mr. JENNER. They were curved? Were they curved in any respect?

Mrs. PAINE. They curved at the ends to attach to the bracket that held them up on the wall.

Mr. JENNER. May I use the chalk on the board, Mr. Chairman. Perhaps it might be better for you, Mrs. Paine, so I don't influence you. Would you draw a picture of the rods?

Mrs. PAINE. You are looking down from the top. It attaches here, well, over a loop thing on the wall. Looking from the inside, it curves over a slight bit, and then this is recessed.

Mr. JENNER. I am going to have to have you do that over on a sheet of paper. Will you remain standing for the moment. We will give it an exhibit number. But I would like to have you proceed there. What did you say this was, in the lower diagram?

Mrs. PAINE. You are looking down.

Mr. JENNER. Now, where was the break?

Mrs. PAINE. The break?

Mr. JENNER. You said they were extension.

Mrs. PAINE. That is right. When they are up on the window, it would be like that.

Mr. JENNER. You have drawn a double line to indicate what would be seen if you were looking down into the U-shape of the rod?

Mrs. PAINE. Yes.

Mr. JENNER. The double line indicates what on either side?

Mrs. PAINE. That the lightweight metal, white, turned over, bent around, something less than a quarter of an inch on each side.

Mr. JENNER. Now, would you be good enough to make the same drawing. We will mark that sheet as Commission Exhibit No. 449 upon which the witness is now drawing the curtain rod.

(Commission Exhibit No. 449 was marked for identification.)

Mr. JENNER. While you are doing that, Mrs. Paine, would you be good enough when you return to Irving, Tex., to see if those rods are at hand, and some of our men are going to be in Irving next week. We might come out and take a look at them, and perhaps you might surrender them to us.

Mrs. PAINE. You are perfectly welcome to them.

Mr. JENNER. Would you in that connection, Mrs. Paine, do not open the package until we arrive?

Mrs. PAINE. I won't even look, then.

Mr. JENNER. All right. Now, would you mark "A" in the upper elevation and "B" in the lower elevation. The elevation in the drawing you have indicated as "A" is a depiction of what?

Mrs. PAINE. The curtain rod, as you might look at it from the top when it is hanging in its position, when it is placed in position on the window.

Mr. JENNER. And "B"?

Mrs. PAINE. "B" is as it might appear if you could look at it from outside the house; the window.

Mr. JENNER. While the rod was in place?

Mrs. PAINE. While the rod was in place.

Mr. JENNER. You have written to the left-hand side "Place at which it attaches to wall fixture," indicating the butt end of the curved side of the rod?

Mrs. PAINE. Yes.

Mr. JENNER. And the two oblongs, each of which you have put at the ends of depiction "B," represent the upturned ends of the fixtures at each end?

Mrs. PAINE. Right.

Mr. JENNER. Would you put a little line as to where the break was in the rod.

I offer in evidence, Mr. Chairman, as Commission Exhibit No. 449 the drawing that the witness has just made, and about which she has testified.

Senator COOPER. It will be admitted as part of the evidence.

(Commission Exhibit No. 449 was received in evidence.)

Mr. JENNER. Had there been any conversation between you and Lee Oswald, or between you and Marina, or any conversation taking place in your presence prior to this occasion, in which the subject of curtain rods was mentioned?

Mrs. PAINE. No; there was no such conversation.

Mr. JENNER. Was the subject of curtain rods—had that ever been mentioned during all of these weekends that Lee Oswald had come to your home, commencing, I think you said, with his first return on October 4, 1963?

Mrs. PAINE. It had not been mentioned.

Mr. JENNER. Never by anybody?

Mrs. PAINE. By anybody.

Mr. JENNER. Had the subject of curtain rods been mentioned even inadvertently, let us say, by some neighbor talking about the subject, as to whether you had some curtain rods you weren't using?

Mrs. PAINE. No.

Mr. JENNER. That might be loaned? I think you had testified that the curtain rods, when unextended, were 36 inches long, approximately?

Mrs. PAINE. That is a guess. I would say, thinking further about it, it must be shorter than that. One went over a window that I am pretty sure was 30 inches wide, and one went over a window that was 42 inches wide, so it had to extend between these. They were identical, and had served at these different windows.

Mr. JENNER. The rods were identical in length when unextended?

Mrs. PAINE. Or when fully extended; yes.

Mr. JENNER. What?

Mrs. PAINE. Or when fully extended.

Mr. JENNER. Or when fully extended; yes. They could be extended to as great as 42 inches?

Mrs. PAINE. At least that. I am just saying what windows they were used for.

Mr. JENNER. If the rods are still available, we will be able to obtain them?

Mrs. PAINE. Yes.

Mr. JENNER. And we will know exactly their length, extended and unextended. Now, as you think further about it, the rods when not extended, that is, when pushed together, might be but 30 inches long?

Mrs. PAINE. Yes.

Mr. JENNER. Because you recall that you have a 30-inch-wide window.

Mrs. PAINE. I believe it is more that width than 36.

Mr. JENNER. Would you hold up your hands to indicate what you think the width or the length of the rods is when not extended?

Mrs. PAINE. Oh, I don't recall. Maybe like this.

Mr. JENNER. Would you measure that, Mr. Liebeler, please?

Mr. LIEBELER. About 28 inches.

Mr. JENNER. I intend to leave the subject of the curtain rods, gentlemen, if you have any questions.

Mr. McCLOY. May I ask a question. Did the FBI question you about the curtain rods any, or the Dallas police officials?

Mrs. PAINE. Not the Dallas police.

Mr. McCLOY. Not the Dallas police?

Mrs. PAINE. No. It is possible the FBI did. I don't recall such question.

Mr. McCLOY. They didn't take any rods from the garage that you are aware of?

Mrs. PAINE. You are aware what the police took. I never did know exactly what they took. I have never heard any mention of the rods having left.

Mr. McCLOY. You are not conscious of the Dallas police ever talking to you about curtain rods?

Mrs. PAINE. Absolutely no.

Mr. McCLOY. But possibly some member of the FBI did?

Mrs. PAINE. Possibly. I can't recall.

Mr. McCLOY. You can't recall?

Mr. JENNER. Did you ever mention to the FBI anything, or anybody else up until recently, the existence of the curtain rods about which you have now testified?

Mrs. PAINE. I have already said Michael and I discussed it.

Mr. JENNER. When?

Mrs. PAINE. A week or two after the assassination would be my guess.

Mr. JENNER. And did you discuss those particular curtain rods about which you have now testified?

Mrs. PAINE. We were particularly interested in seeing if the wrapping paper that we used to wrap these things was there, and it was. I recall that.

Representative FORD. Did Lee Oswald know where you kept this roll of wrapping paper?

Mrs. PAINE. To the best of my knowledge, he did not know where I kept it. I had never wrapped something when he was around. Neither he nor Marina had ever asked to use this paper or the string that I had.

Representative FORD. Where did you keep it? I don't recall precisely.

Mrs. PAINE. I can be very clear. There is a picture here of a large secretary desk on Commission Exhibit No. 435. It is in the bottom drawer, you see, in that desk. This is not the secretary desk upon which——

Mr. JENNER. The note was found?

Mrs. PAINE. The note was found.

Representative FORD. You kept it in the lower drawer?

Mrs. PAINE. Along with some gum tape and string.

Representative FORD. And this is the section shown on Commission Exhibit 435?

Mrs. PAINE. That is right.

Mr. JENNER. Mr. Reporter, you caught the measurement by Mr. Liebeler, 28 inches. Mrs. Paine, what is your best recollection as to how many curtain rods there were?

Mrs. PAINE. Two, I am certain.

Mr. JENNER. Just two? And you wrapped the package yourself, did you?

Mrs. PAINE. Yes.

Mr. JENNER. When you and Michael undertook your discussion about curtain rods, did you or did he open up this package?

Mrs. PAINE. I don't recall.

Mr. JENNER. Is it your present best recollection that as far as you know, the package, as far as wrapping is concerned, is in the same condition now as when you wrapped it initially?

Mrs. PAINE. Certainly very similar.

Senator COOPER. What was the answer?

Mrs. PAINE. Certainly very similar. I don't recall making any change.

Mr. JENNER. Is there a possibility that the package was unwrapped at anytime?

Mrs. PAINE. In connection with this inquiry of Michael's; yes.

Mr. JENNER. You think he might have but you don't know.

Mrs. PAINE. Or I might have. I don't recall. I recall that it wasn't something that interested me as much as the other things I had to get done.

Mr. JENNER. But the rods about which you have testified as far as you know are on the shelf in your garage at your home?

Mrs. PAINE. Yes.

Mr. JENNER. Do you recall whether when the FBI discussed this subject with you, if you can recall that, that you advised the FBI of these particular curtain rods?

Mrs. PAINE. I am not perfectly certain that they discussed it with me.

Mr. JENNER. You just have no recollection of any interview with the FBI on this particular subject?

Mrs. PAINE. It seems to me they brought it up, but I don't recall the content nor whether they went out. I certainly think I would remember if I had gone out to the garage with an FBI representative.

Mr. JENNER. But you do not?

Mrs. PAINE. But I do not remember such an occasion.

Mr. JENNER. Unless the members of the Commission have any further questions with respect to the curtain rods, I will return to the afternoon.

Senator COOPER. I want to ask just two questions. Before the assassination, did you know where the package with the curtain rods in it was situated within the garage?

Mrs. PAINE. I gave it no attention but yes, it is my impression that I did go out to see if things were where I expected to find them. They were wrapped in brown paper, the curtain rods and venetian blinds. And found things there. I don't recall that I looked into the package.

Mr. JENNER. You did find the package?

Mrs. Paine. Yes.

Mr. Jenner. What was the size of the package in length and width if you can remember at the time you wrapped it?

Mrs. Paine. I suppose about like this, not closed but just wrapping paper folded over.

Mr. Jenner. Would you hold your hands there please.

Mrs. Paine. Yes. But by no means a neat package, just enough to keep the dust off.

Mr. Liebeler. Thirty-two and a half inches.

Senator Cooper. What was the width of the package?

Mrs. Paine. Like so.

Senator Cooper. That you wrapped?

Mrs. Paine. Now I am not certain. I am really thinking now of the package with the venetian blind. I don't recall exactly the package with the rods, whether they were included in this other or whether they warranted a package of their own.

Mr. Liebeler. The witness indicated a width of approximately 7½ inches.

Senator Cooper. I will ask one other question. The ends of the rod which are at right angles to the long surface, how long? What is their approximate size?

Mrs. Paine. Two and a half inches to three inches.

Senator Cooper. What?

Mrs. Paine. Two and a half to three inches.

Senator Cooper. All right, go ahead.

Mr. Jenner. Anyone entering your home from the outside walking up your driveway and looking in the windows, would they see anybody sitting on the sofa you have described?

Mrs. Paine. No.

Mr. Jenner. Do you sit on the sofa to look at your television set?

Mrs. Paine. Yes.

Mr. Jenner. Would you take the ground floor plan that is before you and indicate——

Mrs. Paine. Do you want me to draw in the sofa and the television set?

Mr. Jenner. No; I just want you to put an "X" as to where the sofa is, and put a double "X" as to where the television set is. Now the opening that appears to the left of the double "X," is that a window or a door?

Mrs. Paine. That is the front door.

Mr. Jenner. And is there any window in that wall, in the living room wall.

Mrs. Paine. Practically the rest of the wall is window.

Mr. Jenner. And on this drawing it appears as a solid wall?

Mrs. Paine. Yes.

Mr. Jenner. The fact is that is a picture window?

Mrs. Paine. That is right. It is just your printing filled in. It is exactly like this. There it is.

Mr. Jenner. Turning to Commission Exhibit 431, the picture window is shown there, is it not?

Mrs. Paine. Yes.

Mr. Jenner. Now it would be possible, would it not, if someone walked along the sidewalk and was intent on peering in to see if anyone is there, to see somebody sitting at the sofa looking at the television set?

Mrs. Paine. Oh, yes.

(Discussion off the record.)

Mr. McCloy. I am very anxious to hear your story before we leave.

Senator Cooper. I can stay here while the details are filled in.

Mr. Jenner. The police arrived and what occurred.

Mrs. Paine. I went to the door. They announced themselves as from both the sheriff's office and the Dallas Police Office, showed me at least one package or two. I was very surprised.

Mr. Jenner. Did you say anything?

Mrs. Paine. I said nothing. I think I just dropped my jaw. And the man in front said by way of explanation "We have Lee Oswald in custody. He is charged with shooting an officer." This is the first I had any idea that Lee might be in trouble with the police or in any way involved in the day's events. I asked them to come in. They said they wanted to search the house. I asked if they had a warrant. They said they didn't. They said they could get the sheriff out here right away with one if I insisted. And I said no, that was all right, they could be my guests.

They then did search the house. I directed them to the fact that most of the Oswald's things were in storage in my garage and showed where the garage was, and to the room where Marina and the baby had stayed where they would find the other things which belonged to the Oswalds. Marina and I went with two or three of these police officers to the garage.

Mr. JENNER. How many police officers were there?

Mrs. PAINE. There were six altogether, and they were busy in various parts of the house. The officer asked me in the garage did Lee Oswald have any weapons or guns. I said no, and translated the question to Marina, and she said yes; that she had seen a portion of it—had looked into—she indicated the blanket roll on the floor.

Mr. JENNER. Was the blanket roll on the floor at that time?

Mrs. PAINE. She indicated the blanket roll on the floor very close to where I was standing. As she told me about it I stepped onto the blanket roll.

Mr. JENNER. This might be helpful. You had shaped that up yesterday and I will just put it on the floor.

Mrs. PAINE. And she indicated to me that she had peered into this roll and saw a portion of what she took to be a gun she knew her husband to have, a rifle. And I then translated this to the officers that she knew that her husband had a gun that he had stored in here.

Mr. JENNER. Were you standing on the blanket when you advised——

Mrs. PAINE. When I translated. I then stepped off of it and the officer picked it up in the middle and it bent so.

Mr. JENNER. It hung limp just as it now hangs limp in your hand?

Mrs. PAINE. And at this moment I felt this man was in very deep trouble and may have done——

Mr. McCLOY. Were the strings still on it?

Mrs. PAINE. The strings were still on it. It looked exactly as it had at previous times I had seen it. It was at this point I say I made the connection with the assassination, thinking that possibly, knowing already that the shot had been made from the School Book Depository, and that this was a rifle that was missing, I wondered if he would not also be charged before the day was out with the assassination.

Mr. JENNER. Did you say anything?

Mrs. PAINE. No; I didn't say that.

Mr. JENNER. When the officer picked up the blanket package, did you hear any crinkling as though there was paper inside?

Mrs. PAINE. No crinkling.

Mr. JENNER. None whatsoever. When you stepped on the package, did you have a feeling through your feet that there was something inside the package in the way of paper.

Mrs. PAINE. Not anything in the way of paper.

Mr. JENNER. Or wrapping.

Mrs. PAINE. Or anything that crinkled; no. I did think it was hard but that was my cement floor.

Mr. JENNER. But definitely you had no sensation of any paper inside?

Mrs. PAINE. No such sensation.

Mr. JENNER. Of the nature or character of the wrapping paper you identified yesterday.

Mrs. PAINE. No; and when he picked it up I would think such paper would rattle, but there was no such sound. Marina said nothing at this time. She was very white, and of course I judged——

Mr. JENNER. Did she blanch?

Mrs. PAINE. She is not a person to immediately show her feelings necessarily. She was white. I wouldn't say that it was a sudden thing. I can't be certain that it was sudden at that point.

Representative FORD. How close was she standing to it.

Mrs. PAINE. From here to there, about 6 feet.

Mr. JENNER. Proceed.

Mrs. PAINE. The officers then said they would like me and Marina to go down to the police station, and I said well, I would seek to try to get a baby-sitter to come to stay with the children so that we might accompany them. About this time, we then left the garage as I recall, because then Michael Paine arrived at the front door. I was in the living room when he came. And I said "Did you know to come" and he said that he had heard Oswald's name mentioned on the radio, and had come over directly, for which I may say I was very glad.

Mr. JENNER. How far away from your home—where did he live?

Mrs. PAINE. It would take about a half hour drive—he was working—from where he was working to come, 20 minutes perhaps.

Mr. JENNER. Do you have the address at the tip of your tongue?

Mrs. PAINE. Where he works; no. I don't know the address. I know how to get to it.

Mr. JENNER. Do you know where he lived?

Mrs. PAINE. Yes.

Mr. JENNER. What was the address?

Mrs. PAINE. He lived at the Villa Fontaine Apartments, apartment 217, 2377 Dalworth.

Mr. JENNER. D-A-L-W-O-R-T-H?

Mrs. PAINE. D-A-L-W-O-R-T-H, in Grand Prairie, Tex.

Mr. JENNER. Where is Grand Prairie, Tex.

Mrs. PAINE. Grand Prairie is suburban to Dallas, between Dallas and Fort Worth, nearer to Dallas, and it was a location very near to where he worked.

Mr. JENNER. What distance in miles from your home?

Mrs. PAINE. You measure distance in minutes in Texas; driving time. I don't know; 20 minutes to where he lived.

Mr. JENNER. All right, proceed.

Mrs. PAINE. The police officers then asked if Michael would also accompany us to the police station and he said he would. I changed clothes to a suit from slacks, and went to the house of my babysitter. She has no telephone. I need to walk to her.

Mr. JENNER. Where was Marina in the meantime?

Mrs. PAINE. Marina remained in the house with the children. Lynn by this time had awakened as I recall. Christopher was still sleeping and I think June was also. And I said I would walk over to my neighbors to ask if—there was something that intervened I just remembered. I first went and asked my immediate neighbor, Mrs. Roberts, if she could keep the children for a short time in the afternoon, but she was just on her way to go somewhere. She couldn't. So then I went to the home of the person I normally have for a baby-sitter. It was now after school or this babysitter would not have been there, which brings us to 3:30 perhaps. And I asked the mother if the young girl, teenage girl, could come and stay at the house. I was accompanied to the house by one of the officers. As we left the house I said "Oh, you don't have to go with me." Oh, he said, he'd be glad to. And then it occurred to me he had been assigned to go with me, and I said "come along." It was the first I have ever experienced being in the company of people who suspected me of anything, and of course that is their business.

We did arrange then for the girls to come back, one or two, I forget whether it was two of the daughters or one that came then to my house to stay with the children. As I came back, I noticed the officers carrying a number of things from the house, and I looked into the back of one of the cars. It was across the street from my house, and saw he had three cases of 78 records of mine, and I said, "You don't need those and I want to use them on Thanksgiving weekend. I have promised to lead a folk dance conference on the weekend. I will need those records which are all folk dance records and I doubt that you might get them back at that time."

And I said, "that is a 16 mm projector. You don't want that. It is mine."

And he took me by the arm and he said, "We'd better get down to the station. We have wasted too much time as it is." And I said, "I want a list of what you are taking, please." Or perhaps that was before. As much answer as I ever got was "We'd better get to the station." Then I evidently had made them nervous because when we got back from this car to the house, Marina wanted to change from slacks as I had already done to a dress. They would not permit her to do that. I said "She has a right to, she is a woman, to dress as she wishes before going down." And I directed her to the bathroom to change. The officer opened the bathroom door and said no, she had no time to change. I was still making arrangements with the babysitters, arranging for our leaving the children there, and one of the officers made a statement to the effect of "we'd better get this straight in a hurry Mrs. Paine or we'll just take the children down and leave them with juvenile while we talk to you."

And I said "Lynn, you may come too" in reply to this. I don't like being threatened. And then Christopher was still sleeping so I left him in the house and Lynn, my daughter, and Marina took her daughter and her baby with her to the police station, so we were quite a group going into town in the car. Michael was in one car, Marina and I and all the children were in another with three police officers as I recall. One of them spoke some Czech, tried to understand what was being said. The one in the front seat turned to me and said "Are you a Communist," and I said, "No, I am not, and I don't even feel the need of a Fifth Amendment." And he was satisfied with that. We went on then to the police station, and waited until such time as they could interview us. They interviewed Michael at one point separately.

Mr. JENNER. Separately?

Mrs. PAINE. And they interviewed Marina while I was present.

Mr. JENNER. Did you interpret for her?

Mrs. PAINE. They had an interpreter there, a Mr. Ilya Mamantov whom I was very glad to see. He is the son-in-law of a woman who has tutored me in Dallas, so I had met him before. I was very glad to have someone whose skill in Russian was greater than mine, and Marina had said even in the car going down to the station, "your Russian has suddenly become no good at all." She had asked me again in the car, "isn't it true that the penalty for shooting someone in Texas is the electric chair" and I said "yes, that is true."

Then at the police station——

Representative FORD. May I ask this. Was there any interrogation other than what you have mentioned by police officers in the car?

Mrs. PAINE. No; none that I recall.

Representative FORD. You and Marina talked back and forth freely or to a limited degree?

Mrs. PAINE. We talked back and forth freely and then she wanted me to translate to the officer, to the one who understood some Czech, to help him understand. Then in the room where we were asked questions, what I particularly recall was they wanted Marina to say what she had said in the garage to the effect that she had seen a rifle in that wrapped blanket, and she made the statement again and it was made up into an affidavit for her to sign with Mr. Mamantov making very clear the translation of each sentence, each word, and I recall her statement was to the effect that she had looked in and seen a portion of the gun, of something which she took to be the gun she knew her husband had; that she had not opened the package, but had just looked into it.

They then brought in ——

Mr. JENNER. Mrs. Paine, a slight interruption.

Mrs. PAINE. Yes.

Mr. JENNER. Was the occasion when Mrs. Oswald, Marina, made the remark of having seen a weapon inside the blanket, was that the first notice that you had of any kind or character that there was a weapon in your garage?

Mrs. PAINE. That is absolutely the first. Indeed it was contrary to my expectation as I said. When the officer asked me I answered his question before I even translated it, answered it in the negative, and then translated it and found that indeed there had been a gun there.

Mr. JENNER. All right, go ahead.

Mrs. PAINE. They then showed a gun, a rifle to Marina, and asked her if she could identify the gun as being her husband's.

She said her husband had a dark gun, dark in color, that she wasn't absolutely certain that this was the gun. She couldn't definitely recall the sight on the top of it.

Mr. JENNER. The telescope sight?

Mrs. PAINE. Yes. Then I also was asked to make an affidavit which I signed, to the effect that I had heard her say in the garage that she had looked into this package and seen what she took to be a rifle she knew her husband had. It was after they had finished with this session that I went back in the same room where Michael was, and Mrs. Oswald, senior, came in, Mrs. Marguerite Oswald.

Mr. JENNER. Had you met her at anytime up to that moment?

Mrs. PAINE. No. I had never met her before.

Mr. JENNER. Had you ever talked with her at anytime up to that moment?

Mrs. PAINE. I had never talked with her.

Mr. JENNER. Were you advised in advance of anything that had been said that she was to come?

Mrs. PAINE. No. She said she had heard on her car radio, on her way to work in the afternoon.

Mr. JENNER. What time was this about?

Mrs. PAINE. She heard it?

Mr. JENNER. No; that she came?

Mrs. PAINE. It was, it was certainly supper time. We had eaten no lunch.

Mr. JENNER. All right.

Mrs. PAINE. And she said she heard on her car radio that Lee Oswald had been in custody in Dallas and had come over. Previously during October and November Marina had told me she regretted that Lee didn't wish to keep up contact with his mother because she thought it was only proper to tell the mother of the coming grandchild, and then she wanted to announce the birth when the baby had come but she said Lee didn't try to keep her address, and Marina didn't know how to contact her or didn't want to do so around her husband certainly. There was a warm greeting in the police station.

Mr. JENNER. Between whom?

Mrs. PAINE. Between Marguerite Oswald and Marina Oswald and I recall both wept and Mrs. Marguerite Oswald exclaimed over the new baby, and then held the baby. I then also met Robert Oswald.

Mr. JENNER. When did he come with relation to when Marguerite Oswald entered?

Mrs. PAINE. It seemed to me later.

Mr. JENNER. Had you met Robert Oswald at anytime up to that moment?

Mrs. PAINE. No; I had not.

Mr. JENNER. Was there any discussion that had taken place during the course of the day up to that moment indicating to you that Robert Oswald might or would arrive on the scene?

Mrs. PAINE. No; nothing that day about Robert at all.

Mr. JENNER. When he entered was there an indication to you at all that none of the people, in addition to yourself, was aware that he was about to—that they had any advance advice that he was going to be present?

Mrs. PAINE. There was no indication of any advance advice to any of the people.

Mr. JENNER. Was there any indication to the contrary?

Mrs. PAINE. I don't think anyone was really surprised that he had come.

Mr. JENNER. There was this lack of prior notice?

Mrs. PAINE. Lack of prior notice. We then talked about where to go.

Mr. JENNER. Excuse me, does the "we" include your husband all the time?

Mrs. PAINE. The "we" then was a group at this point of my husband, Marguerite Oswald, Marina Oswald, Robert Oswald, and myself, three children.

Mr. JENNER. Did your husband know Robert Oswald prior to this time?

Mrs. PAINE. No.

Mr. JENNER. Were they introduced to each other on this occasion?

Mrs. PAINE. They were in the same room and they might have been. It was agreed that Robert was to stay in a hotel. Marguerite Oswald asked if she could come out and stay with Marina at my home, and it was agreed.

Mr. JENNER. Was it agreed that Marina would stay at your house that night?

Mrs. PAINE. Yes; certainly all her baby things were there. So, we went back there. We were taken back by police officers.

Mr. JENNER. Everybody assumed she would return back to your home?

Mrs. PAINE. Oh, yes.

Mr. JENNER. Was there any discussion that would indicate any reluctance on the part of anybody that she return to your home?

Mrs. PAINE. None.

Mr. JENNER. None whatsoever by anybody?

Mrs. PAINE. That is correct, none whatsoever by anybody.

The police officers brought us back to my home. It was by this time dark, and I think it was about 9 o'clock in the evening. I asked Michael to go out and buy hamburgers at a drive-in so we wouldn't have to cook, and we ate these as best we could, and began to prepare to retire. We talked. I have a few specific recollections of that period that I will put in here.

Just close to the time of retiring Marina told me that just the night before Lee had said to her he hoped they could get an apartment together again soon. As she said this, I felt she was hurt and confused, wondering how he could have said such a thing which indicated wanting to be together with her when he must have already been planning something that would inevitably cause separation. I asked her did she think that Lee had killed the President and she said, "I don't know." And I felt that this was not something to talk about really anyway. But my curiosity overcame my politeness.

Now, back a little bit to the time in the living room, Mrs. Oswald and Michael and Marina and I were all there, and Mrs. Oswald, I recall, said, I mean of course Mrs. Marguerite Oswald——

Mr. JENNER. Yes.

Mrs. PAINE. That if they were prominent people there would be three of the lawyers down in the city jail now trying to defend her son, and coming to his aid.

She felt that since they were just small people that there wouldn't—they wouldn't get the proper attention or care, and I tried to say this was not a small case. That most careful attention would be given it, but she didn't feel that way.

Mr. JENNER. You made no impression on her?

Mrs. PAINE. I made no impression on her.

Mr. JENNER. I take it——

Mrs. PAINE. She made an impression on me.

Mr. JENNER. I think we would prefer if you would call her Marguerite. It would avoid confusion.

Mrs. PAINE. All right. Somewhere in that evening before we retired, and after we had eaten, the doorbell rang and two men from Life Magazine appeared. I was——

Mr. JENNER. Had you had any advance notice?

Mrs. PAINE. We had had no advance notice.

Mr. JENNER. Nobody did?

Mrs. PAINE. Nobody did.

Mr. JENNER. You in particular and none of the others in the room?

Mrs. PAINE. None of the others.

Mr. JENNER. That was your impression?

Mrs. PAINE. I would be quite certain that none of the others and myself——

Mr. JENNER. At least that was your impression at the moment?

Mrs. PAINE. That they had no prior information that these people might come. I will say I was not surprised that anyone of the press found his way to our door at that point. If anything, I was surprised there weren't more. Life Magazine was the only company or group to appear that evening. I permitted them to come in, and I felt that Mrs. Marguerite Oswald was interested in the possibility of their buying the story or paying for what information she and Marina might give them.

Mr. JENNER. Had that occurred to you?

Mrs. PAINE. Had that occurred to me? No. But then, too, I wasn't thinking about pay for lawyers but she made that connection verbally in my presence.

Mr. JENNER. What connection?

Mrs. PAINE. Between the need for money.

Mr. JENNER. Yes.

Mrs. PAINE. The availability of Life Magazine and the need to pay for a lawyer.

Mr. JENNER. And she was the one who raised that subject?

Mrs. PAINE. Yes; she raised it.

Mr. JENNER. For commercialization of the story?

Mrs. PAINE. I recall now she raised it definitely enough that Mr. Tommy Thompson of Life called, I believe still that evening, to see if he could offer anything or what he might be empowered to offer.

Mr. JENNER. That was all instigated by her?

Mrs. PAINE. Yes; very much so. I noticed that the other man, whose name I forget, had a camera and I was amazed, and I also saw he took a picture and I was amazed, he tried with a dim light in the room.

Mr. JENNER. When you say he took a picture, you don't mean he took a picture from your living room?

Mrs. PAINE. He took a picture in my living room. He photographed. I saw him wind his roll.

Mr. JENNER. Thank you.

Mrs. PAINE. I made the mistake I now think of turning on another light simply as an act of hostess, it was dim in the living room but I hadn't realized until later that I was making it possible for him to take a picture.

I didn't know what was best for me to do as hostess. It seemed to me that Mrs. Oswald, Sr., Mrs. Marguerite Oswald, was both interested in encouraging the Life Magazine representatives and still didn't really want her picture taken, and I had no personal objection to their being there. But I considered the Oswalds my guests and I didn't want to have the Life Magazine people there if they didn't want them. But they left fairly promptly, saying that they would come back in the morning.

Mr. JENNER. Did they say anything about your talking or not talking to any other news media representatives until they had talked with you?

Mrs. PAINE. Not to me.

Mr. JENNER. Nothing of that implied?

Mrs. PAINE. No. It was after this that the conversation I have already related with Marina took place, and we finished our preparations for bed. She said to me she didn't think she would sleep fairly soon and asked if she could borrow my hair dryer, she would stay up and take a shower, which she often said renewed her spirits, and I then went to bed, having given her my hair dryer. We woke perhaps something after 7 the next morning or closer to 8.

Mr. JENNER. When you say "we", who do you mean?

Mrs. PAINE. The household. I think we had not yet—we pretty much woke all at once.

Mr. JENNER. Did your husband remain at your home?

Mrs. PAINE. Yes; he remained at my home that night, the first time he had been there in a great long time. We were still eating breakfast or had just begun when the two Life people arrived again, this time with an interpreter, a woman doctor whose name I don't remember, and Marguerite Oswald and Marina Oswald, with her two little girls went with these two Life Magazine people to downtown Dallas for the purpose of seeing Lee, and Marguerite Oswald wanted to see that he got legal counsel immediately.

They were acting, the Life people were acting in this case as shovers, I feel, and I also thought Marguerite Oswald was hoping that something could be arranged between them, that would be financially helpful.

Mr. JENNER. Did she say anything that further stimulated your thoughts and reaction in that direction?

Mrs. PAINE. Yes. I don't recall specifically but I have the clear impression that——

Mr. JENNER. From her conversation with the Life representatives?

Mrs. PAINE. From her conversation. Yes. They left quite soon, I remember wishing Marina had taken more time to have more breakfast since it was going to be a trying day, and that is the last I saw her until March 9, in the evening, very recently.

Mr. JENNER. March 9, 1964?

Mrs. PAINE. Yes.

Mr. JENNER. Just a week or so ago?

Mrs. PAINE. That is right. She left, of course, expecting to come back. She took only the immediate needs of the baby's diapers and bottle, and I fully expected her to come back later that same day. I don't really recall. I think there must have been some newsmen out then that morning, later that morning.

Mr. JENNER. To see you, at your home?

Mrs. PAINE. At my home. I would be certain of that. The Houston Post—well, yes. And Michael was there also, at least in the morning as I recall, and talked with these people.

I believe the local paper, Irving News, was there. Then Michael, as I recall, went to do something related to his work or had to do some shopping.

Mr. JENNER. He left your home?

Mrs. PAINE. Anyway, in the afternoon I was the only one there and I felt I had better get some grocery shopping done so as to be prepared for a long stay home just answering the doorbell and telling what I could to the people who wanted to know. I was just preparing to go to the grocery store when several officers arrived again from the Dallas Police Office and asked if they could search.

This time I was in the yard, the front yard on the grass, and asked if they could search and held up their warrant and I said, yes, they could search. They said they were looking for something specific and I said, "I want to go to the grocery store, I'll just go and you go ahead and do your searching."

I then went to the grocery store and when I came back they had finished and left, locking my door which necessitated my getting out my key, I don't normally lock my door when I go shopping.

Representative FORD. Did you take your children shopping?

Mrs. PAINE. Always. Then about 3:30 or 4 I got a telephone call.

Mr. JENNER. The phone rang?

Mrs. PAINE. The phone rang; I answered it.

Mr. JENNER. Did you recognize the voice?

Mrs. PAINE. I recognized the voice but I don't recall what he said?

Mr. JENNER. What did the voice say?

Mrs. PAINE. The voice said: "This is Lee."

Mr. JENNER. Give your best recollection of everything you said and if you can, please, everything he said, and exactly what you said.

Mrs. PAINE. I said, "Well, Hi." And he said he wanted to ask me to call Mr. John Abt in New York for him after 6 p.m. He gave me a telephone number of an office in New York and a residence in New York.

Mr. JENNER. Two telephone numbers he gave you?

Mrs. PAINE. Yes.

Mr. JENNER. One office and one residence of Mr. John Abt. Did he say who Mr. John Abt was?

Mrs. PAINE. He said he was an attorney he wanted to have.

Mr. JENNER. Represent him?

Mrs. PAINE. To represent him. He thanked me for my concern.

Mr. JENNER. Did he tell you or ask you what you were to do or say to Mr. Abt if you reached him?

Mrs. PAINE. I carried the clear impression I was to ask him if he would serve as attorney for Lee Oswald.

Mr. JENNER. All right.

Have you given the substance of the conversation in as much detail, of the entire conversation, as you now can recall?

Mrs. PAINE. There is a little more that is——

Senator COOPER. Why don't you just go ahead and tell it as you remember it, everything that he said and you said?

Mrs. PAINE. I can't give the specific words to this part but I carry a clear impression, too, that he sounded to me almost as if nothing out of the ordinary had happened.

I would make this telephone call for him, would help him, as I had in other ways previously. He was, he expressed gratitude to me. I felt, but did not express, considerable irritation at his seeming to be so apart from the situation, so presuming of his own innocence, if you will, but I did say I would make the call for him.

Then he called back almost immediately. I gather that he had made the call to me on the permission to make a different call and then he got specific permission from the police to make a call to me and the call was identical.

Mr. JENNER. This is speculation?

Mrs. PAINE. This is speculation but the content of the second call was almost identical.

Mr. JENNER. The phone rang?

Mrs. PAINE. He asked me to contact John Abt.

Mr. JENNER. He identified himself and he asked you to make the call?

Mrs. PAINE. Yes.

Mr. JENNER. What did he say?

Mrs. PAINE. He wanted me to call this lawyer.

Mr. JENNER. Did you express any surprise for him to call back almost immediately giving you the same message that he had given previously?

Mrs. PAINE. I think somebody must have said, that the officers had said he could call, make this call.

Mr. JENNER. Did you say anything about the fact that he had already just called you about the same subject matter?

Mrs. PAINE. He may have added.

Mr. JENNER. Did you, please?

Mrs. PAINE. No. I was quite stunned that he called at all or that he thought he could ask anything of me, appalled, really.

Mr. McCLOY. Did he say he was innocent, or did he just have this conversation with respect to the retention of a counsel?

Mrs. PAINE. That is all.

Mr. JENNER. At no time during either of those conversations did he deny that he was in any way involved in this situation?

Mrs. PAINE. He made no reference to why he was at the police station or why he needed a lawyer.

Mr. JENNER. He just assumed that you knew he was at the police station, did he?

Mrs. PAINE. That is right.

Mr. JENNER. That was your impression?

Mrs. PAINE. That is right.

Mr. JENNER. He didn't say where he was?

Mrs. PAINE. No.

Mr. JENNER. He just started out saying what you now say he said?

Mrs. PAINE. That is right.

Mr. JENNER. But in no respect did he say to you that he was entirely innocent of any charges that had been made against him?

Mrs. PAINE. He did not say that.

Mr. JENNER. Did he mention the subject at all of the assassination of the President or the slaying of Officer Tippit?

Mrs. PAINE. No; he did not.

Mr. JENNER. What you have given is your best recollection of the entire conversation?

Mrs. PAINE. That is correct.

Representative FORD. This was Saturday afternoon, November 23?

Mrs. PAINE. Yes.

Representative FORD. About what time?

Mrs. PAINE. Four, perhaps in the afternoon.

Representative FORD. Had you seen him the day before?

Mrs. PAINE. No.

Mr. McCLOY. Who was in the house with you when that call came in?

Mrs. PAINE. Just my children.

Mr. McCLOY. Just your children.

Representative FORD. While you were shopping and after the officers had come with a warrant, they went in the house, no one was in the house?

Mrs. PAINE. For a portion of the time they were looking, no one was in the house.

Representative FORD. They were there alone?

Mrs. PAINE. That is right.

Mr. McCLOY. Did they indicate—were they still there when you got back?

Mrs. PAINE. No; they were not. Remember the door was locked.

Mr. McCLOY. Yes; the door was locked, that is what I gather. Do you know what they took on this occasion, or did they tell you what they were coming for?

Mrs. PAINE. No; I do not. Before I left they were leafing through books to see if anything fell out but that is all I saw.

Mr. McCLOY. All right.

Mrs. PAINE. In this interim then, I suppose I talked to some more news people but I want to get to the next important point which was that Lee called again.

Mr. JENNER. A third time?

Mrs. PAINE. I really call the first two one, but it was twice dialed.

Mr. JENNER. Fix the time, please.

Mrs. PAINE. It was around 9:30 in the evening.

Mr. JENNER. Who was home? Was your husband there on that occasion?

Mrs. PAINE. I don't recall.

Mr. JENNER. Was anyone else other than your children and yourself in your home at the time of the receipt of the call in the evening?

Mrs. PAINE. It could only have been Michael. I would remember someone else.

Mr. JENNER. But you have no definite recollection that even he was present?

Mrs. PAINE. No.

Mr. JENNER. All right. The phone rang, you answered it.

Mrs. PAINE. Yes.

Mr. JENNER. Did you recognize the voice?

Mrs. PAINE. I recognized the voice.

Mr. JENNER. Whose was it?

Mrs. PAINE. It was Lee Oswald's.

Mr. JENNER. What did he say and what did you say?

Mrs. PAINE. He said, "Marina, please," in Russian.

Mr. JENNER. Please, Mrs. Paine, did he speak to you in English in the conversations in the afternoon or in Russian?

Mrs. PAINE. He spoke in English the entire conversation.

Mr. JENNER. The two in the afternoon?

Mrs. PAINE. Yes.

Mr. JENNER. Now, however, he resorted to Russian, did he?

Mrs. PAINE. Yes. He planned to speak to Marina.

Mr. JENNER. I beg your pardon?

Mrs. PAINE. He planned to speak to Marina, and this opening phrase was one he normally used calling as he had many previous times to speak to her.

Mr. JENNER. He was under the assumption, you gathered, that Marina was in your home?

Mrs. PAINE. He certainly was.

Mr. JENNER. All right.

Mrs. PAINE. And I would be fairly certain that I answered him in English. I said she was not there, that I had a notion about where she might be, but I wasn't at all certain. That I would try to find out. He said, he wanted me to—he said he thought she should be at my house. He felt irritated at not having been able to reach her. And he wanted me to——

Mr. JENNER. Did he sound irritated?

Mrs. PAINE. Yes; he sounded just a slight edge to his voice. And he wanted me to deliver a message to her that he thought she should be at my house.

Mr. JENNER. And he so instructed you?

Mrs. PAINE. Yes.

Mr. JENNER. That is what he said?

Mrs. PAINE. Yes. That was so far as I remember, the entire conversation.

Mr. JENNER. What response did you give to his direction?

Mrs. PAINE. I said I would try to reach her.

Mr. JENNER. His direction——

Mrs. PAINE. And tell her his message.

Mr. JENNER. All right.

Mrs. Paine, in the meantime, had you sought to reach John Abt?

Mrs. PAINE. I had, after 6 o'clock, thank you. I had dialed both numbers and neither answered.

Mr. JENNER. Neither answered. Was there any conversation between you and Lee Oswald in the evening conversation to which you reported to him your inability to reach Mr. Abt?

Mrs. PAINE. I do not specifically recall.

Mr. JENNER. Or the subject of Mr. Abt at all?

Mrs. PAINE. I don't want to get into rationalization. I can judge that something was said but I do not recall it specifically.

Mr. JENNER. Now, have you given the full extent of that conversation?·

Mrs. PAINE. To the best of my recollection.

Mr. JENNER. At anytime during that conversation with Lee Harvey Oswald did he assert or intimate in any form or fashion his innocence of any charges against him?

Mrs. PAINE. No; he did not.

Mr. JENNER. Was the assassination mentioned at all?

Mrs. PAINE. No; it was not.

Mr. JENNER. Was the shooting or murder of Officer Tippit mentioned?

Mrs. PAINE. No.

Mr. JENNER. You have given everything that was said in that conversation as best you are able to recall it at the moment?

Mrs. PAINE. That is right. I then tried the only thing I knew to do, to try to reach Marina. I had heard one of the FBI agents try to find her when he was at my home, had dialed the hotel where the Life people were staying and asked to be put in contact with Marina and was told, I judge, because he repeated it and wrote it down. Executive Inn. Here I am turning detective in this small way.

Mr. JENNER. You also mentioned now for the first time there were FBI agents in your home?

Mrs. PAINE. That day.

Mr. JENNER. During the course of the day?

Mrs. PAINE. Yes. I then dialed——

Mr. JENNER. You shook your head, did you shake your head in the affirmative?

Mrs. PAYNE. Yes; there were FBI agents in my home during the day. One I recalled made this telephone call. I was waiting to hear from Marina to see if she wanted to talk with me. I had no desire to press her or to attempt to reach her unless she wanted to reach me, but then with this message, I went ahead and dialed the Executive Inn and asked for Tommy Thompson, and Marguerite Oswald answered, and I said I would like to talk to Marina, and she said, "Well, Marina is in the bathroom," and I said to Marguerite that Lee had called me, that he wanted me to deliver a message to Marina, that he wished for her to be at my home, and Marguerite Oswald said, "Well, he is in prison, he don't know the things we are up against, the things we have to face. What he wants doesn't really matter," which surprised me. And again I asked to speak to Marina and waited until I did speak to her and delivered the same message in Russian to her but there was no further——

Mr. JENNER. What response did Marina make to the message that you conveyed to her?

Mrs. PAINE. She said she was very tired and wanted to get to bed, as I recall, and thought it was certainly best to stay there that night.

Mr. JENNER. Is that your best recollection?

Mrs. PAINE. Yes. And I certainly agreed with her.

Mr. JENNER. Did she say anything in response to your delivery of Lee Oswald's message about Marina staying with you, of the possibility of her staying with you, say, the next day?

Mrs. PAINE. Nothing of that nature was said. I think I remember that we did discuss whether she had seen Lee during the day, and on that occasion it seems to me I learned that she had seen him around noon but I may be wrong about when I learned that. I knew she had seen him.

Mr. JENNER. Either in that conversation or any other conversation with Marina that you may have had, was the subject of Lee Oswald's attitude or any comments he made mentioned?

Mrs. PAINE. No.

Mr. JENNER. Nobody reported to you anything about any conversation they might or did have with Lee Oswald either on the 22d or 23d or even on the 24th of November 1963?

Mrs. PAINE. No. I am of the impression I again tried the home telephone of John Abt on Sunday morning, but I am not certain, and there was no answer. That I certainly remember.

Mr. McCLOY. Did you ever reach Abt?

Mrs. PAINE. No.

Mr. JENNER. Did you ever attempt to report to Lee Oswald that you had been unable to reach Mr. Abt?

Mrs. PAINE. Not unless such transpired in our 9:30 conversation Saturday evening, but I made no effort to call the police station itself.

Mr. JENNER. Excuse me?

Mrs. PAINE. I made no effort to call the police station.

Mr. JENNER. Did you have at anytime any further conversations with Lee Oswald?

Mrs. PAINE. No.

Mr. JENNER. Other than what you have now related?

Mrs. PAINE. That is right.

Mr. McCLOY. Did you have any impression as to why he wanted Marina to come back with you? Was it in order to make her available for telephone calls from him or what?

Mrs. PAINE. What is distinctly my impression is that he thought she should be available. That it was she wasn't where he could find her that irritated him rather than that he thought this was the best place for her.

Representative FORD. Did you know of Mr. Abt or was this just——

Mrs. PAINE. I had never heard of Mr. Abt before.

Representative FORD. Never heard of him?

Mrs. PAINE. That is right.

Senator COOPER. Did Marguerite Oswald explain any further, in the statement you said she made, about having too many obstacles or having obstacles or having troubles?

Mrs. PAINE. Are you referring to the statement on Friday night when she was at my home?

Senator COOPER. No. I think you said a few mintues ago when she went to the hotel you called her and told her what Lee Oswald had told you to tell Marina.

Mrs. PAINE. Yes.

Senator COOPER. I think you said she said something about——

Mrs. PAINE. "Well, he doesn't understand the things we are up against or things of this nature." What I remember most clearly is that she didn't seem to care whether he was told the truth or not.

Mr. JENNER. What?

Mrs. PAINE. Well, that is perhaps a further statement, told the truth about— had it seemed to me a lack of respect on her part. She didn't care what his wishes were in the situation, in other words. And this sticks in my mind.

Mr. JENNER. Did you have any conversation with Robert Oswald on the 22d, subsequent to the time that you met him when he first come to the police station?

Mrs. PAINE. No.

Mr. JENNER. Did you on the 23d of November?

Mrs. PAINE. No.

Mr. JENNER. The 24th?

Mrs. PAINE. I believe the only other time I saw Robert was some 3 weeks or more later when he came with two other people to pick up the rest of Marina's things.

89

Mr. JENNER. Then from the 22d of November until he came sometime in December you had no conversation with him and you had not seen him?

Mrs. PAINE. That is right.

Mr. JENNER. You had no contact at all with him?

Mrs. PAINE. That is my best recollection. Marina called me around noon on Sunday, the 24th. She said she was with the police, and, of course, this was said in Russian; I don't know whether she meant Secret Service or Irving Police or Dallas Police or what sort, but official. Her husband had already been shot at this time, so it was just after. He had been shot and I had the television on and I knew that.

Representative FORD. Did she know it?

Mrs. PAINE. I am certain she did. What makes me certain I can't recall definitely. I felt that she was confining herself in her conversation to the things she just had to say.

Senator COOPER. What did she say?

Mrs. PAINE. She was directing me how to find certain things she needed to have. A winter coat, things for the baby, a little purse with some money in it that she left either on top of the dresser or in a drawer in the bedroom where they had stayed.

Mr. JENNER. Did she sound less than cordial——

Mrs. PAINE. Oh, no, she sounded, as I recall it, as a call from a woman who was doing her best to simply achieve the things she had to do but was under a tremendous strain.

Mr. JENNER. Was any mention made of the death of her husband?

Mrs. PAINE. He was not yet dead, he had been shot but he was not yet dead.

Mr. JENNER. Was any mention made between you in this conversation of the fact that Lee Oswald had been shot?

Mrs. PAINE. I don't recall such.

Mr. JENNER. You didn't mention it?

Mrs. PAINE. I did not tell her; no.

Mr. JENNER. Did you—it might be natural that you would express sympathy. Did you mention the subject at all, sympathetical or otherwise?

Mrs. PAINE. I don't recall mentioning the subject and as I say, I have this distinct feeling that she knew, and I knew she knew but what caused that, I can't identify.

Mr. JENNER. Did you have the feeling, if I may use some vernacular, that she was "under wraps" or rather she was bereft and just seeking to do——

Mrs. PAINE. I had no feeling she was restraining herself from saying any particular things.

Mr. JENNER. Was under restraint?

Mrs. PAINE. No.

Mr. JENNER. From some outside source?

Mrs. PAINE. I had no such feeling.

Mr. JENNER. All right.

Mrs. PAINE. I then, well, I should say there were one or two officers from the Irving Police Department there who were waiting to take the things that she directed——

Mr. JENNER. The police officers had already arrived at your home?

Mrs. PAINE. Yes; I guess I remembered it as virtually simultaneous. I might fill in, whether it is important to your inquiry or not, the moment the television announced that Lee Oswald had been shot, an Irving Police patrol car that had been going by my house and had hesitated in front, stopped and the officer got out carrying a rifle and came into my house, closed the curtains and said he was here to protect me. I later learned that he thought Mrs. Oswald, Marina Oswald, was in the house, and he had been directed by his car radio to come in, and he then closed all the blinds and peered out. And it was in the midst of this time that Marina called, so you see the officers were there already on other business.

Mr. JENNER. The officer was in your home when you talked with Marina?

Mrs. PAINE. Yes; when Marina made the call.

Mr. JENNER. Did you say anything to the officers that Marina had called when you finished that conversation?

Mrs. PAINE. Yes.

Mr. JENNER. You told them?

Mrs. PAINE. Yes.

Mr. JENNER. Did you tell them anything of the substance of the call?

Mrs. PAINE. Yes; that I was to get some things and I think they had the same information separately a different way from a car radio or something at the same time, which was to put some things together to take to her. I did then pack one or two, or even three of the suit cases we talked about yesterday with baby things.

Mr. JENNER. Excuse me, Mrs. Paine. You keep referring to one or two or three. Were there as many as three?

Mrs. PAINE. I think there were as many as three, including a very small, you might say, cosmetic case, only more, not as fancy as that. This was in her room, and I recall looking in it and seeing a family album of photographs and thinking this had better be in her hands, and included that along with clothes. I sent a childs toy, some things that I thought might be helpful to her in keeping her children happy as well as the individual items she had asked for specifically.

Mr. McCLOY. Did you sense any note of estrangement at all between you and Marina when she telephoned you?

Mrs. PAINE. No; the situation was strained.

Mr. McCLOY. Strained because she hadn't reappeared, you mean?

Mrs. PAINE. No; because her husband had been shot.

Mr. McCLOY. No; I meant in your conversation with her was there any indication of any coolness between you?

Mrs. PAINE. No; none I detected.

Mr. JENNER. Had you noticed any when you were in the police station?

Mrs. PAINE. Oh, no.

Mr. JENNER. On the previous day?

Mrs. PAINE. Oh, no.

Mr. JENNER. None at all. So that up to the moment of this telephone conversation and after you finished you had no feeling there was any estrangement, any coolness, any change in attitude on the part of Marina toward you as a person?

Mrs. PAINE. No.

Mr. McCLOY. Have you felt any evidence of that since?

Mrs. PAINE. Yes; and that has several parts to it and I could easily go into it now.

Mr. JENNER. I was going to ask her some general questions and Senator Cooper asked me if I would permit her just to go through the day as she has without, with a minimum of, interruptions so that you and he might, and Representative Ford, might ask some general questions before you left, so that is what I have done.

Mr. McCLOY. Have you completed your report?

Mrs. PAINE. That brings us to the 24th so that all else is really quite post the assassination.

Mr. McCLOY. There is one thing I would like to ask before I go, if I may, and that is your husband testified that several times he had moved this blanket when it was in the garage. Can you fix the date when he was in your house and working in the garage so that he was compelled to move the blanket? When did he come to——

Mrs. PAINE. He normally came on Friday evening. He would sometimes come on a Sunday afternoon, and either of those times could have been times that he had worked in the garage.

Mr. McCLOY. That was all through September, October?

Mrs. PAINE. Yes; September, October; yes.

Mr. McCLOY. But when he had been working there he never mentioned to you any—about the existence of this blanket, package which he had been compelled to move?

Mrs. PAINE. No. That didn't come up until after the assassination.

Mr. McCLOY. It didn't come up until after the assassination.

Mr. JENNER. Excuse me, you are seeking to refresh your recollection from what document, please?

Mrs. PAINE. I am looking at a calendar to see if there is anyway that I can tell when Michael was in the house.

Mr. JENNER. That is Commission exhibit number what?

Mrs. PAINE. 401. But it has not helped me in refreshing my memory.

Mr. McCLOY. Did you have contacts with the FBI and if so what were they before the assassination?

Mrs. PAINE. An FBI agent was out, I have learned since, on November 1. I made no note of the day for myself. Sat down and talked in a relaxed way and for sometime in my living room. He said that the FBI liked to make it plain to people who have been in this country sometime, immigrated from an iron curtain country if they were experiencing any blackmail pressure from their home country, that they were welcome, and invited to discuss it with the FBI if they so choose.

Mr. JENNER. Excuse me, Marina was present?

Mrs. PAINE. Marina was present.

Mr. JENNER. Did she overhear?

Mrs. PAINE. I am not certain—I tried to translate some of this conversation, I am not certain how good my translation was or how well I conveyed it, or even if I conveyed it to her.

Mr. JENNER. But you do recall translating some of the conversation to her?

Mrs. PAINE. I do recall translating some of the conversation indeed.

Mr. JENNER. Were you at times asked to address Marina to convey something that the FBI agent asked you to convey to her and then to translate in the reverse to him?

Mrs. PAINE. I don't recall anything as formal as that; no. The agent and I conversed some in English. He said, for instance, that, well he was interested in knowing if Lee Oswald lived here. I told him he did not, that he had a room in town; he asked if I knew where the room was and I said I did not. He asked if he was working and I said yes, and that he was working at the Texas School Book Depository. I haven't gone over any of this yet, it must have been in conversation with you.

Mr. JENNER. You testified to this yesterday afternoon?

Mrs. PAINE. I thought I did. It sounds familiar.

Mr. McCLOY. I just wanted to fix for my own benefit the number of times you saw FBI agents prior to the assassination in the company of Marina.

Mr. JENNER. There was a succeeding date?

Mrs. PAINE. There was a succeeding date which again I have been told by the FBI was November 5, the first time.

Mr. JENNER. Do you recall it was a few days after the first man came?

Mrs. PAINE. I recall——

Mr. JENNER. Do you recall it was in your home?

Mrs. PAINE. I recall it was in the early part of the week.

Mr. JENNER. Did the same gentleman call?

Mrs. PAINE. The same gentleman. He had someone else along.

Mr. JENNER. That was Mr. Hosty, the gentleman whom you now have in mind?

Mrs. PAINE. Yes; I now know his name as Hosty.

Mr. McCLOY. From that you knew that the FBI was still interested in the activity of Oswald?

Mrs. PAINE. Oh, indeed.

Mr. McCLOY. That is what I want to bring out. I think that is all I have, the questions I have.

Are you going to take up later this estrangement as to how it developed?

Mr. JENNER. Yes; I shall do that this afternoon. Representative Ford has afforded me a list of subjects upon which to make inquiry and I will do so this afternoon. Perhaps Representative Ford and Senator Cooper, you would have some questions of this lady before we adjourn for the luncheon period?

Senator COOPER. Are you going to continue this afternoon?

Mr. JENNER. Yes.

Senator COOPER. I will postpone mine until this afternoon. I think Mr. McCloy and Congressman Ford have to go.

Representative FORD. Mr. Jenner, I will give you these questions and use those, if any, that are other than what you planned to use yourself. I am a little interested and I would like to hear you tell it, if I could, Mrs. Paine, how much did you know about the finances of Lee and Marina?

Mrs. PAINE. It seemed to me they lived on a very small budget. In March of the year, at either the first or second visit with her, she told me she lived on something under, around $200 a month and this was more than they had been, because they had just finished paying a debt that they had incurred for their passage to this country and they were feeling rich on $200 a month, and I could see she was a good planner in what she bought. I could see they seldom, if ever, bought clothes for themselves or even for June. In the fall then Lee never volunteered or gave any money for the cost of her being at my house. He did on one occasion buy a few things at the grocery store for, at Marina's request, which he paid for, and on another occasion I was aware that he had given her some money to buy shoes. Did I mention this previously?

Representative FORD. Yes.

Mr. JENNER. Yesterday afternoon you did; yes.

Representative FORD. But even after he gained employment at the Texas School Book Depository and was being paid he never gave her any money for her to contribute to you?

Mrs. PAINE. No; he did not.

Representative FORD. Did Marina ever express any concern about this?

Mrs. PAINE. Periodically she expressed her embarrassment at having to receive always from me. I tried to convince her how useful and helpful it was to me to have her conversation, but I never felt I had convinced her of that. I would have to say I am guessing that she hoped Lee would contribute. It would have been like her to think that he should.

Mr. JENNER. You gather that from the fact that she did raise the subject occasionally?

Mrs. PAINE. Just from the fact that she raised her embarrassment? Yes.

Mr. JENNER. Yes.

Representative FORD. I think that is all now. Mr. Jenner, you can use those to supplement or as you see fit during the interrogation this afternoon. Thank you.

Mr. McCLOY. I have no more questions.

I would like to say this though, perhaps, Mrs. Paine, that you understand we are not trying to punish anybody here. We are not——

Mrs. PAINE. I do understand.

Mr. McCLOY. This is not a court of law. We are trying to get at the facts. Anything that you can contribute before you complete your testimony which would help us to get the facts we would like to receive, whether it be in the form of hunches or anything that you have, and you must not, I suggest that you don't, assume that merely because we haven't examined you on a particular fact that if there is anything that you do have in mind that you advance it and volunteer it for the benefit of the further security of the country.

Mrs. PAINE. I have tried very hard to think of the things that I thought would be useful to you, especially as we had so little time in advance of testifying to help me recall in thinking about it.

Mr. JENNER. May I say, Mr. McCloy, that Mrs. Paine yesterday and the day before, when I had an opportunity to talk with her, she did volunteer several matters of which we had no notice whatsoever. For example, the telephone calls by Lee Harvey Oswald to her, we had not known of that. And the existence of the curtain rods.

Mr. McCLOY. Anything that is in the background that you have——

Mrs. PAINE. I did want to amend my testimony of yesterday in one small particular. I spoke, indeed, during the testimony I recalled this incident of Lee having gotten into my car, started it, and did the driving from my home to the parking lot where we practiced, pretty much over my objection in a sense but I did not object strongly enough. I said this was about three blocks. That would appear that it was walking distance. It was longer than that.

If you have someone out there in time, why I could go with the person to show just exactly what the distance was.

Representative FORD. What was his reaction when you objected? First, was your objection just oral, was it strong, was it admonition, of what kind?

Mrs. PAINE. I felt that, and this is what you are getting at too and I think something we haven't yet discussed, is the matter of what kind of person this was or how I reacted to the kind of person he was. He seemed to me prickly, all sharp points and edgy, and I wished he could be more relaxed and more at ease. I didn't want to confront him with a statement of, "Lee, I didn't want you to start this car and take it yourself", so I simply said, "my father is an insurance man and he certainly would not want me to be permitting you to drive in the street when you don't even have a learner's permit yet, and I will certainly drive it home."

From the time I had first known him he had changed in his attitude toward me, I felt. I felt in the spring he expected to be disliked, that he carried a shell of proud disdain around him to protect himself from human contact, and this was falling away from him at my home.

Mr. JENNER. In the fall you mean?

Mrs. PAINE. In the fall of the year, in October and November. He began to appear much more at ease, and as if he had some confidence in how he would be treated. It is a whole subject really.

Representative FORD. Can you give us a little more information on what you said to him and what he, or how he responded in this incident involving the car?

Mrs. PAINE. I would say he clearly wanted to do the driving and to drive in the street. I felt that this, my not permitting him to, was one of the things that was helping to get him to the office where he could get a learner's permit, and he was eager to be driving, and to learn to drive on the street.

Representative FORD. Did he just slough off, so to speak, your admonition that he shouldn't drive?

Mrs. PAINE. I didn't make it a requirement that he stop right there so he didn't have to stop.

Representative FORD. You just suggested it might be better?

Mrs. PAINE. I just made it clear I was uncomfortable and on the way home I would drive.

Mr. McCLOY. There is one thing we haven't had testimony about, I imagine, except implicitly.

It is alleged that Lee possessed a .38 caliber revolver. Do you, in the light of hindsight, perhaps, do you have any feeling now that he was secreting that weapon on your premises?

Mrs. PAINE. I had no idea that it was there or ever was there.

Mr. McCLOY. Nothing now makes you feel that it was there other than the finding of the rifle?

Mrs. PAINE. That is right.

Representative FORD. Thank you very much, Mrs. Paine.

Senator COOPER. The Commission will recess until 2 o'clock today.

(Whereupon, at 12:20 p.m., the Commission recessed.)

Afternoon Session

TESTIMONY OF RUTH HYDE PAINE RESUMED

The President's Commission reconvened at 2 p.m.

The CHAIRMAN. We will start now. We will continue until Senator Cooper comes and then he will preside the rest of the afternoon. I will be busy with Mr. Rankin some of the time.

Mr. JENNER. Thank you, Mr. Chief Justice.

Mrs. Paine, this morning I was seeking to qualify and introduce in evidence Commission Exhibit 425, which, at the time I had it in my hand, consisted of one page. You called my attention to the fact that it was a letter dated October 14, 1963, to your mother by you in your handwriting, but that you had only given me the first page or sheet, which consists front and reverse of two pages. Then you tendered me the second page or sheet, and indicated some reluctance about the need for its use in this connection.

During the noon recess you have afforded me the possession of the second page, and my recollection is you have voiced no objection to its introduction in evidence.

Mrs. PAINE. I have no objection to its introduction. It refers just to personal matters, but if you don't have it, you will have to wonder what it is. It is better not to wonder.

Mr. JENNER. Yes. And it does give the full context of the really pertinent statements that you made in the first two pages and to which you made allusion yesterday in your testimony.

Mrs. PAINE. That is right.

Mr. JENNER. I direct your attention to the second sheet, the first of which is numbered three and the reverse side numbered four.

Is the handwriting on both of those sheets yours?

Mrs. PAINE. Yes it is.

Mr. JENNER. And it is the third and fourth pages of the letter to which you referred yesterday and again this morning, Commission Exhibit No. 425?

Mrs. PAINE. It is.

Mr. JENNER. And that page is in the same condition now as when—that is pages three and four, as when—you dispatched the entire letter to your mother?

Mrs. PAINE. That is right.

Mr. JENNER. Mr. Chief Justice, I offer Commission Exhibit No. 425 in evidence. It has been heretofore marked.

The CHAIRMAN. It may be admitted.

(Commission Exhibit No. 425 was marked and received in evidence.)

Mr. JENNER. There have been marked as Commission's exhibits in this series 451 and 453 to 456, a series of five colored photographs purporting to be photographs of one Curtis LaVerne Crafard, taken on the 28th day of November 1963. Mrs. Paine would you be good enough to look at each of those, and after you have looked at them, I wish to ask you a question.

Mrs. PAINE. I have looked at them all.

Mr. JENNER. Calling on your recollection of the physiognomy and appearance of Lee Oswald, do you detect a resemblance between the man depicted in those photographs, the exhibit numbers of which I have given, and Lee Oswald?

Mrs. PAINE. Yes; I do.

Mr. JENNER. To the best of your present recollection, do you recall whether you have ever seen the person whose features are reflected on those photographs?

Mrs. PAINE. No; I have not seen him.

The CHAIRMAN. May I see those, please?

Mrs. PAINE. Should I say that one picture in particular struck me as looking similar to Lee?

Mr. JENNER. Yes. When the Chief Justice has concluded his examination I will have you pick out that one in particular. Thank you, sir. When you select it will you give the exhibit number which appears on the reverse side?

Mrs. PAINE. Exhibit No. 453. Clearly the shoulders are broader than with Lee, but it is a quality about the face that recalls Oswald to my mind.

Mr. JENNER. And the jacket?

Mrs. PAINE. And the attire.

Mr. JENNER. The attire that is shown on the exhibit which is the first one you have before you, what is the number of that?

Mrs. PAINE. Exhibit 451.

Mr. JENNER. I asked you to describe Lee Oswald, his general attire. Did he normally wear a zipper jacket of the character shown on that exhibit?

Mrs. PAINE. Yes.

Mr. JENNER. And referring to the other photographs, you say that man's attire is similar to that Lee Oswald normally effected and employed.

Mrs. PAINE. Yes. It certainly is.

Mr. JENNER. I offer Commission Exhibits Nos. 451 and 453 through 456.

The CHAIRMAN. They may be admitted.

(Commission Exhibits Nos. 451 and 453 through 465 were received in evidence.)

Mr. JENNER. Mrs. Paine, the Commissioners this morning, had especially directed questions to you evidencing their interest in FBI interviews.

The CHAIRMAN. Senator, will you now continue to preside please, so I will be free to work with Mr. Rankin a little this afternoon. I will remain here though for a while.

Senator Cooper. Thank you.

Mr. Jenner. I gather the first interview by any FBI agent to your knowledge was on the first day of November 1963?

Mrs. Paine. Yes; and I don't really think interview is a fully accurate word.

Mr. Jenner. What word would you like to use?

Mrs. Paine. I felt that the agent stopped to see whether the Oswalds, either Mrs. Oswald or Mr., were living there, and to make the acquaintance of me. He said that he had talked with my immediate neighbor, Mrs. Roberts, the previous time.

Mr. Jenner. The pronoun you are using refers to the FBI agent.

Mrs. Paine. He, the FBI agent.

Mr. Jenner. Yes.

Mrs. Paine. Said that he had inquired of my next door neighbor, Mrs. Roberts, whether the Oswalds lived here, and she had said that she didn't know the last name but knew that the wife of the family was living there, and that there had just been a baby girl born, and that the husband came out some week ends.

Mr. Jenner. Is this what the agent told you?

Mrs. Paine. No, the neighbor told me.

Mr. Jenner. I see. All right.

Mrs. Paine. And I judged he wanted to find out directly.

Mr. Jenner. Had you finished?

Mrs. Paine. Yes.

Mr. Jenner. Have you subsequently learned the name of the gentleman who interviewed you or conversed with you?

Mrs. Paine. I have subsequently learned his name, yes. It was James Hosty.

The Chairman. What was the name?

Mrs. Paine. James Hosty, H-O-S-T-Y.

Mr. Jenner. I don't wish you to give that full interview again because you touched on it yesterday and again at greater length this morning. But I do wish to ask you with respect to that interview, did you give Agent Hosty the telephone numbers that you had received from Lee Oswald as to where he might be reached in Dallas?

Mrs. Paine. No; I didn't. He asked me if I knew where Lee lived. I did think of these phone numbers, but——

Mr. Jenner. During the course of the——

Mrs. Paine. Or later.

Mr. Jenner. Of the interview?

Mrs. Paine. At least between that time and the time he came again, but I have been impressed with what I have now concluded was a mistaken impression I have which effected my behavior; namely, that the FBI was in possession of a great deal of information, or so I thought, and certainly would find it very easy to find out where Lee Oswald was living. I really didn't believe they didn't know or needed to find out from me. This is a feeling stemming from my understanding of the difficulties they faced working in a free society. I would behave quite differently now, but I have learned a lot from this particular experience.

Mr. Jenner. Now was there a subsequent interview?

Mrs. Paine. There was an interview a few days later, yes, interview to the extent that he came to the door, walked in the door. We didn't as much as sit down. But he asked again about an address. I had none. I did say that I expected——

Mr. Jenner. An address as to where Lee resided?

Mrs. Paine. In town where he resided. I did say that I expected that when Marina moved into an apartment with Lee again, as we all thought would occur, that I would be in contact with her, and that I would be perfectly willing to give him information as to that address when I had such, but that my contact was with her and therefore through that way I would have the address.

Mr. Jenner. Were you again interviewed by telephone or otherwise by any FBI agent prior to November 22, 1963.

Mrs. PAINE. I have mentioned two times.

Mr. JENNER. Yes.

Mrs. PAINE. And that was all.

Mr. JENNER. That was all. So up to the time of the assassination, the only interviews with the FBI to your knowledge were on the first?

Mrs. PAINE. That is right.

Mr. JENNER. You will recall your testimony yesterday, Mrs. Paine, of the incident in which a telephone call was made by you at the request of Marina using the telephone number that has been left with you by Lee Oswald, and your inability to locate him, in fact the person who answered the telephone stated that there was no Lee Oswald living there. Do you recall your testimony on that score?

Mrs. PAINE. Yes.

Mr. JENNER. Did you report that to the FBI?

Mrs. PAINE. No; I did not.

Mr. JENNER. You also recall your testimony with respect to the draft of the proposed letter which I think is before you, and that is Commission exhibit number?

Mrs. PAINE. 130.

Mr. JENNER. Did you call the FBI and advise them of that incident?

Mrs. PAINE. No; I did not.

Mr. JENNER. And without seeking to have you repeat your testimony, were your reasons for not doing so the same as the one that you gave when I asked you whether you had given Agent Hosty the telephone number?

Mrs. PAINE. No; not identical. Certainly I didn't think that they had any information of such a letter, whereas I did think they knew where he lived or could easily find out, and of course they could also come to the house and see him at my house as he came on weekends.

Mr. JENNER. You did say to the FBI?

Mrs. PAINE. I did.

Mr. JENNER. That he would be at your home on weekends.

Mrs. PAINE. And I judged by the fact they didn't come that this was not someone they were terribly worried about talking to immediately. Both this letter, and the telephone conversation really, the one that followed it, where Marina reported to me that he was using a different name, were something new and different in the situation that made me feel this was a man I hadn't accurately perceived before.

I have said my impression in reading the letter was—I have said something similar to this—that of a small boy wanting to get in good with the boys, trying to use words that he thought would please. I didn't know to whom he addressed himself, but it struck me as something out of Pravda in his terminology. And I knew, as I have testified, that several of the statements in it were flatly false, and I wondered about the rest, and then when I heard that he was using a different name, that again was indication of a great disregard for truth on the part of Lee Oswald.

Mr. JENNER. Now what time of day did the interview on November 1 take place?

Mrs. PAINE. Afternoon.

Mr. JENNER. Late?

Mrs. PAINE. Middle of the afternoon. My memory is there were no children around which means it was nap time.

Mr. JENNER. It couldn't have been along about 5 o'clock in the afternoon?

Mrs. PAINE. It was a Friday, wasn't it?

Mr. JENNER. Yes, it was.

Mrs. PAINE. And he probably came out that Friday.

Mr. JENNER. You were just telling the agent, you had told the agent, had you not, that he came on weekends.

Mrs. PAINE. I did.

Mr. JENNER. And he arrived on Fridays?

Mrs. PAINE. I did.

Mr. JENNER. And this was a Friday?

Mrs. PAINE. It was, and you will recall yesterday——

Mr. JENNER. And you did tell the agent that?

Mrs. PAINE. Yes. It had to have been that session. I know I certainly told him, and it had to have been that time because the second meeting was very brief and had only to do with the address.

Mr. JENNER. And that was not on a Friday?

Mrs. PAINE. No; it was not.

Mr. JENNER. Was anything said about the agent remaining because Lee Oswald would be along, he was expected?

Mrs. PAINE. No. May I interject here to recall to your mind that as I looked through my calendar trying to find if there was any time, any weekend other than the weekend of October 12, that Lee arrived on a Saturday instead of a Friday, it had to be that weekend by deduction. And I don't recall whether he arrived that Friday evening.

I do recall when he arrived we told him about this meeting and I gave him the piece of paper on which I had written Mr. Hosty's name and the normal telephone number for the FBI in Dallas.

Mr. JENNER. But you recall no conversation. May I suggest this to you as possibly refreshing your recollection. That on that Friday afternoon, which I may say to you now, Mrs. Paine, is reported by Agent Hosty as having taken place on November 1, and he has made his report accordingly, was there any discussion of a suggestion that Lee Oswald would be out that weekend, that is either that you told him he would not be or that he would be, that you would expect him?

Mrs. PAINE. My recollection is that I said he came out here on weekends and he could be seen then.

Mr. JENNER. Go ahead.

Mrs. PAINE. And I have no recollection of ever thinking he was not going to come that weekend.

Mr. JENNER. You have also testified that you were also advised in advance when he was coming?

Mrs. PAINE. Yes.

Mr. JENNER. He asked permission. So if he were coming on the 1st of November, that very day, you would have been advised in advance that he was coming, would you not, according to your testimony.

Mrs. PAINE. Yes; I would think so.

Mr. JENNER. But you don't recall saying anything to Agent Hosty that he was coming that evening, at least that you expected him to be there.

Mrs. PAINE. I may have. I don't specifically recall.

Mr. JENNER. But you do have a recollection that you told him at least generally that Lee Oswald came to your home on weekends?

Mrs. PAINE. I feel certain of that.

Mr. JENNER. In any event, Agent Hosty did not remain?

Mrs. PAINE. He did not remain. I don't think it was very close to 5 when he left. It was earlier in the afternoon.

Mr. JENNER. You are inclined to think the interview took place earlier in the afternoon, that is prior to 5 o'clock?

Mrs. PAINE. Yes; more likely 2 to 3 or 3:30.

Mr. JENNER. During the slumber hours of your children?

Mrs. PAINE. That is right.

Mr. JENNER. Now you are certain in your own mind that you had no interview or no FBI agent interviewed you prior to November 1?

Mrs. PAINE. That is right.

Mr. JENNER. And if an FBI agent did interview you, you were not aware that you were being interviewed?

Mrs. PAINE. That is absolutely correct.

Mr. JENNER. Do you have a recollection that on October 29, that would be 2 days before the Friday session that you have testified about, that some sales person or purporting to be a sales person or a drummer or somebody came to your door and made some inquiries of you about the Oswalds?

Mrs. PAINE. October 29 is a Tuesday. I don't recall any such encounter. Written on my calendar is "Dal" for Dallas "Junie" meaning we went to a clinic in Dallas in the morning. It doesn't say about the rest of the day.

Mr. JENNER. Now when you reported to Lee Oswald the name of the agent and the telephone number, you put that on a slip of paper.

Mrs. PAINE. I did.

Mr. JENNER. And handed the slip of paper to him?

Mrs. PAINE. Yes; I did.

Mr. JENNER. Was there any conversation between you then as to FBI agents having at any time prior thereto interviewed Lee Oswald.

Mrs. PAINE. There may have been. I am certainly clear that I was told probably by Marina that he had been interviewed, or by both of them, that he had been interviewed in Fort Worth when they first returned from the Soviet Union. This I knew before the time of the assassination.

Mr. JENNER. Did Marina say whether she had been interviewed in Fort Worth?

Mrs. PAINE. No.

Mr. JENNER. This was only that Lee Oswald had been interviewed at Fort Worth?

Mrs. PAINE. Yes.

Mr. JENNER. But you recall no conversation in which either Lee or Marina said or intimated to you that they had, either of them had been interviewed either in New Orleans or in Dallas.

Mrs. PAINE. Nothing was mentioned of having been interviewed in New Orleans or Dallas.

Mr. JENNER. You made some reference yesterday, and I want to keep it in context, to the license number of the FBI agent.

Mrs. PAINE. Not in testimony. Did I?

Mr. JENNER. I thought you had.

Mrs. PAINE. Perhaps.

Mr. JENNER. It would be well if we went into that. Would you please recite what that incident was?

Mrs. PAINE. I am confused by the question.

Mr. JENNER. Do you recall the matter of the taking of the agent's license number from his automobile?

Mrs. PAINE. I was told by Agent Hosty well after the assassination that they had found in Oswald's room in Dallas a slip of paper which included not only Hosty's name and the telephone number of the FBI in Dallas, but also the license plate number with one letter incorrect, one number incorrect, of the car that Hosty had driven out. This was the first I had heard anything about their having been a license plate.

Mr. JENNER. You did not take——

Mrs. PAINE. Number taken down.

Mr. JENNER. You did not take the number down and place it on that piece of paper?

Mrs. PAINE. I did not.

Mr. JENNER. Or give it to Lee Harvey Oswald or to Marina?

Mrs. PAINE. I did not. I was never at any time interested in the license plate number. I wondered why anyone else would have been.

Mr. JENNER. In any event, the first you heard of the license number was after the assassination?

Mrs. PAINE. That is right.

Mr. JENNER. Under the circumstances you have now related?

Mrs. PAINE. I might describe the second meeting with Mr. Hosty a little more in detail.

Mr. JENNER. That is November 1?

Mrs. PAINE. That is the only way I can guess as to how this license plate number was in Oswald's room.

Mr. JENNER. All right.

Mrs. PAINE. Hosty and I, and a second agent was with him, I don't know the name, stood at the door of my home and talked briefly, as I have already described, about the address of Oswald in Dallas. Marina was in her room feeding the baby, or busy some way. She came in just as Hosty and I were closing the conversation, and I must say we were both surprised at her entering.

He then took his leave immediately, and as he has told me later, drove to the end of my street which curves and then drove back down Fifth Street.

Mr. JENNER. Now you are reporting something agent Hosty has told you?

Mrs. PAINE. Yes.

Mr. JENNER. Were you aware of the fact that he drove to the end of the street?

Mrs. PAINE. Not at that time, no. I was aware that he had parked his car out in front of my house. My best judgment is that the license plate was not visible, however, while it was parked; not visible from my house.

Mr. JENNER. Did you see the car?

Mrs. PAINE. I saw the car.

Mr. JENNER. Parked?

Mrs. PAINE. Yes. I noticed it particularly. Because the first time he had come on the 1st of November, he had parked down the street, and he made reference to the fact that they don't like to draw attention for the neighborhood to any interviews that they make, and in fact my neighbor also commented when she had talked with him a few days previously that his car was parked down the street and wasn't in front of my house. So I noticed the change that he had parked directly in front. But to the best of my recollection, in back of the Oldsmobile of my husband's.

Mr. JENNER. Did you attempt to look to see what his license number was?

Mrs. PAINE. What?

Mr. JENNER. Did you attempt to look at his automobile to see what the license number was?

Mrs. PAINE. No; nor could I have seen it from my house without my glasses on. I am nearsighted, and I was not wearing them.

Mr. JENNER. But the license plate would have been visible to anybody walking down the street or who desired?

Mrs. PAINE. Walking down the street, yes.

Mr. JENNER. Or looking out your garage.

Mrs. PAINE. I don't think so, because to the best of my recollection, an Oldsmobile that my husband bought was also in front of the house, so that the cars would have been close at the bumpers.

Mr. JENNER. So the license plates would have been screened by the Oldsmobile?

Mrs. PAINE. Yes.

Mr. JENNER. Have you given us all you have in mind with respect to the incidents?

Mrs. PAINE. There is one other thing which is a little different, and I had forgotten it but it is recalled by our conversation. I have already said that I said to Agent Hosty that if in the future Marina and Lee are living together, and I know, or I have correspondence with them I would give him his address if he wished it. Then it was the next day or that evening or sometime shortly thereafter Marina said to me while we were doing dishes that she felt their address was their business. Now my understanding is she doesn't understand English well. The word in Russian for address is "adres," and she made it plain that this was a matter of privacy for them. This surprised me. She had never spoken in this way to me before, and I didn't see that it made any difference.

Mr. JENNER. Did this arise out of, or in connection with, or was it stimulated, by any discussion between the two of you of the visit of Agent Hosty?

Mrs. PAINE. So far as I could see, it arose separately.

Mr. JENNER. So far as you can recall?

Mrs. PAINE. As far as I can recall.

Mr. JENNER. Did you make any effort to obtain Lee Oswald's address so that you could give it to the FBI?

Mrs. PAINE. No. As I have testified, I really thought they had it.

Mr. JENNER. When you made the telephone call to Lee Oswald and learned he apparently was living under an alias, and certainly in that weekend immediately preceding the assassination when the argument occurred between Marina and Lee Oswald on which he upbraided her for having made the call, you still weren't activated to call the FBI and tell them that he was living under an assumed name, is that true?

Mrs. PAINE. That is true. I did expect to give this copy which I had made of his "Dear Sirs," letter which you have marked Commission Exhibit 103 to the FBI agent at the next meeting.

Mr. JENNER. At the time he called if he did call?

Mrs. PAINE. I thought he would.

Mr. JENNER. During the interview on November 1, you have testified that Marina was present some of the time.

Mrs. PAINE. She was present virtually all of that time.

Mr. JENNER. All of the time?

Mrs. PAINE. And virtually none of the next time.

Mr. JENNER. Virtually none.

Mrs. PAINE. Just came in at the end, on the 5th.

Mr. JENNER. Was she out in the yard? Did you get that impression any time during that second interview?

Mrs. PAINE. No; she had to have been in her room the entire time.

Mr. JENNER. Are you firm, reasonably firm that Marina, even if she desired to learn of the license number on Agent Hosty's car, that she could not have seen or detected it while remaining in the house?

Mrs. PAINE. She might possibly—oh, I wouldn't say that. It is conceivable, depending on where it was parked, it is conceivable that she could have seen it from the bedroom window.

Mr. JENNER. You are holding up exhibit number?

Mrs. PAINE. 430.

Mr. JENNER. And you are pointing to what on that exhibit?

Mrs. PAINE. The window of the bedroom which she occupied, which is the southeast bedroom of my house, looks directly out to where I thought the car was parked. From that position, if I am correct about where the car was parked, she couldn't have seen the license plate, but she could have seen it if as Agent Hosty described to me later she saw it while the car was moving along the street.

Mr. JENNER. When he pulled away?

Mrs. PAINE. When he pulled away and then he came back and went the other way.

Mr. JENNER. So it is possible that she may have seen the license?

Mrs. PAINE. It is possible.

Mr. JENNER. This date that you are now talking about when he parked the car in front of your house, that was November 5?

Mrs. PAINE. Yes, it was.

Mr. JENNER. Whereas on November 1, he parked the car down the street.

Mrs. PAINE. That is right. I might add a little more detail here if you want it. Marina and I talked about whether to tell Lee that the FBI had been out a second time, and the 5th was a Tuesday. We didn't see Lee until the 8th. She said to me that he had been upset by the FBI's coming out and inquiring about him, and he felt it was interference with his family. And I said there is no reason for him to be upset, or I think conveyed that idea. But the question of whether to tell him was settled by Marina who told him on Friday evening, the 8th, and then Lee inquired of me about that meeting, and he said—I don't think I have yet said for the record—he said to me then he felt the FBI was inhibiting his activities. This is what he said. Has this been said?

Mr. JENNER. Not yet.

Mrs. PAINE. All right, I have said it. I said to him "Don't be worried about it. You have your rights to your views, whether they are popular or not." But I could see that he didn't take that view but rather was seriously bothered by their having come out and inquired about him. At this time or another, I don't recall certainly, I asked whether he was worried about losing his job, and he was.

Mr. JENNER. Did he say so, Mrs. Paine?

Mrs. PAINE. I recall particularly a telephone conversation with him. On one of those in which he called out to talk to Marina, I judge, and perhaps she was busy still changing a baby and I talked. I don't recall the exact circumstances but I do recall it, and I said to him if his views, not any references now to the FBI or their interest in him, but if his political views were interfering with his ability to hold a job, that this might be a matter of interest to the

101

American Civil Liberties Union, that he should in our country have a right to unpopular views or any other kind.

This I believe was after he had been to an American Civil Liberties Union meeting with my husband, that meeting having been October 25.

Mr. JENNER. What was his response?

Mrs. PAINE. He was pleased, I felt. He felt in a sense reassured. And indeed I think his response was to join, because it was later reported in the press that he had, which makes me think that this telephone conversation was quite close to the time of the assassination.

Mr. JENNER. Mrs. Paine——

Mrs. PAINE. I am putting in a lot of guesswork.

Mr. JENNER. Am I interrupting you?

Mrs. PAINE. No. It is just that I wonder if you want me to dredge this deeply into things I cannot be absolutely certain about.

Mr. JENNER. We would like your best recollection. We do hesitate about speculation.

Mrs. PAINE. Indeed.

Mr. JENNER. When we are asking about factual matters. We do ask for your speculation occasionally, but to try to make it quite deliberate when we are asking for that rather than for facts. Have you now stated all that comes to mind with respect to the advice to Lee Oswald of the visit of FBI agents or any discussion with Mr. Oswald at any time while he visited your home during this period in 1963 prior to November 22 with respect to FBI agent visits?

Have you now exhausted your recollection on the subject?

Mrs. PAINE. I think one other thing. Agent Hosty asked me, and I am not certain which time, but more likely the second, since so far as I can recall Marina wasn't present, if I thought this was a mental problem, his words referring to Lee Oswald, and I said I didn't understand the mental processes of anyone who could espouse the Marxist philosophy, but that this was far different from saying he was mentally unstable or unable to conduct himself in normal society.

I did tell Lee that this question had been asked. He gave no reply, but more a scoffing laugh, hardly voiced.

Mr. JENNER. Have you now exhausted your recollection?

Mrs. PAINE. I have clearly exhausted it.

Senator COOPER. Who asked the question?

Mrs. PAINE. Hosty asked the question "Is this a mental problem?"

Senator COOPER. Did you ever hear Oswald express any anger toward either the agents or the FBI, as an agency?

Mrs. PAINE. He expressed distinct irritation that he was being bothered. That is how he looked upon it.

Senator COOPER. You said that you thought he was concerned about its effect upon his job, but did he express any emotion other than that?

Mrs. PAINE. And he was being inhibited in what he wanted to do.

Senator COOPER. Any irritation or anger because they had interviewed?

Mrs. PAINE. In tone of voice, yes.

Senator COOPER. What would it be like?

Mrs. PAINE. Well, irritated. He said, "They are trying to inhibit my activities."

Senator COOPER. Did he swear at all?

Mrs. PAINE. No.

Senator COOPER. He used no language.

Mrs. PAINE. No; he didn't.

Senator COOPER. Did he raise the tone of his voice?

Mrs. PAINE. No.

Senator COOPER. Did he show——

Mrs. PAINE. Nothing more than an edge to his voice I would say.

Senator COOPER. Did he direct it against any individual FBI agent.

Mrs. PAINE. No; he didn't. I have one other recollection that possibly should be put in regarding the conversation with Agent Hosty the first time when Marina was present. We discussed many things, just as you would having coffee in the afternoon with a visitor, and——

Mr. JENNER. Is this a discussion between you and Marina with the agent present or not present.

Mrs. PAINE. He was present.

Mr. JENNER. All right.

Mrs. PAINE. Discussion between the three of us.

Mr. JENNER. Thank you.

Mrs. PAINE. And I can't recall certainly who brought it up, but I think Marina asked of Hosty what did he think of Castro, and he said, "Well, he reads what is printed and from the view given in the American newspapers of Castro's activities and intentions, he certainly didn't like those intentions or actions."

And Marina expressed an opinion subsequently, but contrary, that perhaps he was not given much chance by the American press, or that the press was not entirely fair to him. This I translated.

Mr. JENNER. Is that the extent of it? Now have you exhausted your recollection?

Mrs. PAINE. I hope so. I have exhausted myself.

Mr. JENNER. Mr. Chairman, do you have another question?

Senator COOPER. Not on this subject.

Mr. JENNER. I would like to return to your furnishing of the name and the telephone number of Agent Hosty. In Commission Exhibit No. 18, which is in evidence, which was Lee Oswald's diary—by the way, may I hand the exhibit to the witness, Mr. Chairman?

Senator COOPER. Yes.

Mr. JENNER. This is an address book. In any event it is in evidence as Exhibit No. 18. Have you ever seen that booklet before?

Mrs. PAINE. No.

Mr. JENNER. Examine the outside of the booklet. Have you seen this?

Mrs. PAINE. I have never seen this.

Mr. JENNER. You have never seen that in Lee Oswald's possession?

Mrs. PAINE. I have never seen it at all.

Mr. JENNER. There is an entry as follows. Would you help me Mr. Redlich. Would you read it please?

Mr. REDLICH. "November 1, 1963 FBI agent James P. Hosty."

Mrs. PAINE. Junior?

Mr. REDLICH. Just above the word "Hosty" appears in parentheses "RI 1–1121," and underneath "James P. Hosty" appears "MU 8605." Underneath that is "1114 Commerce Street Dallas." I would just like to correct upon the record that the phone number originally read is "RI–11211."

Mrs. PAINE. That is correct.

Mr. JENNER. What is that phone number?

Mrs. PAINE. That phone number I recognize from my own use of it is to the FBI in Dallas, my use since the assassination.

Mr. JENNER. And the series of numbers rather than phone numbers, series of numbers "MU 8605."

Mrs. PAINE. Is not known to me.

Mr. JENNER. What is the system of license plate numbering and lettering employed in Texas?

Mrs. PAINE. I am not acquainted with any particular system. They use both letters and numbers.

Mr. JENNER. I call your attention in connection with this entry that it is dated November 1, 1963, and there does appear in it the license number.

Mrs. PAINE. Oh, yes.

Mr. JENNER. Your recollection is firm that you didn't furnish it?

Mrs. PAINE. May I point out also that he must have put this down after November 1st, or at least that evening. He could not have written it down with——

Mr. JENNER. It had to be after the fact as you furnished him the name.

Mrs. PAINE. That is right.

Mr. JENNER. And the agent's address.

Mrs. PAINE. I would think he could as well have added—you don't want my thinking—this number.

Mr. JENNER. The reason I call that to your attention, Mrs. Paine, it still does not stimulate your recollection.

Mrs. PAINE. No.

Mr. JENNER. Any differently than before. You did not furnish the license number.

Mrs. PAINE. I certainly did not. To the best of my recollection I did not put down the address either.

Mr. JENNER. Now during the course of that interview of November 5th, did you not say to Agent Hosty that Lee had visited at your home November 2 and 3?

Mrs. PAINE. It is entirely possible, likely.

Mr. JENNER. And in this connection I am at liberty to report to you that Agent Hosty's report is that you did advise him that Oswald had visited at your home on November 2 and November 3. Does that serve to refresh your recollection that you did so advise him?

Mrs. PAINE. I don't recall that.

Mr. JENNER. Now did you express an opinion to Agent Hosty that Oswald was "an illogical person?"

Mrs. PAINE. Yes, I did, in answer to his question was this a mental problem, as I have just described to you.

Mr. JENNER. Yes; that is all right. And did you also say to Agent Hosty that Oswald himself had "Admitted being a Trotskyite Communist."

Mrs. PAINE. Oh, I doubt seriously I said Trotskyite Communist. I would think Leninist Communist, but I am not certain.

Mr. JENNER. Do you remember making a remark of similar import?

Mrs. PAINE. Reference to Trotsky surprises me. I have come since the assassination to wonder if he had Trotskyite views. I have become interested in what such views are since the assassination.

Mr. JENNER. To the best of your recollection you don't recall making that comment?

Mrs. PAINE. I wouldn't think that I had the knowledge by which to make such a statement even.

Mr. JENNER. Now after this rationalization you have made, Mrs. Paine, it is your recollection that you did not make such a comment?

Mrs. PAINE. I can't recall. What was the second item that I told Hosty he had been out on the second and third? I am just trying to clarify here.

Mr. JENNER. You had told him that Lee Oswald had been at your home November 2 and 3, that you told him that Lee Oswald was an illogical person?

Mrs. PAINE. That is it.

Mr. JENNER. And third, that you told him that Oswald had admitted being a Trotskyite Communist.

Mrs. PAINE. I may have said that. I don't recall.

Mr. JENNER. You may have said the latter.

Mrs. PAINE. I don't recall, that is right.

Mr. JENNER. It is possible that you did say it?

Mrs. PAINE. It is possible. I am surprised, however, by the word at that point.

Mr. JENNER. Now do you recall a telephone interview or call by Agent Hosty on the 27th of January 1964? Perhaps I had better put it this way to you. Do you recall subsequent telephone calls after the assassination that you received from Agent Hosty, that you did receive such telephone calls?

Mrs. PAINE. I did, and visits also, at the house.

Mr. JENNER. Do you recall he called you on the 27th of January 1964 and that he inquired whether you had given Lee Oswald the license number of his automobile when he had been at your home? You stated that you had not.

Mrs. PAINE. That is right.

I would have thought that was a face to face interview but I don't recall.

Mr. JENNER. But you also told Agent Hosty on that occasion, "However, this license number could have easily been observed by Marina Oswald since her bedroom is located only a short distance from the street where this car would have been parked."

Mrs. PAINE. I doubt I said "easily."

104

Mr. JENNER. But you could have said that the license number could have been observed by Marina from her bedroom?

Mrs. PAINE. My recollection of this, that it was not a telephone interview.

Mr. JENNER. Telephone or otherwise, there was an interview of you at which you made that statement, that Marina could have seen the license?

Mrs. PAINE. That Marina could have?

Mr. JENNER. You do recall the incident. You don't recall whether it was at your home or whether it was by telephone?

Mrs. PAINE. I certainly recall talking with Agent Hosty and on at least one occasion about how that license number got in Oswald's possession.

Mr. JENNER. Do you recall a telephone interview by an FBI agent Lee, Ivan D. Lee on the 28th of December 1963?

Mrs. PAINE. The name is not familiar to me. A great many FBI agents——

Mr. JENNER. Do you recall an incident in which you reported to an FBI agent that you had just talked with a reporter from the Houston Post?

Mrs. PAINE. Right.

Mr. JENNER. You recall that?

Mrs. PAINE. I do.

Mr. JENNER. Now during the course of that interview, you made reference to a newspaper reporter, did you not?

Mrs. PAINE. I did. His name is Lonny Hudkins.

Mr. JENNER. Did you say that the reporter whom you have now identified had advised you that Lee Harvey Oswald's mother had been working for a party in Forth Worth during September and October 1962 as a practical nurse, and according to the reporter, Mrs. Oswald, mother of Lee Harvey Oswald, advised this party during her employment that her son was doing important anti-subversive work?

Mrs. PAINE. That is correct.

Mr. JENNER. Would you please relate that incident so we will have the facts insofar as you participated in them stated of record?

Mrs. PAINE. I will. I would not have recalled the date, but I knew it to be toward the end of 1963. I was called on the telephone by Lonny Hudkins, whom I had never met, announced himself as from the Houston Post, said there was a matter of some importance that he wanted to talk with me about, could he come out to the house? And he then indicated the nature of what he wanted to talk about to the extent very accurately reported in what you have just read. I called the FBI really to see if they could advise me in dealing with this man. It struck me as a very unresponsible thing to print, and I wanted to be able to convince Hudkins of that fact. I was hopeful that they might be willing to make a flat denial to him, or in some way prevent the confusion that would have been caused by his printing this.

Now shall I go on to tell about the encounter which followed with Mr. Hudkins, and something of that content?

Mr. JENNER. I am a little at a loss. Why don't you start because I can't anticipate.

Mrs. PAINE. Whether it is important?

Mr. JENNER. You haven't related this to me. Are these statements you made to the FBI that you are about to relate?

Mrs. PAINE. If they asked. I don't recall specifically. I certainly recall that the content of the telephone conversation reported there is accurate and is in sum the conversation that then followed with Lonny Hudkins too, except that it doesn't say what I said in the situation.

Mr. JENNER. Did you report to the FBI that Mr. Hudkins had said to you that the primary purpose of seeing you was an effort to get some confirmation if possible of the possibility Oswald was actually working on behalf of the United States Government prior to the assassination?

Mrs. PAINE. I was aware that was his purpose.

Mr. JENNER. That you knew of no such situation, and ventured the opinion to the reporter that the story was wholly unlikely, that you could not imagine anyone having that much confidence in Oswald?

Mrs. PAINE. That is accurate. I went on to say that Mrs. Oswald, senior, Mrs. Marguerite Oswald, could well have said to this matron a full year back

105

and more that her son was doing important anti-subversive work for the government. This was 1962 he was talking about, but that this was her opinion or what she may have wished to have true. And I did not consider it terribly creditable, and said to him "You don't think you have a story here, do you?"

Mr. JENNER. You also recall——

Mrs. PAINE. May I put in another point here?

Mr. JENNER. In connection with this subject matter?

Mrs. PAINE. Yes.

Mr. JENNER. All right.

Mrs. PAINE. I called and the man to whom I talked, I don't know if it was Lee, or I think it was someone else who answered first, I am not certain at all.

Mr. JENNER. Odum?

Mrs. PAINE. Odum? It certainly was not Odum. I know him. But someone answered the phone and I told this to him, and perhaps it was Lee. He said to me in response to my inquiring "What shall I do, here is this man coming," he said "well you don't know anything of this nature do you?" I said, "No".

"Then anything you might have to say is sheer conjecture on the subject?" "Yes."

"Then you should certainly make that plain in talking with him."

Mr. JENNER. Did you do so?

Mrs. PAINE. Yes; I certainly did. And I felt as though I really shouldn't have bothered them. This was not of interest to them. But then I was called back later by the FBI on the same subject.

Mr. JENNER. And you reported that conversation, the subsequent call back by the FBI?

Mrs. PAINE. No. You have content of the first conversation I think there, isn't that so, or it might have been?

Mr. JENNER. There are a series, Mrs. Paine, that run in this order. The first was on December 28, 1963. The conversation occurred between you and an Agent Lee, and it was a telephone interview?

Mrs. PAINE. Yes.

Mr. JENNER. I have asked you about that, and I have read from the report and you have affirmed that you so reported to the agent. And on the next day, December 29, 1963, you had a telephone conversation, whether you called or whether the agent called, with Kenneth C. Howe.

Mrs. PAINE. What is his name?

Mr. JENNER. Kenneth C. Howe, on this same subject. I have questioned you about that, and I have read from the report, and you have affirmed as to that. Then on January 3, 1964, this apparently was an interview at your home by Agent Odum? Do you recall that?

Mrs. PAINE. Agent Odum has been out a great deal.

Mr. JENNER. In which you say, did you not, that this reporter Hudkins of the Houston Post newspaper in his contact with you on the previous Saturday, December 28 had stated that the FBI was foolish to deny that Agent Joseph Hosty, being a reference to the FBI agent we have been talking about today, had tried to develop Lee Harvey Oswald as an informant. You stated you had made no comment one way or the other to Hudkins regarding this remark, and furthermore that you knew that——

Mrs. PAINE. Would you please repeat that, that I stated?

Mr. JENNER. I will read it all to you then. You advised that Lonny Hudkins, the reporter of the Houston Post in his contact that he had with you on the previous Saturday, December 28, 1963, had stated to you that the FBI was foolish to deny that Agent Hosty had tried to develop Lee Harvey Oswald as an informant. Did you make that statement?

Mrs. PAINE. Not in just those terms.

Mr. JENNER. Did you make the further statement that you made no comment one way or the other to Hudkins regarding this remark of his to you? In order to get this in the proper posture, Mrs. Paine——

Senator COOPER. Do you understand the question?

Mrs. PAINE. I understand what is said, but it doesn't check strictly with my recollection, that is the confusion.

Mr. JENNER. What the agent is reporting is your report of what Lonny Hudkins had said to you, and your report to the agent of your response to what Lonny Hudkins had said to you. Do we have it now in the proper posture?

Mrs. PAINE. This is by no means an accurate description of the conversation or my response.

Mr. JENNER. You don't have to accept this report, of course, Mrs. Paine. Tell us what occurred in that interview?

Mrs. PAINE. All right.

Mr. JENNER. What you said and what Agent Odum said to you.

Mrs. PAINE. Oh, I don't recall that so well. I was going to tell you what I said to Hudkins. I do recall this, and it may be the foundation for what appears in your report there. I made no comment on Mr. Hudkins saying that there was a Joe Hosty, and that this agent had been in contact with Oswald. I observed that Hudkins had inaccurate information.

Mr. JENNER. Didn't you tell the agent what this reporter had said to you that was inaccurate, to wit, that the reporter had stated to you that the FBI was foolish to deny that Agent Hosty had tried to develop Lee Harvey Oswald as an informant?

Mrs. PAINE. What is totally inaccurate is the following, that implies that I made no comment to Hudkins regarding such a remark.

Mr. JENNER. No please, that has not been suggested. I am trying to take this chronologically. Did you first report to the agent that Hudkins had said to you that the FBI was foolish to deny that Agent Joseph Hosty had tried to develop Lee Harvey Oswald as an informant.

Mrs. PAINE. Certainly what Hudkins said was of this nature.

Mr. JENNER. And you so reported to the agent?

Mrs. PAINE. Yes.

Mr. JENNER. Then did you make the further remark, which is what I think you are trying to say, that you made no comment one way or the other to Hudkins when he made that remark, his remark to you?

Mrs. PAINE. I made a great deal of comment and I will say what those comments were.

Mr. JENNER. You did to the reporter.

Mrs. PAINE. To the reporter, yes.

Mr. JENNER. Please say what you said, and did you report this to the FBI, Mr. Odum?

Mrs. PAINE. Inadequately clearly, judging from the——

Mr. JENNER. Why don't you do it this way?

Mrs. PAINE. Yes I reported it.

Mr. JENNER. Let us have first what you said to the FBI agent on the subject?

Mrs. PAINE. I can't recall what I said to the FBI agent. It is much easier for me to recall what I said to Hudkins. But I do recall clearly that I said to the FBI agent "I made no correction of his inaccuracies about Hosty's name." This is where I made no comment.

Mr. JENNER. I am at a loss now.

Mrs. PAINE. Joe is not his name.

Mr. JENNER. I see. His name is James?

Mrs. PAINE. Yes.

Mr. JENNER. Did you indicate to the agent that you had raised an issue with the reporter?

Mrs. PAINE. He also spelled it with an "i", Hudkins.

Mr. JENNER. With respect to the other phase, that is to what the reporter had said to you.

Mrs. PAINE. I would guess that I reported to Mr. Odum other things about——

Mr. JENNER. Present recollections Mrs Paine.

Mrs. PAINE. I don't recall the particular conversation with Mr. Odum at all. I talked with him a great deal.

Mr. JENNER. Did you deny this state to Mr. Hudkins, the reporter?

Mrs. PAINE. To Mr. Hudkins?

Mr. JENNER. Did you say to him that you did not agree with his statement?

Mrs. PAINE. To Mr. Hudkins I said many things, which I hoped would convince him that he had no story, that his information was very shaky, that Oswald was not in my view a person that would have been hired by the FBI or by Russia. I said to him "You are the other side of the coin from a Mr. Guy Richards of the New York Journal-American who is certain that Oswald was a paid spy for the Soviet Union, and just as inaccurate," and coming to, in my opinion, and of course I made it clear this was my opinion, to conclusions just as wrong.

Mr. JENNER. That is, it was your opinion that Lee Oswald was neither a Russian agent nor an agent of any agency of the United States?

Mrs. PAINE. That is right. I said indeed to Mr. Hudkins, I had said to Mr. Richards that if the so-called great Soviet conspiracy has to rest for its help upon such inadequate people as Lee Oswald, there is no hope of their achieving their aims. I said I simply cannot believe that the FBI would find it necessary to employ such a shaky and inadequate person.

Mr. JENNER. And is that still your view?

Mrs. PAINE. Indeed it is.

Mr. JENNER. Did you also say to Mr. Odum on that occasion that you knew that Agent Hosty had not interviewed Lee Harvey Oswald?

Mrs. PAINE. Probably.

Senator COOPER. Did you read the statements after they had been written?

Mrs. PAINE. What statements?

Senator COOPER. The statements of the FBI.

Mrs. PAINE. Oh, no; I have never.

Senator COOPER. You have never seen them?

Mrs. PAINE. Never seen anything of it. I knew they must write something, but I have never seen any of these statements.

Senator COOPER. You never asked them to show you the statements?

Mrs. PAINE. No.

Mr. JENNER. Did you ever make a statement to anybody that you can recall that Lee Harvey Oswald in your opinion was doing underground work?

Mrs. PAINE. That has never been my opinion. I would be absolutely certain that he never——

Mr. JENNER. Please, did you say it?

Mrs. PAINE. And I would be absolutely certain that I never said such a thing.

Mr. JENNER. To anybody, including when I say anybody, Mrs. Dorothy Gravitis?

Mrs. PAINE. Absolutely certain. Never said to anyone that I thought Lee was doing undercover work.

Senator COOPER. What is that name?

Mr. JENNER. Gravitis, G-r-a-v-i-t-i-s.

Senator COOPER. Do you know this person?

Mrs. PAINE. She is my Russian tutor in Dallas.

Senator COOPER. What?

Mrs. PAINE. Russian tutor and the mother-in-law of the translator that was at the police station.

Mr. JENNER. To conclude this series——

Mrs. PAINE. Would you clarify for me, someone is of the opinion that I thought that Oswald was an undercover agent for whom?

Mr. JENNER. That you said so.

Mrs. PAINE. For whom?

Mr. JENNER. For the Russian government.

Mrs. PAINE. Oh. I have certainly never said anything of the sort.

Mr. JENNER. Did you ever say to anybody including Mrs. Gravitis that you thought Lee Harvey Oswald was a Communist?

Mrs. PAINE. Well, it is possible I said that. I thought he considered himself a Communist by ideology, certainly a Marxist. He himself always corrected anyone who called him a Communist and said he was a Marxist.

Mr. JENNER. When you use the term communist do you think of a person as a member of the Communist Party or a native of Russia?

Mrs. PAINE. I seldom use the term at all, but I would confine it to people who were members or considered themselves in support of Communist ideology.

Mr. JENNER. A person in your mind may be a Communist, and yet not a member of the Communist Party, even in Russia?

Mrs. PAINE. I might use the word in that loose way.

Mr. JENNER. The last of these interviews was on, may I suggest, and if not would you correct me, January 27, 1964, by Agent Wiehl, and Agent Hosty. It appears, and would you please correct me if I am wrong, to have been an interview in your home at the very tail end of January 1964?

Mrs. PAINE. I have no specific recollection.

Mr. JENNER. Do you recall an interview in which you reported to the FBI, these two agents, that agent Hosty—no, that you gave Lee Harvey Oswald the name of agent James P. Hosty together with the Dallas FBI telephone number which you had obtained on November 1, 1963, that you did not give him the license number of the automobile driven by agent Hosty, however, and that, as I have asked you before, the license number could have been observed by Marina Oswald on November 1?

Mrs. PAINE. That is my recollection of the occurrence.

Mr. JENNER. And it could have been observed on November 5th?

Mrs. PAINE. That is right.

Senator COOPER. Did you yourself see the license plate?

Mrs. PAINE. No.

Senator COOPER. You don't know the numbers or letters that were on the license plate?

Mrs. PAINE. No.

Mr. JENNER. Mrs. Paine, you testified yesterday and you testified again today, this morning, that you had no recollection of Lee Oswald having gone into the garage of your home on Thursday, November 21. Do you recall that testimony?

Mrs. PAINE. Well, that I did not see him there or see him go through the door to the garage. I was clear in my own mind that it was he who had left the light on, and I tried to describe that.

Mr. JENNER. It may have been a possibility and you were inferring from that that he was in the garage.

Mrs. PAINE. I definitely infer that.

Mr. JENNER. Were you interviewed by the FBI agents Hosty and Abernathy on the 23d of November 1963?

Mrs. PAINE. Yes.

Mr. JENNER. And in the course of that interview, do you recall having stated to these agents that on the evening of November 21, Lee Oswald went out to the garage of your home, where he had many of his personal effects stored, and spent considerable time, apparently rearranging and handling his personal effects.

Mrs. PAINE. I don't recall saying exactly that.

Mr. JENNER. Could you have said that to the agents.

Mrs. PAINE. I could have said as far as spending considerable time.

Mr. JENNER. Now that your recollection is possibly further refreshed, please tell us what you did say to the agents as you now recall?

Mrs. PAINE. You have refreshed nothing. You have got all there was of my recollection in previous testimony.

Mr. JENNER. Based on the fundamentals, the specifics which you have given us yesterday and today, you did report to the FBI on the 23d of November in the interview to which I have called your attention that on the evening of the 21st Oswald went out to the garage where he had many of his personal effects stored, and spent considerable time apparently rearranging and handling his personal effects.

Mrs. PAINE. I don't recall ever saying "apparently rearranging and handling."

Mr. JENNER. Other than the word "apparently" that is a reasonable summary of what you did say to the FBI agents, is it?

Mrs. PAINE. I don't recall. I think my best recollection is as I have given it to you in the testimony, was it this morning, that I certainly was of the opinion that he had been out there. I had been busy for some time with my children, and I could easily, and of course that was the day after, and this several months after, have been of the opinion, been informed as to how long he had been out there, but my recollection now doesn't give me any length of time.

Mr. JENNER. You have heretofore given us yesterday and today your very best recollection after full reflection on all the course of events.

Mrs. PAINE. I certainly have.

Mr. JENNER. I notice that during the course of the interview, and perhaps you will recall, that you did call attention of the FBI, these two agents, to the Mexico City letter about which you have testified, is that correct?

Mrs. PAINE. Yes; I gave it to them.

Mr. JENNER. Mr. Chairman, that is all I intend to cover with respect to the FBI. Do you have any questions? We will go on to another subject.

Senator COOPER. This would be going back into the subject on which you have already testified, but with reference to this last statement, this letter, where it is reported, you said, Lee Oswald did go into the garage and spend some time, did you make a statement to the FBI after the agents had been in the garage, or the police had been in the garage, and had found the blanket with nothing in it.

Mrs. PAINE. Yes, certainly, this was the next day that Hosty was out with Abernathy.

Senator COOPER. And you did remember of course that you found the light on?

Mrs. PAINE. Yes.

Senator COOPER. You did not expect it to be on in the garage? Do you think it is correct then that at the time you made this statement, recognizing the importance of the garage, that you did say at that time that he had been in the garage on the night before the President was assassinated?

Mrs. PAINE. Yes. I think I said that.

Senator COOPER. You think you made that statement?

Mrs. PAINE. I think I made that statement. This was certainly my impression.

Mr. JENNER. You have already related the arrival of your husband, Michael Paine, at your home in mid-afternoon of the day of the assassination?

Mrs. PAINE. Yes.

Mr. JENNER. Now would you please tell me exactly to the best of your recollection the words of your husband as he walked in the door?

Mrs. PAINE. I don't recall his saying anything.

Mr. JENNER. Now his words if any with respect to why he had come.

Mrs. PAINE. I asked him before he volunteered. I said something to the effect of "how did you know to come?"

Mr. JENNER. And what did he say?

Mrs. PAINE. He said he had heard on the radio at work that Lee Oswald was in custody, and came immediately to the house.

Mr. JENNER. And that is what you recall he said?

Mrs. PAINE. That is right.

Mr. JENNER. Did he say, and I quote: "I heard where the President was shot, and I came right over to see if I could be of any help to you.'"

Mrs. PAINE. No.

Mr. JENNER. Did he also say to you that he "Just walked off the job."

Mrs. PAINE. No. He said he had come from work. I might interject here one recollection if you want it.

Mr. JENNER. Please.

Mrs. PAINE. Of Michael having telephoned to me after the assassination. He wanted to know if I had heard.

Mr. JENNER. Did he call you before he arrived at your home?

Mrs. PAINE. He called. He knew about the assassination. He had been told by a waitress at lunchtime. I don't know whether he knew any further details, whether he knew from whence the shots had been fired, but he knew immediately that I would want to know, and called simply to find out if I knew, and of course I did, and we didn't converse about it, but I felt the difference between him and my immediate neighbor to whom I have already referred. Michael was as struck and grieved as I was, and we shared this over the telephone.

Mr. JENNER. And his appearance in mid-afternoon, as you have related, was, according to what he said activated as you have related, that he had heard that Lee Oswald was now involved.

Mrs. PAINE. That is right.

Mr. JENNER. How did you and Marina look at the parade, that is as the motorcade went along were you and Marina——

Mrs. PAINE. This was not shown on television.

Mr. JENNER. Oh, it wasn't?

Mrs. PAINE. To the best of my recollection they had cameras at the convention center, whatever it was, that the President was coming to for dinner, and for his talk.

Mr. JENNER. And was the motorcade being described, broadcast by radio?

Mrs. PAINE. The motorcade was being described.

Mr. JENNER. Were you and Marina listening to that?

Mrs. PAINE. Well, it was coming through the television set, but it wasn't being shown.

Mr. JENNER. Were you listening?

Mrs. PAINE. We were.

Mr. JENNER. Did she show an interest in this?

Mrs. PAINE. Oh, yes.

Mr. JENNER. And it being broadcast in English, I assume you were doing some interpreting for her?

Mrs. PAINE. Yes.

Mr. JENNER. Is that correct?

Mrs. PAINE. Yes.

Mr. JENNER. Most of this has been covered, Senator Cooper, and I am getting through pages fortunately that we don't have to go over again.

Senator COOPER. After you knew that the President was dead, and Marina knew, do you know, from that time on, whether she ever went into her room, left you and went into her room?

Mrs. PAINE. I would think it highly likely that she did. The announcement that the President was actually dead came, oh, I think around 1:30 or close to 2. I already related that my little girl wept and fell asleep on the sofa. This was a time therefore that Marina would have been putting Junie to bed in the bedroom.

Senator COOPER. Between the time that you heard the President had been shot and the news came that he died, did she ever leave you and go into her room, do you remember?

Mrs. PAINE. I don't remember specifically, but you must understand that the little baby was already born. She would have had many occasions, needs to go into the room.

Senator COOPER. Do you know whether she went into the garage?

Mrs. PAINE. I don't know.

Senator COOPER. What?

Mrs. PAINE. I don't know whether she went into the garage.

Mr. JENNER. You have no impressions in that respect?

Mrs. PAINE. None.

Mr. JENNER. Do you recall an incident involving Lee Oswald's wedding ring?

Mrs. PAINE. I do.

Mr. JENNER. Would you relate that, please?

Mrs. PAINE. One or two FBI agents came to my home, I think·Odum was one of them, and said that Marina had inquired after and wanted Lee's wedding ring, and he asked me if I had any idea where to look for it. I said I'll look first in the little tea cup that is from her grandmother, and on top of the chest of drawers in the bedroom where she had stayed. I looked and it was there.

Mr. JENNER. Calling on your recollection of this man, was he in the habit of wearing his wedding ring?

Mrs. PAINE. Yes.

Mr. JENNER. Did this strike you as unusual that the wedding ring should be back in this cup on the dresser in their room?

Mrs. PAINE. Yes, quite.

Mr. JENNER. Elaborate as to why it struck you as unusual?

Mrs. PAINE. I do not wear my wedding ring. Marina has on several occasions said to me she considers that bad luck, not a good thing to do.

I would suspect that she would certainly have wanted Lee to wear his wedding ring, and encouraged him to do it.

Mr. JENNER. In face of the fact that he regularly wore his wedding ring, yet on this occasion, that is being home the evening before, you received this call, you went to the bedroom and you found the wedding ring. Did it occur to you that that might have been in the nature of a leave-taking of some kind by Lee Oswald, leaving his wedding ring for Marina?

Mrs. PAINE. It occurred to me that that might have been a form of thinking ahead. I had no way of knowing whether or not Marina had known that he left it. I was not instructed where to look for it.

Mr. JENNER. You were not?

Mrs. PAINE. No.

Mr. JENNER. But Marina did say to you "would you look for Lee's wedding ring?"

Mrs. PAINE. No, Odum did.

Mr. JENNER. Odum did.

Mrs. PAINE. And of course clearly they would know whether he had it.

Mr. JENNER. Yes, I see. It was not Marina. It was one of the FBI agents. And it is your clear recollection that he was in the habit of wearing that wedding ring all the time. Do you ever recall an occasion when he left the wedding ring at home?

Mrs. PAINE. No.

Mr. JENNER. To your knowledge?

Mrs. PAINE. To my knowledge, no.

Mr. JENNER. When you obtained the wedding ring did you examine it?

Mrs. PAINE. No.

Mr. JENNER. I mean did you look inside to see if there was an inscription on it or were you curious about that?

Mrs. PAINE. I gave it to Mr. Odum who was with me in the room.

Mr. JENNER. Mr. Odum accompanied you?

Mrs. PAINE. Went with me to the bedroom. I am pretty sure he was the one.

Senator COOPER. The morning of the day that the President was killed, did Mrs. Oswald, after she got up, say anything to you about any unusual characteristics of Lee Oswald's taking leave of her that morning?

Mrs. PAINE. Absolutely none.

Senator COOPER. Did she talk about him leaving? Did she tell you anything at all about what happened when he did get up?

Mrs. PAINE. I have a recollection that must be from her that she woke enough to feed the baby, to nurse the baby in the morning, when he was getting up to go, but she then went back to sleep after that, and she must have told me that. But that is all I know, that she had been awake, and nursed the baby early in the morning, and then went back to sleep.

Senator COOPER. And Lee Oswald went back to sleep?

Mrs. PAINE. No, no, Marina went back to sleep.

Senator COOPER. Oh, Marina went back to sleep. Was he leaving then?

Mrs. PAINE. I judge so.

Senator COOPER. What?

Mrs. PAINE. I judge so.

Senator COOPER. But I mean did she say anything else about him?

Mrs. PAINE. No; nothing about his leaving at all.

Mr. JENNER. What were his habits with respect to breakfast? For example on the Monday mornings of the weekends which he visited your home, did he prepare his own, and if so, what kind of a breakfast did he prepare?

Mrs. PAINE. I would say his habit was to have a cup of instant coffee only.

Mr. JENNER. And you have a clear recollection that on the morning of the 21st when you went into the kitchen——

Mrs. PAINE. The 22d.

Mr. JENNER. The 22d, I am sorry, the 22d you saw a plastic coffee cup or tea cup, and you looked at it and you could see the remains of somebody having prepared instant coffee?

Mrs. PAINE. That is right.

Mr. JENNER. And that is clear in your mind?

Mrs. PAINE. Perfectly clear. I looked especially for traces of Lee having been up, since I wondered if he might be still sleeping, having overslept.

Mr. JENNER. Was he in the habit on these weekends of making himself a sandwich which he would take with him?

Mrs. PAINE. No; there is no such habit. Perhaps once Marina prepared something for him to take with him, I think more for him to put in his room, partly for lunch, partly for him to have at his room in town and use the refrigerator.

Mr. JENNER. But in any event, on the morning of the 22d you saw no evidence of there having been an attempt by anybody to prepare?

Mrs. PAINE. No.

Mr. JENNER. Sandwiches for lunch or to take anything else in the way of food from your home?

Mrs. PAINE. I saw no evidence, and I saw nothing that was missing.

Mr. JENNER. At any time during all the time you knew the Oswalds, up to and including November 22, was any mention ever made of any attempt on the life of Richard Nixon?

Mrs. PAINE. None.

Mr. JENNER. Just that subject matter, was it ever mentioned?

Mrs. PAINE. Never.

Mr. JENNER. To the best of your recollection did they ever discuss Richard Nixon as a person?

Mrs. PAINE. I can't recall Richard Nixon coming into the conversation at any time.

Mr. JENNER. And to the present day—well, I want to include the time that you spoke here a couple weeks ago with Marina, let us say up to and including that day had there ever been any discussion with you by Marina of the possibility of Lee Oswald contemplating making an attack upon the person of Richard Nixon?

Mrs. PAINE. No; no such discussion.

Mr. JENNER. Did anyone else ever talk to you about that up to that time, talk to you on that subject?

Mrs. PAINE. Well, after it was rumored in the paper, someone asked me if I thought there was anything to it but that is something else.

Mr. JENNER. When you say recently some rumor to that effect that is what you are talking about?

Mrs. PAINE. That is right.

Mr. JENNER. Up to that time?

Mrs. PAINE. Absolutely none.

Mr. JENNER. I take it from your testimony this morning that you have seen and talked with Robert Oswald but once?

Mrs. PAINE. And you recall also when he came to pick up her things?

Mr. JENNER. Oh, yes.

Mrs. PAINE. Twice.

Mr. JENNER. So you saw him once for the first time in the city police station?

Mrs. PAINE. That is right.

Mr. JENNER. You talked with him on that occasion. You saw him on one occasion when not so long after that he came out to pick up her things?

Mrs. PAINE. That is right.

Mr. JENNER. And had some conversation with him then. Have there ever been any other occasions that you have had a conversation with him directly or by telephone?

Mrs. PAINE. No. I made one attempt to have such a conversation and drove out to his home in Denton and talked with his wife.

Mr. JENNER. And what occurred then? When was that?

Mrs. PAINE. Possibly in January.

Mr. JENNER. Of 1964?

Mrs. PAINE. Right.

Mr. JENNER. Why did you go out there?

Mrs. PAINE. I had been writing letters to Marina and receiving no reply, and I wanted to go and talk with both Robert and his wife to inquire what was the best way to be a friend to Marina in this situation, whether it was better to write letters or better not to, whether she wanted to hear from me or whether she didn't, and knowing that they had seen her, I felt they might be able to help me with this.

I was told by Mrs. Robert Oswald that Robert had a bad cold, and she didn't want to expose my children who were with me, and she and I talked through the screen, and I explained what I wanted. But I didn't feel helped by the visit.

Mr. JENNER. You did not.

Mrs. PAINE. No.

Mr. JENNER. Did you feel that there was a lack of cordiality?

Mrs. PAINE. She apologized for not having me in, and she was friendly and said, "what nice children you have," but it is somewhat hard to communicate through a screen.

Mr. JENNER. That was the only difficulty that you observed, the difficulty in talking through the screen door, the screen of the door?

Mrs. PAINE. I felt that she could have asked me whether I cared if my children were exposed. I felt that she preferred for me not to come in.

Senator COOPER. Was Marina staying with them?

Mrs. PAINE. I don't believe so. I am pretty certain she was at that time at the Martin's home.

Senator COOPER. Did you get any impression in your talk with Mrs. Robert Oswald that they were not interested in finding out the information that you were asking for?

Mrs. PAINE. She offerered the opinion that she didn't think there was any particular point to writing letters at this time, but she offered no reason.

Mr. JENNER. By the way, do you have copies of those letters, Mrs. Paine?

Mrs. PAINE. At home.

Mr. JENNER. I know now that I will be to see you on Monday.

Mrs. PAINE. Monday?

Mr. JENNER. Yes. Are you going to be home on Monday?

Mrs. PAINE. I am flying Monday morning. Shall we go together? I am not leaving until Monday morning.

Mr. JENNER. I am going down Sunday night. So may I see those letters on that occasion?

Mrs. PAINE. As soon as I get home.

Mr. JENNER. Would you be good enough——

Mrs. PAINE. I will have to translate them.

Mr. JENNER. All right.

Mrs. PAINE. That will take a while.

Mr. JENNER. With respect to the curtain-rod package, would you be good enough to leave it intact, don't touch it, just leave it where it is without touching it at all.

Mrs. PAINE. Yes.

Mr. JENNER. Now you have related to us the Texas School Book Depository employment, the ability to operate an automobile. I am going to read a list of names to you, and you stop me every time I read a name that is familiar to you. There are some of the Russian emigré group in and around Dallas. Some of them may not be Russian emigré group people, but some of the members of the staff want these particular persons covered.

George Bouhe.

Mrs. PAINE. I don't know him.

Mr. JENNER. I want also your response that you didn't hear these names discussed by either Marina or Lee.

Mrs. PAINE. I have never heard that name discussed by Marina or Lee Oswald.

Mr. JENNER. Mr. and Mrs. Frank Ray.

Mrs. PAINE. I did not hear that name discussed by either of them. I have since learned from Mrs. Ford that it was to Mrs. Ray's home that Marina went from Mrs. Ford's home in the fall of 1962.

Mr. JENNER. Mr. and Mrs. Thomas Ray.

Mrs. PAINE. No.

Mr. JENNER. I won't ask you—well, I have Mr. and Mrs. De Mohrenschildt on my list.

You have already testified about them.

Mrs. PAINE. I have met them once; yes.

Mr. JENNER. Only on that one occasion?

Mrs. PAINE. To the best of my recollection; that is right.

Mr. JENNER. John and Elena Hall?

Mrs. PAINE. No; I don't know them.

Mr. JENNER. Did you ever hear them discussed by either Marina or Lee?

Mrs. PAINE. I have never at any time heard that name.

Mr. JENNER. All right.

I think I pronounce this correctly, Tatiana Biggers?

Mrs. PAINE. I am not familiar with that name, and I never heard it.

Mr. JENNER. Mr. Teofil Meller?

Mrs. PAINE. I am not familiar with that name.

Mr. JENNER. Lydia Dymitruk?

Mrs. PAINE. I met a Lydia who was working as a clerk at a grocery store in Irving, and I had met Marina previously. I am not certain of her last name. I am certain that Marina told me not to learn Russian from her, it was not grammatical.

Mr. JENNER. I see.

By the way, did Marina go out by herself occasionally and shop?

Mrs. PAINE. No.

Mr. JENNER. Mr. and Mrs. Daniel F. Sullivan?

Mrs. PAINE. I don't know that name.

Mr. JENNER. Mr. and Mrs. Alan A. Jackson III?

Mrs. PAINE. I don't know that name.

Mr. JENNER. Peter Gregory?

Mrs. PAINE. I know that name; yes. That name was mentioned by, to the best of my recollection first in my presence by, Marguerite Oswald, who told us that she had just started at the police when I first met her——

Mr. JENNER. I would like that. The first time there came to your attention and your consciousness the name Peter Gregory was when Marguerite Oswald mentioned it at the police station on the 22d of November 1963, is that correct?

Mrs. PAINE. Yes; because she had just begun a course of study with him in order to try to learn the Russian language at the public library.

Mr. JENNER. She so said?

Mrs. PAINE. She so said. I don't recall having heard the name previously. Although I am not certain.

Mr. JENNER. Paul Gregory.

Mrs. PAINE. I would be absolutely certain I had never heard the name from either of the Oswalds.

Mr. JENNER. All right. Is that likewise true of Paul Gregory who is the son I may tell you of Peter Gregory?

Mrs. PAINE. I am not familiar with that name.

Mr. JENNER. Mr. and Mrs., I know you are familiar with this name, Mr. and Mrs. Declan Ford. When did you first hear of the name of those people with respect to November 22, 1963, before or after or on that very day?

Mrs. PAINE. Mrs. Ford was mentioned to me by name by Marina in the fall of 1963 before the time of the assassination. Marina described to me a party at Mrs. Ford's home, and described the decor of the house and how much she admired Mrs. Ford's tastes, and said that Mrs. Ford had done most of the decorating herself.

Let me just say Marina also told me she had stayed at someone's home in the fall of 1962, but she did not tell me the name of Mrs. Ford in that connection. It came up in this other connection. It is only since the assassination that I learned she had stayed briefly at Mrs. Ford's.

Mr. JENNER. I see.

That is the extent of your information with respect to the Fords at least up to November 22?

Mrs. PAINE. Up to the time of the assassination that is the extent of it.

Mr. JENNER. I wish to be certain of this and I don't recall whether I asked you and, therefore, I will risk repetition.

Did Marina and Lee, with you or even without you, visit any people, to your knowledge, while Marina was living with you in the fall of 1963, just social visit, go out and make a social visit?

Mrs. PAINE. No.

Mr. JENNER. I meant to include whether either together as a couple or separately.

Mrs. PAINE. I recall no such visit.

Mr. JENNER. I think your testimony was when Lee Oswald came home on the weekends, from what you have described he remained on the premises?

Mrs. PAINE. Yes.

Mr. JENNER. With the possible exception of one instance when he went off and bought some groceries or am I wrong about that exception?

Mrs. PAINE. He went with my children to buy some popsicles while I was teaching a student, so I was not at home that time.

Mr. JENNER. All right.

We have a report, Mrs. Paine, and you might help us with it on this subject, of a barber in your community, who recounts to the FBI that in his opinion Lee Harvey Oswald or what he thinks a gentleman who was that man, came to his shop reasonably regularly and had a haircut on Saturday, on Saturdays, and accompanying him was what he judged to be a 14-year-old boy. Do you recall Lee Oswald ever obtaining a haircut over any weekend while he was at your home?

Mrs. PAINE. No.

Mr. JENNER. To the best of your recollection, subject to his being off the premises while you were away shopping, it is your present firm recollection he never left the premises once he arrived, save this one instance that you knew of when he went to get popsicles?

Mrs. PAINE. Of course, I was away during that instance.

Mr. JENNER. You were?

Mrs. PAINE. Yes.

Mr. JENNER. But you anticipated?

Mrs. PAINE. Yes. Now, the morning of the 11th of November I was not home from something before 9 o'clock until about 2 that afternoon. I don't know what transpired during that time.

Mr. JENNER. Were there other occasions when you were off ministering to your children, that is taking them to the dentist or something of that nature, on a Saturday or to church on Sunday or to the local park on Sunday, that Lee Oswald may have been, that is periods of time when you would not have known whether he was on or off your premises?

Mrs. PAINE. I can think only of grocery shopping which would have been an hour to an hour and a half period, and the two times that I can recall in the Saturday afternoon, on a Saturday afternoon that I went to Dallas to teach one Russian student a lesson. I can't think of any other spaces of time, hours that I was away.

Mr. JENNER. Now, this gentleman also says——

Mrs. PAINE. Except the one I have just mentioned, of course, the one of November 11.

Mr. JENNER. He also says that the man he thinks was Lee Harvey Oswald not only regularly came to his shop on Friday evenings or Saturday mornings for a haircut, but that he occasionally drove a station wagon.

Do you know of any occasion to your certain knowledge that Lee drove your station wagon other than the one occasion you have already related?

Mrs. PAINE. Absolutely none.

Mr. JENNER. Do you know whether Lee Oswald subscribed to any newspapers?

Mrs. PAINE. Yes; I do.

Mr. JENNER. What newspapers, excuse me, did he or did he not subscribe?

Mrs. PAINE. Yes. They came to my door. They sat around the house until the weekend when he arrived.

Mr. JENNER. Tell us what newspapers those were?

Mrs. PAINE. I noticed a paper which I was told was from Minsk.

Mr. JENNER. Was it in Russian?

Mrs. PAINE. In Russian.

Mr. JENNER. Did you ever see it in the sense of glancing at it out of idle curiosity if nothing else?

Mrs. PAINE. Yes.

Mr. JENNER. And it was in Russian?

Mrs. PAINE. Yes.

Mr. JENNER. Was there something about it that indicated to you that it came from Minsk?

Mrs. PAINE. Marina told me.

Mr. JENNER. She told you. Was it a political tract or was it a newspaper as we understand newspapers?

Mrs. PAINE. It was a newspaper as Russians understand newspapers which makes it a borderline political tract.

Mr. JENNER. All right.

In addition to that Russian newspaper from Minsk was there anything——

Mrs. PAINE. There was a Russian magazine, small, Reader's Digest size.

Mr. JENNER. The witness is indicating in her hands about a page size of about nine by——

Mrs. PAINE. Six.

Mr. JENNER. Nine by six.

Is that about the size?

Mrs. PAINE. Something like that, called the Agitator, the name written in Russian.

Mr. JENNER. The word "Agitator" was written in Russian, printed in Russian?

Mrs. PAINE. That is right.

Mr. JENNER. On the face or cover page of this document, is that true?

Mrs. PAINE. Yes.

Mr. JENNER. Was the entire document in Russian?

Mrs. PAINE. Yes.

Mr. JENNER. Did you have occasion to look at it?

Mrs. PAINE. Just the outside.

Mr. JENNER. Your curiosity or intellectual interest never went beyond reading any portion of one of the issues?

Mrs. PAINE. It never did.

Mr. JENNER. But you do recall definitely the title page?

Mrs. PAINE. Yes.

Mr. JENNER. Any others?

Mrs. PAINE. Crocodile, which is a Russian satirical humor magazine.

Mr. JENNER. Was that in Russian?

Mrs. PAINE. Yes.

Mr. JENNER. Did you have occasion to read it and to observe Russian humor?

Mrs. PAINE. Yes.

Mr. JENNER. It was not political in character?

Mrs. PAINE. Being satirical, of course, it made political reference but it was not particularly political in nature.

Mr. JENNER. It was not designed as a political tract, put it that way.

Mrs. PAINE. No.

Mr. JENNER. Anything else?

Mrs. PAINE. Yes. The Russian magazine Ogonok.

Mr. JENNER. What does that mean in Russian?

Mrs. PAINE. It means "bonfire" or "fire".

Mr. JENNER. Was that printed in Russian?

Mrs. PAINE. Yes.

Mr. JENNER. Did you have—did your curiosity lead you to read any portion of it?

Mrs. PAINE. Or it may be—let's see, I am not certain in my translation, but go ahead with the question.

Mr. JENNER. You are not certain of your translation of the word?

Mrs. PAINE. Of that single word?

Mr. JENNER. Of the title of this document about which you are now speaking?

Mrs. PAINE. Yes.

Mr. JENNER. But you think it means what you said it meant?

Mrs. PAINE. It has something to do with fire; yes.

Mr. JENNER. Did you read any portion of any of those issues?

Mrs. PAINE. Yes; I did.

Mr. JENNER. And what was the nature of it with respect to whether it was political or otherwise?

Mrs. PAINE. It was not political.

Mr. JENNER. What was its nature?

Mrs. PAINE. Narrative, special articles of interest to the general population. Marina enjoyed reading this one.

Mr. JENNER. She enjoyed it?

Mrs. PAINE. She expressed herself as disliking the Agitator. She interpreted some of the things in Crocodile for me which I had difficulty understanding.

Mr. JENNER. Anything else?

Mrs. PAINE. Yes. He subscribed to Time magazine.

Mr. JENNER. Here in America?

Mrs. PAINE. Yes.

Mr. JENNER. And did he read it when he come out on weekends?

Mrs. PAINE. Yes; he did. He read that first.

Mr. JENNER. Sat down and read that first.

Did he take the issue away with him when he left every week?

Mrs. PAINE. It is my impression he did.

Mr. JENNER. Are there any others?

Mrs. PAINE. Yes. He subscribed to the Militant.

Mr. JENNER. Militant. What is the Militant?

Mrs. PAINE. It is a paper in English, newspaper style and I would say these next two——

Mr. JENNER. Published by whom?

Mrs. PAINE. I don't know.

Mr. JENNER. Socialist Worker's Party?

Mrs. PAINE. I have been so told.

Mr. JENNER. You just don't know?

Mrs. PAINE. I don't know.

Mr. JENNER. But was it a political tract?

Mrs. PAINE. I don't know that.

Mr. JENNER. Did you read it?

Mrs. PAINE. No.

Mr. JENNER. Why didn't you?

Mrs. PAINE. I wasn't interested.

Mr. JENNER. Because of the nature of the document?

Mrs. PAINE. If I had had time to do much reading, I might have taken an interest but I had no time, insufficient time to do the reading I really wanted to do. He also subscribed to the Worker.

Mr. JENNER. Is that the publication of the Communist Party USA?

Mrs. PAINE. I have been told so.

Mr. JENNER. Did you read that?

Mrs. PAINE. No.

Mr. JENNER. Did you observe—have you now concluded the list of newspapers, periodicals or magazines to which he was a subscriber?

Mrs. PAINE. I believe so. I might say that my awareness of his subscribing to these last two, the Militant and the Worker, came after the assassination. There was mail awaiting for him for that weekend which he did not pick up on the 21st, and after the assassination, indeed, after Saturday evening, the 23d, when it was announced on television that they had a photograph of Lee Oswald holding two papers. I looked at this pile of mail waiting for him which consisted of these two newspapers, the Militant and the Worker, and I threw them away.

Mr. JENNER. You threw them away?

Mrs. PAINE. Without opening them.

Mr. JENNER. Why did you throw them away?

Mrs. PAINE. I was pleased to throw away anything I could. I just didn't want it.

Mr. JENNER. Well, my question or query, and I think expression of surprise, is activated by what I am about to ask you as to whether you might call that to the attention of the FBI?

Mrs. PAINE. Oh, I am sure they knew.

Mr. JENNER. How are you sure they knew?

Mrs. PAINE. Because mail stopped coming on the spot, nothing came after the assassination, I was certain it was still coming to some place.

Mr. JENNER. But this was almost instantaneously after you heard a broadcast that a photograph of him had been found in which he had been holding up the Militant.

But you immediately went to see if he had that mail and there was a copy of the Militant and you threw it away?

Mrs. PAINE. Why not?

Mr. JENNER. Well, it occurred to me you might have called the FBI's attention to the fact that it had come to the house. But you didn't in any event?

Mrs. PAINE. No; I didn't.

Mr. JENNER. Did you report it to the FBI in any of these interviews you had subsequently with them, or did they ask? It is two questions, if you will answer both.

Mrs. PAINE. If so, it was quite recently.

Mr. JENNER. When did the other papers begin to arrive? Did I interrupt you before you had a chance to complete your answer to my question?

Mrs. PAINE. No.

Mr. JENNER. The papers different from the Worker and the Militant, when did they begin to arrive at your home?

Mrs. PAINE. Well, they began to arrive, I would say, some time after October 4th. That is, of course, my judgment. That is a rationalization.

Mr. JENNER. These magazines and newspapers you have recounted first appeared at your home after Lee Oswald came to Dallas and became employed or came to Dallas to live at your house and to seek employment?

Mrs. PAINE. He came to Dallas, he lived in Dallas, but he used my house.

Mr. JENNER. He came to your house?

Mrs. PAINE. As a residence, mailing address. Never asked to and I never complained but I noticed, of course, that he was using it as a mailing address.

Mr. JENNER. Up to that time and even though Marina was living with you nothing of that nature came to your home?

Mrs. PAINE. What?

Mr. JENNER. Prior to the time that Lee arrived at your home on or about or on the 4th of October 1963, none of these newspapers or periodicals had come to your home, is that correct?

Mrs. PAINE. That is correct.

Mr. JENNER. Was he a reader of the local newspaper?

Mrs. PAINE. Yes.

Mr. JENNER. You were a subscriber to what?

Mrs. PAINE. To the Irving newspaper and the Sunday Dallas Morning News.

Mr. JENNER. Did he read both of those?

Mrs. PAINE. He was very interested in seeing the Sunday paper edition especially. He read both, to the best of my recollection.

Mr. JENNER. He also read the daily papers?

Mrs. PAINE. Well, he wasn't there daily.

Mr. JENNER. When he was there he read it?

Mrs. PAINE. The Irving paper didn't come out on Saturday, so it was only the Sunday papers.

Mr. JENNER. But there were occasions when you had issues, the Friday issue around or Thursday issue around your home?

Mrs. PAINE. I don't recall his being interested in back issues.

Mr. JENNER. Are there any letters and communications between you and Marina or between you and Lee Oswald to which you have not called my attention?

Mrs. PAINE. There never were any letters of any sort between me and Lee Oswald except unless you could include this English portion to which I have already called your attention in a letter to Marina.

Mr. JENNER. Yes.

Mrs. PAINE. The only other letters—I have called your attention to all such letters, but I will have to wait until you are in Dallas to see the letters written since the assassination to Marina.

Mr. JENNER. Then I will ask you this question.

You produced for my inspection all of these letters other than the ones that I will see when I am in Dallas which you have identified as having been written subsequent to, subsequently to, November 22, 1963, is that correct?

Mrs. PAINE. That is right, you have all the correspondence.

Mr. JENNER. All right.

Mrs. PAINE. Wait, we did omit one letter which you have from Marina.

Mr. JENNER. Yes; I have it here.

Mrs. PAINE. You have no gaps that I could supply you.

Mr. JENNER. I appreciate the fact I have that letter which we found not relevant and, therefore, I did not tender it. You have tendered to me everything other than those I will see when I reach Dallas.

Mrs. PAINE. That is right.

Mr. JENNER. Now, do you recall having a conversation with Dr. Froelich Rainey——

Senator COOPER. May I ask, just a moment, the letter which has not been tendered and which was said not to be relevant——

Mrs. PAINE. You have a copy of it.

Senator COOPER. To whom was that letter addressed?

Mr. JENNER. That is addressed to Marina.

Senator COOPER. May I ask, does counsel have a copy of that letter?

Mr. JENNER. Yes; I have a copy of the letter and I have preserved the original and I also have a typewritten copy.

Senator COOPER. It has not been offered as part of evidence?

Mr. JENNER. It has not been offered because it is irrelevant to anything referred to here and it also has a personal remark in it that Mrs. Paine would prefer not to have spread on the record.

Mrs. PAINE. A remark not pertinent to the assassination or to the Oswalds but to my marriage.

Mr. JENNER. Is the name——

Senator COOPER. Let me just say for the record I think that will have to be a matter which will have to be considered by the members of the Commission.

Mr. JENNER. All right.

The letter to which you have reference you have exhibited to me, it is in your handwriting and it is in the same condition now as it was, a copy of a letter as I recall?

Mrs. PAINE. Which letter are you referring to?

(Short recess.)

Senator COOPER. On the record.

Mr. JENNER. I will do some jumping around because we have some tag ends to cover, I hope in a hurry.

You left New Orleans on September 23, was that in the morning or afternoon?

Mrs. PAINE. It was early morning.

Mr. JENNER. Early morning.

Did you drive right straight through to Irving?

Mrs. PAINE. No.

Mr. JENNER. You stopped then the evening of September 23, is that right?

Mrs. PAINE. That is right.

Mr. JENNER. And where, in Texas?

Mrs. PAINE. Yes; it was just over the line into Texas.

Mr. JENNER. Do you remember the name of the town?

Mrs. PAINE. No; I don't.

Mr. JENNER. Did you pay for that lodging?

Mrs. PAINE. Yes; I did.

Mr. JENNER. By the way, was there ever any financial arrangement agreed on with respect to Marina's stay with you in the fall of 1963 which would involve your giving her $10 a week or any other sum?

Mrs. PAINE. No; nothing was said beyond this attempt in the letter that I made to make her feel that she would not be having to ask for every need.

120

Mr. JENNER. We have those letters now in evidence and you testified about them yesterday?

Mrs. PAINE. Yes.

Mr. JENNER. Returning your attention to the time that Mr. Oswald, Lee Oswald, came to Irving in October of 1963, that is October 4, and reported to you he hitchhiked, you recall that?

Mrs. PAINE. Yes.

Mr. JENNER. He remained overnight the night of the 4th of October, is that correct?

Mrs. PAINE. Yes; he did.

Mr. JENNER. Did he return to Dallas the following day?

Mrs. PAINE. No.

Mr. JENNER. Was he driven back to Dallas within the next couple of days by you?

Mrs. PAINE. My recollection is that I took him to the bus station around noon on the 7th of October, that is a Monday.

Mr. JENNER. You did not drive him all the way into downtown Dallas?

Mrs. PAINE. No; I don't believe so.

Mr. JENNER. Marina has testified, or at least when interviewed by the FBI stated, that you did drive Lee to downtown Dallas.

Mrs. PAINE. I have given you all my recollections on this matter, haven't I, for the record?

Mr. JENNER. Yes.

Mrs. PAINE. With——

Mr. JENNER. Even after further reflection last night your recollection is as you have already stated?

Mrs. PAINE. That there was an occasion that we were going in with a Russian typewriter on an errand of mine to get that fixed, and I drove him to Ross Street and some crossroad, and he said was near to the employment office.

Mr. JENNER. I see.

What occasion was this?

Mrs. PAINE. What day?

Mr. JENNER. Day, yes; please?

Mrs. PAINE. I don't recall but I would be fairly certain it was a Monday.

Mr. JENNER. And had he been out at your home over the weekend?

Mrs. PAINE. Yes; that is my best recollection.

Mr. JENNER. Was it after he had become employed with the Book Depository?

Mrs. PAINE. No; he was on his way to the employment office. This was his purpose.

Mr. JENNER. So it was sometime prior to the weekend, was it, that the matter of employment by the Texas Book Depository had arisen?

Mrs. PAINE. I would judge that it has to have been on the 14th, which was Monday prior and indeed morning prior to the conversation at Mrs. Roberts about this.

Mr. JENNER. I see.

Mrs. PAINE. But I may be wrong about that, but it is my best recollection.

Mr. JENNER. Did the conversation at Mrs. Roberts take place on the 15th of October?

Mrs. PAINE. No; on the 14th.

Mr. JENNER. On the 14th. That was what day of the week?

Mrs. PAINE. Monday.

Mr. JENNER. Did you drive him into Dallas on that day?

Mrs. PAINE. I can't think when else it could have been.

Mr. JENNER. And to the best of your recollection that is probably the day then?

Mrs. PAINE. That is right.

Mr. JENNER. Did you indicate—did Marina accompany you?

Mrs. PAINE. Yes.

Mr. JENNER. Did she or you indicate any interest in driving by and seeing his apartment or room?

Mrs. PAINE. No.

Mr. JENNER. Was there any discussion at any time, Mrs. Paine, in your home or otherwise, with Marina or with Lee, as to the appearance of his rooming house, curtains flooring, what it was like?

Mrs. PAINE. The only thing I recall is that he described it as more comfortable than the $7 room he had occupied, told me the cost of it, said that he could watch television and had privileges to use the refrigerator.

Mr. JENNER. But other than that he didn't describe it?

Mrs. PAINE. No.

Mr. JENNER. Was there ever any discussion of any need on his part for curtains, that he liked to brighten up his room or in any respect, any additional appointments?

Mrs. PAINE. There was no such conversation at any time.

Mr. JENNER. You are acquainted with Dr. Froelich Rainey?

Mrs. PAINE. I am.

Mr. JENNER. He is—what is his position with the University of Pennsylvania. He has a position with the University of Pennsylvania Music Department, has he not?

Mrs. PAINE. He is the curator, the head man, as I understand it.

Mr. JENNER. You are acquainted with his wife Penelope?

Mrs. PAINE. I am.

Mr. JENNER. Does Penelope speak Russian fluently?

Mrs. PAINE. She has a very good command of the language. I think she has not had very much opportunity to use it in speech.

Mr. JENNER. Have you had occasion to inquire of Mrs. Rainey as to whether she might assist you with your Russian studies?

Mrs. PAINE. Well, there was never any discussion of assisting me in the role of tutor. She did some years ago loan me a record which I taped that was in Russian, and we visited this fall as part of my trip in the east.

Mr. JENNER. You mean, summer, not fall.

Mrs. PAINE. Well, it was, yes, August probably or early September that I saw her.

Mr. JENNER. And you do recall during the course of your summer trip before you went, that is you wound up in New Orleans from that trip?

Mrs. PAINE. Yes.

Mr. JENNER. So we are talking about the same trip.

Mrs. PAINE. That is the same trip.

Mr. JENNER. You did see her?

Mrs. PAINE. I did.

Mr. JENNER. Where in Philadelphia?

Mrs. PAINE. At her home.

Mr. JENNER. Where is her home?

Mrs. PAINE. Her home is not far from the residence where I was staying in Paoli. It is suburban Philadelphia.

Mr. JENNER. Did you have occasion then to report to her that—about Marina?

Mrs. PAINE. Yes; I did.

Mr. JENNER. And advise her in that respect, that she was married to an American who is now residing in New Orleans?

Mrs. PAINE. Yes.

Mr. JENNER. Did you say to her that the, I will call the, lady, Marina, but it is stated differently here, appeared to be having marital difficulties with her husband.

Mrs. PAINE. Yes.

Mr. JENNER. And would you state what your remarks were to Mrs. Rainey in that connection? That is the treatment of Marina by Lee?

Mrs. PAINE. I don't recall exactly what I said as to the treatment, but that Marina was unhappy, and that I thought she should have some alternative to living with him, and that I would probably, when down there, offer for her to live at my home. She asked me what Michael thought of that, and I said we had discussed it but that Michael and I were not living together, and this was news to Mrs. Rainey, and concerned her deeply.

And I said that I was lonely. I recall one important thing in what I said to Mrs. Rainey, that I never said in conversation to anyone else, that I was worried about offending Lee, that if offended, or if he felt I was taking his wife or not doing what he wanted in the situation, that he might be angry with me, and that I didn't want to subject myself or my children to possible harm from him.

She is the only person to whom I mentioned my thought that he might possibly be a person who could cause harm, and there was a very, not a strong thought in my thinking at all, but should be registered as having at least occurred to me, that he could be angry to the point of violence in relation to me.

Mr. JENNER. To the point of physical violence in relation to you?

Mrs. PAINE. In relation to me in this situation and I wanted to be perfectly sure before I made any offer definite that he was not, in fact, angry at my offer.

Mr. JENNER. Do you recall visiting your sister Sylvia?

Mrs. PAINE. Yes; indeed.

Mr. JENNER. You were there about 3 days?

Mrs. PAINE. Yes.

Mr. JENNER. Did you discuss Marina when you were with your sister?

Mr. PAINE. Very probably.

Mr. JENNER. And in substance did you say to your sister that you intended to go to New Orleans in the course of your trip within about 2 weeks to pick up Marina who was pregnant, she was the wife of an American, and she was to live with you in your home in Texas?

Did you say that much to her?

Mrs. PAINE. Well, I probably said it depended on whether she wanted to go.

Mr. JENNER. Other than that have I stated the substance in that connection?

Mr. PAINE. Yes.

Mr. JENNER. Did you also say to her that Marina wanted to leave her husband who was not supporting her, and was a jerk as far as his husband's role was concerned?

Mrs. PAINE. No.

Mr. JENNER. You did not.

What did you say, did you say anything of similar import?

Mrs. PAINE. Similar?

Mr. JENNER. That is, you did imply to your sister, did you, that Marina wished to leave Lee?

Mrs. PAINE. No. I would guess that was her interpretation.

Mr. JENNER. What did you say in this connection, please?

Mrs. PAINE. I don't recall exactly.

Mr. JENNER. Well, did you say, did you express your personal opinion to your sister as to Lee Oswald?

Mrs. PAINE. Yes.

Mr. JENNER. What did you say in that connection.

Mrs. PAINE. My opinion of Lee Oswald was quite negative all the way up to——

Mr. JENNER. This is what you have told your sister now, that is what I want.

Mrs. PAINE. I can't recall exactly what I told my sister at all.

Mr. JENNER. Yes.

Mrs. PAINE. I talked with virtually everyone I saw this summer, and there were a great many people, about this friend because it was important to me. I have already testified that I thought Lee didn't care enough about his wife and wasn't being a proper husband in the spring and through the summer, therefore, and it wasn't until I was in New Orleans that I thought he cared at all.

Mr. JENNER. I am just confining myself to this period. During this period as you visited your friends you did have occasion to express a negative opinion on your part with respect to Lee Oswald?

Mrs. PAINE. Indeed.

Mr. JENNER. Is that correct?

Mrs. PAINE. That is correct.

Mr. JENNER. It might have been more or less forceful in that expression of your opinion depending on the person with whom or to whom you were talking.

Mrs. PAINE. I would say that my sister's reaction to what I said was more forceful than what I said.

Mr. JENNER. But you did express a negative opinion.

Mrs. PAINE. Yes.

Mr. JENNER. You testified that—are you acquainted with a Dr. Carl Hyde?

Mrs. PAINE. He is my brother.

Mr. JENNER. Did you discuss Marina and Lee with him when you visited there in September of 1963?

Mrs. PAINE. I recall particularly an evening discussion with his wife where I told quite a lot about the contact that I had had with Marina.

Mr. JENNER. Did you state to either or both of them that Marina's husband was a Communist?

Mrs. PAINE. That is possible. I think it is more likely that I referred to him as a Marxist.

Mr. JENNER. Now, what is the distinction between a Marxist and a Communist in your mind?

Mrs. PAINE. Distinction is not clear to me, but I judged that Lee felt there was a distinction as he——

Mr. JENNER. What was your impression as to what Lee thought a Marxist was as distinguished from a Communist?

Mrs. PAINE. I have no clear impression.

Mr. JENNER. If I suggested the possibility of, that a Marxist tenet was the change in government by violent means rather than gradual process?

Mrs. PAINE. This is not something I ever heard from him.

Mr. JENNER. Was it anything that you ever thought of?

Mrs. PAINE. No.

Mr. JENNER. A concept that you ever had?

Mrs. PAINE. In describing Marxism?

Mr. JENNER. Yes.

Mrs. PAINE. No.

Mr. JENNER. Did you ever discuss with Lee why he was—he always took care to distinguish to say that he was a Marxist as distinguished from a Communist?

Mrs. PAINE. No; I never did.

Mr. JENNER. Did you form an impression as to what he intended to convey by that description?

Mrs. PAINE. He intended to convey that he was more pure, I felt, that was my impression.

Mr. JENNER. More pure than what?

Mrs. PAINE. Than a Communist.

Mr. JENNER. Did you also say to your brother or your sister or both of them that Lee had not permitted her to learn English, that is Marina?

Mrs. PAINE. Very probably.

Mr. JENNER. And that Marina was experiencing marital difficulties with Lee?

Mrs. PAINE. Very probably.

Mr. JENNER. Did you ever say that Marina did not share her husband's political views?

Mrs. PAINE. Yes; I did.

Mr. JENNER. Excuse me, that is to your brother or sister or both of them?

Mrs. PAINE. To the best of my recollection.

Mr. JENNER. Speaking of the marital difficulties, did you ever have the feeling that Marina was in some measure a contribution—contributed toward those, causing those difficulties or a catalyst from which those difficulties resulted?

Mrs. PAINE. I didn't have that feeling.

Mr. JENNER. You did not.

What feeling did you have in that direction, assuming you had one?

Mrs. PAINE. All the time I knew her or at least any references from her of the matter to their marriage left me with the impression that it was hopeful that though it was difficult they could work out their difficulties.

Mr. JENNER. And that she was desirous of attempting to do so?

Mrs. PAINE. She was desirous of attempting to do so though still leaving open the possibility that in time she would have to conclude that she couldn't.

She by no means simply gave in to him on every point or let him walk on her, but that, I would say, is a healthy thing for the marriage rather than anything contributive to any fundamental difficulty in it.

Mr. JENNER. Have you completed your answer?

Senator COOPER. May I ask a question?

Mr. JENNER. Yes.

Senator COOPER. Did Marina ever indicate to you in any way whether or not she felt, after she came to the United States and saw Lee Oswald in his country in which he had been born and reared, that she found him unintelligent or a person of mean ability, small ability or poor background?

Did she ever have any comment in any way on his being inferior?

Mrs. PAINE. I don't recall her ever commenting in that way.

Mr. JENNER. Was she disappointed in any way after he returned to the United States?

Mrs. PAINE. I don't recall her ever saying that.

I had heard Mrs. Ford express such an opinion.

Mr. JENNER. That would be hearsay?

Mrs. PAINE. That would be hearsay.

Mr. JENNER. Did you know, are you familiar with the report that appeared in the Fort Worth Press on January 15, 1964, reporting that you had told Marvin Lane that Lee could not have taken the rifle from your garage and gone to practice without your knowledge?

Do you recall that?

Mrs. PAINE. I do.

Mr. JENNER. Mark Lane.

Mrs. PAINE. It is Mark but that perhaps was in the Fort Worth Press. I recall that.

Mr. JENNER. Did you ever make that statement to a reporter for the Fort Worth Press?

Mrs. PAINE. Yes, I did; with slight variation. It always came out a more definite statement in the press than I meant to make it.

Mr. JENNER. What did you say to the reporter then?

Mrs. PAINE. I said I did not see how he could have taken the gun from the garage without my knowing it. There were two weekends particularly in question which had been reported in the Press that someone had seen him at a firing range, one being the weekend of the 9th and 10th, and I was home virtually all of that weekend except Monday the 11th as I have already described.

The other being the following weekend, and I didn't see how he could have— the weekend he was not out at my house, I didn't see how he could have come out, taken the gun, gone away without my knowledge, and if the gun had not been in that garage that weekend, I didn't see what the purpose of his coming out the 21st of November was in the situation.

And this is what I told Mr. Tackett of the Fort Worth Press.

Mr. JENNER. Did you also tell Mr. Tackett in addition to, that his reasons for his not engaging in rifle practice that weekend or any other weekend was that he couldn't drive an automobile?

Mrs. PAINE. Very probably.

Mr. JENNER. And also that he couldn't have walked that far for rifle practice?

Mrs. PAINE. Yes. By that far I mean there is no place you can walk to from my house, not only not to the firing range, but to an open enough place where you could fire. It would be difficult to walk that far.

Mr. JENNER. Where was the firing range at which it was suggested he practiced?

Mrs. PAINE. I don't know exactly. It was in the Grand Prairie area, just south of where we are located. But it would be a 15-minute car drive I would expect.

Mr. JENNER. From your home to the firing range. Do you know, did you ever go to the firing range to see where it really was located?

Mrs. PAINE. No; I never did.

Mr. JENNER. You are relying on the newspapers, are you?

Mrs. PAINE. That is right.

Mr. JENNER. When you say thinking of its location you are thinking of the general location of Grand Prairie, Tex.

Mrs. PAINE. Yes.

Senator COOPER. Were you asked to give your opinion on that?

Mrs. PAINE. I think so.

Senator COOPER. Why would you submit that as your conclusion that he could not have taken the rifle away, could not have got to a firing range?

Mrs. PAINE. The only thing—well—it had been reported in the press that he had been seen at a firing range or someone said he had seen him, Oswald, at a firing range on the weekend of the 9th, 10th, and the following weekend and it seemed to me important to say what I could on the subject if I had any contrary information, and I did any time the reporters asked me about it.

Senator COOPER. When you made a statement about the rifle, were you considering the fact that he had left your house on the morning of the 21st before you got up?

Mrs. PAINE. I don't understand the question.

Senator COOPER. The 22d, yes.

Mrs. PAINE. Let me say in making such a statement to the Press, I was not implying that I didn't think Oswald had taken a gun from my house on the morning of the 22d. Now, you ask the question again and perhaps I will understand it better.

Senator COOPER. Were you referring to two weekends when he left your house in saying that he couldn't take the gun or were you including also the morning of the 22d?

Mrs. PAINE. I was definitely not including the morning of the 22d.

Mr. JENNER. May I proceed, Mr. Chairman.

Senator COOPER. Yes.

Mr. JENNER. Do you know of any occasion when Lee and Marina did or might have visited the welfare office of the Salvation Army on your return from Dallas?

Mrs. PAINE. No.

Mr. JENNER. Having in mind all your contact with them during that period, do you have an opinion as to whether that could have taken place, that they did visit the Salvation Army Welfare Office?

Mrs. PAINE. It was suggested that this was in the fall of the year?

Mr. JENNER. Yes.

Mrs. PAINE. I don't know of any time that they could have.

Mr. JENNER. Do you recall in your discussion with Mr. Randle when the matter of the Texas School Book Depository possible employment came up, did you make a statement to Mrs. Randle suggesting that she not mention to anyone that Marina was of Russian birth?

Mrs. PAINE. After he had been hired I told Mrs. Randle that Lee was worried about losing his job, and asked her if she would mention to Wesley that he was worried about this, and would prefer for it not to be talked about where he worked, that he had a Russian wife as that would, therefore, bring up the subject of his having been in Russia and, therefore, the subject of his having tried to change his citizenship there, and she said to me oh, she was certain that Wesley would not talk about it.

Mr. JENNER. That was the extent of the conversation?

Mrs. PAINE. That is right.

Mr. JENNER. And its thrust, rather than the cryptic thrust I have given it?

Mrs. PAINE. Yes.

Mr. JENNER. Do you know a Frank Krystinik?

Mrs. PAINE. I do.

Mr. JENNER. He is an associate of your husband?

Mrs. PAINE. Yes.

Mr. JENNER. Did you have occasion to say to him at any time that Lee Oswald was not properly taking care of his wife and children?

Mrs. PAINE. I could well have given him that impression or given him that impression through Michael. I didn't very often see Frank.

Mr. JENNER. But you could have made that remark to him?

Mrs. PAINE. Yes.

Mr. JENNER. You made similar remarks to others?

Mrs. PAINE. Indeed, I have.

Mr. JENNER. During the time you visited with your mother-in-law, Mrs. Young, did you say to her that Lee wished his wife to return to Russia alone?

Mrs. PAINE. I very probably did.

Mr. JENNER. And also that he did not wish his wife to learn to speak English?

Mrs. PAINE. I would judge that I did.

Mr. JENNER. And that Marina did not wish to return to Russia?

Mrs. PAINE. That is correct.

Senator COOPER. While you are getting your papers together can I ask a few questions?

Mr. JENNER. Surely.

Senator COOPER. I refer to November 22 when the police came and you and Marina went into the garage with the police, you testified about that. Then you discovered that there wasn't anything in the blanket.

Now, at a later time, I believe you testified that the police showed Marina a rifle and asked her if she could identify this rifle that she had seen in Lee's possession.

What did she say about it?

Mrs. PAINE. She said that her husband's rifle had been a dark gun, that she was not certain that that was the one. That she could not absolutely recall whether there had been a telescopic sight on his gun or not.

Senator COOPER. Was she speaking in Russian?

Mrs. PAINE. That is right.

Senator COOPER. Were you translating?

Mrs. PAINE. No, Mr. Mamantov.

Senator COOPER. Were you following what she said?

Mrs. PAINE. Yes; indeed.

Senator COOPER. How did she designate the sight? What words?

Mrs. PAINE. It is a Russian word that sounded to me like binocular, as I recall.

Senator COOPER. Did she refer to it as a sighting device not in the words sighting device, but did her language in substance as she described it give reference to it as a sight on the rifle?

Mrs. PAINE. My judgment is that Mr. Mamantov used the word in reference to it first, you see, and then she simply used the same word.

Asking her was she acquainted with this, and giving the word in Russian, and she said she wasn't certain she had seen that binocular or whatever the word used was on the gun.

Senator COOPER. Now, at any time on the 22d, after she had admitted that she had seen a rifle before, and in your talk with her, either on the way into the police station or any other time, did she say anything more about having seen the rifle before?

Mrs. PAINE. No; she didn't.

Senator COOPER. To you? What?

Mrs. PAINE. No.

Senator COOPER. Did you know who brought Lee Oswald to your house from Dallas when he would come for his visits?

Mrs. PAINE. After he had gotten his job it was my understanding that he came with Wesley Frazier.

Senator COOPER. Did you ever hear him say that anyone else brought him to your house?

Mrs. PAINE. No; I didn't.

Senator COOPER. Did he ever say that any fellow worker at the Depository brought him to the house?

Mrs. PAINE. Other than Wesley Frazier; no.

Senator COOPER. Did he ever mention by name or any description any of the people with whom he worked at the Depository?

Mrs. PAINE. Except for Wesley; no.

Senator COOPER. He never mentioned any one of his fellow workers, associates there?

Mrs. PAINE. None.

Senator COOPER. Did he ever refer to them in any way as liking or disliking them as a group or as individuals?

Mrs. PAINE. No; he didn't.

Senator COOPER. In your talks with him or in hearing him talk did he ever refer to any persons who were friends of his or associates?

Mrs. PAINE. I never heard him mention anyone.

Senator COOPER. He never mentioned the name of any person?

Mrs. PAINE. Not anyone. He mentioned a friend in Houston as I have already testified, no name and I was wondering whether there was any such friend, I recall that. That is absolutely the only reference I can recall.

Senator COOPER. You said that you told someone that Marina did not agree with his political views?

Mrs. PAINE. Yes.

Senator COOPER. How did you know that?

Mrs. PAINE. She told me she wasn't interested in politics. She told me indeed that Lee complained about her lack of interest.

Senator COOPER. That is something different from saying that she didn't agree with them.

Mrs. PAINE. Well, she did say that she didn't like his having passed out leaflets in New Orleans. This is still different from saying she disagreed, though. But that is the most I can say.

Senator COOPER. Did she ever tell her what her political views were, if any?

Mrs. PAINE. She said she didn't consider herself a person interested in politics. She——

Senator COOPER. Did she ever refer to Lee being a Marxist or a Communist?

Mrs. PAINE. I don't recall such a reference ever.

Senator COOPER. Did she ever tell you whether or not she was a Marxist or a Communist?

Mrs. PAINE. No. I assumed she was not either.

Senator COOPER. What?

Mrs. PAINE. I assumed she was not either. She did at one point poke fun at the Party faithful who attended a Young Communist meeting in Minsk, whom she considered a dull lot and the meetings quite dull.

Senator COOPER. I missed the early part of your testimony so you may have testified to this, but I thought that I recalled that you did answer a question addressed to you by someone, a member of the Commission or counsel, in which you said that you were attracted to the Oswalds when you first met them, one, because you wanted to perfect your own Russian, and did you say, too, that you were interested because of the fact that he had been a defector and had returned and it was an unusual circumstance which interested you?

Mrs. PAINE. It made him an odd person.

Senator COOPER. What?

Mrs. PAINE. It made him an odd person. I was interested in the curious sense of what could have motivated him to do this.

Senator COOPER. Having that interest, didn't you ever talk to him about it, inquire about his experience?

Mrs. PAINE. I guess I wasn't interested enough.

Senator COOPER. What led him to do it?

Mrs. PAINE. And as I have already testified he always wanted to speak Russian to me, which shortens my tongue. I can't say as much or raise as many questions.

Senator COOPER. Well, did you try to search out the reasons for his defection and the reasons for returning?

Mrs. PAINE. No; I didn't.

Senator COOPER. And his political views, his economic views, that kind of thing?

Mrs. PAINE. No; I regret now that I didn't take any interest, but I did not.

Senator COOPER. You said that, in answer to counsel that, you either did tell people or probably told them that you believed Lee Oswald was a Communist.

Mrs. PAINE. It is my impression I spoke of him as he spoke of himself as a Marxist.

Senator COOPER. And you think, you believe, that has some relationship to communism?

Mrs. PAINE. Oh; yes.

Senator COOPER. I think you have stated that you didn't believe it was necessary for a person to actually be a member of the Communist Party to be a Communist in his views?

Mrs. PAINE. Yes. But that I considered it something less than actually accurate to call such a person a Communist that went on being——

Senator COOPER. Other than the persons you have named in your testimony as having come to your house, was there anyone else who ever came to your house, who talked to Lee Oswald or Marina?

Mrs. PAINE. I recall no one other than the people I have mentioned, sir.

Senator COOPER. Knowing that he was as you have described in your own words, a Marxist, were you concerned at all about that or worried about that, as being in your home?

Mrs. PAINE. Well, as I have described in testimony, I asked myself whether or not he might be a spy. I was not at all worried about ideology contrary to my own or with which I disagreed, and it looked to me that he was a person of this ideology or philosophy which he calls Marxism, indeed nearly a religion.

But not that he was in any way dangerous because of these beliefs.

Senator COOPER. Thinking now and then that he might be a spy or in the employ of the Soviet Union, were you concerned about the fact that such person who might be a spy or an agent of the Soviet Union was living in your house?

Mrs. PAINE. Well, if you recall my testimony I concluded that he was not, and also I was pleased that the FBI had come and I felt that they would worry about that, and that I didn't need to worry about any risk to me of public censure for my befriending such a person.

Senator COOPER. You told about the newspapers and periodicals that he received and read.

Mrs. PAINE. Yes.

Senator COOPER. Did he also have any books that he read while he was at your house?

Mrs. PAINE. I don't recall his reading books while he was at my house. He watched television a great deal but I don't recall his reading books.

Senator COOPER. You said that he did not have very ample means, financial means.

Were you struck with the fact that he was able to have these newspapers sent to him from Russia, England, New York?

Mrs. PAINE. Yes, I observed——

Senator COOPER. The Communist Worker comes from New York.

Mrs. PAINE. Yes, nothing from England, I recall, but he certainly considered these valuable. He was willing to spend money on these, I observed that, yes. It was rather unusual or unlike the rest of his behavior in that he did spend money for these periodicals.

Senator COOPER. Did you ever lend any money to either Marina or Lee Oswald?

Mrs. PAINE. No.

Senator COOPER. What?

Mrs. PAINE. No.

Mr. JENNER. Did you ever give them any money?

Mrs. PAINE. Cash money; no.

Senator COOPER. What?

Mrs. PAINE. Cash; no.

Of course, I bought groceries but that is not what you are asking.

Senator COOPER. You gave no money in the sense that you turned over physical possession of it?

Mrs. PAINE. I did not.

Senator COOPER. To either Lee or Marina?

Mrs. PAINE. No; not at any time to either one.

Senator COOPER. You did help them in the sense that you provided a home for Marina and on occasion provided food for Lee?

Mrs. PAINE. That is right.

Senator COOPER. I have just one or two more.

You said at one time you came to the conclusion that he wasn't an agent or spy because you didn't think he was intelligent enough.

I believe you said that.

Mrs. PAINE. That and the fact that as far as I could see had no contacts or any means of getting any information that would have been of any interest to the Soviet Union.

Senator COOPER. Yet he was intelligent enough that he had learned to speak Russian.

Mrs. PAINE. His Russian was poor. His vocabulary was large, his grammar never was good.

Senator COOPER. You said that he had, I believe, had the initiative to go to Russia, not as a tourist but as for reasons that he had developed himself, and that he came back when he made up his mind to come and was able to bring his wife.

You knew he moved around rather quickly, didn't you? He was in New Orleans——

Mrs. PAINE. In this country?

Senator COOPER. Yes.

Mrs. PAINE. No, I knew he had been in Fort Worth and had come to Dallas to seek work and then losing work had gone back to New Orleans and then back to Dallas.

Senator COOPER. What made you willing to have this man, you have said, this very curious man, from all you have described about him, to have him in your house?

Mrs. PAINE. He was Marina's husband and I like her, and I, as I have described, was both lonely and interested in learning the Russian language. I would have been happy had he never come out, indeed happier had he not come out on the weekends.

But they were not separated as a married couple nor contemplating such separation, and I didn't feel that this—it was appropriate for him to have to stay away. I did not ask that.

Senator COOPER. Prior to the time that Marina left your home—the day of the assassination, wasn't it?

Mrs. PAINE. She left the next day.

Senator COOPER. The next day.

Had you and Marina ever had any disputes or quarrels between yourselves?

Mrs. PAINE. I have referred to just one time when she in a sense was taking me to task on the matter of whose property their address was, I just mentioned that, that is the only time I recall.

Mr. JENNER. That is the incident in which you——

Mrs. PAINE. Following the November 5th meeting with Mr. Hosty.

Mr. JENNER. Mr. Hosty.

Mrs. PAINE. Yes.

Senator COOPER. You had said that, I believe you said, prior to the assassination you considered Lee Oswald as being violent or dangerous?

Mrs. PAINE. Well, now I have said that the thought crossed my mind once in relation to myself.

Senator COOPER. What caused that?

Mrs. PAINE. That he might be violent, because I thought he might resent my stepping in to do for his wife what he was not doing.

Senator COOPER. What made you think he would be violent about it if he wasn't caring about taking care of her?

Mrs. PAINE. Well, I wanted to satisfy myself, and I did then. The thought crossed my mind before I went to New Orleans for the second time as I have referred to it in a conversation with Mr. Rainey, before I went to New Orleans and then seeing him and changing my opinion some about him, I felt that he would not be violent or angry with me for this offer, and then proceeded with it, and this is the only——

Senator COOPER. I can understand why a person might be angry about something. But what about him led you to believe that he might be violent?

Mrs. PAINE. There was nothing that I could put my finger on. On the contrary my general impression was not of a man who would break out in sudden marked violence. He argued with his wife, and was distinctly unpleasant with her.

Senator COOPER. I believe you said the other day in answer to a question by Congressman Boggs that you held the opinion now that he did fire the rifle at the President.

Mrs. PAINE. Yes; I believe that is so but I don't know.

Senator COOPER. From this vantage point, is there anything about him now which you think of which seems consistent with the fact that he, that you believe he did shoot the President, President Kennedy?

Mrs. PAINE. Well, what has led me to the conclusion that he did shoot President Kennedy is the massive circumstantial evidence that surrounds his relationship or where he was, what he had at the time of the assassination. Perhaps we should get into the matter of motive.

Senator COOPER. In other words, a person's personality, is there anything you can think of now which would change your mind or change the viewpoint that you held previously that he wasn't violent?

Mrs. PAINE. No; I still can recall no incident that I saw, nothing or thought at the time, with this small exception of the one reference to Mrs. Rainey that—and that was a conjecture in reference to myself. Nothing that violent or indeed that insane.

Senator COOPER. Was it your opinion that Mrs. Oswald was shaken by the assassination and by the fact that her husband was charged with it?

Mrs. PAINE. She was certainly shaken on the afternoon when the policemen were out there, when he was at that time just charged with the shooting of Tippit. I never saw her after he was charged with the shooting of the President.

Senator COOPER. One other question: I think you said when Marguerite Oswald, Lee Oswald's mother, came to your house, and the Life people later appeared, you spoke of that, did you say that both of them, both Marina and Marguerite, seemed to be interested in making some kind of a deal with Life in order to get money?

Mrs. PAINE. No.

Senator COOPER. Or were you speaking only of Marguerite Oswald?

Mrs. PAINE. I was speaking only of Marguerite Oswald. I could add here that Marina appeared to me to want to be courteous and polite toward her mother-in-law, and wished to go along with whatever wishes Marguerite had on the subject.

Senator COOPER. Has anyone tried to make any kind of a business transaction for your statement or story?

Mrs. PAINE. At that time or since?

Senator COOPER. Since.

Mrs. PAINE. Yes.

Senator COOPER. What?

Mrs. PAINE. Yes. The Commission has a copy of an article that was written for Look which was not published and will not be.

Senator COOPER. Has that been testified?

Mr. JENNER. Will not be what?

Mrs. PAINE. Published. It is now my property and I don't plan to, I have no plans presently, at least.

Senator COOPER. Just for the record, have you entered into any kind of business transaction by which you would be paid for a story about this assassination?

Mrs. PAINE. I will not be paid for any story I write, and I am certain now I don't want to write any such story. I have, however, worked with Miss Jessamyn West, who is an author for an article which will appear in Time and Red Book magazine, or I expect it will. She is writing that, she talked to me.

Mr. JENNER. She approached you on that article?

Mrs. PAINE. No one approached me in that article. Was already decided before I was asked. But that is——

Mr. JENNER. Who decided it?

Mrs. PAINE. I had implied that I would be willing to do this, but not to anyone I thought was making an offer. This is aside.

Mr. JENNER. This was an offer to help the subject of the interview being interviewed?

Mrs. PAINE. All I really should say in clarification here is that there was bad communication between Red Book, Miss West and myself, and she was under the impression that I had agreed to do this before she had in fact been contacted, but then the fact of Red Book and Miss West thinking that this was something I had agreed to I then did agree to do it.

(Discussion off the record.)

Senator COOPER. Back on the record.

Have you been paid or promised any monetary consideration for any article that you might write or you might assist someone else in writing about your experiences connected with the Oswalds?

Mrs. PAINE. The complete answer to that would be that I received a $300 advance from Look magazine for helping in the writing of that article which will not appear, and that I have been told I will receive $500 from Red Book magazine for helping Miss West in writing that, and if you want, I will tell you what I think about what I want to do with this money but perhaps that is not pertinent.

Senator COOPER. If you want to?

Mrs. PAINE. Well, I plan to give it away.

Mr. JENNER. You mean give it to charity?

Mrs. PAINE. To charity.

Senator COOPER. That is all I have.

Mr. JENNER. You have referred to a Look magazine article in the preparation of which you have assisted. I have marked as Commission Exhibit No. 460 a document which I received from Mr. George Harris, after you had authorized me to call him and ask for it.

Would you glance through that and verify that that is the article in the final form?

You have examined Commission Exhibit 460. Is that the Look article to which you have made reference in your testimony here this afternoon?

Mrs. PAINE. Yes.

Mr. JENNER. And that article, however, is not one to be published?

Mrs. PAINE. That is right.

Mr. JENNER. Did you look over that article in this final form and approve it as to text and statements made in it?

Mrs. PAINE. Yes; although I don't think the final draft had been done or final approval given before it was decided that it would not be used.

Mr. JENNER. But as this exhibit stands, Commission Exhibit No. 460, the text and statements that are made in there had your approval?

Mrs. PAINE. Yes; they are, of course, not all of my words.

Mr. JENNER. Of course, not. The article was written by?

Mrs. PAINE. By George Harris, who is a senior editor on Look magazine, and he wrote it from typed copy he had directly as he had taken it from my telling.

Mr. JENNER. So it is, to use somewhat of a vernacular, it is ghost written?

Mrs. PAINE. It is ghost written but most of it is my words.

Mr. JENNER. I offer in evidence, as Commission Exhibit No. 460, the document we have just identified.

Senator COOPER. It will be received in evidence.

(The document referred to, heretofore identified as Commission Exhibit No. 460, was received in evidence.)

Mr. JENNER. Do you have an interest in the Russian language as has appeared from your testimony?

Mrs. PAINE. Yes.

Mr. JENNER. Mrs. Paine, are you now or have you ever been a member of the Communist Party?

Mrs. PAINE. I am not now and have never been a member of the Communist Party.

Mr. JENNER. Do you now or have you ever had any leanings which we might call Communist Party leanings.

Mrs. PAINE. No; on the contrary.

Mr. JENNER. Are you now or have you ever been a member of any groups which you consciously recognize as being, let us say, Communist front groups?

Mrs. PAINE. No; I have not and I would be quite certain I had not been unconsciously a member of any such groups.

Mr. JENNER. I take it from your response that you have an aversion to communism?

Mrs. PAINE. Yes; I do.

Mr. JENNER. And would be at pains and have been at pains during your adult life, at least, to avoid any association with or any advancement of communism as we know and abhor it?

Mrs. PAINE. Yes; that is right.

If I may say here, I am offended by the portion of the Communist doctrine that thinks violence is necessary to achieve its aims. I am likewise offended by the doctrine that any means to what is considered a good end is legitimate.

I, on the contrary, feel that there is no justification at any time for deception, and the Communists, as I have observed their activity, have no reluctance to deceive, and this offends me seriously.

Mr. JENNER. In that thinking, violence also impels you against the Communist faith?

Mrs. PAINE. It certainly does.

Mr. JENNER. Or political doctrine?

Mrs. PAINE. Yes; their espousal of violence repels me.

Mr. JENNER. You have an interest in the Russian language?

Mrs. PAINE. Yes; I do.

Mr. JENNER. Now, the members of the Commission, all of them are interested in how you came to have your interest in the Russian language, and they would like to have you indicate when it first arose and under what circumstances and what impelled you to have an interest in the Russian language; start from the very beginning of your life in that connection—that episode in your life?

Mrs. PAINE. All right. To be really the very beginning I will start and say I have been interested in other languages before being interested in Russian. I studied French in high school, German in college, and got a tutor to study Yiddish when I was working with a group that spoke that language.

Mr. JENNER. That is the Golden Age group of the Young——

Mrs. PAINE. Men and Young Women——

Mr. JENNER. Hebrew Association in Philadelphia?

Mrs. PAINE. That is correct.

Mr. JENNER. At that time you were employed by?

Mrs. PAINE. That organization.

Mr. JENNER. By that organization. And were you doing work in connection with this plan of Antioch College?

Mrs. PAINE. No; that was after I had completed my work at Antioch.

Mr. JENNER. I see.

Mrs. PAINE. Well, I do believe I did get some credit for that year at Antioch although I had completed my academic work, I was still getting some credit for my job credit, that is.

Mr. JENNER. All right, proceed.

Mrs. PAINE. And then I was working with a group of young Quakers, had been indeed for sometime.

Mr. JENNER. Please fix a little more definite time, please?

Mrs. PAINE. I began my interest in young Quakers in 1947.

Mr. JENNER. In 1947?

Mrs. PAINE. Yes.

Mr. JENNER. As quite a young girl?

Mrs. PAINE. When my interest also began in the Quaker church.

Mr. JENNER. You were then what, you were 19 years old?

Mrs. PAINE. I was going on 15, as a matter of fact.

Mr. JENNER. Going on 15?

Mrs. PAINE. That is right.

Mr. JENNER. You were going to high school?

Mrs. PAINE. Yes.

Mr. JENNER. Where were you living then?

Mrs. PAINE. I was living in Columbus, Ohio.

Mr. JENNER. And you became interested in the Quaker faith then or at least in the Quaker activity?

Mrs. PAINE. Both.

Mr. JENNER. And were you a member of the Friends Society, young people's society in Columbus at that time?

Mrs. PAINE. I attended the meeting which is the Quaker church in Columbus. They didn't have enough young people to have a society in that particular meeting. But then in college I became active in the national young Friends group.

Mr. JENNER. What is the official name of that?

Mrs. PAINE. The name at that time was the Young Friends Committee of North America. It included Canada young Friends. And in this connection I was, I served, as Chairman or Conference Coordinator for a conference of young friends that was held in 1955.

Mr. JENNER. Where?

Mrs. PAINE. At Quaker Haven, Ind.

Mr. JENNER. Did you attend that?

Mrs. PAINE. I did. It was at this conference, toward the latter part, part of really arising out of a discussion of the need for communication and more of it between the United States and the Soviet Union by no means the bulk of the business of this conference, but a small committee of interested people, was working on this matter.

Mr. JENNER. Are these interested young people?

Mrs. PAINE. These are all young Friends.

Mr. JENNER. And you were then of what age, 1955. 23?

Senator COOPER. 9 years ago?

Mrs. PAINE. 22, going on 23, that is right.

Mr. JENNER. 22 going on 23. Was this in the summer time?

Mrs. PAINE. Yes.

Mr. JENNER. Vacation period?

Mrs. PAINE. Yes.

Mr. JENNER. I see. By the way, Mrs. Paine, you had been to England, had you not, in some activity of the Friends Society back in 1952?

Mrs. PAINE. Yes.

Mr. JENNER. That was what meeting did you attend, and as a delegate of what?

Mrs. PAINE. I was selected as a delegate of the Lake Erie Association which is the larger group to which my meeting in Columbus belonged.

Mr. JENNER. Your Quaker meeting?

Mrs. PAINE. My Quaker meeting. To go as a delegate to the Friends world conference held at Oxford, England, in the summer of 1952. I also attended a young Friends conference held in Reading, England, just before the larger conference. Shall I return now to the conference at Quaker Haven in 1955?

Mr. JENNER. Yes.

Mrs. PAINE. I felt a calling in Friends terminology at that conference.

Mr. JENNER. An impulse, a desire, is that what you mean, a pulling?

Mrs. PAINE. More than that, that God asked of me that I study language, and I can't say that it was specifically said what language. This was at the time that plans first began for encouraging an exchange of young people between the Soviet Union and the United States, and I became active with the committee planning that, and from that planning there was an exchange, three Soviet young people came to this country and four young Quakers went to the Soviet Union, and I was very much impressed with the dearth of people in this country who could speak Russian. Here was a need for communication with people we had to live with, although we disagreed with them, certainly disagreed with the government, and the first elements of communication, the language, was not available among most young people, and even among older people in the country. My letter of June 18, 1959, marked Commission Exhibit No. 459-1 contains a statement of my motivation to study Russian. So it was this really that started me upon a course of study in Russian. Then once started, I was more propelled by my interest in the language itself. Shall I describe what training I have had?

Mr. JENNER. Well, please. I want to cover something else before that. I offer Commission Exhibit No. 459-1 in evidence.

The CHAIRMAN. It is received.

Mr. JENNER. Was there a movement also in this connection which you are now describing of a pen pal communication between young people here in America and young people in Russia?

Mrs. PAINE. Yes.

Mr. JENNER. Did you have anything to do with that?

Mrs. PAINE. There was a subcommittee of this Young Friends Committee of North America which was called East-West Contact Committee.

Mr. JENNER. Were you the leader of that committee?

Mrs. PAINE. I was not. But I was chairman of a committee of that committee, which was called Correspondence, and I helped make contact between young people in this country who wished to write to someone in the Soviet Union, and an organization of young people in Moscow which found pen pals for these young Americans.

We particularly wanted to go through an official organization so as to be certain we were not endangering or putting suspicion upon anyone, any young person in the Soviet Union to whom we were writing. We felt if they picked their own people that would lessen the suspicion of the Soviet person.

Mr. JENNER. Were you active in that group?

Mrs. PAINE. I was chairman of that for sometime.

Mr. JENNER. Did you take part in the pen pal correspondence yourself?

Mrs. PAINE. Yes; I did.

Mr. JENNER. And do you recall now the names of the Russian young people or Russian young person with whom you communicate, or sought communication?

Mrs. PAINE. I recall I wrote a few letters to a person named Ella, I have forgotten her last name, and I don't believe I have the correspondence still. If I did, I don't any more.

Mr. JENNER. If you once had it?

Mrs. PAINE. If I once had it, I don't have it now in my possession, and then that stopped because she stopped writing. I wrote and got another correspondent whose name is Nina Aparina, with whom I corresponded up to last spring, I would say, and I haven't—yes; and I haven't heard anything from her for about a year.

Mr. JENNER. What was the nature of the correspondence, particularly with respect to subject matter?

Mrs. PAINE. We discussed?

Mr. JENNER. In this letter period?

Mrs. PAINE. We discussed our mutual interest in language. She was a teacher of the English language. She married an engineer during the time of our correspondence.

Mr. JENNER. Russian?

Mrs. PAINE. Yes; of course.

Mr. JENNER. Russian citizen?

Mrs. PAINE. Yes. We exchanged a magnetic tape recording one time. I sent her one and she sent one with music and readings, hers were music and readings in Russian, and mine was similar in English as part of language study aid.

My last communication said she was expecting a baby last June but I haven't heard anything from her since that communication, as I say, probably a year ago that came.

Mr. JENNER. Now all of your activity, this activity, of correspondence between you and any citizen in Russia, was part of it, originated in the Young Friends group, an activity to supply here a meeting with, communication by, Americans with citizens in Russia, and then latterly in your communication with the lady you have last mentioned, a mutual exchange between the two of you here to improve her English and you to improve your Russian?

Mrs. PAINE. That is right. The committee was formed much the same time that our State Department made arrangements with the Soviets for cultural exchange, and I think our purposes were similar but, of course, outside the government.

Mr. JENNER. Now the three Russian students who came over here, did you have any contact with them?

Mrs. PAINE. I met them once at an open meeting in North Philadelphia.

Mr. JENNER. Were a number of other people present?

Mrs. PAINE. Oh, yes.

Mr. JENNER. And that is the only contact you had with them?

Mrs. PAINE. Yes.

Mr. JENNER. All right. Proceed.

Mrs. PAINE. Except that I read a book that was written by one of these students nearly a year after he had gone back to the Soviet Union which I found most disillusioning, I must say, in which it was pure propaganda.

135

Mr. JENNER. He sought to report what his experiences here were in America?

Mrs. PAINE. He sought to report on this trip that he had taken, that we had worked to achieve.

Mr. JENNER. Did you regard him as fair or accurate, that is, what you read?

Mrs. PAINE. What I read of the book he wrote was extremely inaccurate and unfair.

Mr. JENNER. Did it misrepresent America as you knew it?

Mrs. PAINE. Misrepresented America, certainly.

Mr. JENNER. All right.

Mrs. PAINE. Shall I go on now to what I have studied?

Mr. JENNER. Yes. Have you had any formal education in the study of the Russian language?

Mrs. PAINE. Yes; I have. I attended a concentrated summer course at the University of Pennsylvania in the summer of 1957 where, during the course of 6 weeks, we completed a first year college Russian text.

Mr. JENNER. What year did you say that was?

Mrs. PAINE. I believe that was 1957.

Mr. JENNER. All right.

Mrs. PAINE. And then I had difficulty keeping that up, keeping Russian up over the next year, but the following year I was no longer teaching and took a course at Berlitz School of Languages in Philadelphia in Russian, and improved by ability to converse, and it helped me to recall what I had gone through rather too fast in this accelerated course.

I then applied for the summer course at the Middlebury College summer language school in Middlebury, Vt., in the summer of 1959 and attended that 7-week course. At Middlebury they required that you speak nothing but the language you are studying the entire time, both in class and out. This was very valuable though very difficult.

Mr. JENNER. Who was your instructor?

Mrs. PAINE. There?

Mr. JENNER. Yes.

Mrs. PAINE. I took three courses. Natalie Yershov.

Mr. JENNER. You were relating, Mrs. Paine, you recalled one of your instructors at Middlebury?

Mrs. PAINE. Yes.

Mr. JENNER. Do you recall the name of any other?

Mrs. PAINE. Offhand I can't recall. I recall certainly the director of the school but he was not an instructor of mine.

Mr. JENNER. Did you have a roommate?

Mrs. PAINE. Yes; I did.

Mr. JENNER. What was your roomate's name?

Mrs. PAINE. Her name was Helen Mamikonian.

Mr. JENNER. Is that correct?

Mrs. PAINE. Yes.

Mr. JENNER. Do you still have contact with her?

Mrs. PAINE. It has been a long time since I have written but we have exchanged Christmas cards.

Mr. JENNER. Christmas cards and an occasional letter?

Mrs. PAINE. Yes.

Mr. JENNER. Where does she live?

Mrs. PAINE. She lives and works in Boston where she is a teacher of Russian langauge at Simmons College, as I recall.

Mr. JENNER. Did she at one time live in New York City?

Mrs. PAINE. Yes; her home is New York. She spent her high school years there after having immigrated from France, and I believe her mother still lives there, is a tutor for the Berlitz School in Russian in New York.

Mr. JENNER. Her mother is?

Mrs. PAINE. Yes.

Mr. JENNER. All right.

Now we have your study at Pennsylvania, University of Pennsylvania, and your study at the Berlitz School in Philadelphia, was it?

Mrs. PAINE. Yes.

Mr. JENNER. And your study at Middlebury College. What additional formal or at least let us say semiformal instruction or education have you had in the Russian language?

Mrs. PAINE. I then moved to the Dallas area to the place where I presently live in Irving, and then I would guess it was early in 1960 I took up some study again at the Berlitz School in Dallas, completed a course which I had paid for in Philadelphia, and then went on after that with private lessons with Mrs. Gravitis, who has already been mentioned.

Mr. JENNER. Is Mrs. Gravitis also an instructor in the Berlitz School in Dallas?

Mrs. PAINE. I met her because she was an instructor for a short time there and I think is yet on call to them as an instructor.

Mr. JENNER. Does that cover your formal education in the Russian language?

Mrs. PAINE. Yes; it does.

Mr. JENNER. Now, are you a teacher of Russian?

Mrs. PAINE. I have one student whom I teach beginning Russian.

Mr. JENNER. Is that a connection with an established institution?

Mrs. PAINE. It began in connection with an established institution during the summer of 1963, at the Saint Marks School of Texas in Dallas, Tex.

Mr. JENNER. And you were the teacher of Russian in the Saint Marks School during that quarter or summer term?

Mrs. PAINE. Summer term.

Mr. JENNER. And arising out of that has been your engagement as a tutor, is that correct?

Mrs. PAINE. That is correct.

Mr. JENNER. Who is your student?

Mrs. PAINE. My student's name is Bill H-U-T-K-I-N-S.

Mr. JENNER. Is he, what is he, a young man?

Mrs. PAINE. I am sorry, it is H-O-O-T-K-I-N-S.

Mr. JENNER. How old is he?

Mrs. PAINE. He turned 15 in the summer.

Mr. JENNER. Is he a native American so far as you know?

Mrs. PAINE. As far as I know, yes.

Mr. JENNER. Is it your—has it been also your desired objective on your part to teach Russian as a regular instructor or teacher in the public or private schools?

Mrs. PAINE. Yes; I would like to do that.

Mr. JENNER. That is still your hope and desire?

Mrs. PAINE. It interests me very much.

Mr. JENNER. And it has been for sometime an objective of yours, has it?

Mrs. PAINE. Yes.

Mr. JENNER. I will ask you a couple of general questions. First, I will probably repeat this when I examine you in your deposition also, Mrs. Paine, but I desire to have it on this record before the Commission, is there anything that has come to your mind that you would like to relate to the Commission which you think might be helpful to it in its deliberations in consideration of the serious problems and events into which they are inquiring?

Mrs. PAINE. There are a few small items I hope we will get into tomorrow.

Mr. JENNER. Would you please state them as to subject matter, at least. Would they take very long for you to state?

Mrs. PAINE. I will make an attempt to be brief here. I recall that Lee once used my typewriter to type something else beside this note, is that what you want?

Mr. JENNER. Yes; would you turn and direct your remarks to the Chairman, to Senator Cooper, so we can all hear you and you might speak up a little bit, your voice has been dropping.

Mrs. PAINE. I am tired.

I recall that Lee once asked to borrow my typewriter and used it to type something I judged was a letter at sometime prior to this day November 9, when he typed a letter which we have a rough draft. This is probably no use to you.

Mr. JENNER. That is what I call the Mexico letter?

Mrs. PAINE. That is what you call it, all right.

Mr. JENNER. All right. Give the exhibit.

Mrs. PAINE. It is Exhibit No. 103.

Mr. JENNER. Thank you.

Mrs. PAINE. I want to know whether you want to inquire of me my account of Secret Service agents having come and asked me, having come out to the house after the assassination to ask me if I had ever seen a particular note which they had. And I have later assumed that this is what has been referred to in the press as the note written by Oswald at the time of the attempt on Walker and if you want I will make it clear all I know in relation to that.

Mr. JENNER. Yes; I recall that incident and I wish you would, please.

Mrs. PAINE. And then the other thing is simply to invite the members of the Commission, but if it is a deposition I can't do that then, to feel free to ask me any questions that are not settled in their mind or clear regarding the separation which existed between myself and my husband, if that is troublesome in any way or if there is anything in which——

Mr. JENNER. Mrs. Paine, if that doesn't embarrass you, members of the Commission have voiced to me some interest in that, that is an interest only to the extent they are seeking to resolve in their mind who Ruth Paine is and if I may use the vernacular, what makes her tick, so would you relate that now on the Commission record, please?

Mrs. PAINE. All right. I might say that I think it is important and relevant here because if I had not been separated from my husband I would have not as I think I have already testified, made an invitation to anyone to join the family circle, especially in such a small house.

Really, I might ask if you have questions it might be easier for me to answer them.

Mr. JENNER. Perhaps we can bring it along in this fashion. What was the cause of the separation between your husband and yourself, in your view?

Mrs. PAINE. In my view, of course, yes. He expressed himself as not really interested in remaining married to me. We never quarreled. We never indeed have had any serious difference of opinion except I want to live with him and he is not that interested in being with me, would be our single difference of opinion.

And in the spring of 1962 I felt that something more definite should be done, and asked Michael why he continued to live with me if he felt that way about it, and he said that it was easier and cost less, and I said that wasn't a good enough reason for a marriage, and asked him to be out of the house in the fall when I returned from summer vacation that year.

Mr. JENNER. That was 1962?

Mrs. PAINE. 1962, yes. I would say our marriage is marked both by mutual honesty, that is exceptional, and by a lack of overt or interior strife except that it hasn't quite come together as a mutual partnership.

My mother recently said to me that "If you would just look only at what Michael does there is nothing wrong with your marriage at all. It is just what he says", and I concur with her opinion on that, that he is so scrupulously honest with his own feelings that, and really too hard on himself in a sense, that he states verbally this is not feeling that he loves me or loves me enough, but in fact his actions toward me are totally acceptable to me.

Mr. JENNER. Is he gracious and kind and attentive to you?

Mrs. PAINE. Yes.

Mr. JENNER. Has he always been?

Mrs. PAINE. Insufficiently attentive, I would say, but he is always kind and thoughtful.

Mr. JENNER. Have you had any financial differences of opinion?

Mrs. PAINE. We have not.

Mr. JENNER. He even during this period of time when you were separated, he voluntarily supported the household and you lived in a manner and style that suited you or to which you had become accustomed?

Mrs. PAINE. Yes, that is right.

Mr. JENNER. You had no arguments about matters of that nature?

Mrs. PAINE. That is right.

Mr. JENNER. Your husband has returned to your home?

Mrs. PAINE. He is living there now.

Mr. JENNER. How long has that been?

Mrs. PAINE. He has been staying there since the night of November 22. He didn't move his belongings in until the middle of the following week.

Mr. JENNER. Would you say this is a reconciliation?

Mrs. PAINE. I can't say that.

Mr. JENNER. You cannot.

Do you wish to say any more in the statement of yours?

Mrs. PAINE. Not unless you have questions. I think it is an accurate statement of the marriage.

Mr. JENNER. All right.

What brought this forth was my asking you if you had anything you would like to bring before the Commission.

Mrs. PAINE. That is correct.

Mr. JENNER. Are there any others?

Mrs. PAINE. I can think of nothing else.

Mr. JENNER. To the best of your present recollection are the statements and the testimony you gave, you have given so far, before the Commission consistent with statements you have given to the FBI, to Secret Service, to magazine reporters, editors, to anyone?

Mrs. PAINE. The statements I have given here are fully consistent with anything I have said before except that the statement here has been much fuller than any single previous statement.

Mr. JENNER. And you have testified to matters and things before the Commission about which, which you did not relate or even had occasion to relate in your mind, at least, to FBI agents, to Secret Service agents and to the others that you have identified in general terms?

Mrs. PAINE. Yes.

Mr. JENNER. Mrs. Paine, you and I had the opportunity, you afforded me the privilege of speaking with you before your testimony commenced, before the Commission. And also I think the first day of your testimony you were gracious enough to return here to the Commission room and we spent several hours talking?

Mrs. PAINE. Yes.

Mr. JENNER. As a matter of fact, we left around 12:30, a quarter of one in the morning, did we not?

Mrs. PAINE. Yes, that is right, we did.

Mr. JENNER. Now, recalling back to those periods of conferences with me, do you have any feeling or notion whatsoever that any of your testimony before the Commission was in any degree whatsoever, inconsistent with anything you related to me?

Mrs. PAINE. Oh, no; I don't think so, not in any way.

Mr. JENNER. Not in any way. Do you have any feeling whatsoever that during the course of my conferences with you, outside this Commission, that I influenced or sought to shape your testimony in any respect?

Mrs. PAINE. No. Clearly I felt no influence from you.

Mr. JENNER. All of the statements that you related to me were free and voluntary on your part, and not given under any coercion, light or heavy, as the case might be, on my part.

Mrs. PAINE. That is right.

Mr. JENNER. Mr. Chairman, there are some additional matters we wish to examine the witness about and Representative Ford has given me a rather long list of questions he asked me to cover. He regretted that was necessary because of his enforced absence, and Mrs. Paine has agreed that she would be available in the morning, and I may examine her by way of deposition before a reporter under oath, and with that understanding of the Commission, of you, Mr. Chairman, I would at this moment as far as the staff is concerned, close the formal testimony of Mrs. Paine before the Commission, with advice to you, sir, that tomorrow morning I will cover additional matters by way of deposition.

Senator COOPER. As I understand the matters you will go into by deposition will not be any new evidence in the sense of substance but more to——

Mr. JENNER. I can tell you what they are, it will be her background, some of which she has now given in regard to her study of the Russian language.

More formal proof of her calendar, and her address book. Also her general background which I have already mentioned. Some correspondence between herself and her mother, and the items that Mrs. Paine has now mentioned she would like to relate herself.

Mrs. PAINE. One of which we took care of already.

Mr. JENNER. One of which we took care of. We will cover those and I was going to ask her questions tomorrow, some of which we have already covered of Lee Harvey Oswald's personality and habits and actions.

I am going to ask here about Mrs. Shirley Martin, who has appeared on the scene since the assassination, and appears to be a self-appointed investigator, and to the extent that there has been any contact between Mrs. Paine and Mrs. Shirley Martin, and then inquire, I may not even do this because we have covered a very great deal of the conversations and discussions between Marina and Mrs. Paine on various possible subjects, and I can see from my list we have covered many of them already.

Senator COOPER. Let it be ordered that evidence will be taken this way, with this reservation, of course, if the Commission determines after studying the deposition that it would be necessary for her to be called again, you would be willing to come again before the Commission to testify.

Mrs. PAINE. I would certainly be willing if there is any need for my coming.

Mr. JENNER. In addition to this, Mr. Chairman, as I think already appears of record, I will come to Mrs. Paine's home in Irving, Tex., sometime on Monday or Monday evening or if she finds it more convenient, on Tuesday of next week to inquire of her with a court reporter present relative to the curtain rod package, and I also will make a tour of her home and as we move about her home the reporter will record the conversation between us, questions and answers.

Senator COOPER. Are there any further questions?

Mr. JENNER. That is all. Thank you, sir.

Senator COOPER. All right, then we will stand in recess subject to the call of the Chairman of the Commission.

(Translations of letters introduced in evidence in the course of Mrs. Paine's testimony are reproduced in the exhibit volumes.)

Tuesday, March 24, 1964

TESTIMONY OF HOWARD LESLIE BRENNAN, BONNIE RAY WILLIAMS, HAROLD NORMAN, JAMES JARMAN, JR., AND ROY SANSOM TRULY

The President's Commission met at 9 a.m., on March 24, 1964, at 200 Maryland Avenue NE., Washington, D.C.

Present were Chief Justice Earl Warren, Chairman; Representative Gerald R. Ford, John J. McCloy, and Allen W. Dulles, members.

Also present were J. Lee Rankin, general counsel; Joseph A. Ball, assistant counsel; David W. Belin, assistant counsel; Norman Redlich, assistant counsel; and Charles Murray, observer.

TESTIMONY OF HOWARD LESLIE BRENNAN

The CHAIRMAN. The Commission will come to order.

Mr. Brennan, in keeping with our statements, so you will know just what the purpose of the session is, I will read a little statement to you.

The purpose of today's hearing is to hear the testimony of Howard Leslie Brennan, Bonnie Ray Williams, James Jarman, Jr., Harold Norman, Roy S. Truly.

These witnesses were all in the vicinity of the Texas School Book Depository Building at the time of the assassination of President John F. Kennedy. They will be asked to provide the Commission with their knowledge of the facts concerning the assassination of President Kennedy.

Would you please rise and be sworn?

Do you solemnly swear that the testimony you give before this Commission will be the truth, the whole truth, and nothing but the truth, so help you God?

Mr. BRENNAN. I do.

The CHAIRMAN. You may be seated, Mr. Brennan.

Mr. Belin will conduct the interrogation.

Mr. BELIN. Mr. Brennan, will you state your name for the record, please?

Mr. BRENNAN. Howard Leslie Brennan.

Mr. BELIN. Where do you live?

Mr. BRENNAN. 6814 Woodward, Dallas 27.

Mr. BELIN. And how old a man are you?

Mr. BRENNAN. 45.

Mr. BELIN. Are you married?

Mr. BRENNAN. Yes.

Mr. BELIN. Family?

Mr. BRENNAN. Two children. One grandson.

Mr. BELIN. What is your occupation, Mr. Brennan?

Mr. BRENNAN. Steamfitter.

Mr. BELIN. And for whom are you employed, or by whom are you employed?

Mr. BRENNAN. Wallace and Beard.

Mr. BELIN. Is that a construction company?

Mr. BRENNAN. Yes.

Mr. BELIN. And let me ask you this: How long have you been a steamfitter?

Mr. BRENNAN. Since 1943, I believe.

Mr. BELIN. Do you work for one employer, or do you go from job to job?

Mr. BRENNAN. I go from job to job.

Mr. BELIN. Is that at your direction or at the direction of any union?

Mr. BRENNAN. Local 100 in Dallas.

Mr. BELIN. Mr. Brennan, where were you on the early part of the afternoon of November 22, 1963, say around noon or so?

Mr. BRENNAN. I left a position behind the Book Store, which is a leased part of Katy Yards, which we have fabrication for pipe for the Republic Bank Building. At 12 o'clock I went to the cafeteria on the corner of Main and Record. I believe that is it.

Mr. BELIN. That would be at Main and Record Streets in Dallas?

Mr. BRENNAN. Yes.

Mr. BELIN. And did you have your lunch there?

Mr. BRENNAN. Yes.

Mr. BELIN. And then after lunch, where did you go?

Mr. BRENNAN. I finished lunch and I glanced at a clock—I don't know exactly where the clock is located—and noticed it was 12:18. So I thought I still had a few minutes, that I might see the parade and the President.

I walked to the corner of Houston and Elm.

Mr. BELIN. What route did you take to get to Houston and Elm?

Mr. BRENNAN. I went west on Main.

Mr. BELIN. You went west on Main from Record Street to——

Mr. BRENNAN. Houston.

Mr. BELIN. Houston

Mr. BRENNAN. And on the east side of Houston, I walked to Elm.

Mr. BELIN. All right.

Mr. BRENNAN. Crossed the street to the southwest corner of Houston and Elm.

Mr. BELIN. Do you have any estimate about how long it took you to get there?

Mr. BRENNAN. A possibility I would say more or less 4 minutes.

Mr. BELIN. And then what did you do when you got to the southwest corner of Houston and Elm?

Mr. BRENNAN. I stayed around a couple of minutes. There was a man having an epileptic fit, a possibility of 20 yards east—south of this corner. And they

141

were being attended by some civilians and officers, and I believe an ambulance picked him up.

Mr. BELIN. All right.

Mr. BRENNAN. And I walked over to this retainer wall of this little park pool and jumped up on the top ledge.

Mr. BELIN. You jumped up on the retaining wall?

Mr. BRENNAN. Yes.

Mr. BELIN. Now, I hand you what has been marked as Exhibit 477.

(The document referred to was marked Commission Exhibit No. 477 for identification.)

Mr. BELIN. I ask you to state if you know what this is.

Mr. BRENNAN. Yes.

Mr. BELIN. Will you please tell the Commission what this is?

Mr. BRENNAN. That is the Book Store at the corner of Houston and Elm.

Mr. BELIN. By the Book Store, you mean the Texas School Book Depository Building?

Mr. BRENNAN. Right.

Mr. BELIN. Now, do you know what——

Mr. BRENNAN. That is the retainer wall which I perched on.

Mr. BELIN. All right. This is the retaining wall on which you perched. I believe that this is actually you sitting on this retaining wall in a picture that we took in Dallas pursuant to your showing us where you were November 22; we took that picture on this past Friday.

Mr. BRENNAN. That is correct.

Mr. BELIN. Which would be the 20th of March. Is that correct?

Mr. BRENNAN. That is correct.

Mr. BELIN. All right. I hand you now what the reporter has marked as Commission Exhibit 478.

(The document referred to was marked Commission Exhibit No. 478 for identification.)

Mr. BELIN. I ask you to state, if you know, what this is.

Mr. BRENNAN. Yes. That is the retaining wall and myself sitting on it at Houston and Elm.

Mr. BELIN. You remember that the photographer was standing on the front steps of the Texas School Book Depository when that picture was taken on the 20th of March?

Mr. BRENNAN. Yes; I do.

Mr. BELIN. And the camera is pointed in what direction?

Mr. BRENNAN. South.

Representative FORD. Are those the positions where you were sitting on November 22?

Mr. BRENNAN. Yes, sir.

Representative FORD. At about 12——

Mr. BRENNAN. From about 12:22 or 12:24 until the time of the assassination.

Representative FORD. In both pictures, that is a true——

Mr. BRENNAN. True location.

Representative FORD. True location of where you were sitting November 22d?

Mr. BRENNAN. Yes, sir.

Mr. BELIN. Mr. Brennan, I am going to hand you a negative, which has been marked as Commission Exhibit 479.

(The document referred to was marked Commission Exhibit No. 479 for identification.)

Mr. BELIN. This appears to be a negative from a moving picture film. And I will hand you a magnifying glass—the negative has been enlarged. This negative appears to be a picture of the Presidential motorcade on the afternoon of November 22d. I ask you to state if you can find yourself in the crowd in the background in that picture.

Mr. BRENNAN. Yes. I am sitting at the same position as I was in the picture taken Friday, with the exception, I believe, my hand is resting on the wall, and Friday my hand, I believe, was resting on my leg.

Mr. BELIN. Well, your legs in this picture, Exhibit 479, I notice, are not dangling on the front side there, is that correct?

Mr. BRENNAN. No.

Mr. BELIN. What were you wearing on November 22d? What clothes were you wearing?

Mr. BRENNAN. Gray khaki work clothes, with a dark gray hard helmet.

Mr. BELIN. Your head here appears to be the highest in the group, a little bit left of center in the upper part of the picture, is that correct?

Mr. BRENNAN. Yes, sir.

Mr. BELIN. Does this scene depict the scene as you recollect it on that day, November 22d?

Mr. BRENNAN. It does.

Mr. BELIN. Mr. Brennan, could you please tell the Commission what happened from the time you sat on that retaining wall, what you saw?

Mr. BRENNAN. Well, I was more or less observing the crowd and the people in different building windows, including the fire escape across from the Texas Book Store on the east side of the Texas Book Store, and also the Texas Book Store Building windows. I observed quite a few people in different windows. In particular, I saw this one man on the sixth floor which left the window to my knowledge a couple of times.

Mr. BELIN. Now, you say the window on the sixth floor. What building are you referring to there?

Mr. BRENNAN. That is the Texas Book Store.

Mr. BELIN. I am going to ask you to circle on Exhibit 477 the particular window that you said you saw a man leave and come back a couple of times.

Mr. BRENNAN. Well, I am confused here, the way this shows. But I believe this is the sixth floor, the way those windows are built there right at the present. I am confused whether this is the same window.

Mr. BELIN. You mean because some windows are open below it?

Mr. BRENNAN. No. The way the building is built, it seems like this is more or less a long window with a divider in the middle.

Mr. BELIN. Here is a marking pencil. Will you just mark the window that you believe you saw the man.

All right.

And do you want to put a letter "A", if you would, by that.

All right, now you have marked on Commission Exhibit 477 a circle with the letter "A" to show the window that you saw a man in, I believe you said, at least two times come back and forth.

Mr. BRENNAN. Yes.

Mr. BELIN. Did you see any other people in any other windows that you can recollect?

Mr. BRENNAN. Not on that floor.

There was no other person on that floor that ever came to the window that I noticed.

There were people on the next floor down, which is the fifth floor, colored guys. In particular, I only remember two that I identified.

Mr. BELIN. Do you want to mark the window with the circle that you believe you saw some Negro people on the fifth floor. Could you do that with this marking pencil on Exhibit 477, please?

Mr. BRENNAN. The two that I identified, I believe, was in this window.

Mr. BELIN. You want to put a "B" on that one?

Now, after you saw the man—well, just tell what else you saw during that afternoon.

Mr. BRENNAN. Well, as the parade came by, I watched it from a distance of Elm and Main Street, as it came on to Houston and turned the corner at Houston and Elm, going down the incline towards the railroad underpass. And after the President had passed my position, I really couldn't say how many feet or how far, a short distance I would say, I heard this crack that I positively thought was a backfire.

Mr. BELIN. You thought it was backfire?

Mr. BRENNAN. Of a motorcycle.

Mr. BELIN. Then what did you observe or hear?

Mr. BRENNAN. Well, then something, just right after this explosion, made me think that it was a firecracker being thrown from the Texas Book Store. And

I glanced up. And this man that I saw previous was aiming for his last shot.

Mr. BELIN. This man you saw previous? Which man are you talking about now?

Mr. BRENNAN. The man in the sixth story window.

Mr. BELIN. Would you describe just exactly what you saw when you saw him this last time?

Mr. BRENNAN. Well, as it appeared to me he was standing up and resting against the left window sill, with gun shouldered to his right shoulder, holding the gun with his left hand and taking positive aim and fired his last shot. As I calculate a couple of seconds. He drew the gun back from the window as though he was drawing it back to his side and maybe paused for another second as though to assure hisself that he hit his mark, and then he disappeared.

And, at the same moment, I was diving off of that firewall and to the right for bullet protection of this stone wall that is a little higher on the Houston side.

Mr. BELIN. Well, let me ask you. What kind of a gun did you see in that window?

Mr. BRENNAN. I am not an expert on guns. It was, as I could observe, some type of a high-powered rifle.

Mr. BELIN. Could you tell whether or not it had any kind of a scope on it?

Mr. BRENNAN. I did not observe a scope.

Mr. BELIN. Could you tell whether or not it had one? Do you know whether it did or not, or could you observe that it definitely did or definitely did not, or don't you know?

Mr. BRENNAN. I do not know if it had a scope or not.

Mr. BELIN. I believe you said you thought the man was standing. What do you believe was the position of the people on the fifth floor that you saw—standing or sitting?

Mr. BRENNAN. I thought they were standing with their elbows on the window sill leaning out.

Mr. BELIN. At the time you saw this man on the sixth floor, how much of the man could you see?

Mr. BRENNAN. Well, I could see—at one time he came to the window and he sat sideways on the window sill. That was previous to President Kennedy getting there. And I could see practically his whole body, from his hips up. But at the time that he was firing the gun, a possibility from his belt up.

Mr. BELIN. How much of the gun do you believe that you saw?

Mr. BRENNAN. I calculate 70 to 85 percent of the gun.

Mr. BELIN. Do you know what direction the gun was pointing.

Mr. BRENNAN. Yes.

Mr. BELIN. And what direction was the gun pointing when you saw it?

Mr. BRENNAN. At somewhat 30 degrees downward and west by south.

Mr. BELIN. Do you know down what street it was pointing?

Mr. BRENNAN. Yes. Down Elm Street toward the railroad underpasses.

Mr. BELIN. Now, up to the time of the shots, did you observe anything else that you have not told us about here that you can think of right now?

Mr. BRENNAN. Well, not of any importance. I don't remember anything else except——

Mr. BELIN. Let me ask you this. How many shots did you hear?

Mr. BRENNAN. Positively two. I do not recall a second shot——

Mr. BELIN. By a second shot, you mean a middle shot between the time you heard the first noise and the last noise?

Mr. BRENNAN. Yes; that is right. I don't know what made me think that there was firecrackers throwed out of the Book Store unless I did hear the second shot, because I positively thought the first shot was a backfire, and subconsciously I must have heard a second shot, but I do not recall it. I could not swear to it.

Mr. BELIN. Could you describe the man you saw in the window on the sixth floor?

Mr. BRENNAN. To my best description, a man in his early thirties, fair complexion, slender but neat, neat slender, possibly 5-foot 10.

Mr. BELIN. About what weight?

Mr. BRENNAN. Oh, at—I calculated, I think, from 160 to 170 pounds.

Mr. BELIN. A white man?

144

Mr. BRENNAN. Yes.

Mr. BELIN. Do you remember what kind of clothes he was wearing?

Mr. BRENNAN. Light colored clothes, more of a khaki color.

Mr. BELIN. Do you remember the color of his hair?

Mr. BRENNAN. No.

Mr. BELIN. Now, I believe you said that after the last shot you jumped off this masonry structure on which you were sitting. Why did you jump off?

Mr. BRENNAN. Well, it occurred to me that there might be more than one person, that it was a plot which could mean several people, and I knew beyond reasonable doubt that there were going to be bullets flying from every direction.

Mr. BELIN. Then what did you do after that? Or what did you see?

Mr. BRENNAN. I observed to my thinking that they were directing their search towards the west side of the building and down Houston Street.

Mr. BELIN. When you say "they", who do you mean?

Mr. BRENNAN. Law-enforcement officers.

Mr. BELIN. By the west side of the building, you mean towards the underpass or railroad tracks?

Mr. BRENNAN. Yes.

Mr. BELIN. After you saw that, what did you do?

Mr. BRENNAN. I knew I had to get to someone quick to tell them where the man was. So I ran or I walked—there is a possibility I ran, because I have a habit of, when something has to be done in a hurry, I run. And there was one officer standing at the corner of the Texas Book Store on the street. It didn't seem to me he was going in any direction. He was standing still.

Mr. BELIN. What did you do or what did you say to him?

Mr. BRENNAN. I asked him to get me someone in charge, a Secret Service man or an FBI. That it appeared to me that they were searching in the wrong direction for the man that did the shooting.

And he was definitely in the building on the sixth floor.

I did not say on the sixth floor. Correction there.

I believe I identified the window as one window from the top.

Mr. BELIN. All right.

Mr. BRENNAN. Because, at that time, I did not know how many story building it was.

Representative FORD. But you did say to the policeman it was a window on the second floor from the top?

Mr. BRENNAN. Right.

Mr. BELIN. And then what happened?

Mr. BRENNAN. He——

The CHAIRMAN. May I ask there. By the second floor from the top, do you mean the one directly underneath the top floor?

Mr. BRENNAN. Underneath the top floor, excluding the roof, yes, sir.

Mr. BELIN. And then what happened, sir?

Mr. BRENNAN. He said, "Just a minute." And he had to give some orders or something on the east side of the building on Houston Street. And then he had taken me to, I believe, Mr. Sorrels, an automobile sitting in front of the Texas Book Store.

Mr. BELIN. And then what happened there?

Mr. BRENNAN. I related my information and there was a few minutes of discussion, and Mr. Sorrels had taken me then across the street to the sheriff's building.

Mr. BELIN. Did you describe the man that you saw in the window?

Mr. BRENNAN. Yes; I believe I did.

Mr. BELIN. Mr. Brennan, later that afternoon, or the next day, did you have occasion to go down to the Dallas Police Station to try to identify any person?

Mr. BRENNAN. That evening, the Secret Service picked me up, Mr. Patterson, I believe, at 6 o'clock, at my home, and taken me to the Dallas Police Station.

Mr. BELIN. All right. Could you tell us what happened there, please?

Mr. BRENNAN. If I might add a part, that I left out a couple of minutes ago——

Mr. BELIN. Go right ahead, sir.

Mr. BRENNAN. As Mr. Sorrels and some more men were discussing this, I mentioned these two colored guys.

Mr. BELIN. Yes.

Mr. BRENNAN. Came out of the book store, running down the steps.

Mr. BELIN. You mean the two——

Mr. BRENNAN. That I had previously saw on the fifth floor.

Mr. BELIN. All right.

Mr. BRENNAN. And I immediately identified these two boys to the officers and Mr. Sorrels as being on the fifth floor.

Mr. BELIN. Do you have anything else you wish to add now?

Mr. BRENNAN. No; that concludes that.

Mr. McCLOY. They were running out of the building?

Mr. BRENNAN. They came running down the front steps of the building on the Elm street side.

Mr. McCLOY. Did they then disappear in the crowd?

Mr. BRENNAN. No; they took them in custody, I suppose, and questioned them.

Representative FORD. The law enforcement officers stopped them, and you did what, then?

Mr. BRENNAN. No. I believe Mr. Sorrels or the Secret Service man stopped them.

I am not sure, but I don't believe an officer of the police department stopped them.

Representative FORD. But you were standing on the steps of the Texas School Book Depository Building talking to whom?

Mr. BRENNAN. Mr. Sorrels and another man, and I believe there was an officer standing there, a police officer.

Representative FORD. And these two Negroes came out of the front door?

Mr. BRENNAN. Yes, sir.

Representative FORD. And you did what then?

Mr. BRENNAN. I——

Representative FORD. Spoke to Mr. Sorrels?

Mr. BRENNAN. Spoke to Mr. Sorrels, and told him that those were the two colored boys that was on the fifth floor, or on the next floor underneath the man that fired the gun.

Representative FORD. You positively identified them?

Mr. BRENNAN. I did, at that time.

Mr. BELIN. Is there anything else now up to the time you got down to the Dallas Police Station?

Mr. BRENNAN. Well, nothing except that up until that time, through my entire life, I could never remember what a colored person looked like if he got out of my sight. And I always thought that if I had to identify a colored person I could not. But by coincidence that one time I did recognize those two boys.

Representative FORD. Did those two Negro men say in your presence that they had been in the fifth floor window?

Mr. BRENNAN. I don't recall. I don't recall.

Mr. BELIN. Is there anything else, sir, now up to the time you got down to the Dallas Police Station?

Mr. BRENNAN. On Friday evening, you are speaking of?

Mr. BELIN. Yes.

Mr. BRENNAN. No.

Mr. BELIN. All right.

What happened when you got down to the Dallas Police Station?

Mr. BRENNAN. Mr. Patterson, if I am correct in the Secret Service that picked me up, directed me to go to the fourth floor, a certain room on that floor.

(At this point, Mr. Warren and Representative Ford withdrew from the hearing room.)

Mr. BRENNAN. I later was introduced to several men—Captain Fritz in Mr. Sorrels' office, and several more men. I do not remember their names.

Mr. BELIN. All right.

Before I go any further, do you remember the name of the officer you talked to in front of the School Book Depository Building?

Mr. BRENNAN. I don't believe I ever heard it. I do not remember his name.

Mr. BELIN. Are you sure of the names of the Secret Service men you talked to? I believe you mentioned the name Sorrels.

Mr. BRENNAN. I do not know the other man's name.

Mr. BELIN. You believe one of them was Sorrels?

Mr. BRENNAN. I believe one of them was Sorrels.

Mr. BELIN. I think for the record——

Mr. BRENNAN. That is at the building.

Mr. BELIN. Yes, sir.

I think we should offer and introduce Commission Exhibits 477, 478, and 479.

Mr. DULLES. The Chief Justice has asked me to preside in his absence this morning.

They shall be admitted.

(The documents heretofore marked for identification as Commission Exhibits Nos. 477, 478 and 479, were received in evidence.)

Mr. BELIN. By the way, Mr. Brennan, I note that you have glasses with you here today.

Were you wearing glasses at the time of the incident that you related here?

Mr. BRENNAN. No. I only use glasses to see fine print and more especially the Bible and blueprint.

Mr. BELIN. And have you had your eyes checked within the past 2 or 3 years?

Mr. BRENNAN. These here were prescriptioned, I believe, a possibility less than a year before the incident.

Mr. DULLES. Does that mean you are farsighted?

Mr. BRENNAN. Yes.

(At this point, Representative Ford entered the hearing room.)

Mr. BELIN. Has there been anything that has happened since the time of November 22, 1963, that has changed your eyesight in any way?

Mr. BRENNAN. Yes, sir.

Mr. BELIN. What has happened?

Mr. BRENNAN. The last of January I got both eyes sandblasted.

Mr. BELIN. This is January of 1964?

Mr. BRENNAN. Yes. And I had to be treated by a Doctor Black, I believe, in the Medical Arts Building, through the company. And I was completely blind for about 6 hours.

Mr. BELIN. How is your eyesight today?

Mr. BRENNAN. He says it is not good.

Mr. BELIN. But this occured January of this year, is that correct?

Mr. BRENNAN. Yes.

Mr. BELIN. Now, taking you down to the Dallas Police Station, I believe you said you talked to Captain Fritz. And then what happened?

Mr. BRENNAN. Well, I was just more or less introduced to him in Mr. Sorrels' room, and they told me they were going to conduct a lineup and wanted me to view it, which I did.

Mr. BELIN. Do you remember how many people were in the lineup?

Mr. BRENNAN. No; I don't. A possibility seven more or less one.

Mr. BELIN. All right.

Did you see anyone in the lineup you recognized?

Mr. BRENNAN. Yes.

Mr. BELIN. And what did you say?

Mr. BRENNAN. I told Mr. Sorrels and Captain Fritz at that time that Oswald—or the man in the lineup that I identified looking more like a closest resemblance to the man in the window than anyone in the lineup.

Mr. BELIN. Were the other people in the lineup, do you remember—were they all white, or were there some Negroes in there, or what?

Mr. BRENNAN. I do not remember.

Mr. BELIN. As I understand your testimony, then, you said that you told him that this particular person looked the most like the man you saw on the sixth floor of the building there.

Mr. BRENNAN. Yes, sir.

Mr. BELIN. In the meantime, had you seen any pictures of Lee Harvey Oswald on television or in the newspapers?

Mr. BRENNAN. Yes, on television.

Mr. BELIN. About when was that, do you believe?

Mr. BRENNAN. I believe I reached home quarter to three or something of that, 15 minutes either way, and I saw his picture twice on television before I went down to the police station for the lineup.

Mr. BELIN. Now, is there anything else you told the officers at the time of the lineup?

Mr. BRENNAN. Well, I told them I could not make a positive identification.

Mr. BELIN. When you told them that, did you ever later tell any officer or investigating person anything different?

Mr. BRENNAN. Yes.

Mr. BELIN. When did that happen?

Mr. BRENNAN. I believe some days later—I don't recall exactly—and I believe the Secret Service man identified hisself as being Williams, I believe, from Houston. I won't swear to that—whether his name was Williams or not.

Mr. BELIN. All right.

Mr. BRENNAN. And he could have been an FBI. As far as I remember, it could have been FBI instead of Secret Service.

But I believe it was a Secret Service man from Houston.

And I——

Mr. BELIN. What did he say to you and what did you say to him?

Mr. BRENNAN. Well, he asked me—he said, "You said you couldn't make a positive identification."

He said, "Did you do that for security reasons personally, or couldn't you?"

And I told him I could with all honesty, but I did it more or less for security reasons—my family and myself.

Mr. BELIN. What do you mean by security reasons for your family and yourself?

Mr. BRENNAN. I believe at that time, and I still believe it was a Communist activity, and I felt like there hadn't been more than one eyewitness, and if it got to be a known fact that I was an eyewitness, my family or I, either one, might not be safe.

Mr. BELIN. Well, if you wouldn't have identified him, might he not have been released by the police?

Mr. BRENNAN. Beg pardon?

Mr. BELIN. If you would not have identified that man positively, might he not have been released by the police?

Mr. BRENNAN. No. That had a great contributing factor—greater contributing factor than my personal reasons was that I already knew they had the man for murder, and I knew he would not be released.

Mr. BELIN. The murder of whom?

Mr. BRENNAN. Of Officer Tippit.

Mr. BELIN. Well, what happened in between to change your mind that you later decided to come forth and tell them you could identify him?

Mr. BRENNAN. After Oswald was killed, I was relieved quite a bit that as far as pressure on myself of somebody not wanting me to identify anybody, there was no longer that immediate danger.

Mr. BELIN. What is the fact as to whether or not your having seen Oswald on television would have affected your identification of him one way or the other?

Mr. BRENNAN. That is something I do not know.

Mr. BELIN. Mr. Brennan, could you tell us now whether you can or cannot positively identify the man you saw on the sixth floor window as the same man that you saw in the police station?

Mr. BRENNAN. I could at that time—I could, with all sincerity, identify him as being the same man.

Mr. BELIN. Was the man that you saw in the window firing the rifle the same man that you had seen earlier in the window, you said at least a couple of times, first stepping up and then going back?

Mr. BRENNAN. Yes, sir.

Mr. BELIN. About how far were you away from that window at the time you saw him, Mr. Brennan?

Mr. BRENNAN. Well, at that time, I calculated 110-foot at an angle. But closer surveillance I believe it will run close to 122 to 126 feet at an angle.

Mr. BELIN. I believe that on Friday we paced the distance between the place where you were sitting and the front door of the Texas School Book Depository Building, and it ran about——

Mr. BRENNAN. 93-foot.

Representative FORD. This doesn't have to be now, but I think some time he ought to step by step on a diagram trace his movements from the restaurant until he left the scene of the shooting.

Mr. BELIN. On that particular diagram, Congressman Ford, which is Exhibit No. 361, the intersection of Main and Houston, and of Record and Main is not shown. It would be a little bit to the south.

Representative FORD. But he might be able to show the direction from which he came to get on to the scene.

Mr. BELIN. Yes; that he can do.

Representative FORD. And then his movements from there on until he left the area. I think it would be very helpful to tie down the precise places he was from time to time.

Mr. BELIN. I think he might do that right now.

Mr. Brennan, I place in front of you Exhibit 361, and I call to your attention that the top appears to be south rather than north, and the arrow north is pointed towards the bottom. And you will notice at the top here, running in what would be an east-west direction, is Elm Street. And you can see running in a north-south direction Houston Street, with the Texas School Book Depository Building noted here in black.

Do you see that?

Mr. BRENNAN. It should be here.

Mr. BELIN. I will turn the map around to show you north and south; we can keep it upside down for the moment.

This is Elm Street. To the north is Pacific. Main would be down here off the bottom of the map. And here is Record Street right here. And I believe you said you were at lunch at Record and Main, and then you walked to the south.

I wonder if you might take this pen and kind of, off the street markings, you might start maybe down here at the bottom as to where you had your lunch.

Mr. BRENNAN. This is Main here.

Mr. BELIN. Main would be running there, yes.

If you would, put a "D" at that point.

Now, if you would kind of on a line trace your course that you took that day. All right.

Mr. BRENNAN. I didn't go to the corner.

Mr. BELIN. You didn't go to the corner of Elm and Houston. That would be the southeast corner?

Mr. BRENNAN. I noticed this man having a fit. And I came across at this corner.

Mr. BELIN. Now, would you put the letter "E" where you ended up sitting. This is on Exhibit No. 361.

Mr. BRENNAN. "E"?

Mr. BELIN. Yes.

Mr. BRENNAN. I believe that would be just about where the retainer wall is.

Mr. BELIN. All right.

So you have put on Exhibit 361 the letter "E" where you were sitting facing the School Book Depository Building.

Representative FORD. I think that it might be helpful to trace it where he went subsequent to that.

Mr. BELIN. All right.

Subsequent to the time of the shooting, would you put a line from your point at point "E" to where you went to talk to the police officers and the Secret Service officers?

Mr. BRENNAN. The retaining wall come around here and straight across here.

Mr. BELIN. Will you put an "F" where you talked to him?

Mr. BRENNAN. The car was sitting here. That is where I talked to him. This is where I contacted the officer.

Mr. BELIN. You contacted the officer at "F".

Mr. BRENNAN. Yes.

Mr. BELIN. And then you went over to a car.

Mr. BRENNAN. Yes.

Mr. BELIN. Would you put your direction to the car and put a "G" on there?

Mr. BRENNAN. I walked down the street hereaways with this officer.

Mr. BELIN. All right, the point from "F" where you walked down the street, that would be walking north on Houston?

Mr. BRENNAN. I don't know; however, we walked down this way, but I do remember going in that direction with the officer.

Mr. BELIN. You went to the north on Houston?

Mr. BRENNAN. Yes. And then back to——

Mr. BELIN. Well, just put a mark in there, and cut it back, if you could, just to show the route of you going north.

Mr. BRENNAN. I don't know exactly however.

Mr. BELIN. All right.

Will you put a mark to "G" at the end? And I believe you said that the car that you talked to the Secret Service agent in was at point "G" approximately?

Mr. BRENNAN. Right.

Mr. BELIN. Now, are these accurate or approximate locations, Mr. Brennan?

Mr. BRENNAN. Well, don't you have photographs of me talking to the Secret Service men right here?

Mr. BELIN. I don't believe so.

Mr. BRENNAN. You should have. It was on television before I got home— my wife saw it.

Mr. BELIN. On television?

Mr. BRENNAN. Yes.

Mr. BELIN. At this time we do not have them.

Do you remember what station they were on television?

Mr. BRENNAN. No. But they had it. And I called I believe Mr. Lish who requested that he cut those films or get them out of the FBI. I believe you might know about them. Somebody cut those films, because a number of times later the same films were shown, and that part was cut.

Mr. BELIN. Who would Mr. Lish be with?

Mr. BRENNAN. The FBI.

Mr. BELIN. All right.

We thank you very much for that information.

Is there anything else that you did at point "G" or anywhere else after the time of the assassination before you went to the Sheriff's office?

Mr. BRENNAN. I walked up the steps and stood on the outside of the doorway.

Mr. BELIN. Of what building?

Mr. BRENNAN. Of the Texas Book Store, while the officers or the men that I was with gave some more orders. And then Mr. Sorrels taken me across to the Sheriff's office.

Mr. DULLES. You did not go inside the building?

Mr. BRENNAN. No; I did not.

Mr. BELIN. Did you notice any people coming out of the front stairs of the building after these two Negroes came out?

Mr. BRENNAN. Well, I recall people going in and out, but a different picture I cannot remember.

Representative FORD. Where were you standing when you identified the two Negroes?

Mr. BRENNAN. On the edge of the street, outer side of the sidewalk, when the two colored boys came out of the building and came down the steps.

Mr. BELIN. Was that at point "G"?

Mr. BRENNAN. Yes, sir.

Mr. BELIN. All right.

Now, perhaps on Exhibit No. 478 you can trace your route at least along Houston Street to the time—to the place where you were sitting. You recognize the intersection of Main and Houston there?

Mr. BRENNAN. Yes.

Mr. BELIN. All right.

Could you start there and kind of trace—well, I don't know if you can see all of it.

Mr. BRENNAN. No.

Mr. BELIN. Do the best you can, you can trace along here.

Here would be the intersection of Main and Houston.

Mr. BRENNAN. I came down that side. Now, this street was open at that time.

Mr. BELIN. By this street you mean Houston Street?

Mr. BRENNAN. Yes. I don't recall any parked cars there.

Mr. BELIN. Could you make that line a little darker, sir, that you have put on. All right. Now, at that first point, this would be——

Mr. BRENNAN. I believe I walked a little south there, just observing them picking the man up.

Mr. BELIN. All right.

You have marked a line on Exhibit No. 478 heading a little bit south on the west side of Houston street, commencing at the southwest corner of the intersection, which is where you say you walked to watch the man with the epileptic fit, is that it?

Mr. BRENNAN. Well, I didn't go up—he was almost center way of the block here. I didn't go up that far.

Mr. BELIN. All right.

And will you put the letter "H" there, if you would?

Mr. BRENNAN. Where I was standing watching the man?

Mr. BELIN. Where you were standing watching the man; yes.

Mr. BRENNAN. Right there.

Mr. BELIN. And then where did you go from there?

Mr. BRENNAN. Right there.

Mr. BELIN. All right.

Now, you have taken a line which would be running along the south side of Elm Street there towards the point where you are sitting, and that is in the picture Exhibit 478. And that was the route that you took?

Mr. BRENNAN. Yes.

Mr. BELIN. Put the letter "I", if you would, there, please.

Now, on Exhibit No. 477, I wonder if you would perchance show us after the assassination, or the shooting—you said you first went over to another side of the wall.

Would it be to the east or to the west there?

Mr. BRENNAN. To the east. This right here is solid concrete.

Mr. BELIN. Is this where you went?

Mr. BRENNAN. Yes.

Mr. BELIN. All right.

On Exhibit 477, could you put the letter "J" where you went right after the shooting?

All right.

Now, I believe you said you later stood up and eventually walked across the street to get a police officer. On Exhibit 477, could you put a letter "K" where you believe you went to talk to this police officer, where he was.

It looks like there is a car there now.

So you went from point "J" to point "K", and point "K", on Exhibit 477, would correspond with "F" on Exhibit 361, is that right?

Mr. BRENNAN. Right.

Mr. BELIN. All right.

Now, I wonder if you could perchance show on Exhibit 477 the point that corresponds with point "G" on Exhibit 361, which is where you said you went to the car.

Mr. BRENNAN. This car here—letter what?

Mr. BELIN. "L".

Mr. BRENNAN. That is this car here, sitting approximately where——

Mr. BELIN. I note that this car that you have marked the "L" is not actually on the extreme north part of Elm, but really appears to be on that part which is going down to the Freeway.

Mr. BRENNAN. Oh, is that right?

Yes; you are correct there.

Mr. BELIN. Now, is this accurate, or was it one that you saw parked right in front of the building?

Mr. BRENNAN. Right next to the curb in front of the building.

Mr. BELIN. Would it be behind—you might put the letter "M" to show the car which it is behind now.

Mr. BRENNAN. All right.

Mr. BELIN. You have put the letter "M" on Exhibit 477 to show the car behind the one which the Secret Service car was parked.

Mr. BRENNAN. Yes.

Mr. BELIN. At this time I believe Exhibits 477, 478 and 479 should be reoffered to show all of the markings that the witness has made on these exhibits.

Mr. DULLES. They shall be admitted as remarked.

(The documents referred to, previously marked for identification as Commission's Exhibit Nos. 477, 478, and 479 were readmitted into evidence.)

Mr. BELIN. And also Exhibit 361 should be reoffered.

Mr. DULLES. What is 361?

Mr. BELIN. It is the large chart which also has been marked on.

Mr. DULLES. It shall be admitted again, remarked.

(The chart referred to, previously marked as Commission's Exhibit No. 361 for identification, was readmitted into evidence.)

Mr. BELIN. Mr. Brennan, in this sixth floor window, where you saw the gun fired, did you see any objects of any kind in the window, or near the window?

Mr. BRENNAN. Yes. Through the window, which I referred to as back in the book store building, I could see stacks of boxes.

Mr. BELIN. Now, I hand you what has been marked as Exhibit 480, which appears to be a picture of the Texas School Book Depository Building, which was taken shortly after this time.

I believe on the fifth floor you can see on two of the open windows there some people looking out, and Exhibit 481 is a picture of the east windows on the south side of the fifth and sixth floors, and Exhibit 482 is an enlargement of 481.

First of all, on Exhibits 481 and 482, do you recognize any of these two persons in the fifth floor window as people you saw there?

Mr. BRENNAN. No; I do not recognize them.

As positive identification I cannot recognize them.

Now, I see where there is a possibility I did make a mistake. I believe these two colored boys was in this window, and I believe I showed on that other exhibit that they were in this window.

Mr. BELIN. All right.

I am going to hand you now——

Mr. BRENNAN. The only thing I said is that they were one window over below the man that fired the gun.

Mr. BELIN. Well, I hand you Commission Exhibit 477, where you marked a "B" at the point there you first said you saw the Negro men. Is this the one you say now you might have been mistaken?

Mr. BRENNAN. Yes; I believe I was mistaken. I believe the two men that I identified was in this window.

Mr. BELIN. You are pointing to the window to the east of where you have now marked "B"?

Mr. BRENNAN. That I am not positive of. I just remember that they were over one window from below him, which at that time I might have thought this was one window over.

Mr. BELIN. All right. Let me ask you this. On Exhibit 481, does the condition of the opening of the windows in the fifth floor appear to be that which you saw on the afternoon of November 22?

Mr. BRENNAN. Yes. These do.

Mr. BELIN. You are pointing to the fifth-floor windows now?

Mr. BRENNAN. But I don't recall this window at the time of the shooting being that low.

Mr. BELIN. Now, by this window you are pointing to the window on the sixth floor?

Mr. BRENNAN. Right.

Mr. BELIN. On Exhibit 481. I wonder if you would mark that with the letter "A"—if you would circle that window. And could you put an "A" on that, if you would.

Now, window A, on Exhibit 481, when you saw it, how high do you believe it was open?

Mr. BRENNAN. I believe that at the time he was firing, it was open just like this.

Mr. BELIN. Just like the windows on the fifth floor immediately below?

Mr. BRENNAN. That is right.

Mr. BELIN. I note in window "A" there appear to be some boxes in the window. To the best of your recollection, what is the fact as to whether or not those boxes as shown in this exhibit appear to be similar to the ones you saw on November 22?

Mr. BRENNAN. No; I could see more boxes.

Mr. BELIN. In the window or behind the window?

Mr. BRENNAN. Behind the window.

Mr. BELIN. I am talking in the window itself.

Mr. BRENNAN. No, no. That is—I don't remember a box in the window, these boxes I remember are stacked up behind the window, and they were zigzagged, kind of step down, and there was a space it looked like back of here.

Mr. BELIN. Now, you are pointing to a space which would be on the east side, is that right?

Mr. BRENNAN. Yes.

Mr. BELIN. When you say you don't remember——

Mr. BRENNAN. Well, I can see those boxes there now. I don't know whether you can see them or not. It seems like I can see the boxes in that picture. Am I right?

Mr. BELIN. I don't know, sir. I can't see them on Exhibit 471. That could be the dirty window here.

Mr. BRENNAN. Here they are here. Those boxes there.

Mr. BELIN. Well, here is Exhibit 482.

First of all, I see a box on Exhibit 482, right in the window.

Mr. BRENNAN. Yes; I don't recall that box.

Mr. BELIN. Do you recall that it definitely was not there, or just you don't recall whether it was or was not there.

Mr. BRENNAN. I do not recall that being there. So, therefore, I could not say it definitely wasn't there.

Mr. BELIN. You cannot say whether it was or was not?

Mr. BRENNAN. No.

Mr. BELIN. On Exhibit 482, do you want to point an arrow to where you believe you can see boxes back there. Or where you saw boxes.

All right.

Let the record show that Exhibits 480, 481, and 482 were taken by, I believe it is, Underwood or—just a second. Thomas C. Dillard, Chief Photographer of the Dallas Morning News, who was riding in the car with Robert H. Jackson, who has already testified before the Commission, and the deposition of Mr. Dillard will be taken by Mr. Ball and me in Dallas in the first part of April.

And that Exhibits 480, 481, and 482 were taken shortly after the firing of the third shot. I think that this should appear in the record.

I think it should also appear in the record that Exhibit 479 is one of the frames from the Abraham Zapruder movie film.

Mr. Brennan, from the time you first saw the Presidential motorcade turning north on Houston from Main, did you observe the window from which you say you saw the last shot fired at any time prior to the time you saw the rifle in the window?

Mr. BRENNAN. Yes.

Mr. BELIN. Well, what I am saying is this. You saw the motorcade turn?

Mr. BRENNAN. No; not after I saw the motorcade, I did not observe a man or rifle in the window.

Mr. BELIN. Did you observe the window at all until after you heard that first sound which was a backfire or firecracker, at least you thought it was?

Mr. BRENNAN. No.

Mr. BELIN. So you did not observe the window and would not know whether or not there was any man in the window during that period?

Mr. BRENNAN. No.

Mr. BELIN. Well, let the record be clear. The first sound you first thought was what?

Mr. BRENNAN. Backfire of a motorcycle.

Mr. BELIN. And then you later said something about a firecracker.

Did that have reference to the first shot, or something in between the first and last?

Mr. BRENNAN. I positively thought that the first shot was a backfire of a motorcycle. And then something made me think that someone was throwing firecrackers from the Texas Book Store, and a possibility it was the second shot. But I glanced up or looked up and I saw this man taking aim for his last shot. The first shot and last shot is my only positive recollection of two shots.

Mr. McCLOY. Did you see the rifle explode? Did you see the flash of what was either the second or the third shot?

Mr. BRENNAN. No.

Mr. McCLOY. Could you see that he had discharged the rifle?

Mr. BRENNAN. No. For some reason I did not get an echo at any time. The first shot was positive and clear and the last shot was positive and clear, with no echo on my part.

Mr. McCLOY. Yes.

But you saw him aim?

Mr. BRENNAN. Yes.

Mr. McCLOY. Did you see the rifle discharge, did you see the recoil or the flash?

Mr. BRENNAN. No.

Mr. McCLOY. But you heard the last shot.

Mr. BRENNAN. The report; yes, sir.

Mr. DULLES. Could you see who or what he was aiming at? You testified as to the declination of the rifle, the angle of the rifle. But could you see what he was firing at?

Mr. BRENNAN. Subconsciously I knew what he was firing at. But immediately I looked towards where President Kennedy's car should be, and there was something obstructing my view. I could not see the President or his car at that time.

And I still don't know what was obstructing my view, because I was high enough that I should have been able to see it. I could not see it.

Mr. BELIN. Mr. Brennan, on one of your interviews with the FBI, they record a statement that you estimated your distance between the point you were seated and the window from which the shots were fired as approximately 90 yards.

At that time did you make that statement to the FBI—and this would be on 22 November. To the best of your recollection?

Mr. BRENNAN. There was a mistake in the FBI recording there. He had asked me the question of how far the shot was fired from too, and also he had asked me the question of how far I was from the shot that was fired. I calculated the distance at the angle his gun was resting that he must have been firing 80 to 90 yards.

Now, I——

Mr. BELIN. You mean 80 or 90 yards from where?

Mr. BRENNAN. From Kennedy's position.

Mr. BELIN. But could you see Kennedy's position?

Mr. BRENNAN. No; I could not. But I could see before and after.

Mr. BELIN. In that same interview, you stated that you attended a lineup at the Dallas Police Department at which you picked Lee Harvey Oswald as the person most closely resembling the man you observed with the rifle in the window of the Texas School Book Depository, but you stated you could not positively identify Oswald as the person you saw fire the rifle.

Now, is this an accurate recording of the statement you made to the FBI on or about November 22?

Mr. Brennan. Yes; I believe——

Mr. Belin. In other words, that part of the FBI statement is correct, as to what you told them?

Mr. Brennan. Yes.

Mr. Belin. What was the fact as to whether you could or could not identify the person, apart from what you told them?

Mr. Brennan. Why did I——

Mr. Belin. No.

What was the fact. Could you or could you not actually identify this person as the man you saw firing the rifle?

Mr. Brennan. I believed I could with all fairness and sincerity. As you asked me the question before, had I saw those pictures of Oswald prior, which naturally I don't know whether it confused me or made me feel as though I was taking unfair advantage or what. But with all fairness, I could have positively identified the man.

Mr. Belin. Now, on December 17 there appears to be another interview that you had with an agent of the FBI in which you at that time, according to this report, stated that you could now say that you were sure that Lee Harvey Oswald was the person you saw in the window at the time of the assassination, but that when you first saw him in a lineup you felt positive identification was was not necessary, because it was your understanding that Oswald had already been charged with the slaying of Officer Tippit, and you also said that another factor was that you had observed his picture on television prior to the time of identification, and that that tended to cloud any identification you made of Oswald at the police department.

Now, does this December 17 interview accurately record what you told the FBI with regard to that matter of identification?

Mr. Brennan. I believe it does.

Mr. Belin. Now, later we have an interview on January 7 with the FBI in which at that time the interview records that while you were at home and before you returned to view the lineup, which included the possible assassin of President Kennedy, you observed Lee Harvey Oswald's picture on television, and that you said that this, of course, did not help you retain the original impression of the man in the window with the rifle, but that upon seeing Lee Harvey Oswald in the police lineup, you felt that Oswald most resembled the man whom you had seen in the window.

Now, is that what you told the man on January 7—that Oswald most resembled the man that you had seen in the window?

Mr. Brennan. Yes.

Mr. Belin. Does that mean you could not give him a positive identification at that time, but could merely say he most resembled the man in the window?

Mr. Brennan. Well, I felt that I could. But for personal reasons I didn't feel like that at that moment it was compulsory and I did not want to give a positive identification at that time.

Mr. Belin. Now, this last interview was on January 7th. You still felt these personal reasons as recently as January 7th, then?

Mr. Brennan. No. I felt better about it. This is the first guy that——

Mr. Belin. No. I am referring now to the last interview you had on January 7th, in which it says that you felt that Oswald most resembled the man you had seen in the window.

Is that what you told them?

Mr. Brennan. Yes.

You mean told this man?

Mr. Belin. On January 7th; yes, sir.

Mr. Brennan. No; I don't believe I told this man in those words. I told him what I had said at the lineup. But he might have misinterpreted that I was saying that again.

Mr. Belin. In other words—well, I don't want to say in other words.

155

When you said on January 7th that upon seeing Lee Harvey Oswald in the lineup you felt that Oswald most resembled the man whom you had seen in the window?

Mr. BRENNAN. Yes.

Mr. BELIN. Now, I am referring to a statement to the FBI on January 7th of this year.

Mr. BRENNAN. All right.

Mr. BELIN. By that, did you have reference to your own personal recollection, or what you said at the time of the Dallas Police Department lineup?

Mr. BRENNAN. I believe I was referring to what I said at the Dallas Police Department.

Mr. BELIN. On January 7th of this year, what is the fact as to whether or not you could give—whether or not you felt on November 22d that the man you saw in the window was the man you saw in the police lineup—not what you told him, but what was the fact?

Mr. BRENNAN. On January 7th, at that time I did believe that I could give positive identification as well as I did later.

Mr. BELIN. You mean in the December interview?

Mr. BRENNAN. Yes.

Mr. BELIN. Let me ask you this: You said you saw the man with the rifle on the sixth floor, and then you said you saw some Negroes on the fifth floor.

Mr. BRENNAN. Yes.

Mr. BELIN. Did you get as good a look at the Negroes as you got at the man with the rifle?

Mr. BRENNAN. Yes.

Mr. BELIN. Did you feel that your recollection of the Negroes at that time was as good as the one with the man with the rifle?

Mr. BRENNAN. Yes—at that time, it was. Now—the boys rode up with me on the plane—of course I recognize them now. But as far as a few days later, I wouldn't positively say that I could identify them. I did identify them that day.

Mr. BELIN. Well, for instance, when I showed you Exhibit 482, you said that you could not identify——

Mr. BRENNAN. Well, the picture is not clear enough, as far as distinct profiles.

Mr. DULLES. Mr. Belin, I don't think you have asked they be admitted as yet.

Mr. BELIN. No, sir. I have one more mark to make on them, sir.

Mr. BRENNAN. The pictures there are not clear enough, the profile is not distinct enough.

Mr. BELIN. All right.

Now, I wonder if you would take on Exhibit 482, if you can kind of mark the way the rifle was at the time you saw it.

Here is a red pencil. If you could put on Exhibit 482 the direction that you saw the rifle pointing, sir.

Mr. BRENNAN. I would say more at this angle. Maybe not as far out as this.

Mr. BELIN. You have put a line, and I have tried to make a little bit darker line.

Mr. BRENNAN. That is as close as I can get it.

Mr. BELIN. This is on Exhibit 482—as to the angle at which you saw the rifle. And you say perhaps it wasn't out of the window as far as this line goes on Exhibit 482, is that correct?

Mr. BRENNAN. Right.

Representative FORD. That is the angle that you believe the rifle was pointed?

Mr. BRENNAN. Yes.

Mr. DULLES. And that is from the area in the window from which the rifle was pointing?

Mr. BRENNAN. Right.

Mr. BELIN. Could you tell whether or not any part of the rifle was protruding out of the window?

Mr. BRENNAN. On a straight view like that it looked like it was.

But as I have told investigating officers prior, a person would have to be at an angle to tell how much was protruding out of the window. It did look at that time that as much was protruding out of the window as there was in the window.

Mr. BELIN. At this time, we offer and introduce into evidence Exhibits 480, 481, and 482.

Mr. DULLES. They will be accepted.

(The documents heretofore marked for identification as Commission Exhibits Nos. 480, 481, and 482 were received in evidence.)

Mr. McCLOY. I have one or two questions, if you are finished, Mr. Belin.

Mr. BELIN. One more question, sir.

Did you ever tell anyone that you were 90 yards away from that window where you saw the gun?

Mr. BRENNAN. No. It was a misunderstanding. My first calculation was that I was about 75-foot out from the window, and the calculation of the window 75-foot up. So the hypotenuse there would be approximately 110-foot. That was my first calculation.

But since we made a step of the grounds Friday, I was farther out than 75 feet. Approximately 93 feet is what we calculated Friday.

Mr. BELIN. One additional question, sir.

When did you first see Exhibit 479?

Mr. BRENNAN. This morning.

Mr. BELIN. This morning here.

And on Exhibit 479, who picked the person out as being you in that picture? Was it you or was it I?

Mr. BRENNAN. I did.

I might add that prior to Friday, no one had ever gave me any information on your evidence whatsoever.

Mr. BELIN. Well, on Friday you and I met for the first time in Dallas—that would be on March 20th.

Mr. BRENNAN. Right.

Mr. BELIN. And we sat down and I asked you just to tell me what happened, is that correct?

Mr. BRENNAN. That is right.

Mr. BELIN. Did I ask you a general question and say, "What happened?" Or did I just ask you repeated questions?

Mr. BRENNAN. No.

Well, you more or less told me to tell it in my own way exactly what happened.

Mr. BELIN. And you just started to tell it, is that correct?

Mr. BRENNAN. Yes. I believe that sums it up.

Mr. BELIN. And then we then went outside where you pointed out the place where you were sitting?

Mr. BRENNAN. Yes.

Mr. BELIN. Do you remember the doctor that examined your eyes when you had them examined?

Mr. BRENNAN. He is in Port Lavaca. He is the only leading optometrist there.

Mr. BELIN. Would it be Dr. Howard R. Bonar?

Mr. BRENNAN. That is right.

How did you find that out?

Mr. BRENNAN. Well, sir, it is on one of your interviews here.

Mr. BRENNAN. Had that question been asked me before?

Mr. BELIN. Yes, it had. On November 22, when you advised that you wore glasses for reading purposes only.

Mr. BRENNAN. That is right, the FBI, Mr. Lish, right?

Mr. BELIN. Yes, sir.

Mr. McCLOY. That examination was before the sand blasting, of course.

Mr. BRENNAN. Oh, yes, sir. The sandblasting wasn't until January or early February of this year.

Representative FORD. Did you have your glasses on at the time of the assassination?

Mr. BRENNAN. No.

Mr. McCLOY. You can see better at that distance without your glasses than with them?

Mr. BRENNAN. Oh, yes, much better. Oh, I could put these glasses on and it is just like looking through a window pane. The upper part is just regular clear.

Mr. DULLES. Do you have some questions, Mr. McCloy?

Mr. McCLOY. Yes; I have some questions.

You said you went across the street after having sort of jumped off this retaining wall in order to protect yourself against the possible fusilade of shots.

Mr. BRENNAN. Right.

Mr. McCLOY. Then you went across and picked up a police officer, is that right?

Mr. BRENNAN. Right, sir.

Mr. McCLOY. And then you went with him to the steps of the Texas School Book Depository?

Mr. BRENNAN. Eventually, yes.

Mr. McCLOY. How long did it take you, do you think, from the time of the—when you first got up—from the time of the last shot, how long would you estimate it would be before you got to the steps of the Texas Book Depository?

Mr. BRENNAN. I could not calculate that, because before I got to the steps of the Texas Book Store, I had already talked to this officer, and he had taken me to the Secret Service men, I had talked to them.

Mr. McCLOY. And you stayed behind the retaining wall for a little while until you saw the coast was clear?

Mr. BRENNAN. Just seconds. I would say from the time the last shot was fired, and me diving off the wall there, and getting around on the solid side, and then running across to the officer, the time element is hard to figure, but it would still be in seconds.

Mr. McCLOY. Then when you got to the officer he took you to a Secret Service man, and then the Secret Service man and you were on the steps of the depository?

Mr. BRENNAN. Yes.

Well, we talked at the car, and then when these two colored guys came down the stairway onto the street, I pointed to them, and identified them as being the two that was in the floor below that floor. And then Mr. Sorrels, I think, had to give some orders to someone in the book store. He walked me up the steps, and I stood on the top landing.

Mr. McCLOY. When you were standing on those steps, did you see anyone pass you, or anyone that you could recognize as being—as looking somewhat like the man that you had seen in the window with the rifle?

Mr. BRENNAN. No, I did not.

Mr. DULLES. Did you give any estimate—was it a matter of 5 minutes, 6 minutes, 7 minutes? In general, how long did it take you from the time that you left where you were protecting yourself to the time you were on the front steps? What order of magnitude? 10 minutes?

Mr. BRENNAN. No; it was a shorter time than that.

I talked to Mr. Sorrels—I believe it was Mr. Sorrels—and the Secret Service men there—I don't believe I talked to them more than 3 to 5 minutes.

Mr. McCLOY. But you had prior to that time talked to the police officer?

Mr. BRENNAN. Yes.

Mr. McCLOY. You said the police officer said, "Wait a minute."

Mr. BRENNAN. Yes.

Mr. McCLOY. How long was that?

Mr. BRENNAN. That was quick, too. He gave his orders to some one on that side of the building, and then he had taken me to the Secret Service man.

Mr. McCLOY. Did you have the feeling that the police had put a cordon around the building, and were they keeping people in, or were people coming in and out while you were there?

Mr. BRENNAN. Well, I did, by the time I got on the steps of the Texas Book Store—I felt like that the place was completely surrounded and blocked by then. But at the time I ran across to this officer, I may have been completely wrong, they may have—the Secret Service men and police department, too, may have been directing their search to the building, but I felt as though they were directing their search to the west side of the building.

Mr. McCLOY. You testified, I believe, that you saw them directing their search towards the wrong side of the building, so to speak?

Mr. BRENNAN. Yes. That was my thoughts.

Mr. McCLOY. And so that would indicate that at that time they were not blocking that particular entrance at the east side of the building, below the window that you saw the shot fired from?

Mr. BRENNAN. Not according to my calculations.

Mr. DULLES. Any other questions?

Representative FORD. Mr. Chairman, I would suggest that perhaps in the case of Mr. Brennan and other witnesses, if a biography prepared by the individual, looked over by the staff, would not be helpful to include in the record—I don't mean a biography in great depth, but at least an outline of the individual's background—I think it would be helpful for the record.

Mr. DULLES. We have certain information.

Mr. BELIN. We have certain information in the record right now which we took at the very beginning of the session here this morning.

Representative FORD. Yes, I was present. But I think it is important to have more of a background of his education, experience, and I think it is wise to have it for all of the witnesses—not in great depth, but at least a background to show some biographical information.

Mr. BELIN. Would you care to have that prepared by the witness himself, or here in the record?

Representative FORD. I would suggest that it be prepared initially by the witness, checked over by the staff, and then mutually agreed as acceptable through the witness, and then insert it in the record.

Mr. DULLES. Prior to his testimony?

Representative FORD. Yes.

Mr. BELIN. Would you be willing to furnish us with some kind of an autobiographical sketch of yourself—your date and place of birth, where you went to school, your education, your jobs that you have had, and perhaps it also should include some kind of a physical description as to your approximate height and weight and what-have-you?

Mr. BRENNAN. Not at all. But you sure going to be confused on my jobs, sir.

Mr. BELIN. Because you have gone from one job to another?

Mr. BRENNAN. Well, I worked under the union constitution for the last 20 years, and I have worked for many a contractor.

Mr. BELIN. You mean you just work on contract, and when you are through with that particular construction job, the union would send you to another construction job?

Mr. BRENNAN. Yes. Usually a contractor wants me to go to the State of Washington, like I did in California, or he wants me to go to Utah or somewhere like that.

Mr. DULLES. I don't think we need all that detail.

Mr. BELIN. In other words, you have been a steamfitter.

Mr. BRENNAN. Yes, sir.

With the exception of the possibility of 2 years I was in business in California, private business.

Mr. McCLOY. Are you a member of a church?

Mr. BRENNAN. Yes, sir.

Mr. McCLOY. What church are you a member of?

Mr. BRENNAN. Baptist.

Mr. McCLOY. You testified you were a Bible reader.

Mr. BRENNAN. Well, I don't read it as much as I should.

Mr. McCLOY. When you do, you have to wear glasses?

Mr. BRENNAN. Yes, sir.

Mr. DULLES. Any other questions?

Mr. BELIN. There have been two or three other questions that have come up here, sir.

One question—when we visited on Friday in Dallas, what is the fact as to whether or not I told you what to say or you yourself just told me what you wanted to tell me?

Mr. BRENNAN. I told you—you did not instruct me what to say at all. I told you in the best words I could to explain exactly my movements and what happened.

Representative FORD. And here today you have testified freely on your own?

Mr. BRENNAN. Right, I have.

Mr. DULLES. Anything you would like to add?

Mr. BELIN. One other question, sir.

For the record, would you repeat what I would say would be a full statement of the reasons which caused you to state in your December interview to the FBI that you had always been convinced that the man you saw in the lineup was the man you saw firing the rifle, whereas on November 22d you declined to give positive identification. Could you give all of the reasons, please?

Mr. BRENNAN. Well, as I previously have said, I had saw the man in the window and I had saw him on television. He looked much younger on television than he did from my picture of him in the window—not much younger, but a few years younger—say 5 years younger.

And then I felt that my family could be in danger, and I, myself, might be in danger. And since they already had the man for murder, that he wasn't going to be set free to escape and get out of the country immediately, and I could very easily sooner than the FBI or the Secret Service wanted me, my testimony in, I could very easily get in touch with them, if they didn't get in touch with me, and to see that the man didn't get loose.

Representative FORD. When you got home, about 3 o'clock, on November 22d, that is when you did get home——

Mr. BRENNAN. Yes.

Representative FORD. Was your wife there?

Mr. BRENNAN. Yes.

Representative FORD. Did you and your wife discuss any aspects of the assassination and your being present, more or less, at the scene of the assassination?

Mr. BRENNAN. Yes; we discussed it. We talked—I talked of moving her and my grandson, which was living with us at that time and my daughter—moving them out of town somewhere in secrecy.

Representative FORD. Why did you talk about moving your wife and your grandson out of town on this afternoon on November 22d?

Mr. BRENNAN. Because I had already more or less given a detailed description of the man, and I talked to the Secret Service and gave them my statement, and they had convinced me that it would be strictly confidential and all that. But still I felt like if I was the only eyewitness, that anything could happen to me or my family.

So that was just about the length of our discussion of it.

She seemed to think that a person can't get away—wherever they go.

Representative FORD. Did you talk to anybody else between 3 p.m., November 22d and the time when one of the law enforcement agents came out and picked you up that day?

Mr. BRENNAN. Not to tell—not to give any information out.

My wife and I went to the bank in Mesquite that evening, and my daughter was at home. And I told her if anyone called to first have them identify themselves, and find out the nature of their business that they wanted me for, and if it was the FBI or the Secret Service, to tell them where they could contact me.

And so we were in the bank, I believe, talking to the vice president that evening. My daughter called and said Mr. Sorrels had called, and that he had requested her to get the word to me to call him. And she called me at the bank, and then I asked the secretary to get the number for me. And I called Mr. Sorrels, and Mr. Sorrels told me there would be a man to pick me up at 6 o'clock promptly.

Representative FORD. 6 p.m., November 22d.

Mr. BRENNAN. Yes; that is right.

Representative FORD. And he did pick you up, and you did go down to the police station?

Mr. BRENNAN. Yes, sir.

Mr. BELIN. When you got back from the police station, did you have any further conversation with your wife about what you saw in the police station?

Mr. BRENNAN. Yes. But I don't believe I explained to her full details. She probably remembers whether I did or not, but I don't. I believe I just told her that I would not identify, make positive identification. I believe that is all I told her.

Mr. BELIN. That you would not, or that you could not?

Mr. BRENNAN. I believe I told her I would not.

Mr. BELIN. Do you remember the specific color of any shirt that the man with the rifle was wearing?

Mr. BRENNAN. No, other than light, and a khaki color—maybe in khaki. I mean other than light color—not a real white shirt, in other words. If it was a white shirt, it was on the dingy side.

Mr. BELIN. I am handing you what the court reporter has marked as Commission Exhibit 150.

Does this look like it might or might not be the shirt, or can you make at this time any positive identification of any kind?

Mr. BRENNAN. I would have expected it to be a little lighter—a shade or so lighter.

Mr. BELIN. Than Exhibit 150?

Mr. BRENNAN. That is the best of my recollection.

Mr. BELIN. All right.

Could you see the man's trousers at all?

Do you remember any color?

Mr. BRENNAN. I remembered them at that time as being similar to the same color of the shirt or a little lighter. And that was another thing that I called their attention to at the lineup.

Mr. BELIN. What do you mean by that?

Mr. BRENNAN. That he was not dressed in the same clothes that I saw the man in the window.

Mr. BELIN. You mean with reference to the trousers or the shirt?

Mr. BRENNAN. Well, not particularly either. In other words, he just didn't have the same clothes on.

Mr. BELIN. All right.

Mr. BRENNAN. I don't know whether you have that in the record or not. I am sure you do.

Mr. DULLES. Any further questions?

I guess there are no more questions, Mr. Belin.

Mr. BELIN. Well, sir, we want to thank you for your cooperation with the Commission.

Mr. DULLES. Thank you very much for coming here.

TESTIMONY OF BONNIE RAY WILLIAMS

Mr. BELIN. Our next witness is Mr. Bonnie Ray Williams.

Mr. DULLES. Mr. Williams, the purpose of the hearing today is to take the testimony of you and certain others whose names are mentioned here.

You and the other witnesses were all in the vicinity of the Texas School Book Depository Building at the time of the assassination of President John F. Kennedy.

You will be asked to provide the Commission with your knowledge of the facts concerning the assassination of President Kennedy.

Mr. WILLIAMS. Yes, sir.

Mr. DULLES. Would you rise, sir?

Do your swear that the evidence you will give is the truth, the whole truth, and nothing but the truth, so help you God?

Mr. WILLIAMS. Yes, I do.

Mr. BALL. Mr. Williams, how old are you?

Mr. WILLIAMS. I am 20 years old.

Mr. BALL. Where do you live?

Mr. WILLIAMS. I live in Dallas, Tex.

Mr. BALL. What is your address?

Mr. WILLIAMS. 1502 Avenue B, Apartment B.

Mr. BALL. Are you married?

Mr. WILLIAMS. Yes, I am.

Mr. BALL. Where were you born?

Mr. WILLIAMS. I was born in Carthage, Tex.

Mr. BALL. Did you go to school in Texas?

Mr. WILLIAMS. Yes, I did.

Mr. BALL. How far through school?

Mr. WILLIAMS. All the way.

Mr. BALL. Graduated from high school?

Mr. WILLIAMS. Yes.

Mr. BALL. Where?

Mr. WILLIAMS. Marshall, Tex., and I finished high school summer course in Dallas, Texas, Madison High.

Mr. BALL. What year did you get out of high school?

Mr. WILLIAMS. 1962.

Mr. BALL. And where did you go to work after that?

Mr. WILLIAMS. I went to work at Marriott's Motor Hotel.

Mr. BALL. What did you do there?

Mr. WILLIAMS. Well, I started off as a dishwasher. Then they put me on as a fry cook.

Mr. BALL. And how long did you stay there?

Mr. WILLIAMS. About 6 or 7 months.

Mr. BALL. Then where did you go to work?

Mr. WILLIAMS. I went to work at Union Terminal Building, baggage department.

Mr. BALL. How long did you work there?

Mr. WILLIAMS. I worked there about a year.

Mr. BALL. What kind of work did you do there?

Mr. WILLIAMS. I was a mail separator.

Mr. BALL. Then where did you go?

Mr. WILLIAMS. Then I found this job at the Texas School Book Depository.

Mr. BALL. When did you get that job?

Mr. WILLIAMS. Around about September 8th.

Mr. BALL. What year?

Mr. WILLIAMS. 1963.

Mr. BALL. How did you happen to go there to get the job?

Mr. WILLIAMS. Well, my wife was expecting, and I just wanted a day job— I was working at night. So I just went looking for a day job, and I happened to come down that way.

Mr. DULLES. Were you going to school in the daytime?

Mr. WILLIAMS. No.

Mr. DULLES. This is after you finished school?

Mr. WILLIAMS. All this took place after I finished school.

Mr. BALL. You finished school when?

Mr. WILLIAMS. 1962.

Mr. BALL. And you had these three——

Mr. WILLIAMS. Yes, sir; and I had a part-time job at a construction company. I don't remember the name of it. But it was just for about a week.

Mr. BALL. When you were going to school?

Mr. WILLIAMS. No. That was the same time I was working at Marriott's Motel.

Mr. BALL. Did you work while you went to school?

Mr. WILLIAMS. I delivered the Dallas morning newspaper sometimes, and little odd jobs.

Mr. BALL. Well, did anybody tell you you might get a job at the Texas School Book Depository before you went down there?

Mr. WILLIAMS. No, sir.

Mr. BALL. You were just looking for a job?

Mr. WILLIAMS. I just put in applications everywhere.

Mr. BALL. What kind of work did you do when you first went with the Texas School Book Depository?

Mr. WILLIAMS. I think the first day I started work there they started me off as a wrapper. Then the fellows told me that I had qualifications to be a checker, so they put me on as a checker there.

Mr. BALL. What are you doing now?

Mr. WILLIAMS. At the present time I do anything—check, pack, fill orders, anything.

Mr. BALL. When you went to work there, did you work at the building on the corner of Houston and Elm?

Mr. WILLIAMS. No, sir. The first time I went there I was hired on at the other warehouse, the lower part of Houston Street.

Mr. BALL. By lower part, do you mean north of the main building?

Mr. WILLIAMS. Yes, sir. Down further, the big white building.

Mr. BALL. That is sort of a warehouse?

Mr. WILLIAMS. Yes, sir.

Mr. BALL. You went to work there. That is about a block, a block and a half north?

Mr. WILLIAMS. A block and a half.

Mr. BALL. North of the corner of Houston and Elm?

Mr. WILLIAMS. Yes, sir.

Mr. BALL. And how long did you work at that place?

Mr. WILLIAMS. Well, I worked there until business began to get slow. I think that was—it was before November. I think it was some time during October. I am not sure.

Mr. BALL. And what did they put you to work at at that time?

Mr. WILLIAMS. They called me up to help lay a floor on the fifth floor, they wanted more boards over it. As I say, business was slow, and they were trying to keep us on without laying us off at the time.

So I was using the saw, helping cut wood and lay wood.

Mr. BALL. You were laying a wood floor over the old floor?

Mr. WILLIAMS. Yes, sir.

Mr. BALL. On the fifth floor?

Mr. WILLIAMS. Yes, sir.

Mr. BALL. And when you finished on the fifth floor, what did you do?

Mr. WILLIAMS. After we finished on the fifth floor, we started to move up to the sixth floor. But at the time we didn't complete the sixth floor. We only completed just a little portion of it.

Mr. BALL. By the time, you are talking about November 22d?

Mr. WILLIAMS. Yes, sir.

Mr. BALL. Before November 22d, how long had you been laying floor in the building at Houston and Elm?

Mr. WILLIAMS. Before November 22d, I think we had been working on the fifth floor, I think, about 3 weeks. I think altogether I had been up there just about 4 weeks, I think.

Mr. BALL. And how long had you been on the sixth floor before—how long have you been working on the sixth floor before November 22d?

Mr. WILLIAMS. Let's see. Before November 22d, I think it might have been 2 days—it might have been 2 days. I would say about 2 days, approximately 2 days.

Mr. BALL. Before you started to lay the floor, did you have to move any cartons?

Mr. WILLIAMS. Yes; we did.

Mr. BALL. From what part of the sixth floor did you move the cartons?

Mr. WILLIAMS. We moved cartons from, I believe, the west side of the sixth floor to the east side of the sixth floor, because I think there was a vacancy in there.

Mr. BALL. Clear over to the east side?

Mr. WILLIAMS. Yes, sir.

Mr. BALL. Were there cartons stacked up between the west side and the east side—were there cartons on the floor?

Mr. WILLIAMS. Yes; there was.

Mr. BALL. After you moved the cartons, then did you start laying the floor?

Mr. WILLIAMS. After we moved the cartons, we started laying the floor.

Then we had to move the cartons.

As we go we would move cartons to vacate the space, so we could lay the floor.

Mr. BALL. On November 22d, what time did you go to work?

Mr. WILLIAMS. November 22d, I went to work at 8 o'clock.

Mr. BALL. Were you late or on time that morning?

Mr. WILLIAMS. I believe I was on time that morning. I always get there a little before eight.

Mr. BALL. Did you know Lee Oswald, Lee Harvey Oswald?

Mr. WILLIAMS. I didn't know him personally, but I had seen him working. Never did say anything to anyone. He never did put himself in any position to say anything to anyone.

He just went about his work. He never said anything to me. I never said anything to him.

Mr. BALL. Did you ever have lunch with him?

Mr. WILLIAMS. No.

The only time he would come into the lunchroom sometimes and eat a sandwich maybe, and then he would go for a walk, and he would go out. And I assume he would come back. But the only other time he would come in and read a paper or nothing, and laugh and leave again.

Mr. DULLES. But he would never say good morning or good evening?

Mr. WILLIAMS. He never would speak to anyone. He was just a funny fellow. I don't know what kind of a fellow he was.

Mr. BALL. Did you notice what he read in the newspaper?

Mr. WILLIAMS. I believe one morning I noticed he was reading something about politics, and as he was reading this he acted like it was funny to him. He would read a paragraph or two, smile, or laugh, then throw the paper down and get up and walk out.

Representative FORD. Where did this go on?

Mr. WILLIAMS. This was going on in what we call the domino room. This is where we would eat our lunch and play dominoes. Some fellow would bring newspapers, to read the sports or something. He never would read the sports.

Mr. BALL. The domino room is a little recreation room on the first floor?

Mr. WILLIAMS. Yes; it is.

Mr. BALL. Now, you see the map there which has been marked Commission Exhibit 362. Will you point on that map the location of the domino room?

Mr. DULLES. Would it be easier if we put the map up there, and then everybody could see.

Mr. WILLIAMS. In the front entrance—I could explain the way I know the best.

As I said, this would be the main entrance from Elm Street. Well, this would be—the domino room is in the same line with Mr. Shelley's office, and Mr. Truly's office. The domino room would be right in here. Because two bathrooms, a large one and a small one right in this vicinity here.

Mr. BALL. That is marked on the map—the domino room is marked on the map as rec room, and the toilet is shown there?

Mr. WILLIAMS. Yes, sir. And there is a small one on the other side.

Mr. BALL. That is on Exhibit 362.

Mr. DULLES. What floor is this we are looking at now?

Mr. WILLIAMS. That is the first floor.

Representative FORD. And it was in the rec room or domino room where you saw Oswald read the paper on this occasion?

Mr. WILLIAMS. Yes, sir.

Mr. DULLES. And you said he read some of it to you and smiled about it?

Mr. WILLIAMS. No; he didn't read it to me. We were waiting turns to play dominoes, and I happened to glance over. And I just noticed what he was reading.

Mr. BALL. Now, this morning, did you see Oswald on the floor at any time?

Mr. WILLIAMS. This morning of November 22d?

Mr. BALL. 22d.

Mr. WILLIAMS. The morning of November 22d Oswald was on the floor. The only time I saw him that morning was a little after eight, after I had started working. As usual, he was walking around with a clipboard in his hands, I believe he was.

Mr. BALL. That is on the first floor?

Mr. WILLIAMS. Yes. He had a clipboard in his hand.

Mr. BALL. That is the only time you saw him that morning?

Mr. WILLIAMS. That is the only time I saw him that morning. I saw him again between 11:30 and maybe 10 until 12:00.

Mr. BALL. We will come to that in a moment.

Where did you work that morning?

Mr. WILLIAMS. That morning I worked on the sixth floor. I think we went directly up to the sixth floor and I got there.

Mr. BALL. And how many were working on the sixth floor with you?

Mr. WILLIAMS. I believe there were five.

Mr. BALL. What are their names?

Mr. WILLIAMS. Well, Bill Shelley, Charles Givens, and there was a fellow by the name of Danny Arce.

Mr. BALL. He is a Mexican boy?

Mr. WILLIAMS. Yes. And a fellow by the name of Billy Lovelady, and myself. And there was a fellow that came up—his name was Harold Norman. He really wasn't working at the time, but there wasn't anything to do, he would come around to help a little bit, and then back down.

Mr. DULLES. Was he in the employ of the company?

Mr. WILLIAMS. Yes; he had been working there at the time about 2 years, I think.

Mr. DULLES. But he wasn't on this particular detail on the sixth floor that you are speaking of?

Mr. WILLIAMS. Well, he had been helping us on the fifth floor. When the orders would come in, he would go down and help with the orders, and when he didn't have anything else to do he would come back and help us move stock around.

I think that was him.

Mr. BALL. What part of the sixth floor were you working that morning?

Mr. WILLIAMS. On the west side.

Mr. BALL. Were you moving stock or laying floor that morning?

Mr. WILLIAMS. We were doing both.

Mr. BALL. You were doing both?

Mr. WILLIAMS. Yes, sir.

Mr. BALL. The west side of the sixth floor—you mean the whole west side, or was there a certain part—northwest or southwest or middle?

Mr. WILLIAMS. I believe it was the whole west side, because we had to go from window to window—from the elevator to the front window facing Elm Street— we were laying the floor parallel.

Mr. BALL. Did you see Oswald on the sixth floor that morning?

Mr. WILLIAMS. I am not sure. I think I saw him once messing around with some cartons or something, back over the east side of the building. But he wasn't in the window that they said he shot the President from. He was more on the east side of the elevator, I think, messing around with cartons, because he always just messed around, kicking cartons around.

Mr. BALL. What was his job?

Mr. WILLIAMS. His job was an order filler.

Mr. BALL. What do you mean by that?

Mr. WILLIAMS. I mean by that an order filler—when orders come in for the State schools mostly, from Austin, he would take the orders and fill the orders.

If the orders called for a certain amount of books, he would fill that order, and turn it in to be checked, to be shipped out.

Mr. BALL. You say he would fill the order. He would go and get books?

Mr. WILLIAMS. He would get books. As an order filler you had access to all the floors, all seven floors.

Mr. BALL. And were the cartons that you are talking about containers of books?

Mr. WILLIAMS. Yes, they were.

Mr. BALL. Would a checker—would an order filler go to the different floors and take books out of cartons?

Mr. WILLIAMS. Yes, sir. The order filler would have to, in order to fill the order—he would have to move around to each floor, and take the books that he needs.

Mr. BALL. Then where would he take the books?

Mr. WILLIAMS. Down to the first floor.

Mr. BALL. And what was on the first floor?

Mr. WILLIAMS. The first floor is where the checkers, the freight, and all—they are checking the books to go out, and also where they wrap the books.

Mr. BALL. And were there certain men down there wrapping books?

Mr. WILLIAMS. Certain men wrapping, checking, weighing, et cetera.

Mr. DULLES. Did you have a schedule somewhere posted up so that you knew which books were on which floor when an order came in? You would know whether to go to the sixth floor or what floor to go to get the particular books that were wanted?

Mr. WILLIAMS. Well, as I remember, I don't know too much about the building.

Mr. DULLES. You were not in the order filling business?

Mr. WILLIAMS. No, sir; not in that department.

At the other building. I was just transferred to that building.

I don't think you really had any schedule to go by, or anything to show you where the books were. You just asked the older fellows that had been there were certain books—if you are looking for a certain book, they would tell you where to find it.

Mr. BALL. This morning, when you think you saw Oswald on the sixth floor, can you tell us about where he was?

Mr. WILLIAMS. Well, as I said before, I am not sure that he was really on the sixth floor. But he was always around that way. In the place I think I saw him was as the east elevator come up to the sixth floor, he was on that side of the elevator.

Mr. BALL. I have here a diagram of the sixth floor which I will have marked as Exhibit 483.

(The document referred to was marked Commission Exhibit No. 483 for identification.)

Mr. BALL. First of all, this is Houston Street, and the top is north—east and west. Here is Elm Street.

Mr. WILLIAMS. This would be the east elevator.

Mr. BALL. This is the east elevator, west elevator and the stairway.

Now, can you take this and show us about where your men were working laying floor on that sixth floor?

Mr. WILLIAMS. I would say——

Mr. BALL. First of all, you take this pencil and put it down there, and then we will make the markings afterwards.

Mr. WILLIAMS. This is the west side of the building.

Mr. BALL. The area where you were laying floor. Make the outside limits of the area.

Mr. WILLIAMS. We were working in this area down there like that.

Mr. BALL. In other words, from there to the west, or where?

Mr. WILLIAMS. We were working from the west coming this way, coming to the east. And we had got about just so much.

Mr. BALL. Well, let's draw a dark line down there. This marks the area that you saw?

Mr. WILLIAMS. Yes, sir.

Mr. BALL. You had already laid floor from the west side to the dark line?

Mr. WILLIAMS. Yes, sir.

Mr. BALL. And you were working right around in the dark line area, were you?

Mr. WILLIAMS. Yes, sir.

Mr. BALL. That morning?

Mr. WILLIAMS. Yes, sir.

Mr. BALL. Now, take your pencil and show us about where it was that you saw Oswald that morning.

Mr. WILLIAMS. I think I saw Oswald somewhere around in this vicinity.

As I was up by this other elevator, I think one time I saw him over there. I am not really sure.

Mr. BALL. You have drawn a line here. This is a sort of general area where you say you saw Oswald, is that right?

Mr. WILLIAMS. Yes, sir.

Mr. BALL. We will mark that as "O". That is on the north side of the floor near the east elevator.

Mr. WILLIAMS. Yes, sir.

Mr. BALL. We will mark that "O".

Now, these lines you have marked show your area where you were working.

Mr. WILLIAMS. Yes, sir.

Mr. BALL. We will mark that W-1 and W-1.

Mr. DULLES. Mr. Williams, were all the boxes of books moved out of this area while you were working, or as you finished a part of it, were some boxes put back in?

Mr. WILLIAMS. To begin with, I think we were working on the wall first. I don't think we moved too many books in this area. I think we just moved them out and right back in, as I remember.

But I think after we got a little further over, I think we had to move some books. We had to move these books to the east side of this building, over here, and those books—I would say this would be the window Oswald shot the President from. We moved these books kind of like in a row like that, kind of winding them around.

Mr. DULLES. That is moving them from the west towards the east of the building?

Mr. WILLIAMS. Yes, sir.

Mr. McCLOY. The window was here?

Mr. BALL. That is right.

Mr. DULLES. Any other questions on this?

Mr. BALL. About what time of day do you think it was you saw Oswald, if you can remember? If you can't remember, don't guess.

Mr. WILLIAMS. I cannot remember.

Mr. BALL. What time did you knock off work for the lunch hour?

Mr. WILLIAMS. Well, approximately—between 11:30 to 12, around in there. I wouldn't say the exact time, because I don't remember the exact time.

Mr. BALL. What time do you usually quit for lunch?

Mr. WILLIAMS. We always quit about 5 minutes before time.

During the rush season we quit about 5 minutes before time and washup.

Mr. BALL. Wash your hands and face before you eat lunch?

Mr. WILLIAMS. That is right.

Mr. BALL. You say quit 5 minutes before time. What is the time?

Mr. WILLIAMS. Five before 12.

Mr. BALL. Did you quit earlier this day?

Mr. WILLIAMS. I believe this day we quit about maybe 5 or 10 minutes, because all of us were so anxious to see the President—we quit a little ahead of time, so that we could wash up and we wanted to be sure we would not miss anything.

Mr. BALL. Now, did you go downstairs?

Mr. WILLIAMS. We took two elevators down. I mean, speaking as a group, we took two down.

Mr. BALL. Was there some reason you took two down?

Mr. WILLIAMS. We always had a little kids game we played racing down with the elevators. And I think one fellow, Charles Givens, had the east elevator, and me, and I think two or three more fellows had the west elevator. And we was racing down.

Mr. BALL. Who was driving the west side elevator?

Mr. WILLIAMS. I don't remember exactly who was.

Mr. BALL. You were not?

Mr. WILLIAMS. I don't think I was. I don't remember.

Mr. BALL. Who was driving the east side elevator?

Mr. WILLIAMS. I think that was Charles Givens.

Mr. BALL. Now, did something happen on the way down—did somebody yell out?

Mr. WILLIAMS. Yes; on the way down I heard Oswald—and I am not sure whether he was on the fifth or the sixth floor. But on the way down Oswald hollered "Guys, how about an elevator?" I don't know whether those are his exact words. But he said something about the elevator.

And Charles said, "Come on, boy," just like that.

And he said, "Close the gate on the elevator and send the elevator back up." I don't know what happened after that.

Representative FORD. Had the elevator gone down below the floor from which he yelled?

Mr. WILLIAMS. Yes; I believe it was. I assume it was the fifth or the sixth.

The reason I could not tell whether it was the sixth or the fifth is because I was on the opposite elevator, and if you are not thinking about it it is kind of hard to judge which floor, if you started moving.

Representative FORD. The elevator did not go back up to the floor from which he yelled?

Mr. WILLIAMS. No, sir.

Mr. DULLES. Did he ask the gate be closed on the elevator?

Mr. WILLIAMS. I think he asked Charles Givens—I think he said, "Close the gate on the elevator, or send one of the elevators back up."

I think that is what he said.

Mr. McCLOY. That is in order that he would have an elevator to come down when he wanted to come down?

Mr. WILLIAMS. Yes, sir.

Mr. BALL. On the 23d of November 1963, you talked to two FBI agents according to the record I have here, Bardwell Odum and Will Griffin, and they reported that you said that as they were going down, that you saw Lee on the fifth floor.

Mr. WILLIAMS. I told him the fifth or the sixth. I told him I wasn't sure about it.

Mr. BALL. And were you sure at that time?

Mr. WILLIAMS. About which floor it was?

Mr. BALL. Yes.

Mr. WILLIAMS. No; I wasn't.

Mr. BALL. Are you sure today?

Mr. WILLIAMS. I am not sure today.

Mr. BALL. But you think it was the fifth or the sixth floor?

Mr. WILLIAMS. Yes, sir.

Mr. BALL. Are you sure it was Oswald you talked to?

Mr. WILLIAMS. I am sure it was Oswald. I didn't talk to him.

Mr. BALL. But you heard him?

Mr. WILLIAMS. I heard him.

Mr. BALL. You went down to the first floor.

What did you do?

Mr. WILLIAMS. We went down to the first floor. I think the first thing I did, I washed up, then I went into the domino room where I kept my lunch, and I got my lunch, came back out and went back up.

Mr. BALL. Did you carry your lunch that day?

Mr. WILLIAMS. Yes; I did.

Mr. BALL. Do you usually carry your lunch to work?

Mr. WILLIAMS. Yes; I do.

Mr. BALL. That was your habit, carrying your lunch?

Mr. WILLIAMS. Yes, sir.

Mr. BALL. And that day, on November 22d, how did you carry your lunch from home to work?

Mr. WILLIAMS. I carried my lunch from home to work in a brown paper bag. I believe it was size No. 6 or maybe 8—paper bag.

Mr. BALL. Number 6 or 8 size paper bag?

Mr. WILLIAMS. Yes, sir.

Mr. BALL. Small bag?

Mr. WILLIAMS. Yes, sir.

Mr. BALL. Like you get in the grocery store?

Mr. WILLIAMS. Yes, sir.

Mr. BALL. What did you have in your lunch?

Mr. WILLIAMS. I had a chicken sandwich.

Mr. BALL. Describe the sandwich. What did it have in it besides chicken?

Mr. WILLIAMS. Well, it just had chicken in it. Chicken on the bone.

Mr. BALL. Chicken on the bone?

Mr. WILLIAMS. Yes.

Mr. BALL. The chicken was not boned?

Mr. WILLIAMS. It was just chicken on the bone. Just plain old chicken.

Mr. BALL. Did it have bread around it?

Mr. WILLIAMS. Yes, it did.

Mr. BALL. Before you went upstairs, did you get anything to drink?

Mr. WILLIAMS. I got a small bottle of Dr. Pepper from the Dr. Pepper machine.

Mr. BALL. Did you have anything else in your lunch besides chicken?

Mr. WILLIAMS. I had a bag of Fritos, I believe it was.

Mr. BALL. Anything else?

Mr. WILLIAMS. No; I believe that was all.

Mr. BALL. You say you went back upstairs. Where did you go?

Mr. WILLIAMS. I went back up to the sixth floor.

Mr. BALL. Why did you go to the sixth floor?

Mr. WILLIAMS. Well, at the time everybody was talking like they was going to watch from the sixth floor. I think Billy Lovelady said he wanted to watch from up there. And also my friend; this Spanish boy, by the name of Danny Arce, we had agreed at first to come back up to the sixth floor. So I thought everybody was going to be on the sixth floor.

Mr. BALL. Did anybody go back?

Mr. WILLIAMS. Nobody came back up. So I just left.

Mr. BALL. Where did you eat your lunch?

Mr. WILLIAMS. I ate my lunch—I am not sure about this, but the third or the fourth set of windows, I believe.

Mr. BALL. Facing on what street?

Mr. WILLIAMS. Facing Elm Street.

Mr. McCLOY. What floor?

Mr. WILLIAMS. Sixth floor.

Mr. DULLES. You ate your lunch on the sixth floor?

Mr. WILLIAMS. Yes, sir.

Mr. DULLES. And you were all alone?

Mr. WILLIAMS. Yes, sir.

Mr. BALL. What did you sit on while you ate your lunch?

Mr. WILLIAMS. First of all, I remember there was some boxes behind me. I just kind of leaned back on the boxes first. Then I began to get a little impatient, because there wasn't anyone coming up. So I decided to move to a two-wheeler.

Mr. BALL. A two-wheeler truck, you mean?

Mr. WILLIAMS. Yes, sir. I remember sitting on this two-wheeler.

By that time, I was through, and I got up and I just left then.

Mr. DULLES. How much of the room could you see as you finished your lunch there? Was your view obstructed by boxes of books, or could you see a good bit of the sixth floor?

Mr. WILLIAMS. Well, at the time I couldn't see too much of the sixth floor, because the books at the time were stacked so high. I could see only in the path that I was standing—as I remember, I could not possibly see anything to the east side of the building.

But just one aisle, the aisle I was standing in I could see just about to the west side of the building. So far as seeing to the east and behind me, I could only see down the aisle behind me and the aisle to the west of me.

Representative FORD. Have you ever had any trouble with the law at all?

Mr. WILLIAMS. No, sir.

Representative FORD. No difficulty as far as the law is concerned?

Mr. WILLIAMS. I have never been inside of a courthouse before.

169

Mr. BALL. I have an exhibit here marked 484.

(The document referred to was marked Commission Exhibit No. 484 for identification.)

Mr. BALL. Do you recognize that?

Mr. WILLIAMS. Yes, sir; I recognize that.

Mr. BALL. What do you see?

Mr. WILLIAMS. I see a two-wheeler, a Dr. Pepper bottle, and some boxes in the windows.

Mr. BALL. And is that anywhere near where you were sitting?

Mr. WILLIAMS. Yes, sir; that is the exact place I was sitting.

Mr. BALL. That is the two-wheeler you were sitting on?

Mr. WILLIAMS. Yes, sir.

Mr. BALL. Now, when you were on the two-wheeler, as you were sitting there, did you have a view, could you see down towards the southeast corner?

Mr. WILLIAMS. No, sir; I couldn't see anything as I remember there. About the only thing that I could see from there would be just the top edge of the window, because the boxes were stacked up.

Mr. BALL. The boxes were stacked up high?

Mr. WILLIAMS. Yes, sir.

Mr. BALL. Let me show you another picture here.

Mr. DULLES. You are not introducing that at this time?

Mr. BALL. I will. I am going to introduce them all.

Let's go back to the diagram, which is 483. Could you mark on this diagram the window that is shown in this picture 484—that is, the place where you were sitting and eating your lunch?

Mr. WILLIAMS. That would be facing Elm Street. I would say right around in this.

Mr. BALL. In other words, you are marking here something between—some area between the third and the fourth window.

Mr. WILLIAMS. Yes, sir.

Mr. BALL. You are not able to tell exactly?

Mr. WILLIAMS. No; I am not.

Mr. BALL. The witness has drawn a red rectangle to show the approximate area which runs from about the center of the second row of windows from the southeast corner over to about the fourth pane of windows.

Mr. WILLIAMS. I would say about right in here, third or fourth.

Mr. BALL. Third or fourth?

Mr. WILLIAMS. Yes, sir.

Mr. BALL. Now, you have made two marks, so I will identify the last mark. Between the third and fourth, is that right?

Mr. WILLIAMS. Yes, sir.

Mr. BALL. We will mark the rectangle, and we will mark it "W-3" and "W-4" the end of the lines.

Mr. McCLOY. What time of day was this, when you were eating your lunch?

Mr. WILLIAMS. About 12.

Mr. McCLOY. Just 12?

Mr. WILLIAMS. Yes, sir.

Mr. BALL. Now, as you looked towards the southeast corner from where you were sitting, could you see the windows in the southeast corner?

Mr. WILLIAMS. In the southeast—that is—the southeast. I really don't remember if I seen anything—it would be just the top edge of the window, as I remember.

Mr. BALL. Did you see anyone else up there that day?

Mr. WILLIAMS. No, I did not.

Mr. BALL. How long did you stay there?

Mr. WILLIAMS. I was there from—5, 10, maybe 12 minutes.

Mr. BALL. Finish your lunch?

Mr. WILLIAMS. Yes, sir. No longer than it took me to finish the chicken sandwich.

Mr. BALL. Did you eat the chicken?

Mr. WILLIAMS. Yes, I did.

Mr. BALL. Where did you put the bones?

Mr. WILLIAMS. I don't remember exactly, but I think I put some of them back in the sack. Just as I was ready to go I threw the sack down.

Mr. BALL. What did you do with the sack?

Mr. WILLIAMS. I think I just dropped it there.

Mr. BALL. Anywhere near the two-wheeler?

Mr. WILLIAMS. I think it was.

Mr. BALL. What did you do with the Dr. Pepper bottle?

Mr. WILLIAMS. Just set it down on the floor.

Mr. BALL. There is a pop bottle that you see in the picture, 484—does that look like anything like the pop bottle that you were drinking from that day?

Mr. WILLIAMS. I believe that was the bottle—I believe. I am not sure. But it looks like it.

Mr. BALL. Did you leave the bottle somewhere near the point shown of the bottle shown on 484?

Mr. WILLIAMS. I am really not sure about it. I don't think I left it there. I am not sure. I think I left it sitting up on top of the boxes, right to the side of the two-wheeler. As I remember—I am not sure about it. It is possible that I could have put it there.

Mr. BALL. Your memory is that the Dr. Pepper bottle was left on top of the boxes?

Mr. WILLIAMS. Beg pardon?

Mr. BALL. Your memory is that you left the Dr. Pepper bottle on top of some of the cartons?

Mr. WILLIAMS. As I remember. I am not sure.

Mr. BALL. It is shown there on the floor.

Mr. WILLIAMS. Yes, sir.

Mr. BALL. Where did you go when you left there?

Mr. WILLIAMS. I went down to the fifth floor.

Mr. BALL. How did you get down there?

Mr. WILLIAMS. I took an elevator down.

Mr. BALL. You didn't go down the stairs?

Mr. WILLIAMS. No, sir.

Mr. BALL. Which elevator did you take?

Mr. WILLIAMS. I took the east elevator down.

Mr. BALL. Is that the one that is worked with a hand——

Mr. WILLIAMS. Yes, sir. That is the one with the one gate, and works with the hand pedal.

Mr. BALL. How does the other one work?

Mr. WILLIAMS. The other one worked by push button. You have two gates to pull. That is the one you can pull two gates on and it will come back up by itself. The east side elevator won't come up unless someone is operating.

Mr. BALL. You took the elevator from the sixth floor to the fifth floor?

Mr. WILLIAMS. Yes, sir.

Mr. BALL. Where did you intend to go when you left the sixth floor?

Mr. WILLIAMS. I intended to stop on the fifth floor, and if there wasn't anyone there, I intended to get out of the building, go outside.

Mr. BALL. Well, you stopped on the fifth floor. Why?

Mr. WILLIAMS. Beg pardon?

Mr. BALL. Why did you stop on the fifth floor?

Mr. WILLIAMS. To see if there was anyone there.

Mr. BALL. Did you know there was anyone there before you started down?

Mr. WILLIAMS. Well, I thought I heard somebody walking, the windows moving or something. I said maybe someone is down there, I said to myself. And I just went on down.

Mr. BALL. Did you find anybody there?

Mr. WILLIAMS. As I remember, when I was walking up, I think Harold Norman and James Jarman—as I remember, they was down facing the Elm Street on the fifth floor, as I remember.

Mr. BALL. Now, I want to call your attention to another report I have here. On the 23d of November 1963, the report of Mr. Odum and Mr. Griffin, FBI agents, is that you told them that you went from the sixth floor to the fifth

171

floor using the stairs at the west end of the building. Did you tell them that?

Mr. WILLIAMS. I didn't tell them I was using the stairs. I came back down to the fifth floor in the same elevator I came up to the sixth floor on.

Mr. BALL. You did?

Mr. WILLIAMS. Yes, sir.

Mr. BALL. Now, also, on January 14th, did you remember talking to a couple of agents named Carter and Griffin?

Mr. WILLIAMS. I can't remember their names, but I am sure I did.

Mr. BALL. You talked to a good many of them?

Mr. WILLIAMS. Yes, sir.

Mr. BALL. Well, they reported here that you went down to the fifth floor, and you did so by going down on the west elevator.

Mr. WILLIAMS. The east elevator. The reason I was able to determine whether it was the east elevator is because I think when you questioned us the other day, the other fellows—I told you I didn't remember which elevator first. But the other fellows said they had the west elevator. There are only two elevators. If they are sure they had the west elevator up, that only leaves the east elevator.

Mr. BALL. When you got to the fifth floor and left the elevator, at that time were both elevators on the fifth floor?

Mr. WILLIAMS. Yes, sir.

Mr. BALL. Both west and east?

Mr. WILLIAMS. Yes, sir, as I remember.

Mr. BALL. The other day, when I talked to you in Dallas, on Friday 20 March——

Mr. WILLIAMS. Yes, sir.

Mr. BALL. And at that time were you able—did you remember which elevator it was?

Mr. WILLIAMS. Which elevator I had?

Mr. BALL. What you had come down from six to five on.

Mr. WILLIAMS. As I remember, I first said I wasn't sure. After the fellows said they brought the west elevator up, I said I must have the east elevator.

Mr. BALL. Is it fair to say now that you don't have any definite memory as to whether it was the east or west elevator?

Mr. WILLIAMS. Yes, sir. I believe that would be true.

Mr. BALL. But you did bring an elevator up?

Mr. WILLIAMS. Yes, sir; I did.

Mr. BALL. Now, when you came down there and got off that elevator, did you notice that the other elevator was also on that floor?

Mr. WILLIAMS. Well, at the time I didn't notice it.

Mr. BALL. Did you, later?

Mr. WILLIAMS. No, sir; as I remember.

Mr. BALL. You don't remember?

Mr. WILLIAMS. No, sir; I don't remember.

Mr. BALL. When you got off the elevator, you went over to the front of the building, the Elm Street side.

Mr. WILLIAMS. Yes, sir; I did.

Mr. BALL. And you saw Norman and——

Mr. DULLES. Mr. Ball, could we get the time element?

Mr. BALL. I am going to bring that in.

Mr. DULLES. All right. I will bide my time.

Mr. BALL. You went over to the front of the building, did you?

Mr. WILLIAMS. Yes.

Mr. BALL. And you saw your two friends, Norman and Jarman?

Mr. WILLIAMS. Yes.

Mr. BALL. You had known them before?

Mr. WILLIAMS. Yes, sir.

Mr. BALL. Now, do you know what time that was?

Mr. WILLIAMS. I do not know the exact time.

Mr. BALL. It was——

Mr. WILLIAMS. It was after I had left the sixth floor, after I had eaten the chicken sandwich. I finished the chicken sandwich maybe 10 or 15 minutes after 12. I could say approximately what time it was.

Mr. BALL. Approximately what time was it?

Mr. WILLIAMS. Approximately 12:20, maybe.

Mr. BALL. Well, now, when you talked to the FBI on the 23d day of November, you said that you went up to the sixth floor about 12 noon with your lunch, and you stayed only about 3 minutes, and seeing no one you came down to the fifth floor, using the stairs at the west end of the building.

Now, do you think you stayed longer than 3 minutes up there?

Mr. WILLIAMS. I am sure I stayed longer than 3 minutes.

Mr. BALL. Do you remember telling the FBI you only stayed 3 minutes up there?

Mr. WILLIAMS. I do not remember telling them I only stayed 3 minutes.

Mr. BALL. And then on this 14th of January 1964, when you talked to Carter and Griffin, they reported that you told them you went down to the fifth floor around 12:05 p.m., and that around 12:30 p.m. you were watching the Presidential parade.

Now, do you remember telling them you went down there about 12:05 p.m.?

Mr. WILLIAMS. I remember telling the fellows that—they asked me first, they said, "How long did it take you to finish the sandwich?" I said, "Maybe 5 to 10 minutes, maybe 15 minutes." Just like I said here. I don't remember saying for a definite answer that it was 5 minutes.

Mr. BALL. Well, is it fair to say that you do not remember the exact time now?

Mr. WILLIAMS. Yes, sir.

Mr. BALL. You do remember, though, that you ate your lunch and drank your pop, your Doctor Pepper, before you came down?

Mr. WILLIAMS. Yes, sir.

Mr. BALL. Were you there any length of time before the Presidential parade came by?

Mr. WILLIAMS. Well, sir, on the fifth floor?

Mr. BALL. On the fifth floor, yes, with your two friends, Norman and Jarman.

Mr. WILLIAMS. I was there a while before it came around.

Mr. BALL. You were at what window?

Mr. WILLIAMS. Well, I believe we was on the east side of the window, and I think Hank was—I think he was directly under the sixth floor window where Oswald was supposed to have shot the President from. And I think I was a window over. And I think James Jarman was two or three windows over.

Mr. BALL. I will show you a picture here, which is 482. Do you see yourself in that picture?

Mr. WILLIAMS. Yes, sir; I am right here.

Mr. BALL. All right. Draw a dark line down there towards you and put an arrow on the end. I will mark that W; the arrow W on 482 points to you, Bonnie Ray Williams.

Mr. WILLIAMS. Yes, sir.

Mr. BALL. Is that about the way you were sitting in the window?

Mr WILLIAMS. Yes, sir.

Mr. BALL. And you were watching the parade?

Mr. WILLIAMS. I don't remember whether I was watching the parade here or not. But I was in the window, that window.

Mr. BALL. Do you recognize the man in the window to the right of us as we look at the picture?

Mr. WILLIAMS. Yes, sir; that is Harold Norman.

Mr. BALL. Now, here is another photograph which is 480, giving more of the front of the building. Can you tell us in what window your friend Jarman was sitting, or watching?

Mr. WILLIAMS. I believe this is James Jarman right here.

Mr. BALL. All right. Draw a line down to that on 480. Draw an arrow to the window.

Mr. WILLIAMS. Yes, sir.

Mr. BALL. We will mark that W on 480.

Now, were you boys sitting down or standing up?

Mr. WILLIAMS. Are you referring to the picture?

Mr. BALL. No, I am talking about your memory now as to what you were doing at the time you were watching for the Presidential parade.

Mr. WILLIAMS. At the time we were watching for the President's parade, I believe I was in a squat position. But I don't remember whether I was on my knees or just squatting on the balls of my feet.

Mr. BALL. When the parade went by, how were you—squatting?

Mr. WILLIAMS. As the parade went by, I was in a squat position.

Mr. BALL. Last Friday you went up to the sixth floor, or the fifth floor with us, and a photographer, and you three men got into position, did you not?

Mr. WILLIAMS. Yes, sir.

Mr. BALL. To have your pictures taken.

Mr. WILLIAMS. Yes; we did.

Mr. BALL. I can only ask you about your position. First of all, we will mark this as 485.

(The photograph was marked Commission Exhibit No. 485 for identification.)

Mr. BALL. I will mark this photograph as 486.

(The photograph was marked Exhibit No. 486 for identification.)

Mr. BALL. 485 is a picture of three men. You were there when that picture was taken?

Mr. WILLIAMS. Yes, sir.

Mr. BALL. Who are the men who are there?

Mr. WILLIAMS. First of all in the corner of the east of the building is Harold Norman. Secondly, the fellow over from me, that would be James Jarman.

Mr. BALL. Who is the man in the center?

Mr. WILLIAMS. That is me.

Mr. BALL. Is that about the way you were sitting when you watched the parade?

Mr. WILLIAMS. I believe it was at the time.

Mr. BALL. Now, I show you 486 and who are the men in that position?

Mr. WILLIAMS. In this picture here, 486—this fellow—the other fellow in the corner, in the east of the building, is Harold Norman. I am in the window next to him.

Mr. BALL. Your back is to the picture?

Mr. WILLIAMS. Yes, sir.

Mr. BALL. Is that about the position you were in when the President's parade went by?

Mr. WILLIAMS. I believe it was.

Mr. BALL. Now, what do you remember happened when the President's parade went by?

Mr. WILLIAMS. Well, to the best of my ability, what I remember was first coming off of—I believe it was Main Street—well, two motorcycle policemen came around. I think it was two or maybe three. They came around first. And then I think the President's car followed. And I believe a car was behind it carrying the Vice President, as I remember. I am not sure about it. President Kennedy was sitting in the back seat. I believe his wife was in the back seat. I believe Governor Connally was sitting in the front seat of the car as it was going down the street—I believe——

Mr. McCLOY. What street are you talking about there? Are you talking about Main Street, Houston Street, or Elm Street?

Mr. WILLIAMS. First of all, as I say, they was coming off of Main Street. Then as it turned the corner, the corner which I am speaking of, most people refer to it as Elm Street. But it is not really Elm Street. I believe it is the start of the turnpike, because Elm Street runs parallel with the building, but comes to a dead end.

Mr. BALL. Did you see the parade come up Houston, north on Houston?

Mr. WILLIAMS. Yes, sir; I did.

Mr. BALL. And then you saw it turn to the left in front of your building?

Mr. WILLIAMS. Yes, sir.

Mr. BALL. Now tell us what happened after the President's car had passed your window.

Mr. WILLIAMS. After the President's car had passed my window, the last thing I remember seeing him do was, you know—it seemed to me he had a habit of pushing his hair back. The last thing I saw him do was he pushed his hand up like this. I assumed he was brushing his hair back. And then the thing that happened then was a loud shot—first I thought they were saluting the President, somebody—even maybe a motorcycle backfire. The first shot—there was two shots rather close together. The second and the third shot was closer together than the first shot and the second shot, as I remember.

Mr. BALL. Now, was your head out the window?

Mr. WILLIAMS. I could not say for sure. I do not remember.

Mr. BALL. Did you notice—where did you think the shots came from?

Mr. WILLIAMS. Well, the first shot—I really did not pay any attention to it, because I did not know what was happening. The second shot, it sounded like it was right in the building, the second and third shot. And it sounded—it even shook the building, the side we were on. Cement fell on my head.

Mr. BALL. You say cement fell on your head?

Mr. WILLIAMS. Cement, gravel, dirt, or something, from the old building, because it shook the windows and everything. Harold was sitting next to me, and he said it came right from over our head. If you want to know my exact words, I could tell you.

Mr. BALL. Tell us.

Mr. WILLIAMS. My exact words were, "No bull shit." And we jumped up.

Mr. BALL. Norman said what?

Mr. WILLIAMS. He said it came directly over our heads. "I can even hear the shell being ejected from the gun hitting the floor." But I did not hear the shell being ejected from the gun, probably because I wasn't paying attention.

Mr. BALL. Norman said he could hear it?

Mr. WILLIAMS. He said he could hear it. He was directly under the window that Oswald shot from.

Mr. BALL. He was directly under. He told you as he got up from the window that he could hear the shells ejected from the gun?

Mr. WILLIAMS. Yes; he did.

Mr. BALL. After he made the statement that you mentioned, he thought it came from overhead, and you made some statement, did Jarman say anything?

Mr. WILLIAMS. I think Jarman, he—I think he moved before any of us. He moved towards us, and he said, "Man, somebody is shooting at the President." And I think I said again, "No bull shit." And then we all kind of got excited, you know, and, as I remember, I don't remember him saying that he thought the shots came from overhead. But we all decided we would run down to the west side of the building.

Mr. BALL. You ran down to the west side of the building?

Mr. WILLIAMS. Yes, sir.

Representative FORD. Ran down to the west side? You mean you were still on the fifth floor?

Mr. WILLIAMS. Yes; we were on the fifth floor, the east side of the building. We saw the policemen and people running, scared, running—there are some tracks on the west side of the building, railroad tracks. They were running towards that way. And we thought maybe—well, to ourself, we know the shots practically came from over our head. But since everybody was running, you know, to the west side of the building, towards the railroad tracks, we assumed maybe somebody was down there. And so we all ran that way, the way that the people was running, and we was looking out the window.

Mr. BALL. When the cement fell on your head, did either one of the men notice it and say anything about it?

Mr. WILLIAMS. Yes, sir. I believe Harold was the first one.

Mr. BALL. That is Hank Norman?

Mr. WILLIAMS. I believe he was the first one. He said "Man, I know it came from there. It even shook the building." He said, "You got something on your head." And then James Jarman said, "Yes, man, don't you brush it out." By that time I just forgot about it. But after I got downstairs I think I brushed it out anyway.

Mr. BALL. Jarman is called Junior?

Mr. WILLIAMS. Yes, sir.

Mr. BALL. Well, did Norman say anything about hearing the bolt of the rifle?

Mr. WILLIAMS. I don't remember him saying anything about it.

Mr. BALL. But you heard him say he could hear the cartridges?

Mr. WILLIAMS. I heard Harold Norman—pardon me, I thought you were saying James Jarman.

Mr. BALL. Did Norman say anything about the bolt?

Mr. WILLIAMS. Yes. He said he could hear the rifle, and it sounded like it was right above. He said he could hear the rifle being ejected, the shells hitting the floor.

Mr. BALL. But you could not hear this?

Mr. WILLIAMS. No; I could not hear it.

Mr. BALL. That was an old floor, wasn't it?

Mr. WILLIAMS. Yes; it was.

Mr. BALL. Could you see light through the floor from the fifth to the sixth floor as you would look above your window?

Mr. WILLIAMS. Well, at the time, that day of November 22d, I did not notice that. But the other day when you were questioning me, even after the thick new floor that was put over the old floor on the sixth floor, well, you still could see light. And the new floor extended a little beyond the old floor. So therefore I would say that you could see light much more when the old floor was there.

Mr. BALL. When you were there the other day, you looked up through a crack in the ceiling of the fifth floor?

Mr. WILLIAMS. Yes, sir.

Mr. BALL. Could you see the new floor?

Mr. WILLIAMS. You could. You could see daylight through.

Mr. BALL. Now, where was that crack with reference to the wall of the fifth floor?

Mr. WILLIAMS. With reference to the wall of the fifth floor, the crack that I was speaking about was directly over my head, and also directly over Norman's head.

Mr. BALL. And that would be where the floor would ordinarily make a joint with the wall?

Mr. WILLIAMS. With the wall.

Mr. BALL. You say you ran down to the west window.

Mr. WILLIAMS. Yes, sir.

Mr. BALL. From where you were?

Mr. WILLIAMS. Yes, sir. First of all——

Mr. BALL. I will take this same diagram——

Mr. WILLIAMS. First of all we made a stop before we got to the last stop that we was when the policeman came up.

Mr. BALL. Yes. That is where I want you to show me now, where you made the stop. This is the fifth floor diagram.

We will mark the fifth floor diagram as Exhibit 487.

(The document so described was marked Commission Exhibit No. 487 for identification.)

Mr. BALL. This is Elm Street on 487, and here are the windows where you have shown us you were standing.

Mr. WILLIAMS. Yes, sir.

Mr. BALL. Now, will you show us the direction that you ran and also point to the window?

Mr. WILLIAMS. The direction that we ran after we heard the shots was—I would say I was in about this position here, this window. And we left like this. Harold was coming from here.

Mr. BALL. Let me show you the diagram. Here are these two pair of windows that are shown here on this diagram. This is the corner. Here is the next window, and here is the next window.

Now, take the pencil and show where you were and where you ran to.

Mr. WILLIAMS. I was right here.

Mr. BALL. Mark an X, and bring it on down, and show us.

Mr. WILLIAMS. I left here, and I came like this. The other fellows followed like this. We all was running this direction here. And I believe when we got to this point here, we stopped. And I am not sure, but I think James Jarman, he raised this window, this corner window here, and we all huddled in this corner window.

Mr. BALL. We will mark that window Y. And then you ran from X to Y, you three men?

Mr. WILLIAMS. Yes, sir.

Mr. BALL. Was the window open or closed?

Mr. WILLIAMS. I think it was closed at the time.

Mr. BALL. Was it opened then?

Mr. WILLIAMS. I believe James Jarman opened the window.

Mr. BALL. Now, the other day, when you were up here, you three men went to that window and stood there and had your picture taken, did you not?

Mr. WILLIAMS. Yes, sir.

Mr. BALL. This window which you have shown as Y, in 487, the diagram of the fifth floor.

Mr. WILLIAMS. That's right.

Mr. BALL. Here is 488.

(The document so described was marked Commission Exhibit No. 488 for identification.)

Mr. BALL. Is that the window?

Mr. WILLIAMS. Yes; it is.

Mr. BALL. And is that about the way you were standing as you looked out to the west?

Mr. WILLIAMS. That is about the way we were standing.

Mr. BALL. Did you run fast towards the west?

Mr. WILLIAMS. We did. We moved rather fast. We was at a trotting pace.

Mr. DULLES. Was that to get a better view of the President's party in the car?

Mr. WILLIAMS. No, sir: I don't think—we knew the President had been shot at at that time. The car was gone, you know. It has speeded up and left. But the people, as I said before, the policemen and people were running towards the tracks. The tracks are at this side of the building. We wondered why they were running that way.

Mr. DULLES. How did you know the President was shot at this time?

Mr. WILLIAMS. We heard the shots, and we assumed somebody had shot him. And we decided to run down that way.

Representative FORD. Why didn't you go up to the sixth floor?

Mr. WILLIAMS. I really don't know. We just never did think about it. And after we had made this last stop, James Jarman said, "Maybe we better get the hell out of here." And so we just ran down to the fourth floor, and came on down. We never did think about it, going up to the sixth floor. Maybe it was just because we were frightened.

Mr. DULLES. Did you know the President had been hit?

Mr. WILLIAMS. Well, personally I did not know he had been hit, but I think Harold—I remember—I don't know whether he said or not—but I think he said he saw him slump. So from that I think we all assumed he had been shot at.

Mr. DULLES. One of the other two?

Mr. WILLIAMS. Yes, sir; I think it was.

Mr. DULLES. Said that?

Mr. WILLIAMS. Yes, sir; I believe that is what he said. Anyway, we knew he had been shot at.

Mr. BALL. After you left this corner window in the southwest corner that we have shown you the picture of as 488, where did you go?

Mr. WILLIAMS. Then we moved over to another window on the west side of the building.

Mr. BALL. Let's go back to the diagram of the fifth floor, 487, and you show me where that window was.

Mr. WILLIAMS. It was one of these windows, I believe it was this window here, I believe. Maybe it was this window. I would say this window.

Mr. BALL. All right. We will mark that Z—window Z.

Mr. WILLIAMS. Yes, sir.

Mr. BALL. And the other day, Friday, March 20th, when we were in Dallas, you three men went to that same window, didn't you?

Mr. WILLIAMS. Yes, sir.

Mr. BALL. And you had your picture taken?

Mr. WILLIAMS. Yes, sir.

Mr. BALL. That is 489.

(The described document was marked Commission Exhibit No. 489 for identification.)

Mr. BALL. Is that about it?

Mr. WILLIAMS. Yes, sir.

Mr. BALL. Why did you go there and look in that direction?

Mr. WILLIAMS. Because, as I said before, the policeman was running toward the tracks.

Mr. BALL. The tracks shown in this picture?

Mr. WILLIAMS. Yes, sir. I believe that is the parking lot right here.

Mr. BALL. And the tracks are shown in there, aren't they?

Mr. WILLIAMS. Yes, sir.

Mr. BALL. And were people running towards the tracks?

Mr. WILLIAMS. Yes, sir; the policemen were.

Representative FORD. Mr. Ball, I hate to interrupt, but I do have to go to a call of the House. I wonder if I could ask one question right here. I dislike breaking up the sequence.

Mr. Williams, when did you first know that the President's motorcade would come by the Texas School Book Depository?

Mr. WILLIAMS. Well, I never did know the exact time. But I think my wife had mentioned it before that Friday. She had told me, because I never did have too much time reading the paper. And that morning, that Friday morning, we was on the sixth floor, and I think some fellows mentioned it to me again, some of the fellows working with me.

Representative FORD. You did not know the motorcade was coming by your building until Friday morning?

Mr. WILLIAMS. No, sir; I didn't know the exact way it was coming, because I hadn't been reading the papers.

Representative FORD. You had not read the paper the day before?

Mr. WILLIAMS. About the only thing I would read in the paper in the mornings before I leave home would be the sports.

Representative FORD. Was it discussed in the building that morning of November 22d that the motorcade was coming by the Texas School Book Depository?

Mr. WILLIAMS. I believe I heard a couple of fellows say—I don't remember exactly who it was—but I believe I heard them say the motorcade was coming around that way.

Representative FORD. But it was not until Friday that you personally knew it was coming by the building?

Mr. WILLIAMS. Yes, sir.

Mr. DULLES. I would like to ask one question here.

When you were on the sixth floor eating your lunch, did you hear anything that made you feel that there was anybody else on the sixth floor with you?

Mr. WILLIAMS. No, sir; I didn't hear anything.

Mr. DULLES. You did not see anything?

Mr. WILLIAMS. I did not see anything.

Mr. DULLES. You were all alone as far as you knew at that time on the sixth floor?

Mr. WILLIAMS. Yes, sir.

Mr. DULLES. During that period of from 12 o'clock about to—10 or 15 minutes after?

Mr. WILLIAMS. Yes, sir. I felt like I was all alone. That is one of the reasons I left—because it was so quiet.

Mr. McCLOY. When you saw Oswald that morning, was he carrying any package? Did you see any bundle or package with him?

Mr. WILLIAMS. No, sir; I didn't see anything other than the clipboard with the orders on it that he was filling, as I remember.

Mr. McCLOY. How many shots did you hear fired?

Mr. WILLIAMS. I heard three shots. But at first I told the FBI I only heard two—they took me down—because I was excited, and I couldn't remember too well. But later on, as everything began to die down, I got my memory even a little better than on the 22d, I remembered three shots, because there was a pause between the first two shots. There was two real quick. There was three shots.

Mr. BALL. Did you hear anything upstairs at all?

Mr. WILLIAMS. No, sir; I didn't hear anything.

Mr. BALL. Any footsteps?

Mr. WILLIAMS. No, sir. Probably the reason we didn't hear anything is because, you know, after the shots we were running, too, and that was making a louder noise.

Mr. BALL. You really ran?

Mr. WILLIAMS. Yes, sir; we ran. And that was probably making a lot of noise.

Mr. BALL. Now, I'm going to hold this up. I don't know whether everybody can see it or not——

Mr. DULLES. Could I ask one question in connection with your last question?

Did you hear either of the elevators going up or down while you were eating your meal?

Mr. WILLIAMS. No, sir; I did not.

Mr. DULLES. You didn't hear the elevators at all?

Mr. WILLIAMS. No, sir.

Mr. DULLES. If an elevator had come to that floor, would you have heard it then?

Mr. WILLIAMS. That all depends——

Mr. DULLES. Were they noisy elevators? The operation of the doors and so forth?

Mr. WILLIAMS. Yes, sir. The elevator that I came up on to the sixth floor, if you would listen—say you were listening for the boss, you could hear, because you would be paying attention. The elevator is worked by hand pedal. When you release the hand pedal it makes a noise. It bangs—or maybe you can hear the old elevator when it is first coming up. But at that time I did not hear anything.

(At this point, Representative Ford left the hearing room.)

Mr. BALL. I would like to point out over in the northwest corner there is a stairwell. And the elevators are shown here. And the witness has placed himself at point "Z" on Exhibit 487, which is near a pair of west windows.

Now, you are oriented there, are you not?

Mr. WILLIAMS. Yes, sir.

Mr. BALL. All right. When you were at "Z" were you able to see the stairwell?

Mr. WILLIAMS. No, sir.

Mr. BALL. Why?

Mr. WILLIAMS. You could not see the stairs from that point because this other—this is the stairway, and it has some shelves made out of some old wooden boxes. Those old wooden boxes come out to about right here. And they come out maybe 5 feet, even more than that, past the stairway. And that would block your view of the stairway from that point.

Mr. BALL. Mark it in there with your pencil.

Mr. WILLIAMS. These are the stairs. I would say the bookcase would come out like that.

Mr. BALL. The shelf we will mark "WX", both ends of the shelf. How high is the shelf?

Mr. WILLIAMS. Pretty high.

Mr. BALL. Does it go to the ceiling?

Mr. WILLIAMS. As I remember, they do not go exactly to the ceiling. But I am 6 feet, and they are way over me, I think.

Mr. BALL. Now, could you see all of the elevators from there?

Mr. WILLIAMS. Well, by me being the tallest, I saw——

Mr. BALL. I am not going into what you saw. But could you see either elevator from where you were standing at "Z"?

Mr. WILLIAMS. Yes, sir; you could see this pretty plainly.

Mr. BALL. You mean the west elevator?

Mr. WILLIAMS. Yes, sir.

Mr. BALL. Could you see the east elevator?

Mr. WILLIAMS. No, sir; you could not see it exactly.

Mr. BALL. Now, when you were questioned by the FBI agents, talking to Mr. Odum and Mr. Griffin, they reported in writing here that while you were standing at the west end of the building on the fifth floor, a police officer came up on the elevator and looked all around the fifth floor and left the floor. Did you see anything like that?

Mr. WILLIAMS. Well, at the time I was up there I saw a motorcycle policeman. He came up. And the only thing I saw of him was his white helmet.

Mr. BALL. What did he do?

Mr. WILLIAMS. He just came around, and around to the elevator.

Mr. BALL. Which elevator?

Mr. WILLIAMS. I believe it was the east elevator.

Mr. BALL. Did you see anybody with him?

Mr. WILLIAMS. I did not.

Mr. BALL. You were only able to see the top of his helmet?

Mr. WILLIAMS. Yes, sir.

Mr. BALL. You could only see the top of his helmet?

Mr. WILLIAMS. Yes, sir; that is the only thing I saw about it.

Mr. BALL. They reported that you told them on the 23d of November that you and Hank, that is Hank Norman, isn't it——

Mr. WILLIAMS. Yes, sir.

Mr. BALL. And Junior—that is Junior Jarman—were standing where they would have seen anyone coming down from the sixth floor by way of the stairs. Did you tell them that?

Mr. WILLIAMS. I could not possibly have told him that, because you cannot see anything coming down from that position.

Mr. BALL. And that you did not see anyone coming down.

Mr. WILLIAMS. No, sir. An elephant could walk by there, and you could not see him.

Mr. BALL. That day we were out there, Friday, March 20th, we took some pictures.

Mr. WILLIAMS. Yes, sir.

Mr. BALL. I show you 490.

(The document described was marked Exhibit No. 490 for identification.)

Mr. BALL. We took a picture from where you were standing towards the stairs. Do you recognize that?

Mr. WILLIAMS. Yes, sir.

Mr. BALL. What is that?

Mr. WILLIAMS. This is the side we were on. I believe these are the bookshelves I was speaking of.

Mr. BALL. That is the ones that hide the stairwell?

Mr. WILLIAMS. That is right.

Mr. BALL. And the camera is—you saw where the camera was set, didn't you?

Mr. WILLIAMS. Yes, sir.

Mr. BALL. You saw these pictures taken?

Mr. WILLIAMS. Yes, sir.

Mr. BALL. Where was the camera?

Mr. WILLIAMS. The camera was located about the exact place I was standing looking out this window.

Mr. BALL. That would be "Z" on 487?

Mr. WILLIAMS. That's right.

Mr. BALL. And was pointed toward what direction?

Mr. WILLIAMS. It was pointed towards the stairway and the bookcase.

Mr. BALL. The way you would have been looking on that day?

Mr. WILLIAMS. Right.

Mr. BALL. And this shows those shelves.

Mr. WILLIAMS. Yes, sir.

Mr. BALL. I have two other pictures I would like to show, and I would like to show the Commissioners all three at the same time.

Now, do you recall that we had you three men stand near the stairwell?

Mr. WILLIAMS. Yes, sir.

Mr. BALL. Now, on this picture here, on 487, that would be what location?

Mr. WILLIAMS. On this picture here, that would be about right in here.

Mr. BALL. Near the "up", is that right?

Mr. WILLIAMS. Yes, sir.

Mr. BALL. I would like to have the Commissioners note that—that the man was standing near the "up" part of the stairwell.

We took your pictures three in a row, is that right?

Mr. WILLIAMS. That is right.

Mr. BALL. And then do you recall the picture was taken?

Mr. WILLIAMS. Yes, sir; I recall this picture. This picture was taken from the position we were standing, and it gave the view of—the only thing you would be able to see from this point. And this picture here was James Jarman, which we were standing shoulder to shoulder.

Mr. BALL. Also were the cartons piled at that time so that—as they were here—on the day, November 22d, were the cartons piled somewhat like they are here?

Mr. WILLIAMS. They were piled somewhat like here, because they have been rearranged since that time.

Mr. BALL. Now, in both pictures, 492 and 490, you see two windows, do you not?

Mr. WILLIAMS. Yes, sir.

Mr. BALL. And those windows are shown on the diagram of the fifth floor, 487, as where?

Mr. WILLIAMS. Right here.

Mr. BALL. The windows next to the west elevator?

Mr. WILLIAMS. Yes, sir.

Mr. BALL. And in this picture, are you able to see either elevator?

Mr. WILLIAMS. In this picture?

Mr. BALL. This picture—490 and 492—are you able to see either elevator?

Mr. WILLIAMS. No, sir; you cannot see exactly the elevator.

Mr. BALL. Now, in this picture, 491, where is the downstairs?

Mr. WILLIAMS. The downstairs come right in here.

Mr. BALL. Are you able to see the opening of the downstairs from this view, 492?

Mr. WILLIAMS. No, sir.

Mr. BALL. And the thing that obstructs your view is this shelving, is that right?

Mr. WILLIAMS. Yes, sir; that's right.

Mr. DULLES. How long has that shelving been there—for quite a long while? Or was it put there recently?

Mr. WILLIAMS. I think it was there from the time I started, as far as I can remember.

Mr. DULLES. That goes back to the time you were first employed there?

Mr. WILLIAMS. Yes, sir. At the time I came to the building.

Mr. DULLES. So it could not have been put up a day or two before.

Mr. WILLIAMS. No, sir.

Mr. BALL. Did you hear anyone going up or down the stairs?

Mr. WILLIAMS. No, I didn't.

Mr. BALL. Did you pay any attention to that?

Mr. WILLIAMS. No, sir.

Mr. BALL. As you were standing at the window, did you hear any footsteps?

Mr. WILLIAMS. No, sir.

Mr. BALL. Up above—hear any movement up above?

Mr. WILLIAMS. No, sir; I don't remember.

Mr. BALL. Were you paying any attention whether or not there was anyone up above?

Mr. WILLIAMS. No, sir; we wasn't paying any attention.

Mr. BALL. Now, in this FBI report that we have dated the 23d of November 1963, the report that you said that someone might have been coming down on the elevator and you would not have noticed that. Did you say that?

Mr. WILLIAMS. I think I remember saying that.

Mr. BALL. After you stood at the west window for a while, what did you do?

Mr. WILLIAMS. After we stood at the west window for a while, we decided to go down. Then we left.

Mr. BALL. How did you go down?

Mr. WILLIAMS. By stairs.

Mr. BALL. Where did you go?

Mr. WILLIAMS. We went to the fourth floor first. Then we paused for a minute there, where we saw these women looking out of the window. Then we decided to go down to the first floor, and we ran on down.

Mr. BALL. When you got to the first floor, what did you see there?

Mr. McCLOY. How did you get to the first floor?

Mr. WILLIAMS. By stairs.

Mr. DULLES. There were some people on the fourth floor?

Mr. WILLIAMS. Yes, sir. I remember seeing maybe two or three women standing in the window, looking out the window.

Mr. DULLES. Looking out the window?

Mr. WILLIAMS. Yes, sir.

Mr. McCLOY. Which stairway did they take, west or east?

Mr. BALL. There was only one stairway, and that is the one in the corner. Did you run down stairs?

Mr. WILLIAMS. Yes, sir; we ran.

Mr. BALL. When you got to the first floor, what did you see?

Mr. WILLIAMS. When we arrived to the first floor, the first thing I noticed was that the policemen had rushed in. I think some firemen came in with a water hose. And then the next thing that happened, these detectives, or maybe FBI—anyway, they stopped us all and they said, "Do you work here?" And we told them yes. And they took our name, address, and they searched everybody. And then the other fellow—I think one fellow asked whether we had been working upstairs. I think we told him yes. They got out all the fellows I think that was working on the sixth floor at the time, and they took us all down to the courthouse, I think, and we had to fill out some affidavits and things.

Mr. BALL. You made out an affidavit there?

Mr. WILLIAMS. Yes, sir.

Mr. BALL. Did you go out of the building shortly after you came downstairs?

Mr. WILLIAMS. They wouldn't let anybody out of the building.

Mr. BALL. How long after you came down from the first floor were you taken over to the Police Department?

Mr. WILLIAMS. I couldn't give you the exact time, but it wasn't long.

Mr. BALL. You can't give me any estimate in minutes?

Mr. WILLIAMS. No, sir; I would not want to say.

Mr. DULLES. Did you see Lee Oswald at any time during this period?

Mr. WILLIAMS. No, sir; I don't remember seeing him.

Mr. BALL. Were the police with you?

Mr. WILLIAMS. Yes; they were.

Mr. BALL. Were your two friends with you, Jarman and——

Mr. WILLIAMS. No; they wasn't with me. First I think they took me and another fellow, Danny—they took us in one car. Then they took some other fellows in another car, and then another car, I think.

Mr. BALL. You were with Danny Arce and one or two police officers?

Mr. WILLIAMS. Yes, sir.

Mr. BALL. Anybody else?

Mr. WILLIAMS. That's all.

Mr. BALL. Do you know when Norman and Jarman went out?

Mr. WILLIAMS. Well, at the time I don't think Norman and Jarman came down right then. They brought Bill Shelley and Bill Lovelady, a fellow by the name of Jack Dougherty, and Charles Givens later on, they brought them right behind us.

Mr. BALL. When you left the first floor with the officers, was Norman still there?

Mr. WILLIAMS. Yes, sir; he was in the building.

Mr. BALL. And was Jarman still there?

Mr. WILLIAMS. Yes, sir.

Mr. BALL. I would like to offer all of the exhibits that we marked so far into evidence.

Mr. DULLES. Could you give me the numbers?

Mr. BALL. I think they run 483 to 492, inclusive.

Mr. DULLES. Was 481 introduced?

Mr. BALL. If 481 and 482 were not, we offer them. 483 is a diagram of the sixth floor. We offer that. Everything this morning from 477 to 492 we offer in evidence. The last number is 492.

Mr. DULLES. All exhibits subsequent to the last exhibit noted in the record up to and including 492 will be admitted.

(The material heretofore marked Exhibits Nos. 481 through 492, inclusive, previously marked for identification, were received in evidence.)

Mr. McCLOY. I have some questions.

When you came downstairs, do you remember seeing a man named Brennan, and did a man named Brennan identify you downstairs?

Mr. WILLIAMS. No, sir; I don't remember that.

Mr. McCLOY. No one that you know—no one said, "This is the man I have seen on the fifth floor window?"

Mr. WILLIAMS. No, sir.

Mr. McCLOY. Were you physically kept from leaving the building when you got downstairs? Did you try to go out of the building?

Mr. WILLIAMS. No, sir; I wasn't trying to go out of the building because there wasn't any use of trying to, because at the time we arrived on the first floor, I heard an officer shout out and say, "No one leave the building."

Mr. McCLOY. Have you got any appreciation of the time that elapsed between your hearing the first shot and the time that you got finally down to the first floor, after you had been on the fifth floor and the fourth floor?

Mr. WILLIAMS. No, sir; I could not give you any time.

Mr. McCLOY. Well, you did not give us any time. Do you have any recollection now of about how long that was? Was it 15 minutes, 10 minutes, 20 minutes? How long did it take from the time that you were looking out that window and you heard that shot until you did get down to the first floor?

Mr. WILLIAMS. Well, I could say approximately 15 minutes, maybe a little before then, maybe after. I could not say exactly.

Mr. DULLES. Do you know what time it was when you went off and left for the police station?

Mr. WILLIAMS. I could not give you the exact time.

Mr. McCLOY. Do you know whether or not anybody got out of the building before the police could get there? Did any of your friends or the people you were working with, did you hear whether any of them had left the building before the building was closed?

Mr. WILLIAMS. Yes, sir; I heard Mr. Truly—he said that—he mentioned that—he said, "Where is Lee?" That is what everybody called him. "Where is Lee?", he said, and therefore I assume he did not know where Lee was, that he was out of the building, because everybody else was there. And there was another colored fellow by the name of Charles Givens. He wasn't in the building at the time. He was downtown somewhere.

Mr. McCLOY. Had he been at the building at the time of the shooting—Givens?

Mr. WILLIAMS. I don't believe he had.

Mr. DULLES. What did Mr. Truly say about Lee not being there?

Mr. WILLIAMS. The only thing I heard him say is—I think an officer asked him, "Is everyone here?" And he said, "Where is Lee?"—like that, you know.

Mr. DULLES. Mr. Truly said that?

Mr. WILLIAMS. Yes, sir.

Mr. McCLOY. Do you know the name of the first policeman that accosted you, who stopped you?

Mr. WILLIAMS. No, sir.

Mr. McCLOY. Are you familiar with firearms?

Mr. WILLIAMS. No, sir.

Mr. McCLOY. Do you ever do any hunting?

Mr. WILLIAMS. No, sir; I never go hunting.

Mr. McCLOY. But you have heard shots fired?

Mr. WILLIAMS. Yes, sir; I heard my grandfather try a gun out, something like that.

Mr. McCLOY. You were not in the army?

Mr. WILLIAMS. No, sir; I have never been in the army.

Mr. McCLOY. I think that is all I have.

Mr. DULLES. I have one question.

You have referred to three explosions that—one you thought was a backfire or a firecracker.

Mr. WILLIAMS. Yes, sir.

Mr. DULLES. Was there any difference in the sound of those three explosions?

Mr. WILLIAMS. As far as I remember, there wasn't any difference in the sound. It was just the time between the sound.

Mr. McCLOY. As I heard you testify, you said there was a larger pause between the first and the second shot than there was between the second and the third.

Mr. WILLIAMS. Yes, sir.

Mr. McCLOY. Let me get this clear. Did you see the President crumple after the shot? Did you see the President hit?

Mr. WILLIAMS. Personally, I did not see him, because I was kind of jumping.

Mr. DULLES. Are there any other questions?

Thank you very much, and we appreciate your coming. We will recess at this time until 2 o'clock this afternoon.

(Whereupon, at 12:40 p.m., the President's Commission recessed.)

Afternoon Session

TESTIMONY OF HOWARD LESLIE BRENNAN RESUMED

The President's Commission reconvened at 2:05 p.m.

Mr. McCLOY. The purpose of today's hearing is to have the testimony of Mr. Brennan here and you gentlemen.

Mr. Williams has already appeared before us, and Mr. Norman and Mr. Jarman and also Mr. Truly who will be on the stand later.

You were all witnesses, you were all in the vicinity of the Texas School Book Depository Building at the time of the assassination of President Kennedy, and we are going to ask you to give us your knowledge of the facts such as they come within your knowledge of that event and we will have some questions that we will wish to ask you.

Mr. BALL. The record will show that Harold Norman, whose nickname is Hank, is present and Bonnie Ray Williams and James Jarman, whose nickname is Junior. Mr. Brennan is also.

Mr. BELIN. Mr. Brennan, you testified here this morning, is that correct?

Mr. BRENNAN. Right.

Mr. McCLOY. You are still under oath, Mr. Brennan.

Mr. BELIN. I believe that you testified that you thought you recognized two of the people that you saw looking out of the fifth floor of the School Book Depository Building you thought you recognized outside of the building sometime after the assassination, is that correct?

The two people that you saw, are they any of these three people here?

Mr. BRENNAN. Yes. I believe it is the one on the end and this one here, I am not sure.

Mr. BELIN. By that you would mean——

Mr. BRENNAN. I don't know which of those two.

Mr. BALL. Let's identify.

Mr. BELIN. Which person do you mean, you mean Mr. Norman sitting opposite?

Mr. BRENNAN. Yes; I believe he was one of them.

Mr. BELIN. And you believe it was Mr. Jarman together?

Mr. BRENNAN. Jarman.

Mr. BELIN. Were they with some policeman as they came out of the building or in custody of some plainclothesman?

Mr. BRENNAN. I don't believe they were.

Mr. BELIN. You saw them together come out of the building?

Mr. BRENNAN. I don't believe they were. I don't recall seeing any officer bring them out or with them.

Mr. BELIN. Now you do not believe then that it was Mr. Williams?

Mr. BRENNAN. No; I won't say for sure. I can't tell which of those two it was.

Mr. BELIN. In other words, you say that you can't, when you say you can't tell whether it was Mr. Williams or Mr. Norman, did you just see one person or two?

Mr. BRENNAN. I saw two but I can't identify which one it was.

Mr. BELIN. Could it have been neither one of these persons that you saw?

Mr. BRENNAN. I think it was one of them. I think it was this boy on the end.

Mr. BELIN. You thought it was Mr. Norman. And what about Mr. Jarman?

Mr. BRENNAN. I believe it was him, too. Am I right or wrong?

Mr. BALL. I don't know.

Mr. BRENNAN. I explained that to you this morning.

Mr. BALL. I understand.

Any questions?

Mr. McCLOY. Did you recognize anyone in this room that you saw in the fifth floor window while you were sitting on the masonry opposite the school book depository?

Mr. BRENNAN. That is the two boys that I am speaking of now.

Mr. McCLOY. That you are speaking of now?

Mr. BRENNAN. Yes.

Mr. McCLOY. You saw these two men in the fifth floor window and you saw them again on the first floor?

Mr. BRENNAN. Coming out of the building down the stairway, coming out on the street, those were the only two people I could identify.

Mr. BELIN. I hand you——

Mr. BRENNAN. I recall seeing three people with you I——

Mr. BELIN. I hand you Exhibit 477 which you testified to this morning was a recent picture taken of the Texas School Book Depository Building on March 20. This is you sitting on that concrete wall?

Mr. BRENNAN. Right.

Mr. BELIN. At first I believe this morning you thought that you saw one person or two people at the point marked B, and then you later said it was to the window which would be to the——

Mr. BRENNAN. Left.

Mr. BELIN. Well, let's talk about directions. This direction here would be to the east and this direction here would be to the west?

Mr. BRENNAN. Right.

Mr. BELIN. Would it be a window to the east or west?

Mr. BRENNAN. I believe it was a window to the east.

Mr. BELIN. So you saw, you believe you saw two people in this window here to the east of the window that you first marked B?

Mr. BRENNAN. Yes. I am not positive.

Mr. BELIN. You are not positive?

Mr. BRENNAN. No.

Mr. REDLICH. Mr. McCloy, may I have permission to ask this question of this witness?

Mr. McCLOY. Very well.

Mr. REDLICH. You stated that you saw two employees walking down the steps of the building?

Mr. BRENNAN. Yes.

Mr. REDLICH. Do you recall whether the two employees that you saw walking down the steps of the building were the same two employees that you saw on the window, in the window on the fifth floor at the easterly most end of the building?

Mr. BRENNAN. Yes; as far as on the fifth floor and at one of these two windows. The one I circled or this window here.

Mr. REDLICH. You mean two of the people that you——

Mr. BRENNAN. At one of the windows I saw two, two of those people, employees that came down.

Mr. REDLICH. But you are not prepared to state which of these three possible windows?

Mr. BRENNAN. That is right.

Mr. REDLICH. By three, I mean the two windows to the east, plus the one window which is circled and marked with a B.

Mr. BRENNAN. Nothing makes me think that they were in this window but I am in question whether it was this window or this window.

Mr. REDLICH. And of the two people that you saw, it is possible you are saying that one might have been in the window marked B and another might have been in a window to the east?

Mr. BRENNAN. Yes.

Mr. REDLICH. Thank you.

Mr. BELIN. Mr. Brennan, are you basing your recollection on what you saw during the moments that the shots were fired or on what you saw when you observed these windows prior to the time the motorcade arrived?

Mr. BRENNAN. What I saw prior. There was no significance to the fact at all. In other words, there is a little difference in your memory there on this.

Mr. BALL. No questions.

You may be excused, Mr. Brennan.

You two men can also be excused and we will call you in a few moments, Mr. Jarman.

Mr. REDLICH. We don't need Mr. Williams at all.

Mr. BALL. We don't need you at all.

Mr. REDLICH. We may want him back.

Mr. BELIN. Don't get too far away.

TESTIMONY OF HAROLD NORMAN

I will ask you if you will please stand and hold up your right hand.

Do you solemnly swear that the testimony you give in this case will be the truth, the whole truth, and nothing but the truth, so help you God?

Mr. NORMAN. I do.

Mr. BALL. Mr. Norman.

Mr. NORMAN. Yes, sir.

Mr. BALL. Where do you live?

Mr. NORMAN. 4858 Beulah Place, Dallas, Tex.

Mr. BALL. Are you married?

Mr. NORMAN. Yes.

Mr. BALL. How old are you?

Mr. NORMAN. 26. I will be.

Mr. BALL. Where were you born?

Mr. NORMAN. Clarksville, Tex.

Mr. BALL. Were you raised in Clarksville?

Mr. NORMAN. Yes, sir.

Mr. BALL. Go to school there?

Mr. NORMAN. Yes, sir.

Mr. BALL. How far did you go to school?

Mr. NORMAN. I graduated there.

Mr. BALL. From high school?

Mr. NORMAN. Yes, sir.

Mr. BALL. In Clarksville?

Mr. NORMAN. Yes, sir.

Mr. BALL. What kind of work did you do after you got out of school?

Mr. NORMAN. Well, I remember working in Salina. I did a car washing job at the McElroy Chevrolet Co., and after I left there I came to Dallas and I started working at the depository, the School Book Depository.

Mr. BALL. That was about what year did you start working there?

Mr. NORMAN. In 1961, I believe.

Mr. BALL. 1961?

Mr. NORMAN. Yes, sir.

Mr. BALL. How long did you work there?

Mr. NORMAN. Well, I think this coming October would have made 3 years.

Mr. BALL. And you work there now?

Mr. NORMAN. No, sir.

Mr. BALL. Where do you work now?

Mr. NORMAN. The Foxboro Co.

Mr. BALL. What kind of business is that?

Mr. NORMAN. Engineer instrumentation.

Mr. BALL. What kind of work do you do?

Mr. NORMAN. Porter.

Mr. BALL. When did you leave the Texas School Book Depository for this new job?

Mr. NORMAN. I left during the Christmas holidays and the New Year's leave after we got off for New Year's.

Mr. BALL. In November 1963, this is this last fall, what kind of work were you doing at the Texas School Book Depository?

Mr. NORMAN. I was employed as an order filler.

Mr. BALL. Is that the same kind of a job that Lee Oswald had?

Mr. NORMAN. Yes, sir.

Mr. BALL. Did you know him?

Mr. NORMAN. No; just as an employee, that is all.

Mr. BALL. You didn't know him before he came to work there?

Mr. NORMAN. No, sir.

Mr. BALL. Did you get acquainted with him after he was there?

Mr. NORMAN. No. Just knew his name. I mean, you know, he wouldn't talk to anybody so I didn't——

Mr. BALL. He didn't talk to anybody?

Mr. NORMAN. No.

Mr. BALL. Did you ever engage him in conversation at the time he was there?

Mr. NORMAN. No, sir. I just, you know, speak to him, that is all. I wouldn't engage in conversation.

Mr. BALL. Are you the boys that use clipboards?

Mr. NORMAN. Yes, sir.

Mr. BALL. The order fillers?

Mr. NORMAN. Yes, sir.

Mr. BALL. Somebody gives you orders by way of papers?

Mr. NORMAN. Yes, sir.

Mr. BALL. What do you do after you get an order on a paper?

Mr. NORMAN. We had a different publisher in the building, and each individual, he had a publisher that he would take, maybe I would take to a publisher and the other orders would and we would fill orders and bring them down to the first floor for them to be checked and shipped out.

Mr. BALL. You have to go up and get the books out of cartons, do you?

Mr. NORMAN. Yes. If we didn't have enough down in the bins down on the first floor we would have to go upstairs, to complete the orders.

Mr. BALL. Do you fill some of your orders from the first floor?

Mr. NORMAN. Yes.

Mr. BALL. How many floors did you go to that morning yourself, November 22? Can you remember that?

Mr. NORMAN. I believe I went as far as the fifth floor that morning.

Mr. BALL. That is as far——

Mr. NORMAN. Yes.

Mr. BALL. Did you ever go to the sixth floor that day, that morning?

Mr. NORMAN. I can't—yes, I went up that morning during the time I think they were laying the floor up there when I went up there.

Mr. BALL. Did you help them?

Mr. NORMAN. No; I was just up there shooting the breeze.

Mr. BALL. Now what about Lee Oswald. Do you know what publisher he filled orders for?

Mr. NORMAN. I knew Scott-Foresman.

Mr. BALL. Scott-Foresman.

Mr. NORMAN. Yes.

Mr. BALL. That was the publisher assigned to him?

Mr. NORMAN. Yes. Well, I don't know if he was assigned to him but he filled, you know.

Mr. BALL. He filled those orders?

Mr. NORMAN. Yes.

Mr. BALL. You say then he filled Scott-Foresman book orders?

Mr. NORMAN. Yes.

Mr. BALL. Do you know where those books were kept?

Mr. NORMAN. The majority of them were on the sixth floor.

Mr. BALL. They were?

Mr. NORMAN. Yes.

Mr. BALL. And did you also keep a stock of Scott-Foresman books on the first floor?

Mr. NORMAN. Yes.

Mr. BALL. What time did you get to work on the morning of November the 22d?

Mr. NORMAN. I got there I would say about 5 minutes of 8 o'clock, 5 minutes until 8 in the morning.

Mr. BALL. You weren't late?

Mr. NORMAN. No; I wasn't.

Mr. BALL. Did you see Lee Oswald when you got to work?

Mr. NORMAN. No; I don't recall seeing him when I got to work.

Mr. BALL. Did you remember seeing him at any time that morning?

Mr. NORMAN. Yes; around about 10 or 10:15, somewhere in the neighborhood of that.

Mr. BALL. Where did you see him?

Mr. NORMAN. Over in the bins by the windows, I mean looking out, you know, at Elm Street, towards Elm Street.

Mr. BALL. On what floor?

Mr. NORMAN. The first.

Mr. BALL. Looking out on Elm through windows, is that right?

Mr. NORMAN. Yes, sir. I was looking out the window. He happened to come by to fill orders.

Mr. BALL. Did he say anything to you?

Mr. NORMAN. No; he didn't.

Mr. BALL. Did you say anything to him?

Mr. NORMAN. No.

Mr. BALL. Did you see him at any time after that?

Mr. NORMAN. No; no more. I don't recall seeing him any more that day.

Mr. BALL. What time did you quit for lunch?

Mr. NORMAN. I believe I quit around 11:45, I think.

Mr. BALL. And what did you do after you quit?

Mr. NORMAN. Well, I went in, washed up and I——

Mr. BALL. When you go in and wash up, where did you go to wash up?

Mr. NORMAN. In the men's bathroom.

Mr. BALL. Is that bathroom near the domino room or off the domino room?

Mr. NORMAN. Yes; that is the one off the domino room.

Mr. BALL. It is the one near the domino room?

Mr. NORMAN. Yes; one near the domino room.

Mr. BALL. Right next to it?

Mr. NORMAN. Yes.

Mr. BALL. After you washed up, what did you do?

Mr. NORMAN. Well, I got my lunch, I ate my lunch in the domino room.

Mr. BALL. Did you bring your lunch from home that day?

Mr. NORMAN. Yes; I believe I did.

188

Mr. BALL. And in what kind of a package did you bring it?

Mr. NORMAN. A brown paper sack, paper bag.

Mr. BALL. Where did you keep your lunch or leave your lunch from 8 in the morning until you got it at noon?

Mr. NORMAN. I left it in the window of the domino room.

Mr. BALL. Did you notice any other packages in that window that morning?

Mr. NORMAN. I can't say that I noticed any that morning but I know that some of the fellows did keep their lunches in there.

Mr. BALL. Did you notice anything, any unusual package in there that day?

Mr. NORMAN. No; I didn't.

Mr. BALL. You got your lunch and did you eat your lunch?

Mr. NORMAN. Yes; I ate my lunch.

Mr. BALL. Where were you when you ate your lunch?

Mr. NORMAN. In the domino room, as I recall.

Mr. BALL. Who was with you at that time?

Mr. NORMAN. I can't remember who ate in the lunchroom, I mean the domino room, with me.

Mr. BALL. Did some other employees eat there?

Mr. NORMAN. I think there was someone else in there because we usually played dominoes in there but that particular day we didn't play that morning.

Mr. BALL. Why didn't you play that morning?

Mr. NORMAN. Well, didn't nobody show up there to play like the guys usually come in to play.

Mr. BALL. You usually play dominoes during the noon hour?

Mr. NORMAN. Noon hour and the break period.

Mr. BALL. After you ate your lunch, what did you do?

Mr. NORMAN. I got with James Jarman, he and I got together on the first floor.

Mr. BALL. Where was James Jarman when you got together with him?

Mr. NORMAN. He was somewhere in the vicinity of the telephone, I believe. I am not for sure.

Mr. BALL. Out near the bins?

Mr. NORMAN. Yes.

Mr. BALL. What do you call James Jarman?

Mr. NORMAN. Junior.

Mr. BALL. And you and Junior did what?

Mr. NORMAN. We went outside.

Mr. BALL. You went out the front door, did you?

Mr. NORMAN. Yes.

Mr. BALL. That is the Elm Street?

Mr. NORMAN. Yes, sir.

Mr. BALL. Where did you stand?

Mr. NORMAN. We stood on the Elm Street sidewalk.

Mr. BALL. On the sidewalk?

Mr. NORMAN. Yes. We didn't go any further than that point.

Mr. BALL. What time was it that you went out there?

Mr. NORMAN. Oh, I would say, I don't know exactly, around 12 or 12:10, something like that.

Mr. BALL. Who was standing with you when you were standing on the sidewalk, on the Elm Street sidewalk?

Mr. NORMAN. I remember it was Danny Arce.

Mr. BALL. And who else?

Mr. NORMAN. I remember seeing Mr. Truly and Mr. Campbell. They were standing somewhere behind us, not exactly behind us but they were back of us.

Mr. BALL. Anybody else?

Mr. NORMAN. Well, I believe Billy Lovelady, I think. He was sitting on the steps there.

Mr. BALL. He was?

Mr. NORMAN. Yes. That is about all the employees I remember seeing out there. There were more people out there.

Mr. BALL. Did you stay there?

189

Mr. NORMAN. Well, we stayed there I believe until we got the news that the motorcade was coming down, let's see, is that Commerce, no Main, because Commerce—we went back in the building, James Jarman and I.

Mr. BALL. Where did you go when you went in the building?

Mr. NORMAN. We got the east elevator. No; the west.

Mr. BALL. The west elevator?

Mr. NORMAN. The west elevator. And went to the fifth floor.

Mr. BALL. The west elevator is the one you use the push button on?

Mr. NORMAN. Yes; the one you pull the gate.

Mr. BALL. That is right. It is a push button elevator.

Mr. NORMAN. Yes.

Mr. BALL. And you went up to the fifth floor?

Mr. NORMAN. Fifth floor.

Mr. BALL. Why did you go to the fifth floor?

Mr. NORMAN. Usually, one reason was you usually fill orders, I fill quite a few orders from the fifth floor and I figured I could get, you know, a better view of the parade or motorcade or whatever it is from the fifth floor because I was more familiar with that floor.

Mr. BALL. And what did you and Junior do after you got off the elevator?

Mr. NORMAN. We walked around to the windows facing Elm Street and I can't recall if any were open or not but I remember we opened some, two or three windows ourselves.

Mr. BALL. Did somebody join you there?

Mr. NORMAN. Bonnie Ray, I can't remember if he was there when we got there or he came later. I know he was with us a period of time later.

Mr. BALL. And then did he come down before the President's motorcade came by?

Mr. NORMAN. Yes; he was with us before the motorcade came by.

Mr. BALL. Did you move around any from one window to another before the motorcade?

Mr. NORMAN. Well, if I did I didn't move no further than those three windows that were open in the front there. I didn't move any further than that.

Mr. BALL. I show you some pictures here. This is Commission Exhibit No. 482. Do you recognize anybody in that window?

Mr. NORMAN. That is myself and that is Bonnie Ray Williams.

Mr. BALL. "Myself" is pointed to as to the window in the extreme southeast corner of the fifth floor, is that right?

Mr. NORMAN. Yes.

Mr. BALL. And Bonnie Ray is in the window next to you?

Mr. NORMAN. Yes.

Mr. BALL. I show you 480. Do you see the window in which you were looking?

Mr. NORMAN. That window is where I was looking.

Mr. BALL. In other words, you were looking in the extreme southeast corner?

Mr. NORMAN. Yes.

Mr. BALL. Put over here a red arrow which shows the window from which you were looking.

Mr. NORMAN. Yes.

Mr. BALL. Here is 482. Do you see your picture in that window?

Mr. NORMAN. Yes.

Mr. BALL. The same picture?

Mr. NORMAN. Yes.

Mr. BALL. Point out your picture on 482.

Mr. NORMAN. That is myself.

Mr. BALL. I will point that out with a red arrow on 482. Now were you standing up or sitting down?

Mr. NORMAN. I was sitting. I wasn't at all standing up.

Mr. BALL. At the time the President's motorcade went by, how were you sitting?

Mr. NORMAN. I believe I wasn't on my knees I don't think, but I was in a hunched over position somewhat like this.

Mr. BALL. Last Friday afternoon, that is March 20, you and Junior Jarman and Bonnie Ray Williams went up on the fifth floor with me, didn't you?

Mr. NORMAN. Yes, sir.

Mr. BALL. And a photographer?

Mr. NORMAN. Yes.

Mr. BALL. And you took a position; did you?

Mr. NORMAN. Yes.

Mr. BALL. What position did you take at the window? First of all, what did I ask you to do? What position did I ask you to take?

Mr. NORMAN. I believe you told us to take the position that we thought we were in during the time of the motorcade.

Mr. BALL. And do you recognize this picture, 486? Do you show in the picture?

Mr. NORMAN. Yes, sir; that is myself there.

Mr. BALL. You are sitting there looking out a window. How does that picture compare with what you remember as to your position when the President's motorcade went by?

Mr. NORMAN. Well, I don't think—I think I was facing the window more straight during that time, I mean the motorcade, that I am in this position here.

Mr. BALL. That picture shows you looking out the window down the street, is that right?

Mr. NORMAN. Yes.

Mr. BALL. And this is a picture of Bonnie Ray also, isn't it?

Mr. NORMAN. Yes.

Mr. BALL. Now you saw the President go by, did you?

Mr. NORMAN. Yes.

Mr. BALL. What happened then?

Mr. NORMAN. About the time that he got past the window where I was, well, it seems as though he was, I mean you know, brushing his hair. Maybe he was looking to the public.

Mr. McCLOY. Saluting?

Mr. NORMAN. Yes.

Mr. BALL. With which arm?

Mr. NORMAN. I believe it was his right arm, and I can't remember what the exact time was but I know I heard a shot, and then after I heard the shot, well, it seems as though the President, you know, slumped or something, and then another shot and I believe Jarman or someone told me, he said, "I believe someone is shooting at the President," and I think I made a statement "It is someone shooting at the President, and I believe it came from up above us."

Well, I couldn't see at all during the time but I know I heard a third shot fired, and I could also hear something sounded like the shell hulls hitting the floor and the ejecting of the rifle, it sounded as though it was to me.

Mr. BALL. How many shots did you hear?

Mr. NORMAN. Three.

Mr. BALL. Do you remember whether or not you said anything to the men then as to whether or not you heard anything from above you?

Mr. NORMAN. Only I think I remember saying that I thought I could hear the shell hulls and the ejection of the rifle. I didn't tell I think I hear anybody moving, you know.

Mr. BALL. But you thought, do you remember you told the men then that you thought you heard the ejection of the rifle?

Mr. NORMAN. Yes, sir.

Mr. BALL. And shells on the floor?

Mr. NORMAN. Yes, sir.

Mr. BALL. Falling?

Mr. NORMAN. Yes.

Mr. BALL. Did anybody say anything as to where they thought the shots came from?

Mr. NORMAN. Well, I don't recall of either one of them saying they thought where it came from.

Mr. BALL. But you did?

Mr. NORMAN. Yes.

Mr. BALL. And you said you thought it came from where?

Mr. NORMAN. Above where we were, above us.

Mr. BALL. Did you see any dust or dirt falling?

Mr. NORMAN. I didn't see any falling but I saw some in Bonnie Ray Williams' hair.

Mr. BALL. Did anybody say anything about it?

Mr. NORMAN. I believe Jarman told him that it was in his hair first. Then I, you know, told him it was and I believe Jarman told him not to brush it out his hair but I think he did anyway.

Mr. BALL. After that happened, what did you do?

Mr. NORMAN. Well, we ran to the farthest window facing the expressway.

Mr. BALL. The farthest window, is that right?

Mr. NORMAN. Yes.

Mr. BALL. I have here a diagram of this fifth floor.

Mr. McCLOY. May I interrupt there.

Mr. BALL. Go right ahead.

Mr. McCLOY. You spoke about seeing the President sort of slump over after the first shot?

Mr. NORMAN. Yes; I believe the first.

Mr. McCLOY. Did you see the President hit on any subsequent shots?

Mr. NORMAN. No; I don't recall seeing that.

Mr. BALL. Here is a diagram of the sixth floor.

Mr. NORMAN. The sixth floor?

Mr. BALL. Of the fifth floor rather, which is Commission's 487, and this is the southeast corner window. To what window did you and your two friends run?

Mr. NORMAN. This is the south. This is the window we were in. We came to this last, I believe it is the next to the last or the last window on this end here, right here.

Mr. BALL. And the other day when you were up on the fifth floor with a photographer, you ran to that window, did you?

Mr. NORMAN. Well, we ran to the window, we thought it was the window we ran to.

Mr. BALL. And you opened that window?

Mr. NORMAN. Yes.

Mr. BALL. And had your picture taken?

Mr. NORMAN. Yes.

Mr. BALL. Here is 485. Is that the window as you remembered it that you ran to?

Mr. NORMAN. I can't say it was that particular window that day but it was between these two windows here.

Mr. BALL. One of the two windows?

Mr. NORMAN. Yes.

Mr. BALL. This is marked Y here on 487, is that correct?

Mr. NORMAN. Yes.

Mr. BALL. Why did you run down to that window?

Mr. NORMAN. Well, it seems as though everyone else was running towards the railroad tracks, and we ran over there. Curious to see why everybody was running that way for. I thought maybe——

Mr. BALL. Did anybody say anything about going up to the sixth floor?

Mr. NORMAN. I don't remember anyone saying about going up to the sixth floor.

Mr. BALL. Then did you leave that window that you have marked Y on 487?

Mr. NORMAN. Yes.

Mr. BALL. And you went to what window?

Mr. NORMAN. To the west window.

Mr. BALL. Look on the diagram and tell me what window you went to, as you remember it?

Mr. NORMAN. It was between this point here, these two right here.

Mr. BALL. That is marked Z?

Mr. NORMAN. Yes.

Mr. BALL. Is that correct?

Mr. NORMAN. Yes.

Mr. BALL. What did you do when you went to that window?

Mr. NORMAN. I don't remember if we raised the window or not but I remember looking out the window that day.

Mr. BALL. Here is a picture 489 taken last Friday when you were with me on that floor?

Mr. NORMAN. Yes.

Mr. BALL. Do you show in the picture?

Mr. NORMAN. Yes, sir.

Mr. BALL. Is that the window you looked out of?

Mr. NORMAN. Yes, sir; I believe that is the one.

Mr. BALL. What did you look at when you looked out that window?

Mr. NORMAN. We saw the policeman, and I guess they were detectives, they were searching the empty cars over there. I remember seeing some guy on top of them.

Mr. BALL. On top of the cars?

Mr. NORMAN. Yes. They were going through there.

Mr. BALL. You saw police officers searching cars over on the railroad tracks?

Mr. NORMAN. Yes.

Mr. BALL. And how long did you stay at that window?

Mr. NORMAN. I don't remember, but it wasn't very long.

Mr. BALL. Then where did you go?

Mr. NORMAN. We ran down to the first floor.

Mr. BALL. As you were at the fifth floor, looking west as shown in Exhibit No. 489, were you able to see the stairwell?

Mr. NORMAN. No.

Mr. BALL. Why?

Mr. NORMAN. Because there is a row of bins there that prevents you standing in a position that I was in to keep you from seeing it.

Mr. BALL. There is 492. Does that show the row of bins?

Mr. NORMAN. Yes; the row of bins.

Mr. BALL. They block off the stairwell.

Mr. NORMAN. Yes.

Mr. BALL. Do you remember that we tried an experiment when you were there by putting you three men in line and then taking a picture to see if we could see any one of you?

Mr. NORMAN. Yes, sir.

Mr. BALL. This is a picture 491. That is your picture, isn't it?

Mr. NORMAN. Yes, sir.

Mr. BALL. Where are you?

Mr. NORMAN. In the middle.

Mr. BALL. And who is that on the end?

Mr. NORMAN. Which end? Oh, this is Bonnie Ray Williams.

Mr. BALL. Who is this one?

Mr. NORMAN. James Jarman.

Mr. BALL. And then a picture, do you remember another picture was taken, 492?

Mr. NORMAN. Yes, sir; I remember that picture.

Mr. BALL. Can you see anyone in that picture?

Mr. NORMAN. I see one person.

Mr. BALL. Can you make him out?

Mr. NORMAN. Yes. I recognize him as James Jarman.

Mr. BALL. Jarman, the one on the end?

Mr. NORMAN. Yes, sir.

Mr. BALL. Now did you see any police officer come up on that floor?

Mr. NORMAN. I didn't.

Mr. BALL. You didn't.

Mr. NORMAN. No, sir.

Mr. BALL. Or did you see Mr. Truly come up?

Mr. NORMAN. No, sir; I didn't.

Mr. BALL. Or did you hear any elevator operator?

Mr. NORMAN. No; I don't recall.

Mr. BALL. Going up or down?

Mr. NORMAN. No, sir; I don't recall anyone.

Mr. BALL. When you were brought to the first floor or when you came to the first floor how did you go down there?

Mr. NORMAN. We came down the stairway. I remember we came down the stairway.

Mr. BALL. When you got to the first floor did someone talk to you, police officers?

Mr. NORMAN. I don't remember a police officer talking to me as soon as we got down there. I don't.

Mr. BALL. Did anyone talk to you later?

Mr. NORMAN. Yes.

Mr. BALL. Who?

Mr. NORMAN. I guess they were Secret Service men. But I know they talked to us.

Mr. BALL. Did they take you over to the police station later?

Mr. NORMAN. No; they didn't carry me to the police station.

Mr. BALL. When did you leave the place?

Mr. NORMAN. Oh, I would say somewhere around 2 o'clock, somewhere in the vicinity of that.

Mr. BALL. Who did you leave with?

Mr. NORMAN. Mr. James Jarman. I can't remember who.

Mr. BALL. From the time that you went down on the first floor until you left the building to go home did you leave the building at all?

Mr. NORMAN. No; I didn't.

Mr. BALL. Where did you stay?

Mr. NORMAN. They kept us on the first floor.

Mr. BALL. You did make a statement later to the Secret Service, didn't you?

Mr. NORMAN. Yes.

Mr. BALL. I have here a document 493, which is a copy of a statement made by this witness, which I now mark 493.

(The document referred to was marked Commission Exhibit No. 493, for identification.)

Mr. BALL. The document that I have here shows the date 4th of December 1963. Do you remember having made a statement to Mr. Carter, Special Agent of the Secret Service, on that day?

Mr. NORMAN. I can't remember the exact date but I believe I remember Mr. Carter.

Mr. BALL. I want to call your attention to one part of the statement and I will ask you if you told him that:

"Just after the President passed by, I heard a shot and several seconds later I heard two more shots. I knew that the shots had come from directly above me, and I could hear the expended cartridges fall to the floor. I could also hear the bolt action of the rifle. I also saw some dust fall from the ceiling of the fifth floor and I felt sure that whoever had fired the shots was directly above me."

Did you make that statement to the Secret Service man?

Mr. NORMAN. I don't remember making a statement that I knew the shots came from directly above us. I didn't make that statement. And I don't remember saying I heard several seconds later. I merely told him that I heard three shots because I didn't have any idea what time it was.

Mr. BALL. I see. Did you tell them that you heard the bolt action of the rifle?

Mr. NORMAN. Yes.

Mr. BALL. And that you heard the expended cartridges fall to the floor?

Mr. NORMAN. Yes; I heard them making a sound.

Mr. BALL. I would like to offer this into evidence.

Mr. McCLOY. It may be admitted.

(The document referred to, heretofore identified as Commission Exhibit No. 493 for identification, was received in evidence.)

Mr. McCLOY. You used the expression you heard the ejection. This refers to the bolt action?

Mr. NORMAN. Yes.

Mr. McCLOY. Those are the same things?

Mr. NORMAN. Yes, sir; that is what I mean.

Mr. McCLOY. That is what you meant by that?

Mr. NORMAN. Yes, sir.

Mr. BALL. What language did you use when you talked to the Secret Service man, do you know? Did you say you heard the ejection or that you heard the bolt action? Which did you use?

Mr. NORMAN. I probably said the ejection.

Mr. BALL. That is what you think you said?

Mr. NORMAN. Yes.

Mr. BALL. The same thing you said here?

Mr. NORMAN. Yes.

Mr. BALL. Do you remember Friday that we conducted an experiment to see whether or not you could hear?

Mr. NORMAN. Yes, sir.

Mr. BALL. From the sixth floor?

Mr. NORMAN. Yes.

Mr. BALL. And where did you put yourself in order to conduct the experiment?

Mr. NORMAN. In the same window. I may not have been in the same position but I was in the same window.

Mr. BALL. The same window?

Mr. NORMAN. Yes, sir.

Mr. BALL. And that window was open?

Mr. NORMAN. Yes, sir.

Mr. BALL. And the window, was the window on the sixth floor also open?

Mr. NORMAN. Yes, sir; they told me it was open. I didn't see it.

Mr. BALL. And a Secret Service man went upstairs with a rifle, didn't he?

Mr. NORMAN. Yes.

Mr. BALL. What did you hear on the fifth floor?

Mr. NORMAN. Well, I heard the same sound, the sound similar. I heard three something that he dropped on the floor and then I could hear the rifle or whatever he had up there.

Mr. BALL. You could hear the rifle, the sound of an ejection?

Mr. NORMAN. Yes, sir.

Mr. BALL. Did you hear the sound of the bolt going back and forth?

Mr. NORMAN. Yes, sir; I sure did.

Mr. BALL. You could hear it clearly, could you?

Mr. NORMAN. Yes, sir.

Mr. BALL. Now there has been a new floor put in on the sixth floor, hasn't there?

Mr. NORMAN. Yes, sir.

Mr. BALL. The day that you were there on November 22, what was the condition of the ceiling and the floor of the sixth floor?

Mr. NORMAN. I would say that you could see daylight through there because during the times they put the plywood down you can see the plywood, some portion of the plywood, so I would say you could see a little daylight during that time.

Mr. BALL. When you were there Friday afternoon, did you look up at the ceiling from where you were sitting at the southeast window on the fifth floor?

Mr. NORMAN. Yes, sir.

Mr. BALL. What could you see on the ceiling?

Mr. NORMAN. There was one place I could see the plywood and then another place you could still see a little daylight, I mean peering through the crack.

Mr. BALL. What about the joint where the upper floor or the floor of the sixth and ceiling of the fifth floor comes against the wall. Could you see daylight through there?

Mr. NORMAN. Against the wall?

Mr. BALL. Yes.

Mr. NORMAN. Yes; in one place you could see a small amount of daylight.

Mr. BALL. Now the day of the experiment last Friday when you heard the cartridges eject, the bolt action and the cartridges ejecting——

Mr. NORMAN. Yes.

Mr. BALL. Was there any noise outside?

Mr. NORMAN. Yes; there was.

Mr. BALL. What was it?

Mr. NORMAN. There was a train and there were trucks and cars.

Mr. BALL. Was there more noise or less noise on the day you conducted the experiment last Friday, March 20, than on November 22, at 12:30?

Mr. NORMAN. It was more noise last Friday than it was November 22.

Mr. BALL. Was there any train going by on November 22?

Mr. NORMAN. No, sir.

Mr. BALL. Were there any trucks going by on November 22?

Mr. NORMAN. No, sir.

Mr. BALL. I have no further questions.

Mr. McCLOY. How did you get your job at the Texas School Book Depository?

Mr. NORMAN. Well, as I remember the time that I told you before I used to live in Salina and washing cars at the Chevrolet company I had a friend that lived in Dallas and he was working down there, and he told me that he thought that I could get a job down there, and that is how I got familiar with the place. I did go by there and Mr. Truly gave me a job.

Mr. McCLOY. Were you getting better pay there than you had at your former job?

Mr. NORMAN. At the Chevrolet company?

Mr. McCLOY. Yes.

Mr. NORMAN. Yes, sir; I was getting better pay there.

Mr. McCLOY. Do you have any rough recollection of the amount of time that passed between the time you heard the first shot and when you ran down to the west end of the building and looked out the window there and the time when you left the fifth floor and finally came down to the first floor where the police officers were? Can you give me a general estimate of about how much time that took?

Mr. NORMAN. To come down from the fifth floor?

Mr. McCLOY. Yes. From the time you first heard the shot and saw what was going on in the motorcade and then ran down toward the western end of the building and then as I understand your testimony, you left there and went down to the—did you go down to the fourth floor first or did you go all the way down?

Mr. NORMAN. I believe we went all the way.

Mr. McCLOY. Until you got down to the first floor, how much would you say was the entire length of that time, from the first shot until you got down on the first floor?

Mr. NORMAN. Oh, I would say somewhere between 10 or 15 minutes, somewhere like that.

Mr. McCLOY. I don't think I have any other questions.

Mr. BALL. I have one question.

On the 26th of November, an FBI agent named Kreutzer advises us in a report that he talked to you. Do you remember that?

Mr. NORMAN. Yes, sir.

Mr. BALL. You remember?

Mr. NORMAN. Yes; I remember talking to him. I don't know his name.

Mr. BALL. He reports that you told him that you heard a shot and that you stuck your head from the window and looked upward toward the roof but could see nothing because small particles of dirt were falling from above you. Did you tell him that?

Mr. NORMAN. I don't recall telling him that.

Mr. BALL. Did you ever put your head out the window?

Mr. NORMAN. No, sir; I don't remember ever putting my head out the window.

Mr. BALL. And he reports that you stated that two additional shots were fired after you pulled your head back in from the window. Do you remember telling him that?

Mr. NORMAN. No, sir; I don't.

Mr. BALL. I have no further questions.

Mr. McCloy. Have you ever had any difficulty with the law? Have you ever been convicted of a crime?

Mr. Norman. No, sir.

Mr. McCloy. At the time after you heard the shots, did you have any thought that you might run upstairs and see if anybody was up there where the shots were coming from there?

Mr. Norman. No, sir.

Mr. McCloy. Did you feel that it might be dangerous to go upstairs?

Mr. Norman. Yes, sir.

Mr. McCloy. You testified that you had not seen Oswald except this one occasion in the morning. Did you hear any of your friends or coworkers say whether they had seen Oswald on that morning?

Mr. Norman. Not until after——

Mr. McCloy. After the assassination?

Mr. Norman. Yes, sir; that is the only time.

Mr. Belin. Off the record.

(Discussion off the record.)

The Chairman. Did you see Brennan down there when you came downstairs? Did you come out the front door?

Mr. Norman. Yes, sir; I came out the front door and I remember seeing Mr. Brennan.

Mr. Belin. About how long after the shooting was that?

Mr. Norman. It wasn't very long because—I can't remember the time but it wasn't too long a period of time, and I remember seeing him because he had on a steel helmet, a little steel helmet.

Representative Ford. Was he standing with another man and they called you over?

Mr. Norman. I don't know if he was exactly standing with another man, but it was several people standing around there, and I remember him talking and I believe I remember him saying that he saw us when we first went up to the fifth floor window, he saw us then. I believe I heard him say that, but otherwise I don't know if he was standing by. There was quite a few people standing around there.

Representative Ford. You were stopped and Mr. Brennan made these comments?

Mr. Norman. Yes, sir; I remember.

Representative Ford. On the front entrance steps?

Mr. Norman. Yes, sir.

Representative Ford. Of the Depository Building?

Mr. Norman. Yes.

The Chairman. Then did you go out of the building, away from the building or come back?

Mr. Norman. No, sir; we had to go back inside.

The Chairman. You had to go back?

Mr. Norman. Yes, sir.

Mr. Ball. In other words, you went out in front?

Mr. Norman. Yes, sir.

Mr. Ball. And then came back?

Mr. Norman. Yes, sir.

Mr. Ball. After you had gone to the first floor?

Mr. Norman. Yes, sir.

Representative Ford. Did law enforcement officers make you go back or did you do it on your own initiative?

Mr. Norman. I remember, I don't know if this is the only time or not, but I remember the law enforcement saying not to let anybody leave from the building and I can't remember if that is the time we went back in the building or before or what.

Mr. Ball. Who did you go out with?

Mr. Norman. I know James Jarman and I went out. I can't remember.

Representative Ford. May I ask did we get into the testimony enough of his background and biography?

Mr. BALL. Clear from where he was born, through high school and all his jobs through high school.

He is 26 years old, married, and never been in any trouble in his life. I think that is all.

Mr. McCLOY. Thank you, Mr. Norman.

The CHAIRMAN. Thank you very much for coming.

Off the record.

(Discussion off the record.)

TESTIMONY OF JAMES JARMAN, JR.

Mr. BELIN. Chief Justice Warren, this is Mr. Jarman.

The CHAIRMAN. How do you do. Glad to see you.

Mr. BELIN. Congressman Ford——

Mr. McCLOY. Would you hold up your right hand. Do you solemnly swear that the testimony you give in this case will be the truth, the whole truth, and nothing but the truth, so help you God?

Mr. JARMAN. I do.

Mr. BALL. The statement has been read to you as to the purpose of your examination before the Commission?

Mr. JARMAN. Yes, sir.

Mr. BALL. Hasn't it, Mr. Jarman?

Mr. JARMAN. Yes.

Mr. BALL. State your name, please?

Mr. JARMAN. James Jarman, Junior.

Mr. BALL. What do they call you, Junior?

Mr. JARMAN. Junior.

Mr. BALL. Where do you live?

Mr. JARMAN. 4930 Echo.

Mr. BALL. Are you married?

Mr. JARMAN. Yes.

Mr. BALL. What is your age?

Mr. JARMAN. 34.

Mr. BALL. Where were you born?

Mr. JARMAN. Dallas, Tex.

Mr. BALL. Have you lived there all your life?

Mr. JARMAN. Yes; I have.

Mr. BALL. You still live there?

Mr. JARMAN. Yes.

Mr. BALL. And did you go to school in Dallas?

Mr. JARMAN. Yes; I did.

Mr. BALL. How far did you go through school?

Mr. JARMAN. To the 10th grade and went to California in 1947 and stayed there for about a year.

Mr. BALL. What did you do in California?

Mr. JARMAN. I was living with my aunt at the time.

Mr. BALL. Did you work?

Mr. JARMAN. No; I was still in school.

Mr. BALL. What school did you go to?

Mr. JARMAN. Alameda High.

Mr. BALL. Then where did you go after you came back, after you left California?

Mr. JARMAN. I came back to Dallas.

Mr. BALL. Did you go to school any more?

Mr. JARMAN. No, sir. I went into service.

Mr. BALL. What year did you go in the service?

Mr. JARMAN. 1948.

Mr. BALL. How long were you in the service?

Mr. JARMAN. I was in the service up until 1952.

Mr. BALL. What service?

Mr. JARMAN. U.S. Army.

Mr. BALL. And did you enlist in 1948?

Mr. JARMAN. Yes.

Mr. BALL. Enlisted?

Mr. JARMAN. Yes.

Mr. BALL. Did 4 years in the Army?

Mr. JARMAN. Yes; I did.

Mr. BALL. Did you receive an honorable discharge from the Army?

Mr. JARMAN. Yes.

Mr. BALL. And then what did you do?

Mr. JARMAN. I came out and stayed out for about until July of 1953.

Mr. BALL. Then what?

Mr. JARMAN. And reenlisted in the service again.

Mr. BALL. How long did you stay in the Army this time?

Mr. JARMAN. Until 1956.

Mr. BALL. And were you discharged then?

Mr. JARMAN. Yes, I was.

Mr. BALL. Did you get an honorable discharge?

Mr. JARMAN. Yes, sir.

Mr. BALL. And what did you do after that?

Mr. JARMAN. Well, I started working at the Texas School Book Depository for about 2 months after.

Mr. BALL. After you got out of the Army?

Mr. JARMAN. Yes.

Mr. BALL. You are still there; are you?

Mr. JARMAN. Yes, sir.

Mr. BALL. Was there any period of time since 1956 to 1964 that you didn't work there?

Mr. JARMAN. Yes.

Mr. BALL. How many times?

Mr. JARMAN. I started in 1956. I worked from August up until November, and I was laid off until December the same year and I started back again and I worked up until 1958 I believe, 1958 or 1959, and I quit there and went to Parkland Hospital. From there I went back to the Depository. And I got laid off again and I went to Bakers Hotel, and I think it was in 1961 I went back to the Depository and I have been there ever since.

Mr. BALL. What was your job at the Depository in November of 1963, last fall?

Mr. JARMAN. Checker.

Mr. BALL. What does a checker do?

Mr. JARMAN. He checks various orders, books and things that go out to different schools.

Mr. BALL. Do the order fillers bring the books down to where you have your——

Mr. JARMAN. Right.

Mr. BALL. On a table. You have a table?

Mr. JARMAN. I have a table with a scale and I weigh these books up and put the upholstery on them and put them on a little conveyor and the wrappers wrap them or pack them, whichever one it may be.

Mr. BALL. Did you know Lee Oswald?

Mr. JARMAN. Only as a coworker.

Mr. BALL. Did you ever talk to him while he was working there?

Mr. JARMAN. I have had him to correct orders at various times. That is about all.

Mr. BALL. Did you ever talk to him about politics?

Mr. JARMAN. No.

Mr. BALL. Religion?

Mr. JARMAN. No.

Mr. BALL. Anything at all?

Mr. JARMAN. Not until November the 22d.

Mr. BALL. Not until that day?

Mr. JARMAN. Not until that day.

Mr. BALL. Did Oswald have any friends there?

Mr. Jarman. Well, not that I know of.

Mr. Ball. Did he have any close friend that he would eat lunch with every day?

Mr. Jarman. No, sir; not that I know of.

Mr. Ball. Did you notice whether Oswald brought his lunch most of the time or bought his lunch most of the time?

Mr. Jarman. Most of the time he brought his lunch.

Mr. Ball. Most of the time he brought his lunch?

Mr. Jarman. Yes.

Mr. Ball. Did you ever see him buy his lunch?

Mr. Jarman. Well, occasionally. I don't think so.

Mr. Ball. I don't understand.

Mr. Jarman. I mean sometimes he would go out of the building. One time I know in particular that he went out, but he didn't buy any lunch.

Mr. Ball. There is a catering service that comes by the building every morning at 10 o'clock, isn't there?

Mr. Jarman. Yes, sir.

Mr. Ball. Did you ever see him buy his lunch from this catering service?

Mr. Jarman. I think once or twice he did.

Mr. Ball. Did you ever see him when he was eating his lunch?

Mr. Jarman. Yes.

Mr. Ball. Where?

Mr. Jarman. Sometimes in the, as we called it, domino room, and again over by the coffee table where they make coffee.

Mr. Ball. Is that the first floor?

Mr. Jarman. That is the first floor.

Mr. Ball. Now on November 22, what time did you get to work?

Mr. Jarman. About 5 minutes after 8.

Mr. Ball. Was Oswald there when you got there?

Mr. Jarman. Yes, sir.

Mr. Ball. Where did you see him the first time?

Mr. Jarman. Well, he was on the first floor filling orders.

Mr. Ball. Did you bring your lunch that day?

Mr. Jarman. No, sir; I didn't.

Mr. Ball. What did you do about lunch that day?

Mr. Jarman. I got a sandwich off the carrying truck.

Mr. Ball. About what time of day?

Mr. Jarman. It was about 10 or a little after 10, maybe.

Mr. Ball. Where did you put it, keep it until lunch?

Mr. Jarman. In the domino room.

Mr. Ball. Where in the domino room?

Mr. Jarman. Well, they have two little windows, they have two sets of windows in there and I put it in the window.

Mr. Ball. Did you talk to Oswald that morning?

Mr. Jarman. I did.

Mr. Ball. When?

Mr. Jarman. I had him to correct an order. I don't know exactly what time it was.

Mr. Ball. Oh, approximately. Nine, ten?

Mr. Jarman. It was around, it was between eight and nine, I would say.

Mr. Ball. Between 8 and 9?

Mr. Jarman. Between 5 minutes after 8 and 9.

Mr. Ball. You had him correct an order?

Mr. Jarman. Yes, sir.

Mr. Ball. Did you talk to him again that morning?

Mr. Jarman. Yes, sir. I talked to him again later on that morning.

Mr. Ball. About what time?

Mr. Jarman. It was between 9:30 and 10 o'clock, I believe.

Mr. Ball. Where were you when you talked to him?

Mr. Jarman. In between two rows of bins.

Mr. Ball. On what floor?

Mr. Jarman. On the first floor.

Mr. BALL. And what was said by him and by you?

Mr. JARMAN. Well, he was standing up in the window and I went to the window also, and he asked me what were the people gathering around on the corner for, and I told him that the President was supposed to pass that morning, and he asked me did I know which way he was coming, and I told him, yes; he probably come down Main and turn on Houston and then back again on Elm. Then he said, "Oh, I see," and that was all.

Mr. BALL. Did you talk to him again?

Mr. JARMAN. No, sir.

Mr. BALL. What time did you quit for lunch?

Mr. JARMAN. It was right about 5 minutes to 12.

Mr. BALL. What did you do when you quit for lunch?

Mr. JARMAN. Went in the rest room and washed up.

Mr. BALL. Then what did you do?

Mr. JARMAN. Went and got my sandwich and went up in the lounge and got me a soda pop.

Mr. BALL. Where is the lounge?

Mr. JARMAN. On the second floor.

Mr. BALL. On the second floor?

Mr. JARMAN. Yes.

Mr. BALL. Then where did you go after you got your soda pop?

Mr. JARMAN. Came back and went down to the window.

Mr. BALL. What window?

Mr. JARMAN. Where Oswald and I was talking.

Mr. BALL. Where?

Mr. JARMAN. Between those two rows of bins.

Mr. BALL. Where Oswald and you had been talking?

Mr. JARMAN. Yes.

Mr. BALL. What did you do there?

Mr. JARMAN. I was eating part of my sandwich there, and then I came back out and as I was walking across the floor I ate the rest of it going toward the domino room.

Mr. BALL. You say you ate the rest of it when?

Mr. JARMAN. Walking around on the first floor there.

Mr. BALL. Did you sit down at the window when you ate part of your sandwich?

Mr. JARMAN. No; I was standing.

Mr. BALL. And did you have the pop in your hand, too?

Mr. JARMAN. Yes; I had a sandwich in one hand and pop in the other.

Mr. BALL. You say you wandered around, you mean on the first floor?

Mr. JARMAN. On the first floor.

Mr. BALL. Were you with anybody when you were at the window? Did you talk to anybody?

Mr. JARMAN. No; I did not.

Mr. BALL. Were you with anybody when you were walking around finishing your sandwich?

Mr. JARMAN. No; I wasn't. I was trying to get through so I could get out on the street.

Mr. BALL. Did you see Lee Oswald?

Mr. JARMAN. No; I didn't.

Mr. BALL. After his arrest, he stated to a police officer that he had had lunch with you. Did you have lunch with him?

Mr. JARMAN. No, sir; I didn't.

Mr. BALL. When you finished your sandwich and your bottle of pop, what did you do?

Mr. JARMAN. I throwed the paper that I had the sandwich in in the box over close to the telephone and I took the pop bottle and put it in the case over by the Dr. Pepper machine.

Mr. BALL. And then what did you do?

Mr. JARMAN. Then I went out in front of the building.

Mr. BALL. With who?

Mr. JARMAN. Harold Norman, Bonnie Ray, and Danny Arce and myself.

Mr. BALL. You say Bonnie Ray Williams?

Mr. JARMAN. Bonnie Ray Williams.

Mr. BALL. Do you remember him going with you?

Mr. JARMAN. No; I am sorry. Excuse me, but it was Harold Norman and myself and Daniel Arce.

Mr. BALL. What about Billy Lovelady?

Mr. JARMAN. I didn't go out with them. They came out later.

Mr. BALL. Did you see Billy Lovelady out there?

Mr. JARMAN. Yes, sir.

Mr. BALL. Where was he?

Mr. JARMAN. Standing on the stairway as you go out the front door.

Mr. BALL. Where did you stand?

Mr. JARMAN. I was standing over to the right in front of the building going toward the west.

Mr. BALL. Were you on the sidewalk or curb?

Mr. JARMAN. On the sidewalk.

Mr. BALL. The sidewalk in front of the Texas School Book Depository Building?

Mr. JARMAN. Yes, sir.

Mr. BALL. How long did you stand there?

Mr. JARMAN. Well, until about 12:20, between 12:20 and 12:25.

Mr. BALL. Who do you remember was standing near you that worked with you in the Book Depository?

Mr. JARMAN. Harold Norman and Charles Givens and Daniel Arce.

Mr. BALL. What about Mr. Truly?

Mr. JARMAN. He wasn't standing close to me.

Mr. BALL. Did you see him?

Mr. JARMAN. Yes, sir.

Mr. BALL. Who was he with?

Mr. JARMAN. He was with the Vice President of the company.

Mr. BALL. What is his name?

Mr. JARMAN. O. V. Campbell.

Mr. BALL. Where were they standing?

Mr. JARMAN. They were standing at the corner of the building in front of the mail boxes.

Mr. BALL. You left there, didn't you, and went some place?

Mr. JARMAN. Yes, sir.

Mr. BALL. With whom?

Mr. JARMAN. Harold Norman and myself.

Mr. BALL. Where did you go?

Mr. JARMAN. We went around to the back of the building up to the fifth floor.

Mr. BALL. You say you went around. You mean you went around the building?

Mr. JARMAN. Right.

Mr. BALL. You didn't go through and cross the first floor?

Mr. JARMAN. No, sir; there was too many people standing on the stairway there, so we decided to go around.

Mr. BALL. You went in the back door?

Mr. JARMAN. Right.

Mr. BALL. That would be the north entrance to the building, wouldn't it?

Mr. JARMAN. Right.

Mr. BALL. Did you take an elevator or the stairs?

Mr. JARMAN. We took the elevator.

Mr. BALL. Which elevator?

Mr. JARMAN. The west side elevator.

Mr. BALL. That is the one you use a punch button on, isn't it?

Mr. JARMAN. Right.

Mr. BALL. Where did you go?

Mr. JARMAN. To the fifth floor.

Mr. BALL. Why did you go to the fifth floor?

Mr. JARMAN. We just decided to go to the fifth floor.

Mr. BALL. Was there any reason why you should go to the fifth floor any more than the fourth or the sixth?

Mr. JARMAN. No.

Mr. BALL. Did you know who made the suggestion you go to the fifth floor?

Mr. JARMAN. Well, I don't know if it was myself or Hank.

Mr. BALL. When you got there was there anybody on the fifth floor?

Mr. JARMAN. No, sir.

Mr. BALL. What did you do when you got to the fifth floor?

Mr. JARMAN. We got out the elevator and pulled the gate down. That was in case somebody wanted to use it. Then we went to the front of the building, which is on the south side, and raised the windows.

Mr. BALL. Which windows did you raise?

Mr. JARMAN. Well, Harold raised the first window to the east side of the building, and I went to the second rear windows and raised, counting the windows, it would be the fourth one.

Mr. BALL. It would be the fourth window?

Mr. JARMAN. Yes.

Mr. BALL. Did somebody join you then?

Mr. JARMAN. Yes, sir; a few minutes later.

Mr. BALL. Who joined you?

Mr. JARMAN. Bonnie Ray Williams.

Mr. BALL. And where did he stand or sit?

Mr. JARMAN. He took the window next to Harold Norman.

Mr. BALL. I show you a picture which is 480, a picture of the Texas School Book Depository Building. Can you show me the window before which you were standing and out of which you were looking?

Mr. JARMAN. This window here.

Mr. BALL. It is marked W on this picture. Where was Harold Norman, the window out of which Harold Norman was looking?

Mr. JARMAN. He was first right here.

Mr. BALL. That is the one marked with a red arrow?

Mr. JARMAN. Yes.

Mr. BALL. Where was Bonnie Ray Williams?

Mr. JARMAN. Bonnie Ray Williams was in this one.

Mr. BALL. Next to the window of Norman, is that right?

Mr. JARMAN. Yes, sir.

Mr. BALL. Was——

Mr. BELIN. What exhibit is that?

Mr. BALL. That is 480. This is 482. You recognize those two pictures?

Mr. JARMAN. Yes, sir.

Mr. BALL. Who are they?

Mr. JARMAN. Harold Norman and Bonnie Ray Williams.

Mr. BALL. Now the other day you went up to the fifth floor of the Texas State School Book Depository with me and a photographer, and had your picture taken, did you not?

Mr. JARMAN. Yes.

Mr. BALL. And what did I ask you to do before the picture was taken?

Mr. JARMAN. To try to get in the same position that we were the day the assassination was.

Mr. BALL. And did you do that?

Mr. JARMAN. Yes, sir. We tried to the best of our knowledge.

Mr. BALL. I have a picture here I would like to have marked as Commission Exhibit 494.

Mr. McCLOY. It is so marked.

(The document referred to was marked Commission Exhibit No. 494 for identification.)

Mr. BALL. Is that your picture?

Mr. JARMAN. Yes, sir.

Mr. BALL. Taken last Friday afternoon, March 20th, is that right?

Mr. JARMAN. Yes, sir.

Mr. BALL. Now does it or does it not show your position at about the time, as you were watching the President's motorcade go by?

Mr. JARMAN. Yes, sir; that is the position I had as it was going by.

Mr. BALL. You are on your knees?

Mr. JARMAN. Right, sir.

Mr. BALL. I show this to each member of the Commission. This is a new exhibit. 485, you recognize that picture?

Mr. JARMAN. Yes, sir.

Mr. BALL. What does it show?

Mr. JARMAN. It shows that I was on my knees as the motorcade was passing.

Mr. BALL. And shows the other two men?

Mr. JARMAN. As the motorcade was passing.

Mr. BALL. It shows their position?

Mr. JARMAN. At the time.

Mr. BALL. At the time the motorcade was passing?

Mr. JARMAN. Right, sir.

Mr. BALL. This has been introduced into evidence. I don't believe you have seen that, Congressman.

Representative FORD. This is yourself here?

Mr. JARMAN. Yes.

Representative FORD. The one closest to an individual looking at the photograph.

Mr. JARMAN. Yes.

Mr. BALL. After the motorcade passed, what happened?

Mr. JARMAN. After the motorcade turned, going west on Elm, then there was a loud shot, or backfire, as I thought it was then—I thought it was a backfire.

Mr. BALL. You thought it was what?

Mr. JARMAN. A backfire or an officer giving a salute to the President. And then at that time I didn't, you know, think too much about it. And then the second shot was fired, and that is when the people started falling on the ground and the motorcade car jumped forward, and then the third shot was fired right behind the second one.

Mr. BALL. Were you still on your knees looking up?

Mr. JARMAN. Well, after the third shot was fired, I think I got up and I run over to Harold Norman and Bonnie Ray Williams, and told them, I said, I told them that it wasn't a backfire or anything, that somebody was shooting at the President.

Mr. BALL. And then did they say anything?

Mr. JARMAN. Hank said, Harold Norman, rather, said that he thought the shots had came from above us, and I noticed that Bonnie Ray had a few debris in his head. It was sort of white stuff, or something, and I told him not to brush it out, but he did anyway.

Mr. BALL. He had some white what, like plaster?

Mr. JARMAN. Like some come off a brick or plaster or something.

Mr. BALL. Did Norman say anything else that you remember?

Mr. JARMAN. He said that he was sure that the shot came from inside the building because he had been used to guns and all that, and he said it didn't sound like it was too far off anyway. And so we ran down to the west side of the building.

Mr. BALL. Did Norman say anything about hearing cartridges or ejection or anything like that, do you remember?

Mr. JARMAN. That was after we got down to the west side of the building.

Mr. BALL. After you got down where?

Mr. JARMAN. To the west side of the building.

Mr. BALL. Down the west side?

Mr. JARMAN. Right.

Mr. BALL. Now you ran down to the west side of the building, did you?

Mr. JARMAN. Yes, sir.

Mr. BALL. And when you were up there you showed me the window to which you ran, didn't you?

Mr. JARMAN. Yes, sir.

Mr. BALL. The picture was taken of you at that place?

Mr. JARMAN. Yes, sir.

Mr. BALL. When you ran down there was the window open or closed?

Mr. JARMAN. It was closed.

Mr. BALL. And who opened it?

Mr. JARMAN. I did.

Mr. BALL. And what did you do after you opened the window?

Mr. JARMAN. I leaned out and the officers and various people was running across the tracks, toward the tracks over there where they had the passenger trains, and all, boxcars and things.

Mr. BALL. I show you 488. What does that show?

Mr. JARMAN. That shows me leaning out the window and Bonnie Ray and Harold Norman was over to the side of me.

Mr. BALL. What window?

Mr. JARMAN. The window on the west side of the building.

Mr. BALL. Is that the one to which you ran after you heard the shots?

Mr. JARMAN. Yes, sir.

Mr. BALL. And you looked out that window?

Mr. JARMAN. Yes, sir.

Mr. BALL. How did you happen to run to that window?

Mr. JARMAN. Well, I wanted to see what was going on mostly, because that was after the motorcade car had took off, and I thought they had stopped under the underpass, but they hadn't. So they went on around the bend, and after I couldn't see from there I ran to another, the second window.

Mr. BALL. That second one you ran to, you pointed that out to me last Friday, did you?

Mr. JARMAN. Yes, sir.

Mr. BALL. And the picture was taken of that, is that right?

Mr. JARMAN. Yes, sir.

Mr. BALL. And that window is on which side?

Mr. JARMAN. On the west side of the building also.

Mr. BALL. I show you 489. Is that a picture of the west window?

Mr. JARMAN. Yes, sir.

Mr. BALL. And what did you see when you looked out that window?

Mr. JARMAN. When I looked out that window, I saw the policemen and the secret agents, the FBI men, searching the boxcar yard and the passenger train and things like that.

Mr. BALL. Where were you when you heard Harold Norman say something that he had heard cartridges?

Mr. JARMAN. All that took place right here in this corner after we had went to this window.

Mr. BALL. This corner. What corner do you mean?

Mr. JARMAN. In the corner of the building right after we had looked out this window.

Mr. BALL. Which corner?

Mr. JARMAN. Right here on the west side of the building.

Mr. BALL. On the west side of the building?

Mr. JARMAN. Right.

Mr. BALL. And would that be the window that is shown in 488, or the window that is shown in 489?

Mr. JARMAN. It was between the two windows.

Mr. BALL. Between the two?

Mr. JARMAN. As we was going to this window.

Mr. BALL. To that window?

Mr. JARMAN. Yes.

Mr. BALL. What did you hear him say?

Mr. JARMAN. He said it was something sounded like cartridges hitting the floor, and he could hear the action of the rifle, I mean the bolt, as it were pulled back, or something like that.

Mr. BALL. Had you heard anything like that?

Mr. JARMAN. No, sir; I hadn't.

Mr. BALL. Had you heard any person running upstairs?

Mr. JARMAN. No, sir.

Mr. BALL. Or any steps upstairs?

Mr. JARMAN. No, sir.

Mr. BALL. Any noise at all up there?

Mr. JARMAN. None.

Mr. BALL. I have here a diagram which is 487. This is the southeast corner of the building on this diagram. Do you recognize that?

Mr. JARMAN. Yes, sir.

Mr. BALL. This is the Elm Street side?

Mr. JARMAN. Yes, sir.

Mr. BALL. Will you point out the window to which you three boys ran when you looked out, you opened the window and looked out towards the——

Mr. JARMAN. This one here.

Mr. BALL. The one marked Y on this diagram?

Mr. JARMAN. Yes.

Mr. BALL. Is that right?

Mr. JARMAN. This one right here.

Mr. BALL. That one marked Y.

Mr. JARMAN. Right.

Mr. BALL. Where is the window to which you went afterwards to look out when you saw the police and other agents searching boxcars?

Mr. JARMAN. I went to the second window from the south side of the building on the west.

Mr. BALL. Is that the one marked Z?

Mr. JARMAN. Yes.

Mr. BALL. At that time could you see the stairwell when you stood there at Z?

Mr. JARMAN. No, sir; I couldn't.

Mr. BALL. Why?

Mr. JARMAN. Because there is a row of bins there with books in them.

Mr. BALL. They block your view?

Mr. JARMAN. Yes, sir.

Mr. BALL. And did we conduct an experiment there to see how much you could see from Z?

Mr. JARMAN. Yes, sir.

Mr. BALL. I show you a picture, 491. Do you remember standing in line near the stairwell?

Mr. JARMAN. Yes, sir.

Mr. BALL. That is you on the end, isn't it?

Mr. JARMAN. Right.

Mr. BALL. On the end, the farthest from the stairwell?

Mr. JARMAN. Yes, sir.

Mr. BALL. And we took a picture, is that right?

Mr. JARMAN. Yes, sir.

Mr. BALL. Of that area. Does that show the bins?

Mr. JARMAN. That shows the bins.

Mr. BALL. I am now referring to 492.

Mr. JARMAN. Yes, sir.

Mr. BALL. Now was there any part of the stairwell that you could see when you were along this west wall?

Mr. JARMAN. No, sir.

Mr. BALL. Could you see the elevators?

Mr. JARMAN. I imagine if I had looked over, but I didn't.

Mr. BALL. Do you remember any of the elevators coming up or down as you were standing there at the west window?

Mr. JARMAN. No, sir.

Mr. BALL. Looking toward the railroad track?

Mr. JARMAN. No, sir.

Mr. BALL. Do you remember seeing Mr. Truly?

Mr. JARMAN. No, sir.

Mr. BALL. Or did you see a motorcycle officer come up?

Mr. JARMAN. No, sir.

Mr. BALL. Or did you hear the elevator go up?

Mr. JARMAN. No, sir.

Mr. BALL. What did you men do after you looked out the window toward the railroad tracks from the west window?

Mr. JARMAN. Well, after Norman had made his statement that he had heard the cartridges hit the floor and this bolt action, I told him we'd better get the hell from up here.

Mr. BALL. Did anybody suggest you go up to the sixth floor?

Mr. JARMAN. No, sir.

Mr. BALL. And where did you go then?

Mr. JARMAN. Down. We ran to the elevator first, but the elevator had gone down.

Mr. BALL. Where did you go?

Mr. JARMAN. Then we ran to the stairway and ran downstairs, and we paused a few minutes on four.

Mr. BALL. Which elevator did you run to?

Mr. JARMAN. To the elevator on the west side.

Mr. BALL. On the west. That wasn't there?

Mr. JARMAN. No, sir.

Mr. BALL. When you went downstairs, what did you see on the first floor?

Mr. JARMAN. When we got downstairs on the first floor, I think the first one I seen was Eddie Piper.

Mr. BALL. Eddie Piper works there, does he?

Mr. JARMAN. Yes, sir.

Mr. BALL. And who else did you see?

Mr. JARMAN. And I ran into Roy Edward Lewis, which is also another employee.

Mr. BALL. Did you see anybody else there?

Mr. JARMAN. No, sir. I ran, then we ran to the front door.

Mr. BALL. You ran to the front door?

Mr. JARMAN. Yes, sir; and out on the street.

Mr. BALL. You and who?

Mr. JARMAN. Harold Norman.

Mr. BALL. You and Harold went out there?

Mr. JARMAN. Yes, sir.

Mr. BALL. Did you ever see a fellow named Brennan?

Mr. JARMAN. Yes, sir.

Mr. BALL. Where did you see him first?

Mr. JARMAN. He was talking to a police officer.

Mr. BALL. How was he dressed?

Mr. JARMAN. He was dressed in construction clothes.

Mr. BALL. Anything else, any other way to describe him?

Mr. JARMAN. Well, he had on a silverlike helmet.

Mr. BALL. Hard-hat?

Mr. JARMAN. Yes, sir.

Mr. BALL. Did you stay out there very long?

Mr. JARMAN. Just a few minutes.

Mr. BALL. Then where did you go?

Mr. JARMAN. We heard him talking to this officer about that he had heard these shots and he had seen the barrel of the gun sticking out the window, and he said that the shots came from inside the building, and I told the officer that I believed that they came from inside the building also, and then he rushed us back inside.

Mr. BALL. The officer did?

Mr. JARMAN. Yes, sir.

Mr. BALL. How did you know this fellow was Brennan?

Mr. JARMAN. Well, at that time I didn't know him at all.

Mr. BALL. Have you learned that since?

Mr. JARMAN. Yes, sir.

Mr. BALL. Who told you that the man in the hard-hat was Brennan?

Mr. JARMAN. Well, they have had him down there at the building a couple of times.

Mr. BALL. Were you taken to the police station?

Mr. JARMAN. Yes, sir.

Mr. BALL. Did you make a statement?

Mr. JARMAN. Yes, sir.

Mr. BALL. When?

Mr. JARMAN. That Saturday morning.

Mr. BALL. The next day?

Mr. JARMAN. Yes, sir.

Mr. BALL. How long did you stay in the building, the Texas School Book Depository Building that afternoon?

Mr. JARMAN. I'd say it was somewhere between two and two-thirty when they turned us loose and told us to go home.

Mr. BALL. When you were there did you notice whether any of the employees were missing?

Mr. JARMAN. Yes, sir.

Mr. BALL. When did you notice, and who was missing?

Mr. JARMAN. When we started to line up to show our identification, quite a few of us asked where was Lee. That is what we called him, and he wasn't anywhere around. We started asking each other, have you seen Lee Oswald, and they said no.

Mr. BALL. Was there anybody else missing?

Mr. JARMAN. Yes.

Mr. BALL. Who.

Mr. JARMAN. Charles Douglas Givens, I believe.

Mr. BALL. Charles Givens?

Mr. JARMAN. Yes, sir.

Mr. BALL. Anybody else?

Mr. JARMAN. I can't recall.

Mr. McCLOY. Had Givens been in the Depository that morning?

Mr. JARMAN. Yes, sir; he had.

Mr. McCLOY. He had been there?

Mr. JARMAN. Yes, sir.

Mr. BALL. Did Givens come back later?

Mr. JARMAN. He didn't come back to the building until they picked him up.

Mr. BALL. He did come back to the building before you left, did he?

Mr. JARMAN. No, sir.

Mr. BALL. He didn't?

Mr. JARMAN. No, sir.

Mr. BALL. He was not there when you left?

Mr. JARMAN. No, sir.

Mr. BALL. When you were on the fifth floor, did you pay any attention to whether or not there was noise above you, before the shots were fired?

Mr. JARMAN. No, sir; I didn't.

Mr. BALL. In other words, if there was noise up there—let's put it this way. If there had been any noise up there, you didn't notice it?

Mr. JARMAN. No, sir; I didn't.

Mr. BALL. Now after the shooting, did you hear any noise from upstairs?

Mr. JARMAN. No, sir.

Mr. BALL. Did you listen for any?

Mr. JARMAN. No, sir.

Mr. BALL. How long was it before you ran down to the west end, from the time of the shots until you ran down to the west end, about how much time do you think it was?

Mr. BALL. After the third shot was fired I would say it was about a minute.

Mr. McCLOY. You have had military experience, haven't you?

Mr. JARMAN. Yes, sir.

Mr. McCLOY. And you can recognize rifle shots when you hear them?

Mr. JARMAN. Yes, sir.

Mr. McCLOY. But you didn't hear, you didn't catch the sound of the bolt moving?

Mr. JARMAN. No, sir.

Mr. McCLOY. Did you see the President actually hit by the bullets?

Mr. JARMAN. No, sir. I couldn't say that I saw him actually hit, but after the second shot, I presumed that he was, because I had my eye on his car from the time it came down Houston until the time it started toward the freeway underpass.

Mr. McCLOY. You saw him crumple, you saw him fall, did you?

Mr. JARMAN. I saw him lean his head.

Representative FORD. You actually saw the car lurch forward, did you?

Mr. JARMAN. Yes, sir.

Representative FORD. That is a distinct impression?

Mr. JARMAN. Yes.

Representative FORD. And you had followed it as it turned from Main on to Houston and followed it as it turned from Houston on to Elm?

Mr. JARMAN. Right, sir.

Representative FORD. Had your eye on the car all the time?

Mr. JARMAN. Yes, sir.

Representative FORD. Where did you think the sound of the first shot came from? Do you have a distinct impression of that?

Mr. JARMAN. Well, it sounded, I thought at first it had came from below. That is what I thought.

Representative FORD. As you looked out the window and you were looking at the President's car.

Mr. JARMAN. Yes, sir.

Representative FORD. Did you have a distinct impression as to whether the sound came from your left or from your right?

Mr. JARMAN. I am sure it came from the left.

Representative FORD. But your first reaction, that is was from below.

Mr. JARMAN. Yes, sir.

Representative FORD. When the second shot came, do you have any different recollection?

Mr. JARMAN. Well, they all sounded just about the same.

Representative FORD. You distinctly recall three shots?

Mr. JARMAN. Yes, sir.

Representative FORD. And at what point did you get up from where you were on your knees in the window?

Mr. JARMAN. When the motorcar picked up speed.

Representative FORD. Was this after what you thought was the third shot?

Mr. JARMAN. The third shot; yes.

Representative FORD. Mr. McCloy said you had been in the army 8 years, two 4-year hitches. Was there any doubt in your mind that this was a gunshot, either one of the three?

Mr. JARMAN. Not after the second shot. I didn't have any doubt in my mind then.

Representative FORD. When did you first learn of the President's motorcade route?

Mr. JARMAN. That morning.

Representative FORD. Friday morning, November 22d?

Mr. JARMAN. Yes, sir.

Representative FORD. How did you find out about it?

Mr. JARMAN. The foreman of the employees on the first floor.

Representative FORD. What is his name?

Mr. JARMAN. William Shelley was standing up talking to Mrs. Lee.

Representative FORD. To Mrs. Lee?

Mr. JARMAN. Miss Lee, or Mrs. Lee, I think, and he was discussing to her about the President coming, asked her was she going to stand out there and see him pass.

Representative FORD. About what time Friday morning was this?

Mr. JARMAN. I imagine it would be about—I think it was between 8:30 and 9:00. I am not sure.

Representative FORD. You hadn't read about it in the papers the night before or that morning?

Mr. JARMAN. No, sir.

Representative FORD. When did you have this conversation with Lee Oswald, where he asked you—you told him that the motorcade was coming by the School Book Depository Building?

Mr. JARMAN. It was some time that morning, between 9:30 and 10:30.

Representative FORD. This was after you heard Mr. Shelley and Miss or Mrs. Lee talk?

Mr. JARMAN. Discuss it—yes.

Representative FORD. Did Oswald ask you, or did you initiate the conversation and tell Oswald of the route?

Mr. JARMAN. He asked me.

Representative FORD. What was his reaction?

Mr. JARMAN. After I had told him the route that the President probably would take, he just said, "Oh, I see" and went back to filling orders.

Representative FORD. You testified earlier that you were standing on the steps or in front of the School Depository Building prior to the President's motorcade coming by the building.

Mr. JARMAN. No, sir. I was standing on the sidewalk.

Representative FORD. But in front of the building?

Mr. JARMAN. In front of the building.

Representative FORD. Then you said you went around the building.

Mr. JARMAN. Yes.

Representative FORD. What route did you take? Did you go down Elm or did you go down Houston?

Mr. JARMAN. I went to the corner of the building facing Elm, and turned going north on Houston.

Representative FORD. Can you turn around and—here is the main entrance on Elm Street. And you were standing out on the sidewalk more or less where?

Mr. JARMAN. Right here.

Representative FORD. In which direction did you go then?

Mr. JARMAN. This way.

Representative FORD. You went by the front to the corner of Houston and Elm, and then down Houston towards the loading dock?

Mr. JARMAN. Yes, sir.

Representative FORD. And where did you get on the elevator?

Mr. JARMAN. We walked around to the back entrance and went through this door here, and this elevator here was up on six, I believe. And we walked around the elevator and took the west elevator up.

Representative FORD. How could you tell this elevator was at six?

Mr. JARMAN. Because after we got around to the other side we looked up.

Representative FORD. You could see it was on six?

Mr. JARMAN. Yes.

Representative FORD. This was about what time?

Mr. JARMAN. That was about 12:25 or 12:28.

Representative FORD. You got off the fifth floor?

Mr. JARMAN. Yes, sir.

Representative FORD. As you rode the elevator, you noticed the other one was on the sixth floor?

Mr. JARMAN. Right, sir.

Representative FORD. Have you ever been in any trouble with the police or did you ever have any disciplinary troubles in the Army?

Mr. JARMAN. No, sir.

Mr. BALL. How was Oswald dressed that morning when you saw him at work? Do you remember that?

Mr. JARMAN. I don't exactly recall how he was dressed. I think he had on some dress pants. But I didn't notice the color.

Mr. BALL. What kind of pants?

Mr. JARMAN. Some kind of these slacks you wear.

Mr. BALL. What kind of a shirt?

Mr. JARMAN. Ivy leagues, I believe.

Mr. BALL. What kind of a shirt, do you know?

Mr. JARMAN. He never hardly worked in a shirt. He worked in a T-shirt.

Mr. BALL. Do you remember if he had a T-shirt on that day?

Mr. JARMAN. Yes; he had on a T-shirt that morning.

Mr. BALL. I have no further questions.

Mr. McCloy. Did you see at any time Oswald that morning with a bundle or package of any kind?

Mr. Jarman. No, sir.

The Chairman. When did you first come to the conclusion that any of the shots came from up above you?

Mr. Jarman. After we had ran down to this last window on the west side of the building, and we was discussing it. And then after I got to thinking about all the debris on Bonnie Ray's head, and I thought about that, also. And so I told Hank, I say, "That shot probably did come from upstairs, up over us," and Hank said, "I know it did, because I could hear the action of the bolt, and I could hear the cartridges drop on the floor."

And I told him there we better get the hell from up here.

The Chairman. Now, tell me, when you went downstairs—when you were downstairs and went out the first time, that is, just before you met Brennan, did anyone stop you as you went out the building?

Mr. Jarman. No, sir.

The Chairman. You could have gone right away if you wanted to, could you?

Mr. Jarman. Yes, sir.

The Chairman. And then you happened to run across Brennan, and had this conversation with him?

Mr. Jarman. No. He ran up to the police officer and was telling him about the man sticking a gun out the window. And I heard him telling the officer that.

And I told him that I thought the shots came from inside, too.

The Chairman. I see.

Are you a married man?

Mr. Jarman. Yes, sir.

The Chairman. Do you have a family?

Mr. Jarman. Yes, sir; three children.

The Chairman. I think that is all.

Thank you very much for coming and helping us out. We appreciate it very much.

Mr. Jarman. We are glad to do it.

Mr. Ball. Mr. Chairman, we would like to recall Mr. Brennan.

TESTIMONY OF HOWARD LESLIE BRENNAN RESUMED

Mr. Belin. Mr. Brennan, you are the same Howard Leslie Brennan who testified this morning here?

Mr. Brennan. Yes, sir.

Mr. Belin. Do you know a George Murray, of the National Broadcasting Co.?

Mr. Brennan. I do not.

Mr. Belin. Have you ever worked for the Union Terminal Co.——

Mr. McCloy. You are still under oath, you realize.

Mr. Brennan. Yes, sir.

Mr. Belin. Have you ever worked for the Union Terminal Co. in Dallas?

Mr. Brennan. I have not.

Mr. Belin. Did you ever state to anyone that you heard shots from opposite the Texas School Book Depository and saw smoke and paper wadding come out of boxes on a slope below the railroad trestle at the time of the assassination? Did you ever say that or that, in substance, to anyone?

Mr. Brennan. I did not.

Mr. Belin. That is all.

Mr. Brennan. Is there another Howard Brennan?

Mr. Belin. Well, sir; we don't know. We wanted to know whether or not you ever made this statement to anyone.

Mr. Brennan. No, sir.

The Chairman. Thank you very much, Mr. Brennan.

Mr. Brennan. I would like to ask a question off the record.

The Chairman. Off the record.

(Discussion off the record.)

Mr. BELIN. Next we will call Mr. Truly.

Mr. McCLOY. Will you raise your right hand, and stand?

Do you solemnly swear the testimony you will give in this case will be the truth, the whole truth, and nothing but the truth, so help you God?

Mr. TRULY. I do.

Mr. McCLOY. I would like to state, Mr. Truly, what the purpose of this hearing is.

This is to hear the testimony of several witnesses, or people close to the event of the assassination of the President, to get as much knowledge as we can of the facts concerning that event, which largely centers around the School Book Depository and the people in it, on the afternoon of November 22d.

Will you state for the record your full name?

Mr. TRULY. Roy Sansom Truly.

Mr. BELIN. Mr. Truly, where do you live?

Mr. TRULY. I live at 4932 Jade Drive, Dallas, Tex.

Mr. BELIN. Are you originally from Dallas?

Mr. TRULY. No. I have been in Dallas since 1925.

Mr. BELIN. Where were you born, sir?

Mr. TRULY. Hubbard, Tex.

Mr. BELIN. And what was your birth date?

Mr. TRULY. August 29, 1907.

Mr. BELIN. Mr. Truly, where did you go to school?

Mr. TRULY. I finished high school at Hubbard.

Mr. BELIN. In Texas?

Mr. TRULY. In Texas.

Mr. BELIN. And what did you do after you finished high school?

Mr. TRULY. Well, I came to Dallas in the fall of that year and I have been there ever since.

Mr. BELIN. For whom did you become employed when you came to Dallas?

Mr. TRULY. I believe—my father ran a cafe here in Dallas, and I worked with him a short while. And then in the fall of 1925, I went to work for Higginbotham, Bailey, Logan Co.

Mr. BELIN. What business is that?

Mr. TRULY. That is wholesale drygoods.

Mr. BELIN. And how long did you work with them?

Mr. TRULY. I believe a little less than a year.

Mr. BELIN. And then where did you go?

Mr. TRULY. I went to work for National Casket Co.

Mr. BELIN. And about how long did you work for them?

Mr. TRULY. I couldn't be certain. Several years—maybe 3 or 4 or 5 years.

Mr. BELIN. And in what capacity did you work for them?

Mr. TRULY. Well, I worked in the cloth room, learning the trade of putting in the drapery and things in the caskets.

Mr. BELIN. And from there, where did you go?

Mr. TRULY. I worked a short time at the Dallas Coffin Co., several months. It wasn't very long. And I left there and during the depression I worked for several things. I drove a laundry truck off and on for a couple of years.

(At this point, Representative Ford withdrew from the hearing room.)

Mr. TRULY. I believe I even worked for the WPA back there in those days.

Mr. BELIN. All right.

And after the depression, where did you start working then?

Mr. TRULY. I went to work for the Texas School Book Depository in July 1934.

Mr. BELIN. And have you been employed by the Texas School Book Depository since that date, since July 1934?

Mr. TRULY. That is right.

(At this point, Mr. Dulles entered the hearing room.)

Mr. BELIN. In what capacity have you worked for that company?

Mr. TRULY. First, when I first went to work for this company, I had charge of the miscellaneous order department, which is actually a one-man operation. I filled orders for books other than state-adopted textbooks.

Mr. BELIN. And then what?

Mr. TRULY. I worked on through that time until the present time.

During the war I worked in the North American plant at Arlington.

Mr. BELIN. That is the North American Aviation?

Mr. TRULY. North American Aviation plant at Arlington, for around 14 months, at night. But I continued to hold my job.

Well, I would go down to work 2, 3, 4 hours a day. Shortly after that, I took charge of all the shipping.

Well, I have been superintendent of the operation since some time in the late 1944.

Mr. BELIN. You have been superintendent of the Texas School Book Depository. And do you have any other positions with the company at this time?

Mr. TRULY. I am a director—I am a member of the board of directors of the Texas School Book Depository.

Mr. BELIN. Is that a State organization or a private company?

Mr. TRULY. It is a private corporation.

Mr. BELIN. Mr. Truly, when did you first hear of the name of Lee Harvey Oswald?

Mr. TRULY. I heard the name on or about October 15th.

Mr. BELIN. Of what year?

Mr. TRULY. Of 1963.

Mr. BELIN. And from whom did you hear the name? Could you just relate to the Commission the circumstances, if you would, please?

Mr. TRULY. I received a phone call from a lady in Irving who said her name was Mrs. Paine.

Mr. BELIN. All right.

What did Mrs. Paine say, and what did you say?

Mr. TRULY. She said, "Mr. Truly"—words to this effect—you understand— "Mr. Truly, you don't know who I am but I have a neighbor whose brother works for you. I don't know what his name is. But he tells his sister that you are very busy. And I am just wondering if you can use another man," or words to that effect.

And I told Mrs.—she said, "I have a fine young man living here with his wife and baby, and his wife is expecting a baby—another baby, in a few days, and he needs work desperately."

Now, this is not absolutely—this is as near as I can remember the conversation over the telephone.

And I told Mrs. Paine that—to send him down, and I would talk to him—that I didn't have anything in mind for him of a permanent nature, but if he was suited, we could possibly use him for a brief time.

Mr. BELIN. Was there anything else from that conversation that you remember at all, or not?

Mr. TRULY. No. I believe that was the first and the last time that I talked to Mrs. Paine.

In fact, I could not remember her name afterwards until I saw her name in print, and then it popped into my mind that this was the lady who called me.

Mr. BELIN. All right.

Anything else on—what was this—October 15th—about Lee Harvey Oswald?

Mr. TRULY. Yes, sir; I am sure it was on October 15th.

Mr. BELIN. Anything else you can remember about Lee Harvey Oswald on that day?

Mr. TRULY. She told me she would tell him to come down and see me.

So he came in, introduced himself to me, and I took him in my office and interviewed him. He seemed to be quiet and well mannered.

I gave him an application to fill out, which he did.

Mr. BELIN. Did he fill it out in front of you, or not?

Mr. TRULY. Yes; he did. And he told me—I asked him about experience that he had had, or where he had worked, and he said he had just served his term in the Marine Corps and had received an honorable discharge, and he listed some things of an office nature that he had learned to do in the Marines.

I questioned him about any past activities. I asked him if he had ever had any trouble with the police, and he said, no. So thinking that he was just out of the Marines, I didn't check any further back. I didn't have anything of a permanent nature in mind for him. He looked like a nice young fellow to me—he was quiet and well mannered. He used the word "sir", you know, which a lot of them don't do at this time.

So I told him if he would come to work on the morning of the 16th, it was the beginning of a new pay period. So he filled out his withholding slip, with the exception of the number of dependents.

He asked me if I would hold that for 3 or 4 days, that he is expecting a baby momentarily.

So some 4 days or so later—I don't remember the exact day—he told me that he had this new baby, and he wanted to add one dependent.

He finished filling it out. And I sent it up to Mr. Campbell who makes out the payroll for the company.

Mr. BELIN. Now, on October 15th you saw him fill out the application form for employment in his own writing?

Mr. TRULY. Yes.

Mr. BELIN. You also saw him fill out the withholding slip, except for the number of exemptions, in his own writing, is that correct?

Mr. TRULY. Yes, sir.

Mr. BELIN. Any other conversation that you can remember from your meeting on October 15th?

Mr. TRULY. Well, he told me that he needed a job. He said he had a wife and child to support. And he also repeated that he was expecting a child in a few days.

And I told Lee Oswald that I had some work, that if he could fit in, of a temporary nature, we could put him on. But I didn't have anything in mind of a permanent job at that time, because I didn't have any openings for a permanent person. And he said he would be glad to have any type of work I would give him, because he did need—and he stressed he really needed a job to support his family.

Mr. BELIN. Anything else from that conversation on October 15th?

Mr. TRULY. Nothing that I can recall, except that he seemed to be grateful that I was giving him the chance of a little extra work, if you want to call it that.

He left, and I didn't see him any more until the morning of the 16th.

Mr. BELIN. What were his hours of work to be?

Mr. TRULY. His hours were from 8 in the morning until 4:45 in the afternoon. His lunch period was from 12 to 12:45.

Mr. BELIN. Did you have a time clock there that they punch or not?

Mr. TRULY. No, sir.

Mr. BELIN. The next morning, do you know whether or not he came to work?

Mr. TRULY. He came to work the next morning. I told him what his duties were to be—would be filling book orders. And I told Mr. Shelley, who is on that floor and has charge of the miscellaneous department.

Now, this particular thing as to whether I called a boy or Mr. Shelley did—anyway, we put Lee Oswald with another worker who was experienced in filling orders. This boy showed him the location of the various publishers' stock. He worked with him, it seems to me, like only an hour or two, and then he started filling orders by himself. And from then on he worked alone.

He would occasionally ask the other boys where certain stock items were when he couldn't find them. But he was filling small parcel post and a few freight orders for the various schools—as they would come down from the office.

Mr. BELIN. Well, could you describe how his work progressed as he was working with you?

Mr. TRULY. Well, he seemed to catch on and learn the location of the stock. We have several thousand titles of books in our warehouse. But he was filling mostly one or two publishers' orders.

Mr. BELIN. What publishers were those?

Mr. Truly. The main publisher was Scott, Foresman and Co.

Now, they have quite a lot of small orders, all through the year. They are one of our biggest publishers. So it kept him busy filling mostly their orders, plus some of the smaller publishers. Possibly he filled some of Gregg Publishing Co. and others. But when he would run out of Scott, Foresman orders, he would pick up other orders that might have had several publishers' books on the same order.

Incidentally, not only Scott, Foresman orders were billed separately. There would be other publishers' orders on the same invoice.

Mr. Belin. Well, perhaps you might explain to the Commission just what exactly the nature of your business is, and how an employee would go about filling orders.

Mr. Truly. We are agents for a number of publishers. We furnish offices for those who desire them in Texas. And our business is shipping, inventorying, collecting, doing all the bookkeeping work for the various publishers' books.

Now, we have—most of the publishers' stock is lined up alphabetically by titles or by stock numbers or code numbers, whichever determines that.

And the location of the books—each publisher's books are to themselves. They are not mixed in with several other publishers on the various floors.

On the first floor we have bin stock, shelf stock, we fill a lot of small orders from.

And then in the basement the same.

The fifth and the sixth floor, and part of the seventh floor is overflow stock. It is reserve stock.

But the boys have to go to those floors all during the day to pick up stock and bring it to the first floor in order to process and complete the orders for the checker.

Mr. Dulles. What would reserve stock mean?

Mr. Truly. Actually it is not reserve stock—it is not surplus either. It is part of our stock. But we can carry a limited amount only on the first floor where we do our shipping. So they may get an order for a hundred copies of a certain book and there may only be 10 or 15 or 20 on the shelf on the first floor. They will have to go upstairs and get a carton or two. And they replenish the first floor stock from that.

And many of our freight orders are filled entirely from our reserve stock. And they bring them to the first floor. All orders reach the first floor, where they are checked and processed and packed and shipped from that floor.

Mr. Belin. Where, generally, are Scott, Foresman books kept?

Mr. Truly. On the first floor and the sixth floor. We have a large quantity of their books on the sixth floor.

Mr. Belin. And this is the area where Lee Harvey Oswald worked?

Mr. Truly. That is right.

Mr. Belin. That publisher?

Mr. Truly. That publisher. He had occasion to go to the sixth floor quite a number of times every day, each day, after books.

Mr. Belin. Now, when an order would come in, how would it get to the individual employee, so the employee would go out and pick out the books?

Mr. Truly. The orders came into our office and were processed by our girls, priced and billed by the bill clerks, and then were sent down a little chute to the first floor, a little dumbwaiter, regardless of publisher.

The boys would take them off of this dumbwaiter and carry them over on to a little table near the checker stand.

Various ones would sort out the publishers—sort out the orders by publishers. Scott Foresman could be here, there would be a stock of Gregg and Southwestern over here, we have a number of small publishers, maybe we would group them altogether. And the boys usually know which particular orders they are supposed to fill from, because they know the books, they can tell.

On each order it says, "SF" for Scott, Foresman on each invoice and so forth.

Mr. Belin. Do they just pick up the piece of paper for the order and carry them around with them?

Mr. TRULY. That is right. Most of them use a clipboard. They may have several orders at a time on the clipboard. That saves them going back to the table continually for one order. These orders amount from anything to $3 or $4 to $300 or $400, on up.

But usually if a boy is filling Scott, Foresman's orders, for instance, and he sees half a dozen over there, he will pick up maybe that many.

But during our busy season, when we have stacks and stacks of orders on the table, they don't try to put them all on a clipboard, they take a few at a time—when they go to the sixth floor after stock, they try to be certain what they need for several orders at one trip.

Mr. BELIN. Who else worked on Scott, Foresman other than Lee Harvey Oswald?

Mr. TRULY. Well, I assume that all of our boys, all of our order fillers have worked at some time or other, because when the boys finish up the stocks they are working, the orders they are filling, if there is anything left, regardless of publisher, they go fill it.

But Scott, Foresman was one of our publishers that I would say would be easiest for a new man to learn how to fill.

And we have a lot of those orders.

You can give a new man those orders, once he understands a little about the alphabetical arrangement, the location of the stock, and he can go ahead and fill orders, and you won't have to keep showing him things. They are easier to fill.

Usually the boys that fill a lot of the other orders are the boys that have had more experience overall, they have been there some time, and they will know the general location of all the stock, and it is just easier for an experienced man to fill some other orders.

Mr. BELIN. When they fill the orders, they go and get the books, and bring them down to your wrapping and mailing section?

Mr. TRULY. That is right. And they are checked to see that they are in correct quantities and titles and called for on the order, or the invoice.

Then they are weighed up on parcel post scales, if they go by parcel post, or they are processed over on the floor if they are big enough for freight.

Mr. BELIN. And, as I understand it, they would first look to see if the title would be on the first floor in your bins, and then only if it wasn't on the first floor would they go up to some of the upper floors with your reserve stock, is that correct?

Mr. TRULY. That is right.

Mr. BELIN. Anything else you can think of with regard to the particular nature of the type of work that Lee Harvey Oswald did when he was working for your company?

Mr. TRULY. Nothing—except that we have occasionally—we would check the number of orders that each boy filled per day, to see if he is doing a day's work. And each invoice which is the billing of the order, has a little section for a checker's number. And the order filler's number. Our checker periodically would count at the end of the day the number of orders that each order filler filled that day.

We could tell at that time whether some of them were doing much more work than others.

And we also kept a list of mistakes that he catches a boy making, such as filling the wrong quantity of books, or the wrong title. We didn't do that every day, because it is a top heavy thing, and if we have to keep a check on your boys all the time, it is not worthwhile.

Mr. BELIN. What did you find generally—would you classify Lee Harvey Oswald as an average employee—above average, or below average employee?

Mr. TRULY. I would say for the nature of the work and the time he was there, the work that he did was a bit above average. I wasn't on that floor constantly. The boy, from all reports to me, and what I have seen kept working and talked little to anybody else. He just kept moving. And he did a good day's work.

Mr. BELIN. What was his pay?

Mr. TRULY. $1.25 an hour.

Mr. BELIN. 5-day week?

Mr. TRULY. Yes.

Mr. BELIN. Did he miss many days of work?

Mr. TRULY. We had no record of him missing any days.

Mr. BELIN. By the way, was your company open on Armistice Day, November 11th, or not? If you know.

Mr. TRULY. We usually are closed on that day.

Now, I just cannot remember whether we were closed that day or not.

Mr. BELIN. I hand you what has been marked Commission Exhibit No. 496, which appears to be a photostatic copy of a document, and I ask you to state if you know what that is.

(The document referred to was marked Commission Exhibit No. 496 for identification.)

Mr. TRULY. This is a copy of the application blank that Oswald filled out. I am not familiar with his handwriting, because he didn't do anything that we have records of. All the work that he ever did was put his number or something.

Mr. BELIN. Well, my first question is this: Is this particular form a form of your company?

Mr. TRULY. That is one form; yes. We changed it a little bit, and this might have been just one that I pulled out. I can't recall whether it is the one we use now or the one we did use.

Mr. BELIN. Well, was this a form that you were using at about the time he came for employment?

Mr. TRULY. Yes.

(At this point, Representative Ford entered the hearing room.)

Mr. BELIN. Did you see him fill this out? Was it in your office or not?

Mr. TRULY. Yes. He was sitting opposite me, and he filled it out on my desk.

Mr. BELIN. He filled this Exhibit 496 out on your desk?

Mr. TRULY. Yes.

Mr. BELIN. At this time we offer in evidence Exhibit 496.

495 as yet has not been offered. And I don't know if 494 has been offered or not.

But, in the event it has not, we offer that in evidence.

Mr. McCLOY. It may be admitted.

(The documents heretofore marked for identification as Commission Exhibits Nos. 494, 495, and 496 were received in evidence.)

Mr. BELIN. Mr. Truly, are there any other observations you can give about Lee Harvey Oswald as an employee during the month of October 1963, or during the month of November, prior to November 22, 1963?

Mr. TRULY. Nothing that I can recall.

I would speak to him in the morning when I would come through, and I would say, "Good morning, Lee," and he would say, "Good morning, sir."

I would ask him how he was. Occasionally I would ask about his baby, and he would usually smile a big smile when I asked him how his new baby was. And that was just about the extent of my conversation that I can remember with the boy.

But I usually saw him every morning as I would come through. He would be working around the front part of the Scott, Foresman bins and shelf space.

Mr. BELIN. Did you ever see whether or not he seemed to strike up any friendship or acquaintanceship with the other employees?

Mr. TRULY. No; I never noticed that anywheres. In fact, I would be inclined—well—I never saw him with anyone else, except occasionally talking, maybe asking where books were or something.

I don't know what he would say. But very little conversation he had with anyone.

And he worked by himself. His job was something that he needed no help with, other than to ask occasionally for stock. It wasn't a teamwork job at all.

Consequently, he didn't have much occasion to talk with the other boys. I thought it was a pretty good trait at the time, because occasionally you have to spread your boys out and say, "Quit talking so much, let's get to work."

And it seemed to me like he paid attention to his job.

Mr. BELIN. Did you notice whether or not he brought his lunch to work generally?

Mr. TRULY. I never was aware that he brought a lunch. I would see him occasionally in the shipping department eating some little snack or something—didn't pay much attention. Offhand, it seemed to be not too much—a Coca-Cola, Dr. Pepper, and some little thing.

Maybe he would be sitting there reading a book or a newspaper.

Mr. BELIN. You would see him occasionally reading a newspaper at the lunch hour?

Mr. TRULY. I am sure so; yes.

And occasionally—I didn't always go to lunch at 12—usually a little after. And he would have to pass my door to go out the front. Occasionally I had seen the boy go out, and maybe he would be gone long enough to get across the street and back, with something in his hand. I seem to recall possibly a newspaper, maybe potato chips or something like that.

Mr. BELIN. Did you ever have any discussions with him about politics or anything like that?

Mr. TRULY. Never.

Mr. BELIN. Prior to November 22, did you have any discussion with him about the Presidential motorcade, or hear him talk to anyone about it?

Mr. TRULY. I never heard him talk to anyone, and I didn't talk to him myself.

Mr. BELIN. Any other things about Lee Harvey Oswald prior to November 22 that you can think of?

Mr. TRULY. Offhand I cannot recall a thing.

Just like I said—he seemed to go about his business in a quiet way, didn't talk much, seemed to be doing a satisfactory job.

Mr. BELIN. If you turn behind you, you will see Commission Exhibit No. 362, and it appears to be a floor plan which is entitled, "Texas School Book Depository." You see the room marked Mr. Truly's office?

Mr. TRULY. That is right.

Mr. BELIN. Does that appear to accurately depict where your office is located? This is the front of the building here at the top.

Mr. TRULY. Yes, sir.

Mr. BELIN. And it was in the place marked Mr. Truly's office that Lee Harvey Oswald filled out in front of you on your desk Exhibit 496?

Mr. TRULY. That is right.

Mr. BELIN. And also the withholding slip?

Mr. TRULY. Yes, sir.

Mr. BELIN. Now I want to take you to the morning of November 22d.

First let me ask you when you first heard your employees discussing the fact that the motorcade would be going by the Texas School Book Depository? Was that first on the morning of November 22d that you heard that, or at any prior date?

Mr. TRULY. I don't recall. I don't recall hearing any particular discussion about him coming by. No, sir; I don't.

Mr. BELIN. All right.

What time did you get to work on November 22d?

Mr. TRULY. Around 8 o'clock, or shortly thereafter.

Mr. BELIN. Did you see Lee Harvey Oswald at any time during that day?

Mr. TRULY. I am almost certain that I saw him early that morning as I came in, and spoke to him.

Mr. BELIN. And where was he when you saw him?

Mr. TRULY. I think he was around the front part of the Scott, Foresman bins.

Mr. BELIN. On what floor?

Mr. TRULY. On the first floor.

Mr. BELIN. Was he filling orders?

Mr. TRULY. Apparently; yes, sir. I don't recall too close. But I am almost certain that I talked to him that morning.

218

Mr. BELIN. Do you recall any conversation you might have had with him, or he might have had with you?

Mr. TRULY. No, sir. If there was anything, I just said "Good morning, Lee", and he said, "Good morning, sir" and that would be the extent of my conversation, if I saw him that morning, which I am almost certain I did.

Mr. BELIN. Did you see him any other time during that day?

Mr. TRULY. I cannot recall. I believe I saw him that morning later on, around his work. But I probably wasn't on that floor too much, or out on the floor that morning.

Mr. BELIN. Now, when did you leave for lunch, Mr. Truly?

Mr. TRULY. As near as I know, it was between somewheres around 12:10 or shortly after, possibly 12:15.

Mr. BELIN. At that time did you go out to lunch?

Mr. TRULY. Yes, sir.

Mr. BELIN. Where did you go to eat?

Mr. TRULY. We didn't go anywheres. Mr. Campbell and I——

Mr. BELIN. That is Mr. O. V. Campbell?

Mr. TRULY. Mr. O. V. Campbell, vice president—and I had started out for lunch. I don't know as we had any particular place in mind. We ate at several places around there.

It was around 12:10 or 12:15, I would say, to the nearest of my memory.

As we got to the outside of the building, we noticed that it wouldn't be long until the motorcade would come by, and we decided to wait and watch the President come by.

Mr. BELIN. Do you remember where you were standing with Mr. Campbell?

Mr. TRULY. I would judge out in Elm Street, 10 to 15 or 20 feet from the front steps. We first stood on the steps, the bottom steps a few minutes, and then we walked out in the line of spectators on the side of Elm Street.

Mr. BELIN. I hand you what has been marked Commission Exhibit 495, and ask you to state, if you know, what this is.

Mr. TRULY. This is the front entrance to our building.

Mr. BELIN. In what direction would the camera be pointing?

Mr. TRULY. Almost straight out from it. It would not be—well, it could be on a little angle.

Mr. BELIN. I mean would the camera be pointing east, west, north, or south?

Mr. TRULY. North.

Mr. BELIN. And the camera would be pointing north on Exhibit 495.

I wonder if on that exhibit you would put the place where you and Mr. Campbell first stood, and mark that with the letter "A" if you would.

Mr. TRULY. The street curved there, I suppose. I think possibly along here somewheres.

Mr. BELIN. You have marked a letter "A" on Exhibit 495. Now, I believe you said that afterwards you went and moved out towards the street, is that correct?

Mr. TRULY. That is right.

Mr. BELIN. I am going to put up on the board Commission Exhibit No. 361. The bottom of the picture is relatively north, sir.

And the top faces roughly south.

And here is the Texas School Book Depository Building—located at Houston and Elm.

Mr. TRULY. That is right.

Mr. BELIN. I wonder if you could put on Exhibit 361 with the letter "T" the spot at which you were standing when you moved to a closer position to watch the motorcade.

Mr. TRULY. I could be off a few feet, but I believe possibly over this way just a bit—that is within 3 or 4 or 5 feet of this area.

We were almost out in this. And I think when the motorcade came around, we probably pushed out even a bit farther.

Mr. BELIN. Now, by this, you are referring to the entrance to the parkway, is that correct?

Mr. TRULY. Yes.

Mr. BELIN. And you say that you are either at the spot marked by the letter "T" or perhaps a little bit to the east of that?

Mr. TRULY. That is right.

Mr. BELIN. And that you gradually might have moved a little bit towards the south, towards the parkway, is that correct?

Mr. TRULY. That is correct.

Mr. BELIN. All right.

Do you know approximately what time you got there, Mr. Truly? To the best of your recollection.

Mr. TRULY. 3 or 4 minutes after we reached the entrance, the walkway, we stood on the steps 2 or 3 minutes, and then I don't believe—we just gradually moved out a bit.

And then when the policemen leading the motorcade came off of Main on to Houston, we saw them coming, and then we just moved out a little farther to the edge of the parkway.

Mr. BELIN. Did you notice any other company employees with you other than Mr. Campbell at that time?

Mr. TRULY. Well, I did. I noticed several. Mrs. Reid was standing there close. And it seemed like there were several of the other employees standing out in front of the building. But I cannot—I think Bill Shelley was standing over to my right as I faced the motorcade—somewheres in that area.

I noticed just before the motorcade passed there were, I believe, three of our colored boys had come out and started up, and two of them came back. And I didn't see them when the motorcade passed.

But they had started across Houston Street up Elm, and they came back later on, and I think those were the ones that were—two of them were the ones on the fifth floor. Possibly they could not see over the crowd. They are short boys. I wasn't doing too well at that, myself.

Mr. BELIN. All right.

What did you next see with reference to the motorcade?

Mr. TRULY. Do you mind me——

Mr. BELIN. Do you want to turn that over, sir? Will that be easier for you?

Mr. TRULY. It might be easier for the gentlemen when I point this out.

Now, what was the question?

Mr. BELIN. My question is what did you see with reference to the motorcade?

Mr. TRULY. All right.

We saw the motorcycle escort come off of Main and turn onto Houston Street.

Mr. BELIN. Main would be down here, and it would be coming off Houston, heading towards the building?

Mr. TRULY. Headed towards the building.

Mr. BELIN. All right.

Mr. TRULY. And it went on down this way. And immediately after——

Mr. BELIN. By "this way" you mean the street marked Parkway?

Mr. TRULY. I assume that is the underpass that you have marked Parkway.

Mr. BELIN. The street leading to the expressway, that diagonal street?

Mr. TRULY. That is right.

And the President's car following close behind came along at an average speed of 10 or 15 miles an hour. It wasn't that much, because they were getting ready to turn. And the driver of the Presidential car swung out too far to the right, and he came almost within an inch of running into this little abutment here, between Elm and the Parkway. And he slowed down perceptibly and pulled back to the left to get over into the middle lane of the parkway. Not being familiar with the street, he came too far out this way when he made his turn.

Mr. BELIN. He came too far to the north before he made his curve, and as he curved—as he made his left turn from Houston onto the street leading to the expressway, he almost hit this north curb?

Mr. TRULY. That is right. Just before he got to it, he had to almost stop, to pull over to the left.

If he had maintained his speed, he would probably have hit this little section here.

Mr. BELIN. All right.

Now, what is your best estimate of the speed as he started to go down the street here marked Parkway?

Mr. TRULY. He picked up a little speed along here, and then seemed to have fallen back into line, and I would say 10 or 12 miles an hour in this area.

Mr. BELIN. All right.

Then what did you see happen?

Mr. TRULY. I heard an explosion, which I thought was a toy cannon or a loud firecracker from west of the building. Nothing happened at this first explosion. Everything was frozen. And immediately after two more explosions, which I realized that I thought was a gun, a rifle of some kind.

The President's—I saw the President's car swerve to the left and stop somewheres down in this area. It is misleading here. And that is the last I saw of his car, because this crowd, when the third shot rang out—there was a large crowd all along this abutment here, this little wall, and there was some around us in front—they began screaming and falling to the ground. And the people in front of myself and Mr. Campbell surged back, either in terror or panic. They must have seen this thing. I became separated from Mr. Campbell. They just practically bore me back to the first step on the entrance of our building.

Mr. BELIN. When you saw the President's car seem to stop, how long did it appear to stop?

Mr. TRULY. It would be hard to say over a second or two or something like that. I didn't see—I just saw it stop. I don't know. I didn't see it start up.

Mr. BELIN. Then you stopped looking at it, or you were distracted by something else?

Mr. TRULY. Yes. The crowd in front of me kind of congealed around me and bore me back through weight of numbers, and I lost sight of it.

I think there were a lot of people trying to get out of the way of something. They didn't know what.

Mr. BELIN. Then what did you do or see?

Mr. TRULY. I heard a policeman in this area along here make a remark, "Oh, goddam," or something like that. I just remember that. It wasn't a motorcycle policeman. It was one of the Dallas policeman, I think—words to that effect.

I wouldn't know him. I just remember there was a policeman standing along in this area about 7, 8, or 10 feet from me.

But as I came back here, and everybody was screaming and hollering, just moments later I saw a young motorcycle policeman run up to the building, up the steps to the entrance of our building. He ran right by me. And he was pushing people out of the way. He pushed a number of people out of the way before he got to me. I saw him coming through, I believe. As he ran up the stairway—I mean up the steps, I was almost to the steps, I ran up and caught up with him. I believe I caught up with him inside the lobby of the building, or possibly the front steps. I don't remember that close. But I remember it occurred to me that this man wants on top of the building. He doesn't know the plan of the floor. And that is—that just popped in my mind, and I ran in with him. As we got in the lobby, almost on the inside of the first floor, this policeman asked me where the stairway is. And I said, "This way". And I ran diagonally across to the northwest corner of the building.

Mr. BELIN. Now, let me, if I can—turning to Exhibit 362 again, I wonder if you would, with this—we can first do it with this pen, if you would—trace your route inside there. Point out the place inside the lobby where you talked to the policeman, where he said "where is the stairway."

Mr. TRULY. I believe along right there.

Mr. BELIN. All right. Could you put a "T" on Exhibit 362, if you would.

Mr. TRULY. I could be wrong, but I am almost positive that is the place.

Mr. BELIN. All right.

Now—and this is inside the glass or plastic set of doors shown on Exhibit 495, is that correct?

Mr. TRULY. That is correct.

Mr. BELIN. Now, he said to you what?

Mr. TRULY. Where is the stairway.

Mr. BELIN. And what did you say to him?

Mr. TRULY. I said "This way."

Mr. BELIN. Now, I wonder if you would take this pen and show the route that you took with the policeman, or take your own pen, if you would, sir—starting from point "T" on Exhibit 362.

Mr. TRULY. I ran in front of him.

Mr. BELIN. You better mark on the exhibit, sir.

Mr. TRULY. Took this route. There is a swinging door and a counter, what we call our will call counter right here.

Mr. BELIN. Is it here, or here?

Mr. TRULY. No, wait a minute.

There—right here. We came in this way.

Mr. BELIN. Do you still want to put point "T" up here?

Mr. TRULY. No. This was on the steps, wasn't it? This is where I am sure he asked me.

Mr. BELIN. You better cross out the other one, then.

Mr. TRULY. I saw this thing here, and I thought it was that little swinging door.

Mr. BELIN. That would be the main door?

Now, you have point "T."

Now, will you trace the route from point "T"?

Mr. TRULY. We came through this door here. The policeman right behind me.

Mr. BELIN. All right.

Mr. TRULY. This is a counter and this is a counter built in that cut inside—this is where our customers come that pick up books.

Mr. BELIN. All right.

When you are pointing to the counter on Exhibit 362, you are pointing to a rectangle that appears to be located immediately to the west of the glass—looks like a glass partition to your office, is that correct?

Mr. TRULY. That is right.

Mr. BELIN. You call that the will call counter?

Mr. TRULY. That is right.

Mr. BELIN. What happened when you got there?

Mr. TRULY. There is a little swinging door that swings in and out that we have there. We never keep it locked. But on the bottom is a little bolt that you can lock it to keep people from pulling it out or pushing it in. And this bolt had slid out. It has done that on occasions. I started to run through this little opening, and I ran into the door, and the bolt hung against the side of the counter, and the policeman ran into my back. And so I just pulled it back and continued on through.

Mr. BELIN. All right.

Now, the door didn't swing through. The bolt stuck. So you were stuck by the door. The policeman ran into you. And then you had to stop and pull the door back and go through it.

Mr. TRULY. That is right.

Mr. BELIN. Then where did you go? You might continue with your pen on Exhibit 362, showing the route.

All right.

Now, you have cut sort of diagonally across towards the rear, and you have come to the west elevator in the rear.

Mr. TRULY. That is right.

Mr. BELIN. Let me ask you this, Mr. Truly. I note on Exhibit 362 right where you came in there appears to be some stairs there. Why didn't you go up those stairs, instead of running to the back?

Mr. TRULY. Those stairs only reached to the second floor, and they wouldn't have any way of getting up to the top without going to the back stairway.

Mr. BELIN. All right.

Mr. TRULY. So this is the logical stairway that goes all the way to the seventh floor.

Mr. BELIN. And you are pointing to the stairway in what would be the northwest corner?

Mr. TRULY. That is right.

Mr. BELIN. Now, you got to the elevator, and what did you do then?

Mr. TRULY. I looked up. This is two elevators in the same well. This elevator over here——

Mr. BELIN. You are pointing to the west one?

Mr. TRULY. I am pointing to the west one. This elevator was on the fifth floor. Also, the east elevator—as far as I can tell—both of them were on the fifth floor at that time.

This elevator will come down if the gates are down, and you push a button.

Representative FORD. Which elevator is that?

Mr. TRULY. The west one. But the east one will not come down unless you get on it and bring it down. You cannot call it if the gates are down.

Representative FORD. That is the east elevator?

Mr. TRULY. The east elevator?

There is a button and a little bell here. I pressed——

Mr. BELIN. You might put a "B" on Exhibit 362 by the elevator for "button."

Mr. TRULY. That is right on this surface. There is a little button. I pressed the button and the elevator didn't move.

I called upstairs "Turn loose the elevator."

Mr. BELIN. When you say call up, in what kind of a voice did you call?

Mr. TRULY. Real loud. I suppose in an excited voice. But loud enough that anyone could have heard me if they had not been over stacking or making a little noise. But I rang the bell and pushed this button.

Mr. BELIN. What did you call?

Mr. TRULY. I said, "Turn loose the elevator."

Those boys understand that language.

Mr. BELIN. What does that mean?

Mr. TRULY. That means if they have the gates up, they go pull the gates down, and when you press the button, you can pull it down.

Mr. BELIN. And how many times did you yell that?

Mr. TRULY. Two times.

Mr. BELIN. After you had first pushed the button?

Mr. TRULY. That is right. I had pressed the button twice, I believe, and called up for the elevator twice.

Mr. BELIN. Then what did you do?

First of all, did the elevator come down?

Mr. TRULY. It did not.

Mr. BELIN. All right.

Then what did you do?

Mr. TRULY. I went up on a run up the stairway.

Mr. BELIN. Could you again follow—from Point B, could you show which way you went?

All right.

Mr. TRULY. What is this here?

Mr. BELIN. This is to show this is a stairway, and there is a stairway above it, too. But you went up the stairs right here?

Mr. TRULY. That is right.

Mr. BELIN. Okay. And where was this officer at that time?

Mr. TRULY. This officer was right behind me and coming up the stairway. By the time I reached the second floor, the officer was a little further behind me than he was on the first floor, I assume—I know.

Mr. BELIN. Was he a few feet behind you then?

Mr. TRULY. He was a few feet. It is hard for me to tell. I ran right on around to my left, started to continue on up the stairway to the third floor, and on up.

Mr. BELIN. Now, when you say you ran on to your left, did you look straight ahead to see whether there was anyone in that area, or were you intent on just going upstairs?

Mr. TRULY. If there had been anybody in that area, I would have seen him on the outside. But I was content—I was trying to show the officer the pathway up, where the elevators—I mean where the stairways continued.

Mr. BELIN. Now, I hand you what has been marked Exhibit 497.

(The document referred to was marked Commission Exhibit No. 497, for identification.)

Mr. BELIN. This is entitled "Texas School Book Depository, Diagram of Second Floor."

You can sit down, if you would, please, Mr. Truly.

And would you, on Exhibit 497, if you would kind of take an arrow to show the route that you took going out—or up from the first floor, and starting up the stairs towards the third.

Now, you marked that with pen.

Could you put a "T" on that, if you would, please?

Now, there appears to be some kind of a vestibule or hall of one kind or another with the No. 22 in a circle on it, on Exhibit 497. Is this completely clear, or are there books there from time to time?

Mr. TRULY. No; that is always clear. There is a few cartons of office stock, invoices, blank invoices and stationery and stuff up and down here. But there is always a pathway. There is a post, right about where this 22 is. You can always clear it and come by there. I don't think there would ever be stock here that would obstruct your view of the other area across there.

Mr. BELIN. Now, I hand you what has been marked Commission Exhibit 498.

(The document referred to was marked Commission Exhibit No. 498 for identification.)

Mr. BELIN. I ask you to state, if you know what this is.

Mr. TRULY. Yes. This is the vestibule, when you first come up the stairs on the second floor—this is what you will find right there.

Mr. BELIN. Now, as you take a look at the picture Exhibit 498, is this a post immediately to the left side of the picture, to the extreme left of the picture?

Mr. TRULY. No.

Mr. BELIN. What is this, to the extreme left? Is that the wall for the staircase?

Mr. TRULY. Yes; there is an opening on this side, and the staircase is back over here. This picture is just part of this vestibule out here.

Mr. BELIN. And what direction does the camera appear to be pointing, or what is shown there?

Mr. TRULY. It appears to be pointing east.

Mr. BELIN. And I see a door with a glass in it.

Could you show where on this diagram Exhibit 497 this door with the glass is?

Do you see a number with an arrow pointing to the door?

Mr. TRULY. That is it.

Mr. BELIN. What number is that?

Mr. TRULY. It is number 23.

Mr. BELIN. All right. Number 23, the arrow points to the door that has the glass in it.

Now, as you raced around, how far did you start up the stairs towards the third floor there?

Mr. TRULY. I suppose I was up two or three steps before I realized the officer wasn't following me.

Mr. BELIN. Then what did you do?

Mr. TRULY. I came back to the second floor landing.

Mr. BELIN. What did you see?

Mr. TRULY. I heard some voices, or a voice, coming from the area of the lunchroom, or the inside vestibule, the area of 24.

Mr. BELIN. All right. And I see that there appears to be on the second floor diagram, a room marked lunchroom.

Mr. TRULY. That is right.

Mr. BELIN. What did you do then?

Mr. TRULY. I ran over and looked in this door No. 23.

Mr. BELIN. Through the glass, or was the door open?

Mr. TRULY. I don't know. I think I opened the door. I feel like I did. I don't remember.

Mr. BELIN. It could have been open or it could have been closed, you do not remember?

Mr. TRULY. The chances are it was closed.

Mr. BELIN. You thought you opened it?

Mr. TRULY. I think I opened it. I opened the door back and leaned in this way.

Mr. BELIN. What did you see?

Mr. TRULY. I saw the officer almost directly in the doorway of the lunchroom facing Lee Harvey Oswald.

Mr. BELIN. And where was Lee Harvey Oswald at the time you saw him?

Mr. TRULY. He was at the front of the lunchroom, not very far inside—he was just inside the lunchroom door.

Mr. BELIN. All right.

Mr. TRULY. 2 or 3 feet, possibly.

Mr. BELIN. Could you put an "O" where you saw Lee Harvey Oswald? All right.

You have put an "O" on Exhibit 497.

What did you see or hear the officer say or do?

Mr. TRULY. When I reached there, the officer had his gun pointing at Oswald. The officer turned this way and said, "This man work here?" And I said, "Yes."

Mr. BELIN. And then what happened?

Mr. TRULY. Then we left Lee Harvey Oswald immediately and continued to run up the stairways until we reached the fifth floor.

Mr. BELIN. All right.

Let me ask you this now. How far was the officer's gun from Lee Harvey Oswald when he asked the question?

Mr. TRULY. It would be hard for me to say, but it seemed to me like it was almost touching him.

Mr. BELIN. What portion of his body?

Mr. TRULY. Towards the middle portion of his body.

Mr. BELIN. Could you see Lee Harvey Oswald's hands?

Mr. TRULY. Yes.

Mr. BELIN. Could you see——

Mr. TRULY. I am sure I could, yes. I could see most of him, because I was looking in the room on an angle, and they were this way.

Mr. BELIN. When you say you were looking in the room on an angle——

Mr. TRULY. What I mean—this door offsets the lunchroom door.

Mr. BELIN. By this door, you mean door No. 23 is at an angle to door No. 24?

Mr. TRULY. Yes. One this way and the other one is this way.

Mr. BELIN. All right.

Could you see whether or not Lee Harvey Oswald had anything in either hand?

Mr. TRULY. I noticed nothing in either hand.

Mr. BELIN. Did you see both of his hands?

Mr. TRULY. I am sure I did. I could be wrong, but I am almost sure I did.

Mr. BELIN. About how long did Officer Baker stand there with Lee Harvey Oswald after you saw them?

Mr. TRULY. He left him immediately after I told him—after he asked me, does this man work here. I said, yes. The officer left him immediately.

Mr. BELIN. Did you hear Lee Harvey Oswald say anything?

Mr. TRULY. Not a thing.

Mr. BELIN. Did you see any expression on his face? Or weren't you paying attention?

Mr. TRULY. He didn't seem to be excited or overly afraid or anything. He might have been a bit startled, like I might have been if somebody confronted me. But I cannot recall any change in expression of any kind on his face.

Mr. BELIN. Now, I hand you what the reporter has marked as Exhibit 499.

(The document referred to was marked Commission Exhibit No. 499 for identification.)

Mr. BELIN. I ask you to state if you know what this is.

Mr. TRULY. That is the interior of the lunchroom.

Mr. BELIN. And what direction does the camera appear to be pointing on Exhibit 499?

Mr. TRULY. East.

Mr. BELIN. And does this appear to be the doorway in the very foreground of the picture?

Mr. TRULY. I believe so.

Representative FORD. Which doorway would that be?

Mr. TRULY. Number 24. The camera seems to be right in the doorway when that picture was taken. You cannot see the doorway very well.

Mr. DULLES. May I ask you a question?

Do you know why it was that the officer didn't follow you up the stairs, but instead was distracted, as it were, and went with Lee Harvey Oswald into the lunchroom?

Mr. TRULY. I never knew until a day or two ago that he said he saw a movement, saw a man going away from him.

Mr. DULLES. As he was going up the stairs?

Mr. TRULY. As he got to the second floor landing. While I was going around, he saw a movement.

Mr. DULLES. And he followed that?

Mr. TRULY. That is right.

Representative FORD. He saw a movement in the lunchroom or a man go into the lunchroom?

Mr. TRULY. He saw the back of a man inside the door—I suppose door No. 23. But that isn't my statement. I didn't learn about that, you see, until the other day.

Mr. BELIN. I believe we have some additional pictures of the lunchroom. Perhaps we can just briefly identify them.

Here is a picture which has been marked Commission Exhibit 500.

(The document referred to was marked Commission Exhibit No. 500 for identification.)

Mr. BELIN. I will ask you to state what this is.

Mr. TRULY. This is a picture of the lunchroom.

Mr. BELIN. What direction is the camera facing there?

Mr. TRULY. East.

Mr. BELIN. What about Exhibit 501?

(The document referred to was marked Commission Exhibit No. 501 for identification.)

Mr. TRULY. This picture is part of the lunchroom. And I would say the camera must be facing northeast.

Mr. BELIN. What about Exhibit 502?

Mr. TRULY. This is the lunchroom looking west. Northwest, I would say.

Mr. BELIN. Is this door clear to the left of the picture, the door in which you saw Officer Baker standing when he was talking to Lee Harvey Oswald?

Mr. TRULY. Yes, sir.

Mr. BELIN. Now, Mr. Truly, you then went up to the third floor with Officer Baker.

Mr. TRULY. We continued on until we reached the fifth floor.

Mr. BELIN. Now, by the way, I have used the name Officer Baker.

When did you find out what his name was?

Mr. TRULY. I never did know for sure what his name was until he was down to the building and you were interviewing him last week.

Mr. BELIN. This was on Friday, March 20th?

Mr. TRULY. I had heard his name was Baker or Burton or various other names. But I never did try to find out what his name was.

Mr. BELIN. All right.

(The document referred to was marked Commission Exhibit No. 502 for identification.)

Mr. BELIN. Now, Mr. Truly, did you notice when you got to the third floor—first of all. On the second floor, was there any elevator there?

Mr. TRULY. No, sir.

Mr. BELIN. What about the third floor?

Mr. TRULY. No, sir.

Mr. BELIN. Fourth floor?

Mr. TRULY. No, I am sure not.

Mr. BELIN. What about the fifth floor?

Mr. TRULY. When we reached the fifth floor, the east elevator was on that floor.

Mr. BELIN. What about the west elevator? Was that on the fifth floor?

Mr. TRULY. No, sir. I am sure it wasn't, or I could not have seen the east elevator.

Mr. BELIN. All right.

Mr. TRULY. I am almost positive that it wasn't there.

Mr. DULLES. You said you released the elevator and let it go down?

Mr. TRULY. No; the east elevator was the one on the fifth floor.

Mr. BELIN. Now, Exhibit 487 appears to be a diagram of the fifth floor. As I understand it, you might mark on that diagram the way you went from the stairs over to the east elevator.

Mr. TRULY. Well, I started around towards the stairway, and then I noted that this east elevator was there. So I told the officer, "Come on, here is an elevator," and then we ran down to the east side, and got on the east elevator.

Mr. BELIN. Could you put the letter "T" at the end of that line, please?

All right.

Now, where did you go with the east elevator, to what floor?

Mr. TRULY. We rode the east elevator to the seventh floor.

Mr. BELIN. Did you stop at the sixth floor at all?

Mr. TRULY. No, sir.

Mr. BELIN. What did you do when you got to the seventh floor?

Mr. TRULY. We ran up a little stairway that leads out through a little penthouse on to the roof.

Mr. BELIN. What did you do on the roof?

Mr. TRULY. We ran immediately to the west side of the building. There is a wall around the building that you cannot see over without getting your foot between the mortar of the stones and, or some such toehold. We did that and looked over the ground and the railroad tracks below. There we saw many officers and a lot of spectators, people running up and down.

Mr. BELIN. Did the officer say to you why he wanted to go up to the roof?

Mr. TRULY. No. At that time, he didn't.

Mr. BELIN. Did he ever prior to meeting you again on March 20th tell you why he wanted to go on the roof?

Mr. TRULY. No, sir.

Mr. BELIN. Where did you think the shots came from?

Mr. TRULY. I thought the shots came from the vicinity of the railroad or the WPA project, behind the WPA project west of the building.

Mr. BELIN. Did you have any conversation with the officer that you can remember? About where you thought the shots came from?

Mr. TRULY. Yes. When—some time in the course, I believe, after we reached the roof, the officer looked down over the boxcars and the railroad tracks and the crowd below. Then he looked around the edge of the roof for any evidence of anybody being there. And then looked up at the runways and the big sign on the roof.

He saw nothing.

He came over. And some time about then I said, "Officer, I think"—let's back up.

I believe the officer told me as we walked down into the seventh floor, "Be careful, this man will blow your head off."

And I told the officer that I didn't feel like the shots came from the building. I said, "I think we are wasting our time up here," or words to that effect, "I don't believe these shots came from the building."

Mr. BELIN. Did he say anything to that at all?

Mr. TRULY. I don't recall exactly what he said. I believe he said, yes, or somebody said they did, or some such thing as that. I don't remember. I have heard so many things since, you know.

Mr. BELIN. All right.

Now, Mr. Truly, on March 20th, you and I visited about this particular incident you have related about the running into the building and up the stairs with this officer, is that correct?

Mr. TRULY. That is correct.

Mr. BELIN. And as a matter of fact you and Officer Baker and I tried to reconstruct the incident in an effort to determine how long it took you to do all this, is that correct?

Mr. TRULY. That is correct.

Mr. BELIN. And do you remember watching me getting over with Officer Baker in front of the sheriff's office on Market Street—pardon me—Houston Street, with a stopwatch?

Mr. TRULY. Yes, sir.

Mr. BELIN. And then you saw Officer Baker race his motorcycle over and come in front of the building, and then you ran in with him, is that correct?

Mr. TRULY. That is correct.

Mr. BELIN. And then what is the fact as to whether or not you and Officer Baker and I recreated the incident as you have testified to here, going into the lobby with the conversation you had with Officer Baker, and running into that swinging door, and going back to the elevator and pushing the elevator button, and then calling or yelling twice for the elevator to come down, and then coming up the stairs to the second floor. Do you remember that?

Mr. TRULY. I remember that.

Mr. BELIN. When we recreated that incident, did we walk or run?

Mr. TRULY. We walked. We trotted.

Mr. BELIN. We trotted.

Did we get out of breath, do you remember?

Mr. TRULY. Yes.

Mr. BELIN. Did we go at about the speed that you feel you went on that day with Officer Baker?

Mr. TRULY. I think so—which was a little more than a trot, I would say.

Mr. BELIN. Do you remember offhand what the stopwatch timed us at—I think we did it twice, is that correct?

Mr. TRULY. No, sir—not from the time that he got on his motorcycle, I don't remember.

Mr. BELIN. All right.

Mr. TRULY. But I was thinking it was somewheres under 2 minutes. Between a minute and a half and 2 minutes.

Mr. BELIN. Officer Baker, I think, will be able to testify to that in the morning.

Representative FORD. But in reconstructing the incident, you went more or less at a similar pace, took about the same time you did on November 22d?

Mr. TRULY. As far as I can tell; yes, sir.

Mr. BELIN. You ran at about the same speed, do you believe?

Mr. TRULY. Yes; I believe so.

We tried to—we had a few people we had to push our way through to start in the building the other time, and possibly didn't run quite so fast at first.

Mr. BELIN. Would you say that again?

Mr. TRULY. I said when the officer and I ran in, we were shouldering people aside in front of the building, so we possibly were slowed a little bit more coming in than we were when he and I came in March 20th. I don't believe so. But it wouldn't be enough to matter there.

Mr. BELIN. Would you say that the reconstruction that we did on March 20th was a minimum or a maximum time?

Mr. TRULY. Oh, I would say that would be the minimum time.

Mr. BELIN. Mr. Truly, when you took the elevator to the fifth—from the fifth to the seventh floor, that east elevator did you see the west elevator at all as you passed the sixth floor, when you got to the seventh floor?

Mr. TRULY. No, sir; because—I could not see the west elevator while operating the east elevator.

Mr. BELIN. You mean because you were not looking at it, or you just couldn't see it?

Mr. TRULY. Well, the back of the east elevator is solid metal, and if I passed—yes; I could. I beg your pardon.

I could see it from the fifth floor. I didn't notice it anywheres up there. I wasn't really looking for it, however.

Mr. BELIN. Now, after you got—when did you notice that west elevator next? If you know.

Mr. TRULY. I don't know.

Mr. BELIN. I believe you said when you first saw the elevators, you thought they were both on the same floor, the fifth floor.

Mr. TRULY. Yes, sir.

Mr. BELIN. Then how do you explain that when you got to the fifth floor, one of the elevators was not there?

Mr. TRULY. I don't know, sir. I think one of my boys was getting stock off the fifth floor on the back side, and probably moved the elevator at the time—somewheres between the time we were running upstairs. And I would not have remembered that. I mean I wouldn't have really heard that, with the commotion we were making running up the enclosed stairwell.

Mr. BELIN. Did you see anyone on the fifth floor?

Mr. TRULY. Yes. When coming down I am sure I saw Jack Dougherty getting some books off the fifth floor.

Now, this is so dim in my mind that I could be making a mistake.

But I believe that he was getting some stock, that he had already gone back to work, and that he was getting some stock off the fifth floor.

Mr. BELIN. You really don't know who was operating the elevator, then, is that correct?

Mr. TRULY. That is correct.

Mr. BELIN. What is your best guess?

Mr. TRULY. My best guess is that Jack Dougherty was.

Mr. BELIN. Now, after you got down from the seventh floor, you then went down to the sixth floor with Officer Baker?

Mr. TRULY. Yes.

Mr. BELIN. Did he look around on the sixth floor at all or not?

Mr. TRULY. Just before we got on the elevator on the seventh floor, Officer Baker ran over and looked in a little room on the seventh floor, and glanced around on that floor, which is open, and it didn't take much of a search. And then we reached the sixth floor. I stopped. He glanced over the sixth floor quickly.

Mr. BELIN. Could you see the southeast corner of the sixth floor from there?

Mr. TRULY. I don't think so; no, sir. You could not.

Mr. BELIN. Then what?

Mr. TRULY. Then we continued on down, and we saw officers on the fourth floor.

I don't recall that we stopped any more until we reached the first floor. But I do recall there was an officer on the fourth floor, by the time we got down that far.

Mr. BELIN. All right.

And then you got down eventually to the first floor?

Mr. TRULY. That is right.

Mr. BELIN. About how long after these shots do you think it took you to go all the way up and look around the roof and come all the way down again?

Mr. TRULY. Oh, we might have been gone between 5 and 10 minutes. It is hard to say.

Mr. BELIN. What did you do when you got back to the first floor, or what did you see?

Mr. TRULY. When I got back to the first floor, at first I didn't see anything except officers running around, reporters in the place. There was a regular madhouse.

Mr. BELIN. Had they sealed off the building yet, do you know?

Mr. TRULY. I am sure they had.

Mr. BELIN. Then what?

Mr. TRULY. Then in a few minutes—it could have been moments or minutes at a time like that—I noticed some of my boys were over in the west corner of the shipping department, and there were several officers over there taking their names and addresses, and so forth.

There were other officers in other parts of the building taking other employees, like office people's names. I noticed that Lee Oswald was not among these boys.

So I picked up the telephone and called Mr. Aiken down at the other warehouse who keeps our application blanks. Back up there.

First I mentioned to Mr. Campbell—I asked Bill Shelley if he had seen him, he looked around and said no.

Mr. BELIN. When you asked Bill Shelley if he had seen whom?

Mr. TRULY. Lee Oswald. I said, "Have you seen him around lately," and he said no.

So Mr. Campbell is standing there, and I said, "I have a boy over here missing. I don't know whether to report it or not." Because I had another one or two out then. I didn't know whether they were all there or not. He said, "What do you think"? And I got to thinking. He said, "Well, we better do it anyway." It was so quick after that.

So I picked the phone up then and called Mr. Aiken, at the warehouse, and got the boy's name and general description and telephone number and address at Irving.

Mr. BELIN. Did you have any address for him in Dallas, or did you just have an address in Irving?

Mr. TRULY. Just the address in Irving. I knew nothing of this Dallas address. I didn't know he was living away from his family.

Mr. BELIN. Now, would that be the address and the description as shown on this application, Exhibit 496?

Mr. TRULY. Yes, sir.

Mr. BELIN. Did you ask for the name and addresses of any other employees who might have been missing?

Mr. TRULY. No, sir.

Mr. BELIN. Why didn't you ask for any other employees?

Mr. TRULY. That is the only one that I could be certain right then was missing.

Mr. BELIN. Then what did you do after you got that information?

Mr. TRULY. Chief Lumpkin of the Dallas Police Department was standing a few feet from me. I told Chief Lumpkin that I had a boy missing over here— "I don't know whether it amounts to anything or not." And I gave him his description. And he says, "Just a moment. We will go tell Captain Fritz."

Mr. BELIN. All right. And then what happened?

Mr. TRULY. So Chief Lumpkin had several officers there that he was talking to, and I assumed that he gave him some instructions of some nature—I didn't hear it. And then he turned to me and says, "Now we will go upstairs".

So we got on one of the elevators, I don't know which, and rode up to the sixth floor. I didn't know Captain Fritz was on the sixth floor. And he was over in the northwest corner of the building.

Mr. BELIN. By the stairs there?

Mr. TRULY. Yes; by the stairs.

Mr. BELIN. All right.

Mr. TRULY. And there were other officers with him. Chief Lumpkin stepped over and told Captain Fritz that I had something that I wanted to tell him.

Mr. BELIN. All right. And then what happened?

Mr. TRULY. So Captain Fritz left the men he was with and walked over about 8 or 10 feet and said, "What is it, Mr. Truly," or words to that effect.

And I told him about this boy missing and gave him his address and telephone number and general description. And he says, "Thank you, Mr. Truly. We will take care of it."

And I went back downstairs in a few minutes.

There was a reporter followed me away from that spot, and asked me who Oswald was. I told the reporter, "You must have ears like a bird, or something. I don't want to say anything about a boy I don't know anything about. This is a terrible thing." Or words to that effect.

I said, "Don't bother me. Don't mention the name. Let's find something out." So I went back downstairs with Chief Lumpkin.

Mr. BELIN. When you got on the sixth floor, did you happen to go over to the southeast corner of the sixth floor at about that time or not?

Mr. TRULY. No, sir; I sure didn't.

Mr. BELIN. When did you get over to the southeast corner of the sixth floor?

Mr. TRULY. That I can't answer. I don't remember when I went over there. It was sometime before I learned that they had found either the rifle or the spent shell cases. It could have been at the time I went up and told them about Lee Harvey Oswald being missing. I cannot remember. But I didn't know it. I didn't see them find them, and I didn't know at the time—I don't know how long they had the things.

Mr. BELIN. There has been some testimony here, Mr. Truly, about some bins for storing books on the fifth floor near the stairway. I am going to hand you an exhibit which has been marked as Commission Exhibit 490, and ask you to state, if you know—were you there when these pictures were taken on the fifth floor? On Friday, March 20th?

The CHAIRMAN. The fifth floor?

Mr. BELIN. The fifth floor; yes, sir.

Mr. TRULY. Yes; I was, I believe. Some of them I may not have been when all of them were taken. I was not there when this picture was taken, no, sir.

Mr. BELIN. You are familiar with those bins on the fifth floor, are you not?

Mr. TRULY. Yes, sir.

Mr. BELIN. How long have those bins by the stairway been there?

Mr. TRULY. Well, it would be hard for me to say, but they have been there, I suppose, almost from the time we moved in—nearly 2 years. They were there at the time of November 22.

Mr. BELIN. On Commission Exhibit 487, the line marked "W", will you state whether or not this appears to be the approximate line where the bins are located?

Mr. TRULY. Yes, it would be.

Mr. BELIN. Can you see over those bins?

Mr. TRULY. You cannot.

Mr. BELIN. I mean when you are at the window—say you are in the southwest corner.

Mr. TRULY. No, sir; you cannot. They obscure the stairway.

Mr. BELIN. All right.

Now, there was a floor laying project that was going along on the sixth floor at about the time of November 22, is that correct?

Mr. TRULY. Yes, sir.

Mr. BELIN. Handing you Commission Exhibit 483, could you state, if you know, approximately where on the sixth floor they were laying new plywood floor around November 22d?

Mr. TRULY. This is it——

Mr. BELIN. This is north right here?

Mr. TRULY. They were in this area right here.

Mr. BELIN. Well, there is a blank line that appears to have a "W" at one end or the other. Would that be a fairly accurate——

Mr. TRULY. Yes, sir; in the west end of the building.

Mr. BELIN. Where they were laying the floor?

Mr. TRULY. That is where they were laying the floor.

Mr. BELIN. Now, when you were—were you familiar with the fact that they had moved books in the process of laying that floor?

Mr. TRULY. I knew they had to. I didn't know where they moved them particularly until that time. I don't suppose I had been up on that floor in several days.

Mr. BELIN. By that time, you mean November 22?

Mr. TRULY. Yes, sir.

Mr. BELIN. Where did it appear that they had moved them?

Mr. TRULY. They moved a long row of books down parallel to the windows on the south side, following the building, and had quite a lot of cartons on the north—let's see—the southeast corner of the building.

Mr. BELIN. Sometime on November 22d did you go to the southeast corner of the building?

Mr. TRULY. Yes, sir.

Mr. BELIN. Did you notice anything particularly about the books that were in the southeast corner?

Mr. TRULY. I didn't at that time—with the exception of a few cartons that were moved. But I did not know any pattern that the boys used in putting these cartons up there. They were just piled up there more or less at that time.

Mr. BELIN. Well, handing you what has been marked as Exhibit 503, which is a picture, does this appear to portray the southeast corner of the sixth floor as you saw it on November 22d?

Mr. TRULY. Yes, sir.

(The document referred to was marked Commission Exhibit No. 503 for identification.)

Mr. BELIN. Now, I notice some rows of books along the east wall. Did those books go all the way to the corner or not?

Mr. TRULY. They did not in front of the window extend very much in height, but they did go all the way on the floor to the corner of the building.

Mr. BELIN. Was this prior to November 22d?

Mr. TRULY. Yes, sir.

Mr. BELIN. When you got there on November 22d, did those books still go to the corner of the east wall of the sixth floor?

Mr. TRULY. No, sir. There were several cartons that had been moved out of the corner and apparently placed on top of the cartons next to them in front of the east window.

Mr. BELIN. Do you have any books that are called Rolling Readers?

Mr. TRULY. Yes, sir.

Mr. BELIN. Do you know what floor those Rolling Readers are usually kept on?

Mr. TRULY. The first floor and the sixth floor. Most of them are on the sixth floor.

Mr. BELIN. Do you know where on the sixth floor the Rolling Readers are?

Mr. TRULY. Yes, sir.

Mr. BELIN. Approximately where?

Mr. TRULY. They were—I would say they were thirty or forty feet from the corner. They were not in the area that the boys moved books from.

Mr. BELIN. Well, handing you Exhibit 483, I wonder if you would mark with your pen the letters "RR" for Rolling Readers. Would there have been any occasion at all to move any Rolling Readers from the area you have marked on Exhibit 483 to the southeast corner of the sixth floor?

Mr. TRULY. No, sir; because the boys had not finished much of the plywood work, and they would—none of that stock was moved at that time for any purpose.

Mr. BELIN. Are the Rolling Reader cartons average size or small size or large size?

Mr. TRULY. They are much smaller than the average size cartons on that floor.

Mr. McCLOY. Do you intend to offer all of these exhibits en bloc later on?

Mr. BELIN. Yes, sir.

Now, handing you Commission Exhibit 504, there appear to be some boxes near a window on a floor of your building. And I note that on two of the boxes they are marked "Ten Rolling Readers." Are those the Rolling Reader cartons that you referred to, with the letters "RR" on Commission Exhibit 483?

(The document referred to was marked Commission Exhibit No. 504 for identification.)

Mr. TRULY. Yes, sir; that is right.

Representative FORD. The Rolling Reader boxes were not ordinarily in that southeast corner?

Mr. TRULY. No, sir. That was not the place for them. They were 40 feet or so away.

Representative FORD. May I ask—the job that Oswald had, how did you designate it?

Mr. TRULY. Well, he filled orders.

Representative FORD. He was an order filler?

Mr. TRULY. Order filler.

Representative FORD. Do you keep records of the orders that are filled by each order filler every day?

Mr. TRULY. Not every day; no, sir. Occasionally we would double check on the employees, or the checker would count up the number and give me the number each employee filled in that day, or several days in succession for a whole week.

Representative FORD. Would you know what orders Oswald filled November 22d?

Mr. TRULY. No, sir; I would not.

Representative FORD. You would have no way of checking that?

Mr. TRULY. No. They would have been some orders that he filled the 21st that were not checked and out of the house on the 22d. And I could not tell how many he filled or when he filled his orders, no, sir.

Representative FORD. When an order filler fills an order, does he make his initial or mark on it?

Mr. TRULY. Yes, sir; he does. Up there where it says "L", which is layout, he puts his number, and then the checker puts his number under "C" when he checks the order and sees that it is all right, and sends it on for packing.

Representative FORD. Well, it would seem to me that every order that was filled on a particular day by an order filler could be identified as to the individual.

Mr. TRULY. You see, we don't always get out our orders the same day they are shipped. The order fillers fill lots of orders, and they are filling orders on up to quitting time in the afternoon, and those wouldn't go out until the next day, or sometime, if they get ahead of the checker. They don't put the date on them when they fill them.

Representative FORD. What I am trying to find out—is there any way to trace by the orders that were filled by Oswald on the morning of November 22d as to whether or not in the process of filling orders he was taken to the sixth floor?

Mr. TRULY. No, sir; we could not tell whether he filled any orders that might be dated November 22d—might have been filled—if they were dated November 22d and had Oswald's number on it, we would know that he filled those on November 22d. But if they were billed and dated on the 20th and 21st, and there was a number of those filled, we could not tell how many of those he filled on the 22d.

Representative FORD. Have you ever gone back through your orders for the 22d?

Mr. TRULY. No, sir.

Representative FORD. Just to take a survey?

Mr. TRULY. We have thousands and thousands of accounts, and they run from A to Z alphabetically in our files. We would have to take—we would have to go through every invoice in each file, from A to Z, in order to find any orders he might have filled on that day. And it would be hard to prove that he filled them on that date because, unless we found one that had his number on it and was dated November 22d—because we know he wasn't there after that—but if it was dated November 21st, he could easily have filled a good number of those orders that morning of the 22d. But we could not tell whether he filled them the 21st or the 22d.

Mr. BELIN. Mr. Truly, in line with Congressman Ford's questions, was there ever a clipboard found in your building at all?

Mr. TRULY. Yes, sir. Sometime later there was a clipboard found that had two or three orders on it.

Mr. BELIN. What were those orders dated?

Mr. TRULY. I don't remember, sir.

Mr. BELIN. Do you remember where the clipboard was found?

Mr. TRULY. I later learned it was found up on the sixth floor, near the stairway, behind some cartons. I do not remember just exactly how many orders were on it, but I think it was only two or three.

Mr. BELIN. Do you remember who found it?

Mr. TRULY. A boy by the name of Frankie Kaiser.

Mr. BELIN. Is he still one of your employees?

Mr. TRULY. Yes, sir:

233

Mr. BELIN. Do you know whether this was ever identified as having ever belonged to any particular employee of yours?

Mr. TRULY. Well, he brought the clipboard to Bill Shelley and told him about it, and he said, "This is an old clipboard I used to use. This is the one that Oswald was using." It was a kind of homemade affair.

Mr. BELIN. When you say he brought it to Bill Shelley, who are you referring to?

Mr. TRULY. I am referring to Frankie Kaiser who brought the clipboard with the orders downstairs and told Bill Shelley that he had found Oswald's clipboard with some orders on it.

Mr. BELIN. Had those orders ever been filled or not?

Mr. TRULY. No, sir. You see, when they fill the orders, they take them off the clipboard. They may have 25 on the clipboard, and after a while they will have 15 or 10 or something.

Mr. BELIN. Do you know whether or not those orders were ever eventually filled that were found on the clipboard?

Mr. TRULY. Yes, sir; they were filled.

Mr. BELIN. What did you do with the clipboard and the order blanks that were on there?

Mr. TRULY. I think someone else filled the order blanks and the clipboard lay around there for a while until it was mentioned. I don't recall what happened to it. At the time nobody considered it of too much significance, I suppose—that the boy was just filling orders up there and he had just thrown his clipboard over. I believe that someone from a government agency either got the clipboard or looked at it. I have this thing all mixed up. It hasn't been very long ago, you know, about the clipboard. I don't know the solution of it. They were trying to identify this clipboard just a short while ago for someone—the FBI or the Secret Service, or it could be you, could it?

Mr. BELIN. No, sir.

Mr. TRULY. Just shortly before you.

Mr. BELIN. Well, let me ask you this question?

Are there any ways in which your orders are posted that show anything along the lines that Congressman Ford suggested as to who might fill an order or when an order would be posted? In other words, if you come to an order and you see that the order is dated maybe November 21st, but you do not know whether it was filled on November 21st or November 22d, would your posting system of entries on your ledger or journal in any way show when it was filled?

Mr. TRULY. No, sir. The date that we go by is the date the checker checks the order, and then he puts the date stamp on it. He puts it over on the table in a little conveyor belt, and the boys wrap it. When he separates the packing list and the invoice itself—he puts the packing list and the label with the order. Then he dates the invoice as of that date, and it goes upstairs to be matched with the other copies, and then charged to the customer.

Mr. BELIN. Well, you mentioned earlier that periodically your checkers get a check to ascertain how many orders were filled by the various employees. Do you know of any such check made on the morning of November 22d?

Mr. TRULY. No, sir; I do not recall having made a check in several days before that. We would usually run a check of errors for a week, and then we would run a check occasionally of orders filled. And checking on the errors the various boys made—maybe we have an unusual number for us of teachers writing in saying that they got the wrong book. So we try to check and see which one of these boys possibly was making these errors.

Mr. BELIN. Is it your testimony that you do not recall any check being made on November 22d, or you are sure there was no check on November 22d?

Mr. TRULY. There was no check that I recall. And I am sure there wasn't.

(At this point, the Chairman left the hearing room.)

Representative FORD. Could you tell us the approximate date that this individual found the clipboard and brought it to your attention?

Mr. TRULY. No, sir.

Representative FORD. Was it a few days after the assassination, or several weeks?

Mr. TRULY. I think it was just a few days afterward because—now, we would have to check upstairs. If these orders are not filled and processed and gone upstairs and matched with the copies in several days there, then we go looking for the order like the boys missed them. We have copies in the office, and if they do not come through in a reasonable time, we think that someone has lost some orders, and we get to checking them. If we cannot find them, we have to duplicate the orders.

Representative FORD. In other words, if 2 weeks had passed without the order being filled according to your records, you would have instituted a more thorough search to find out where the unfilled order blank was.

Mr. TRULY. Yes, sir—less than that, I would say, because we do not—our customers would probably write to us before then, if they did not receive it. But the girls on it—usually 3 or 4 days, if those orders have not cleared, they come to check about them, to see if we are holding one back because we do not have the stock, or if we have lost it, the boys have lost it.

(At this point, the Chairman entered the hearing room.)

Representative FORD. Who is the man who brought the clipboard to you?

Mr. TRULY. Bill Shelley called my attention to it. At that time I do not recall anything being done except maybe one of the boys filling the orders and just forgetting about that part of it.

Representative FORD. To your best recollection, who gave the clipboard to Bill Shelley?

Mr. TRULY. Frankie Kaiser.

Representative FORD. Was he an employee of the Texas School Book Depository?

Mr. TRULY. Yes, sir.

Representative FORD. Do you know generally where Kaiser found the clipboard?

Mr. TRULY. Yes, sir.

Representative FORD. Can you point it out to us on one of the exhibits?

Mr. BELIN. The diagram of the sixth floor has been marked as Exhibit No. 483. Perhaps you can mark on Exhibit No. 483 with the letter "C" where you think the clipboard was found.

I might at this point on the record say for the Commission that Exhibit 506 purports to be the position of the clipboard when it was discovered—the clipboard is circled, and the number on the picture, on Exhibit 506, is numbered 36, and on the Exhibit 483 appears at the end of the arrow with the number 36 on it, which is near where Mr. Truly put his "C". And the number 35 on that same exhibit—the number 35 will be shown tomorrow to be the position of the rifle when it was discovered.

Representative FORD. And 36 is the position of the clipboard?

Mr. BALL. I don't think you can take that as evidence.

Mr. BELIN. This is not evidence. This is just background.

Mr. BALL. This is really an offer of proof on our part. That is the most you can consider it—because we intend to take the deposition of Kaiser who found the clipboard.

Representative FORD. Is there someone here, the staff or Mr. Truly, who knows approximately when the clipboard was found?

Mr. BELIN. Yes, sir. I can give you that date in about one minute. According to our records, Frankie Kaiser, when interviewed on December 2d, said that on the morning of December 2d he found a clipboard which he had made and which he had turned over to Lee Harvey Oswald with orders. And we have a list of the orders also in one of the Commission documents. It is Document 7, page 381.

But we are going to have to actually take the deposition of Mr. Kaiser, which we will do when we go to Dallas next week or the week after, or whenever we get to him.

Representative FORD. Off the record.

(Discussion off the record.)

Representative FORD. Back on the record.

Mr. BELIN. Three more pictures, Mr. Truly.

I hand you what the reporter has marked as Exhibit 505.

(The document referred to was marked Commission Exhibit No. 505 for identification.)

I ask you to state if this appears to be the stairway leading from the second to the third floor, or can't you tell?

Mr. TRULY. I believe so; yes.

Mr. BELIN. And that is the stairway that you went up two or threee steps before you came down to get Officer Baker?

Mr. TRULY. Yes, sir.

Mr. BELIN. Now, I note with regard to the floor plan on the second floor that when you want to get to the lunchroom from the elevator, if you want to get to the lunchroom from the west elevator you have to walk in the area through that door marked number 23. Is that correct?

Mr. TRULY. That's right.

Mr. BELIN. If you want to get there from the east elevator, what do you do?

Mr. TRULY. Well, there is a side door. a north door, coming into the lunchroom that they can come through.

Mr. BELIN. Does that north door appear on Exhibit 501?

Mr. TRULY. Yes.

Mr. BELIN. That appears to be located east of the Coca Cola machine, is that correct?

Mr. TRULY. That is correct.

Mr. BELIN. Now, if someone wanted to take an elevator and get off on the second floor, and go through the back door to get to the lunchroom, would there be any way for that elevator to leave the second floor other than for someone to get back on that east elevator and personally operate it?

Mr. TRULY. No, sir.

Mr. BELIN. In other words, the east elevator you have to actually have an operator on it and it cannot be moved by just pushing a button?

Mr. TRULY. That's right.

Mr. BELIN. One other question. Just what are Rolling Readers? Is Rolling a company or what is it?

Mr. TRULY. Well, if you would look at it you wouldn't know what it was after you opened the box. But it is a new concept in material for reading for children in the first grade, kindergarten and so forth. They are little blocks with words on them that roll out, and then you turn them over. It is something like—I know way back in my childhood they would use number blocks and things like that. But it has words and sentences and things they can put together.

Mr. DULLES. A square like dice?

Mr. TRULY. That's right. It looks like dice, only they are bigger. They have the theory that these can interest a lot of children because of the noise they put out here, and they pick them up when they hit the floor and put them together into sentences and things. Something to stimulate the interest of children who are not quite as advanced in their reading.

Mr. BELIN. Are they relatively heavy or light cartons?

Mr. TRULY. They are very light.

Mr. BELIN. The cartons themselves. About how much would a carton of 10 Rolling Readers weigh?

Mr. TRULY. I don't think they would weigh over between five and ten pounds.

Mr. BELIN. And by 10 Rolling Readers you mean there were 10 sets of the Rolling Readers in each of these cartons shown on Exhibit 504?

Mr. TRULY. That's right.

Mr. BELIN. At this time we offer in evidence exhibits 490 through 506 inclusive.

Mr. McCLOY. They may be admitted.

(The documents heretofore marked Commission Exhibits Nos. 490 through 506, inclusive, for identification, were received in evidence.)

Mr. McCLOY. Mr. Truly, I think I heard you say when you were describing the first contact that you had with Oswald that you said, "That is the last time I saw him until November 16th."

Did I hear you say that?

Mr. TRULY. No, sir; I did not. If I did, it was a mistake. I saw him on October 16th, the morning he came to work.

Mr. McCloy. I put down here that was the last time you had seen him until November 16th.

Mr. Truly. For the record, if I said that, that is wrong. I meant October 16th.

The Chairman. Which was the next morning?

Mr. Truly. That was the next morning after he was told to come to work.

Mr. Dulles. Do you recall, Mr. Truly, whether you hired any personnel for work in this particular building, in the School Depository, after the 15th of October and before the 22d of November?

Mr. Truly. No, sir; I don't recall hiring anyone else other than Oswald for that building the same day that I hired Oswald. I believe, if I am not mistaken, I hired another boy for a temporary job, and put him in the other warehouse at 1917 North Houston.

Mr. Dulles. At a different warehouse?

Mr. Truly. At a different warehouse. He was laid off November 15th, I believe—November 15th, or something like that.

Mr. Dulles. What I was getting at is whether an accomplice could have gotten in in that way. That is why I was asking the question.

Mr. Truly. No, sir; I don't recall. Actually, the end of our fall rush— if it hadn't existed a week or 2 weeks longer, or if we had not been using some of our regular boys putting down this plywood, we would not have had any need for Lee Oswald at that time, which is a tragic thing for me to think about.

Mr. McCloy. Mr. Truly, while Oswald was in your employ, did you have any inquiries made of you by any of the United States agencies, such as FBI, regarding him?

Mr. Truly. No, sir; nothing ever.

Mr. Dulles. Did Oswald mention to you anything about his trip to Russia and return from Russia?

Mr. Truly. No, sir; he did not. He just told me that he just recently was discharged from the Marines with an honorable discharge. And I suppose that if he had had some background of a few jobs, skipping here and there, I might have investigated those jobs thoroughly.

Mr. Dulles. He did not tell you about those short-time jobs he had?

Mr. Truly. No. The thing is I thought he was just discharged from the service, and we have worked with boys in the past, and they have gone on and got on their feet and got a better job. And I did not give it a thought that he was really just not discharged from the Marines.

Mr. Belin. Mr. Truly, you mentioned the fact that you thought Jack Dougherty was the one operating that west elevator. Is that correct?

Mr. Truly. Yes, sir.

Mr. Belin. Could you tell us a little bit about Jack Dougherty?

Mr. Truly. Jack Dougherty has been working for us 12 or 14 years. Until we moved into this building, he has been mostly in our State Department, the building at 1917 North Houston. He would fill orders for—that called for many cartons of books on a three-textbook-order basis to the various schools in Texas. And he seemed to be intelligent and smart and a hard worker. The main thing is he just worked all the time.

I have never had any occasion to have any hard words for Jack. A few times he would get a little bit—maybe do a little something wrong, and I would mention it to him, and he would just go to pieces—not anything—but anything the rest of the day or the next day would not be right. [Deletion.] He is a great big husky fellow. I think he is 39 years old. He has never been married. He has no interest in women. He gets flustered, has a small word for it, at times. He has never had any trouble. He is a good, loyal, hard working employee. He always has been.

Mr. Belin. Would you consider him of average intelligence?

Mr. Truly. Yes, sir. I think what is wrong with him mostly is his emotional makeup. I would say that for the work he is doing, he is of average intelligence.

Mr. BELIN. When you got to the fifth floor, as I understand it, the west elevator was not there, but when you started up from the first floor, you thought it was on the fifth floor.

Mr. TRULY. No. When I came down from the second floor—from the seventh floor with the officer, I thought I saw Jack Dougherty on the fifth floor, which he would have had plenty of time to move the elevator down and up and get some stock and come back.

Mr. BELIN. But when you got to the fifth floor that west elevator was not there?

Mr. TRULY. No, sir.

Mr. BELIN. Was it on any floor below the fifth floor?

Mr. TRULY. I didn't look.

Mr. BELIN. As you were climbing up the floors, you did not see it?

Mr. TRULY. No, sir.

Mr. BELIN. And if it wasn't on the fifth floor when you got there, it could have been on the sixth or seventh, I assume.

Mr. TRULY. No, sir; I don't believe so, because I think I would have heard or seen it coming downstairs when I got on the fifth floor elevator, on the east side.

Mr. BELIN. Well, suppose it was just stopped on the sixth floor when you got on the fifth floor elevator. Would you have seen it then?

Mr. TRULY. I think so, yes, sir. As we started up from the fifth floor, you could see the top of it at an angle.

Mr. BELIN. Were you looking in that direction as you rode up on the fifth floor, or were you facing the east?

Mr. TRULY. No, sir. I don't know which way I was looking. I was only intent on getting to the seventh floor.

Mr. BELIN. So you cannot say when you passed the sixth floor whether or not an elevator was there?

Mr. TRULY. I cannot.

Mr. BELIN. When you got to the seventh floor, you got out of the east elevator. Was the west elevator on the seventh floor?

Mr. TRULY. No, sir.

Mr. BELIN. Are you sure it was not on the seventh floor?

Mr. TRULY. Yes, sir.

Mr. BELIN. Did you hear the west elevator running at any time when you were riding the elevator from the fifth to the seventh?

Mr. TRULY. I was not aware of it.

Mr. BELIN. All right. I have no further questions.

The CHAIRMAN. Any other questions?

Representative FORD. How many employees do you have in the building on the corner of Houston and Elm?

Mr. TRULY. I cannot tell you the figures, the total number of the office and all employees. We had about 15, I think. We had 19-warehouse and order-filler boys in both warehouses, and there are only four or five down at the other place. I think we had 15 men working in our warehouse at Houston and Elm on that day.

Representative FORD. On November 22d.

Mr. DULLES. Would all of them normally have had access to the sixth floor, or might have gone to the sixth floor?

Mr. TRULY. Possibly any—possibly so. We have one man that checks. He hardly fills any orders. And we have one or two that write up freight. But any of the order-fillers there might be a possibility—there might be a possibility they might need something off the sixth floor.

Representative FORD. When you noticed the police assembling the employees after the assassination, what prompted you to think that Oswald was not among them?

Mr. TRULY. I have asked myself that many times. I cannot give an answer. Unless it was the fact that I knew he was on the second floor, I had seen him 10 or 15 minutes, or whatever it was, before that. That might have brought that boy's name to my mind—because I was looking over there and he was the only one I missed at that time that I could think of. Subconsciously it

238

might have been because I saw him on the second floor and I knew he was in the building.

Representative FORD. Had there been any traits that you had noticed from the time of his employment that might have made you think then that there was a connection between the shooting and Oswald?

Mr. TRULY. Not at all. In fact, I was fooled so completely by the sound of—the direction of the shot, that I did not believe—still did not believe—maybe I could not force myself to believe, that the shots came from that building until I learned that they found the gun and the shells there. So I had no feeling whatever that they did come from there. I am sure that did not bring Oswald in my mind. But it was just the fact that they were trying to get people's names.

Mr. DULLES. When you reported that Oswald was missing, do you recall whether you told the police that he had been on the second floor?

Mr. TRULY. No, sir; I did not.

Mr. DULLES. You did not?

Mr. TRULY. No, sir; I just said, "I have a man that is missing. I don't know whether it means anything, but this is the name."

Representative FORD. Do you know about what time that was that you told the police?

Mr. TRULY. I could be wrong, but I think it was around 15—between 15 minutes or 20 minutes after the shots, or something. I could be as far off as 5 minutes or so. I don't know. I did not seem to think it was very long. We might have spent more time up on the roof and coming down, and then I might have walked out in the shipping department. Everybody was running up asking questions. Time could fool me. But I did not think it was but about 15 or 20 minutes later.

Representative FORD. In your description of Oswald to Captain Fritz, did you describe the kind of clothes that Oswald had on that day?

Mr. TRULY. I don't know, sir. No, sir; I just told him his name and where he lived and his telephone number and his age, as 23, and I said 5 feet, 9, about 150 pounds, light brown hair—whatever I picked up off the description there. I did not try to depend on my memory to describe him. I just put down what was on this application blank. That's the reason I called Mr. Aiken, because I did not want to mislead anybody as to a description. I might call a man brown-haired, and he might be blonde.

Mr. DULLES. When you and the officer saw Oswald in the luncheon room, did any words pass between you?

Mr. TRULY. No. The officer said something to the boy.

Mr. DULLES. I mean between you and Oswald.

Mr. TRULY. No, sir. Oswald never said a word. Not to me.

Mr. DULLES. What was he doing?

Mr. TRULY. He was just standing there.

Mr. DULLES. Did he have a coke?

Mr. TRULY. No, sir.

Mr. DULLES. No drink?

Mr. TRULY. No drink at all. Just standing there.

Mr. DULLES. Anything about his appearance that was startling or unusual?

Mr. TRULY. No, sir. No, sir; I didn't see him panting like he had been running or anything.

Mr. DULLES. Didn't appear to be doing anything special, moving in any direction?

Mr. TRULY. No, sir. He was standing still facing the doorway to the lunchroom. The officer was there with a gun pointed at him, around towards his middle, almost touching.

Mr. DULLES. How long before the President's actual visit on the 22d of November did you know of the visit and of the route that he was going to take.

Mr. TRULY. Well, I think they said it was announced 72 hours before the assassination that he would take that route.

Mr. DULLES. Was there any discussion, as far as you know, among your employees, of the fact that the procession would go near the School Depository?

Mr. TRULY. No, sir; not that I know of.

Mr. McCLOY. Did you ever have any reason to suspect any other member—any other of your boys of being in any way connected with this affair?

Mr. TRULY. No, sir; I never have found anything or any actions to make me feel that they might be connected with it.

Mr. McCLOY. You never observed Oswald conversing with any strange or unidentified characters during his employment with you?

Mr. TRULY. Never.

Mr. DULLES. Did Oswald have any visitors as far as you know?

Mr. TRULY. Never knew of a one; no, sir.

Mr. McCLOY. Did he have the use of a telephone when he was in the building?

Mr. TRULY. Yes, sir. We have a telephone on the first floor that he was free to use during his lunch hour for a minute. He was supposed to ask permission to use the phone. But he could have used the phone.

Mr. DULLES. Pay telephone or office telephone?

Mr. TRULY. No, sir; it is a regular office telephone. It is a pushbutton type.

Mr. McCLOY. Did he strike you as being a frequent user of that telephone?

Mr. TRULY. I never remember ever seeing him on the telephone.

Mr. DULLES. Would you have any record or be able to find out now whether he had ever used it?

Mr. TRULY. No, sir.

Mr. McCLOY. You did not see him on November 22d with any package or any bundle?

Mr. TRULY. No, sir.

Mr. BELIN. Mr. Truly, when we were there on March 20th, did you take a walk down from the southeast corner window on the sixth floor with Officer Baker and a Secret Service Agent Howlett—we walked along from that window at the southeast corner of the sixth floor, walked along the east wall to the northeast corner of the building, and then across there around the elevators, and Secret Service Agent Howlett simulated putting a rifle at the spot where the rifle was found; and then we took the stairs down to the second floor lunchroom where Officer Baker encountered Lee Harvey Oswald? You remember us doing that?

Mr. TRULY. Yes, sir.

Mr. BELIN. How fast were we going—running, trotting, walking or what?

Mr. TRULY. Walking at a brisk walk, and then a little bit faster, I would say.

Mr. BELIN. You remember what time that was? How long did it take?

Mr. TRULY. It seemed to me like it was a minute and 18 seconds, and a minute and 15 seconds. We tried it twice. I believe that is about as near as I remember.

Mr. BELIN. If a person were in that southeast corner window, just knowing the way the books were laid up there, would that have been the most practicable route to use to get out of there, to get down the stairs?

Mr. TRULY. I believe so. I believe it to be.

Mr. McCLOY. In your judgment, you think that is the route that Oswald took?

Mr. TRULY. I think—he had two possible routes there. One of them, he could come half way down the east wall and down this way, but he would have to make one more turn. But if he came all the way down the east wall to where the rows of books stop, he had a straight run toward the sixth floor stairs.

Mr. DULLES. You do not think he used any of the elevators at any time to get from the sixth to the second floor?

Mr. TRULY. You mean after the shooting? No, sir; he just could not, because those elevators, I saw myself, were both on the fifth floor, they were both even. And I tried to get one of them, and then when we ran up to the second floor—it would have been impossible for him to have come down either one of those elevators after the assassination. He had to use the stairway as his only way of getting down—since we did see the elevators in those positions.

Mr. DULLES. He could not have taken it down and then have somebody else go up to that floor and leave it?

Mr. TRULY. No, sir; I don't believe he would have had time for that.

Representative FORD. He couldn't have taken an elevator down and then sent it up to a higher floor?

Mr. TRULY. No, sir. Yes; he could. I suppose he could put his hand through the slotted bars and touched one of the upper floors.

Mr. BELIN. On both elevators?

Mr. TRULY. That is just the west one only.

Representative FORD. That was feasible, even though it might be a little difficult?

Mr. TRULY. Yes, sir.

Representative FORD. There was no button on the outside that permitted him to send an elevator up to a higher floor?

Mr. TRULY. No, sir. It would take him quite a little job to get his hand all through there and press one.

Mr. DULLES. Would he have to break any glass to do it?

Mr. TRULY. No, sir. The car gate—and then there was an outside gate slatted—slats about this far apart.

Mr. McCLOY. When you entered the building with the officer behind you, when you were presumably trying to get to the roof, there had been no cordon at that time thrown around the building?

Mr. TRULY. No, sir.

Mr. McCLOY. So that Oswald could have slipped out without an officer having been at the doorway at that point?

Mr. TRULY. Yes, sir; I think so. There were many officers running down west of the building. It appears many people thought the shots came from there because of the echo or what.

Mr. DULLES. Is it your view he went out the front door rather than one of the back doors?

Mr. TRULY. Yes, sir; it is. From the nature—from the direction he was walking through the office, and the front stairway, to reach the second floor—it is my view that he walked down the front stairs and just out through the crowd there, probably a minute or two before the police had everything stopped.

Mr. McCLOY. From what you know of these young men who testified before you today, are they trustworthy?

Mr. TRULY. Yes, sir; I think they are. They are good men. They have been with me, most of them, for some time. I have no reason to doubt their word. I do know that they have been rather, as the expression goes, shook up about this thing, especially this tall one, Bonnie Williams. He is pretty superstitious, I would say. For 2 or 3 weeks the work was not normal, or a month. The boys did not put out their normal amount of work. Their hearts were not in it. But after that, they have picked up very well. They are doing their work well.

Mr. BELIN. If we can go off the record for just a moment.

(Discussion off the record.)

The CHAIRMAN. Back on the record.

Mr. TRULY. I thank you very much.

The CHAIRMAN. Thank you, sir. You have helped us a good deal.

We will recess at this time until 9 o'clock tomorrow morning.

(Whereupon, at 6 p.m. the President's Commission recessed.)

Wednesday, March 25, 1964

TESTIMONY OF MARRION L. BAKER, MRS. ROBERT A. REID, LUKE MOONEY, EUGENE BOONE, AND M. N. McDONALD

The President's Commission met at 9:50 a.m. on March 25, 1964, at 200 Maryland Avenue NE., Washington, D.C.

Present were Chief Justice Earl Warren, Chairman; Senator John Sherman Cooper, Representative Hale Boggs, Representative Gerald R. Ford, and Allen W. Dulles, members.

Also present were Joseph A. Ball, assistant counsel; David W. Belin, assistant counsel; Norman Redlich, assistant counsel; Charles Murray, observer; and Waggoner Carr, attorney general of Texas.

TESTIMONY OF MARRION L. BAKER

The CHAIRMAN. Would you raise your right hand and be sworn please?

Do you solemnly swear the testimony you give before this Commission will be the truth, the whole truth and nothing but the truth so help you God?

Mr. BAKER. I do, sir.

The CHAIRMAN. You may be seated. I will read a little short brief statement to you, Mr. Baker, which will indicate the purpose of our meeting today.

The purpose of today's hearing is to hear the testimony of M. L. Baker, Mrs. R. A. Reid, Eugene Boone, Luke Mooney, and M. N. McDonald. Officer Baker and Mrs. Reid were in the vicinity of the Texas School Book Depository Building at the time of the assassination.

Deputy Sheriffs Boone and Mooney assisted in the search of the sixth floor of the Texas School Depository Building shortly after the assassination and Officer McDonald apprehended Lee Harvey Oswald at the Texas theater.

I read this to you just so you will know the general nature of the inquiry we are making today and we will make of you.

Mr. Belin will conduct the examination.

Mr. BELIN. Officer Baker, would you state your legal name, please for the Commission?

Mr. BAKER. Marrion L. Baker.

Mr. BELIN. You are known as M. L. Baker?

Mr. BAKER. That is right, sir.

Mr. BELIN. What is your occupation?

Mr. BAKER. With Dallas Police Department.

Mr. BELIN. How long have you been with the Dallas Police Department?

Mr. BAKER. Almost 10 years.

Mr. BELIN. How old are you, Officer Baker?

Mr. BAKER. Thirty-three.

Mr. BELIN. Where were you born?

Mr. BAKER. In a little town called Blum, Tex.

Mr. BELIN. Did you go to school in Blum, Tex.?

Mr. BAKER. Yes, sir; I think I went to about the sixth grade.

Mr. BELIN. Then where did you go?

Mr. BAKER. We moved to Dallas and I continued schooling at the Roger Q. Mills School, elementary, went to junior high school, I believe it was called Storey, and then I finished high school in Adamson High School.

Mr. BELIN. In Dallas?

Mr. BAKER. Yes, sir.

Mr. BELIN. What did you do after you graduated from high school?

Mr. BAKER. I think I got married.

The CHAIRMAN. Gentlemen, at this time I must go to the court, we have a session of the court today hearing arguments and Mr. Dulles, you are going to be here through the morning, so if you will conduct the meeting from this time on.

Excuse me, gentlemen.

(At this point, the Chief Justice left the hearing room.)

Mr. BELIN. After you got married, sir, what did you do. I mean in the way of vocation?

Mr. BAKER. I took up a job as a sheetmetal man at the Continental Tin Co.

Mr. BELIN. How long did you work for Continental?

Mr. BAKER. Approximately 3 months.

Mr. BELIN. Then what did you do?

Mr. BAKER. At that time I quit this job and went to the Ford Motor Co.

Mr. BELIN. What did you do at Ford?

Mr. BAKER. Well, at that time I stayed there approximately 11 months and they laid me off and I went to the, I believe they call it Chance Vought at that time, aircraft.

Mr. BELIN. What did you do at Ford, sir?

Mr. BAKER. I was a glass installer, I believe that is what you would call it.

Mr. BELIN. All right.

When you went to this aircraft factory what did you do?

Mr. BAKER. I was a material clerk.

Mr. BELIN. How long did you work for them?

Mr. BAKER. I didn't understand?

Mr. BELIN. How long did you work for the aircraft company?

Mr. BAKER. It seemed like somewhere around a year and a half.

Mr. BELIN. All right, then what did you do?

Mr. BAKER. At that time it was uncertain out there whether you would stay there or not, they were laying off a few of the men and I went with the neighbor's trailer company which was located in Oak Cliff there.

Mr. BELIN. What did you do there?

Mr. BAKER. I was, I guess you would call it a mechanic. I did a little bit of everything there, I did all the road work, and did all the delivering at that time.

Mr. BELIN. How long did you stay with them?

Mr. BAKER. A little over 3 years.

Mr. BELIN. Then what did you do?

Mr. BAKER. Then I became, I went with the city of Dallas.

Mr. BELIN. With the police department?

Mr. BAKER. Yes, sir.

Mr. BELIN. Did you take a course of instruction for the police department?

Mr. BAKER. Yes, sir; I went to the Dallas Police Academy School out there.

Mr. BELIN. How long was this schooling period, approximately?

Mr. BAKER. Four months.

Mr. BELIN. After you were graduated from the Dallas Police Academy, did you right away become a motorcycle policeman or were you first a patrolman or what did you do?

Mr. BAKER. No, sir; at first I was a patrolman and I spent some 23 months in radio patrol division. And then I volunteered solo division.

Mr. BELIN. When you were in this radio car, was this a patrol car where two men would be——

Mr. BAKER. That is right, sir.

Mr. BELIN. And have you been a motorcycle policeman then, say, for the last 7 or 8 years?

Mr. BAKER. Yes, sir; that is pretty close to it.

(At this point, Representative Ford left the hearing room.)

Mr. BELIN. By the way, you use the word solo; generally do people in police cars ride in pairs during the daytime or solos or what?

Mr. BAKER. If you are talking about the squad cars at the time that I worked in the radio patrol division, most of them were two-men squads.

Mr. BELIN. Were there some one-man squads, too?

Mr. BAKER. Very few.

Mr. BELIN. What about today, do you know what the situation is?

Mr. BAKER. They still have, say, very few two-men squads and a lot of one-man squads now.

Mr. BELIN. They have a lot of one-man squads now?

Mr. BAKER. Yes, sir.

Mr. DULLES. Is that because of a shortage of men for the jobs to cover?

Mr. BAKER. Yes, sir.

Mr. DULLES. Not because of the procedures?

Mr. BAKER. Now, at night they try to ride them two men.

Mr. BELIN. In the daytime what is the situation now?

Mr. BAKER. Usually the downtown squads which I work are two men, and the outlying squads are one man.

Mr. BELIN. All right.

Coming down to November 22, 1963, what was your occupation on that day?

Mr. BAKER. I was assigned to ride a motorcycle.

Mr. BELIN. And where were you assigned to ride the motorcycle?

Mr. BAKER. At this particular day in the office up there before we went out, I was, my partner and I, we received instructions to ride right beside the President's car.

Mr. BELIN. About when was this that you received these instructions?

Mr. BAKER. Let's see, I believe we went to work early that day, somewhere around 8 o'clock.

Mr. BELIN. And from whom did you receive your original instructions to ride by the side of the President's car?

Mr. BAKER. Our sergeant is the one who gave us the instructions. This is all made up in the captain's office, I believe.

Mr. BELIN. All right.

Mr. DULLES. Captain Curry?

Mr. BAKER. Chief Curry ; our captain is Captain Lawrence.

Mr. BELIN. Were these instructions ever changed?

Mr. BAKER. Yes, sir. When we got to the airport, our sergeant instructed me that there wouldn't be anybody riding beside the President's car.

Mr. BELIN. Did he tell you why or why not?

Mr. BAKER. No, sir. We had several occasions where we were assigned there and we were moved by request.

Mr. BELIN. On that day, you mean?

Mr. BAKER. Well, that day and several other occasions when I have escorted them.

Mr. BELIN. On that day when did you ride or where were you supposed to ride after this assignment was changed?

Mr. BAKER. They just—the sergeant told us just to fall in beyond it, I believe he called it the press, behind the car.

Mr. BELIN. Beyond the press?

Mr. BAKER. Yes, sir.

Mr. BELIN. Did he tell you this after the President's plane arrived at the airport or was it before?

Mr. BAKER. It seemed like it was after he arrived out there.

Mr. BELIN. Had you already seen him get out of the plane?

Mr. BAKER. Yes, sir.

Mr. BELIN. About what time was it before the motorcade left that you were advised of this, was it just before or 5 or 10 minutes before, or what?

Mr. BAKER. It was 5 or 10 minutes before.

Mr. BELIN. All right.

Then the motorcade left and you rode along on a motorcycle in the motorcade?

Mr. BAKER. Yes, sir.

Mr. BELIN. Was it a two-wheeler or a three-wheeler?

Mr. BAKER. It was a two-wheeler.

Mr. BELIN. You rode with the motorcade as it traveled through downtown Dallas?

Mr. BAKER. Yes, sir.

Mr. BELIN. And eventually what is the fact as to whether or not the motorcade got to Main Street?

Mr. BAKER. You say how fast?

Mr. BELIN. No ; did the motorcade get to Main Street in Dallas, was it going down Main Street at anytime?

Mr. BAKER. Yes, sir ; it did.

Mr. BELIN. All right.

I wonder if you would pick up your actions with the motorcade as it went down Main Street commencing at, say, Main and Record Streets.

Mr. BAKER. Well, it was the usual escort. We were traveling about somewhere around 5 to 10 miles an hour.

Mr. DULLES. There is a map right behind you.

(Discussion off the record.)

Mr. BELIN. Back on the record again.

Mr. DULLES. Would you state exactly where you were riding? We know a good deal about this, the cars the way they were paced. There was a car right behind the President's car that followed it, I think 6 or 7 feet right behind the President's car.

Mr. BAKER. That was the Secret Service car.

Mr. DULLES. That is right. Were you in that gap between the two cars or what?

Mr. BAKER. No, sir; I was, it seemed to me like, there was this car.

Mr. DULLES. When you say "this car" what do you mean?

Mr. BAKER. That Secret Service car.

Mr. DULLES. The Secret Service car right behind the President?

Mr. BAKER. And there was one more car in there.

Mr. DULLES. Behind that?

Mr. BAKER. Yes, sir.

Mr. DULLES. That was the Vice President's car, wasn't it?

Mr. BAKER. Yes, sir.

Mr. DULLES. And then?

Mr. BAKER. There were four press cars carrying the press and I was right at the side of that last one.

Representative BOGGS. The last press car?

Mr. DULLES. The last press car?

Mr. BAKER. Yes, sir.

Mr. DULLES. So you were roughly how far behind the President's car at this stage?

Mr. BAKER. Sometimes we got, at this stage we were possibly a half block.

Mr. DULLES. A half block?

Mr. BAKER. Yes, sir; as I say as I turned the corner the front of it was turning the corner at Elm Street.

Mr. BELIN. You mean as you were turning right from Main on to Houston Street heading north onto Houston, the President's car had already turned to the left off Houston heading down that entrance to the expressway, is that correct?

Mr. BAKER. That is right.

Mr. BELIN. All right.

I believe—pardon me, Mr. Dulles, does that answer your question?

Mr. DULLES. That answers my question. I wanted to see where he was.

Mr. BELIN. You said you were going down Main Street at around Record at from 5 to 10 miles an hour?

Mr. BAKER. Yes, sir.

Mr. BELIN. All right.

Will you take up your trip from there, please?

Mr. BAKER. As we approached the corner there of Main and Houston we were making a right turn, and as I came out behind that building there, which is the county courthouse, the sheriff building, well, there was a strong wind hit me and I almost lost my balance.

Mr. BELIN. How fast would you estimate the speed of your motorcycle as you turned the corner, if you know?

Mr. BAKER. I would say—it wasn't very fast. I almost lost balance, we were just creeping along real slowly.

Mr. DULLES. That is turning from Main into Houston?

Mr. BAKER. That is right, sir.

Mr. BELIN. You turned—do you have any actual speed estimate as you turned that corner at all or just you would say very slow?

Mr. BAKER. I would say from around 5 to 6 or 7 miles an hour, because you can't hardly travel under that and you know keep your balance.

Mr. BELIN. From what direction was the wind coming when it hit you?

Mr. BAKER. Due north.

Mr. BELIN. All right.

Now, tell us what happened after you turned on to Houston Street?

Mr. BAKER. As I got myself straightened up there, I guess it took me some 20, 30 feet, something like that, and it was about that time that I heard these shots come out.

Mr. BELIN. All right.

Could you just tell us what you heard and what you saw and what you did?

Mr. BAKER. As I got, like I say as I got straightened up there, I was, I don't know when these shots started coming off, I just—it seemed to me like they were high, and I just happened to look right straight up——

Mr. DULLES. I wonder if you would just tell us on that chart and I will try to follow with the record where you were at this time, you were coming down Houston.

Mr. BELIN. Sir, if you can—I plan to get that actual chart in a minute. If we could——

Mr. DULLES. I want to see where he was vis-a-vis the building on the chart there.

Mr. BAKER. This is Main Street and this is Houston. This is the corner that I am speaking of; I made the right turn here. The motorcade and all, as I was here turning the front car was turning up here, and as I got somewhere about right here——

Mr. DULLES. That is halfway down the first block.

Mr. BELIN. No, sir; can I interrupt you for a minute?

Mr. DULLES. Certainly.

Mr. BELIN. Officer Baker, when we were in Dallas on March 20, Friday, you walked over with me and showed me about the point you thought your motorcycle was when you heard the first shot, do you remember doing that?

Mr. BAKER. Yes, sir.

Mr. BELIN. And then we paced this off measuring it from a distance which could be described as the north curbline of Main Street as extended?

Mr. BAKER. Yes, sir; that would be this one right across here.

Mr. BELIN. And we paced it off as to where you thought your motorcycle was when you heard the first shot and do you remember offhand about where you said this was as to what distance it was, north of the north curbline of Main Street?

Mr. BAKER. We approximated it was 60 to 80 feet there, north of the north curbline of Main on Houston.

Mr. DULLES. Thank you.

Mr. BELIN. Does that answer your question?

Mr. DULLES. That answers my question entirely.

Mr. BELIN. In any event you heard the first shot, or when you heard this noise did you believe it was a shot or did you believe it was something else?

Mr. BAKER. It hit me all at once that it was a rifle shot because I had just got back from deer hunting and I had heard them pop over there for about a week.

Mr. BELIN. What kind of a weapon did it sound like it was coming from?

Mr. BAKER. It sounded to me like it was a high-powered rifle.

Mr. BELIN. All right. When you heard the first shot or the first noise, what did you do and what did you see?

Mr. BAKER. Well, to me, it sounded high and I immediately kind of looked up, and I had a feeling that it came from the building, either right in front of me or of the one across to the right of it.

Mr. BELIN. What would the building right in front of you be?

Mr. BAKER. It would be this Book Depository Building.

Mr. BELIN. That would be the building located on what corner of Houston and Elm?

Mr. BAKER. That would be the northwest corner.

Mr. BELIN. All right. And you thought it was either from that building or the building located where?

Mr. BAKER. On the northeast corner.

Mr. BELIN. All right. Did you see or hear or do anything else after you heard the first noise?

Mr. BAKER. Yes, sir. As I was looking up, all these pigeons began to fly up to the top of the buildings here and I saw those come up and start flying around.

Mr. BELIN. From what building, if you know, do you think those pigeons came from?

Mr. BAKER. I wasn't sure, but I am pretty sure they came from the building right on the northwest corner.

Mr. BELIN. Then what did you see or do?

Mr. BAKER. Well, I immediately revved that motorcycle up and was going up there to see if I could help anybody or see what was going on because I couldn't see around this bend.

Mr. BELIN. Well, between the time you revved up the motorcycle had you heard any more shots?

Mr. BAKER. Yes, sir; I heard—now before I revved up this motorcycle, I heard the, you know, the two extra shots, the three shots.

Mr. BELIN. Do you have any time estimate as to the spacing of any of these shots?

Mr. BAKER. It seemed to me like they just went bang, bang, bang; they were pretty well even to me.

Mr. BELIN. They were pretty well even.

Anything else between the time of the first shot and the time of the last shot that you did up to the time or saw——

Mr. BAKER. No, sir; except I was looking up and I could tell it was high and I was looking up there and I saw those pigeons flying around there.

Mr. BELIN. Did you notice anything in either of those two buildings either on the northeast or northwest corner of Houston and Elm?

Mr. BAKER. No, sir; I didn't.

Mr. BELIN. Were you looking at any of those windows?

Mr. BAKER. I kind of glanced over them, but I couldn't see anything.

Mr. BELIN. How many shots did you hear?

Mr. BAKER. Three.

Mr. BELIN. All right. After the third shot, then, what did you do?

Mr. BAKER. Well, I revved that motorcycle up and I went down to the corner which would be approximately 180 to 200 feet from the point where we had first stated, you know, that we heard the shots.

Mr. BELIN. What distance did you state? What we did on Friday afternoon, we paced off from the point you thought you heard the first shot to the point at which you parked the motorcycle, and this paced off to how much?

Mr. BAKER. From 180 to 200 feet.

Mr. BELIN. That is where you parked the motorcycle?

Mr. BAKER. Yes.

Mr. BELIN. All right.

I wonder if we could go on this plat, Officer Baker, and first if you could put on here with this pen, and I have turned it upside down.

With Exhibit 361, show us the spot at which you stopped your motorcycle approximately and put a "B" on it, if you would.

Mr. BAKER. Somewhere at this position here, which is approximately 10 feet from this signal light here on the northwest corner of Elm and Houston.

Mr. BELIN. All right.

You have put a dot on Exhibit 361 with the line going to "B" and the dot represents that signal light, is that correct?

Mr. BAKER. That is right, sir.

Mr. BELIN. You, on Friday, March 20, parked your motorcycle where you thought it was parked on November 22 and then we paced off the distance from the nearest point of the motorcycle to the stop light and it was 10 feet, is that correct?

Mr. BAKER. That is correct, sir.

Mr. BELIN. All right.

Now, I show you Exhibit 478 and ask you if you will, on this exhibit put an arrow with the letter "B" to this stoplight.

Mr. BAKER. Talking about this one here?

Mr. BELIN. The stoplight from which we measured the distance to the motor-cycle. The arrow with the letter "B" points to the stoplight, is that correct?

Mr. BAKER. That is correct, sir.

Mr. BELIN. And you stopped your motorcycle 10 feet to the east of that stop-light, is that correct?

Mr. BAKER. That is correct, sir.

Mr. BELIN. We then paced off the distance as to approximately how far it was from the place your motorcycle was parked to the doorway of the School Book Depository Building, do you remember doing that, on March 20?

Mr. BAKER. Yes, sir.

Mr. BELIN. And it appears on Exhibit 477 that that doorway is recessed, is that correct?

Mr. BAKER. That is correct, sir.

Mr. BELIN. Do you remember how far that was from the place your motorcycle was parked to the doorway?

Mr. BAKER. Approximately 45 feet.

Mr. BELIN. This same stoplight appears as you look at Exhibit 477 to the left of the entranceway to the building, is that correct?

Mr. BAKER. That is correct, sir.

Mr. BELIN. After you parked your motorcycle, did you notice anything that was going on in the area?

Mr. BAKER. Yes, sir. As I parked here——

Mr. BELIN. You are pointing on Exhibit 361 to the place that you have marked with "B."

Mr. BAKER. And I was looking westward which would be in this direction.

Mr. BELIN. By that, you are pointing down the entrance to the freeway and kind of what I will call the peninsula of the park there?

Mr. BAKER. Yes, sir.

Mr. BELIN. Toward the triple underpass.

Representative BOGGS. Where is the underpass?

Mr. BAKER. The underpass is down here. This is really Elm Street, and this would be Main and Commerce and they all come together here, and there is a triple overpass.

Representative BOGGS. Right.

Mr. BAKER. At this point, I looked down here as I was parking my motorcycle and these people on this ground here, on the sidewalk, there were several of them falling, and they were rolling around down there, and all these people were rushing back, a lot of them were grabbing their children, and I noticed one, I didn't know who he was, but there was a man ran out into the crowd and back.

Mr. BELIN. Did you notice anything else?

Mr. BAKER. Except there was a woman standing—well, all these people were running, and there was a woman screaming, "Oh, they have shot that man, they have shot that man."

Mr. BELIN. All right.

Now, you are on Exhibit 361, and you are pointing to people along the area or bordering the entrance to that expressway and that bit of land lying to the west and north, as to where you describe these people, is that correct?

Mr. BAKER. That is correct, sir.

Mr. DULLES. Would you mark where the overpass would be, right at the end of those lines, just so we get oriented on it.

Mr. BELIN. I am trying to see down here.

Mr. DULLES. I just wanted to get a general idea.

Mr. BELIN. On Exhibit 361, sir, it wouldn't show but it basically would be off in this direction coming down this way. The entrance to the freeway would go down here and the overpass would roughly be down here.

Mr. DULLES. As far as that?

Mr. BELIN. Yes, sir; I think Mr. Redlich is going to get a picture that will better describe it.

Mr. DULLES. All right.

Mr. BELIN. All right.

Is there anything else you saw there, Officer Baker, before you ran to the building?

Mr. BAKER. No, sir; not at that time.

Mr. BELIN. All right.

Then what did you do after surveying the situation?

Mr. BAKER. I had it in mind that the shots came from the top of this building here.

Mr. BELIN. By this building, you are referring to what?

Mr. BAKER. The Book Depository Building.

Mr. BELIN. Go on.

Representative BOGGS. You were parked right in front of the Building?

Mr. BAKER. Yes, sir; ran right straight to it.

Representative BOGGS. Right.

Let me ask you a question. How far away, approximately, were these people who were running and falling and so forth from the entrance to the Building?

Mr. BAKER. Well, now, let me say this. From this position here.

Mr. BELIN. That is position "B" on Exhibit 361?

Mr. BAKER. There were people running all over this here.

Mr. BELIN. And you are pointing to the street and the parkway all in front of the School Building?

Mr. BAKER. You see, it looked to me like there were maybe 500 or 600 people in this area here.

Representative BOGGS. Yes.

Mr. BAKER. As those shots rang out, why they started running, you know, every direction, just trying to get back out of the way.

Mr. DULLES. For the record, by this area right here, you have that little peninsula between the Elm Street extension and the Building?

Mr. BAKER. That is right. This little street runs down in front of the building down here to the property of the railroad tracks and this is all a parkway.

Mr. DULLES. Yes. I just wanted to get it for the record.

Mr. BELIN. You then ran into the Building, is that correct?

Mr. BAKER. That is correct, sir.

Mr. BELIN. What did you see and what did you do as you ran into the Building?

Mr. BAKER. As I entered this building, there was, it seems to me like there was outside doors and then there is a little lobby.

Mr. BELIN. All right.

Mr. BAKER. And then there are some inner doors and another door you have to go through, a swinging door type.

As I entered this lobby there were people going in as I entered. And I asked, I just spoke out and asked where the stairs or elevator was, and this man, Mr. Truly, spoke up and says, it seems to me like he says, "I am a building manager. Follow me, officer, and I will show you." So we immediately went out through the second set of doors, and we ran into the swinging door.

Mr. BELIN. All right.

Now, during the course of running into the swinging door, did you bump into the back of Mr. Truly?

Mr. BAKER. Yes, sir; I did.

Mr. BELIN. Then what happened?

Mr. BAKER. We finally backed up and got through that little swinging door there and we kind of all ran, not real fast but, you know, a good trot, to the back of the Building, I was following him.

Mr. BELIN. All right.

Then what did you do?

Mr. BAKER. We went to the northwest corner, we was kind of on the, I would say, the southeast corner of the Building there where we entered it, and we went across it to the northwest corner which is in the rear, back there.

Mr. BELIN. All right.

Mr. BAKER. And he was trying to get that service elevator down there.

Mr. BELIN. All right. What did you see Mr. Truly do?

Mr. BAKER. He ran over there and pushed the button to get it down.

Mr. BELIN. Did the elevator come down after he pushed the button?

Mr. BAKER. No, sir; it didn't.

Mr. BELIN. Then what did he do?

Mr. BAKER. He hollered for it, said, "Bring that elevator down here."

Mr. BELIN. How many times did he holler, to the best of your recollection?

Mr. BAKER. It seemed like he did it twice.

Mr. BELIN. All right.

Then what did he do?

Mr. BAKER. I said let's take the stairs.

Mr. BELIN. All right. Then what did you do?

Mr. BAKER. He said, "Okay" and so he immediately turned around, which the stairs is just to the, would be to the, well, the west of this elevator.

Mr. BELIN. All right.

Mr. BAKER. And we went up them.

Mr. BELIN. You went up the stairs then?

Mr. BAKER. Yes, sir.

Mr. BELIN. When you started up the stairs what was your intention at that time?

Mr. BAKER. My intention was to go all the way to the top where I thought the shots had come from, to see if I could find something there, you know, to indicate that.

Mr. BELIN. And did you go all the way up to the top of the stairs right away?

Mr. BAKER. No, sir; we didn't.

Mr. BELIN. What happened?

Mr. BAKER. As I came out to the second floor there, Mr. Truly was ahead of me, and as I come out I was kind of scanning, you know, the rooms, and I caught a glimpse of this man walking away from this—I happened to see him through this window in this door. I don't know how come I saw him, but I had a glimpse of him coming down there.

Mr. DULLES. Where was he coming from, do you know?

Mr. BAKER. No, sir. All I seen of him was a glimpse of him go away from me.

Mr. BELIN. What did you do then?

Mr. BAKER. I ran on over there——

Representative BOGGS. You mean where he was?

Mr. BAKER. Yes, sir. There is a door there with a glass, it seemed to me like about a 2 by 2, something like that, and then there is another door which is 6 foot on over there, and there is a hallway over there and a hallway entering into a lunchroom, and when I got to where I could see him he was walking away from me about 20 feet away from me in the lunchroom.

Mr. BELIN. What did you do?

Mr. BAKER. I hollered at him at that time and said, "Come here." He turned and walked right straight back to me.

Mr. BELIN. Where were you at the time you hollered?

Mr. BAKER. I was standing in the hallway between this door and the second door, right at the edge of the second door.

Mr. BELIN. He walked back toward you then?

Mr. BAKER. Yes, sir.

Mr. BELIN. I hand you what has been marked Commission Exhibit 497 which appears to be a diagram of the second floor of the School Book Depository, and you will notice on this diagram there are circles with arrows. I want you to state, if you will, what number or the arrow approximates the point at which you were standing when you told him to "Come here". Is there a number on there at all or not?

Mr. BAKER. This 24 would be the position where I was standing.

Mr. BELIN. The arrow which is represented by No. 24, is that correct?

Mr. BAKER. That is correct.

Mr. BELIN. On Exhibit 497. When you first saw him in which direction was he walking?

Mr. BAKER. He was walking east.

Mr. BELIN. Was—his back was away from you, or not, as you first saw him?

Mr. BAKER. As I first caught that glimpse of him, or as I saw him, really saw him?

Mr. BELIN. As you really saw him.

Mr. BAKER. He was walking away from me with his back toward me.

Mr. DULLES. Can I suggest if you will do this, put on there where the officer was and where Lee Oswald was, or the man who turned out to be Lee Oswald, and which direction he was walking in. I think that is quite important.

Mr. BELIN. Yes, sir. We are going to get to that with one more question, if I can, sir. When you saw him, he then turned around, is that correct, and then walked back toward you?

Mr. BAKER. Yes, sir.

Mr. BELIN. Was he carrying anything in his hands?

Mr. BAKER. He had nothing at that time.

Mr. BELIN. All right. Were you carrying anything in either of your hands?

Mr. BAKER. Yes, sir; I was.

Mr. BELIN. What were you carrying?

Mr. BAKER. I had my revolver out.

Mr. BELIN. When did you take your revolver out?

Mr. BAKER. As I was starting up the stairway.

Mr. BELIN. All right. Now, turning to Exhibit 497, if you would approximate on Exhibit 497 with a pen the point at which you saw this man in the lunch room when you told him to turn around.

Mr. DULLES. Could we get first where he first saw him.

Representative BOGGS. You have that already.

Mr. DULLES. I don't think you have it on the chart where he was.

Mr. BELIN. This is when he first saw him after he got in the room, sir. If I can go off the record.

Mr. DULLES. What I wanted to get is where he first saw him as he was standing down here, as he was going up the stairs and stopped and then in what direction he was—he seemed to be moving at that time before he saw.

Mr. BELIN. Just answer the question, if you will. Where were you when you first caught a glimpse of this man?

Mr. BAKER. I was just coming up these stairs just around this corner right here.

Mr. BELIN. All right. You were coming up the stairs at the point on Exhibit 497 where there are the letters "DN" marking down.

Mr. BAKER. Yes, sir.

Mr. BELIN. And you saw something move through a door which is marked as what number on Exhibit 497?

Mr. DULLES. Where was he when you first saw him?

Mr. BAKER. At this doorway right here, this 23.

Mr. BELIN. At 23.

Representative BOGGS. May I ask a couple of questions because I have to go?

Mr. BELIN. Surely.

Representative BOGGS. Were you suspicious of this man?

Mr. BAKER. No, sir; I wasn't.

Representative BOGGS. And he came up to you, did he say anything to you?

Mr. BAKER. Let me start over. I assumed that I was suspicious of everybody because I had my pistol out.

Representative BOGGS. Right.

Mr. BAKER. And as soon as I saw him, I caught a glimpse of him and I ran over there and opened that door and hollered at him.

Representative BOGGS. Right.

Mr. DULLES. He had not seen you up to that point probably?

Mr. BAKER. I don't know whether he had or not.

Representative BOGGS. He came up to you?

Mr. BAKER. Yes, sir; and when I hollered at him he turned around and walked back to me.

Representative BOGGS. Right close to you?

Mr. BAKER. And we were right here at this position 24, right here in this doorway.

Representative BOGGS. Right. What did you say to him?

Mr. BAKER. I didn't get anything out of him. Mr. Truly had come up to my side here, and I turned to Mr. Truly and I says, "Do you know this man, does he work here?" And he said yes, and I turned immediately and went on out up the stairs.

Mr. BELIN. Then you continued up the stairway?

Representative BOGGS. Let me ask one other question. You later, when you recognized this man as Lee Oswald, is that right, saw pictures of him?

Mr. BAKER. Yes, sir. I had occasion to see him in the homicide office later that evening after we got through with Parkland Hospital and then Love Field and we went back to the City Hall and I went up there and made this affidavit.

Representative Boggs. After he had been arrested?

Mr. Baker. Yes, sir.

Mr. Dulles. Could you tell us anything more about his appearance, what he was doing, get an impression of the man at all? Did he seem to be hurrying, anything of that kind?

Mr. Baker. Evidently he was hurrying because at this point here, I was running, and I ran on over here to this door.

Mr. Belin. What door number on that?

Mr. Baker. This would be 23.

Mr. Belin. All right.

Mr. Baker. And at that position there he was already down here some 20 feet away from me.

Representative Boggs. When you saw him, was he out of breath, did he appear to have been running or what?

Mr. Baker. It didn't appear that to me. He appeared normal you know.

Representative Boggs. Was he calm and collected?

Mr. Baker. Yes, sir. He never did say a word or nothing. In fact, he didn't change his expression one bit.

Mr. Belin. Did he flinch in anyway when you put the gun up in his face?

Mr. Baker. No, sir.

Mr. Dulles. There is no testimony that he put the gun up in his face.

Mr. Baker. I had my gun talking to him like this.

Mr. Dulles. Yes.

Mr. Belin. How close was your gun to him if it wasn't the face whatever part of the body it was?

Mr. Baker. About as far from me to you.

Mr. Belin. That would be about how far?

Mr. Baker. Approximately 3 feet.

Mr. Belin. Did you notice, did he say anything or was there any expression after Mr. Truly said he worked here?

Mr. Baker. At that time I never did look back toward him. After he says, "Yes, he works here," I turned immediately and run on up, I halfway turned then when I was talking to Mr. Truly.

Representative Boggs. That question about time I would like to establish. How long would you say it was from the time that you first heard the shots until that episode occurred?

Mr. Baker. We went back and made two trial runs on that, and——

Mr. Belin. Was that on Friday, March 20?

Mr. Baker. Yes, sir.

Mr. Belin. All right.

Mr. Baker. And the first run we made it was a minute and 30 seconds, and——

Mr. Dulles. Will you say from what time to what time, from the last shot?

Mr. Baker. From the last shot.

Mr. Belin. The first shot.

Mr. Dulles. The first shot?

Mr. Baker. The first shot.

We simulated the shots and by the time we got there, we did everything that I did that day, and this would be the minimum, because I am sure that I, you know, it took me a little longer.

Mr. Dulles. I want to get clear in my mind and for the record, it started at the first shot and when did it terminate, when you saw Oswald?

Mr. Baker. When we saw Oswald.

Mr. Dulles. When you saw Oswald?

Mr. Baker. Yes, sir.

Mr. Dulles. And that time is how much?

Mr. Baker. The first run would be a minute and 30 seconds, and then we did it over, and we did it in a minute and 15 seconds.

(At this point, Representative Boggs left the hearing room.)

Mr. Belin. Were we walking or running when we did this?

Mr. Baker. The first time we did it a little bit slower, and the second time we hurried it up a little bit.

Mr. BELIN. Were we running or walking, when we moved, did we run or walk?

Mr. BAKER. From the time I got off the motorcycle we walked the first time and then we kind of run the second time from the motorcycle on into the building.

Mr. BELIN. All right. When we got inside the building did we run or trot or walk?

Mr. BAKER. Well, we did it at kind of a trot, I would say, it wasn't a real fast run, an open run. It was more of a trot, kind of.

Mr. BELIN. You mentioned the relationship between what we did on March 20 and what actually occurred on November 22. Would you estimate that what we did on March 20 was the maximum or the minimum as for the time you took?

Mr. BAKER. I would say it would be the minimum.

Mr. BELIN. For instance, on March 20 did we do anything about trying to get through any people on the front steps of the building at all? Did we slow down at all for that?

Mr. BAKER. No, sir.

Mr. BELIN. Did we slow down at all on March 20 for the time it took you to look over the scene as to what was happening in the area down Elm Street and the Parkway?

Mr. BAKER. No, sir.

Mr. BELIN. Later did we go to the southeast corner of the sixth floor?

Mr. BAKER. Yes, sir; we did.

Mr. BELIN. With the stopwatch?

Mr. BAKER. Yes, sir.

Mr. BELIN. Did we make any or do any stopwatch tests about any route from the southeast corner of the sixth floor down to the lunchroom?

Mr. BAKER. Yes, sir; we made two test runs.

Mr. BELIN. All right. Do you remember what the route was?

Mr. BAKER. Yes, sir; we started on the sixth floor on the east side of the building.

Mr. BELIN. All right.

Mr. BAKER. We walked down the east wall.

Mr. BELIN. We started at that particular corner?

Mr. BAKER. Yes, sir; we started in the southeast corner.

Mr. BELIN. All right. We walked down the east wall, you say?

Mr. BAKER. That is right.

Mr. BELIN. All right, then where did we go?

Mr. BAKER. To the north wall and then we walked down the north wall to the west side of where the stairs was.

Mr. BELIN. All right, we walked from the southeast corner to the northeast corner?

Mr. BAKER. That is right.

Mr. BELIN. Then along the northeast corner, around the elevators, do you remember who was with us when we did this?

Mr. BAKER. Yes, sir. There was, it seems to me like his name was John— anyway, he was a Secret Service man.

Mr. BELIN. John Howlett.

Mr. BAKER. John Howlett. That is right, sir.

Mr. BELIN. Did Mr. Howlett simulate anyone putting a gun in any particular place?

Mr. BAKER. Yes, sir; he did.

Mr. BELIN. And then what did we do when we got to the—where did he do that, do you remember?

Mr. BAKER. That would be as we approached the stairway, there were some cases of books on the left-hand side there.

Mr. BELIN. All right. And Secret Service Agent Howlett went over to these books and leaned over as if he were putting a rifle there?

Mr. BAKER. That is right, sir.

Mr. BELIN. Then what did he do?

Mr. BAKER. Then we continued on down the stairs.

Mr. BELIN. To the lunchroom?

Mr. BAKER. That is right, sir.

Mr. BELIN. Do you remember how long that took?

Mr. BAKER. The first run with normal walking took us a minute and 18 seconds.

Mr. BELIN. What about the second time?

Mr. BAKER. And the second time we did it at a fast walk which took us a minute and 14 seconds.

Mr. BELIN. You saw the stopwatch on all of these timing occasions when it was started and when it was stopped, is that correct?

Mr. BAKER. Yes, sir; I did.

Mr. BELIN. Now, I want to go back to the sixth floor a minute with Mr. Dulles' questions.

Mr. DULLES. Can we go off the record here one moment?

(Discussion off the record.)

Mr. BELIN. On the record.

Officer Baker, when you related your story earlier you said that as you ran back on the first floor you first ran to the elevator shaft, is that correct?

Mr. BAKER. That is right, sir.

Mr. BELIN. And you stopped at the east or the west elevator door?

Mr. BAKER. That would be the west.

Mr. BELIN. All right. This was on the first floor, and did you look up the elevator shaft at that time?

Mr. BAKER. Yes, sir; at that time I did.

Mr. BELIN. This was while Mr. Truly was calling for the elevator?

Mr. BAKER. Yes, sir.

Mr. BELIN. Was there any kind of a gate between you and the elevator shaft?

Mr. BAKER. Yes, sir; there was.

Mr. BELIN. Wood or metal, do you remember?

Mr. BAKER. It is wood.

Mr. BELIN. What did you see when you looked up the elevator shaft?

Mr. BAKER. At that time I thought there was just one elevator there, you know, one big freight elevator, and to me they looked like they were up there, I didn't know how many floors in that building but you could see them up there, it looked like just at that time, I thought it was just one, when I looked up there, and it looked to me anywhere from three to four floors up.

Mr. BELIN. Was either elevator moving at the time or—pardon me, was there any elevator moving at the time you saw and looked up the shaft?

Mr. BAKER. No, sir.

Mr. BELIN. Did you hear any elevator moving?

Mr. BAKER. No, sir.

Mr. BELIN. Mr. Truly pushed the button, I believe you said.

Mr. BAKER. That is right, sir.

Mr. BELIN. When he pushed the button did any elevator start moving?

Mr. BAKER. No, sir.

Mr. BELIN. When you looked up the elevator shaft did it appear as if there was one elevator covering the complete shaft or did it appear there was one elevator that you saw covering half of the shaft?

Mr. BAKER. Like I say, I thought it was one elevator there and it was covering the whole deal up there so to me it appeared to be one.

Mr. BELIN. It didn't appear to be two elevators on different floors?

Mr. BAKER. No, sir.

Mr. BELIN. All right. Now, you got up to floor number two at the time and you did that with the stairs.

Mr. BAKER. Yes, sir.

Mr. BELIN. At the time you got up there was there any elevator on floor number two that you can remember, if you can remember? Maybe you cannot remember, I don't know.

Mr. BAKER. Evidently—now, I didn't look, evidently it wasn't because it seemed to me like the next floor up Mr. Truly said let's take the elevator.

Mr. BELIN. At some higher floor after that?

Mr. BAKER. Yes, sir.

Mr. BELIN. All right, if we can go off the record for a moment here.

(Discussion off the record.)

Mr. BELIN. Officer Baker, first of all, handing you what the court reporter has marked as Exhibit 498, I would like you to state if you know whether or not this appears to be the door leading from the second floor hallway into the vestibule going into the lunchroom.

Mr. BAKER. Yes, sir; it does.

Mr. BELIN. Is this the door through which you glanced as you came around the stairs coming up from the first floor?

Mr. BAKER. Yes, sir.

Mr. BELIN. What did you see that caused you to turn away from going up to the third floor?

Mr. BAKER. As I came out of that stairway running, Mr. Truly had already gone on around, see, and I don't know, as I come around——

Mr. DULLES. Gone on around and up?

Mr. BAKER. He had already started around the bend to come to the next elevation going up, I was coming out this one on the second floor, and I don't know, I was kind of sweeping this area as I come up, I was looking from right to left and as I got to this door here I caught a glimpse of this man, just, you know, a sudden glimpse, that is all it was now, and it looked to me like he was going away from me.

Mr. BELIN. All right. Then what did you do?

Mr. BAKER. I ran on up here and opened this door and when I got this door opened I could see him walking on down.

Mr. DULLES. Had he meanwhile gone on through the door ahead of you?

Mr. BAKER. I can't say whether he had gone on through that door or not. All I did was catch a glance at him, and evidently he was—this door might have been, you know, closing and almost shut at that time.

Mr. BELIN. You are pointing by "this door" to the door on Exhibit 498?

Mr. BAKER. Yes, sir.

Mr. DULLES. You mean you might have seen him as he was opening and going through the door almost?

Mr. BAKER. Well, to me it was the back of it. Now, through this window you can't see too much but I just caught a glimpse of him through this window going away from me and as I ran to this door and opened it, and looked on down in the lunchroom he was on down there about 20 feet so he was moving about as fast as I was.

Mr. DULLES. How far were you as you left the stairwell, the stairway——

Mr. BAKER. Yes, sir.

Mr. DULLES. From that door through which you eventually went through and then saw Oswald?

Mr. BAKER. I would say that was approximately 15, 20 feet, something like that.

Mr. BELIN. All right. On Exhibit 499 is this a picture of the lunchroom?

Mr. BAKER. Yes, sir; it is.

Mr. BELIN. Do you know what direction the camera is pointing to take this picture?

Mr. BAKER. It would be pointed eastward.

Mr. BELIN. All right. I see a coke machine off on the left. When you saw Oswald after you got to this doorway inside the lunchroom, had he gone as far as the coke machine?

Mr. BAKER. I didn't notice the coke machine or any item in the room there. All I was looking at was the man, and he seemed to be approximately 20 feet down there from me.

Mr. BELIN. As you got to the doorway which on Exhibit 497 is marked as number, what number is that, you are referring to this number 24 here?

Mr. BAKER. Yes, sir.

Mr. BELIN. Now, with relation to Exhibit 497 perhaps you can try to trace your route as you came out from the stairway, as to the route you took and the point you were when you first caught a glimpse of some movement through that window or door?

Mr. BAKER. At the upper portion of this stairway leading to the second floor,

I was just stepping out on to the second floor when I caught this glimpse of this man through this doorway.

Mr. BELIN. Do you want to put a spot there, with the letter "B" at the point you believe you were when you were looking through that door? You put the letter "B" on Exhibit 497 when you first saw the movement.

Mr. BAKER. Yes, sir.

Mr. BELIN. And then you, from that point, could you kind of trace your route to the——

Mr. DULLES. Could I ask one question before you ask this question, and this is a bit of a leading question, and think carefully.

If Oswald had been coming down the stairs and going into the lunchroom would he have been following the course insofar as you saw a course, that he—that you saw him follow?

Mr. BAKER. Yes, sir. The reason I say that, this hallway to the right——

Mr. BELIN. By the right you mean the hallway that goes to the—this is——

Mr. BAKER. This is a hallway right here.

Mr. BELIN. It is a hallway that has the number 27 on it?

Mr. BAKER. Yes, sir; from what I understand these are offices in there.

Mr. DULLES. Yes.

Mr. BAKER. And he had no business in there and the lunchroom would be the only place that he would be going, and there is a door out here that you can get out and to the other part of the building.

Mr. BELIN. I think Mr. Dulles' question relates to whether or not any person would have taken a stairway or elevator to have gotten to that point, is that correct?

Mr. DULLES. Yes; that is correct. I am clear as you come up the stairs you take a certain course you would go into the lunchroom.

Mr. BAKER. Yes, sir.

Mr. DULLES. I am not quite clear as to where you would end up on the second floor as you come down the stairs, is it the same point?

Mr. BELIN. Mr. Dulles, if you will look on Exhibit 497, the stairway appears to be the same stairway. You see the letter, the arrow, 21, points to the stairway going up to the third floor which, of course, would be the same stairway going down from the third floor and on the building.

Mr. DULLES. You would cross if you were going up and down, you would cross right there at the same point?

Mr. BELIN. Yes, sir.

Mr. DULLES. And if a man were going up the stairs and then going to the lunchroom and then coming down the stairs and going to the lunchroom, he would be approximately following the same course from the time he got off the stairs and went into that room before you get to the lunchroom.

Mr. BELIN. Yes, sir.

(Discussion off the record.)

Mr. BELIN. Officer Baker, you had just marked on Exhibit 497 point "B" where you thought you were at about the time you caught a glimpse of something, either through a door or through the window in the door marked 23, is that correct?

Mr. BAKER. That is correct, sir.

Mr. BELIN. Could you trace your route from point "B" to the doorway 23, if you would, sir.

Mr. BAKER. I ran right straight across here and through this doorway and this is approximately where, I would say 23 here, is approximately where I looked through this lunchroom and saw a man on down here.

Mr. BELIN. All right. I am going to put an arrow at that point on Exhibit 497, and this arrow in pen, I am going to put a "B-1" and at that arrow which is just to the left of the circle with the number 24 in it you say you then looked through the doorway and saw a man in the lunchroom, right?

Mr. BAKER. Yes, sir; walking away from me.

Mr. BELIN. Walking away from you. And then where did you move from point "B-1"?

Mr. BAKER. I moved on to this position 24 right here in this doorway.

Mr. BELIN. All right. I am going to put—you have put an "X" there, and

I am going to put that on Exhibit 497 as an arrow pointing to it, with "B-2". Is this where you stood when you called to the man to come back to you?

Mr. BAKER. Yes, sir.

Mr. BELIN. Did you move from that time until the man came up to you?

Mr. BAKER. As I called, I remember moving forward a little bit and meeting him right here in this doorway.

Mr. BELIN. As you called you say you remembered moving forward and meeting him right in the doorway which would be marked with the arrow with number 24 on it on Exhibit 497, is that right?

Mr. BAKER. That is right, sir.

Mr. BELIN. After you got there, did you move until the man came up to you?

Mr. BAKER. No, sir.

Mr. BELIN. Did you notice what clothes the man was wearing as he came up to you?

Mr. BAKER. At that particular time I was looking at his face, and it seemed to me like he had a light brown jacket on and maybe some kind of white-looking shirt.

Anyway, as I noticed him walking away from me, it was kind of dim in there that particular day, and it was hanging out to his side.

Mr. BELIN. Handing you what has been marked as Commission Exhibit 150, would this appear to be anything that you have ever seen before?

Mr. BAKER. Yes, sir; I believe that is the shirt that he had on when he came— I wouldn't be sure of that. It seemed to me like that other shirt was a little bit darker than that whenever I saw him in the homicide office there.

Mr. BELIN. What about when you saw him in the School Book Depository Building, does this look familiar as anything he was wearing, if you know?

Mr. BAKER. I couldn't say whether that was—it seemed to me it was a light-colored brown but I couldn't say it was that or not.

Mr. DULLES. Lighter brown did you say, I am just asking what you said. I couldn't quite hear.

Mr. BAKER. Yes, sir; all I can remember it was in my recollection of it it was a light brown jacket.

Mr. BELIN. Are you referring to this Exhibit 150 as being similar to the jacket or similar to the shirt that you saw or, if not, similar to either one?

Mr. BAKER. Well, it would be similar in color to it—I assume it was a jacket, it was hanging out. Now, I was looking at his face and I wasn't really paying any attention. After Mr. Truly said he knew him, so I didn't pay any attention to him, so I just turned and went on.

Mr. BELIN. Now, you did see him later at the police station, is that correct?

Mr. BAKER. Yes, sir.

Mr. BELIN. Was he wearing anything that looked like Exhibit 150 at the police station?

Mr. BAKER. He did have a brown-type shirt on that was out.

Mr. BELIN. Did it appear to be similar to any clothing you had seen when you saw him at the School Book Depository Building?

Mr. BAKER. I could have mistaken it for a jacket, but to my recollection it was a little colored jacket, that is all I can say.

Mr. DULLES. You saw Oswald later in the lineup or later——

Mr. BAKER. I never did have a chance to see him in the lineup. I saw him when I went to give the affidavit, the statement that I saw him down there, of the actions of myself and Mr. Truly as we went into the building and on up what we are discussing now.

(At this point, Senator Cooper entered the hearing room.)

Mr. BELIN. Officer Baker——

Mr. DULLES. I didn't get clearly in mind, I am trying to check up, as to whether you saw Oswald maybe in the same costume later in the day. Did you see Oswald later in the day of November 22d?

Mr. BAKER. Yes, sir; I did.

Mr. DULLES. Under what circumstances? Don't go into detail, I just want to tie up these two situations.

Mr. BAKER. As I was in the homicide office there writing this, giving this affidavit, I got hung in one of those little small offices back there, while the

Secret Service took Mr. Oswald in there and questioned him and I couldn't get out by him while they were questioning him, and I did get to see him at that time.

Mr. DULLES. You saw him for a moment at that time?

Mr. BAKER. Yes, sir.

Mr. BELIN. Officer Baker, you then left the second floor lunchroom with Mr. Truly, is that correct?

Mr. BAKER. That is right, sir.

Mr. BELIN. How long did you stay in the lunchroom after Truly identified this person as being an employee?

Mr. BAKER. Just momentarily. As he said, "Yes, he works here," I turned and went on up the stairs.

Mr. BELIN. All right. Do you have any time estimate as to the period of time that elapsed between the time that you first got to the head of the stairs and saw some movement through that first doorway and the time you left to go back up the flight of stairs going to the third floor?

Mr. BAKER. I would say approximately maybe 30 seconds, something like that. It was a real quick interview, you know, and then I left.

Mr. BELIN. All right. As you left, did you notice whether or not the man in the lunchroom did anything or started moving anywhere?

Mr. BAKER. No, sir. As I left he was still in the position that he was whenever I was facing him.

Mr. BELIN. You then went where?

Mr. BAKER. I immediately turned and went on, started on, up the stairways.

Mr. BELIN. All right. After going up the stairways, do you know what numbered floor it was—I will ask you this, did you take the stairway all the way to the top?

Mr. BAKER. No, sir; we caught that elevator, it seemed like we went up either one or two floors, and Mr. Truly said "Let's take the elevator, here it is."

Mr. BELIN. Did you take an east or west elevator?

Mr. BAKER. We took the east elevator.

Mr. BELIN. Now, the nearest elevator to you when you got off a flight of stairs would have been the east or the west?

Mr. BAKER. The west.

Mr. BELIN. When you got off the flight of stairs Mr. Truly said, "Here is an elevator," did the west elevator appear to be there?

Mr. BAKER. I didn't notice. I was looking around over the building at the time he said, "Let's take the elevator" and I just followed him on around.

Mr. BELIN. You went to an east elevator?

Mr. BAKER. That is right, sir.

Mr. BELIN. How far did it appear you rode up the elevator?

Mr. BAKER. It was a short ride. We just, either went one or two floors. I couldn't remember. I was still looking at the floors, you know, as we went up.

Mr. BELIN. As you rode up on the elevator, did you notice whether or not you passed the elevator on the west side?

Mr. BAKER. No, sir; I didn't notice.

Mr. BELIN. Did you notice or hear anything to indicate that the elevator on the west side might have been moving?

Mr. BAKER. No, sir.

Mr. BELIN. Did you take the east elevator as far as it would go?

Mr. BAKER. Yes, sir; we did.

Mr. BELIN. And then what did you do?

Mr. BAKER. We had to walk up another flight of stairs to get up to the top floor.

Mr. BELIN. To get up to the roof?

Mr. BAKER. Yes, sir.

Mr. BELIN. When you got off on the seventh floor or the top floor——

Mr. BAKER. Yes, sir.

Mr. BELIN. Did you notice whether or not the other elevator was there?

Mr. BAKER. No, sir; I didn't.

Mr. BELIN. You didn't notice. You got off the east elevator and then what did you do?

Mr. BAKER. We walked up the flight of stairs to the top.

Br. BELIN. To the top. What did you do when you got to the top?

Mr. BAKER. We went out on the roof.

Mr. BELIN. What did you do on the roof?

Mr. BAKER. I immediately went around all the sides of the ledges up there, and after I got on top I found out that a person couldn't shoot off that roof because when you stand up you have to put your hands like this, at the top of that ledge and if you wanted to see over you would have to tiptoe to see over it.

Mr. DULLES. If you look right behind you, Officer, you will see a picture and you might point out what the top wall that is shown on that photograph of the building is how high?

Mr. BAKER. Well, it is about 5 feet. I know I had to put my hand on top of it and tiptoe to see over it.

Mr. BELIN. All right. Mr. Dulles is referring to the picture of the School Book Depository building on Exhibit 362 and in demonstrating before the Commission as to where your hands were about how high are they in relation to your shoulders or mouth or chin or what-have-you?

Mr. BAKER. Approximately 5 feet.

Mr. BELIN. Your hands are 5 feet high? Did you go over just to one roof side or to all sides of the roof?

Mr. BAKER. No, sir; we came out at this northwest corner back behind this sign here.

Mr. BELIN. All right.

Mr. BAKER. And then I ran, kind of running walk, went all the way around. First I glanced over this side here, because the last thing I heard here on the radio was the chief saying, "Get some men up on that railroad track."

Mr. BELIN. Did you hear that on your police radio?

Mr. BAKER. Yes, sir; that was the last thing I heard.

Mr. BELIN. As you were getting off your motorcycle?

Mr. BAKER. Yes, sir.

Mr. BELIN. All right.

Senator COOPER. I didn't hear what he said he heard on the radio?

Mr. BAKER. I heard Chief Curry, the chief of the police over there, say, "Get some men over on the railroad track." I think everyone at that time thought these shots came from the railroad track.

Mr. BELIN. By "everyone" do you include you, too?

Mr. BAKER. No, sir. I had it—I was in a better position due to the wind and you know under it, that I knew it was directly ahead, and up, and it either had to be this building here or this one over here.

Mr. BELIN. You are pointing to either the first building, you are pointing to the School Book Depository Building, and the second one you are pointing to is the one across the street. When you heard this announcement on your radio was it while you were parking your motorcycle?

Mr. BAKER. Yes, sir.

Mr. BELIN. Go ahead, if you would, please. You are on the roof now.

Mr. BAKER. Well, as I looked over here, all these people, there were people all over this railroad track.

Mr. BELIN. You are saying as you are looking over the south and over the west?

Mr. BAKER. Yes, sir.

Mr. BELIN. All right.

Mr. BAKER. Then after I looked to see what was going on down there, and then I figured out that he wouldn't have shot from that ledge he would have shot from this sign or this old room, building back here on the back side.

Mr. BELIN. All right. Now, you are pointing to Exhibit 362 to the sign on the top of the School Book Depository Building, the Hertz sign, and some kind of a structure on the northeast corner of the building, is that correct?

Mr. BAKER. That is correct.

Mr. BELIN. Officer Baker, when you talk, I wonder if you would look at me, we might be able to hear a little bit better. Would you tell us what else you did?

Mr. BAKER. As I finished going all around this building here and then I came to this sign and I looked up there to see if I could find anybody hiding up there and I started up these steps, it is a ladder there on that sign, and I got on, say, 10 feet up there and I came back down, I seen that nobody would shoot from up there. He wouldn't have no place to hold on.

Mr. BELIN. By that you are referring to climbing the ladder to climb up the sign, is that correct?

Mr. BAKER. Yes, sir; this large Hertz sign here.

Mr BELIN. On the top of the School Book Depository Building on Exhibit 362. All right. Then what did you do?

Mr. BAKER. Then I came back down and I went and checked this building right here. It is an old deserted room there of some type.

Mr. BELIN. Some kind of a shack on the northeast corner of the building?

Mr. BAKER. That is right, sir.

Mr. BELIN. Out there. What did you see when you saw that shack?

Mr. BAKER. As I approached it, and looked under it, there wasn't anything under it, and you could tell that pigeons had been roosting there for sometime.

Mr. BELIN. All right. There were indications that pigeons had been roosting there?

Mr. BAKER. Yes, sir.

Mr. BELIN. Then what did you do?

Mr. BAKER. No indications that anyone would be around there.

Mr. BELIN. Did you see any pigeons there as you approached it?

Mr. BAKER. No, sir. They had all—at the time I kind of glanced and they were still flying around in the sky up there.

Mr. BELIN. What did you do?

Senator COOPER. You referred to pigeons, did you see some pigeon droppings?

Mr. BAKER. Yes, sir.

Senator COOPER. Had they been disturbed in any way?

Mr. BAKER. No, sir.

Mr. BELIN. Then what did you do?

Mr. BAKER. At that time I went on back. Mr. Truly was standing over here on this northwest corner and we descended on the stairs there.

Mr. BELIN. You went from the stairs to the roof to where, to the top floor of the building?

Mr. BAKER. Yes, sir.

Mr. BELIN. What did you do when you got to the top floor of the building?

Mr. BAKER. We walked on down one more flight of stairs and then we caught the same elevator back down.

Mr. DULLES. The top floor was the seventh floor, is it not?

Mr. BAKER. Well, you have one flight of stairs going from the top floor on up.

Mr. DULLES. Yes.

Mr. BAKER. And then we caught the elevator back down, the same elevator that we took up.

Mr. BELIN. When you referred to one flight of stairs, are you referring to the flight of stairs from the roof to the top floor that you took or the flight of stairs from the top floor to the next to the top floor?

Mr. BAKER. Well, there are two flights of stairs there. The one from the roof down to the top floor and then there is another one there.

Mr. BELIN. When you took the elevator back did you take it from the top floor down or from the next to the top floor down?

Mr. BAKER. That elevator to me, it didn't go to the top floor, it goes to the next to the top.

Mr. BELIN. Did you take it as far as it went?

Mr. BAKER. Yes, sir.

Mr. BELIN. When—did you take an elevator down or did you take the stairs down?

Mr. BAKER. We took the elevator down.

Mr. BELIN. Did you take the same elevator down you took up or did you take a different elevator down?

Mr. BAKER. We took the same one.

Mr. BELIN. When you went to take that elevator going back down did you notice whether or not the other elevator was there?

Mr. BAKER. I didn't notice. It would be to my back and I was looking out forward.

Mr. BELIN. It would be to your back from where you came off the stairs going to the roof?

Mr. BAKER. Are you talking about when we got on the elevator?

Mr. BELIN. When you got on the elevator to make the return trip?

Mr. BAKER. There wasn't one there whenever we come around out of the stairway, you know, to get on, you know we had to get on the east side instead of just stepping over on the west elevator.

Mr. BELIN. Officer Baker, I am going to hand you what the court reporter, what the Commission reporter, has marked as Exhibit 507 which purports to be a diagram of the seventh floor of the Texas School Book Depository Building and on that diagram you will see at the top the marks of two elevators and then, what looks to be the south, a stairway marked "Ladder to the roof."

Mr. BAKER. Yes, sir.

Mr. BELIN. What is the fact as to whether or not this stairway marked "Ladder to the roof" is the stairway that you took to go to the roof?

Mr. BAKER. Yes, sir; it would be.

Mr. BELIN. All right.

Now, when you got off the elevator which you took up to the top floor, which you said was the east elevator——

Mr. BAKER. Yes, sir.

Mr. BELIN. Did you have any occasion to notice whether or not the west elevator was on this top floor?

Mr. BAKER. No, sir; I didn't notice it.

Mr. BELIN. You didn't notice whether it was or whether it was not?

Mr. BAKER. That is right, sir?

Mr. BELIN. When you got back down from the roof to this top floor, did you have any occasion to notice whether or not the west elevator was on that top floor or not?

Mr. BAKER. No, sir; I still didn't look at the elevator. I was following Mr. Truly and every time I had a chance I would look around over the building.

Mr. BELIN. You would look over the floor itself rather than the other elevator?

Mr. BAKER. That is right.

Mr. BELIN. You then got on the elevator to go on back down?

Mr. BAKER. That is correct.

Mr. BELIN. And I believe you said it was the east elevator, is that correct?

Mr. BAKER. That is correct.

Mr. BELIN. How far did you take the east elevator down?

Mr. BAKER. As we descended, somewhere around—we were still talking and I was still looking over the building.

Mr. BELIN. As the elevator was moving?

Mr. BAKER. Yes, sir; downward.

Mr. BELIN. All right.

Mr. BAKER. The next thing that I noticed was Inspector Sawyer, he was on one of those floors there, he is a police inspector.

Mr. DULLES. City of Dallas Police?

Mr. BAKER. Yes, sir. And he was on, I really didn't notice which floor he was on, but that is the first thing I saw as we descended how this freight elevator, you know, it has got these picket boards in front of it and it has got it open so far, and it seemed to me like we stopped for a moment and I spoke to him and I told him that I had been to the roof, and there wasn't anything on the roof that would indicate anybody being up there, and then we started on down.

Mr. BELIN. Did you stay on the elevator while you spoke to him?

Mr. BAKER. Yes, sir.

Mr. BELIN. Do you remember what floor it was that you spoke to him on or how many floors down that you went from the top before you saw him?

Mr. BAKER. No, sir; not at that time. It seemed to me like it was on either the third or the fourth floor.

Mr. BELIN. Do you remember about how long you stayed on the roof?

Mr. BAKER. It was a little over 5 minutes.

Mr. BELIN. When you continued moving on the elevator after you talked to Inspector Sawyer how far did you go on the elevator?

Mr. BAKER. We went to the, I believe it would be the first floor there.

Mr. BELIN. All right. You got off the elevator then?

Mr. BAKER. Yes, sir.

Mr. BELIN. Did you leave Mr. Truly or did you stay with him?

Mr. BAKER. I left Mr. Truly there.

Mr. BELIN. Then what did you do?

Mr. BAKER. I immediately went on out. I was with this motorcade and I went right on straight through the front door and got on my motorcycle and tried to find out what happened to the motorcade.

Mr. BELIN. Officer Baker, when you left the building had the building been sealed off or not?

Mr. BAKER. Yes, sir; there was an officer at the front door.

Mr. BELIN. The officer at the front door, was he stopping people from coming in and out or what?

Mr. BAKER. I assumed that he was but I, you know, just went on out.

Mr. BELIN. All right.

When you got to the first floor on the east elevator did you notice whether the west elevator was there?

Mr. BAKER. No, sir; I didn't.

Mr. BELIN. Was there anything else that you observed in or about the Texas School Book Depository Building at that day that you haven't told us about that you can think of right now?

Mr. BAKER. No, sir; I can't think of anything else.

Mr. BELIN. From the time you went into the building how long did it take you to go up and make your searches and come on down until the time you left, to the best of your recollection?

Mr. BAKER. I would say that I was in there approximately 15 minutes.

Mr. BELIN. And you left there right at the time that you left Mr. Truly on the first floor?

Mr. BAKER. Yes, sir.

Mr. BELIN. In this time sequence you mentioned you were on the roof more than 5 minutes, that could be 25 or 30 or 10 or 15 or what?

Mr. BAKER. This, to my recollection, it seemed like I shouldn't have stayed up there over 10 minutes anyway, if that long.

Mr. BELIN. So you would say somewhere between 5 and 10 minutes?

Mr. BAKER. I just ran around up there looking for something; I didn't find it and then we came on down.

Mr. BELIN. Mr. Dulles, are there any questions that you have?

Mr. DULLES. I have no more questions. Have you any questions?

Mr. BELIN. Off the record.

(Discussion off the record.)

Mr. BELIN. Officer Baker, I believe you testified that you later saw Lee Harvey Oswald at the police station of the homicide office, is that correct?

Mr. BAKER. That is correct, sir.

Mr. BELIN. Was this later on that same day?

Mr. BAKER. Yes, it was.

Mr. BELIN. Would you state whether or not the man who was shown to you in the police station as Lee Harvey Oswald was or was not the same man that you saw and encountered on the second floor lunchroom of the Texas School Book Depository Building on that day?

Mr. BAKER. He was the same man.

Mr. BELIN. Is there anything else about his clothes that you can remember or his dress that you haven't talked about here?

Mr. BAKER. No, sir; I can't.

Mr. DULLES. Do you recall whether or not he was wearing the same clothes, did he appear to you the same when you saw him in the police station as when you saw him in the lunchroom?

Mr. BAKER. Actually just looking at him, he looked like he didn't have the same thing on.

Mr. BELIN. He looked as though he did not have the same thing on?

Mr. BAKER. He looked like he did not have the same on.

Senator COOPER. Did you say when you first saw this man walking away from you in the lunchroom, walking away in the opposite direction, that you said for him to come toward you.

Mr. BAKER. Yes, sir.

Senator COOPER. Did he turn around?

Mr. BAKER. Yes, sir; he did.

Mr. DULLES. The officer testified he had a pistol in his hand at that time, Officer Baker?

Senator COOPER. He did have a pistol in his hand?

Mr. BAKER. I had the pistol.

Mr. DULLES. Officer Baker had a pistol in his hand.

Senator COOPER. I see. Did he move toward you?

Mr. BAKER. Yes, sir; he did.

Senator COOPER. Was there anything about his appearance that was unusual?

Mr. BAKER. No, sir. Whenever I called to him, well he turned around and I had my gun in my hand, you know, and he started walking back towards me and I walked to meet him, and I met him at that doorway over there and about that time Mr. Truly who had started on up the stairs and then he came back, he found that I wasn't with him, came back, and walked up there aside of him and just about the time we met all three of us got there together and I turned to Mr. Truly and I asked him, and I said, "Do you know this man? Does he work here?"

And he said, "Yes," and that is whenever I turned and went on up the stairs. At that time he didn't say a word, he didn't change the expression or nothing on him.

Mr. DULLES. You testified, I believe, that he did not seem to be out of breath?

Mr. BAKER. That is right, sir.

Senator COOPER. He did not show any evidence of any emotion?

Mr. BAKER. No, sir.

Senator COOPER. Did you see anyone else while you were in the building, other than this man you have identified later as Oswald, and Mr. Truly?

Mr. BAKER. On the first floor there were two men. As we came through the main doorway to the elevators, I remember as we tried to get on the elevators I remember two men, one was sitting on this side and another one betweeen 20 or 30 feet away from us looking at us.

Mr. DULLES. Were they white men?

Mr. BAKER. Yes, sir.

Mr. BELIN. Officer Baker, we have an exhibit here 362 showing the first floor of the School Book Depository Building, and the top part of the exhibit is south. It is a little bit upside down from the usual top being north.

You will notice here the stairway in the front of the building.

Mr. BAKER. Yes, sir.

Mr. BELIN. And then there is a glass swinging door which I believe is shown there.

Could you mark the point at which you believe you were when you called out for someone to tell you where the stairway or elevator was?

Mr. BAKER. Is that the steps on the outside and this is the——

Mr. BELIN. These are the steps on the outside, this is the door, the first door and this is kind of the main lobby here, below the words "Main Entrance."

Mr. BAKER. Well, as you come up the steps, there is a glass door here in front of the building.

Mr. BELIN. Pardon me, this will be the recessed glass door right here swinging?

Mr. BAKER. All of this is the lobby.

Mr. BELIN. Yes, that is all the lobby.

Mr. BAKER. OK. This is the first door that you open to get in.

Mr. BELIN. Yes.

Mr. BAKER. And this is the lobby.

Mr. BELIN. Yes.

Mr. BAKER. And then you have another set of glass doors.

263

Mr. BELIN. There is another door right here, yes.

Mr. BAKER. And on through this one you have a swinging door, a little old counter-type door that swings——

Mr. BELIN. This would be the swinging door which would be to the west of the room marked "Mr. Truly's office" on Exhibit 362?

Mr. BAKER. That is right, sir.

Mr. BELIN. Where would you have been when you were yelling would someone tell you about the stairs or the elevator?

Mr. BAKER. At this point approximately where the "T" is here.

Mr. BELIN. You would be where the "T" is?

Mr. BAKER. I was standing inside the front doors and I wasn't too far from this door here.

Mr. BELIN. That would be the, what I call the, middle set of doors as you come in, between the front set of doors and the doors by the side of Mr. Truly's office, that little half door there.

Mr. BAKER. Yes, sir.

Mr. BELIN. And you were at the point as marked on Exhibit 362 approximately where the word "T" is.

Mr. BAKER. This lobby, to the best of my recollection, it seemed to me like, would—I would say, about 15 feet wide or something like that.

Mr. BELIN. Yes.

Mr. BAKER. And I had come in there, oh, say, 4 or 5 feet whenever I said, "Where is the stairway or the elevator?"

Mr. BELIN. I wonder if you could show us on Exhibit 362 the route that you took from the first floor to the time you went to the elevator?

Mr. BAKER. I came through the first set of doors, the second set and this second little old counter-type here, and kind of ran through that, from the southwest corner here through this swinging door.

Mr. BELIN. That is by Mr. Truly's office?

Mr. BAKER. Yes, sir; to the northwest corner here.

Mr. BELIN. By the west elevator.

Mr. BAKER. West elevator, that is right.

Mr. BELIN. Would this be roughly along the pen line already in there, would you estimate?

Mr. BAKER. Yes, sir; that is pretty close to it.

Mr. BELIN. You then went to the east elevator where Mr. Truly first pushed the button for the elevator?

Mr. BAKER. Yes, sir.

Mr. DULLES. Any further questions? Mr. Attorney General, do you have any questions?

Mr. CARR. There is just one. There were many people around there at that time, and the rest of the day——

Mr. DULLES. You are talking now about the Depository Building?

Mr. CARR. Yes, sir; at the time he has been testifying about. Did you have occasion during the rest of the day either in passing visits or idle conversation or anything of that type with any of the people that were there at the time who might have seen something or told you some theory they had about what might have happened?

Mr. BAKER. Not until last Friday morning. Chief Lunday, which is my chief in traffic, called me and asked me to go down to this Texas Depository Building, and I had—I have worked traffic outside several times but I never did go inside or talk to any of the employees.

Mr. CARR. I am referring to the people who were out there at the time of the shooting. Did you have a chance during that day to talk with any of them or did you overhear any conversations that might be material to the investigation here?

Mr. BAKER. The only ones that I talked to would be the solo officers who were around him.

Mr. DULLES. Around whom?

Mr. BAKER. Around the President's car at that time.

Mr. DULLES. What was the nature of those conversations?

Mr. BAKER. Well, we just were discussing, each one of us had a theory, you know where, how it happened, and really none of us knew how it happened, it just happened, and where they was at in place, you know, in reference to the car, would be about the only thing they could say, and at the time the first shot they didn't know where the shot came from.

The second shot they still didn't know, and then the third shot some of them over to the left-hand side, the blood and everything hit their helmets and their windshields and then they knew it had to come from behind.

Mr. BELIN. Say this again, Officer Baker. When you say some were on the left-hand side?

Mr. BAKER. Yes, I believe Officer B. J. Martin——

Mr. BELIN. Is he a motorcycle policeman?

Mr. BAKER. Yes, sir; he is.

Mr. BELIN. On a one- or two-wheeler or three-wheeler?

Mr. BAKER. He is a solo motorcycle, two-wheeler.

Mr. BELIN. Where was he riding at this time?

Mr. BAKER. He was on the left front.

Mr. BELIN. Of what?

Mr. BAKER. There were five motorcycle officers in front. There were four, two on each right side behind.

Mr. BELIN. When you say in front and behind of what vehicle?

Mr. BAKER. We are referring to the President's car.

Mr. BELIN. All right. He was on the front and to the left of the President's car.

Mr. BAKER. Yes, sir; that is right.

Mr. BELIN. What did he say to you about blood or something?

Mr. BAKER. Like I say, we were talking about where the shot came from, and he said the first shot he couldn't figure it out where it came from. He turned his head backward, reflex, you know, and then he turned back and the second shot came off, and then the third shot is when the blood and everything hit his helmet and his windshield .

Mr. BELIN. Did it hit the inside or the outside of his windshield, did he say?

Mr. BAKER. It hit all this inside. Now, as far as the inside or outside of the windshield. I don't know about that. But it was all on the right-hand side of his helmet.

Mr. BELIN. Of his helmet?

Mr. BAKER. On his uniform also.

Mr. BELIN. On his uniform.

Mr. BAKER. That is right.

Mr. BELIN. And he was riding to the left of the President and you say ahead of the President?

Mr. BAKER. On the left-hand side.

Mr. DULLES. But a little ahead of him?

Mr. BAKER. Yes, sir. They were immediately in front of the car.

Mr. DULLES. Any other conversations—pardon me, does that answer your question?

Mr. CARR. I was more interested, sir, in that, of course, but with the laymen around there. There was a lot of talk and theorizing at the time and I was just wondering what he might have heard from any of the laymen, or just ordinary onlookers of the parade, did you get a chance to talk to any of them?

Mr. BAKER. At that time I didn't get a chance to talk to any of those. At that time I immediately got on my motorcycle and went on down to the Trade Mart down there where he was set up for the luncheon and at the time I got on there I didn't stop until here come a sergeant and a medical examiner and they wanted me to take them code 3 to Parkland, at the time I got there we stood around the President's car there and kept the crowd back, and that is where I stayed until, I think we left after they loaded the body, we went to Love Field and stayed there for, say, 30 minutes or something like that.

Mr. BELIN. Did you talk to—pardon me, sir, does that take care of your questions?

Mr. CARR. Yes, sir; thank you very much.

Mr. DULLES. Any further questions?

Mr. CARR. No; thank you, sir.

Mr. BELIN. Did you talk to any of the other officers who were in or about the President's vehicle at the time of the shooting?

Mr. BAKER. Yes, sir; I talked to several of them and all of them had kind of had the same story, you know. It had to come from above and behind.

Mr. BELIN. When did you talk to these officers, like Officer Martin?

Mr. BAKER. That was—I didn't talk to him until we got back to the city hall, which we got off, we were supposed to get off at 3 o'clock that day, we got off around 4 the same time, they called us all in together.

Mr. BELIN. What other officers did you talk to and what did they say that you remember?

Mr. BAKER. I talked to Jim Chaney, and he made the statement that the two shots hit Kennedy first and then the other one hit the Governor.

Mr. BELIN. Where was he?

Mr. BAKER. He was on the right rear of the car or to the side, and then at that time the chief of police, he didn't know anything about this, and he moved up and told him, and then that was during the time that the Secret Service men were trying to get in the car, and at the time, after the shooting, from the time the first shot rang out, the car stopped completely, pulled to the left and stopped.

Mr. BELIN. The President's car?

Mr. BAKER. Yes, sir. Now, I have heard several of them say that, Mr. Truly was standing out there, he said it stopped. Several officers said it stopped completely.

Mr. DULLES. You saw it stop, did you?

Mr. BAKER. No, sir; I didn't see it stop.

Mr. DULLES. You just heard from others that it had stopped?

Mr. BAKER. Yes, sir; that it had completely stopped, and then for a moment there, and then they rushed on out to Parkland.

Mr. BELIN. Officer Baker, did this Officer Chaney say anything else about, for instance, where he thought the source of the shots was?

Mr. BAKER. Not—he knew they came from behind him but he didn't know where. He said from down there they was kind of going down that hill and said that shot, the sound of it, you couldn't tell just exactly where it came from.

Mr. BELIN. How did he know it came from behind then?

Mr. BAKER. Because he was riding from behind, and whenever it hit the President, he said he would see him fall.

Mr. BELIN. Now, you are giving a motion now, did he see him fall backwards first or forwards or when you say fall what do you mean by that?

Mr. BAKER. Well, he just said, when they hit he kind of fell, so I assumed he went to the left of him.

Mr. BELIN. All right.

Did any other officer say anything to you about what he saw or thought what happened?

Mr. BAKER. I talked to several of them but I can't remember exactly, you know, just what their story was.

Mr. BELIN. Was there anyone you talked to who thought the shots came from the front?

Mr. BAKER. No, sir; not except that the chief of police that is the only one. Now, that, like I say, that is the last thing I heard over that radio is "Get some men up on that railroad." Now, that could mean they either came from the side, which is due north, or right across in front of him. You know——

Mr. BELIN. Well, apart from the statement you testified to that the chief of police made over the radio about the underpass, was there any policeman or patrolman who was in the motorcade who in any way indicated to you that the shots came from the front?

Mr. BAKER. No, sir.

Senator COOPER. I would like to ask a couple of questions.

I think you said when you went inside the depository you saw no one except the man you later identified as Oswald, and Mr. Truly. There were two people sitting down on the first floor.

Mr. BAKER. As I entered that depository building, I was—people were running toward you, I don't know whether they worked there or whether they were just trying to get out of the way.

Mr. DULLES. From inside the building?

Mr. BAKER. No; from the street in. As I ran in I was pushing them aside and running through them, and some way, Mr. Truly got from my back to my front.

Now, he said he was right behind me. I never did see him until I got in and asked the question of where the stairs was, so evidently whenever I went in the door why he came on in. There were several people coming in as I, you know, came in, there were several in front of me and also around my sides and my back. And it seemed to me like a double door deal.

Senator COOPER. As you went up on the elevator could you see out of the elevator onto floors?

Mr. BAKER. Yes, sir. The best that I could, that is the reason I wasn't paying too much attention to the elevator I was looking around all those floors.

Senator COOPER. Did you see anyone?

Mr. BELIN. When you say up on the elevator, he didn't get on the elevator until he had got up on the stairs.

Senator COOPER. I am aware of that.

Mr. BAKER. I was still looking.

Senator COOPER. You went up on the second floor by stairs?

Mr. BAKER. Yes, sir.

Senator COOPER. Then you got on the elevator.

Mr. BELIN. No, sir; he didn't get on the elevator until the fifth floor.

Senator COOPER. Anyway, as you walked up the stairs could you see into each floor space as you passed from floor to floor?

Mr. BAKER. Partly. Now, this building has got pillars in it, you know, and then it has got books, cases of books stacked all in it. And the best that I could, you know, I would look through there and see if I could see anybody.

Senator COOPER. Did you see anyone?

Mr. BAKER. No, sir.

Senator COOPER. When you looked?

Mr. BAKER. Not from the second floor on up.

Senator COOPER. As you approached the building by motorcycle, did you notice whether anyone was looking out of the windows of the Texas School Book Depository?

Mr. BAKER. Yes, sir. Those windows, I would say a number of them were open and I tell you, to the best of my recollection, I scanned those windows, but I can't recall anybody looking out of them, you know. I looked at all them buildings so much and there were people looking out of every one of them, every doorway and every window, and I really was looking high more at the roof of it than I was anything, and I really didn't see nothing in the windows.

Senator COOPER. I may be repeating because I missed the first part of his testimony.

Mr. DULLES. Go ahead.

Senator COOPER. But when you heard the shot, you said later you saw some pigeons fly up.

Mr. BAKER. Yes, sir.

Senator COOPER. What was the sequence of time between the time you saw the flight of the pigeons and you heard the shot?

Mr. BAKER. As I got that motorcycle straightened up, and I hadn't gone just a very few feet there, it didn't seem like, you know, I went very far, but it is possible I went, we figured maybe 80, 60 to 80 feet there, and I looked up, as the shots started, I immediately looked up, you know. I was already facing ahead and I just kind of raised, I sighted up, and while I was looking up, those other two shots came off, and as I come up, I noticed those pigeons start to fly up there, but I really didn't see which, there were so many of them I couldn't tell which building they were coming from but I know they were all over.

Say you were facing north like Houston they were in the sky facing north in the street.

Senator COOPER. Which way were the pigeons going?

Mr. BAKER. They were just coming up, you know.

Senator COOPER. I assume you are a hunter, aren't you, from what you said?

Mr. BAKER. Yes, sir; I try to be.

Senator COOPER. Have you seen birds in flight when they are suddenly startled?

Mr. BAKER. Yes, sir.

Senator COOPER. Well, was this the character of the flight of pigeons you saw?

Mr. BAKER. Yes, sir; that is the way it seemed to me, that these birds, you know, just with a sudden uprush.

Senator COOPER. Did you have any notice of anyone saying there might have been a shot from the railroad until you heard the statement over the radio just before you entered the School Book Depository?

Mr. BAKER. No, sir; that was the only words that I remember that was said over the radio from the time the shots rang out until I started parking that motorcycle, and when I came off of it I heard those words.

Senator COOPER. Could you see the railroad yards?

Mr. BAKER. Yes, sir; I could see it—this track ran under this triple underpass to my left, all out behind this building.

Senator COOPER. Did you see anything there which attracted your attention other than——

Mr. BAKER. Nothing except——

Senator COOPER. Crowd?

Mr. BAKER. There were people all over this track, over this triple underpass, and people just standing all over this sloping bank there, you know, going up.

Senator COOPER. Were there any officers that you saw near the School Book Depository when you went in?

Mr. BAKER. There was an officer working traffic on that corner, and Officer J. W. Williams was——

Mr. DULLES. By that corner you mean the corner of Elm and Houston?

Mr. BAKER. That is right, sir. J. W. Williams who is a motorcycle officer, was, I thought, over on the left-hand side of me, and he was right with me, but as I ran in this building, I found out that I was by myself. I didn't know where anybody went.

Senator COOPER. Did you later see J. W. Williams, Officer Williams?

Mr. BAKER. Yes, sir. He stated that when the motorcade left with the President, and they immediately went code 3 to Parkland, why he was up there with him and he went up there with him. And I later saw him out there at Parkland.

Mr. DULLES. You testified, I believe, that you did not yourself see the President's car stop. You just were told it was stopped by several other officers?

Mr. BAKER. Let me say, as I parked that motorcycle, I looked down there, well, the car had swerved to the left, and I saw this man run out into this crowd and back. I don't know who he was but I saw that and I saw these people following him, and all these pressmen jumping out of their cars and running down the street toward him.

Mr. BELIN. Officer Baker, do you know from where this man ran off into the crowd at all or not?

Mr. BAKER. Apparently he came from one of the cars right there by the President's car. He was, he came from the motorcade, inside the motorcade out to the sidewalk and then back.

Mr. BELIN. All right.

You mentioned the fact that you had gone or come back from deer hunting just prior to November 22, 1963.

Mr. BAKER. Yes, sir.

Mr. BELIN. What kind of a weapon did you have when you went deer hunting?

Mr. BAKER. I had one of these .30-06, I believe the Springfield type.

Mr. BELIN. Is it a rifle?

Mr. BAKER. Yes, sir.

Mr. BELIN. Automatic or bolt action?

Mr. BAKER. Bolt action.

Mr. BELIN. How long have you owned a rifle, any rifle?

Mr. BAKER. This particular one I have had it approximately 7 years.

Mr. BELIN. Have you had much experience to go hunting?

Mr. BAKER. Yes, sir. Every year.

Mr. BELIN. Every year you go deer hunting?

Mr. BAKER. Yes, sir.

Mr. BELIN. You have had occasion to hear shots from your rifle?

Mr. BAKER. That is right, sir.

Mr. BELIN. From other rifles?

Mr. BAKER. Yes, sir.

Mr. BELIN. Did this in any way influence your decisions as to what you did on November 22 as you heard the first sound?

Mr. BAKER. Yes, sir; it did.

Mr. BELIN. In what way did it influence them?

Mr. BAKER. To me it was immediately a rifle shot. A lot of the solo officers said they thought it was the backfire from a motorcycle because you can make those motorcycles pop pretty loud. But that instant it just, I don't know, it just hit me as a rifle shot.

Senator COOPER. How long have you been firing a rifle?

Mr. BAKER. Say, from the time I was about 17 years old.

Senator COOPER. Have you fired other types of rifles other than the one you used?

Mr. BAKER. Yes, sir; the first one I had was a 30–30 Marlin lever type.

Senator COOPER. Have you ever seen the rifle that is alleged to have belonged to Lee Oswald?

Mr. BAKER. I saw it, a photograph of it, in the newspaper.

Senator COOPER. Do you know what kind of rifle it is?

Mr. BAKER. Not offhand. I heard it was some foreign make gun. Most of the boys down there at the police department have had dealings with foreign type guns, rifles, you know of this kind, and a lot of them sell them, and a lot of them rework them, you know, make them into deer rifles.

Senator COOPER. What were the characteristics of the report that you heard, three reports, which made you believe that it was a shot from a rifle?

Mr. BAKER. Well, they were too distinct, you know, to be—I have heard that pop from that motorcycle and I have heard rifle shots, and to me there was just a difference in them.

Mr. BELIN. Officer Baker, did it appear to you that these sounds that you heard were from the same rifle or from possibly more than one rifle?

Mr. BAKER. I would say they was from the same rifle.

Mr. BELIN. Did it appear that the sounds all came from the same source?

Mr. BAKER. Yes, sir.

Mr. BELIN. With regard to the closeness of these sounds together, how fast they came, did it appear that it came from or that it could have come from a weapon that had to be operated by bolt action as opposed to a semiautomatic or an automatic weapon?

Mr. BAKER. It seemed to me like you could either fire a semi or bolt action in about the same time.

Mr. BELIN. Have you had occasion to use a bolt action rifle and fire shots quickly one after the other?

Mr. BAKER. Yes, sir; I have.

Mr. BELIN. Did it appear that, from what you heard, that from your experience you could have operated your own bolt action rifle as quickly as those shots came?

Mr. BAKER. Yes, sir.

Senator COOPER. If you made any judgment, what was the length of time from the time you heard the first report until you heard the third?

Mr. BAKER. I would say just about as fast as you could bolt one of those bolt action rifles which wouldn't be—I don't believe it would be over 3 seconds apart.

Mr. DULLES. Over what?

Mr. BAKER. Three seconds apart.

Mr. BELIN. From each shot?

Mr. BAKER. Yes, sir.

Mr. BELIN. Three seconds from the first to the second and another 3 seconds from the second to the third?

Mr. BAKER. Yes, sir.

Mr. BELIN. You are saying not over 3 seconds?

Mr. BAKER. Not over 3 seconds.

Mr. DULLES. Any further questions?

Thank you very much, Officer Baker. Your testimony has been very helpful. (At this point Senator Cooper left the hearing room.)

TESTIMONY OF MRS. ROBERT A. REID

Mr. DULLES. Mrs. Reid, the Chief Justice had to leave a few moments and he expressed his regret to you.

Mrs. REID. Yes.

Mr. DULLES. So I am presiding over the Commission at the present time.

As you possibly have been informed, the purpose of the testimony this morning has been to hear the testimony of Officer Baker, yourself, and certain others who were in the vicinity of the Texas School Book Depository Building at the time of the assassination of the President, and we will ask you give testimony in that connection and anything else you may know.

Would you please rise, Mrs. Reid, and hold up your right hand.

Do you swear the testimony you will give before this Commission is the truth, the whole truth, so help you God, and nothing but the truth?

Mrs. REID. I do.

Mr. DULLES. Mr. Belin will carry forward the interrogation.

Mr. BELIN. We met in Dallas on Friday, March 20.

Mrs. REID. That is right.

Mr. BELIN. Mrs. Reid, could you state your name for the Commission, please?

Mrs. REID. Mrs. Robert A. Reid.

Mr. BELIN. That is R-e-i-d?

Mrs. REID. R-e-i-d, that is right.

Mr. BELIN. Where do you live, Mrs. Reid?

Mrs. REID. 1914 Elmwood Boulevard, Dallas, Tex.

Mr. BELIN. And are you originally from Dallas?

Mrs. REID. Well, I have been for quite a number of years. I was born out in a little town out from Dallas, Cereal, Tex.

Mr. BELIN. How long did you go to school in Dallas? Did you go through high school?

Mrs. REID. I completed high school there and I married and went to Waxahachie and lived there about 15 years and moved back to Dallas then.

Mr. BELIN. Do you have any family, Mrs. Reid?

Mrs. REID. You mean like sisters or my children?

Mr. BELIN. Well, children.

Mrs. REID. Both, I have six sisters and I have two children and a grandchild.

Mr. BELIN. You have a grandchild?

Mrs. REID. And a husband, and a family.

Mr. BELIN. What is your occupation, Mrs. Reid?

Mrs. REID. I am a clerical supervisor.

Mr. BELIN. For what company?

Mrs. REID. Texas School Book Depository.

Mr. BELIN. How long have you worked for the Texas School Book Depository?

Mrs. REID. I have been 7 years.

Mr. BELIN. Have you been a clerical supervisor all the time?

Mrs. REID. No; I started out in the department on what they call their postage desk and I was appointed to a clerical supervisor.

Mr. BELIN. Mrs. Reid, I am taking you to November 22, 1963.

Mrs. REID. All right.

Mr. BELIN. Where were you on that day commencing with, say, around noon or so?

Mrs. REID. Well, at 12 I went to lunch, and I had my lunch rather hurriedly so that I might go downstairs and watch the parade.

Mr. BELIN. Mrs. Reid, you say you ate your lunch?

Mrs. REID. Yes; I did.

Mr. BELIN. Where did you eat your lunch?

Mrs. REID. In our lunchroom, in the lunchroom.

Mr. BELIN. Where is that?

Mrs. REID. Well——

Mr. BELIN. On what floor?

Mrs. REID. On two, the same floor as our office.

Mr. BELIN. That is on the second floor?

Mrs. REID. Yes, sir.

Mr. BELIN. Did you buy your lunch or bring your lunch?

Mrs. REID. No; I brought my lunch.

Mr. BELIN. Was there anyone in the lunchroom when you were eating lunch?

Mrs. REID. Yes.

Mr. BELIN. Do you remember who was there?

Mrs. REID. Well, the girls that work under me, the young ladies, goodness, it is all hard for me to remember how many there were, but the general ones that usually eat there with me every day.

Mr. BELIN. On Commission Exhibit 497, is this room, this lunchroom, the one that is marked "lunchroom" here with the numbers 25 and 26 in it?

Mrs. REID. That is right.

Mr. BELIN. And that is where you ate?

Mrs. REID. Yes.

Mr. BELIN. And on Commission Exhibit 497 do you work on the second floor also?

Mrs. REID. I do.

Mr. BELIN. In the area marked with the room "office space," somewhere in that room?

Mrs. REID. Over here.

Mr. BELIN. You say you work over near the dumbwaiter which is marked?

Mrs. REID. My desk——

Mr. BELIN. Your desk is near the dumbwaiter on Exhibit 497.

Mr. DULLES. That is the desk there, is it?

Mr. BELIN. That is the dumbwaiter.

Mr. DULLES. Oh, yes.

Mr. BELIN. Now, Mrs. Reid, you left lunch about what time?

Mrs. REID. Well, I left, I ate my lunch hurriedly, I wasn't watching the time but I wanted to be sure of getting out on the streets in time for the parade before he got there, and I called my husband, who works at the records building, and they had a radio in their office and they were listening as the parade progressed and he told me they were running about 10 minutes late. But I went down rather soon and stood on the steps.

Mr. DULLES. Where was your husband working?

Mrs. REID. He works for the records building.

Mr. BELIN. Where is that located?

Mrs. REID. Well, it is off the left-hand side, kind of cater-cornered across from our building.

Mr. BELIN. The records building has one side of it on Elm Street running from Houston to Record Street?

Mrs. REID. Yes.

Mr. BELIN. And I believe it is on, it would run on, the south side of Elm?

Mrs. REID. Yes.

Mr. BELIN. Is that correct?

Mrs. REID. Yes.

Mr. BELIN. All right. Do you know about what time it was that you left the lunchroom, was it 12, 12:15?

Mrs. REID. I think around 12:30 somewhere along in there.

Mr. BELIN. All right. When you left the lunchroom, did you leave with the other girls?

Mrs. REID. No; I didn't. The younger girls had gone and I left alone.

Mr. BELIN. Were you the last person in the lunchroom?

Mrs. REID. No; I could not say that because I don't remember that part of it because I was going out of the building by myself, I wasn't even, you know, connected with anyone at all.

Mr. BELIN. Were there any men in the lunchroom when you left there?

Mrs. REID. I can't, I don't, remember that.

Mr. BELIN. All right.

Mrs. REID. I can't remember the time they left.

Mr. BELIN. Now, you went out from the lunchroom; turning to Exhibit 497, you went from the lunchroom through the door, which would be the west door, and then through the doorway marked number 23 on the exhibit there or did you instead go to the front?

Mrs. REID. No; I came back through the office.

Mr. BELIN. You didn't go through the door marked 24?

Mrs. REID. No; I did not.

Mr. BELIN. You came out through this first door of the lunchroom?

Mrs. REID. That is right.

Mr. BELIN. And then you turned which way?

Mrs. REID. Turned this way.

Mr. BELIN. You turned to your left and went through the door which is between numbers 27 and 28?

Mrs. REID. That is right.

Mr. BELIN. On Exhibit 497, and you went back to your office. Did you go by your desk?

Mrs. REID. I am sure I did because I usually leave my purse in there until I get ready to go out and then pick it up.

Mr. BELIN. All right. You walked toward the number marked 29 on Exhibit 497?

Mrs. REID. That is right.

Mr. BELIN. Then where did you walk?

Mrs. REID. I came over here and got my jacket and scarf out of the closet.

Mr. BELIN. All right.

You are now pointing to the closet on Exhibit 497 which would be located on the east side of the building?

Mrs. REID. That is right.

Mr. BELIN. Toward the front. Then what did you do?

Mrs. REID. I came and went out this door.

Mr. BELIN. You are, you went out the door which is marked on Exhibit 497 as room 200, is that correct?

Mrs. REID. That is right.

Mr. BELIN. What did you do?

Mrs. REID. I got on the elevator.

Mr. BELIN. Now, there is an elevator along the east wall toward the front of the building, is that correct?

Mrs. REID. That is right.

Mr. BELIN. Is this a freight or passenger?

Mrs. REID. It is a passenger.

Mr. BELIN. Do you know how far this elevator goes or how high?

Mrs. REID. Fourth floor.

Mr. BELIN. Fourth floor. You got on the elevator on the second floor?

Mrs. REID. That is right.

Mr. BELIN. Then what did you do?

Mrs. REID. Came down on the first floor.

Mr. BELIN. Then you came on the first floor.

Mrs. REID. Went out the front door of our building.

Mr. BELIN. Went out the front door.

Mrs. REID. I stood on the steps for several minutes.

Mr. BELIN. All right.

Mrs. REID. Shall I continue?

Mr. BELIN. Yes.

Mrs. REID. Until I saw the parade coming around the corner from Main and Houston and when I did I walked out to the street so I would be nearer to the people, and I walked out and was standing by Mr. Truly and Mr. Campbell.

Mr. BELIN. All right. This was in front of the steps, ma'am?

Mrs. REID. Well, no; I had gone out directly in the front but I had gotten nearer to the street than the steps.

Mr. BELIN. You were actually onto the street then as the motorcade came by?

Mrs. REID. Yes; that is right. There is a part in there where our streets, one goes this way and one kind of goes off this way, and the line of parade they were going that way and I got right on the curb and was standing there.

Mr. BELIN. Well, turning to Exhibit 361, the top of Exhibit 361 faces south and this is Houston Street, here is the School Book Depository Building that I am pointing to.

Can you give any estimate as to where you were with relation to this, well, I will call it a peninsula of land between the parkway and the building.

Mrs. REID. You have got me turned around.

Mr. BELIN. The parade was coming along Houston.

Mrs. REID. I was standing about along in here, in here.

Mr. BELIN. You were standing a little bit to the north of the spot marked "B" on Exhibit 361.

Mrs. REID. That is right.

Mr. BELIN. And you would be directly in front of the main entrance of the School Book Depository, is that correct?

Mrs. REID. That is correct.

Mr. BELIN. Now, by "B" I am referring to, on Exhibit 361, I am referring to the pen ink—pen and ink "B" which is directly to the east of what I will call the traffic light on that peninsula of land as Elm goes into the parkway there. All right, what did you see?

Mrs. REID. You mean when I was standing there?

Mr. BELIN. What did you see and hear and do?

Mrs. REID. Well, I was naturally watching for the car as the President came by. I looked at him and I was very anxious to see Mrs. Kennedy, I looked at her and I was going to see how she was dressed and she was dressed very attractive and she put up her hand to her hat and was holding it on, the wind was blowing a little bit and then went on right on by me and that is the last as far as the parade, I mean as far as they were concerned.

I did see Johnson, and that was it. I can't even tell you any more about the parade because after the shots I didn't know any part about that.

Mr. BELIN. What did you see and hear and do after that?

Mrs. REID. Well, when I heard—I heard three shots.

Mr. BELIN. You heard three shots?

Mrs. REID. And I turned to Mr. Campbell and I said, "Oh, my goodness, I am afraid those came from our building," because it seemed like they came just so directly over my head, and then I looked up in the windows, and saw three colored boys up there, I only recognized one because I didn't know the rest of them so well.

Mr. BELIN. Which one did you know?

Mrs. REID. James Jarman.

Mr. BELIN. You recognized James Jarman?

Mrs. REID. Yes; because I had had some dealings with him in the business part and I knew him. I couldn't have told you the other two at all because I didn't know them.

Mr. BELIN. Do you remember that floor you saw them on?

Mrs. REID. Well, I wasn't exactly looking at the floor, I don't know, I would say a couple of floors up. I mean several anyway. I don't know exactly.

Mr. BELIN. You don't remember which floor it was.

Mrs. REID. I couldn't tell you because, you know, I didn't count the floors and I didn't count them, and I made the statement "Oh, I hope they don't think any of our boys have done this" and I had no thoughts of anything like that. I turned and went back in the building.

Mr. BELIN. All right. Now, let me ask you this then.

Mrs. REID. All right.

Mr. BELIN. Before you turned and went back into the building did you—did Mr. Campbell say anything to you?

Mrs. REID. He said, "Oh, Mrs. Reid, no, it came from the grassy area down this way," and that was the last I said to him.

Mr. BELIN. All right. When he said "this way" which direction was he pointing?

Mrs. REID. Well, I hope I get my directions. In the direction of the parade was going, in the bottom of that direction.

Mr. BELIN. Now, did you look around after the shots and notice what people were doing?

Mrs. REID. Well, it was just a mass of confusion. I saw people beginning to fall, and the thought that went through my mind, my goodness I must get out of this line of shots, they may fire some more. And don't ask me why I went into the building because I don't know.

Mr. BELIN. Did you see anything else of people running or doing anything else?

Mrs. REID. No; because I ran into the building. I do not recall seeing anyone in the lobby. I ran up to our office.

Mr. BELIN. All right.

Mr. DULLES. Just 1 second there. How long after the third shot did you run into the building?

Mr. BELIN. Mr. Dulles, we did a reconstruction on that time sequence on Friday and I am going to come to that as soon as I get the route first.

Mr. DULLES. Right.

Mr. BELIN. You went into the building in the main lobby?

Mrs. REID. Yes; I did.

Mr. BELIN. Did you take the elevator or the stairs?

Mrs. REID. No; I went up the stairs.

Mr. BELIN. Was this the front stairs or the back stairs?

Mrs. REID. No; the front stairs.

Mr. BELIN. All right. You went up through the stairs and then what did you do?

Mrs. REID. I went into the office.

Mr. BELIN. You went into your office?

Mrs. REID. Yes.

Mr. BELIN. And then what did you do?

Mrs. REID. Well, I kept walking and I looked up and Oswald was coming in the back door of the office. I met him by the time I passed my desk several feet and I told him, I said, "Oh, the President has been shot, but maybe they didn't hit him."

He mumbled something to me, I kept walking, he did, too. I didn't pay any attention to what he said because I had no thoughts of anything of him having any connection with it at all because he was very calm. He had gotten a coke and was holding it in his hands and I guess the reason it impressed me seeing him in there I thought it was a little strange that one of the warehouse boys would be up in the office at the time, not that he had done anything wrong. The only time I had seen him in the office was to come and get change and he already had his coke in his hand so he didn't come for change and I dismissed him. I didn't think anything else.

Mr. BELIN. When you saw him, I believe you said you first saw him when he was coming through the door?

Mrs. REID. Yes, sir.

Mr. BELIN. Turning to Exhibit 497, what doorway was it where you first saw him?

Mrs. REID. Right here.

Mr. BELIN. You are pointing to the doorway between numbers 27 and 28?

Mrs. REID. That is right.

Mr. BELIN. On Exhibit 497?

Mrs. REID. That is right.

Mr. BELIN. Where were you when you saw him in that doorway?

Mrs. REID. I was coming right through here.

Mr. BELIN. You are pointing to what number there?

Mrs. REID. Well, it is 29.

Mr. BELIN. 29. And then about where were you when you actually passed him or had this exchange?

Mrs. REID. Right along here. I passed my desk.

Mr. BELIN. Why don't you put on Exhibit 496 an "X" as to where you were when you thought you passed him.

Mrs. REID. Here.

Mr. BELIN. I wonder if you would put the initial "R" which we will put for Mrs. Reid.

Mrs. REID. All right.

Mr. BELIN. By the "X" and that is where you were when you passed him.

On March 20 you and I met for the first time, didn't we, Mrs. Reid?

Mrs. REID. That is right.

Mr. BELIN. We sat down and I asked you to tell me what happened and you related the story. Did I keep on questioning you or did you tell me what happened?

Mrs. REID. Well, I more or less told you what had happened.

Mr. BELIN. All right. Then we went out on the street, did we not, in front of the building, with a stopwatch, do you remember that?

Mrs. REID. Yes; I surely do. It was kind of cool.

Mr. BELIN. It was kind of cool wasn't it, and a little bit windy.

Mrs. REID. Yes; it was; yes.

Mr. BELIN. And when in Dallas, we started the stopwatch from the time that the last shot was fired, is that correct?

Mrs. REID. That is right.

Mr. BELIN. And then you went through your actions, what you saw, your conversations that you had, and your actions in going back into the building and up to the point that you saw Lee Harvey Oswald?

Mrs. REID. That is right.

Mr. BELIN. Do you remember how long by the stopwatch it took you?

Mrs. REID. Approximately 2 minutes.

Mr. DULLES. I didn't hear you.

Mrs. REID. Two minutes.

Mr. BELIN. From the time of the last shot the time you and Oswald crossed?

Mrs. REID. Yes; I believe that is the way we timed it.

Mr. BELIN. When you—you saw me start the stopwatch and you saw me stop it there, right?

Mrs. REID. Yes.

Mr. BELIN. When you met in the lunchroom——

Mrs. REID. I didn't meet him in the lunchroom.

Mr. BELIN. Pardon me, when you met in the office, which direction were you going, looking toward Exhibit 497, as you look on it, which direction were you going toward the left or right?

Mrs. REID. You mean as I came in the office? I turned in and turned to my left.

Mr. BELIN. That would be heading in a westerly direction is that right?

Mrs. REID. Yes.

Mr. BELIN. What direction was Oswald walking?

Mrs. REID. He was going east.

Mr. BELIN. Did you see him actually walk through or coming through the door there?

Mrs. REID. He had just gotten to the door, was stepping in as I glanced up.

Mr. BELIN. He was stepping in as you glanced up?

Mrs. REID. Yes.

Mr. BELIN. Had you ever—you said, I will put it this way, had you ever seen Oswald in that second floor office space before apart from the time of getting his pay?

Mrs. REID. Well, one other time he came in, now he might have been in to get that change for this time but I didn't see him going up there, and he made a remark to one of the girls back there and she said, "Well, he sure is calm." And I said, "What did he say to you?"

And she says, "I have a baby," and he stopped and I said, "Well, he is pretty calm just having a new baby," and outside of that I never remember seeing him other than to come in to get change.

Mr. BELIN. What about the other men in the warehouse, did they have occasion to come into that office space?

Mrs. REID. Occasionally they come up to get change.

Mr. BELIN. Apart from getting change or getting paid?

Mrs. REID. No; very seldom unless they are sent up there to get something. I mean they just don't come in there and wander around. It is some business for them.

Now, I did see him in the lunchroom a few times prior to this eating his lunch but I didn't even know his name.

Mr. BELIN. Did you know his name on the day you saw him?

Mrs. REID. No; I did not. When I saw his picture I still didn't know his name until they told us who it was.

Mr. BELIN. How did you know the person you saw was Lee Harvey Oswald on the second floor?

Mrs. REID. Because it looked just like him.

Mr. BELIN. You mean the picture with the name Lee Harvey Oswald?

Mrs. REID. Oh, yes.

Mr. BELIN. But you had seen him in the building?

Mrs. REID. Other than that day, sure.

Mr. BELIN. Do you remember what clothes he had on when you saw him?

Mrs. REID. What he was wearing, he had on a white T-shirt and some kind of wash trousers. What color I couldn't tell you.

Mr. BELIN. I am going to hand you what has been marked Commission Exhibit, first 157 and then 158, and I will ask you if either or both look like they might have been the trousers that you saw him wear or can you tell?

Mrs. REID. I just couldn't be positive about that. I would rather not say, because I just cannot.

Mr. BELIN. Do you remember whether he had any shirt or jacket on over his T-shirt?

Mrs. REID. He did not. He did not have any jacket on.

Mr. BELIN. Have you ever seen anyone working at the book depository wearing any kind of a shirt or jacket similar to Commission Exhibit 150 or do you know?

Mrs. REID. No; I do not. I have never, so far as I know ever seen that shirt. I have been asked about that shirt before, I have seen it once before but not since all this happened.

Mr. BELIN. All right. Mrs. Reid, if a person were in the lunchroom with a coke on the second floor, and then wanted to get to the front stairway or front elevator, would there be only one route to get there or would there be more than one?

Mrs. REID. Yes; he could either go around this hallway, or back here in this hallway or he could have gotten through our office or——

Mr. BELIN. All right.

I wonder if in the first hallway you could mark route 1 there so we have it on 496.

Mrs. REID. Does it matter?

Mr. BELIN. That is fine.

Mrs. REID. You said the front stairway, too?

Mr. BELIN. That is the front stairway. You have put a number 1, I am going to put "R–1".

Mrs. REID. All right.

Mr. BELIN. And that will be one hallway to go down to get from the lunchroom to the front stairway?

Mrs. REID. That is right.

Mr. BELIN. Now, would there be another way to get there?

Mrs. REID. He can come through the office.

Mr. BELIN. You could come through the office?

Mrs. REID. Yes.

Mr. BELIN. Which is the way Lee Harvey Oswald was walking?

Mrs. REID. That is right.

Mr. BELIN. Would any one way be faster than the other or not?

Mrs. REID. It couldn't be very much faster because it is practically the same distance here that it is here and you have got this hallway there.

Mr. BELIN. So, either "R-1" or going through the office marked 29 would be approximately the same?

Mrs. REID. Yes.

Mr. BELIN. Now, where you saw Lee Harvey Oswald is there kind of a pathway through there without any obstructions for desks?

Mrs. REID. Yes; there is, sort of a passageway.

Mr. BELIN. You passed at point what you have marked with an "X"?

Mrs. REID. Yes.

Mr. BELIN. Is that correct?

Mrs. REID. Yes.

Mr. BELIN. With an "R" and "X" to it?

Mrs. REID. Yes.

Mr. BELIN. Did Lee Harvey Oswald walk past you?

Mrs. REID. Yes; he did.

Mr. BELIN. Kept on walking in the same direction?

Mrs. REID. Yes, sir.

Mr. BELIN. How far did you see him go?

Mrs. REID. I didn't turn around to look. He went on straight, he did not go on past the back door because I was facing that way. What he did after that——

Mr. BELIN. But you know he did not go out the same back door he came in?

Mrs. REID. No; he did not.

Mr. BELIN. Do you know whether or not he went into the conference room?

Mrs. REID. Well, I wouldn't think he did because this door off here was locked and I had unlocked it for the policeman myself.

Mr. BELIN. All right, let's put an arrow here to the door that you say was locked, and we will put—do you want to put in the word "locked" in there, if you would, please?

Mrs. REID. All right.

Mr. DULLES. On which side was it locked or did you take the key away, was it locked so that you——

Mrs. REID. I would go in from this way. I wasn't going in from our office into the conference room.

Mr. DULLES. And you locked that door?

Mrs. REID. We did. They had asked me, I went in there with the policeman into the conference room.

Mr. DULLES. Did you take the key?

Mrs. REID. Yes, sir; I did, I got it for Mr. Williams.

Mr. DULLES. No; I mean after you locked the door do you leave the key in the lock?

Mrs. REID. No.

Mr. BELIN. What I want to know is this, Mrs. Reid. When you came back up into the building after the shooting and you walked into the conference room, at that time was the door which you have marked "locked," was it locked at that time when you came in?

Mrs. REID. Yes, sir; it was to—it was locked when I got to it, I will say that.

Mr. BELIN. Let me ask you this. Had you been the one who had locked it before or don't you know?

Mrs. REID. Oh, no, I couldn't say that because too many people used the conference room.

I would have no way of knowing who locked it or if it is left unlocked. The porter locks it in the evening.

Mr. BELIN. All right.

If one is locking that door with a key do you lock the door from the inside of the conference room?

Mrs. REID. Either way.

Mr. BELIN. Or the outside, either way?

Mrs. REID. Either way.

Mr. BELIN. Who has custody of the key?

Mrs. REID. I got that from Mr. Williams' desk, because that is where I got it from, and then the porter has one. I could not say. They all have the keys.

Mr. BELIN. When did you get it to unlock the door?

Mrs. REID. Well, by the time the policeman got there and started searching our floor. I can't recall whether I had taken him into the lounge first because they had me to go in there with him, the ladies' lounge, or whether they went in there because there is a little stand in here that Mr. Cason uses when we have a conference, and he jerked it back because it would have been humanly possible for a person to have gotten in there, but it was up against the wall and there was no one there.

Mr. BELIN. Would this have been more or less than 5 minutes after you got back in the building that you opened the lounge?

Mrs. REID. That is where you all get me in this time because I was not watching the clock that day.

Mr. BELIN. That is all right.

Mrs. REID. Time really didn't mean anything to us because they, the police officers, just came in on us and began to ask so many questions.

Mr. BELIN. When you were at point "RX" and moving, if someone would have walked into the conference room would you have heard him in any way?

Mrs. REID. I could have heard him open the door.

Mr. BELIN. You could hear them open the door. During the time, the period of time you were there and saw Lee Harvey Oswald, did you hear anyone open the door to the conference room?

Mrs. REID. I do not recall any.

Mr. BELIN. From your best judgment, if Lee Harvey Oswald didn't go into the conference room and didn't go back to the door marked around between 27 and 28, how would he have gotten out of the office?

Mrs. REID. Right straight out this door down this stairway and out the front door.

Mr. BELIN. You are saying right down the hallway in the direction in which the arrow number 29 is pointing?

Mrs. REID. That is right.

Mr. BELIN. Down through the hall and down through the front stairway.

Have you ever talked to anyone there who ever saw Lee Harvey Oswald leave the building?

Mrs. REID. No; I haven't.

Mr. BELIN. Do you know of your own personal knowledge how he got out of the building?

Mrs. REID. No; I do not, I do not. I have no idea.

Mr. BELIN. Mrs. Reid, did you notice whether or not the man you ran into on the second floor whom you now identify as Lee Harvey Oswald was carrying anything in either arm other than a coke?

Mrs. REID. No.

Mr. BELIN. Was the coke full or empty?

Mrs. REID. It was full.

Mr. BELIN. It was full.

Was there anything else you noticed about him?

Mrs. REID. No.

Mr. BELIN. Anything about the expression on his face?

Mrs. REID. No; just calm.

Mr. BELIN. Anything about whether or not his clothes were clean or dirty?

Mrs. REID. Well, they were clean.

Mr. BELIN. Anything about whether or not his hair was combed or mussed?

Mrs. REID. No; I did not. There wasn't anything unusual.

Mr. BELIN. You say he mumbled something?

Mrs. REID. He did.

Mr. BELIN. Could you even remember one word that he mumbled?

Mrs. REID. I did not because he kept moving and I did, too, and I was just not interested in what he was saying, it was just the excitement of time and I didn't even say, "What did you say?" because I wasn't interested.

Mr. DULLES. Was he moving fast?

Mrs. REID. No; because he was moving at a very slow pace, I never did see him moving fast at any time.

Mr. BELIN. He was moving just at his normal walk?

Mrs. REID. Yes.

Mr. BELIN. Do you remember whether he was wearing any pieces of jewelry like a watch or bracelet or ring or something?

Mrs. REID. No; I do not remember that.

Mr. BELIN. Mrs. Reid, did you ever have any personal contact with Lee Harvey Oswald about such things as his paycheck or anything like that?

Mrs. REID. No; I did not.

Mr. BELIN. Do you remember what hand he was carrying his coke in?

Mrs. REID. Yes.

Mr. BELIN. In what hand?

Mrs. REID. In his right hand.

Mr. BELIN. Mrs. Reid, we thank you very much.

Mr. DULLES. Just one moment.

Mr. BELIN. Pardon me, do you have a question, sir?

Mr. DULLES. How many times do you think you saw Mr. Oswald during the period he was employed?

Mrs. REID. My goodness.

Mr. DULLES. Roughly.

Mrs. REID. It couldn't have been——

Mr. DULLES. Five times, 10 times?

Mrs. REID. I would say five times. At times I would go down to Mr. Truly's office for some business. I would see him across the floor, but he paid no attention to you and there were times, the few times, he ate lunch up there but he never talked to anyone.

Mr. DULLES. Never talked to anyone?

Mrs. REID. And he was usually reading, I noticed that.

Mr. DULLES. Did he seem to repel ordinary conversational attempts or didn't you try that?

Mrs. REID. I never did try it, I never did.

Mr. DULLES. You never tried it.

Mrs. REID. He seemed to be interested in what he was doing, I would never see anyone talking to him at all in the lunchroom so far as I can recall, not any time.

Mr. DULLES. Who in the organization so far as you know would have handled his paychecks?

Mrs. REID. Mr. Campbell.

Mr. DULLES. Campbell would have handled his paychecks.

Mrs. REID. He makes them out and then he sends them to Mr. Truly and I am sure he distributes it to his employees.

Mr. BELIN. Two questions, Mrs. Reid.

Mrs. REID. All right.

Mr. BELIN. When we reconstructed your actions on Friday, March 20, which you said it took about 2 minutes, would you say that this was a maximum or minimum time?

Mrs. REID. Well, it wasn't any less than that I am sure because 2 minutes time——

Mr. BELIN. Did we kind of run?

Mrs. REID. Yes, we did, three times.

Mr. BELIN. Three times.

Mrs. REID. I remember that.

Mr. BELIN. And we were both huffing and puffing?

Mrs. REID. Yes, we were. I know I was that day, I think.

Mr. BELIN. Mrs. Reid, since the tragedy of November 22, have there been any discussions that you have heard among any employees which might relate to the character insofar as the personal habits or what-have-you of Lee Harvey Oswald?

Mrs. Reid. The only thing I have heard anybody say was he never talked to anybody, he always went about his business, that is the only thing I heard the employees say.

Mr. Belin. Did you ever hear anyone say that he might have been friendly with at least one other employee?

Mrs. Reid. No; I have not.

Mr. Dulles. Did the employees discuss him at all among themselves?

Mrs. Reid. You mean prior to this?

Mr. Dulles. Prior, during the period he was employed there?

Mrs. Reid. No.

Mr. Dulles. At the Book Depository?

Mrs. Reid. I never heard it.

Mr. Dulles. They did not discuss him in your presence, the office employees?

Mrs. Reid. Well, the office employees and the warehouse employees are not connected. We talk to them, naturally some of them have been there a long time.

Mr. Dulles. Was it your usual practice to take lunch in the lunchroom on the second floor?

Mrs. Reid. Yes, it is; every day.

Mr. Dulles. Do you recall whether it was Lee Harvey Oswald's usual practice or how many times possibly you saw him there at lunch with you and the others?

Mrs. Reid. You mean did he come up every day? No, he did not.

Mr. Dulles. Would you think he came up half the days or could you give any—half the working days?

Mrs. Reid. No; I wouldn't say he came that often. I can't recall seeing him up there but three times. We have said since then, since he sat there and didn't say anything and was reading we have often wondered what we discussed before him because we all have a general conversation every day at noon but I don't know we would have said anything that interested him.

But you wondered was he listening to what we were saying, I don't know whether he heard anything but he may have heard what we were saying.

Mr. Dulles. You, of course, knew that Lee Harvey Oswald was an employee of the School Book Depository?

Mrs. Reid. You mean by name before this happened?

Mr. Dulles. That the individual that you later knew was Oswald was one of the employees of the school book?

Mrs. Reid. Yes, because I had seen him working in the building.

Mr. Dulles. Yes. Attorney General Carr, do you have any questions?

Mr. Carr. Mrs. Reid, have you had occasion to visit with any of Oswald's relatives, his wife or mother?

Mrs. Reid. No.

Mr. Carr. Have they been in there since that date to look over the premises?

Mrs. Reid. His mother has been but I didn't see her. She didn't go any further than the first floor I understand, but I have never seen her other than these pictures.

Mr. Dulles. Is it usual for the employees of the depository to have friends visit them during office hours or would that be an unusual practice?

Mrs. Reid. No; that would not be unusual. Family or somebody wanted to drop by to see you they never have objected to that.

Mr. Belin. I think the record should show we are offering in evidence this morning, Mr. Dulles, Commission Exhibit 507 which is the diagram of the seventh floor which Officer Baker testified to.

Mr. Dulles. You want that admitted now?

Mr. Belin. We want that admitted now.

Mr. Dulles. No objection. It will be admitted.

(The diagram referred to was marked Commission Exhibit No. 507 for identification and received in evidence.)

Mr. Belin. I think those are all the questions we have of Mrs. Reid.

We want to thank you very much for your cooperation in coming up here, Mrs. Reid.

Mrs. REID. Thank you.

Mr. DULLES. Thank you very much, Mrs. Reid.

I will tell the Chief Justice of your cooperation and helpfulness.

We will reconvene at 2:30.

(Whereupon, at 12:35 p.m., the President's Commission recessed.)

Afternoon Session

TESTIMONY OF LUKE MOONEY

The President's Commission reconvened at 2:15 p.m.

Senator COOPER. The purpose of today's hearing is to hear the testimony of Officer Baker, whose testimony has been heard; Mrs. Reid, Eugene Boone, Luke Mooney, and M. N. McDonald. Officer Baker and Mrs. Reid were in the vicinity of the Texas School Book Depository Building at the time of the assassination. Deputy Sheriffs Boone and Mooney assisted in the search of the sixth floor of the Texas School Book Depository Building shortly after the assassination, and Officer McDonald apprehended Lee Harvey Oswald at the Texas Theatre.

Officer Mooney, will you raise your right hand?

You do solemnly swear that the testimony your are about to give will be the truth, the whole truth, and nothing but the truth, so help you God?

Mr. MOONEY. I do, sir.

Senator COOPER. You are informed now of the nature and purpose of this inquiry.

Mr. MOONEY. Yes, sir.

Senator COOPER. Do you appear here voluntarily?

Mr. MOONEY. Yes, sir.

Senator COOPER. Do you have counsel with you?

Mr. MOONEY. No, sir.

Senator COOPER. Do you desire counsel?

Mr. MOONEY. No, sir.

Mr. BALL. Mr. Mooney, what is your occupation?

Mr. MOONEY. I am a deputy sheriff, Dallas County, Tex.

Mr. BALL. How long have you been in that job?

Mr. MOONEY. I have been on the force since February 1, 1958.

Mr. BALL. Where were you born?

Mr. MOONEY. Hopkins County, south of Brashear.

Mr. BALL. Did you go to school there?

Mr. MOONEY. I went to school at Middle Grove, Tex.

Mr. BALL. How far did you go through school?

Mr. MOONEY. I finished high school there.

Mr. BALL. And then where did you go?

Mr. MOONEY. Well, I finished making a crop—I was a farm boy. My father passed away. I started school at A. & M. and had to withdraw after my father's death, and come back home to my mother, because I was the only child at home. And later on I took a course in aeronautical work, at Luscomb School of Aeronautics, in Dallas, which is about—at that time was about 75 miles from my home, and finished the course, and worked for Luscomb in Garland, Tex., which is a suburb, or 15 miles out of Dallas.

And I worked there approximately a year before I was drafted into the U.S. armed services. I was 19 years old when I was drafted, one of the first.

Mr. BALL. How long were you in the service?

Mr. MOONEY. From 1942—I went in December, I believe it was, 28th, 1942, and got out February 20, 1946, I believe that is correct.

Mr. BALL. And what did you do then, after that?

Mr. MOONEY. I returned home on discharge, discharged out of the services, honorable discharge. And I went to Dallas again, come back to Dallas.

After a short couple of weeks vacation, so to speak, I took a business course at Drawns Business College in Dallas.

281

I finished the course there and was employed at Johnson Brothers Chevrolet Co. for 10 years, approximately 10 years, as a dispatcher in the service department, in charge of the shops. And for 2 years I worked for an automobile financing company, Associate Investment Co.

And after 2 years of service there, I was employed by the Dallas County Sheriff's Office, because I didn't desire to be transferred out of the city of Dallas.

Mr. BALL. What kind of work did you do for the sheriff's office?

Mr. MOONEY. I worked in the Writ and Execution Department, Civil Law, Writ of Sequestrations and Executions. That is my principal job. However, we do everything that comes down.

Mr. BALL. What do you call that writ?

Mr. MOONEY. Writ of Sequestration, or you might call it sequest.

Mr. BALL. Were you on duty on November 22, 1963?

Mr. MOONEY. Yes, sir; I was.

Mr. BALL. What was your job on that day?

Mr. MOONEY. I didn't have a special assignment. Some of the officers did out at the Market Hall. I was waiting in front of the Dallas Criminal Courts Building, which is the sheriff's office, and we were waiting outside on the front steps there. I was down on the sidewalk, off the steps, on the street level, waiting for the motorcade to approach.

Mr. BALL. Were you standing there when the President went by?

Mr. MOONEY. Yes, sir. I took my hat off.

Mr. BALL. That is on Main Street?

Mr. MOONEY. Right.

Mr. BALL. And that is——

Mr. MOONEY. 505 Main.

Mr. BALL. That is where the cavalcade turned north?

Mr. MOONEY. Made a right turn, yes, sir; on Houston Street.

Mr. BALL. That building is about a block south on Houston, isn't it—south of the Texas School Book Depository?

Mr. MOONEY. Yes, sir; it is a short block there.

Mr. BALL. After the President's car went by, what did you do?

Mr. MOONEY. Well, we were—we was more or less milling around. We just kept standing there, more or less talking to one another.

I don't know how many seconds had elapsed—it wasn't too many.

Mr. BALL. You say "we." Who was with you?

Mr. MOONEY. There was another officer there, Hiram Ingram—he is an officer, also, a deputy sheriff. And I believe Ralph Walters was standing there with me, and I believe there was a lady standing there, by the name of Martha Johnson, who is one of the judges' wife, a JP judge.

I believe Officer Boone was standing near us, also. And I don't recall how many more. There was a number of officers there.

Mr. BALL. What happened, as you remember?

Mr. MOONEY. After that few seconds elapsed, we heard this shot ring out. At that time, I didn't realize it was a shot. The wind was blowing pretty high, and, of course, it echoed. I turned my head this way.

Mr. BALL. You mean to the right?

Mr. MOONEY. To the right; yes, sir. We were facing more or less south. And I turned my head to the right.

Mr. BALL. That would be looking towards Houston Street?

Mr. MOONEY. Looking towards the old court.

Well, when I turned my head to the right; yes, sir. I would be looking west. And there was a short lapse between these shots. I can still hear them very distinctly—between the first and second shot. The second and third shot was pretty close together, but there was a short lapse there between the first and second shot. Why, I don't know. But when that begin to take place—after the first shot we started moving out. And by the time I started running—all of us except Officer Ingram—he had a heart attack, and, of course, he wasn't qualified to do any running.

Mr. BALL. Which way?

Mr. MOONEY. Due west, across Houston Street, went down across this lawn, across Elm Street there—I assume it is approximately the location the President was hit.

Of course the motorcade was gone. There wasn't anything there except a bunch of people, a lot of them laying on the ground, taking on, various things. I was running at full speed.

Mr. BALL. When you ran across Elm, where did you go?

Mr. MOONEY. Across Elm, up the embankment, which is a high terrace there, across—there is a kind of concrete building there, more or less of a little park.

Jumped over the fence and went into the railroad yards. And, of course, there was other officers over there. Who they were, I don't recall at this time. But Ralph Walters and I were running together. And we jumped into the railroad yards and began to look around there.

And, of course, we didn't see anything there. Of course the other officers had checked into the car there, and didn't find anything, I don't believe, but a Negro porter. Of course there were quite a few spectators milling around behind us. We were trying to clear the area out and get all the civilians out that wasn't officers.

Mr. BALL. Why did you go over to the railroad yard?

Mr. MOONEY. Well, that was—from the echo of the shots, we thought they came from that direction.

Mr. BALL. That would be north and west from where you were standing?

Mr. MOONEY. Yes, sir. To a certain extent—northwest. The way the echo sounded, the cracking of the shot. And we wasn't there many seconds—of course I never did look at my watch to see how many seconds it took us to run so many hundred yards there, and into the railroad yard. We were there only a few seconds until we had orders to cover the Texas Depository Building.

Mr. BALL. How did you get those orders?

Mr. MOONEY. They were referred to us by the sheriff, Mr. Bill Decker.

Mr. BALL. Where was he when he gave you those orders?

Mr. MOONEY. They were relayed on to us. I assume Mr. Decker was up near the intersection of Elm and Houston.

Mr. BALL. Did you hear it over a loudspeaker?

Mr. MOONEY. No, sir. It come by word, by another officer.

Mr. BALL. And you were with Walters at that time?

Mr. MOONEY. Right. And where Officer Walters went at that time, I don't know. We split up. I didn't see him any more until later on, which I will refer to later.

Mr. BALL. Where did you go?

Mr. MOONEY. Mr. Webster and Mr. Vickery were there with me at the time that we received these orders from another deputy.

Mr. BALL. They are deputy sheriffs?

Mr. MOONEY. Yes, sir; they were plainclothes officers like myself, work in the same department, and we run right over to the building then, which we were only 150, 200 feet back—I assume it is that distance—I haven't measured it. It didn't take us but a few seconds to get there. When we hit the rear part, these big iron gates, they have cyclone fencing on them—this used to be an old grocery store warehouse—Sachs & Co., I believe is correct. And I says let's get these doors closed to block off this rear entrance.

Mr. BALL. Were the doors open?

Mr. MOONEY. They were wide open, the big gates. So I grabbed one, and we swung them to, and there was a citizen there, and I put him on orders to keep them shut, because I don't recall whether there was a lock on them or not. Didn't want to lock them because you never know what might happen.

So he stood guard, I assume, until a uniformed officer took over.

We shut the back door—there was a back door on a little dock. And then we went in through the docks, through the rear entrance.

Officer Vickery and Webster said, "We will take the staircase there in the corner."

I said, "I will go up the freight elevator." I noticed there was a big elevator there. So I jumped on it. And about that time two women come running and said, "we want to go to the second floor."

I said, "All right, get on, we are going."

Mr. BALL. Which elevator did you get on?

Mr. MOONEY. It was the one nearest to the staircase, on the northwest corner of the building.

Mr. BALL. There are two elevators there?

Mr. MOONEY. I found that out later. I didn't know it at that time.

Mr. BALL. You took the west one, or the east one?

Mr. MOONEY. I would say it was the west elevator, the one nearest to the staircase.

Mr. BALL. Did it work with a push button?

Mr. MOONEY. It was a push button affair the best I can remember. I got hold of the controls and it worked. We started up and got to the second. I was going to let them off and go on up. And when we got there, the power undoubtedly cut off, because we had no more power on the elevator. So I looked around their office there, just a short second or two, and then I went up the staircase myself. And I met some other officers coming down, plainclothes, and I believe they were deputy sheriffs. They were coming down the staircase. But I kept going up. And how come I get off the sixth floor, I don't know yet. But, anyway, I stopped on six, and didn't even know what floor I was on.

Mr. BALL. You were alone?

Mr. MOONEY. I was alone at that time.

Mr. BALL. Was there any reason for you to go to the sixth floor?

Mr. MOONEY. No, sir. That is what I say. I don't know why. I just stopped on that particular floor. I thought I was pretty close to the top.

Mr. BALL. Were there any other officers on the floor?

Mr. MOONEY. I didn't see any at that time. I assume there had been other officers up there. But I didn't see them. And I begin criss-crossing it, round and round, through boxes, looking at open windows—some of them were open over on the south side.

And I believe they had started laying some flooring up there.

I was checking the fire escapes. And criss-crossing back and forth. And then I decided—I saw there was another floor. And I said I would go up. So I went on up to the seventh floor. I approached Officers Webster and Vickery. They were up there—in this little old stairway there that leads up into the attic. So we climbed up in there and looked around right quick. We didn't climb all the way into the attic, almost into it. We said this is too dark, we have got to have floodlights, because we can't see. And so somebody made a statement that they believed floodlights was on the way. And I later found out that probably Officers Boone and Walters had gone after lights. I heard that.

And so we looked around up there for a short time. And then I says I am going back down on six.

At that time, some news reporter, or press, I don't know who he was—he was coming up with a camera. Of course he wasn't taking any pictures. He was just looking, too, I assume. So I went back down ahead of Officers Vickery and Webster. They come in behind me down to the sixth floor.

I went straight across to the southeast corner of the building, and I saw all these high boxes. Of course they were stacked all the way around over there. And I squeezed between two. And the minute I squeezed between these two stacks of boxes, I had to turn myself sideways to get in there—that is when I saw the expended shells and the boxes that were stacked up looked to be a rest for the weapon. And, also, there was a slight crease in the top box. Whether the recoil made the crease or it was placed there before the shots were fired, I don't know. But, anyway, there was a very slight crease in the box, where the rifle could have lain—at the same angle that the shots were fired from.

So, at that time, I didn't lay my hands on anything, because I wanted to save every evidence we could for fingerprints. So I leaned out the window, the same window from which the shots were fired, looked down, and I saw Sheriff Bill Decker and Captain Will Fritz standing right on the ground.

Well, so I hollered, or signaled—I hollered, I more or less hollered. I whistled a time or two before I got anybody to see me. And yet they was all looking that way, too—except the sheriff, they wasn't looking up.

And I told him to get the crime lab officers en route, that I had the location spotted.

So I stood guard to see that no one disturbed anything until Captain Will Fritz approached with his group of officers, city officers. At that time, of course, when I hollered, of course Officers Vickery and Webster, they came across and later on several other deputies—I believe Officers McCurley, A. D. McCurley, I believe he came over. Where he came from—they was all en route up there, I assume.

Mr. BALL. I show you three pictures, Officer; for your convenience I will give you the pictures.

I have a picture here which has been marked as Commission Exhibit 508.

(The document referred to was marked Commission Exhibit No. 508 for identification.)

Mr. BALL. Does that look anything like the southeast corner of the building as you saw it that afternoon?

Mr. MOONEY. Yes, sir.

Mr. BALL. About what time of day was this?

Mr. MOONEY. Well, it was approaching 1 o'clock. It could have been 1 o'clock.

Mr. BALL. Did you look at your watch?

Mr. MOONEY. No, sir; I didn't. I should have, but I didn't look at my watch at the time to see what time it was.

Mr. BALL. Were you the only officer in that corner?

Mr. MOONEY. At that very moment I was.

Mr. BALL. You say you squeezed behind certain boxes. Can you point out for me what boxes you squeezed through?

Mr. MOONEY. If I remember correctly, I went in there from this angle right here—right through here. There could be a space. There is a space there I squeezed in between here, and that is when I got into the opening, because the minute I squeezed through there there lay the shells.

Mr. BALL. All right. Let's make a mark here. Is this the space?

Mr. MOONEY. I believe that is going to be the space; yes, sir.

Mr. BALL. If I make an arrow on that, would that indicate it?

Mr. MOONEY. Yes, sir. There is another picture I have seen later that shows an opening in through here, but I didn't see that opening at that time.

Mr. BALL. That is the opening through which you squeezed? And it is an arrow shown on Exhibit 508.

Now, I will show you 509.

(The document referred to was marked Commission Exhibit No. 509 for identification.)

Is that the way the boxes looked?

Mr. MOONEY. That is the three boxes, but one of them was tilted off just a little, laying down on the edge, I believe, to my knowledge.

Mr. BALL. Now, does that look like——

Mr. MOONEY. That is the three boxes that were there; yes, sir.

Mr. BALL. Are they arranged as they were when you saw them?

Mr. MOONEY. I am not positive. As I remember right, there was one box tilted off.

Mr. BALL. What were the boxes—did they have a label on them, two of the boxes?

Mr. MOONEY. These do. I didn't notice the label at that time.

Mr. BALL. That is a picture of the window?

Mr. MOONEY. Yes.

Mr. BALL. Do I understand that you say that it appeared to you that the top box was tilted?

Mr. MOONEY. The end of it was laying this way.

Mr. BALL. You say there was a crease in a box. Where was that crease?

Mr. MOONEY. This crease was right in this area of this box.

Mr. BALL. You mean over on the edge?

Mr. MOONEY. Yes, sir; on this far ledge here, where I am laying my finger.

Mr. BALL. Did it go into the box?

Mr. MOONEY. Very slight crease, very slight.

Mr. Ball. Can you take this and point out about where the crease was on 509?

Now, was there anything you saw over in the corner?

Mr. Mooney. No, sir; I didn't see anything over in the corner. I did see this one partially eaten piece of fried chicken laying over to the right. It looked like he was facing——

Mr. Ball. Tell us where you found it?

Mr. Mooney. It would be laying over on the top of these other boxes. This here is kind of blurred.

Mr. Ball. We will get to that in a moment. Now, I show you 510.

(The document referred to was marked Commission Exhibit No. 510 for identification.)

Mr. Ball. Is that the empty shells you found?

Mr. Mooney. Yes, sir.

Mr. Ball. Are they shown there?

Mr. Mooney. Yes, sir.

Mr. Ball. Now, will you take this and encircle the shells?

Mr. Mooney. All right.

Mr. Ball. Put a fairly good sized circle around each shell. That is the way they were when you saw them, is that right?

Mr. Mooney. Yes, sir. I assume that this possibly could have been the first shot.

Mr. Ball. You cannot speculate about that?

Mr. Mooney. You cannot speculate about that.

Mr. Ball. Those were empty shells?

Mr. Mooney. Yes, sir.

Mr. Ball. They were turned over to Captain Fritz?

Mr. Mooney. Yes, sir; he was the first officer that picked them up, as far as I know, because I stood there and watched him go over and pick them up and look at them. As far as I could tell, I couldn't even tell what caliber they were, because I didn't get down that close to them. They were brass cartridges, brass shells.

Mr. Ball. Is this the position of the cartridges as shown on 510, as you saw them?

Mr. Mooney. Yes, sir. That is just about the way they were laying, to the best of my knowledge. I do know there was—one was further away, and these other two were relatively close together—on this particular area. But these cartridges—this one and this one looks like they are further apart than they actually was.

Mr. Ball. Which ones?

Mr. Mooney. This one and this one.

Mr. Ball. Now, two cartridges were close together, is that right?

Mr. Mooney. The one cartridge here, by the wall facing, is right. And this one and this one, they were further away from this one.

Mr. Ball. Well——

Mr. Mooney. But as to being positive of the exact distance——

Mr. Ball. You think that the cartridges are in the same position as when you saw them in this picture 510?

Mr. Mooney. As far as my knowledge, they are; pretty close to right.

Mr. Ball. Well, we will label these cartridges, the empty shells as "A", "B", and "C."

Now, I didn't quite understand—did you say it was your memory that "A" and "B" were not that close together?

Mr. Mooney. Just from my memory, it seems that this cartridge ought to have been over this way a little further.

Mr. Ball. You mean the "B" cartridge should be closer to the "C?"

Mr. Mooney. Closer to the "C"; yes, sir.

Mr. Ball. Now, I have another picture here which I should like to have marked as 511.

(The document referred to was marked Commission Exhibit No. 511 for identification.)

Mr. Ball. Does this appear to be—first of all, does that appear——

Mr. MOONEY. There are two cartridges.

Where is the third one?

Mr. BALL. The third one is not in this picture. This is taken from another angle.

Mr. MOONEY. This looks more like it than this angle here.

Mr. BALL. You can see it is a different angle.

Mr. MOONEY. That is right.

Mr. BALL. Now, in this same picture—511, you see a box in the window. Does that seem to be about the angle——

Mr. MOONEY. Yes; that box was tilted.

Mr. BALL. That was tilted in that way?

Mr. MOONEY. Yes, sir.

Mr. BALL. Now, when you made a crease on 509, the box shown in 509——

Mr. MOONEY. The box should have been actually tilted.

Mr. BALL. In other words, it was your testimony, was it, that the box as shown in 509 was not as you first saw it?

Mr. MOONEY. If I recall it right, this box was tilted. It had fallen off—looked like he might have knocked it off.

Mr. BALL. Well, you cannot speculate to that, but you can just tell us what you saw. What about the box in the window shown in 511?

Mr. MOONEY. Yes, sir.

Mr. BALL. Is that the box that had the crease on it?

Mr. MOONEY. Yes, sir; I believe that is correct.

Mr. BALL. Now, the crease was—started from the edge, and came across?

Mr. MOONEY. Yes, sir; just a slight crease.

Mr. BALL. I have another picture. This is 512.

(The document referred to was marked Commission Exhibit No. 512 for identification.)

Mr. BALL. Here is a picture taken, also, from another angle. Does that show the cartridges?

Mr. MOONEY. Yes, sir.

Mr. BALL. Now, compare that with 510.

Mr. MOONEY. Yes, sir.

Mr. BALL. Is that about the way it looked?

Mr. MOONEY. Yes, sir; that is right. It sure is.

Mr. BALL. Now, were the boxes, as you saw them, on the extreme left side of the window, the middle of the window, or the right side.

Mr. MOONEY. Well, they were further over to the left of the window than over to the right. More or less as they are in there in that picture.

Mr. BALL. In 509?

Mr. MOONEY. Yes, sir.

Mr. BALL. Now, the boxes are in about the right position with reference to——

Mr. MOONEY. Yes, sir; because I had room enough to stand right here, and lean out this window, without disturbing the boxes.

Mr. BALL. You could stand on the right of the boxes?

Mr. MOONEY. Yes, sir.

Mr. BALL. And put your head out the window?

Mr. MOONEY. Yes, sir. If I recall, I put my hand on the outside of this ledge.

Mr. BALL. And put your head out the window?

Mr. MOONEY. Yes, sir.

Senator COOPER. Was the window open when you got there?

Mr. MOONEY. Yes, sir.

Mr. BALL. If you stood to the left of the boxes, could you have looked out the window?

Mr. MOONEY. I don't believe I could, without disturbing them. Possibly I might have, could have, but I just didn't try it.

Mr. BALL. Now, I show you Exhibit 513.

(The document referred to was marked Commission Exhibit No. 513, for identification.)

Mr. BALL. This is another view of that window.

Mr. MOONEY. Yes, sir.

Mr. BALL. Did you see it from that angle?

Mr. MOONEY. No, sir; I never did.

Mr. BALL. You don't think you have ever seen it——

Mr. MOONEY. From that angle.

Mr. BALL. Does that show any place where you saw the chicken bone?

Mr. MOONEY. If I recall correctly, the chicken bone could have been laying on this box or it might have been laying on this box right here.

Mr. BALL. Make a couple of marks there to indicate where possibly the chicken bone was lying.

Mr. MOONEY. Yes, sir.

Mr. BALL. Make two "X's". You think there was a chicken bone on the top of either one of those two?

Mr. MOONEY. There was one of them partially eaten. And there was a little small paper poke.

Mr. BALL. By poke, you mean a paper sack?

Mr. MOONEY. Right.

Mr. BALL. Where was that?

Mr. MOONEY. Saw the chicken bone was laying here. The poke was laying about a foot away from it.

Mr. BALL. On the same carton?

Mr. MOONEY. Yes, sir. In close relation to each other. But as to what was in the sack—it was kind of together, and I didn't open it. I didn't put my hands on it to open it. I only saw one piece of chicken.

Senator COOPER. How far was the chicken, the piece of chicken you saw, and the paper bag from the boxes near the window, and particularly the box that had the crease in it?

Mr. MOONEY. I would say they might have been 5 feet or something like that. He wouldn't have had to leave the location. He could just maybe take one step and lay it over there, if he was the one that put it there.

Senator COOPER. You mean if someone had been standing near the box with the crease in it?

Mr. MOONEY. Yes, sir.

Senator COOPER. It would have been that approximate distance to the chicken leg and paper bag?

Mr. MOONEY. Sir?

Senator COOPER. And the paper bag you spoke of?

Mr. MOONEY. Yes, sir; they were in close relation to each other, yes, sir.

Mr. BALL. How big a bag was it?

Mr. MOONEY. Well, as to the number—these bags are numbered, I understand. But it was—I don't know what the number you would call it, but it didn't stand more than that high.

Mr. BALL. About 12 inches?

Mr. MOONEY. About 8 to 10 inches, at the most.

Mr. BALL. What color was the bag?

Mr. MOONEY. It was brown. Just a regular paper bag. Just as a grocery store uses for their produce and what-have-you.

Mr. BALL. Did you see any soda pop?

Mr. MOONEY. No, sir; I did not.

Mr. BALL. Did you see a paper bag at any other window?

Mr. MOONEY. No, sir; I didn't.

Mr. BALL. Any other chicken bones?

Mr. MOONEY. No, sir.

Mr. BALL. Did you see a Dr. Pepper bottle any place?

Mr. MOONEY. No, sir; except in the picture.

Mr. BALL. You didn't see it?

Mr. MOONEY. No, sir.

Mr. BALL. When you say you have seen the picture, I will show you the picture, and let me see if that is the one you mean you have seen. That is Commission 484. This picture has been shown to you, hasn't it?

Mr. MOONEY. Yes, sir.

Mr. BALL. I showed you that.

Mr. MOONEY. Yes, sir.

Mr. BALL. And you did not see that two-wheel truck?

Mr. MOONEY. No, sir.

Mr. BALL. You did not see the Dr. Pepper bottle?

Mr. MOONEY. No, sir.

Mr. BALL. You didn't see a paper sack anywhere near a two-wheel truck or a Dr. Pepper bottle?

Mr. MOONEY. No, sir; in my running around up there, I didn't observe it. Possibly it was there. I am sure it was. But I didn't check it.

Mr. BALL. How long did you stay there?

Mr. MOONEY. Sir?

Mr. BALL. How long did you stay up on the sixth floor? After you found the location of the three cartridges?

Mr. MOONEY. Well, I stayed up there not over 15 or 20 minutes longer—after Captain Will Fritz and his officers came over there, Captain Fritz picked up the cartridges, began to examine them, of course I left that particular area. By that time there was a number of officers up there. The floor was covered with officers. And we were searching, trying to find the weapon at that time.

Mr. BALL. Were you there when it was found?

Mr. MOONEY. Yes, sir. I was searching under these books and between them and up on the ledges and the joists, we was just looking everywhere. And I was about 10 or 15 steps at the most from Officer Boone when he hollered, "Here is the gun."

Mr. BALL. Did you go over there?

Mr. MOONEY. I stepped over there.

Mr. BALL. What did you see?

Mr. MOONEY. I had to look twice before I actually saw the gun laying in there. I had to get around to the right angle before I could see it. And there the gun lay, stuck between these cartons in an upright position. The scope was up.

Mr. BALL. Well, now, I will show you a picture, 514.

(The document referred to was marked Commission Exhibit No. 514, for identification.)

Senator COOPER. May I ask—did you change the position of the shells which you have identified?

Mr. MOONEY. No, sir; I didn't have my hands on them.

Senator COOPER. Or the bag, or chicken leg?

Mr. MOONEY. No, sir.

Senator COOPER. Until—before the chief came?

Mr. MOONEY. Captain Will Fritz; yes, sir; he is the chief.

Senator COOPER. Was there any odor in the area when you first got there?

Mr. MOONEY. I didn't particularly notice any. Now, there could have been a slight powder odor there.

(At this point, Mr. Warren entered the hearing room.)

Senator COOPER. Did you smell any powder?

Mr. MOONEY. No, sir; not to my knowledge. Of course it was musty odor, with all those cartons and books there.

Mr. BALL. Do you see the picture which is 514? Does it look like anything like that?

Mr. MOONEY. Yes, sir; with the exception there was more cartons around it than that. In other words, the way it looked to me, when I walked over there—of course these may have been disturbed at a later date.

Mr. BALL. It looks like there are more cartons?

Mr. MOONEY. No; there is less cartons around it right now. Of course that is looking straight down. Now, there are some more boxes here.

Mr. BALL. I show you a picture which we will mark as 515.

(The document referred to was marked Commission Exhibit No. 515 for identification.)

Mr. MOONEY. But that is in the position the gun was laying.

Mr. BALL. That is about the position of the gun?

Mr. MOONEY. Yes, sir.

Mr. BALL. Now, here is a picture of that marked stairway. Can you orient yourself from that picture?

Mr. MOONEY. Let's see. Here is the staircase right in here. If I remember right, the gun was either in this crack or this one here. I don't remember which.

Mr. BALL. Does that show you about the number of cartons around?

Mr. MOONEY. Yes, sir; that is the way it looked; sure did. Because I had to stand up back here, before I could see over off in there.

Mr. BALL. And when you did look down there between the cartons, was the gun——

Mr. MOONEY. It was sitting in that position. The scope was up.

Mr. BALL. As shown in 514?

Mr. MOONEY. Yes, sir. That is the way it was laying, in that position.

Senator COOPER. It was lying on the floor?

Mr. MOONEY. Yes, sir.

Senator COOPER. With the scope on the upper side?

Mr. MOONEY. The scope in upright position. The stock was back to the east. In other words, the gun was pointed west.

Mr. BALL. Did a photographer come up and take pictures when you were there?

Mr. MOONEY. There was a number of photographers up there shooting pictures. Who they were or who they represented—I assume it was the press.

Mr. BALL. How long were they there?

Mr. MOONEY. They were there when all these officers and everybody was up there.

Mr. BALL. I have no further questions.

Senator COOPER. How far was it from the place where the gun was found, from where you first saw the rifle, to the window?

Mr. MOONEY. You mean how far was it from the gun to the window?

Senator COOPER. Yes; where you saw the shells.

Mr. MOONEY. Well, it was clear across the entire sixth floor, thereabouts. In other words, if you take the location from where the shells were found, they were in the southeast corner. And this was in the far northwest corner. Just right there at the staircase.

And the distance across there, I just don't know how far it is, but it is quite a large warehouse floor.

Mr. BALL. I have no further questions. I would like to offer the exhibits up to 515, inclusive. May this witness be excused?

The CHAIRMAN. Any questions, Senator Cooper?

Senator COOPER. As you examined these exhibits, you gave your best judgment, your recollection of the location of the boxes and the shells.

Mr. MOONEY. Yes, sir. The way I remember, sir, is——

Senator COOPER. The chicken and the paper bag?

Mr. MOONEY. Yes, sir. I do remember that the one box was tilted off, laying partially over on the legs.

Senator COOPER. That was the box which you said you observed a crease in?

Mr. MOONEY. Yes, sir. Just very slight, very slight.

Senator COOPER. Is that the box which was the top box?

Mr. MOONEY. The way I remember, the two boxes and the third one was the one tilted off. It looked like it possibly could have been knocked off from a movement, because it wasn't naturally placed that way by hand for any purpose, because it wouldn't have had any purpose, to my knowledge.

Senator COOPER. Let the exhibits which have been offered be admitted in evidence.

(The documents heretofore marked for identification as Commission Exhibits Nos. 508 through 515, were received in evidence.)

Mr. MOONEY. In other words, if you just run against it, you would have knocked it off.

The CHAIRMAN. Thank you very much for coming, sir. You have been very helpful.

Mr. BALL. Our next witness is Deputy Sheriff Boone.

TESTIMONY OF EUGENE BOONE

The CHAIRMAN. Sit right down, Mr. Boone.

Senator COOPER. The purpose of this hearing is to hear the testimony of M. L. Baker, Mrs. R. A. Reid, Eugene Boone, Luke Mooney, and M. N. McDonald. Officer Baker and Mrs. Reid were in the vicinity of the Texas School Book Depository Building at the time of the assassination. Deputy Sheriffs Boone and Mooney assisted in the search of the sixth floor of the Texas School Book Depository Building shortly after the assassination, and Officer McDonald apprehended Lee Harvey Oswald at the Texas theatre.

Will you be sworn? Do you solemnly swear the testimony you are about to give will be the truth, the whole truth, and nothing but the truth, so help you God?

Mr. BOONE. I do.

Senator COOPER. You understand the purpose of this inquiry?

Mr. BOONE. Yes, sir.

Senator COOPER. You have come here voluntarily to testify?

Mr. BOONE. Yes.

Senator COOPER. Do you have a counsel with you?

Mr. BOONE. No.

Senator COOPER. Do you desire one?

Mr. BOONE. No.

Mr. BALL. What is your business?

Mr. BOONE. I am a deputy sheriff in or for the county of Dallas.

Mr. BALL. How long have you been a deputy sheriff?

Mr. BOONE. A year and a half.

Mr. BALL. Where were you born?

Mr. BOONE. Dallas, Tex.

Mr. BALL. Go to school there?

Mr. BOONE. Yes, sir.

Mr. BALL. How far through school did you go?

Mr. BOONE. High school.

Mr. BALL. In Dallas?

Mr. BOONE. Yes, sir.

Mr. BALL. What did you do after you got out of school?

Mr. BOONE. I was working with the Dallas Times Herald Newspaper there, in the advertising department.

Mr. BALL. How long did you work there?

Mr. BOONE. Well, I worked there part time when I was going to school, up until the time I quit, 8 years.

Mr. BALL. Is that the time you went with the sheriff's office?

Mr. BOONE. Yes, sir.

Mr. BALL. How old are you?

Mr. BOONE. Twenty-six.

Mr. BALL. On the 22d of November, where were you working?

Mr. BOONE. I was working downtown. I was out viewing the parade.

Mr. BALL. Where did you view the parade?

Mr. BOONE. Right in front of the sheriff's office.

Mr. BALL. Had you been assigned a place, a job that day?

Mr. BOONE. No.

Mr. BALL. You were out in front of the sheriff's office on Main Street?

Mr. BOONE. That is correct.

Mr. BALL. Near Houston?

Mr. BOONE. Yes.

Mr. BALL. And who were you with?

Mr. BOONE. Officer Mooney was out there, I believe, and several of the office personnel, women in the office, clerk-typist and what-have-you. Ralph Walters, Buddy Walthers, Allen Sweatt, L. C. Smith. Officer Gramstaff. That is about all I can remember.

Mr. BALL. What happened there?

Mr. BOONE. Well, it was approximately 1 o'clock when we heard the shots. The motorcade had already passed by us and turned back to the north on

Houston Street. And we heard what we thought to be a shot. And there seemed to be a pause between the first shot and the second shot and third shots— a little longer pause. And we raced across the street there.

Mr. BALL. You raced across what street?

Mr. BOONE. Houston Street.

Mr. BALL. You turned to your right and went west?

Mr. BOONE. Well, there is a big cement works out there. We went on west across Houston Street, and then cut across the grass out there behind the large cement works there. Some of the bystanders over there seemed to think the shots came from up over the railroad in the freight yards, from over the triple underpass.

So there was some city officer, I don't know who he was, motorcycle officer had laid his motorcycle down and was running up the embankment to get over a little retaining wall that separates the freight yards there. He went over the wall first, and I was right behind him, going into the freight yards. We searched out the freight yards. We were unable to find anything.

Mr. BALL. A good many officers over there searching?

Mr. BOONE. Yes; there were. Most all of the officers—well, all of the officers in front of the sheriff's office there. There were others that I don't recall. There were other officers in the area. Also, they all ran in that general direction, over around the depository and also down into the freight yards.

Mr. BALL. Any railroad employees around there?

Mr. BOONE. There was one colored boy way on back down in the freight yards. He had been working on one of the pullmans down there.

Mr. BALL. And didn't you talk to somebody that was also in a tower?

Mr. BOONE. Yes; I did.

Mr. BALL. A man named Bowers?

Mr. BOONE. I don't know what his name was. He was up in the tower and I hollered up there to see if he had seen anybody running out there in the freight yards, or heard any shots. And he said he didn't hear any shots, and he hadn't seen anybody racing around out there in the yard.

Mr. BALL. That was a railroad tower?

Mr. BOONE. Yes; it is situated between the tracks and the school book depository. Almost directly west of the building.

Mr. BALL. After that, what did you do?

Mr. BOONE. Well, I finally went around and was talking to some of the spectators that were in the area there, located a boy by the name of Betzer. He had taken what he thought was some photographs, or there were photographs—he thought he might have had a portion of the building.

Later on we were able to ascertain that the shots had come from the building, from that southeast corner over there. And he had some photographs, but they didn't extend past the second floor on the building.

Mr. BALL. Did you go up into the building then?

Mr. BOONE. I took him on over to the sheriff's office, and placed him in the sheriff's office, took his camera, to bring it back to the ID Bureau to be developed. Placed him in the sheriff's office at that time to await somebody to take a statement from him.

Then some other officers, Ralph Walters and Officer Gramstaff, and I don't know whether—I don't remember Officer Mooney was with them or not at that time—they headed back to get some heavy power flashlights. They said they wanted to look around in the attic. And there were a bunch of pallets, that they moved the books around, and it was dark and they couldn't see. So we got the lights and went over to the building.

At that time, we proceeded directly to the sixth floor.

Mr. BALL. Somebody tell you to go to the sixth floor?

Mr. BOONE. Well, that is just where everybody was going. And they said five floors below that—I believe Inspector Sawyer with the city was out there, and he said the other floors were in the process of being searched or had been already searched. This was after Officer Mooney found the shells.

Mr. BALL. Did somebody tell you Officer Mooney had found some shells?

Mr. BOONE. Not him in particular. They said the shells had been found on the sixth floor. At that time, I didn't know he had found them.

Mr. BALL. What did you do after you got up to the sixth floor?

Mr. BOONE. Well, I proceeded to the east end of the building, I guess, and started working our way across the building to the west wall, looking in, under, and around all the boxes and pallets, and what-have-you that were on the floor. Looking for the weapon. And as I got to the west wall, there were a row of windows there, and a slight space between some boxes and the wall. I squeezed through them.

When I did—I had my light in my hand. I was slinging it around on the floor, and I caught a glimpse of the rifle, stuffed down between two rows of boxes with another box or so pulled over the top of it. And I hollered that the rifle was here.

Mr. BALL. What happened then?

Mr. BOONE. Some of the other officers came over to look at it. I told them to stand back, not to get around close, they might want to take prints of some of the boxes, and not touch the rifle. And at that time Captain Fritz and an ID man came over. I believe the ID man's name was Lieutenant Day—I am not sure. They came over and the weapon was photographed as it lay. And at that time Captain Fritz picked it up by the strap, and it was removed from the place where it was.

Mr. BALL. You saw them take the photograph?

Mr. BOONE. Yes.

Mr. BALL. Were you alone at that time?

Mr. BOONE. There was an Officer Weitzman, I believe. He is a deputy constable.

Mr. BALL. Where was the rifle located on the floor, general location?

Mr. BOONE. Well, it was almost—the stairwell is in the corner of the building, something like this, and there is a wall coming up here, making one side of the stairwell with the building acting as the other two sides. And from that, it was almost directly in front or about 3 feet south, I guess, it would be, from that partition wall that made up the stairwell.

Mr. BALL. The rifle was about 3 feet from the——

Mr. BOONE. Yes, sir; behind a row of boxes. There was a row of boxes that came across there. Then the rifle was behind that first row of boxes.

Mr. BALL. I show you 514. Is that the way it looked when you saw it?

Mr. BOONE. Yes.

Mr. BALL. Is that the way it was when the picture was taken?

Mr. BOONE. Yes; I believe so.

Mr. BALL. This shows the rifle as you saw it, does it?

Mr. BOONE. That is right. Then you could kneel down over here and see that it had a scope, a telescopic sight on it, by looking down underneath the boxes.

Mr. BALL. Now, I show you 515. Does that look anything like the area where you found the rifle?

Mr. BOONE. Yes; it did.

Mr. BALL. Will you put that down on the table so that everyone can see where it is, and show us where the rifle was with reference to the stairwell?

Mr. BOONE. This is that retaining wall here that I was talking about here. Now, the rifle was right down in this area right here, almost directly. This is the west end of the building here, this being the north side, as I recall.

Mr. BALL. That is the northwest corner?

Mr. BOONE. Yes. And it is about 3 feet from the edge—you cannot see the edge of it, because it is behind this.

Mr. BALL. The edge of what?

Mr. BOONE. The stairwell wall here. It is about 3 feet from where this partition ends over to—back behind these cases of books here.

Mr. BALL. Can you mark with an arrow there the exact space between the boxes where you found the rifle as shown on this exhibit, which is 514?

Mr. BOONE. What do you mean—the exact space? It was in this space right in here, like this.

Mr. BALL. The arrow marks the space.

Mr. BOONE. I had come around these boxes here, next to the windows over here, and that is when I saw it, looking down across this way.

Mr. BALL. You came along the west wall, near the windows shown in this picture 514?

Mr. BOONE. That is correct.

Mr. BALL. And when you looked in the direction that would be easterly, that is when you saw the rifle?

Mr. BOONE. Northeasterly.

Mr. BALL. Here is another picture which we will mark as 516.

(The document referred to was marked Commission Exhibit No. 516 for identification.)

Mr. BALL. Now, 515 contains the arrow which shows the space between boxes where you found the rifle, is that right?

Mr. BOONE. Yes.

Mr. BALL. Now, I show you an exhibit marked 516. Does that show—what corner of the building does that show? Or do you recognize it?

Mr. BOONE. It appears to be the same general location here.

Mr. BALL. Show——

Mr. BOONE. This is the stairwell back here in the corner. If I am not mistaken, there is a freight elevator over here.

Mr. BALL. That would be the right of the picture?

Mr. BOONE. Yes.

Mr. BALL. Now, point to the boxes where you found the rifle.

Mr. BOONE. Right down in this general direction.

Mr. BALL. Draw another arrow. I show you Exhibit 483, a diagram of the sixth floor. Now, by referring to these numbers, can you show us approximately where the rifle was found?

Mr. BOONE. Roughly in the area here, designated by the arrow No. 35.

Mr. BALL. The diagram on the sixth floor, as the Commission knows, has been correlated with certain pictures. I now have Commission Exhibit 517 marked, which has the figure 35 on it, which corresponds to the position of the camera at the time the picture was taken.

In other words, at about point 35 on this map. And now I show you a photograph marked 517. Is that about the way the rifle looked when you first saw it?

Mr. BOONE. Yes; it is. There was some newsman up there right behind Officer Whitman and myself who took movie film of it, too. I don't know his name.

Mr. BALL. What time was it?

Mr. BOONE. 1:22 p.m., in the afternoon.

Mr. BALL. 1:22?

Mr. BOONE. Yes.

Mr. BALL. You looked at your watch?

Mr. BOONE. That is correct.

Mr. BALL. And made a note of it?

Mr. BOONE. Yes; I did.

Mr. BALL. I show you a rifle which is Commission Exhibit 139. Can you tell us whether or not that looks like the rifle you saw on the floor that day?

Mr. BOONE. It looks like the same rifle. I have no way of being positive.

Mr. BALL. You never handled it?

Mr. BOONE. I did not touch the weapon at all.

Mr. BALL. I would like to offer all the exhibits we have offered with this witness, which is 515 to 516 and 517, into evidence.

Senator COOPER. Let the exhibits be admitted in evidence.

(The documents referred to marked Commission Exhibits Nos. 515, 516, and 517 were received in evidence.)

Mr. BALL. I have no further questions.

The CHAIRMAN. I think you said that the reason you didn't touch it was because of the danger of fingerprints on there, is that right?

Mr. BOONE. That is correct. The city officers had personnel in charge up there. Captain Fritz, I believe, was in charge, senior officer on the floor.

He was called to the location as soon as I found the rifle. He came over, and it was photographed then.

Senator COOPER. Did you notice whether the rifle that you discovered had a telescopic sight?

Mr. BOONE. Yes, it did.

Senator COOPER. Did it have a sling?

Mr. BOONE. Yes, it did. Because Captain Fritz picked it up by the sling when he removed it from its resting place.

Senator COOPER. Looking at Exhibit 483, which represents the floor plan of the sixth floor, you have marked on there the place where you found the rifle. Is that near the stairwell?

Mr. BOONE. Yes, sir; this is the stairwell right here in the northeast corner.

Senator COOPER. Also near the elevators?

Mr. BOONE. Yes, sir.

Mr. BELIN. Pardon me, Senator Cooper, I think you said northeast.

Mr. BOONE. Northwest—I beg your pardon.

Senator COOPER. Do you remember whether Officer Mooney came up after you found the rifle?

Mr. BOONE. I don't recall. There were officers, both city and county officers, and constables officers up in the area on the floor. Now, whether he was among the crowd there, I do not know.

Senator COOPER. When you climbed over the retaining wall at the railroad yard, can you describe what the situation in the railroad yard was at that time? Were there railroad cars in the area?

Mr. BOONE. There were four railroad cars down approximately 100 yards from the retaining wall, right over the Elm Street tunnel, or portion of the triple underpass. Then there were some people down to the south of the triple underpass which had viewed the parade, or were viewing the parade—I don't know. The city officer went back south, as I recall, and I went off to the north, northwest.

Senator COOPER. Thank you.

The CHAIRMAN. Sheriff, thank you very much.

Mr. BALL. There is one question. Did you hear anybody refer to this rifle as a Mauser that day?

Mr. BOONE. Yes, I did. And at first, not knowing what it was, I thought it was 7.65 Mauser.

Mr. BALL. Who referred to it as a Mauser that day?

Mr. BOONE. I believe Captain Fritz. He had knelt down there to look at it, and before he removed it, not knowing what it was, he said that is what it looks like. This is when Lieutenant Day, I believe his name is, the ID man was getting ready to photograph it.

We were just discussing it back and forth. And he said it looks like a 7.65 Mauser.

Mr. BALL. Thank you.

The CHAIRMAN. Thank you very much, Sheriff. You have been very helpful.

Mr. BALL. Call Officer McDonald.

TESTIMONY OF M. N. McDONALD

Senator COOPER. Will you stand up and be sworn? Do you swear that the testimony you shall give will be the truth, the whole truth, and nothing but the truth, so help you God?

Mr. McDONALD. I do.

Senator COOPER. You understand that the purpose of this inquiry is to inquire into the circumstances surrounding the assassination of the late President Kennedy?

Mr. McDONALD. Yes, sir; I do.

Senator COOPER. Today's hearings are to hear testimony of various witnesses, including yourself, who were in the vicinity of the Texas School Book Depository Building at the time of the assassination, and because it is reported you apprehended Lee Harvey Oswald in the Texas theatre.

Mr. McDONALD. Yes, sir.

Senator COOPER. Do you testify here voluntarily?

Mr. McDonald. Yes, sir.

Senator Cooper. Do you have counsel with you?

Mr. McDonald. No, sir.

Senator Cooper. Do you desire counsel?

Mr. McDonald. No, sir.

Mr. Ball. Mr. McDonald, where do you live?

Mr. McDonald. 530 South Port Drive.

Mr. Ball. In Dallas?

Mr. McDonald. Yes, sir.

Mr. Ball. Where were you born?

Mr. McDonald. Camden, Ark.

Mr. Ball. Did you go to school in Arkansas?

Mr. McDonald. Yes, sir.

Mr. Ball. How far through school did you go?

Mr. McDonald. Well, I finished through the 11th grade, took an equivalent for a high school diploma, and I attended 1 year at Arkansas State Teachers College in Conway.

Mr. Ball. What year was that?

Mr. McDonald. 1948 and 1949.

Mr. Ball. What did you do after that?

Mr. McDonald. Well, worked in a printing firm for awhile, after getting out of college a year Then I joined the Air Force. But in a break between high school and college, I entered the Navy, in January 1946. I served 22 months in the Navy, active duty.

Mr. Ball. Then you say in the 1950's you joined the Air Force?

Mr. McDonald. Yes, sir ; December 29, 1950.

Mr. Ball. How long were you in the Air Force?

Mr. McDonald. Four years.

Mr. Ball. What work did you do in the Air Force?

Mr. McDonald. I was a supply sergeant.

Mr. Ball. After that, what did you do?

Mr. McDonald. I became a policeman in the Dallas Police Department.

Mr. Ball. That was in 1956?

Mr. McDonald. March 3, 1955.

Mr. Ball. And you have been a police officer ever since?

Mr. McDonald. Yes, sir.

Mr. Ball. Were you on duty on March—November 22, 1963?

Mr. McDonald. Yes, sir.

Mr. Ball. What was your job that day?

Mr. McDonald. Radio patrol.

Mr. Ball. What were your hours of duty?

Mr. McDonald. From 7 :30 a.m. to 3 :30 p.m.

Mr. Ball. Did you ride alone or have a partner?

Mr. McDonald. No, sir ; I had a partner.

Mr. Ball. What is his name?

Mr. McDonald. T. R. Gregory.

Mr. Ball. Were you cruising about 12 :30 that day?

Mr. McDonald. Yes, sir.

Mr. Ball. In what area?

Mr. McDonald. On the Westmoreland Avenue and Falls Drive intersection.

Mr. Ball. Was your area, an area close to downtown Dallas or outside?

Mr. McDonald. Outside, approximately 8 miles.

Mr. Ball. Did you get an order over the radio about that time to move your car?

Mr. McDonald. Yes, sir.

Mr. Ball. What was the order?

Mr. McDonald. Report to the vicinity of Elm and Houston Streets, code 3.

Mr. Ball. And did you know Officer Tippit?

Mr. McDonald. Yes, sir.

Mr. Ball. Was he also a radio patrol officer?

Mr. McDonald. Yes, sir ; he was.

Mr. Ball. Did he cruise alone or with a partner?

Mr. McDonald. He was cruising alone.

Mr. Ball. Do you know what his area—the area assigned to him on that day?

Mr. McDonald. The southern part of Oak Cliff, nearing the city limits.

Mr. Ball. Was that farther out from the center of town than you?

Mr. McDonald. Yes, sir; approximately 10 to 12 miles.

Mr. Ball. Did Tippit usually cruise alone, or did he ever have a partner sometimes?

Mr. McDonald. Well, working in the daylight hours, which we were assigned that month, it is a custom to work alone—unless he had a trainee, such as I. I don't believe he was a trainer.

Mr. Ball. In other words, you had a trainee with you, and that is the reason you were not alone?

Mr. McDonald. Yes, sir.

Mr. Ball. Did you hear an order over the radio for cars in the outlying district near the city limits, what they were to do?

Mr. McDonald. They were to move in closer to the downtown area, but not directly to the area.

Mr. Ball. You were ordered to move into the downtown area?

Mr. McDonald. Yes, sir.

Mr. Ball. And the cars that were cruising farther out were ordered to move closer to the downtown area?

Mr. McDonald. Yes, sir.

Mr. Ball. Did you hear any other specific orders over the radio that day—that morning, or about 12:30, 1 o'clock?

Mr. McDonald. No, sir.

Mr. Ball. What did you do after you received those orders?

Mr. McDonald. I applied my red lights and sirens, and went code 32, Elm and Houston Streets.

Mr. Ball. About what time did you get there?

Mr. McDonald. Approximately 10 minutes later.

Mr. Ball. What time would that be?

Mr. McDonald. Approximately 12:40.

Mr. Ball. Where did you park your car?

Mr. McDonald. On the right curb, Elm Street, before you enter the triple underpass.

Mr. Ball. And how long did you stay there?

Mr. MoDonald. Approximately 35 minutes.

Mr. Ball. What were you doing there?

Mr. McDonald. Well, after I left the car, my partner and I reported to a supervisor, and he directed us to patrol the crowd and move the crowd around Elm Street, and rope off the area.

Mr. Ball. Now, was your radio on?

Mr. McDonald. Yes, sir. There were several police units around the intersection, and all the radios were on. And after I had moved the crowd around, went back to the entrance of the Texas School Book Depository, I heard this over the police radio, of—the first thing I heard was that President Kennedy had expired at Parkland Hospital.

And the next thing I heard was a voice over the radio that was not familiar to police procedure. He was saying that an officer had been shot, and that he was using car No. 10 radio. Of my own knowledge, I knew that car was driven by Officer Tippit, and that that car was assigned to his district.

Mr. Ball. Did he give you a location?

Mr. McDonald. Yes, sir; 400 block of East 10th Street.

Mr. Ball. What did you do?

Mr. McDonald. I told my partner we were not doing much good here, to go to Oak Cliff, and see if we could help out over there, try to apprehend the person that shot Tippit.

Mr. Ball. Did you?

Mr. McDonald. Yes, sir.

Mr. Ball. Where did you go in Oak Cliff?

Mr. McDonald. Well, we got in the car and went underneath the triple underpass and got on the Stemmons Expressway, which leads into the R. L. Thornton

297

Expressway. I believe we took the Jefferson exit and drove up to the 400 block of East Jefferson.

Mr. BALL. Patton is about a block to the north of Jefferson?

Mr. McDONALD. Patton runs across Jefferson. Tenth and Patton.

Mr. BALL. Patton runs north and south?

Mr. McDONALD. Yes, sir.

Mr. BALL. Tenth Street is a block north of Jefferson?

Mr. McDONALD. Yes, sir.

Mr. BALL. How did you happen to go to the 400 block on Jefferson?

Mr. McDONALD. I was stopped by other officers there. They wanted to search a house. So I relieved my partner to go to help the supervisors search this house, in the 400 block of East Jefferson. Then I went around to the alleys, and started cruising the alley in my squad car.

Mr. BALL. And did you get a call over your radio to go to a certain place?

Mr. McDONALD. Well, there was a report from the dispatcher that a suspect was seen running into the public library at Marsalis and Jefferson.

Mr. BALL. You went down there?

Mr. McDONALD. Yes, sir. I went directly to Denver Street, which is an alley at that point. It is still designated as Denver Street. I parked the squad car, took my shotgun, and went to the west basement entrance to the public library, and ordered the people in the basement, in the library outside. They came out with their hands up.

The boy immediately said that he had just run into the library to tell the people that the President had been shot. He was a much younger person than what was broadcast on description on the radio.

Mr. BALL. You had heard a broadcast?

Mr. McDONALD. Yes.

Mr. BALL. Of a description, of someone to look for?

Mr. McDONALD. Yes, sir.

Mr. BALL. What did you hear?

Mr. McDONALD. White male, approximately 27 years old, 5 foot 10, weight about 145 pounds, wearing light clothing.

Mr. BALL. When did you hear that? About what time?

Mr. McDONALD. It came out on the radio as I was coming to Oak Cliff. There was another general description given on the way to the Texas School Book Depository at Elm and Houston Streets. But it was a vague description.

Mr. BALL. The first description that you heard of a man to look for was on the way downtown to the Texas School Book Depository?

Mr. McDONALD. Yes, sir.

Mr. BALL. What was that description?

Mr. McDONALD. White male, approximately 27, 29 years old, and he had a white shirt on, weighed about 160 pounds.

Mr. BALL. And that was about 12:40 you got that?

Mr. McDONALD. Yes, sir.

Mr. BALL. Now, this later description you got was what point in your travel to Oak Cliff?

Mr. McDONALD. This was approximately 1:20, or 1:17.

Mr. BALL. That was after you had heard that Tippit—that the officer had been shot?

Mr. McDONALD. Yes, sir.

Mr. BALL. And what was that description?

Mr. McDONALD. Well, it was 5 foot 10, white male, 27 years old, wearing a white shirt.

Mr. BALL. Now, as you were cruising the alleys, you had gone into the library basement, and gone to cruising the alleys, did you hear something else over the radio that drew your attention to another part——

Mr. McDONALD. Just to report to the public library.

Mr. BALL. After that. Did you receive a report?

Mr. McDONALD. After I was satisfied that this teenager that had run into the library didn't fit the description, I went back to my squad car, put my shotgun back in the rack. Just as I got into the squad car, it was reported that a suspect was seen running into the Texas Theatre, 231 West Jefferson.

So I reported to that location Code 3. This is approximately seven blocks from the library, seven blocks west.

Mr. BALL. Did you go down there with your partner?

Mr. McDONALD. No, sir; I had let my partner out on arrival; my first arrival in the 400 block.

Mr. BALL. He was on foot?

Mr. McDONALD. Yes, sir; I didn't see him any more that day.

Mr. BALL. You went down to the Texas Theatre?

Mr. McDONALD. Yes, sir.

Mr. BALL. And that is what address?

Mr. McDONALD. 231 West Jefferson.

Mr. BALL. What did you do?

Mr. McDONALD. Well, when I got to the front of the theater there was several police cars already at the scene, and I surmised that officers were already inside the theater.

So I decided to go to the rear, in the alley, and seal off the rear. I parked my squad car. I noticed there were three or four other officers standing outside with shotguns guarding the rear exits. There were three other officers at the rear door. I joined them. We walked into the rear exit door over the alley.

Mr. BALL. What were their names?

Mr. McDONALD. Officer Hawkins, T. A. Hutson, and C. T. Walker. And as we got inside the door, we were met by a man that was in civilian clothes, a suit, and he told us that the man that acted suspiciously as he ran into the theater was sitting downstairs in the orchestra seats, and not in the balcony. He was sitting at the rear of the theater alone.

Officer Walker and I went to the exit curtains that is to the left of the movie screen. I looked into the audience. I saw the person that the shoe store salesman had pointed out to us.

Mr. BALL. Were the lights on or off?

Mr. McDONALD. The lights were up, and the movie was playing at this time.

Mr. BALL. And could you see to the rear of the theater?

Mr. McDONALD. Yes, sir.

Mr. BALL. You could see the man. Did the civilian point out to you the man in one of the rear seats?

Mr. McDONALD. He didn't point out personally. He was pointing out the suspect to another officer with him on the right of the stage, just right of the movie screen.

Mr. BALL. What did you do then?

Mr. McDONALD. Well, after seeing him, I noticed the other people in the theater—there was approximately 10 or 15 other people seated throughout the theater. There were two men sitting in the center, about 10 rows from the front.

I walked up the left center aisle into the row behind these two men, and Officer C. T. Walker was behind me. When I got to these two men, I told them to get on their feet. They got up. I searched them for a weapon.

I looked over my shoulder and the suspect that had been pointed out to me. He remained seated without moving, just looking at me.

Mr. BALL. Why did you frisk these two men in the center of the theater?

Mr. McDONALD. I wanted to make sure that I didn't pass anything or miss anybody. I wanted to make sure I didn't overlook anybody or anything.

Mr. BALL. And you still kept your eye on the suspect?

Mr. McDONALD. Yes, sir. He was to my back. I was looking over my shoulder at him.

Mr. BALL. Was he sitting nearest the right or the left aisle as you came in?

Mr. McDONALD. The right center aisle. He was in the second seat.

Mr. BALL. What did you do then?

Mr. McDONALD. After I was satisfied that these two men were not armed or had a weapon on them, I walked out of this row, up to the right center aisle toward the suspect. And as I walked up there, just at a normal gait, I didn't look directly at him, but I kept my eye on him and any other persons. And to my left was another man and I believe a woman was with him. But he was further back than the suspect.

And just as I got to the row where the suspect was sitting, I stopped abruptly, and turned in and told him to get on his feet. He rose immediately, bringing up both hands. He got this hand about shoulder high, his left hand shoulder high, and he got his right hand about breast high. He said, "Well, it is all over now."

As he said this, I put my left hand on his waist and then his hand went to the waist. And this hand struck me between the eyes on the bridge of the nose.

Mr. BALL. Did he cock his fist?

Mr. McDONALD. Yes, sir: knocking my cap off.

Mr. BALL. Which fist did he hit you with?

Mr. McDONALD. His left fist.

Mr. BALL. What happened then?

Mr. McDONALD. Well, whenever he knocked my hat off, any normal reaction was for me to go at him with this hand.

Mr. BALL. Right hand?

Mr. McDONALD. Yes. I went at him with this hand, and I believe I struck him on the face, but I don't know where. And with my hand, that was on his hand over the pistol.

Mr. BALL. Did you feel the pistol?

Mr. McDONALD. Yes, sir.

Mr. BALL. Which hand was—was his right hand or his left hand on the pistol?

Mr. McDONALD. His right hand was on the pistol.

Mr. BALL. And which of your hands?

Mr. McDONALD. My left hand, at this point.

Mr. BALL. And had he withdrawn the pistol——

Mr. McDONALD. He was drawing it as I put my hand.

Mr. BALL. From his waist?

Mr. McDONALD. Yes, sir.

Mr. BALL. What happened then?

Mr. McDONALD. Well, whenever I hit him, we both fell into the seats. While we were struggling around there, with this hand on the gun——

Mr. BALL. Your left hand?

Mr. McDONALD. Yes, sir. Somehow I managed to get this hand in the action also.

Mr. BALL. Your right hand?

Mr. McDONALD. Yes, sir. Now, as we fell into the seats, I called out, "I have got him," and Officer T. A. Hutson, he came to the row behind us and grabbed Oswald around the neck. And then Officer C. T. Walker came into the row that we were in and grabbed his left arm. And Officer Ray Hawkins came to the row in front of us and grabbed him from the front.

By the time all three of these officers had got there, I had gotten my right hand on the butt of the pistol and jerked it free.

Mr. BALL. Had you felt any movement of the hammer?

Mr. McDONALD. Yes, sir. When this hand—we went down into the seats.

Mr. BALL. When your left hand went into the seats, what happened?

Mr. McDONALD. It felt like something had grazed across my hand. I felt movement there. And that was the only movement I felt. And I heard a snap. I didn't know what it was at the time.

Mr. BALL. Was the pistol out of his waist at that time?

Mr. McDONALD. Yes, sir.

Mr. BALL. Do you know any way it was pointed?

Mr. McDONALD. Well, I believe the muzzle was toward me, because the sensation came across this way. To make a movement like that, it would have to be the cylinder or the hammer.

Mr. BALL. Across your left palm?

Mr. McDONALD. Yes, sir. And my hand was directly over the pistol in this manner. More or less the butt. But not on the butt.

Mr. BALL. What happened when you jerked the pistol free?

Mr. McDONALD. When I jerked it free, I was down in the seats with him, with my head, some reason or other, I don't know why, and when I brought the pistol out, it grazed me across the cheek here, and I put it all the way out to the aisle, holding it by the butt. I gave the pistol to Detective Bob Carroll at that point.

Mr. BALL. Grazed your left cheek?

Mr. McDONALD. Yes, sir.

Mr. BALL. Scratched—noticeable scratch?

Mr. McDONALD. Yes, sir; about a 4-inch scratch just above the eye to just above the lip.

Mr. BALL. Then what happened after that?

Mr. McDONALD. Well, the officers that had come to my aid started handcuffing him and taking him out of the theater.

Mr. BALL. What did he say—anything?

Mr. McDONALD. Well, he was cursing a little bit and hollering police brutality, for one thing.

Mr. BALL. What words did he use?

Mr. McDONALD. I couldn't recall the exact words. It was just mixed up words, people hollering and screaming when they get arrested.

Mr. BALL. What did he say about police brutality?

Mr. McDONALD. One thing, "Don't hit me any more." I remember that.

Mr. BALL. Did somebody hit him?

Mr. McDONALD. Yes, sir; I guess they did.

Mr. BALL. Who hit him, do you know?

Mr. McDONALD. No, sir; I don't, other than myself.

Mr. BALL. You know you hit him?

Mr. McDONALD. Yes, sir.

Mr. BALL. Now, did you go with them outside?

Mr. McDONALD. No, sir.

Mr. BALL. What did you do?

Mr. McDONALD. I was looking for my hat and flashlight.

Mr. BALL. Did you go downtown with them?

Mr. McDONALD. No, sir.

Mr. BALL. Later you went downtown?

Mr. McDONALD. Yes, sir.

Mr. BALL. And did you put a mark on the revolver?

Mr. McDONALD. Yes, sir; I did.

Mr. BALL. And did you look at the ammunition in the revolver, the six rounds in the cylinder?

Mr. McDONALD. Yes, sir.

Mr. BALL. Did you notice anything unusual about any one of them?

Mr. McDONALD. I noticed on the primer of one of the shells it had an indentation on it, but not one that had been fired or anything—not that strong of an indentation.

Mr. BALL. We have here Exhibit 143 for identification. Do you know whether or not this is the revolver that you took from the man that you arrested?

Mr. McDONALD. Yes, sir; this is it. I found the mark here.

Mr. BALL. You found your mark?

Mr. McDONALD. Yes, sir.

Senator COOPER. What mark is it?

Mr. McDONALD. I marked the initial "M".

Mr. BALL. Where?

Mr. McDONALD. Right here, on this steel plate.

Mr. BALL. Of the butt?

Mr. McDONALD. Yes, sir.

Mr. BELIN. Let the record show the witness is pointing to a point on the steel plate directly below the screw on the butt.

Mr. BALL. How many cartridges were in the cylinder?

Mr. McDONALD. Six, fully loaded.

Mr. BALL. I will show you four that are marked as—we will give these four an exhibit number. Do you know whether or not they were shells similar to that?

Mr. McDONALD. Yes, sir; they were .38 caliber. Now, I didn't mark all of these shells, myself.

Mr. BALL. Did you mark any of them?

Mr. McDonald. I recall marking one.

Mr. Ball. The four cartridges, the witness is examining now we will mark collectively as Commission Exhibit 518.

(The articles referred to were marked Commission Exhibit No. 518 for identification.)

Mr. Ball. And there are two cartridges that have been marked as Commission Exhibit 145 that the witness is also examining. Now, on one of the cartridges that have come from Commission's Exhibit 145, consisting of two cartridges, one of these you identify as a cartridge with a dent in it?

Mr. McDonald. Yes, sir.

Mr. Ball. How can you tell this?

Mr. McDonald. From the center of this—of the primer there—it is a small indentation, and some of the metal is blurred or not polished.

Mr. Ball. And your mark is on one of these cartridges?

Mr. McDonald. Yes, sir.

Mr. Ball. I will show you an Exhibit 519.

(The document referred to was marked Commission Exhibit No. 519 for identification.)

Mr. Ball. Is that a picture of the theatre?

Mr. McDonald. Yes, sir.

Mr. Ball. And can you mark on there the seat in which the man was seated who was the suspect?

Mr. McDonald. Yes, sir.

Mr. Ball. Put an arrow down to that seat. Did you see Oswald later that evening?

Mr. McDonald. No, sir.

Mr. Ball. Did you ever see him again?

Mr. McDonald. No, sir.

Mr. Ball. When you saw Oswald, was he bloody any?

Mr. McDonald. Afterwards?

Mr. Ball. Well, when he was being taken from the theatre. Was he bloody?

Mr. McDonald. No, sir; I didn't see any blood.

Mr. Ball. You didn't?

Mr. McDonald. Because whenever they took him, they took him directly out.

Mr. Ball. And you never saw him again?

Mr. McDonald. No, sir.

Mr. Ball. What was he wearing at that time?

Mr. McDonald. At the time he was wearing a dark brown shirt and a T-shirt and dark trousers.

Mr. Ball. A dark brown shirt, a T-shirt, and dark trousers?

Mr. McDonald. Yes, sir.

Mr. Ball. I will show you Commission 150. Does that look anything like the color of the shirt he was wearing?

Mr. McDonald. Yes, sir.

Mr. Ball. I would like to at this time offer all exhibits up to 519 in evidence.

Senator Cooper. They will be admitted in evidence.

(The documents heretofore marked for identification as Commission Exhibits Nos. 518 and 519 were received in evidence.)

Mr. Ball. Did you notice where the pistol was concealed on this man's person?

Mr. McDonald. Yes, sir. It was under his right waist band, right side.

Mr. Ball. Was it under the shirt?

Mr. McDonald. Yes, sir; it was underneath the shirt.

Mr. Ball. Underneath the shirt?

Mr. McDonald. Yes, sir. I would like to correct that, and say it was underneath the brown shirt that he had on. Not underneath the T-shirt.

The Chairman. It was not in a holster?

Mr. McDonald. No, sir; no holster at all.

Mr. Ball. Were—was there an FBI agent there?

Mr. McDonald. I don't know, sir. I was told he was there, but I don't know.

Mr. Ball. The only people that you saw were——

Mr. McDonald. The ones I named there.

Mr. Ball. Dallas Police Department men?

Mr. McDonald. Yes, sir.

Mr. Ball. I have no further questions.

Senator Cooper. Who was it that pointed out to you the suspect when you entered the theatre?

Mr. McDonald. I learned his name later.

Senator Cooper. Did some person there point out to you, though, this man sitting in the row whom you later arrested?

Mr. McDonald. Yes, sir. He was a shoestore salesman. His name was Brewer. He was the one that met us at the rear exit door and said that he saw this person run into the Texas Theatre.

Senator Cooper. Did you hear him say that?

Mr. McDonald. Yes, sir.

Senator Cooper. And have you seen him since?

Mr. McDonald. No, sir.

Senator Cooper. But somebody has identified him to you?

Mr. McDonald. Yes, sir.

Mr. Ball. We will examine him next week, sir.

Senator Cooper. May I ask—if the suspect was pointed out to you, why was it you did not go directly to him, but you searched other persons?

Mr. McDonald. Well, usually on information of that sort, you have to weigh it a little bit to make sure you get the right person. He could have been mistaken. If a suspect was in that theatre, I wanted to make sure I got him, and not overlook him.

Senator Cooper. You said, though, that before you went into the theatre, where the seats were located, that a man pointed out to you a person who he claimed was the suspect.

Mr. McDonald. Yes, sir; he said that that was the man that had acted suspiciously in running into the theatre.

Senator Cooper. That was the man that was identified to you?

Mr. McDonald. Yes, sir.

Senator Cooper. Then, if he was the man identified to you, why did you stop and search these two men before you got to the man you later arrested?

Mr. McDonald. Well, I wanted to make sure he was right.

Senator Cooper. Was it your purpose to search everybody in there?

Mr. McDonald. It was my intention—everybody I came to.

Senator Cooper. Were these the first two that you did search?

Mr. McDonald. Yes, sir; they were the closest ones to me.

Senator Cooper. They were sitting in front of the man you later arrested?

Mr. McDonald. Yes, sir; they were sitting about 10 rows in front of him.

Senator Cooper. At the time you were searching them, you could see the other man that you later arrested?

Mr. McDonald. Yes, sir.

Senator Cooper. What did he do?

Mr. McDonald. Just sat in his seat, with his hands in his lap, watching me.

Senator Cooper. Were there any other police officers in his vicinity?

Mr. McDonald. There were police officers in the balcony, and police officers in the aisle, or in the lobby, you might call it—not in the theatre, except for the other three that I named.

Senator Cooper. You are the only one in the theatre?

Mr. McDonald. Well, there was the other three officers that accompanied me through the rear exit door. Officer Walker went through the curtains with me, and Officers Hawkins and Hutson was on the stage with the man that was identifying the suspect.

Senator Cooper. Then when you told the man you arrested to stand up did he immediately pull his pistol out?

Mr. McDonald. No, sir; he stood up and started raising his hands, "Well, it is all over now." But in my opinion, it was an act of giving up or surrendering. It was just natural that my hand went to his waist for a weapon, which was my intent anyway, whether he raised his hands or not. I didn't command him to raise his hands or anything. It was just a reaction of his.

Senator COOPER. Did he hit you with the pistol?

Mr. McDONALD. No, sir.

Senator COOPER. Did he point it towards you?

Mr. McDONALD. I don't know what position the gun was pointed out, whenever my hand was on it, because we were both grappling around there. But, as I say, the top of my hand was over on top of the pistol.

Senator COOPER. To whom did you turn over the possession of the pistol?

Mr. McDONALD. Detective Bob Carroll. He had come into the aisle. Whenever I hollered, "I got him" immediately I was swarmed by officers.

Senator COOPER. Did you mark the pistol at that time before you turned it over?

Mr. McDONALD. No, sir; I marked it at the police station.

Senator COOPER. But you recognized it then as the same pistol you had identified today?

Mr. McDONALD. Yes, sir.

Senator COOPER. That is all.

The CHAIRMAN. Officer, you were in uniform that day?

Mr. McDONALD. Yes, sir.

The CHAIRMAN. Did the blow he gave you on your nose leave any mark?

Mr. McDONALD. Well, for 2 days I had some swelling. It didn't break the skin or anything. Some of the force was taken by my top. It hit the bill of my cap and my nose.

The CHAIRMAN. And the scratch from the corner of your eye down to the corner of your mouth came from the pistol?

Mr. McDONALD. Yes, sir. As I was taking the pistol away, clearing it from his body. Yes, sir.

The CHAIRMAN. I think that is all. We are very glad you are able to be with us today.

Mr. BALL. There is one thing.

I have marked an exhibit, 520.

(The document referred to was marked Commission Exhibit No. 520 for identification and received in evidence.)

Mr. BALL. As he said he had not seen Oswald since, and I know this was taken—but I would like to ask him one question with reference to 520 for identification, and we will later provide an identification, proper identification for it.

Does that look like the man that you arrested in the Texas Theatre that day?

Mr. McDONALD. Yes, sir.

Mr. BALL. And does it look like—well, of course, he had a shirt over that T-shirt.

Mr. McDONALD. Yes, sir.

Mr. BALL. I have no further questions.

The CHAIRMAN. Thank you very much, officer. We are glad you were able to be with us.

(Whereupon, at 4:30 p.m., the President's Commission recessed.)

Thursday, March 26, 1964

TESTIMONY OF MRS. HELEN MARKHAM, WILLIAM W. SCOGGINS, MRS. JEANETTE DAVIS, AND TED CALLAWAY

The President's Commission met at 9:10 a.m. on March 26, 1964, at 200 Maryland Avenue NE., Washington, D.C.

Present were Chief Justice Earl Warren, Chairman; Representative Gerald R. Ford, and Allen W. Dulles, members.

Also present were Joseph A. Ball, assistant counsel; David W. Belin, assistant counsel; Norman Redlich, assistant counsel; Charles Murray, observer; and Waggoner Carr, attorney general of Texas.

TESTIMONY OF MRS. HELEN MARKHAM

The CHAIRMAN. The purpose of the session of the Commission is for the purpose of taking testimony on the assassination of President Kennedy, and it is our information that you have some evidence concerning it and we want to ask you some questions concerning it. You are willing to testify, are you?

Mrs. MARKMAN. Do all I can.

The CHAIRMAN. All right. Will you stand up and be sworn, please?

Do you solemnly swear the testimony you give before this Commission will be the truth, the whole truth and nothing but the truth, so help you God?

Mrs. MARKHAM. I do.

The CHAIRMAN. You may be seated.

Mr. Ball will ask you the questions.

Mr. BALL. Mrs. Markham, what is your address?

Mrs. MARKHAM. 328 East Ninth.

Mr. BALL. In Dallas, Tex.?

Mrs. MARKHAM. Dallas, Tex.

Mr. BALL. Where were you born, Mrs. Markham?

Mrs. MARKHAM. Where was I born? Dallas.

Mr. BALL. The Commission would like to know something of your past life and experience, where you were born and your education so I will just ask you a few questions like that.

Take it easy, this is just——

Mrs. MARKHAM. I am very shook up.

Mr. BALL. This is a very informal little conference here.

Mrs. MARKHAM. Well, do you want me to tell you about my life?

Mr. BALL. Yes. Just tell us briefly where you were born and where you went to school and things of that kind.

Mrs. MARKHAM. I was born in Dallas, Dallas County. My father was a farmer. I was very small when my mother died, I was 6 years old; and my brothers and I were separated which they were put in the State orphans home, and I went to live with my aunt.

Mr. DULLES. Are your brothers older or younger?

Mrs. MARKHAM. I have one older than I. And I went to live with my aunt and uncle in Grand Prairie. I went to Grand Prairie school.

Mr. BALL. How far did you go through school?

Mrs. MARKHAM. Eighth grade.

Mr. BALL. Then did you go to work?

Mrs. MARKHAM. No; I got married. I got married.

Mr. BALL. How long were you married?

Mrs. MARKHAM. Me——

Mr. BALL. I understand you are not married at the present time?

Mrs. MARKHAM. No. I am not married. I would have been married 25 years this past July.

Mr. BALL. Were you a housewife for a while while you were married?

Mrs. MARKHAM. Yes; I was.

Mr. BALL. How many years?

Mrs. MARKHAM. Let me see, about 8 years.

Mr. BALL. Did you have any children?

Mrs. MARKHAM. Yes, I did.

Mr. BALL. How many children did you have?

Mrs. MARKHAM. Well, I have five children.

Mr. BALL. Do they live with you now or what?

Mrs. MARKHAM. I have one son who stays with me.

Mr. BALL. What has been your work most of your life since you were divorced, what kind of work have you done?

Mrs. MARKHAM. Waitress work.

Mr. BALL. You have done waitress work?

Mrs. MARKHAM. Yes, sir.

Mr. BALL. Where do you work now?

Mrs. MARKHAM. Eat Well Restaurant, 1404 Main Street, Dallas, Tex.

Mr. BALL. Were you working there on November 22, 1963?

Mrs. MARKHAM. I was.

Mr. BALL. What hours did you work?

Mrs. MARKHAM. I was due at work from 2:30 in the evening until 10:30 at night.

Mr. BALL. Straight shift?

Mrs. MARKHAM. Yes, sir.

Mr. BALL. Did you leave your home some time that morning to go to work?

Mrs. MARKHAM. That evening?

Mr. BALL. Morning.

Mrs. MARKHAM. That morning?

Mr. BALL. You left your home to go to work at some time, didn't you, that day?

Mrs. MARKHAM. At one.

Mr. BALL. One o'clock?

Mrs. MARKHAM. I believe it was a little after 1.

Mr. BALL. Where did you intend to catch the bus?

Mrs. MARKHAM. On Patton and Jefferson.

Mr. BALL. Patton and Jefferson is about a block south of Patton and 10th Street, isn't it?

Mrs. MARKHAM. I think so.

Mr. BALL. Well, where is your home from Patton and Jefferson?

Mrs. MARKHAM. I had came—I come one block, I had come one block from my home.

Mr. BALL. You were walking, were you?

Mrs. MARKHAM. I came from 9th to the corner of 10th Street.

Mr. BALL. And you were walking toward Jefferson?

Mrs. MARKHAM. Yes, sir.

Mr. BALL. Tenth Street runs the same direction as Jefferson, doesn't it?

Mrs. MARKHAM. Yes, sir.

Mr. BALL. It runs in a generally east and west direction?

Mrs. MARKHAM. Yes, sir.

Mr. BALL. And Patton runs north and south?

Mrs. MARKHAM. Yes, sir; up and down this way.

Mr. BALL. So you were walking south toward Jefferson?

Mrs. MARKHAM. Yes, sir.

Mr. BALL. You think it was a little after 1?

Mrs. MARKHAM. I wouldn't be afraid to bet it wasn't 6 or 7 minutes after 1.

Mr. BALL. You know what time you usually get your bus, don't you?

Mrs. MARKHAM. 1:15.

Mr. BALL. So it was before 1:15?

Mrs. MARKHAM. Yes, it was.

Mr. BALL. When you came to the corner of Patton and 10th Street—first of all, what side of the street were you walking on?

Mrs. MARKHAM. Now you have got me mixed up on all my streets. I was on the opposite of where this man was.

Mr. BALL. Well, you were walking along the street——

Mrs. MARKHAM. On the street.

Mr. BALL. On Patton, you were going toward Jefferson?

Mrs. MARKHAM. Yes, sir.

Mr. BALL. And you were on the right- or left-hand side of the street as you were walking south?

Mrs. MARKHAM. That would be on the left.

Mr. BALL. Your right.

Mrs. MARKHAM. Yes, it would be right.

Mr. BALL. Right-hand side, wouldn't it? When you came to the corner did you have to stop before you crossed 10th Street?

Mrs. MARKHAM. Yes, I did.

Mr. BALL. Why?

Mrs. MARKHAM. On account the traffic was coming.

Mr. BALL. And you stopped there on the corner?

Mrs. MARKHAM. Yes, sir.

Mr. BALL. That would be the northwest corner, wouldn't it?

Mrs. MARKHAM. Northwest corner.

Mr. BALL. Is that right?

Mrs. MARKHAM. I believe it is. I believe it is the northwest corner.

Mr. BALL. Did you see any man walking at that time?

Mrs. MARKHAM. Yes; I seen this man on the opposite side, across the street from me. He was almost across Patton Street.

Mr. BALL. Almost across Patton?

Mrs. MARKHAM. Yes, sir.

Mr. BALL. Walking in what direction?

Mrs. MARKHAM. I guess this would be south.

Mr. BALL. Along 10th, east? Was it along 10th?

Mrs. MARKHAM. Yes, sir.

Mr. BALL. Walking away from you, wasn't he?

Mrs. MARKHAM. He was walking up 10th, away from me.

Mr. BALL. To your left?

Mrs. MARKHAM. Well, he was on the opposite side of the street to me like that.

Mr. BALL. Had he reached the curb yet?

Mrs. MARKHAM. Almost ready to get up on the curb.

Mr. BALL. What did you notice then?

Mrs. MARKHAM. Well, I noticed a police car coming.

Mr. BALL. Where was the police car when you first saw it?

Mrs. MARKHAM. He was driving real slow, almost up to this man, well, say this man, and he kept, this man kept walking, you know, and the police car going real slow now, real slow, and they just kept coming into the curb, and finally they got way up there a little ways up, well, it stopped.

Mr. BALL. The police car stopped?

Mrs. MARKHAM. Yes, sir.

Mr. BALL. What about the man? Was he still walking?

Mrs. MARKHAM. The man stopped.

Mr. BALL. Then what did you see the man do?

Mrs. MARKHAM. I saw the man come over to the car very slow, leaned and put his arms just like this, he leaned over in this window and looked in this window.

Mr. BALL. He put his arms on the window ledge?

Mrs. MARKHAM. The window was down.

Mr. BALL. It was?

Mrs. MARKHAM. Yes, sir.

Mr. BALL. Put his arms on the window ledge?

Mrs. MARKHAM. On the ledge of the window.

Mr. BALL. And the policeman was sitting where?

Mrs. MARKHAM. On the driver's side.

Mr. BALL. He was sitting behind the wheel?

Mrs. MARKHAM. Yes, sir.

Mr. BALL. Was he alone in the car?

Mrs. MARKHAM. Yes.

Mr. BALL. Then what happened?

Mrs. MARKHAM. Well, I didn't think nothing about it; you know, the police are nice and friendly, and I thought friendly conversation. Well, I looked, and there were cars coming, so I had to wait. Well, in a few minutes this man made——

Mr. BALL. What did you see the policeman do?

Mrs. MARKHAM. See the policeman? Well, this man, like I told you, put his arms up, leaned over, he—just a minute, and he drew back and he stepped back about two steps. Mr. Tippit——

Mr. BALL. The policeman?

Mrs. MARKHAM. The policeman calmly opened the car door, very slowly, wasn't angry or nothing, he calmly crawled out of this car, and I still just thought a friendly conversation, maybe disturbance in the house, I did not know; well, just as the policeman got in——

Mr. BALL. Which way did he walk?

Mrs. MARKHAM. Towards the front of the car. And just as he had gotten even with the wheel on the driver's side——

Mr. BALL. You mean the left front wheel?

Mrs. MARKHAM. Yes; this man shot the policeman.

Mr. BALL. You heard the shots, did you?

Mrs. MARKHAM. Yes, sir.

Mr. BALL. How many shots did you hear?

Mrs. MARKHAM. Three.

Mr. BALL. What did you see the policeman do?

Mrs. MARKHAM. He fell to the ground, and his cap went a little ways out on the street.

Mr. BALL. What did the man do?

Mrs. MARKHAM. The man, he just walked calmly, fooling with his gun.

Mr. BALL. Toward what direction did he walk?

Mrs. MARKHAM. Come back towards me, turned around, and went back.

Mr. BALL. Toward Patton?

Mrs. MARKHAM. Yes, sir; towards Patton. He didn't run. It just didn't scare him to death. He didn't run. When he saw me he looked at me, stared at me. I put my hands over my face like this, closed my eyes. I gradually opened my fingers like this, and I opened my eyes, and when I did he started off in kind of a little trot.

Mr. BALL. Which way?

Mrs. MARKHAM. Sir?

Mr. BALL. Which way?

Mrs. MARKHAM. Towards Jefferson, right across that way.

Mr. DULLES. Did he have the pistol in his hand at this time?

Mrs. MARKHAM. He had the gun when I saw him.

Mr. BALL. Did you yell at him?

Mrs. MARKHAM. When I pulled my fingers down where I could see, I got my hand down, he began to trot off, and then I ran to the policeman.

Mr. BALL. Before you put your hands over your eyes, before you put your hand over your eyes, did you see the man walk towards the corner?

Mrs. MARKHAM. Yes.

Mr. BALL. What did he do?

Mrs. MARKHAM. Well, he stared at me.

Mr. BALL. What did you do?

Mrs. MARKHAM. I didn't do anything. I couldn't.

Mr. BALL. Didn't you say something?

Mrs. MARKHAM. No, I couldn't.

Mr. BALL. Or yell or scream?

Mrs. MARKHAM. I could not. I could not say nothing.

Mr. BALL. You looked at him?

Mrs. MARKHAM. Yes.

Mr. BALL. You looked at him?

Mrs. MARKHAM. Yes, sir. He looked wild. I mean, well, he did to me.

Mr. BALL. And you say you saw him fooling with his gun?

Mrs. MARKHAM. He had it in his hands.

Mr. BALL. Did you see what he was doing with it?

Mrs. MARKHAM. He was just fooling with it. I didn't know what he was doing. I was afraid he was fixing to kill me.

Mr. BALL. How far away from the police car do you think you were on the corner when you saw the shooting?

Mrs. MARKHAM. Well, I wasn't too far.

Mr. BALL. Can you estimate it in feet? Don't guess.

Mrs. MARKHAM. I would just be afraid to say how many feet because I am a bad judgment on that.

Mr. BALL. When you looked at the man, though, when he came toward the corner, you were standing on one corner, were you?

Mrs. MARKHAM. Yes, sir

Mr. BALL. Where was he standing with reference to the other corner?

Mrs. MARKHAM. After he had shot——

Mr. BALL. When he looked at you.

Mrs. MARKHAM. After he had shot the policeman?

Mr. BALL. Yes.

Mrs. MARKHAM. He was standing almost even to that curb, not very far from the curb, from the sidewalk.

Mr. BALL. Across the street from you?

Mrs. MARKHAM. Yes, sir.

Mr. BALL. Did he look at you?

Mrs. MARKHAM. Yes, sir.

Mr. BALL. And did you look at him?

Mrs. MARKHAM. I sure did.

Mr. BALL. That was before you put your hands over your eyes?

Mrs. MARKHAM. Yes, sir; and he kept fooling with his gun, and I slapped my hands up to my face like this.

Mr. BALL. And then you ran to the policeman?

Mrs. MARKHAM. After he ran off.

Mr. BALL. In what hand did he have his gun, do you know, when he fired the shots?

Mrs. MARKHAM. Sir, I believe it was his right. I am not positive because I was scared.

Mr. BALL. When he came down the street towards you, in what hand did he have his gun?

Mrs. MARKHAM. He had it in both of them.

Mr. BALL. He had it in both of them?

Mrs. MARKHAM. Yes, sir.

Mr. BALL. When he went towards Jefferson you say he went at sort of a trot?

Mrs. MARKHAM. Yes, sir.

Mr. BALL. Did he cross Patton?

Mrs. MARKHAM. Yes, sir.

Mr. DULLES. Were there many other, or other people in the block at that time, or were you there with Officer Tippit almost alone?

Mrs. MARKHAM. I was out there, I didn't see anybody. I was there alone by myself.

Mr. DULLES. I see. You didn't see anybody else in the immediate neighborhood?

Mrs. MARKHAM. No; not until everything was over—I never seen anybody until I was at Mr. Tippit's side. I tried to save his life, which was I didn't know at that time I couldn't do something for him.

Mr. DULLES. Mr. Tippit, Officer Tippit, didn't say anything to you?

Mrs. MARKHAM. He tried to.

Mr. DULLES. He tried to?

Mrs. MARKHAM. Yes, sir.

Mr. DULLES. But he didn't succeed?

Mrs. MARKHAM. No, I couldn't understand. I was screaming and hollering and I was trying to help him all I could, and I would have. I was with him until they put him in the ambulance.

Mr. BALL. Did you make an estimate of how far you were from this man with the gun when he came—after the shooting, and when he came down to the corner, did you make an estimate of that?

Mrs. MARKHAM. No. To anyone——

Mr. BALL. We measured it the other day. We were out there, weren't we?

Mrs. MARKHAM. Now I couldn't tell you how many feet or nothing because I have never had no occasions to measure that.

Mr. DULLES. Was it further than this table, the length of this table?

Mrs. MARKHAM. It was across the street.

Mr. DULLES. Across the street. It was two or three times the length of this table?

Mrs. MARKHAM. Across from the street. That was too close.

Mr. BALL. We have a map coming from the FBI. We thought it would be here this morning.

Mrs. Markham, you were taken to the Police Department, weren't you?

Mrs. MARKHAM. Yes, sir.

Mr. BALL. Immediately.

Mrs. MARKHAM. Yes, sir.

Mr. BALL. Later that day they had a showup you went to?

Mrs. MARKHAM. A lineup?

Mr. BALL. A lineup.

Mrs. MARKHAM. Yes.

Mr. BALL. How many men were in the lineup?

Mrs. MARKHAM. I believe there were, now I am not positive, I believe there were three besides this man.

Mr. BALL. That would be four people altogether?

Mrs. MARKHAM. I believe that is correct.

Mr. BALL. Were they of anywhere near similar build or size or coloring?

Mrs. MARKHAM. Yes, they were all about the same height.

Mr. BALL. Who were you in the lineup room with?

Mrs. MARKHAM. Who was I in the room where they had this man?

Mr. BALL. Yes.

Mrs. MARKHAM. Policemen.

Mr. BALL. More than one?

Mrs. MARKHAM. The room was full.

Mr. BALL. It was. In this lineup room, the room was full of policemen. Weren't there just one or two men with you?

Mrs. MARKHAM. One or two with me, but I don't know who they were.

Mr. BALL. But there were other officers?

Mrs. MARKHAM. There were all policemen sitting in the back of me, and aside of me.

Mr. BALL. In this room?

Mrs. MARKHAM. Yes, sir. They were doing something.

Mr. BALL. Before you went into this room were you shown a picture of anyone?

Mrs. MARKHAM. I was not.

Mr. BALL. Did you see any television?

Mrs. MARKHAM. I did not.

Mr. BALL. Did a police officer say anything to you before you went in there, to tell you——

Mrs. MARKHAM. No, sir.

Mr. BALL. That he thought "We had the right man," or something of that sort? Anything like that?

Mrs. MARKHAM. No, sir.

Mr. BALL. No statement like that?

Mrs. MARKHAM. No, sir.

Mr. BALL. Did anybody tell you that the man you were looking for would be in a certain position in the lineup, or anything like that?

Mrs. MARKHAM. No, sir.

Mr. BALL. Now when you went into the room you looked these people over, these four men?

Mrs. MARKHAM. Yes, sir.

Mr. BALL. Did you recognize anyone in the lineup?

Mrs. MARKHAM. No, sir.

Mr. BALL. You did not? Did you see anybody—I have asked you that question before—did you recognize anybody from their face?

Mrs. MARKHAM. From their face, no.

Mr. BALL. Did you identify anybody in these four people?

Mrs. MARKHAM. I didn't know nobody.

Mr. BALL. I know you didn't know anybody, but did anybody in that lineup look like anybody you had seen before?

Mrs. MARKHAM. No. I had never seen none of them, none of these men.

Mr. BALL. No one of the four?

Mrs. MARKHAM. No one of them.

Mr. BALL. No one of all four?

Mrs. MARKHAM. No, sir.

Mr. BALL. Was there a number two man in there?

Mrs. MARKHAM. Number two is the one I picked.

Mr. BALL. Well, I thought you just told me that you hadn't——

Mrs. MARKHAM. I thought you wanted me to describe their clothing.

Mr. BALL. No. I wanted to know if that day when you were in there if you saw anyone in there——

Mrs. MARKHAM. Number two.

Mr. BALL. What did you say when you saw number two?

Mrs. MARKHAM. Well, let me tell you. I said the second man, and they kept asking me which one, which one. I said, number two. When I said number two, I just got weak.

Mr. BALL. What about number two, what did you mean when you said number two?

Mrs. MARKHAM. Number two was the man I saw shoot the policeman.

Mr. BALL. You recognized him from his appearance?

Mrs. MARKHAM. I asked—I looked at him. When I saw this man I wasn't sure, but I had cold chills just run all over me.

Mr. BALL. When you saw him?

Mrs. MARKHAM. When I saw the man. But I wasn't sure, so, you see, I told them I wanted to be sure, and looked at his face is what I was looking at, mostly is what I looked at, on account of his eyes, the way he looked at me. So I asked them if they would turn him sideways. They did, and then they turned him back around, and I said the second, and they said, which one, and I said number two. So when I said that, well, I just kind of fell over. Everybody in there, you know, was beginning to talk, and I don't know, just——

Mr. BALL. Did you recognize him from his clothing?

Mrs. MARKHAM. He had on a light short jacket, dark trousers. I looked at his clothing, but I looked at his face, too.

Mr. BALL. Did he have the same clothing on that the man had that you saw shoot the officer?

Mrs. MARKHAM. He had these dark trousers on.

Mr. BALL. Did he have a jacket or a shirt? The man that you saw shoot Officer Tippit and run away, did you notice if he had a jacket on?

Mrs. MARKHAM. He had a jacket on when he done it.

Mr. BALL. What kind of a jacket, what general color of jacket?

Mrs. MARKHAM. It was a short jacket open in the front, kind of a grayish tan.

Mr. BALL. Did you tell the police that?

Mrs. MARKHAM. Yes, I did.

Mr. BALL. Did any man in the lineup have a jacket on?

Mrs. MARKHAM. I can't remember that.

Mr. BALL. Did this number two man that you mentioned to the police have any jacket on when he was in the lineup?

Mrs. MARKHAM. No, sir.

Mr. BALL. What did he have on?

Mrs. MARKHAM. He had on a light shirt and dark trousers.

(Representative Ford is now in the Commission hearing room.)

Mr. BALL. Did you recognize the man from his clothing or from his face?

Mrs. MARKHAM. Mostly from his face.

Mr. BALL. Were you sure it was the same man you had seen before?

Mrs. MARKHAM. I am sure.

Mr. BALL. Now, what time of day was it that you saw this man in the lineup?

Mrs. MARKHAM. I would say it was four, a little after.

Mr. BALL. That was four in the afternoon?

Mrs. MARKHAM. I was so upset I couldn't even tell you the time. In fact, I wasn't interested in the time.

Mr. BALL. Yes.

Mr. DULLES. Could I ask just one question?

Mr. BALL. Yes.

Mr. DULLES. You referred to his eyes; they were rather striking. Can you give any impression of how his eyes looked to you? I realize that is a very vague question.

Mrs. MARKHAM. Yes. He looked wild. They were glassy looking, because I could see——

Mr. DULLES. He had no glasses on?

Mrs. MARKHAM. No. When we looked at each other, he just stared, just like that. I just don't know. I just seen him—I would know the man anywhere, I know I would.

Mr. DULLES. Thank you.

Mr. BALL. I have here an exhibit, Commission Exhibit 162, a jacket. Did you ever see this before?

Mrs. MARKHAM. No; I did not.

Mr. BALL. Does it look like, anything like, the jacket the man had on?

Mrs. MARKHAM. It is short, open down the front. But that jacket it is a darker jacket than that, I know it was.

Mr. BALL. You don't think it was as light a jacket as that?

Mrs. MARKHAM. No, it was darker than that, I know it was. At that moment I was so excited——

Mr. BALL. I show you a shirt here, which is Exhibit 150. Did you ever see a shirt the color of this?

Mrs. MARKHAM. The shirt that this man had, it was a lighter looking shirt than that.

Mr. BALL. The man who shot Tippit?

Mrs. MARKHAM. Yes, sir; I think it was lighter.

Mr. BALL. All right. I have some pictures here that I would like to show you. I have Exhibits 521 and 522, which have been marked as Exhibits. Here is one picture, 521. Do you recognize that as the sign down?

Mrs. MARKHAM. This is the corner of Patton and 10th.

Mr. BALL. Patton and 10th.

Mrs. MARKHAM. This is on the corner of Patton and 10th.

Mr. BALL. Yes. Was the man anywhere near that corner when you saw him?

Mrs. MARKHAM. Yes, he was.

Mr. BALL. After the shooting?

Mrs. MARKHAM. Yes, sir; he was.

Mr. BALL. All right. Now, take this pen and put an X as to the point when he looked at you and you looked at him.

Mrs. MARKHAM. He was right along here.

Mr. BALL. Put an X.

Mrs. MARKHAM. I don't know. I am too nervous.

Mr. BALL. At the time the man was standing at X in this picture, at this location, which is shown in 521, where were you?

Mrs. MARKHAM. I was on the opposite corner, across over here, like this.

Mr. BALL. Were you as close to the curb as—were you close to the curb at that time?

Mrs. MARKHAM. Yes, I was.

Mr. DULLES. Where was the car, where this car is?

Mr. BALL. No, I have another picture I will show her. I have here Exhibit 522; do you recognize the white house in the picture?

Mrs. MARKHAM. Yes.

Mr. BALL. And the driveway next to it?

Mrs. MARKHAM. Yes, sir.

Mr. BALL. Does that show the location of the police car at the time it stopped?

Mrs. MARKHAM. Yes, sir. That is the big old white house, 404.

Mr. BALL. That is right.

Mrs. MARKHAM. 10th Street, and this driveway and this house.

Mr. DULLES. Will you give us an idea, Mr. Ball, as to where she said she was on this picture? Was she over here?

Mr. BALL. We have a picture. There is a booklet here that has been prepared by a succession of witnesses. We have a general diagram here which I will show the witness at this time.

Mrs. Markham, there is a diagram here which shows 10th Street going in an easterly and westerly direction, Patton running north and south.

(Marked Commission Exhibit No. 523 for identification.)

Mrs. MARKHAM. Yes, sir.

Mr. BALL. Do you understand that?

Mrs. MARKHAM. This would be the corner I would be at.

Mr. BALL. No, this would be Patton. This is north and south. Jefferson is down here. Can you locate yourself?

Mrs. MARKHAM. This is 10th?

Mr. BALL. That is 10th.

Mrs. MARKHAM. And this Patton?

Mr. BALL. That is right.

Mrs. MARKHAM. I was standing on the corner of 10th and Patton.

Mr. BALL. That is right. But which corner?

Mrs. MARKHAM. Northeast corner is where I was standing.

Mr. BALL. Northeast or northwest? This would be northeast and this would be northwest. Here is where the squad car would be. Right there. Here is 404.

Mrs. MARKHAM. It would be this corner then.

Mr. BALL. Well, that is northeast and that is northwest. Were you kitty-cornered?

Mrs. MARKHAM. I was kitty-cornered from it like this.

Mr. BALL. Like that?

Mrs. MARKHAM. Yes, sir.

Mr. BALL. Well, this is northwest, this is northeast, southeast, southwest, and here is the car. We are going down the street now.

Mrs. MARKHAM. It would be this—that would be on the opposite side.

Mr. BALL. That is right. Look at a number on that and tell me where you were standing.

Mrs. MARKHAM. I was standing right at the curb.

Mr. BALL. Do you see a number?

Mrs. MARKHAM. Number 5.

Mr. BALL. Number 5 on this diagram would be indicating the place where you would be standing, is that right?

Mrs. MARKHAM. I was standing on the opposite corner from that.

Mr. BALL. I know, but I have got to get you to tell me where you were standing. Picture yourself going down Patton towards Jefferson.

Mrs. MARKHAM. Going down Patton?

Mr. BALL. You were coming from this direction. Your home was up here.

Mrs. MARKHAM. I was coming down Patton. It would be this corner.

Mr. BALL. That corner, all right. Take this pen and show your course down the sidewalk.

Mrs. MARKHAM. Just draw it right on it?

Mr. BALL. Down to where you stood.

Mrs. MARKHAM. Right on the edge.

Mr. BALL. Is there a number there that shows where you were?

Mrs. MARKHAM. Yes.

Mr. BALL. Near 5, is that right?

Mrs. MARKHAM. Yes.

Mr. DULLES. That is the northwest corner?

Mr. BALL. Northwest corner; that is the northwest corner. Here is a picture. Do you recognize that?

Mrs. MARKHAM. Yes, sir.

Mr. BALL. That is picture number 3 in the booklet. Does that show where you were?

(Marked Commission Exhibit No. 524 for identification.)

Mrs. MARKHAM. Yes, sir.

Mr. BALL. Where was the man shot?

Mrs. MARKHAM. Right here.

Mr. BALL. Put a mark where you first saw him. Mark that A. Then he went which direction down the street?

Mrs. MARKHAM. He went this way.

Mr. BALL. In other words, he went in a direction—draw a line and then put an arrow showing what direction.

Mrs. MARKHAM. From here——

Mr. BALL. Yes.

Mrs. MARKHAM. Right on down the side.

Mr. BALL. Make a mark and put an arrow. That was the direction he was walking?

Mrs. MARKHAM. Yes, sir.

Mr. BALL. The police car had not come into sight yet?

Mrs. MARKHAM. That is right.

Mr. BALL. Put an X where the police car was when you first saw it, put an X there and we will mark that B. Now, after the shooting, where was the man when you looked at him?

Mrs. MARKHAM. He turned and came back this way.

Mr. BALL. Where did he stand and look at you?

Mrs. MARKHAM. Right here.

Mr. BALL. Put a mark there. We will mark that C. Where were you standing when he was looking at you?

Mrs. MARKHAM. The same position.

Mr. BALL. The same position as the girl shown on this picture?

Mrs. MARKHAM. Yes, sir.

Mr. BALL. Is that your picture?

Mrs. MARKHAM. Yes, sir.

Mr. BALL. That is you there in that picture?

Mrs. MARKHAM. Yes, sir.

Mr. BALL. Did you stand there for the photographer to show him where you were standing?

Mrs. MARKHAM. Yes, sir.

Mr. BALL. I would like to offer into evidence the diagram in this book, together with the picture which illustrates the diagram.

The CHAIRMAN. Under what numbers?

Mr. BALL. As 523, which is the diagram, and 524, which is the picture.

The CHAIRMAN. They may be admitted.

(The documents identified as Commission Exhibits Nos. 521–524 were received in evidence.)

Mr. BALL. You went out there in picture number 3. Now, Mr. Dulles, I think this will explain it.

Mr. DULLES. Yes, Mr. Ball.

Mr. BALL. I have some other pictures here that might illustrate. Do you recognize this?

Mrs. MARKHAM. Yes.

Mr. BALL. You were here the time the picture was taken?

Mrs. MARKHAM. Yes, sir.

Mr. BALL. You told the parties where to put the squad car?

Mrs. MARKHAM. Yes, sir.

Mr. BALL. Does this show the place where the police car was when this happened?

Mrs. MARKHAM. Yes, sir.

Mr. BALL. The place at the arrow?

Mrs. MARKHAM. Yes, sir.

Mr. BALL. It shows a corner.

Mrs. MARKHAM. Yes, sir.

Mr. BALL. On the picture make a mark where the man was when he came back and looked at you.

Mrs. MARKHAM. Yes, sir. He was a little behind this.

Mr. BALL. Just make an X there in general.

Mrs. MARKHAM. That is supposed to be on the sidewalk.

Mr. BALL. I would like to have this marked as Commission Exhibit 525. The X marks the position of the man who did the shooting on the corner after the shooting, and the arrow points to the squad car. Here is another picture marked 4 in this book which I will mark as Commission Exhibit 526. Is that you in the picture?

Mrs. MARKHAM. Yes, sir.

Mr. BALL. You went out there the day the picture was taken?

Mrs. MARKHAM. Yes, sir.

Mr. BALL. Is that where you were standing?

Mrs. MARKHAM. Yes, sir.

314

Mr. BALL. Is that where you were when you saw the shooting?

Mrs. MARKHAM. Yes, sir.

Mr. BALL. Did you move from that place from the time of the shooting until the time you saw the man on the corner?

Mrs. MARKHAM. No, sir.

Mr. DULLES. I wonder, Mrs. Markham, if you would repeat for me, I would like to hear it, and Congressman Ford would like to hear it, the scene that you saw where the man now known to be Oswald went up and put his arms on the door of the police car, as I understand it.

Mrs. MARKHAM. Yes.

Mr. DULLES. Would you tell that once again. I would like to hear it again.

Mrs. MARKHAM. He calmly walked to the car. He wasn't in no hurry.

Mr. DULLES. May I ask, was he called, were there any words that you heard?

Mrs. MARKHAM. No, I did not. I seen the police car stop.

Mr. DULLES. You didn't hear the policeman say, "Come here," or anything of that kind?

Mrs. MARKHAM. No.

Mr. DULLES. He might have done it, but you didn't hear it?

Mrs. MARKHAM. That is right. And the man went over to the car, put his hands on the window——

Mr. DULLES. The window was open?

Mrs. MARKHAM. Leaned over like this.

Mr. DULLES. Let me see. Was that on the right-hand side of the car, or where the driver was?

Mrs. MARKHAM. It was on the opposite side of the car.

Mr. DULLES. Opposite side of the car from the driver, yes.

Mrs. MARKHAM. Yes. The window was down, and I know it was down, I know, and he put his arms and leaned over, I don't know what they were talking about, I didn't hear it. Then he stepped back in a few minutes, stepped back two steps.

Mr. DULLES. He stepped back two steps from the car?

Mrs. MARKHAM. Just stepped back twice. Mr. Tippit, of course, the policeman—I didn't know it was Mr. Tippit——

Mr. DULLES. Yes.

Mrs. MARKHAM. He calmly opened the door. He calmly crawled out like he wasn't angry.

Mr. DULLES. Did he have a weapon in his hands?

Mrs. MARKHAM. I didn't see one.

Mr. DULLES. And what happened?

Mrs. MARKHAM. He was just calmly walking to the front of the car and when he got even with the wheel on the driver's side, front, you know, that man shot him.

Mr. DULLES. Did you see him draw his revolver?

Mrs. MARKHAM. He shot him like this.

Mr. DULLES. I see.

Mr. BALL. Like this, you mean from the hip or from the waist?

Mrs. MARKHAM. Yes. In the wink of your eye, before you could ever—just like that. It didn't seem like it bothered him, disturbed him.

Mr. DULLES. The policeman hadn't made, as far as you could see, any menacing gestures toward him? He wasn't trying to grab him or anything of that kind?

Mrs. MARKHAM. No. He was very calm, very. I would say like in slow motion, you know, like he was getting out to talk with the man, or go in the house for disturbance or something, I don't know.

Mr. BALL. He shot across the hood of the car?

Mrs. MARKHAM. Across the hood.

Mr. BALL. The policeman was in the street, walking in the street around to the front of the car?

Mrs. MARKHAM. Yes.

Mr. DULLES. The policeman then got out on the opposite side of where Oswald was?

Mrs. MARKHAM. Yes, I guess he was coming around.

Representative FORD. It appeared as though he was walking around the front of the car?

Mrs. MARKHAM. He had started around, and then he was going over to the man.

Mr. BALL. He had only reached the left front wheel though when he was shot?

Mrs. MARKHAM. Yes, sir.

Mr. BALL. And he fell into the street?

Mrs. MARKHAM. He fell into the street, his hat fell off his head. He didn't fall, just clumped down like that.

Representative FORD. Did the man with the gun move at all as the officer started to go around the car?

Mrs. MARKHAM. No. He didn't move. I mean, walked back or anything like that, no, sir.

Representative FORD. He didn't appear to run?

Mrs. MARKHAM. No. I didn't know anything was going to happen. If I had I would have kept walking, not walking, running.

Mr. DULLES. He had walked slowly around the car to meet the other man?

Mrs. MARKHAM. The policeman was.

Mr. DULLES. Slow?

Mrs. MARKHAM. Yes, sir.

Mr. BALL. Was there a pool of blood where Mr. Tippit fell in the street?

Mrs. MARKHAM. Yes, sir.

Mr. BALL. I show you this picture, Exhibit 533 (renumbered as Exhibit 527, see p. 321). Will you look at that picture and tell me whether it shows the approximate position where Mr. Tippit fell after he was shot?

Mrs. MARKHAM. He fell right out this way.

Mr. BALL. Look at the discoloration in the street. Is that anywhere near where Tippit fell?

Mrs. MARKHAM. It don't seem to me it was out that far.

Mr. BALL. It doesn't?

Mrs. MARKHAM. It seemed like to me it was over this way because he fell this way.

Mr. BALL. He fell this way? These people can't see what you are showing here. Here is the pool of blood. Which way do you think he fell?

Mrs. MARKHAM. See the wheel would be right down under here, back right this way. He fell this way.

Mr. BALL. Into the street?

Mrs. MARKHAM. Yes, and his head was like this, you know, it was laying like this.

Mr. DULLES. Is this splotch out here in front of the car the pool of blood?

Mr. BALL. Out to the left.

Mrs. MARKHAM. It seems to me it ought to be here.

Mr. BALL. But there was a pool of blood?

Mrs. MARKHAM. Yes, sir.

Mr. BALL. I will pass this out to the Commissioners.

Representative FORD. May I ask this, Mr. Ball, the place where you pointed, where you thought the pool of blood different from where it is shown on here was only a matter of what, a foot or two?

Mrs. MARKHAM. Yes, sir; just about a little, back a little. It seems his hat was this way.

Representative FORD. So it is a difference of a foot or two, at the most?

Mrs. MARKHAM. Yes.

Mr. BALL. That is right.

Mr. DULLES. Could you see the blood at this time or just see him fall? Did you actually see blood?

Mrs. MARKHAM. Did I actually see it, sir? I was there.

Mr. DULLES. I know you were there.

Mrs. MARKHAM. I was standing over it.

Mr. DULLES. You were standing right over the officer?

Mrs. MARKHAM. Yes. Just as soon as, just as quick as I could get to him; and the blood was coming from here like this and like that, in an oval shape. It did not splutter on his face too much, his mouth. It was here, coming out here.

Representative FORD. The blood was?

Mrs. MARKHAM. Yes, just gushes. I had my workshoes in my hand. I laid them up on the squad car. I had my purse, which I can't remember where I put it, but this, I had a head scarf around my head, I had my coat on.

Mr. BALL. I would like to offer all of these into evidence at this time, up to 526, inclusive.

The CHAIRMAN. They may be received.

(The items identified as Commission Exhibits Nos. 525 and 526 were received in evidence.)

The CHAIRMAN. Mr. Dulles, will you preside in my absence, please. I must attend a session of the Court.

Mr. DULLES. I will, sir.

(The Chairman left the hearing room at this point.)

Mr. BALL. Mrs. Markham, the police car, did the police car go beyond the man who was walking along the sidewalk, or did it stop opposite him?

Mrs. MARKHAM. Almost even with him.

Mr. BALL. And when the police car stopped, did the man stop?

Mrs. MARKHAM. Yes, sir; and walked over to the policeman.

Mr. BALL. The police car was going in the same direction as the man?

Mrs. MARKHAM. Yes, sir.

Mr. BALL. And caught up with him?

Mrs. MARKHAM. Yes, sir.

Mr. BALL. Mrs. Markham, do you know a man named Mark Lane?

Mrs. MARKHAM. No; I do not.

Mr. BALL. Did you ever hear of the name?

Mrs. MARKHAM. Did not.

Mr. BALL. Did you ever talk to a New York lawyer who says he was from New York?

Mrs. MARKHAM. No, sir.

Mr. BALL. Did you ever talk to a lawyer who was investigating the case in behalf of the deceased man, Lee Oswald?

Mrs. MARKHAM. No, sir.

Mr. BALL. Did you ever talk to a man who said he was representing the mother of Lee Oswald?

Mrs. MARKHAM. No, sir.

Mr. BALL. You don't remember ever talking to a man named Mark Lane?

Mrs. MARKHAM. No, sir.

Mr. BALL. In an appearance before this Commission, a man named Mark Lane has testified this way. Let me read it to you. That was on Wednesday, March 4, 1964, Vol. II of a public hearing before this Commission, page 51. This is what he said:

"I spoke with the deponent"—he is talking about an affidavit that you made to the Dallas Police Department—"I spoke with the deponent, the eyewitness, Helen Louise Markham, and Mrs. Markham told me—Miss or Mrs., I didn't ask her if she was married—told me she was 100 feet away from the police car, not the 50 feet which appears in the affidavit."

Do you recall ever stating that to Mr. Lane or anyone else?

Mrs. MARKHAM. No, sir; no, sir.

Mr. BALL. He testified: "She gave me a more detailed description of the man who she said shot Officer Tippit. She said he was short, a little on the heavy side, and his hair was somewhat bushy." Did you say that to Mark Lane?

Mrs. MARKHAM. No, sir; I don't even know the man.

Mr. BALL. Or anybody else?

Mrs. MARKHAM. No, sir.

Mr. BALL. Did you ever tell anyone that the man who shot Tippit was short, a little on the heavy side, and his hair was somewhat bushy?

Mrs. MARKHAM. No, sir.

Mr. BALL. Was the man, is it your memory now that the man who shot Tippit was short, a little on the heavy side?

Mrs. MARKHAM. No, sir. He wasn't too heavy.

Mr. BALL. Is it your memory that his hair was bushy?

Mrs. MARKHAM. It wasn't so bushy. It was, say, windblown or something. What I mean, he didn't have a lot of hair.

Mr. BALL. He didn't have a lot of hair?

Mrs. MARKHAM. No, sir; that I could see. I don't even know that man; I never talked to nobody.

Representative FORD. You didn't talk to him by telephone or any other means?

Mrs. MARKHAM. No, sir.

Representative FORD. Did you ever get an anonymous phone call from a person who asked you these questions?

Mrs. MARKHAM. No.

Mr. BALL. Now, he also says, and he testified as follows:

"Helen Markham said to me she was taken to the police station on that same day, that she was very upset. She, of course, had never seen anyone killed in front of her eyes before, and in the police station she identified Oswald as the person who had shot Officer Tippit in the lineup, including three other persons. She said no one pointed Oswald out to her, and she said she was just shown four people, and she picked Oswald. She said when he asked her how she could identify him, she said she was able to identify him because of his clothing, a gray jacket and dark trousers."

Did you ever make that statement to him?

Mrs. MARKHAM. I did not, sir.

Mr. BALL. Or to anyone else?

Mrs. MARKHAM. Not to anybody.

Mr. BALL. When you identified Oswald—it was the number 2 man—were you told the number 2 man whom you identified in the lineup?

Mrs. MARKHAM. No, I was not.

Mr. BALL. Were you ever told his name?

Mrs. MARKHAM. No.

Mr. BALL. Ever told his name later?

Mrs. MARKHAM. Nobody, nobody told me nothing.

Mr. BALL. Well, the man that you identified as the number 2 man in the lineup in the police station, you identified him as the man you had seen shoot Officer Tippit?

Mrs. MARKHAM. Yes, I did.

Mr. BALL. Did you identify him because of his clothing that he had on at that time in the lineup.

Mrs. MARKHAM. Just like I told you. I mostly looked at his face, his eyes, and his clothing, too.

Mr. BALL. He said here you were able to identify him, Mark Lane testified that you told him you were able to identify him because of his clothing, a gray jacket. First, did the man in the lineup have a gray jacket on?

Mrs. MARKHAM. No, sir.

Mr. BALL. What did he have on?

Mrs. MARKHAM. He had on this light shirt, dark trousers.

Mr. DULLES. You have considered your answers very carefully, have you, on this point?

Mrs. MARKHAM. I am doing my best.

Mr. DULLES. Yes, I know you are, and you are quite sure you never talked to anyone who purported to be Mr. Lane?

Mrs. MARKHAM. Never in my life. I talked to two men, and this man who told me he was from Paris, France. He came down on my job. I was scared to death. I wasn't going to talk to him. I work for a Greek.

Mr. DULLES. Let's get this a little more clearly, Mrs. Markham. You say you talked with someone who came from France?

Mrs. MARKHAM. Yes.

Mr. DULLES. Did he represent a French newspaper?

Mrs. MARKHAM. Yes.

Mr. DULLES. You don't know what newspaper?

Mrs. MARKHAM. No. He told—you see, I didn't understand this man, but my boss could.

Mr. DULLES. He came to you in the restaurant?

Mrs. MARKHAM. Yes. And I was scared, which I was scared of everybody. I was upset and trying to work, too, and he was—he come to me and he asked for me and, of course, they knew who I was because I was there so long.

Mr. DULLES. When was that?

Mrs. MARKHAM. I don't recall the date.

Mr. DULLES. Was it 2 or 3 days after the assassination or was it right after?

Mrs. MARKHAM. It was quite some time after.

Mr. DULLES. Some time after?

Mrs. MARKHAM. Yes.

Mr. DULLES. A week or more, maybe?

Mrs. MARKHAM. Yes.

Representative FORD. Can you describe this man?

Mrs. MARKHAM. He had—he was dark complected, very nice man, black horn-rimmed glasses, black-headed, and he was build kind of——

Mr. DULLES. What did he ask you—excuse me.

Representative FORD. Was he tall or short, heavy set?

Mrs. MARKHAM. About medium, I guess. I didn't pay much attention to the man.

Representative FORD. Did he have an accent?

Mrs. MARKHAM. Yes, he did.

Representative FORD. Was it difficult for you to understand him because of this accent?

Mrs. MARKHAM. Yes. This is what this man told me. He told me—he told my boss and my boss also told me, my boss stood right beside me.

Representative FORD. Did he speak in English with an accent?

Mrs. MARKHAM. Yes. But this man told me the Government sent him.

Representative FORD. Did he identify which government?

Mrs. MARKHAM. He had—he showed me who he was. He was a news reporter.

Mr. DULLES. Did he say whether he was a foreigner or an American citizen?

Mrs. MARKHAM. I can't remember. I was too scared. But he did show me his identification, his picture and everything. The Government had sent him to me, which he was coming to Washington. He was supposed to be here, and then back somewhere in Dallas, I think he told me.

Mr. DULLES. Could you recall the questions he asked you?

Mrs. MARKHAM. He just asked me very few questions. This man asked me about if the police had taken me down to the police station and did I see anything after I went into the police station, hear any TV, or see any TV, any radio, newspapers, or anybody talked to me, and I said they did not.

Representative FORD. Did your employer listen to the questions and answers?

Mrs. MARKHAM. Yes, James Gambolis listened to it.

Mr. DULLES. We will take a moment's recess.

(A short recess was taken.)

Mr. BALL. On the 22d of November, 1963, that is the day of the shooting, did you talk to an FBI agent named Odum? Do you remember?

Mrs. MARKHAM. I talked to some people, men, down at the police station.

Mr. BALL. That is right. He says that you described the man who shot Tippit as a white male, about 18, black hair, red complexion, wearing black shoes, tan jacket, and dark trousers. Do you remember that?

Mrs. MARKHAM. I never said anything about his shoes because I never did look at his feet.

Mr. BALL. Did you say about 18?

Mrs. MARKHAM. I said he was young looking.

Mr. BALL. Did you give that age, 18?

Mrs. MARKHAM. No, I don't believe I did.

Mr. BALL. Did you say he had black hair?

Mrs. MARKHAM. Yes, sir.

Mr. BALL. You thought he was black-haired?

Mrs. MARKHAM. Yes, that is what I told him. I thought he was black-haired. I remember saying that.

Mr. BALL. Red complexion?

Mrs. MARKHAM. No, not red complexioned.

Mr. BALL. You didn't say that?

Mr. DULLES. Mrs. Markham, did you say you talked to two persons, one person whom you are now describing from a foreign newspaper, and one other?

Mrs. MARKHAM. Yes.

Mr. DULLES. Who was the other one with whom you talked?

Mrs. MARKHAM. I don't recall. He was a newspaper reporter by Life magazine.

Mr. DULLES. Life magazine?

Mrs. MARKHAM. Yes. I remember, which they did print the picture in Life magazine.

Mr. DULLES. And Life magazine printed what you told them?

Mrs. MARKHAM. Yes.

Mr. DULLES. And printed it accurately as far as you recall?

Mrs. MARKHAM. Very little of what I told him did he put in.

Mr. DULLES. What they put in was accurate more or less?

Mrs. MARKHAM. Yes.

Representative FORD. It coincided with what you told him?

Mrs. MARKHAM. Yes, just a little old paragraph or two.

Mr. DULLES. Except for those two persons, you don't recall talking with anyone about your testimony or your appearance in the lineup?

Mrs. MARKHAM. No, sir.

Mr. DULLES. Just those two?

Mrs. MARKHAM. Yes, sir.

Mr. BALL. Just a few more questions, Mrs. Markham. You ran immediately over to where the police officer was lying in the street?

Mrs. MARKHAM. I did.

Mr. BALL. Was he alive?

Mrs. MARKHAM. Yes, sir.

Mr. BALL. Did he say anything?

Mrs. MARKHAM. He was trying to, but he just couldn't. I just couldn't make out what he was trying to say.

Mr. BALL. Did some man come up immediately thereafter?

Mrs. MARKHAM. Yes.

Mr. BALL. What kind of a car did he have?

Mrs. MARKHAM. Not immediately.

Mr. BALL. Soon?

Mrs. MARKHAM. Soon.

Mr. BALL. In a pickup truck?

Mrs. MARKHAM. Yes. I very frankly remembered this truck, but I remember it the way it took off.

Mr. BALL. He stopped though, didn't he?

Mrs. MARKHAM. Yes.

Mr. BALL. That is the man who called over the police radio, wasn't he?

Mrs. MARKHAM. I don't recall.

Mr. BALL. What did he look like, the man in the pickup truck?

Mrs. MARKHAM. This man had a hat on. I thought he was a policeman.

Mr. BALL. A dark man, looked somewhat Spanish?

Mrs. MARKHAM. I don't recall. I was screaming and crying and trying to get help, begging for somebody to help me.

Mr. BALL. When did you start screaming?

Mrs. MARKHAM. I started screaming by the time I left where I was standing and screamed plumb across the street.

Mr. BALL. Do you remember what you said?

Mrs. MARKHAM. "The man has killed a policeman," I remember, "Somebody help. He has killed him, he has killed him," I was saying that, I was pulling my hair almost. It is a wonder he did not turn and kill me, really it was.

Mr. BALL. Did you see Mr. Scoggins?

Mrs. MARKHAM. I don't remember——

Mr. BALL. The taxicab driver.

Mrs. MARKHAM. Yes, I saw the taxicab driver.

Mr. BALL. Where was the taxicab?

Mrs. MARKHAM. Parked on Patton.

Mr. BALL. On Patton?

Mrs. MARKHAM. Yes, sir.

Mr. BALL. Did you see the man later, did you see him before the shooting?

Mrs. MARKHAM. Yes, he was sitting in his cab.

Mr. BALL. He was. Then you saw him afterward, didn't you?

Mrs. MARKHAM. Yes, sir.

Mr. BALL. Those are all the questions I have of this witness. Do you have something additional?

Mrs. MARKHAM. Believe me, it was just like——

Mr. DULLES. I believe Mr. Ford would like to have the witness repeat what she saw the man, now known as Oswald, do after the shooting. Will you just repeat that for Congressman Ford?

Mrs. MARKHAM. After he shot the policeman——

Mr. DULLES. After he shot the policeman.

Mrs. MARKHAM. After he shot the policeman he turned around, came back around toward Patton Street. He wasn't he didn't seem to be in a no hurry. I thought he hadn't done anything, and he was fooling with his gun in his hands, and he seen me, and he stops.

Mr. DULLES. He stopped?

Mrs. MARKHAM. When he saw me. That is the reason we were looking at each other.

Mr. DULLES. He hadn't seen you before so far as you could tell?

Mrs. MARKHAM. I put my hands over my face and closed my eyes, because I knew he was going to kill me. I couldn't scream, I couldn't holler. I froze.

Mr. DULLES. I think you testified about that then he began to run slowly.

Mrs. MARKHAM. Then——

Mr. DULLES. Was that after he saw you?

Mrs. MARKHAM. Yes; after I put my hands up, and when I had opened my fingers and my eyes and slowly pulled them down, he was trotting off.

Mr. DULLES. Trotting off?

Mrs. MARKHAM. Yes, sir. He wasn't out of sight when I started running to this police car. He was not out of sight.

Mr. DULLES. You didn't see which way he turned at the end of this run?

Mrs. MARKHAM. No; he cut across like this, across Patton, and went out like that.

Mr. DULLES. Like this means to the right or to the left?

Mrs. MARKHAM. It means to the right, sir.

Mr. BELIN. To his right, to the man's right, as he was running?

Mrs. MARKHAM. He ran back, turned and came back down 10th to Patton Street. He cut across Patton Street like this.

Mr. BELIN. Heading toward what street?

Mrs. MARKHAM. Toward Jefferson; yes, sir. Then he was still in sight when I began to scream and holler and run to this police car, well, to Mr. Tippit.

Mr. DULLES. Thank you.

Mr. BALL. Are there any more questions?

You can be excused, Mrs. Markham.

Mr. DULLES. Do you have any questions you would like to ask, Mr. Attorney General?

Mr. CARR. No; I have not.

Mr. DULLES. Could you wait for just a moment. We are sorry to detain you. There is something that might come up with the next witness, and we might wish to ask you another question. I do not think we will. We are very grateful to you, Mrs. Markham.

Mr. BALL. Exhibit previously marked "533," which is the squad car, Tippit, showing the street and blood spot in the street, I would like to have marked as "Exhibit 527." It was marked by mistake.

Mr. DULLES. Is that our last exhibit?

Mr. BALL. That is our last exhibit, 527 is our last exhibit now.

(The item identified as Commission Exhibit No. 527 was received in evidence.)

Mr. DULLES. You might stand for just a moment, Mr. Scoggins. The witnesses are sworn before they can give testimony before this Commission.

Do you swear, Mr. Scoggins, that the testimony that you will give before this Commission is the truth, the whole truth, so help you God?

Mr. SCOGGINS. To the best of my knowledge; yes.

Mr. DULLES. Be seated, please.

Mr. Scoggins, the Commission is taking testimony, and the Chief Justice asked me to preside in his absence, he has to be away in the Court this morning.

The purpose of today's hearing is to hear your testimony and that of certain others who were in the vicinity of the shooting of Officer Tippit, and we will want your testimony on that particular point this morning.

Will you proceed?

Mr. BALL. Mr. Belin is going to examine this witness.

Mr. DULLES. Mr. Belin will carry on the examination on behalf of the Commission.

Will you proceed, please?

TESTIMONY OF WILLIAM W. SCOGGINS

Mr. BELIN. Yes, sir. Will you please state your name, sir, for the record.

Mr. SCOGGINS. William W. Scoggins.

Mr. BELIN. Where do you live, Mr. Scoggins?

Mr. SCOGGINS. 3138 Alaska.

Mr. BELIN. In what city and State is that?

Mr. SCOGGINS. Dallas.

Mr. BELIN. Dallas, Tex.?

Mr. SCOGGINS. Yes, sir.

Mr. BELIN. How old a gentleman are you?

Mr. SCOGGINS. Forty-nine.

Mr. BELIN. What is your occupation?

Mr. SCOGGINS. Taxicab driver, operator.

Mr. BELIN. For what company?

Mr. SCOGGINS. The Dallas Transit Co. I drive out of Oak Cliff.

Mr. BELIN. You drive out of Oak Cliff?

Mr. SCOGGINS. Yes, sir; Oak Cliff, yes, sir.

Mr. BELIN. Where were you born, Mr. Scoggins?

Mr. SCOGGINS. Hillsboro, Hill County.

Mr. BELIN. Is that in Texas?

Mr. SCOGGINS. Yes, sir.

Mr. BELIN. Did you go to school there?

Mr. SCOGGINS. Well, I went most of the time in McLennan County; most of my schooling was down in McLennon County.

Mr. BELIN. How far did you get through school before you started to work?

Mr. SCOGGINS. Eighth grade.

Mr. BELIN. Now what did you do after school?

Mr. SCOGGINS. Well, while I was going to school, and that time we lived on a farm, you know, and then after that, well, that would be a hard problem there. I left home when I was rather young, stayed with some of my brothers some, and then done odd jobs around for quite a while. My first job, I guess you might say, would be automobile paint job.

Mr. BELIN. Automobile paint job?

Mr. SCOGGINS. Yes, New York City.

Mr. BELIN. New York City. How long did you stay in New York?

Mr. SCOGGINS. Approximately 3 years.

Mr. BELIN. And then where did you go?

Mr. SCOGGINS. I went back to Texas.

Mr. BELIN. Then what did you do there?

Mr. SCOGGINS. Done farmwork.

Mr. BELIN. And about how long did you do farmwork, approximately?

Mr. SCOGGINS. Well now, after—let's see, my life was kind of mixed up. I have been around quite a while in different places and things. After I left New York I went to Connecticut to join the CCC camp and stayed there 3 years.

Mr. BELIN. CCC camp?

Mr. SCOGGINS. Yes, sir. And then I went back to Texas.

The first thing I done was open up a cafe down there and operated it about a year, and from there went to Waco and worked in a cotton mill, and then I moved back to west Texas to a little town about 18 miles out of Waco, and lived there, and done farmwork for a couple or 3 years, and then I moved to Dallas.

I think late in 1941, and I worked for Newhoff Packers in Dallas for 2 years, and then I went into the aircraft business and worked for North American approximately 3 years, and then I went into the contracting business for about a year, and went to General Dynamics, worked there approximately 15½ years, and then I have been working for the company, taxicab company, for a couple of years.

Mr. BELIN. You have been driving a cab for 2 years?

Mr. SCOGGINS. No, not quite 2 years.

Mr. BELIN. A little bit less than 2 years?

Mr. SCOGGINS. A year and 9 months. I don't know exactly when I started.

Mr. BELIN. Where were you driving your cab in the early part of the afternoon of November 22, 1963, if you remember?

Mr. SCOGGINS. Well, I picked up a gentleman at Love Field at approximately 12:35, I would say, and I discharged him at 1 o'clock at 321 North Ewing.

Mr. BELIN. Then where did you go?

Mr. SCOGGINS. I went around by the Gentlemen's Club which I believe is 125 Patton.

Mr. BELIN. What did you do there?

Mr. SCOGGINS. I pulled up and parked at the corner of Patton and 10th and went back down to the club. At first, whenever I passed by, one of the guys hollered at me and asked me did I know the President had been shot, and I made the remark that I had not heard that one. I found a place to park and I came back, and he came back there in a couple of minutes and told me the facts about it. I thought it was some kind of a joke.

So I had to go plumb up to the corner of 10th before I could find a parking place, and I parked right there on the corner and went back and got me a coke and watched the deal, watched the television.

Mr. DULLES. Would you speak a little louder, please; I can't quite hear.

Mr. SCOGGINS. I got me a coke and watched television for a few mnutes, I would say 10, 12, 15 minutes, there, and went out to eat my lunch.

Mr. DULLES. What were you seeing on television?

Mr. SCOGGINS. The deal about the President getting assassinated; and when I got back to my cab and got my lunch, and, well, I noticed a police car cruising east there on 10th Street.

Mr. BELIN. Where was your cab parked with relationship to the intersection of Patton and 10th?

Mr. SCOGGINS. Well, it was headed north on Patton, facing 10th Street, on the right-hand side of the street, right close to where the stop sign had been.

Mr. BELIN. Now, the right-hand side of the street would be the east or the west?

Mr. SCOGGINS. It would be the east side. I was headed north.

Mr. BELIN. All right. Were you on the north side of the intersection or the south side of the intersection?

Mr. SCOGGINS. South side.

Mr. DULLES. How near the intersection were you?

Mr. SCOGGINS. Right near. They had a stop sign there and someone had had a wreck previously, I don't know, the sign was down. It was laying there, it had been bent over.

Representative FORD. Was this a normal stop for you, or how did you happen to be stopped there?

Mr. SCOGGINS. Well, I just went around just like I say. We can take our lunch hour anytime, you know; we can call in and say we are going to be out of service for lunch or for anything we might want to be out for, and that is what I had done.

Representative FORD. This was not a regular place where you waited for calls?

Mr. SCOGGINS. No. You see the way we operate there, just where we discharge a passenger, then we call in and tell them where we are at on our radio, and if they have anybody in that vicinity who needs a cab, they give us their address, you see. Of course, now in the downtown area we do have stands to operate from, at the hotels, and then we have some stands at the medical buildings and the depot and the bus stations; and if we want to pick up there, we can pick up and we don't need to call in. But if we want to sit there we can call in that we are in this neighborhood. If they have got someone who has requested a cab, they give us the address, you see.

Mr. BELIN. Mr. Scoggins, showing you Commission Exhibit 528, I would like to ask you to state, if you know, what this is.

Mr. SCOGGINS. Yes, sir; that is the corner where I was sitting right here, you see, on 10th.

Mr. BELIN. You are pointing to something in the front-center part of the picture. What is that?

Mr. SCOGGINS. That is the stop sign that had been knocked over.

Mr. BELIN. That is the knocked-over stop sign?

Mr. SCOGGINS. Yes.

Mr. BELIN. What intersection is that?

Mr. SCOGGINS. Tenth and Patton.

Mr. BELIN. Now, we offer in evidence remarked Exhibit 527 and also Exhibit 528.

(The items identified as Commission Exhibits Nos. 527 and 528 were received in evidence.)

Mr. BELIN. Mr. Scoggins, handing you what has been marked as Commission Exhibit 523, which purports to be a plat, you see the streets of Patton Avenue there and East 10th. Do you see any number on that exhibit, Exhibit 523, which would indicate the approximate location of your car during the period that you are describing here?

Mr. SCOGGINS. Well, it looks to me like this number 10.

Mr. BELIN. You are not pointing to number 10.

Mr. SCOGGINS. Eleven, isn't it?

Mr. BELIN. It is 11, and here is 9.

Mr. SCOGGINS. It looked like a 10 to me. Number 11.

Mr. BELIN. Number 11 is, you think, where you were with regard to——

Mr. SCOGGINS. Within the general area.

Mr. BELIN. Within the general area of Number 11 on Exhibit 523.

Now, Mr. Scoggins, you stated you were sitting in your cab as you stopped at your intersection. You had a coke and your lunch.

Mr. SCOGGINS. Yes, sir.

Mr. BELIN. What were you doing, eating your lunch?

Mr. SCOGGINS. I was in the process of eating it.

Mr. BELIN. You were in the process?

Mr. SCOGGINS. I had taken one or two bites of my sandwich and drank a couple of swallows out of my coke.

Mr. BELIN. All right.

Mr. DULLES. What time was this, approximately, as far as you can recall?

Mr. SCOGGINS. Around 1:20 in the afternoon.

Mr. BELIN. All right. Will you please state then what happened, what you saw, what you did, what you heard?

Mr. SCOGGINS. Well, I first seen the police car cruising east.

Mr. BELIN. About how fast was it cruising?

Mr. SCOGGINS. Not more than 10 or 12 miles a hour, I would say.

Mr. BELIN. It was going east on what street?

Mr. SCOGGINS. On Tenth.

Mr. BELIN. All right. Did you see the police car go across right in front of yours?

324

Mr. SCOGGINS. Yes; he went right down the street. He come from the west, going east on east Tenth.

Mr. BELIN. Then what did you see?

Mr. SCOGGINS. I noticed he stopped down there, and I wasn't paying too much attention to the man, you see, just used to see him every day, but then I kind of looked down the street, saw this, someone, that looked to me like he was going west, now, I couldn't exactly say whether he was going west or was in the process of turning around, but he was facing west when I saw him.

Mr. BELIN. All right.

Mr. SCOGGINS. And he was—he stopped there.

Mr. BELIN. Let me ask you this now. When you first saw this man, had the police car stopped or not?

Mr. SCOGGINS. Yes; he stopped. When I saw he stopped, then I looked to see why he was stopping, you see, and I saw this man with a light-colored jacket on.

Mr. BELIN. Now, you saw a man with a light-colored jacket. With relation to the police car, was the man east of the police car, west of the police car, or kind of——

Mr. SCOGGINS. Just a little east is the best I can remember.

Mr. BELIN. He was a little bit east of the police car?

Mr. SCOGGINS. Yes; he was just a little bit forward. The police car headed east and he was a little bit, maybe not more than the front end of the car.

Mr. BELIN. You thought the man was at the front end of the car?

Mr. SCOGGINS. Yes; approximately.

Mr. BELIN. But by that you mean the front wheel or front bumper area?

Mr. SCOGGINS. Yes.

Mr. BELIN. Was he on the sidewalk?

Mr. SCOGGINS. At the time I saw him; yes.

Mr. BELIN. When you first saw him, I believe you said you saw the man's face, or did you not say that?

Mr. SCOGGINS. I couldn't see the man's face from there. I saw the face when he passed the cab.

Mr. BELIN. What led you to believe that he was walking west?

Mr. SCOGGINS. Well, he was facing west.

Mr. BELIN. You mean he was facing west when you first saw him?

Mr. SCOGGINS. Yes; he was kind of facing that way.

Mr. BELIN. Was it due west the way the sidewalk was, or was it——

Mr. SCOGGINS. Yes; west in relation to the sidewalk.

Mr. BELIN. All right. Then what did you see the man do?

Mr. SCOGGINS. I saw him turn facing the street, and then I didn't see him any more after that because he went behind some shrubbery.

Mr. BELIN. Did you see the police officer do anything?

Mr. SCOGGINS. I saw him get out of the police car.

Mr. BELIN. Did you see what side he went out of?

Mr. SCOGGINS. He got out of the driver's side, left-hand side.

Mr. BELIN. Then what did you see happen?

Mr. SCOGGINS. Then he took about a step, I would say, or approximately one or two steps, and then I wasn't really—you know—I went back to my eating, and about that time I heard the shots.

Mr. BELIN. How many shots did you hear?

Mr. SCOGGINS. Three or four, in the neighborhood. They was fast.

Mr. BELIN. They were fast shots?

Mr. SCOGGINS. Yes; they were fast.

Mr. BELIN. Then what did you do or say or hear?

Mr. SCOGGINS. Then I saw the man falling, grab his stomach and fall.

Mr. BELIN. Which man did you see fall?

Mr. SCOGGINS. The policeman. I was excited when I heard them shots, and I started to get out—since we went back over there the other day and reenacted that scene, I must have seen him fall as I was getting out of my cab, because I got out of the cab, and in the process of getting out of the cab I seen this guy coming around, so I got out of sight. I started to cross the street, but I seen I didn't have enough time to cross the street before he got down there, so I got back behind the cab, and as he cut across that yard I heard him running into some bushes, and I looked up and seen him going south on Patton and then when I jumped back in my cab I called my dispatcher.

Mr. BELIN. Why did you jump out of your cab first when you heard the shots?

Mr. SCOGGINS. Because anytime that there is anything going on that is one thing the cab driver wants to do is to get away from that cab, because the man is going to try—if he had ever seen the cab, he looked back over his left shoulder, and I don't think he even seen the cab—he would have probably jumped in the cab and had me take him somewhere or maybe shot me, too, you know, and I didn't want to be around the cab at anytime while he was in the neighborhood, you know, when there was anything like that going on, or anything, robbery, or anything.

Mr. BELIN. I believe you said you saw the officer fall. Did you see where he fell?

Mr. SCOGGINS. Yes; he fell right by the side of the front, about, a little bit forward of the door, right about the door.

Mr. BELIN. Did you ever later go up and view the officer?

Mr. SCOGGINS. Yes. I went up there, but by the time I got up there the ambulance had already got there. You see I got my dispatcher and was telling him about it, just by that time the ambulance got there.

Mr. BELIN. Did you notice anything in the street to indicate where the officer fell?

Mr. SCOGGINS. There was blood there, of course. They picked the man up by the time I got there, the ambulance did.

Mr. DULLES. Could I ask one question? You were in touch with your dispatcher over your radio contact?

Mr. SCOGGINS. Yes, sir.

Mr. DULLES. What did you tell your dispatcher?

Mr. SCOGGINS. I told him there had been a policeman shot at 10th and Patton, and you see they have a number of cars they are talking to, you know, and I had to holler about three or four times before I got his attention, and then I seen I wasn't going to get through to him, so I just hollered there had been a policeman shot at 10th and Patton, and then they went to talking to me then.

Mr. DULLES. What did they say to you then?

Mr. SCOGGINS. The first thing they says is do they need an ambulance, and I says, "Sure." And they wanted to know the exact location, and I said right off east of 10th and Patton, and the ambulance was only a block and a quarter or so from the scene, you see, and they just come on right around there.

Mr. DULLES. And this conversation took you a minute or two, would you estimate?

Mr. SCOGGINS. Yes, a couple of minutes, I would say. It was pretty close.

Mr. BELIN. Mr. Scoggins, handing you what the Commission reporter has marked, or what has been marked as Commission Exhibit 527, I ask you to state if this substance on the street here appears to be anything you had ever seen before.

Mr. SCOGGINS. Yes; that appears to be the officer's blood, blood from the officer.

Mr. BELIN. Is that located in approximate location to this car in the same relative position that you saw the blood when you were there, or is it any different, if you know?

Mr. SCOGGINS. I was kind of excited there, a little bit, and I could be mistaken, but I was thinking he was a little bit closer to the car than that.

Mr. BELIN. You thought he was a little bit closer to the car than that?

Mr. SCOGGINS. Yes. I thought he was, but I could be mistaken.

Mr. BELIN. Handing you what has been marked Commission Exhibit 529, which shows a picture of a car and appears to be some kind of a stain in the street, does that look to you any closer to the car than Exhibit 527, or does that look to be about the same place?

Mr. SCOGGINS. It looks to be about the same place as that one there does.

Mr. BELIN. All right. You thought it was a little bit closer to the front?

Mr. SCOGGINS. All right. I thought it was.

Mr. BELIN. Did the officer fall, did he fall forward or backward in any way?

Mr. SCOGGINS. He fell forward.

Mr. BELIN. He fell forward?

Mr. SCOGGINS. Yes.

Mr. BELIN. Do you remember where his head was lying as he fell forward, if you know?

Mr. SCOGGINS. I wouldn't be sure about that. He kind of fell in a crumpled manner, I would say.

Mr. BELIN. When you saw the officer fall, when was the next place that you saw the man, or did you see him at the same time you saw the officer fall, the other man?

Mr. SCOGGINS. No. I saw him coming kind of toward me around that cutoff through there, and he never did look at me. He looked back over his left shoulder like that, as he went by. It seemed like I could see his face, his features and everything plain, you see.

Mr. BELIN. Was he walking or running or trotting?

Mr. SCOGGINS. Kind of loping, trotting.

Mr. BELIN. Kind of loping or trotting?

Mr. SCOGGINS. Not in too big a hurry. It didn't seem like at first.

Mr. BELIN. At first not too big a hurry?

Mr. SCOGGINS. Yes.

Mr. BELIN. Did he change that at all?

Mr. SCOGGINS. Never did change his pace as long as I saw him. I don't know where he went after he passed the cab and got down a little piece, because then I was busy trying to get my dispatcher, and I never did look and never did get to see him.

Mr. BELIN. Did he have anything in his hand?

Mr. SCOGGINS He had a pistol in his left hand.

Mr. BELIN. Did the pistol appear to be—did he appear to be doing anything with the pistol or not?

Mr. SCOGGINS. Yes. He had it, holding it, in his left hand in a manner that the barrel was up like this, and the stock was down here, curved back in here.

Mr. BELIN. Did it look like the gun had been flipped open at all or not?

Mr. SCOGGINS. I wouldn't say.

Mr. BELIN. You don't know?

Mr. SCOGGINS. No; I don't.

Mr. DULLES. You said he had it in his left hand?

Mr. SCOGGINS. Yes, sir.

Mr. BELIN. Did you see where his right hand was?

Mr. SCOGGINS. He was kind of running, kind of like this, in this manner.

Mr. BELIN. Did you hear the man say anything?

Mr. SCOGGINS. I heard him mutter something like, "poor damn cop," or "poor dumb cop." He said that over twice, and the last, I don't know whether the middle word was "damn" or "dumb," but anyway, he muttered that twice.

Mr. BELIN. Did you hear him say any other word or phrase?

Mr. SCOGGINS. No.

Mr. BELIN. Did you hear anyone else making any noise at about that time?

Mr. SCOGGINS. No; I didn't. Of course, there were people coming up there, around there, but I didn't—I didn't notice any.

Mr. BELIN. Recently in Dallas you were asked to go to the scene of the Tippit shooting to try to reconstruct the positions of the various people at this time; is that correct?

Mr. SCOGGINS. Yes, yes; I was over there——

Mr. BELIN. And you parked your cab in what spot?

Mr. SCOGGINS. There on Patton, facing 10th at approximately the place I thought I was parked at, the reasonable area where I thought I was. I wouldn't say I was exactly on that spot, but within a foot or so.

Mr. BELIN. Does Exhibit 530 appear to be a picture of your cab at that point?

Mr. SCOGGINS. Yes, sir.

Mr. BELIN. I also hand you Commission Exhibit 531 and ask you if there is another view of your cab also at that same point?

Mr. SCOGGINS. Yes; it appears to be.

Mr. BELIN. You were there when those two pictures were taken?

Mr. Scoggins. Yes, sir; I was there whenever they took some picture. I couldn't swear these were the ones, but I imagine it was.

Mr. Belin. These are pictures numbered 7 and 22 in that sequence there. Mr. Scoggins, at the time of November 22, 1963, were there as many cars parked along Patton Street as appear to be in these Exhibits 530 and 531?

Mr. Scoggins. There wasn't as many on this side here.

Mr. Belin. You are speaking now when you say "This side here," you are pointing to the east or west side of the street?

Mr. Scoggins. On the west side.

Mr. Belin. There weren't as many on the west side?

Mr. Scoggins. There wasn't as many here as where the pickup truck is setting here.

Mr. Belin. That would be down below the second or third car south of East 10th, is that right.

Mr. Scoggins. Yes; on this other side it was taken up solid, and the only place I could found is here is the reason I come up here and parked, because the club is down here at this other end, and I would have taken the first parking place I found because, you know, the closest to the club.

Mr. Dulles. As far as you know, there were no people in these cars that were parked there?

Mr. Scoggins. No; there was no one in those cars.

Mr. Belin. Did you see any people in any cars parked on either side of Patton Street?

Mr. Scoggins. None.

Mr. Belin. Mr. Scoggins, handing you Exhibit 162, have you ever seen any jacket on any person in that area of East 10th and Patton that looks familiar to, or looks anything similar to this exhibit, or does this appear to be lighter or darker than the jacket?

Mr. Scoggins. It appears to be a little lighter, but the sleeves look familiar all right, the type of sleeve. He had on a jacket, the type of sleeve of that, but I thought it was a little darker.

Mr. Belin. Do you remember whether it was a zipper or button jacket or don't you——

Mr. Scoggins. No; I couldn't tell you that.

Mr. Belin. Do you remember what kind of trousers the man was wearing?

Mr. Scoggins. The best I can remember they was dark, not too dark, and he had on a light shirt.

Mr. Belin. A light shirt?

Mr. Scoggins. I wouldn't say it was white, but——

Mr. Belin. Would the shirt be lighter than Exhibit 150 or about the same color or darker or would Exhibit 150 look anything like the shirt you thought he was wearing, if you know?

Mr. Scoggins. No, I don't, so I couldn't answer that.

Mr. Belin. And you say you don't know, or you think this is different than what he was wearing?

Mr. Scoggins. I couldn't say about the shirt.

Mr. Belin. All right.

Mr. Scoggins. I just couldn't.

Mr. Belin. Mr. Scoggins, when you were in Dallas the other day and they took these pictures, they also tried to take a picture through your car windows toward the place where the car of Officer Tippit was parked, is that correct?

Mr. Scoggins. Yes, sir.

Mr. Belin. Do you remember where the car of Officer Tippit was parked on November 22d?

Mr. Scoggins. Well, it was parked approximately between the first and second houses and across the driveway between the houses, pretty well across the driveway.

Mr. Belin. Was it parked across a driveway?

Mr. Scoggins. Yes, sir. As well as I remember, it was.

Mr. Belin. Handing you what has been marked Exhibit 522, which purports to be a picture taken of a squad car, and I don't know if you can see through the window a little driveway——

Mr. SCOGGINS. Yes.

Mr. BELIN. Does that appear to be the driveway in front of which the squad car was parked?

Mr. SCOGGINS. Yes, sir.

Mr. BELIN. Does that appear to be the two houses between which the driveway ran?

Mr. SCOGGINS. Yes. This would be the two houses—and the other one I didn't know.

Mr. BELIN. We have a magnifying glass here, and I believe with it we might be able to see the number on that house. Can you see the number over the doorway of that house?

Mr. SCOGGINS. 404.

Mr. BELIN. That would be which street?

Mr. SCOGGINS. That would be on East 10th, on the south side.

Mr. BELIN. This appears to be, or does not appear to be, the position of the car on November 22?

Mr. SCOGGINS. Yes; that appears to be the approximate position; I would say it was.

Mr. BELIN. Now, handing you what has been marked Exhibit 532, do you remember when this picture was taken?

Mr. SCOGGINS. I remember the day. I don't remember the date of it.

Mr. BELIN. But you remember it was taken?

Mr. SCOGGINS. I remember it was taken.

Mr. BELIN. Sometime in March of this year?

Mr. SCOGGINS. Yes.

Mr. BELIN. You saw the photographer point the camera through the window?

Mr. SCOGGINS. Yes.

Mr. BELIN. Is this about the view that you had toward the police car on November 22d?

Mr. SCOGGINS. Yes.

Mr. BELIN. As you were eating your lunch?

Mr. SCOGGINS. Yes.

Mr. BELIN. And it appears that you can see through one of the windows there the police car, is that correct?

Mr. SCOGGINS. Yes.

Mr. BELIN. Was the police car at the time Exhibit 532 was taken, was it in the approximate same position that the car of Officer Tippit was on November 22?

Mr. SCOGGINS. I would think so, yes.

Mr. BELIN. Well, you saw the police car there?

Mr. SCOGGINS. Yes.

Mr. BELIN. Was it parked about in front of that driveway?

Mr. SCOGGINS. Yes; I would say in the same area. You know, it may not be on the same inch.

Mr. BELIN. Within a foot or two?

Mr. SCOGGINS. Yes.

Mr. BELIN. I wonder if you would take Exhibit 523 and see if there is any number on Exhibit 523 which corresponds to the position of the man who was walking along East 10th Street, or wherever he was when you first saw him.

Mr. SCOGGINS. Approximately where 16 is.

Mr. BELIN. Yes; you are pointing to the position where the arrow is in number 16?

Mr. BALL. Mr. Belin, he didn't see him walking.

Mr. SCOGGINS. I saw him there.

Mr. BELIN. I used the word "walking." Pardon me. When you first saw him he was on point 16. Where did you see him when you next saw him, where did you see him when he moved?

Mr. SCOGGINS. When I next saw him he was in the process of running up 10th Street.

Mr. BELIN. You next saw him after the shooting then?

Mr. SCOGGINS. Yes; I did.

Mr. BELIN. About where was he on 10th Street when you next saw him?

329

Mr. Scoggins. He was on the sidewalk when I saw him, about, I would say, about—I am trying to figure out now—about number 21 or back a little piece from 21.

Mr. Belin. Here is the squad car and 21 would be just east of the squad car?

Mr. Scoggins. Yes.

Mr. Belin. All right. You saw him there?

Mr. Scoggins. Yes.

Mr. Belin. What was he doing when you saw him in the area of 21 in Exhibit 523?

Mr. Scoggins. He was proceeding west on 10th and had——

Mr. Belin. All right. I wonder if you would just take this pen and on Exhibit 523 mark the route that you think this man took.

Mr. Scoggins. This is a sidewalk here.

Mr. Belin. That is the sidewalk.

Mr. Scoggins. This is the house back here.

Mr. Belin. This is the corner house, this is the second house, this is the third house, 400, 404, and 410.

Mr. Dulles. What does that line show, Mr. Belin?

Mr. Belin. This is to show the movement of the man from point 21.

Mr. Dulles. Along the sidewalk going west?

Mr. Belin. Yes.

Mr. Scoggins. He ran to the point in the shrubbery.

Mr. Belin. Is that as far as you have seen him go?

Mr. Scoggins. Yes.

Mr. Belin. You have now marked by ink line commencing on Exhibit 523 to a point that I will mark is the route that you believe you saw the man take. Where were you when you saw him take this route?

Mr. Scoggins. When I first saw him coming, you see, over here, I got out of my cab and I started to cross the street to find a place to get behind, and I got midway across the street, and then I got back and hid behind the cab. I didn't see him in here, but I saw him when he hit the shrubbery, when he hit that shrubbery.

Mr. Belin. There is an opening in part of that shrubbery?

Mr. Scoggins. Yes, and I heard that when he hit that, and he was looking over his left shoulder at that time. I first saw him and then I got out——

Mr. Belin. I wonder if you would show us on Exhibit 531, if you would put an X there, the approximate location you were when you saw this man.

Mr. Scoggins. When I first saw him?

Mr. Belin. No; when you first—yes, you can put where you first saw him.

Mr. Scoggins. I was sitting inside my cab when I first saw him.

Mr. Belin. I mean after the shooting.

Mr. Scoggins. After the shooting I guess when I first saw him, right along about here.

Mr. Belin. All right, we are going to put—you had gotten out of your car, and we are going to put a letter "A" with an arrow there. Where were you when you saw him coming through the bushes, or by the bushes?

Mr. Scoggins. I was back there beside my cab.

Mr. Belin. You were still at that same point?

Mr. Scoggins. No, when I first saw him I left the cab and I went out to the middle of the street.

Mr. Belin. Where were you when you first saw him and he was at the point you marked, position 21 here on Exhibit 523?

Mr. Scoggins. Here.

Mr. Belin. At point "A." Then you went to the—you went out to the street, in the street, and came back to point "A" on Exhibit 531—were you standing or were you crouched?

Mr. Scoggins. I was kind of crouched down behind the cab.

Mr. Belin. All right. How did you see him if you were crouched?

Mr. Scoggins. Well, whenever he run through those bushes I looked up again, you see.

Mr. Belin. You looked through your cab window?

Mr. Scoggins. I heard him—whenever I heard him hit those bushes——

Mr. Belin. Did you stand or just look through your cab window?

Mr. Scoggins. I just looked and saw he was going down there.

Mr. Belin. About how close was this man to you when you saw him, the closest when you saw him coming through the bushes, approximately.

Mr. Scoggins. Oh, I would say from here to that chair down there.

Mr. Belin. Pardon?

Mr. Scoggins. About that chair down there.

Mr. Belin. 12 feet?

Mr. Scoggins. Yes.

Mr. Dulles. Referring to your tracing of the path that the man later found to be Oswald followed, he went through the lower of these two bushes there, did he? He went right through it?

Mr. Scoggins. Yes, sir. You see there is an opening in there.

Mr. Dulles. But he didn't apparently take the opening, according to this, because he went right through the bushes.

Mr. Scoggins. Well, because I didn't see any opening in there. Was there an opening in there?

Mr. Belin. Mr. Dulles, for the record, when you are referring to 523, there is an opening between the shrubbery, but within the shrubbery itself there is an opening, and I think it will appear if you——

Mr Dulles. I think the witness testified he heard the bushes move.

Mr. Scoggins. Yes.

Mr. Belin. Yes. But the opening within the bushes, is it a large opening or a small opening between the bushes?

Mr. Scoggins. It is not too large, but a man can get through very easily by going through.

Mr. Dulles. But he hits the bushes as he goes through?

Mr. Scoggins. Yes.

Mr. Dulles. I see. That makes it clear.

Mr. Belin. It is not the wide opening between the two sets of bushes.

Mr. Dulles. It is not quite as wide.

Mr. Scoggins. It is an opening between the bushes themselves, like maybe someone had planted three bushes and maybe one of them had died to break the shrubbery.

Mr. Dulles. That has happened to me.

Mr. Belin. What I am saying, Mr. Dulles, on Exhibit 523 there are two groups of bushes. Within the lower group of bushes there is a slight space to which the witness is referring.

Mr. Dulles. I see. It is not the space here.

Mr. Belin. It is not the space between the two sets of bushes.

Mr. Dulles. At this point do you recall whether he was running or walking or what pace was he going at?

Mr. Scoggins. He was going at a kind of lope.

Mr. Dulles. Lope?

Mr. Scoggins. Yes, what you might call a little trot. He did not seem in too big a hurry, but he wasn't walking.

Mr. Belin. Mr. Scoggins, you last saw the man when he was at the point that you let the line stop at on Exhibit 523, is that correct?

Mr. Scoggins. Yes, sir. That would be in the approximate location.

Mr. Belin. What did you do?

Mr. Scoggins. I got on my radio.

Mr. Belin. And then you told us about calling your dispatcher?

Mr. Scoggins. Yes.

Mr. Belin. What did you do after that?

Mr. Scoggins. Well, I got back in my cab to call my dispatcher, you see.

Mr. Belin. Yes.

Mr. Scoggins. And then I got out of the cab and run down there; the ambulance had already arrived by the time I got there, and they were in the process of picking the man up, and they had done had him, was putting him on the stretcher when I got there, and they put him in the ambulance and took him away, and there was someone that got on the radio at that time and they told him he was going to report it, so they told him to get off the air, that it had already been reported, and he picks up the officer's pistol that was laying on the ground, apparently fell out of his holster when he fell, and says, "Come on, let's go see if we can find him."

Mr. DULLES. Before you ask the next question, I wonder if I can ask one question here. Do you know whether the ambulance came as a result of the message you sent?

Mr. SCOGGINS. No, I sure don't.

Mr. DULLES. You do not know?

Mr. SCOGGINS. No.

Mr. DULLES. From the time angle, do you think that could have happened?

Mr. SCOGGINS. It was awful fast if it did. They got there awfully quickly if they did.

Mr. DULLES. You don't know of any other warning going in; you put your warning in, and that is all you know about it?

Mr. SCOGGINS. That is all I know about it at that time, and I do know this other gentleman called after I got up to the car, he called in, and they told him it had already been.

(Off the record discussion.)

Mr. BELIN. Mr. Scoggins, I started to ask you about the revolver of the policeman when you came and saw him. This was in his holster or on the street?

Mr. SCOGGINS. It was on the street whenever I saw it.

Mr. BELIN. Do you know where it was with relation to the policeman's body?

Mr. SCOGGINS. It was there pretty close to his body, you know, like kind of under his body when they picked him up. It either fell out of his holster or was laying on the ground, one, I don't know which.

Mr. BELIN. What did you see him do? This man came up and picked up the policeman's gun. He picked it up and said, "Let's go see if we can find him?"

Mr. SCOGGINS. I thought the man was a kind of police, Secret Service or something, I didn't know, and I take him and we drove around over the neighborhood looking, and I still didn't know what kind—I still thought he was connected with the police department in some way.

Mr. BELIN. What route did you take as you drove over the neighborhood?

Mr. SCOGGINS. I couldn't tell you.

Mr. BELIN. You can't tell us the route you took over the neighborhood?

Mr. SCOGGINS. I was doing the driving and he was doing the directing.

Mr. BELIN. He directed you where to go?

Mr. SCOGGINS. Actually, I couldn't say where he was going.

Mr. BELIN. All right.

Representative FORD. Were you in your cab?

Mr. SCOGGINS. Yes.

Representative FORD. When you saw the pistol it wasn't in Officer Tippit's hands?

Mr. SCOGGINS. No, sir; oh, he never did have a pistol in his hand, as far as I know.

Mr. BELIN. You saw him when he was falling?

Mr. SCOGGINS. Yes; he was holding his stomach.

Mr. BELIN. You saw him holding his stomach as he fell?

Mr. SCOGGINS. Yes.

Mr. BELIN. Did he have anything in his hands?

Mr. SCOGGINS. If he did I couldn't see it, and I don't think he ever got to his pistol from what I saw.

Mr. BELIN. Did you see the man with the gun as he opened his gun, as he was going to the west on—up 10th Street at all after the shooting?

Mr. SCOGGINS. No, I didn't see him.

Mr. BELIN. After you went around to look for the man, did you find him at all?

Mr. SCOGGINS. No. We drove around and asked several people, but we did not see anybody that looked like him.

Mr. BELIN. Then what did you do?

Mr. SCOGGINS. Well, by that time there was more policemen there than you can shake a stick at. They were all over that place, and we stopped the cab.

Mr. BELIN. At about what time, do you know offhand?

Mr. SCOGGINS. About 1:30, I guess, approximately 1:30; between 1:30 and 1:35, I would say. We cruised around several blocks looking for him, and we—one of these police cars came by and this fellow who was with me stopped it, and we got back in the car and went back up to the scene, and he give them the pistol, and that time is when I found out he wasn't an officer.

Mr. BELIN. Then what happened, or what did you do?

Mr. SCOGGINS. Well, they was questioning a lot of people and questioning everybody, and they was talking, and so I went back and got on my radio and contacted my supervisor, and they wanted me to come into the office and make a statement, and so I did, the cab company. One of the supervisors got a statement of it, and he asked me did the police, did I give them a statement, and I told him no because, and he said, "Well, why didn't you?" I said, "They didn't ask me. They talked with everybody else."

So the next day they took me down and put me through a lineup, showed me a lineup of four people, and I identified the one that I had seen the day before.

Mr. BELIN. Now, let me ask you this question. First of all, do you remember, or can you describe the man you saw on November 22 with the gun?

Mr. SCOGGINS. He was a medium-height fellow with, kind of a slender look, and approximately, I said 25, 26 years old, somewhere along there.

Mr. BELIN. Do you remember the color of his hair?

Mr. SCOGGINS. Yes. It was light; let's see, was it light or not—medium brown, I would say.

Mr. BELIN. Pardon?

Mr. SCOGGINS. Medium brown, I would say—now, wait a minute. Now, medium brown or dark.

Mr. BELIN. Medium brown or dark hair?

Mr. SCOGGINS. Yes.

Mr. BELIN. Was he a Negro or a white man?

Mr. SCOGGINS. White, light complected, not real brown.

Mr. BELIN. Was he fat, average build or thin?

Mr. SCOGGINS. No, he was slender; not real slender, but you know——

Mr. BELIN. Was he wearing glasses or not?

Mr. SCOGGINS. No.

Mr. BELIN. Pardon?

Mr. SCOGGINS. No.

Mr. BELIN. That he had on?

Mr. SCOGGINS. No.

Mr. BELIN. Anything else you remember about him, the color of his shoes?

Mr. SCOGGINS. No, I can't say that.

Mr. BELIN. Do you remember any jewelry he might have had on?

Mr. SCOGGINS. No.

Mr. BELIN. You say you went down to the police station when, Mr. Scoggins, approximately?

Mr. SCOGGINS. You mean the time of day it was?

Mr. BELIN. Was it the same day of the shooting or the next day?

Mr. SCOGGINS. No, it was the next day.

Mr. BELIN. Morning, afternoon, or evening, if you remember?

Mr. SCOGGINS. Well, the best I can remember, they called me down from the cab stand, the police came down to the office and picked me up. Well, the other guy—I was close to the downtown area, and it didn't take me long to get there, and I waited quite a while before the other man, he was quite out a ways, and it was before dinner.

Mr. BELIN. It was before dinner?

Mr. SCOGGINS. Yes, whenever they called me in.

Mr. BELIN. Would it have been on the afternoon of November 23, to the best of your recollection?

Mr. SCOGGINS. When they took me down there it was along about dinner time.

Representative FORD. What do you mean by dinner time? In various parts of the country dinner and supper get confused a little bit. Was it the noon meal or the evening meal?

Mr. SCOGGINS. Yes.

Representative FORD. Yes what? It was the noon meal?

Mr. SCOGGINS. Yes.

Mr. BELIN. They took you down about the time of the noon meal, is that correct; they took you to the police station?

Mr. SCOGGINS. I would think that would be about the time.

Mr. BELIN. Sometime after you got there after the noon meal you saw the lineup, is that correct?

Mr. SCOGGINS. Yes.

Mr. BELIN. How many people were in the lineup, if you can remember?

Mr. SCOGGINS. Four.

Mr. BELIN. Four? Did any one of the people look anything like—strike that. Did you identify anyone in the lineup?

Mr. SCOGGINS. I identified the one we are talking about, Oswald. I identified him.

Mr. BELIN. You didn't know his name as Oswald at that time, did you, or did you not?

Mr. SCOGGINS. Yes, the next day I did. But, of course I didn't know what his name was the day that I picked him out.

Mr. BELIN. You saw a man in the lineup?

Mr. SCOGGINS. Yes.

Mr. BELIN. Did anyone tell you any particular man was Oswald in the lineup?

Mr. SCOGGINS. No.

Mr. BELIN. Well, describe what happened in the police station with regard to the lineup, what they did to you, what they said to you, and what you said to them, and so on.

Mr. SCOGGINS. Well, they had the four men up there in the lineup, and before they brought them in they told us what they wanted us to do, to look them over and be sure we was, in our estimation, we was right on the man, and which one it was, the one that we saw, the one that I saw.

Mr. BELIN. Did they tell you one of the men was the man you saw or not, or did they tell you "See if you can"—just what did they say? Did they say "Here is a lineup, see if you can identify anyone," or did they say, "One of the men in the lineup"——

Mr. SCOGGINS. Yes, I believe those are the words they used. I am not——

Mr. BELIN. Did all of these men look different to you? Were most of them fat, or were most of them thin, or some fat, some thin, some tall, some short?

Mr. SCOGGINS. There were two of them—the one that I identified as the one I saw over at Oak Cliff, and there was one I saw similar to him, and the other two was a little bit shorter.

Mr. DULLES. Had you been looking at television or seeing television prior to your appearance here at the lineup?

Mr. SCOGGINS. No.

Mr. DULLES. You had not?

Mr. SCOGGINS. No, sir.

Representative FORD. Had you been working this Saturday morning with your cab?

Mr. SCOGGINS. Yes, sir.

Representative FORD. In other words, you went to work Saturday morning at the regular time?

Mr. SCOGGINS. Yes.

Representative FORD. And were working when they asked you to come down to the cab stand to go over to the police station?

Mr. SCOGGINS. Yes, sir.

Representative FORD. All right.

Mr. BELIN. Had you seen any pictures of Lee Harvey Oswald in the newspapers prior to the time you went to the police station lineup?

Mr. SCOGGINS. I think I saw one in the morning paper.

Mr. BELIN. Do you subscribe to the morning or evening paper?

Mr. SCOGGINS. I take the evening paper myself.

Mr. BELIN. You went down and bought a morning paper?

Mr. SCOGGINS. No; I didn't go out. I was looking at one of the—some of the cab drivers had it.

Mr. BELIN. Did you see any television picture on the morning of November 23 of Lee Harvey Oswald?

Mr. SCOGGINS. I have never until this day seen it.

Mr. BELIN. On television?

Mr. SCOGGINS. I never have.

Representative FORD. Do you have a television in your home?

Mr. SCOGGINS. Yes sir; I do. But I don't—when I get home I will read the paper, and after you work about 12 hours you don't feel like fooling around with television too much.

Mr. BELIN. What number man in the lineup did you identify as having seen on November 22?

Mr. SCOGGINS. Number 3.

Mr. BELIN. Did you have the man turn around, or could you——

Mr. SCOGGINS. Yes, they turned him around.

Mr. BELIN. Did they turn just one man around or all of them?

Mr. SCOGGINS. No; they had them all.

Mr. BELIN. Do you remember if the number 3 man in the lineup was wearing the same clothes that the man you saw at the Tippit shooting wore?

Mr. SCOGGINS. He had on a different shirt, and he didn't have a jacket on. He had on kind of a polo shirt.

Mr. BELIN. Before you went to view the lineup, did any of the police officers show you a picture of this man?

Mr. SCOGGINS. No.

Mr. BELIN. Sometime later, after the lineup, did any investigator come up to you with a picture of anyone and ask you if you could identify him?

Mr. SCOGGINS. Yes.

Mr. BELIN. Do you remember if he was an FBI man or a Dallas policeman or a Secret Service agent?

Mr. SCOGGINS. He was an FBI or a Secret Service.

Mr. BELIN. What did he ask you and what did you tell him?

Mr. SCOGGINS. He gave me some pictures, showed me several pictures there. which was, some of them were, pretty well resembled him, and some of them didn't, and they looked like they was kind of old pictures, and I think I picked the wrong picture. I am not too——

Mr. BELIN. What did he say to you and what did you say to him, if you remember?

Mr. SCOGGINS. I don't really—I know he showed me his credentials.

Mr. BELIN. Did he say to you something like "These are pictures we have of Lee Harvey Oswald"? Did he use that name in front of you, or did he say, "Here are some pictures. See if you can identify them"—if you remember?

Mr. SCOGGINS. I don't remember, but after I got through looking at them and everything, and I says, I told them one of these two pictures is him, out of this group he showed me, and the one that was actually him looked like an older man than he was to me. Of course, I am not too much on identifying pictures. It wasn't a full shot of him, you know, and then he told me the other one was Oswald.

Representative FORD. Had you narrowed the number of pictures from more than two to two?

Mr. SCOGGINS. Yes.

Representative FORD. In other words, they showed you pictures of how many people altogether, how many different people, your best estimate?

Mr. SCOGGINS. I would say 4 or 5.

Representative FORD. And you narrowed the number of 4 or 5 down to 2?

Mr. SCOGGINS. Down to two; yes.

Mr. BELIN. Mr. Scoggins, at the time of the shooting, did you see any pedestrians standing at the corner of East 10th and Patton, any of the corners there?

335

Mr. Scoggins. I didn't see anybody. I was kind of excited.

Mr. Belin. Did you see any other person walking along the street there?

Mr. Scoggins. Not at the time of the shooting, I didn't.

Mr. Belin. Is there anything you can think of that you haven't told us here that might be relevant to what you saw in connection with the Tippit shooting?

Mr. Scoggins. No, I can't—nothing that I know of. That is the first time I ever seen anything like that happen. and I was pretty well excited and mixed up, and not knowing what to do or what not to do. But actually, of course, right after the shooting, I saw a number of people come running over, you see, from everywhere.

Mr. Belin. Were they all men?

Mr. Scoggins. No, they were just people.

Mr. Belin. General Carr, do you have any questions?

Mr. Carr. No, sir. I was exploring with him, but I guess we won't get into it.

Mr. Belin. Those are all the questions I have. Just a second. When you saw a picture in the morning paper of Lee Harvey Oswald, did this look similar to the man you saw at the Tippit shooting, or did it look different?

Mr. Scoggins. I would say similar; yes.

Mr. Belin. Did it look like the same man?

Mr. Scoggins. Yes.

Representative Ford. What kind of eyesight do you have?

Mr. Scoggins. I had my eyes examined when I went to work for the cab company and the lady said I had remarkable eyesight. You know, they have—after I went to work, after a while, I had to go get my eyes examined.

Representative Ford. You had your eyes examined subsequent to your employment with the cab company?

Mr. Scoggins. Well, it was sometime after, maybe 6 months after.

Mr. Dulles. How many years ago was that?

Mr. Scoggins. Oh, about a year, approximately.

Representative Ford. At that time what did the eye examiner tell you?

Mr. Scoggins. She said I had excellent eyesight and vision.

Representative Ford. You don't wear glasses?

Mr. Scoggins. No.

Representative Ford. What about your hearing?

Mr. Scoggins. I can hear. I got good hearing. I never did have it examined or anything, but I can hear everything.

Representative Ford. Have you ever had any difficulty with the law, have you ever had any trouble with officers of the law?

Mr. Scoggins. I got a ticket for parking that I had to pay.

Representative Ford. That is a traffic violation.

Mr. Scoggins. Yes. No; I really haven't had any problems that amount to anything otherwise than traffic violations.

Representative Ford. Nothing other than traffic violations?

Mr. Scoggins. Well, I was picked up one time in New York City for stowing away on a tugboat.

Mr. Belin. Stowing away on a boat?

Mr. Scoggins. Actually what happened——

Mr. Dulles. How old were you then?

Mr. Scoggins. 17 or 18. I was sleeping in a boxcar and they put that boxcar on a tugboat and sent it across the river.

Mr. Dulles. You stowed away without knowing it.

Mr. Scoggins. Yes.

Mr. Dulles. I don't think that is a very grave offense.

Mr. Scoggins. No. I never have been in any grave trouble.

Mr. Belin. One more question, Mr. Scoggins. You rode up here to Washington on an airplane with Mrs. Markham, did you not?

Mr. Scoggins. Yes.

Mr. Belin. Before you saw Mrs. Markham the other day, did you ever recognize her as having seen her from the time of the Tippit shooting at all or not?

Mr. Scoggins. Yes, I saw her down there talking to the policemen after I came back. You see, I saw her talking to them.

Mr. Belin. You never actually saw her standing on the street, did you?

Mr. Scoggins. I never actually observed her there.

Mr. Belin. All right.

Mr. Dulles. When you say, "I came back" is that when you got into your car?

Mr. Scoggins. After I had got in the car and toured the neighborhood and then the policemen came along and I left my cab setting down there and got in a car with them and left the scene.

Mr. Dulles. At what stage did you see Mrs. Markham?

Mr. Scoggins. After I had gotten back up there. After I had drove around in the neighborhood looking for Oswald or looking for this guy.

Mr. Dulles. It was after that?

Mr. Scoggins. It was after that.

(Discussion off the record.)

Mr. Belin. Mr. Scoggins, when you identified the man in the lineup at the police station on November 23, was there any other person who at the same time was asked to identify a man in that lineup?

Mr. Scoggins. Yes, one other.

Mr. Belin. Do you know—one other person?

Mr. Scoggins. Yes.

Mr. Belin. Do you know what that man's name is or what his occupation is?

Mr. Scoggins. Yes, he drives a taxicab.

Mr. Belin. Do you know his name?

Mr. Scoggins. Yes; his name is Bill Whaley.

Mr. Belin. Whaley?

Mr. Scoggins. I think it is Whaley. I didn't know him from Adam until that day, you know, and he said his name was Whaley.

Mr. Belin. When you were there and identified a man, had Whaley already identified that man or not? I mean, did you hear Whaley or see Whaley identify that man?

Mr. Scoggins. No. He was sitting over on my left.

Mr. Belin. He was on your left?

Mr. Scoggins. Yes. It was dark. They turned the lights out where we were sitting. We could see the man with lights up there.

Mr. Belin. Could you see Mr. Whaley at the time he made the identification?

Mr. Scoggins. Well, I suppose if I would have looked over there I could have seen that there was a man there, that I could have recognized him.

Mr. Belin. Were you looking at Mr. Whaley at the time?

Mr. Scoggins. No.

Mr. Belin. Did you make your identification by your voice or by your hands?

Mr. Scoggins. By my hands, using—I put up three fingers.

Mr. Belin. Did they tell you ahead of time to hold up the number of fingers for the man that you saw?

Mr. Scoggins. Yes, sir.

Mr. Belin. How many fingers did you hold up?

Mr. Scoggins. Three.

Mr. Belin. At the time you held up your three fingers, did you know how many fingers Mr. Whaley was holding up?

Mr. Scoggins. No.

Mr. Belin. Then did you know whether or not Mr. Whaley had identified the man?

Mr. Scoggins. No, I sure don't.

Mr. Belin. Was there any person or were there any persons standing between you and Mr. Whaley?

Mr. Scoggins. That I don't know because I did not look over there.

Mr. Dulles. Could Mr. Whaley, in your opinion, see you holding up these fingers?

Mr. Scoggins. No, no. I made sure of that because I had my hand down like this.

Mr. BELIN. When you had your hand down you are putting it in front of your belt?

Mr. SCOGGINS. As well as I could remember I had it down kind of like this here. I don't know whether I used my right or my left hand, but I didn't hold up three fingers like this, but I held them down just about like this.

Mr. BELIN. You are pointing to your right hand and putting it somewhat about a few inches above the buckle of your belt; it that about where you held up your fingers?

Mr. SCOGGINS. About as well as I could remember.

Mr. BELIN. What happened after you held up your fingers, did someone see you holding your fingers up there?

Mr. SCOGGINS. Yes.

Representative FORD. Where were they standing beside you so that they could see your fingers?

Mr. SCOGGINS. Well, this gentleman was standing over back a piece to my left, sir.

Representative FORD. Was it close to you, sir?

Mr. SCOGGINS. There was one man on my right. He was Secret Service or FBI, I think FBI; and the other man was a policeman, Dallas policeman.

Mr. DULLES. Do you know whether Mr. Whaley was making his identification at the same time that you did or did he make it before or after?

Mr. SCOGGINS. No. All I know is that we viewed them at the same time.

Mr. DULLES. He viewed them at the same time?

Mr. SCOGGINS. Yes.

Mr. DULLES. You don't know at what time Mr. Whaley made his identification?

Mr. SCOGGINS. Yes.

Mr. DULLES. You didn't see him make the identification?

Mr. SCOGGINS. I didn't even see him.

Mr. DULLES. You don't know what his identification was?

Mr. SCOGGINS. No. I never asked him which one or nothing, because I never did discuss it with him at all after that.

Representative FORD. When you brought your cab up to the corner of 10th and Patton, did you just conclude or had you just concluded dropping a passenger?

Mr. SCOGGINS. Well, approximately five minutes before that.

Representative FORD. Do you keep a record of the trips that you take?

Mr. SCOGGINS. Yes, sir.

Representative FORD. During your working day?

Mr. SCOGGINS. Yes, sir. If I pick up a passenger, say, like 28 minutes to 12 o'clock, we put 20 minutes to 12. We don't put the odd minutes down.

If we let him out 2 minutes after 12, we put down 12 o'clock. I know I let him out at 1 o'clock, maybe a minute or two after. We do put the destination we leave from and the destination he is going to on our records sheet.

Representative FORD. What does your record show about this last trip?

Mr. SCOGGINS. Well, I picked him up at Love Field and carried him to 321 North Ewing, as well as I can remember now, that was the address.

Representative FORD. And your record shows that?

Mr. SCOGGINS. When I picked him up, the mileage started from, the mileage I let him out on the speedometer. When I picked him up we put the mileage down. We don't put the tenth down, and when we let him out we put the mileage and the time; and when we pick him up we put the mileage and the time, and the destination where we start and where we let him off, and the amount the fare was.

Representative FORD. And your last entry shows what for that day?

Mr. SCOGGINS. I don't know what the last entry was. Up until then that was the one where I let the man off at. It was an apartment building. Of course, I don't have the apartment number, anything like that. The guy says, "I want to go to 321 North Ewing," and that is where I take him. It is an apartment. Of course now, if somebody calls in for a cab at a certain address, if it is an apartment, they have to give their apartment number so we could find it.

Representative FORD. How far was this last destination to the point of 10th and Patton?

Mr. SCOGGINS. It was less than a mile, about a half mile or maybe—well, let's see, it was closer to a mile, I would say.

Representative FORD. Was there any particular reason why you went to the corner of 10th and Patton?

Mr. SCOGGINS. Yes. I belong to that club there, and I was going around there to get me a coca cola that I could have gotten anywhere else, but I know a lot of the guys.

Representative FORD. What is the club called?

Mr. SCOGGINS. It is a gentleman's club, a domino parlor where we play dominos.

Representative FORD. It is at what address?

Mr. SCOGGINS. 123 or 125 South Patton.

Mr. BELIN. About where is it in relation to East 10th and Patton, how far away, a block, two blocks?

Mr. SCOGGINS. It is not a block. It is just about, I would say, just—if it was measured it would be a little over a half block from where I was parked at to the place, you see.

Mr. BELIN. I wonder, perhaps, if we can see it on any of these pictures, Mr. Scoggins. Do you see it in this picture, Exhibit 530?

Mr. SCOGGINS. Yes; I can see the building.

Mr. BELIN. Let's see the building here.

Mr. SCOGGINS. That is it up there.

Mr. BELIN. I wonder if we can't, perhaps, put on Exhibit 530 an arrow which points to this building, and we will put "G" for the gentleman's club; is that correct? Is that the building to which you are referring?

Mr. SCOGGINS. Yes.

Mr. BELIN. Mr. Scoggins, we have another picture that we would like to have you identify, Commission Exhibit 534. This is a picture in which the camera appears to be heading in what direction?

Mr. SCOGGINS. It would be heading east—I mean west on 10th Street.

Mr. BELIN. That picture was taken the other day at the time you drove your cab back to that scene, is that correct?

Mr. SCOGGINS. I would think it was; yes.

Mr. BELIN. Does this appear to be the position your cab was in at the time of the shooting of Officer Tippit?

Mr. SCOGGINS. Yes.

Mr. BELIN. All right. At this time we offer and introduce into evidence all exhibits up through 534, except we do not have a 533 because we renumbered the original Exhibit 533, so we do not have a 533.

Do you have anything more, Congressman Ford?

Representative FORD. Those exhibits will be admitted.

(Items identified as Commission Exhibits through No. 534, with the exception of Exhibit No. 533, were admitted in evidence.)

Mr. DULLES. Mr. Scoggins, you have referred, I believe, to a conversation you had with Mr. Whaley, I think his name is, and I would like to have you just recount what you recall of what Mr. Whaley said to you, and where he said it, and at what time.

Mr. SCOGGINS. Well now, this conversation we are talking about, while we were down there waiting.

Mr. DULLES. Down where, down at the police station?

Mr. SCOGGINS. No; down at the cab office—it is a cab office at 610 South Akard Street, you know.

Mr. DULLES. A cab stand?

Mr. SCOGGINS. Yes. We call it our main office.

Mr. DULLES. And Mr. Whaley's cab belonged to the same company as your cab?

Mr. SCOGGINS. Yes, sir. Only he drives out of downtown, which office is 610 South Akard Street, that is the number. They have a building there, a large building, with all the dispatching offices and everything, and mine, of course,

I have got the same dispatchers, we all belong to the same company. I drive an Oak Cliff cab, and he drives downtown.

Mr. DULLES. Relate what Mr. Whaley said to you.

Mr. SCOGGINS. He didn't relate it to me. He was talking to the others.

Mr. DULLES. He was talking to cabdrivers?

Mr. SCOGGINS. He was talking to one of the——

Mr. DULLES. Where did this take place?

Mr. SCOGGINS. It was down at the cabstand.

Mr. DULLES. Was this on Saturday after the assassination?

Mr. SCOGGINS. And he was telling them where he picked him up and where he took him to.

Mr. DULLES. And that is what you recall?

Mr. SCOGGINS. Yes; because I didn't know him. I wasn't acquainted with the man.

Mr. DULLES. You were not acquainted with Mr. Whaley?

Mr. SCOGGINS. No. Before he came down there that morning I wouldn't have known him from Adam, you know, just wouldn't have had any idea who he was.

Mr. DULLES. Would you recall what he said as to where he picked up the man and where he took him?

Mr. SCOGGINS. He said he picked him up at the Greyhound bus and carried him to a neighborhood, no particular address, on North Beckley, the 500 block.

Mr. DULLES. Have you anything more on that, Mr. Belin?

Mr. BELIN. No, sir. I do have one other question.

Mr. DULLES. Proceed then.

Mr. BELIN. Do you remember whether or not your dispatcher recorded any time on his sheets as to the time you called in after the Tippit shooting?

Mr. SCOGGINS. When I was down there giving my statement to my supervisor, he asked me what time it was, and I said I don't have any idea, so he picked up the phone and called the dispatcher, and he said it was 1:23.

Mr. BELIN. That is the time that he recorded it?

Mr. SCOGGINS. Yes. He must have recorded it up there because he said it was 1:23 in the afternoon.

Mr. BELIN. When you called in after the shooting?

Mr. SCOGGINS. Yes.

Mr. DULLES. Anything else?

Mr. BELIN. No, sir.

Mr. DULLES. Any further questions? Well, thank you very much, Mr. Scoggins.

TESTIMONY OF HELEN MARKHAM RESUMED

Mr. DULLES. You were sworn when you previously were before us, and this testimony of yours will be covered by the oath you previously have given. Will you be seated?

Mr. BALL. I have two Commission Exhibits, 535 and 536. I will show them to you, Mrs. Markham, and I will ask you if you have ever seen the man who is pictured there, whose picture is shown on these two exhibits.

Mrs. MARKHAM. No.

Mr. BALL. Never have seen him before. Do you think he might have been one of the men you talked to before?

Mrs. MARKHAM. No, no.

Mr. BALL. They are pictures of the same man.

Mrs. MARKHAM. No.

Mr. DULLES. We are inquiring whether you had ever seen him after the assassination.

Mrs. MARKHAM. Yes, I know. No; not this man. This man I have never seen—I have never seen this man in my life.

Mr. BALL. I have no further questions.

Mr. DULLES. Do you know who he is?

Mrs. MARKHAM. No; I don't. It is just a picture of a man; I don't know him.

Mr. DULLES. Mr. Ball, do you have any further questions?

Mr. BALL. No further questions.

Representative FORD. Have you ever had any difficulty with the law, Mrs. Markham?

Mrs. MARKHAM. No.

Representative FORD. None whatsoever?

Mrs. MARKHAM. No, sir.

Representative FORD. Traffic violations?

Mrs. MARKHAM. No, sir.

Mr. DULLES. You are lucky.

Mrs. MARKHAM. I have never been in trouble.

Representative FORD. No difficulties whatsoever with the law?

Mrs. MARKHAM. No, sir.

Mr. BALL. That is all, Mrs. Markham. You can be excused.

Mr. DULLES. Thank you very much, Mrs. Markham.

Mr. BALL. I offer Exhibits 535 and 536 in evidence at this time.

Mr. DULLES. They will be received.

(The items identified as Commission Exhibits Nos. 535 and 536 were received in evidence.)

Mr. BALL. They were taken from a newspaper, they were taken from newspaper accounts which purported to be, to show, the picture of a man named Mark Lane.

Mr. DULLES. Yes, because he appeared before this Commission, did he not?

Mr. BALL. Yes.

Mr. DULLES. Mr. Redlich, can you identify him? Were you present when Mr. Lane appeared before this Commission?

Mr. REDLICH. Yes; I was.

Mr. DULLES. Can you identify these pictures as pictures of Mr. Lane?

Mr. REDLICH. Yes; I can identify these as pictures of Mr. Lane. I would also like for the record to indicate where they came from. Commission Exhibit No. 535 is taken from—Commission Exhibit 536 came from the San Francisco Chronicle, and dated February 8, 1964, and purports to be a photograph of Mark Lane.

Commission No. 535 is a photograph from a newspaper clipping which was in the Commission files, and it is an Associated Press photograph, and appeared, it is taken from the New York Herald Tribune of March 5, 1964, and purports to be a photograph of Mark Lane. I have met Mr. Lane once or twice prior to his appearance before this Commission, and I was present during his testimony before this Commission.

Mr. DULLES. You identify these as pictures of Mr. Lane?

Mr. REDLICH. These are photographs of Mark Lane.

Mr. DULLES. And these Exhibits 535 and 536 were the exhibits which were presented to Mrs. Markham?

Mr. BELIN. I think the record should show how they were presented. They were clipped out so there was not any writing or anything to indicate whom they were pictures of on their face.

Mr. DULLES. That is on the record.

Mrs. Markham, there is a short question that Congressman Ford wanted to put to you.

Representative FORD. What kind of eyesight do you have, Mrs. Markham?

Mrs. MARKHAM. I have always had good eyesight.

Representative FORD. Do you wear glasses?

Mrs. MARKHAM. No; I don't.

Representative FORD. Have your eyes tested recently?

Mrs. MARKHAM. No; I haven't. I have no cause to.

Representative FORD. You have never worn glasses in your lifetime?

Mrs. MARKHAM. No.

Mr. DULLES. Are you farsighted, nearsighted, or neither, just good-sighted?

Mrs. MARKHAM. Just good-sighted. I did a lot of writing and a cashier and everything. I see pretty good.

Representative FORD. If you go to a movie can you see the picture easily and well?

Mrs. MARKHAM. Oh, yes; yes, sir; real well.

Representative FORD. You can see things at a distance quite well?

Mrs. MARKHAM. Yes, sir. I have never had glasses.

Representative FORD. Thank you very much.

TESTIMONY OF MRS. BARBARA JEANETTE DAVIS

Mr. BALL. Mrs. Davis, you didn't get the notice through the mail asking you to appear here?

Mrs. DAVIS. No, sir.

Mr. BALL. We told you orally in Washington, or in Dallas last Friday, didn't we?

Mrs. DAVIS. Yes, sir.

Mr. DULLES. She has not been sworn. Will you kindly raise your right hand? Do you solemnly swear the testimony you will give to this Commission is the truth, the whole truth, and nothing but the truth, so help you God?

Mrs. DAVIS. I do.

Mr. BALL. Mrs. Davis, you didn't get a letter from the Commission asking you to appear here?

Mrs. DAVIS. No, sir.

Mr. BALL. But when Mr. Belin and I were in Dallas on Friday of last week we asked you to appear?

Mrs. DAVIS. On Saturday.

Mr. BALL. On Saturday, was it?

Mrs. DAVIS. Yes.

Mr. BALL. That is right. And you voluntarily agreed to come up here, didn't you?

Mrs. DAVIS. That is right.

Mr. BALL. Without any notice from the Commission?

Mrs. DAVIS. That is right.

Mr. BALL. Where do you live?

Mr. DULLES. May we thank you for that.

Mrs. DAVIS. Athens, Tex.

Mr. BALL. Where do you live?

Mrs. DAVIS. Athens, Tex.

Mr. BALL. You are married, are you?

Mrs. DAVIS. Yes.

Mr. BALL. You have some children?

Mrs. DAVIS. Two.

Mr. BALL. What is your husband's name?

Mrs. DAVIS. Troy.

Mr. BALL. Troy Davis?

Mrs. DAVIS. Troy Lee Davis.

Mr. BALL. What is your business or what is his business?

Mrs. DAVIS. He is a roofer.

Mr. BALL. Beg pardon?

Mrs. DAVIS. He is a roofer.

Mr. BALL. Where were you born, Mrs. Davis?

Mrs. DAVIS. Athens.

Mr. BALL. Athens?

Mrs. DAVIS. Yes.

Mr. BALL. Live there all your life?

Mrs. DAVIS. Yes; part of it I have lived in Dallas some.

Mr. BALL. Where did you go to school?

Mrs. DAVIS. Athens.

Mr. BALL. How far through school did you go?

Mrs. DAVIS. Halfway through the 10th midterm.

Mr. BALL. Then did you get married?

Mrs. DAVIS. Yes.

Mr. BALL. You were living in Dallas on November 22, were you?

Mrs. DAVIS. Yes.

Mr. BALL. What was your address there in Dallas?

Mrs. DAVIS. 400 East 10th.

Mr. BALL. Who was living with you at that time?

Mrs. DAVIS. You mean in the apartment or in the building?

Mr. BALL. In the apartment with you.

Mrs. DAVIS. Just my husband and two children.

Mr. BALL. You had a sister, did you?

Mrs. DAVIS. Sister-in-law.

Mr. BALL. What is her name?

Mrs. DAVIS. Virginia.

Mr. BALL. Was she living there at the time, too?

Mrs. DAVIS. They lived around the side of the apartment house.

Mr. BALL. In the same building?

Mrs. DAVIS. Yes.

Mr. BALL. That was your husband's sister?

Mrs. DAVIS. No; it was my husband's brother's wife.

Mr. BALL. Husband's brother's wife. I see.

Mrs. DAVIS. Yes.

Mr. BALL. I have got some pictures here so we will understand. I will show you Exhibit 525. Is the house in which you were living on November 22d shown in the picture?

Mrs. DAVIS. Here.

Mr. BALL. It is the one on the corner? The southeast corner of 10th and Patton, isn't it?

Mrs. DAVIS. I don't know anything about that, but I know where it is.

Mr. BALL. I will show you Commission Exhibit 524. Is the house shown in that picture?

Mrs. DAVIS. Yes; sir.

Mr. BALL. And I show you 534, is the house shown in that picture?

Mrs. DAVIS. Yes, sir.

Mr. BALL. I am showing you 528 and there is a lawn there, that is the lawn of what house?

Mrs. DAVIS. Of the house I lived in.

Mr. BALL. The house you lived in.

On that day did something unusual happen that you observed, on November 22d?

Mrs. DAVIS. Those gunshots.

Mr. BALL. Gunshots? Where were you when you heard gunshots?

Mrs. DAVIS. In bed.

Mr. DULLES. Did you say gunshot or gunshots?

Mrs. DAVIS. Shots.

Mr. DULLES. Plural? How many did you hear?

Mrs. DAVIS. Just two, they were pretty close together.

Mr. BALL. You were lying on the bed. What did you do?

Mrs. DAVIS. I got up, put my shoes on to see what it was.

Mr. BALL. Did you ever go outdoors?

Mrs. DAVIS. At first, I didn't.

Mr. BALL. When you went to the door, did you open the door?

Mrs. DAVIS. I opened the door and held the screen opened.

Mr. BALL. What did you see?

Mrs. DAVIS. Mrs. Markham standing across the street over there, and she was standing over there and the man was coming across the yard.

Mr. BALL. A man was coming across what yard?

Mrs. DAVIS. My yard.

Mr. BALL. And what did you see the man doing?

Mrs. DAVIS. Well, first off she went to screaming before I had paid too much attention to him, and pointing at him, and he was, what I thought, was emptying the gun.

Mr. BALL. He had a gun in his hand?

Mrs. DAVIS. Yes.

Mr. BALL. And he was emptying it?

Mrs. DAVIS. It was open and he had his hands cocked like he was emptying it.

Mr. DULLES. Which hand did he have it?

Mrs. DAVIS. Right hand.

Mr. BALL. To his left palm?

Mrs. DAVIS. Yes.

Mr. BALL. Did you see him throw anything away?

Mrs. DAVIS. No.

Mr. BALL. You didn't?

Mrs. DAVIS. Yes.

Mr. BALL. What did you do next?

Mrs. DAVIS. He looked at her first and looked at me and then smiled and went around the corner.

Mr. BALL. Was he running or walking?

Mrs. DAVIS. He was walking at his normal pace.

Mr. BALL. And he went around the corner?

Did he go on the sidewalk?

Mrs. DAVIS. Yes. He was on the sidewalk right beside the house.

Mr. BALL. Did he go, did he cut across your lawn at all?

Mrs. DAVIS. Yes.

Mr. BALL. Where?

Mrs. DAVIS. He cut across the middle of the yard.

Mr. BALL. Here is a diagram, 523, this is 400—that is your home.

Mrs. DAVIS. He came right across like this.

Mr. BALL. Came across like this?

Mrs. DAVIS. Ran beside the sidewalk.

Mr. BALL. There is already a mark on there.

Mrs. DAVIS. He left the sidewalk about here, just on the other side of this.

Mr. BALL. Well, mark on the picture now, photo 21 which is Commission Exhibit 534, and you just take this and mark with it and show where he left the sidewalk and what course he took.

Mrs. DAVIS. He was just parallel to the side of this and right around this little bush and around the corner.

Mr. BALL. Around the corner?

Mrs. DAVIS. Yes.

Mr. BALL. The black mark from the sidewalk on 534 marks the course that the man took?

Representative FORD. Could you tell us where you were standing when you saw him?

Mrs. DAVIS. I was standing on the porch.

Mr. BALL. Put an "X" there.

Mrs. DAVIS. I can't see the porch. The door is right between these two things here.

Mr. BALL. These two things—what do you mean?

Mrs. DAVIS. Between the two posts.

Mr. BALL. Two posts?

Mrs. DAVIS. Yes.

Mr. BALL. Let's get a better view.

Mr. DULLES. It seems to be the best.

Mr. BALL. You are right.

That is 525.

Now mark where he cut across on that with a line.

Mrs. DAVIS. Right across like this, only it would be on the other side of the bushes here.

Mr. BALL. Yes.

And where were you?

Mrs. DAVIS. Standing right—here is the door right here.

Mr. BALL. Put an "X" there. That "X" is a mark to locate your position and we will give a symbol to it. "D." Now, the line you have drawn from the sidewalk through the bushes is the course the man took. Where was he when you saw him emptying his gun?

Mrs. DAVIS. He was right here on the other side of this bush.

Mr. BALL. Draw a line through the course there.

Mrs. DAVIS. Just about along in here.

Mr. DULLES. Did you know at the time he was emptying his gun?

Mrs. DAVIS. That is what I presumed because he had it open and was shaking it.

Mr. DULLES. I see. Just right there.

Mr. BALL. In other words, there is a cross you make across the line that he took which marks the place where he was emptying the gun.

Mrs. DAVIS. Just about halfway there.

Mr. BALL. Mark it also on 21, 534.

Mrs. DAVIS. Not quite half, not quite to the bushes there.

Representative FORD. Mr. Ball, even though she cannot pinpoint the point where she was standing because of the photograph, she might draw an arrow showing about where she was standing.

Mr. BALL. Show an arrow about where you were standing.

Mrs. DAVIS. About there.

Mr. BALL. That is 21, photo 21 and Commission Exhibit 534.

After the man left, what did you do, after he went out of sight what did you do?

Mrs. DAVIS. I went back in and phoned the police.

Mr. BALL. Then what did you tell the police?

Mrs. DAVIS. I just told them that a policeman had been shot.

Mr. BALL. Then what did you do?

Mrs. DAVIS. I came back outside and walked down to where the policeman's car was out.

Mr. BALL. Did you see the policeman?

Mrs. DAVIS. Yes.

Mr. BALL. Where was he?

Mrs. DAVIS. He was laying on the left-hand side of the car on the ground, by the left-hand fender.

Mr. BALL. Was he alive or what?

Mrs. DAVIS. I don't know.

Mr. BALL. Did he talk?

Mrs. DAVIS. No.

Mr. BALL. You didn't know whether he was alive or dead?

Mrs. DAVIS. No, sir; I didn't get that close.

Mr. BALL. How long did you stay there?

Mrs. DAVIS. Not 5 minutes, I would imagine, because the police cars started coming, so I went back to my yard.

Mr. BALL. Did you see a man coming and get the policeman's gun?

Mrs. DAVIS. No, I didn't.

Mr. BALL. Did you later look in the bushes and find something?

Mrs. DAVIS. Yes; in the grass beside the house.

Mr. BALL. The grass beside the house. What did you find?

Mrs. DAVIS. We found one shell.

Mr. BALL. One shell?

Mrs. DAVIS. Yes.

Mr. BALL. And your sister-in-law, did your sister-in-law find something else?

Mrs. DAVIS. She found one later in the afternoon.

Mr. BALL. One, later?

Mrs. DAVIS. Yes, sir.

Mr. BALL. Can you show me on one of these pictures here where you found one shell?

Mrs. DAVIS. Under the window here. That would be the only one I could tell.

Mr. BALL. The only one that shows, it is photo 3, it is Commission Exhibit 534. Draw an arrow down.

Mrs. DAVIS. Right under that window there.

Mr. BALL. Under that window.

The arrow which is marked "D-1" shows the position where you found one shell. Did you see your sister-in-law find the other shell?

Mrs. DAVIS. Yes.

Mr. BALL. Where was that found?

Mrs. DAVIS. There is a little cement walk right here by her door, it was right there, not too far from there.

Mr. BALL. Could you draw an arrow down to show the approximate position?

Mrs. DAVIS. It was almost in front of her door, there is a little cement porch to step up to her door.

Mr. BALL. The arrow which we marked as "D–2" marks the place where your sister-in-law found the second shell?

Mrs. DAVIS. Yes.

Mr. BALL. You only found two shells, did you, you one and your sister-in-law one?

Mrs. DAVIS. Yes.

Mr. BALL. What time of day did you find the one shell?

Mrs. DAVIS. I don't know. This was probably an hour and a half, maybe 2 hours, after the officer was shot.

Mr. BALL. What time of day did your sister-in-law find her shell, find the shell that she found?

Mr. DAVIS. Somewhere around 4:30, 5, somewhere in there.

Mr. BALL. Did you later go down to the police station?

Mrs. DAVIS. Yes, sir.

Mr. BALL. Were you shown a group of people in the police station and asked if you could identify the man?

Mrs. DAVIS. Yes.

Mr. BALL. Were you alone in that room when you were shown these people?

Mrs. DAVIS. No, sir.

Mr. BALL. Who was with you?

Mrs. DAVIS. My husband, my sister-in-law was with me, and some other men.

Mr. BALL. That is your husband Troy, your sister-in-law Virginia Davis, and yourself, and other men?

Mrs. DAVIS. Yes.

Mr. BALL. Did you know those men?

Mrs. DAVIS. No, sir.

Mr. BALL. Were police officers there?

Mrs. DAVIS. They were all in suits, some sat at the back of the room.

Mr. BALL. When those—how many men were shown to you in this lineup?

Mrs. DAVIS. Four.

Mr. BALL. Were they of the same size or of different sizes?

Mrs. DAVIS. Most of them was about the same size.

Mr. BALL. All white men, were they?

Mrs. DAVIS. Yes.

Mr. BALL. Did you recognize anyone in that room?

Mrs. DAVIS. Yes, sir. I recognized number 2.

Mr. BALL. Number 2 you recognized? Did you tell any policeman there anything after you recognized them?

Mrs. DAVIS. I told the man who had brought us down there.

Mr. BALL. What did you tell him?

Mrs. DAVIS. That I thought number 2 was the man that I saw.

Mr. BALL. That you saw?

Mrs. DAVIS. Yes.

Mr. BALL. By number 2, was the man you saw the man you saw doing what?

Mrs. DAVIS. Unloading the gun.

Mr. BALL. And going across your yard?

Mrs. DAVIS. Yes, sir.

Mr. BALL. That was about what time of day that you were at the lineup?

Mrs. DAVIS. It was after 8, I am sure.

Mr. BALL. After when?

Mrs. DAVIS. After 8 o'clock.

Mr. BALL. On what day?

Mrs. DAVIS. On Friday, the same day.

Mr. BALL. The same day? It was after 8 o'clock on Friday, the same day that you had seen the man unloading the gun?

Mrs. DAVIS. Yes, sir.

Mr. DULLES. Have you any way of fixing the time of when the man ran across your lawn, approximately?

346

Mrs. DAVIS. No, sir; not exactly because I had laid down with the children and I didn't pay any attention to what time it was.

Representative FORD. You saw him take the shells out of the gun?

Mrs. DAVIS. No, sir; he was shaking them.

Representative FORD. He was shaking them?

Mrs. DAVIS. He was shaking them. I didn't see him actually use his hand to take them out. I mean he was sort of shaking them out.

Representative FORD. Did you find this one bullet at the point where you saw him shake the gun?

Mrs. DAVIS. No, sir; it was around the side of the house.

Representative FORD. About how many feet?

Mrs. DAVIS. I don't know. Not too far.

Representative FORD. But he had moved from the one point to where you found the bullets?

Mrs. DAVIS. Yes, sir.

Representative FORD. Yes.

Mrs. DAVIS. That is where they started looking for it.

Representative FORD. I meant the shells rather than the bullets.

Mrs. DAVIS. Yes.

Mr. BALL. Was he dressed the same in the lineup as he was when you saw him running across the lawn?

Mrs. DAVIS. All except he didn't have a black coat on when I saw him in the lineup.

Mr. BALL. Did he have a coat on when you saw him?

Mrs. DAVIS. Yes, sir.

Mr. BALL. What color coat?

Mrs. DAVIS. A dark coat.

Mr. BALL. Now, did you recognize him from his face or from his clothes when you saw him in the lineup?

Mrs. DAVIS. Well, I looked at his clothes and then his face from the side because I had seen him from a side view of him. I didn't see him fullface.

Mr. BALL. Now answer the question. Did you recognize him from seeing his face or from his clothes?

Mrs. DAVIS. From his face because that was all I was looking at.

Mr. BALL. I see. Now, when you heard the shots you were lying down, were you?

Mrs. DAVIS. Yes, sir.

Mr. BALL. Was anyone lying with you?

Mrs. DAVIS. Virginia was laying on the couch.

Mr. BALL. In the same room with you?

Mrs. DAVIS. Yes, sir.

Mr. BALL. Did she go to the door with you when you went to the door?

Mrs. DAVIS. She went right behind me.

Mr. BALL. I have a jacket, I would like to show you, which is Commission Exhibit No. 162. Does .this look anything like the jacket that the man had on that was going across your lawn?

Mrs. DAVIS. No, sir.

Mr. BALL. How is it different?

Mrs. DAVIS. Well, it was dark and to me it looked like it was maybe a wool fabric, it looked sort of rough. Like more of a sporting jacket.

Mr. BALL. I show you a shirt which is Commission Exhibit No. 150. Was that—does that shirt look anything like something he had on, that the man had on who went across your lawn?

Mrs. DAVIS. I thought that the shirt he had on was lighter than that.

Mr. BALL. I have no further questions. Where was Mrs. Markham when you first saw her?

Mrs. DAVIS. She was standing right here on this corner.

Mr. BALL. That picture?

Mrs. DAVIS. Yes, sir.

Mr. BALL. That picture that you refer to is photo number 3, Commission Exhibit 524.

It is as shown on the corner here, as the woman who is shown in the corner?

Mrs. Davis. That was her position.

Representative Ford. Do you wear glasses, Mrs. Davis?

Mrs. Davis. No, sir.

Representative Ford. Have you had your eyes examined recently?

Mrs. Davis. I believe it was in October when I applied for some driver's license.

Representative Ford. In October of 1963?

Mrs. Davis. Yes.

Representative Ford. You applied for a driver's license?

Mrs. Davis. I believe it was the first—some time in October, I believe.

Representative Ford. When you applied for a driver's license in Texas you have to take an examination?

Mrs. Davis. Yes, sir.

Representative Ford. And you did take one?

Mrs. Davis. Yes, sir.

Representative Ford. Did they recommend that you wear glasses?

Mrs. Davis. No, sir. He said my eyes are all right.

Representative Ford. He said your eyes were all right?

Mr. Dulles. Have you had any problems with the law at any time?

Mrs. Davis. No, sir.

Mr. Dulles. Except for traffic violations?

Mrs. Davis. No.

Mr. Dulles. Thank you. What is your husband's occupation?

Mrs. Davis. He is a roofer.

Mr. Dulles. What?

Mrs. Davis. Puts shingles and roofs on houses.

Mr. Dulles. Oh, yes, surely.

Mr. Ball. Mrs. Davis, before you went down to look at the man at the police station at 8 o'clock that night, had you seen television pictures of the man on television that he had been arrested?

Mrs. Davis. As far as I can remember I don't remember seeing it because I was out in the yard all the time that was going on, and I don't believe the TV was on.

Mr. Ball. Before you saw the man in the lineup were you shown a picture of any man by a police officer?

Mrs. Davis. No, sir.

Mr. Ball. Did you read a newspaper and see any pictures in a newspaper, picture of a man in the newspaper, before you went down there?

Mrs. Davis. I don't really know. I couldn't be quite sure. I can't remember whether I did or not.

Mr. Ball. Do you take an evening or a morning paper?

Mrs. Davis. We take an afternoon paper, we took an afternoon paper then.

Mr. Ball. Do you recall whether or not you did see a picture in the paper of the man?

Mrs. Davis. I don't remember. I don't even remember whether I read it or not. There was so much excitement.

Mr. Ball. When the man ran over the lawn, can you give me an estimate of how far away he was from you?

Mrs. Davis. I can't.

Mr. Ball. Make a judgment about it as to this room. Is it as far away from you to me?

Mrs. Davis. It was about as far as here to the corner of the room out there, or just a little bit more, the far corner.

Representative Ford. Just a little less, did you say?

Mrs. Davis. About like that.

Mr. Belin. About seven or eight steps?

Mr. Ball. About 20, 25 feet, is that right?

Mrs. Davis. I believe so.

Mr. Ball. There is an affidavit that has been filed with us, a statement you made to the Secret Service men on the first of December 1963. And in that affidavit, it says, after describing that "The man was on the sidewalk directly in front of me and shaking shells from a pistol into his hand as he walked,"—this says here, "The man was walking in a normal direction and walked across the corner of my property towards Patton Street."

Did you ever tell anyone that you saw the man walking in a normal direction?

Mrs. DAVIS. No; I showed them where it was at, and they done that.

Mr. BALL. I see. He was walking—what direction?

Mrs. DAVIS. I didn't know. And so they figured that out.

Mr. BALL. He was walking towards what street?

Mrs. DAVIS. He was going down Patton.

Mr. BALL. Towards what street?

Mrs. DAVIS. Jefferson. And so they figured it out for me.

Mr. BALL. However—when—did you see the man after he went around the corner of your house?

Mrs. DAVIS. No, sir.

Representative FORD. Did you see the taxicab parked on the corner?

Mrs. DAVIS. Yes, sir.

Mr. BALL. Let's go back to that afternoon, and you give your best memory of what the man looked like. Don't think of what anybody has told you or what has happened in between. Try to remember the vision you had of that man—the color of his hair, the size of his build and so forth.

Mrs. DAVIS. You mean weight and like that?

Mr. BALL. He was white, wasn't he?

Mrs. DAVIS. Yes, sir.

Mr. BALL. Light complexioned, or dark?

Mrs. DAVIS. He was more light complected than he would have been dark.

Mr. BALL. Color of his hair?

Mrs. DAVIS. It was either dark brown or black. It was just dark hair.

Mr. BALL. And the color of his clothes?

Mrs. DAVIS. Well, I said he had on—he looked to me that he had on dark trousers, and it looked like a light colored shirt, with a dark coat over it.

Mr. BALL. About what age would you say the man was?

Mrs. DAVIS. I am not very good on that. I don't know. I would say he was about 23, 24.

Mr. BALL. And what about his weight and height?

Mrs. DAVIS. I——

Mr. BALL. You have to be general, I know that.

Mr. DULLES. Just your best recollection. If you haven't any, just tell us.

Mrs. DAVIS. I just don't know.

Mr. BALL. Was he fat or slender?

Mrs. DAVIS. He was slender built, and not very heavy.

Mr. BALL. Was he a tall man, or a real short man, or average?

Mrs. DAVIS. Oh, he wasn't especially tall. I would say he was about medium height or a little taller. I mean he wasn't extra tall.

Mr. BALL. Now, did you have some difficulty in identifying this No. 2 man in the showup when you saw him?

Mrs. DAVIS. Well, they made us look at him a long time before they let us say anything.

Mr. BALL. What about you? I am not talking about what you told them. What was your reaction when you saw this man?

Mrs. DAVIS. Well, I was pretty sure it was the same man I saw. When they made him turn sideways, I was positive that was the one I seen.

Mr. BALL. I have no further questions.

Mr. BELIN. Thank you, Mrs. Davis.

Mr. DULLES. Did your sister-in-law go with you to the lineup?

Mrs. DAVIS. Yes, sir.

Mr. DULLES. Did she make an identification?

Mrs. DAVIS. Yes, sir.

Mr. DULLES. At the same time as you did?

Mrs. DAVIS. Yes, sir.

Mr. DULLES. Did you see her identification?

Mrs. DAVIS. We didn't discuss it.

Mr. DULLES. I mean, but after she had made it, did you see what identification she had made?

Mrs. DAVIS. Do you mean—I don't understand what you mean.

Mr. DULLES. Well, let me start over again.

Did you identify the man in the lineup before your sister-in-law?

Mrs. DAVIS. Yes, sir.

Mr. DULLES. Before your sister-in-law?

Mrs. DAVIS. Yes, sir; I was the first one.

Mr. DULLES. All right.

Did your sister-in-law, to your knowledge, make the same identification?

Mrs. DAVIS. Yes, sir; she was there with me at the same time.

Mr. DULLES. She was standing with you. And she saw the identification you had made?

Mrs. DAVIS. All I done was just lean over and tell the man.

Mr. DULLES. How did you make your identification? By pointing or holding up your fingers.

Mrs. DAVIS. The man that was sitting next to me just asked me which one I thought it was, and I leaned over and told him. And then he leaned around me and asked her.

Mr. DULLES. He did what?

Mrs. DAVIS. He leaned around—he was behind me, and asked her.

Mr. DULLES. I see.

Mrs. DAVIS. I sort of set up where he could talk to her.

Mr. DULLES. And did you identify the man by number or by pointing?

Mrs. DAVIS. By number.

Mr. DULLES. Do you remember what number it was?

Mrs. DAVIS. It was number 2. From the left.

Mr. DULLES. Have you any questions?

Representative FORD. Did you whisper this information to the man behind you?

Mrs. DAVIS. Well, we were all sitting in a line, and he was sitting on this side of me. He just leaned over and asked me which one I thought it was.

Representative FORD. He was sitting on your right?

Mrs. DAVIS. Yes.

Representative FORD. And you turned to your right and told him?

Mrs. DAVIS. Yes, sir.

Representative FORD. And your sister-in-law was sitting on your left?

Mrs. DAVIS. On the other side, yes.

Representative FORD. When you spoke to him, you were speaking away from her?

Mrs. DAVIS. Yes, sir.

Representative FORD. Did you speak in a loud voice or a whisper?

Mrs. DAVIS. No, sir; very quietly.

Representative FORD. You think your sister-in-law heard you say the number?

Mrs. DAVIS. I don't know.

Mr. DULLES. Mr. Attorney General, have you any questions?

Mr. CARR. Thank you, I do not.

Mr. MURRAY. I have no questions.

Mr. BELIN. I think the record should show that although the witness did not receive the letter notifying her of our request for an appearance, we mailed it to her last known address at 400 East 10th Street, and the letter came back here. But the notice was mailed to the witness. It was just that it was not forwarded to where she now lives in Athens.

Mr. DULLES. You had moved from this house where these incidents took place?

Mrs. DAVIS. Yes.

Mr. DULLES. Off the record.

(Discussion off the record.)

Mr. DULLES. You are excused. Thank you very much.

Mr. BALL. Our next witness is Mr. Ted Callaway.

Mr. DULLES. Mr. Callaway, in the absence of the Chief Justice, I am presiding over the meeting of the Commission this morning.

Would you kindly raise your right hand?

Do you swear that the testimony that you will give to this Commission is the truth, the whole truth, so help you God?

Mr. CALLAWAY. Yes, sir.

Mr. DULLES. And nothing but the truth?

Mr. CALLAWAY. That is correct.

Mr. DULLES. You may be seated.

Mr. Ball, will you proceed?

Mr. BALL. Mr. Callaway, we are investigating the assassination of President Kennedy. We are going to ask you questions with regard to what you saw on the day of November 22, 1963, in Dallas.

Where do you live?

Mr. CALLAWAY. 805 West Eighth.

Mr. BALL. What is your business?

Mr. CALLAWAY. Car salesman.

Mr. BALL. We would like to know something about your background. We ask most of the witnesses these questions.

Where were you born?

Mr. CALLAWAY. In Dallas.

Mr. BALL. Were you raised in Dallas?

Mr. CALLAWAY. Yes, sir.

Mr. BALL. Went to school in Dallas?

Mr. CALLAWAY. Yes, sir.

Mr. BALL. How old are you?

Mr. CALLAWAY. Forty.

Mr. BALL. How far through school did you go?

Mr. CALLAWAY. Two years of college.

Mr. BALL. What college?

Mr. CALLAWAY. S.M.U.

Mr. BALL. And what did you do after you got out of college?

Mr. CALLAWAY. I worked part time as a clothing salesman downtown, and then my uncle was a painter, and I worked for him for awhile. Then I went back in the Marines for 3 years.

And I have been selling cars since '56.

Mr. BALL. You are a used-car salesman?

Mr. CALLAWAY. Yes.

Mr. BALL. Where were you employed—have you had any trouble with the police of any sort?

Mr. CALLAWAY. No.

Mr. BALL. Any difficulty at all in your life?

Mr. CALLAWAY. No, sir; never.

Mr. BALL. You were discharged from the Marines, were you?

Mr. CALLAWAY. Yes, sir.

Mr. BALL. What year?

Mr. CALLAWAY. 1954.

Mr. BALL. Received an honorable discharge from the service?

Mr. CALLAWAY. Yes, sir.

Mr. BALL. On November 22, 1963, where were you working?

Mr. CALLAWAY. At Harris Bros., auto sales.

Mr. BALL. And what was your job?

Mr. CALLAWAY. I was used-car manager.

Mr. BALL. Now, Harris Bros. Auto Sales is located where?

Mr. CALLAWAY. 501 East Jefferson.

Mr. BALL. Where is that from 10th and Patton?

Mr. CALLAWAY. Just one block.

Mr. BALL. One block south?

Mr. CALLAWAY. Yes, sir.

Mr. BALL. What corner?

Mr. CALLAWAY. It would be on the northeast corner.

Mr. BALL. So that we can orient ourselves from 10th and Patton—I have marked this diagram as Commission Exhibit 537.

(The document referred to was marked Commission Exhibit No. 537 for identification.)

Mr. BALL. Now, Mr. Callaway, will you, on 537, take this and mark the location of the used car lot with an "X"?

Mr. CALLAWAY. All right, sir.

Right here.

Mr. BALL. The "X" marks the position of the used-car lot?

Mr. CALLAWAY. Yes, sir.

Mr. BALL. Now, Mr. Callaway, around 1:15 or so of that day, where were you?

Mr. CALLAWAY. I was standing on the front porch of our office.

Mr. BALL. That is at 401 East Jefferson?

Mr. CALLAWAY. No; 501.

Mr. BALL. I will show you a picture which we will mark as 538.

(The document referred to was marked Commission Exhibit No. 538 for identification.)

Mr. BALL. Does this show a picture of the office?

Mr. CALLAWAY. Yes, sir. That is it.

Mr. BALL. Now, you went down there one day last week to have some pictures taken.

Mr. CALLAWAY. Yes, sir.

Mr. BALL. Did you attempt to stand in the same place you were at the time?

Mr. CALLAWAY. Yes, sir.

Mr. BALL. Where you were standing November 22d around 1 o'clock or so?

Mr. CALLAWAY. Yes, sir.

Mr. BALL. What did you hear at that time?

Mr. CALLAWAY. I heard what sounded to me like five pistol shots.

Mr. BALL. Five pistol shots?

Mr. CALLAWAY. Five shots, yes, sir.

Mr. BALL. From the sound, could you tell the source of the sound?

Mr. CALLAWAY. Yes, sir, I could tell it was back of the lot over toward 10th Street.

Mr. BALL. And what did you do?

Mr. CALLAWAY. I ran out to the sidewalk on Patton.

Mr. BALL. And what did you see?

Mr. CALLAWAY. Well, I could see—I was still—before I got to the sidewalk, I could see this taxicab parked down on Patton. I saw the cabdriver beside his cab, and saw a man cutting from one side of the street to the other. That would be the east side of Patton and over to the west side of Patton. And he was running. And he had a gun in his hand, his right hand.

Mr. BALL. And how was he holding the gun?

Mr. CALLAWAY. We used to say in the Marine Corps in a raised pistol position.

Mr. BALL. That would be with the muzzle pointed upward, and with the arm bent at the elbow, is that right?

Mr. CALLAWAY. Yes, sir; just like this.

Mr. BALL. I have a picture here, 539.

(The document referred to was marked Commission Exhibit No. 539 for identification.)

Mr. BALL. When this picture was taken, did you try to represent the place you were standing when you saw the man?

Mr. CALLAWAY. Yes, sir.

Mr. BALL. How did you get there?

Mr. CALLAWAY. I ran.

Mr. BALL. You ran from the place on the porch, is that right?

Mr. CALLAWAY. That is right. From right here, to there.

Mr. BALL. Now, you were at the place shown on 538, on the porch?

Mr. CALLAWAY. Yes.

Mr. BALL. And when you heard the shots, what did you do?

Mr. CALLAWAY. I just hurried—I don't know whether I really ran or not. But I hurried off the side of this porch and came to this position.

Mr. BALL. All right. When you came to this position, you say you saw a taxicab?

Mr. DULLES. Where is this position on this chart? Right here?

Mr. CALLAWAY. It would be about right here. I come off the porch here.

Mr. DULLES. Point 29?

Mr. CALLAWAY. Yes.

Mr. BALL. You saw a taxicab where, on photo 29?

Mr. CALLAWAY. Right here.

Mr. BALL. Let's mark an arrow there, about where you saw the taxicab. The arrow marks the position of the taxicab. You saw a man?

Mr. CALLAWAY. Yes, sir.

Mr. BALL. He was crossing Patton?

Mr. CALLAWAY. Yes, sir.

Mr. BALL. Was that to the south or the north of the taxicab? Closer to you than the taxicab?

Mr. CALLAWAY. Yes.

Mr. BALL. Was he running or walking?

Mr. CALLAWAY. He was running.

Mr. BALL. And where were you when you noticed he had the gun? Or where was he when you noticed he had the gun?

Mr. CALLAWAY. When I first saw the gun, he had already crossed from here to here and was coming up this sidewalk.

Mr. BALL. Coming up the sidewalk on which side of Patton?

Mr. CALLAWAY. West side of Patton.

Mr. BALL. And did he continue to come?

Mr. CALLAWAY. Yes.

Mr. BALL. And did you say anything to him?

Mr. CALLAWAY. Yes.

Mr. BALL. What did you say?

Mr. CALLAWAY. I hollered "Hey, man, what the hell is going on?" When he was right along here.

Mr. BALL. Make a mark there where he was when you yelled, "What the hell is going on?" "X" marks the place where the man with the gun was when you yelled at him?

Mr. CALLAWAY. That is right.

Mr. DULLES. Would you mark it on this chart, too—Exhibit 537?

Mr. CALLAWAY. Right along here—about 27, I guess. That would be it. You see, here is where I was, sir. And then he was right there when I hollered at him.

Mr. DULLES. I don't get this. There is an alleyway there, apparently.

Mr. CALLAWAY. That is right.

Mr. DULLES. But here is where the squad car was.

Mr. CALLAWAY. That is right.

Mr. DULLES. And here is where the cab was.

Mr. CALLAWAY. That is right.

Mr. DULLES. He had come all the way down?

Mr. CALLAWAY. He had come from there through this yard and cut behind this taxicab, over to this side of the street.

Mr. DULLES. So he was there, then?

Mr. CALLAWAY. No, sir. I didn't holler at him until he came up to here. He was running up this sidewalk.

Mr. DULLES. He was going south on Patton?

Mr. CALLAWAY. On the west side of the street.

Representative FORD. You saw him run from about the taxicab——

Mr. CALLAWAY. Across the street, up this sidewalk.

Mr. DULLES. About how far is that? Fifty feet or more?

Mr. CALLAWAY. Oh, it is more than that. From here down to there, I think is about 300 feet.

Mr. BALL. Mark on this diagram, which is 537, where the man was, and the course he took.

Mr. CALLAWAY. Well, now, when I first saw him he was right here. Then he came across here, down this way.

Mr. BALL. Down to the point where you spoke to him?

Mr. CALLAWAY. That is right.

Mr. BALL. What did he do when you hollered at him?

Mr. CALLAWAY. He slowed his pace, almost halted for a minute. And he said something to me, which I could not understand. And then kind of shrugged his shoulders, and kept on going.

Mr. BALL. Show the course he took on the map, if you will.

Mr. CALLAWAY. All right.

Right on down here, and he cut through this front yard.

Mr. BALL. And where was he when you last saw him?

Mr. CALLAWAY. Right here.

Mr. BALL. Right at that point?

Mr. CALLAWAY. Yes.

Mr. BALL. Now, the first "X" marks the position of the parking lot—we will mark that 1. The place of the taxicab we will mark as 2. The place where the man was with the gun when you yelled at him, we will mark that as 3. The last place you saw the man, that we will mark 4.

Mr. CALLAWAY. Yes, sir.

Mr. BALL. All right. Now——

Mr. DULLES. May I ask what course he was taking when you last saw him?

Mr. CALLAWAY. He was going west on Jefferson Street.

Mr. DULLES. West on Jefferson Street?

Mr. CALLAWAY. Yes, sir.

Mr. BALL. What did you do?

Mr. CALLAWAY. I hollered to this guy behind—B. D. Searcy.

Mr. BALL. What did you say to Mr. Searcy?

Mr. CALLAWAY. I told him to keep an eye on that guy, I says, "Keep an eye on that guy, follow him. I am going to go down there and see what is going on." So I ran, a good hard run, from here down around the corner.

Mr. BALL. 10th and Patton?

Mr. CALLAWAY. Yes.

Mr. BALL. When you got there what did you see?

Mr. CALLAWAY. I saw a squad car, and by that time there was four or five people that had gathered, a couple of cars had stopped. Then I saw—I went on up to the squad car and saw the police officer lying in the street. I see he had been shot in the head. So the first thing I did, I ran over to the squad car. I didn't know whether anybody reported it or not. So I got on the police radio and called them, and told them a man had been shot, told them the location, I thought the officer was dead. They said we know about it, stay off the air, so I went back.

By this time an ambulance was coming. The officer was laying on his left side, his pistol was underneath him. I kind of rolled him over and took his gun out from under him. The people wonder whether he ever got his pistol out of his holster. He did.

Mr. BALL. The pistol was out of the holster?

Mr. CALLAWAY. Yes, sir; out of the holster, and it was unsnapped. It was on his right side. He was laying with the gun under him.

Mr. BALL. What did you do?

Mr. CALLAWAY. I picked the gun up and laid it on the hood of the squad car, and then someone put it in the front seat of the squad car. Then after I helped load Officer Tippit in the ambulance, I got the gun out of the car and told this cabdriver, I said, "You saw the guy didn't you?" He said, yes.

I said, "If he is going up Jefferson, he can't be very far. Let's see if we can find him." So I went with Scoggins in the taxicab, went up to 10th, Crawford, from Crawford up to Jefferson, and down Jefferson to Beckley. And we turned on Beckley. If we had kept going up Jefferson, we probably—there is a good chance we would have seen him, because he was headed right towards the Texas Theatre. But then we circled around several blocks, and ended up coming back to where it happened.

Mr. BALL. And the ambulance—had the ambulance been there by that time?

Mr. CALLAWAY. Oh, yes; the ambulance already left before I ever left with the cabdriver.

Mr. BALL. Did you go down to the police station later?

Mr. CALLAWAY. That evening.

Mr. BALL. What time?

Mr. CALLAWAY. I think it was around 6:30 or 7 o'clock. I remember it was after dark.

Mr. BALL. Did you go down there alone?

Mr. CALLAWAY. No. I went with Sam Guinyard, a colored porter of ours. He saw him, also.

(At this point, Representative Ford withdrew from the hearing room.)

Mr. CALLAWAY. We drove down. Officer—Detective Jim Leavelle met us, and took us into this room where they showed us the lineup.

Mr. BALL. Now, before you went down there, had you seen any newspaper accounts of this incident?

Mr. CALLAWAY. No, sir; I had been out there on the lot. I hadn't seen a newspaper, hadn't even heard a radio, really.

Mr. BALL. Had you seen any television?

Mr. CALLAWAY. No, sir.

Mr. BALL. Had you seen a picture of a man?

Mr. CALLAWAY. No.

Mr. BALL. The officer show you any pictures?

Mr. CALLAWAY. No, sir.

Mr. BALL. You went into a police lineup, in a room where they had a lineup of men?

Mr. CALLAWAY. Yes.

Mr. BALL. How many?

Mr. CALLAWAY. Four.

Mr. BALL. And were they all the same size, or different sizes?

Mr. CALLAWAY. They were about the same build, but the man that I identified was the shortest one of the bunch.

Mr. BALL. Were they anywhere near the same age?

Mr. CALLAWAY. They were about the same age, yes, sir. They looked— you know.

Mr. BALL. And you say you identified a man. How did you do that?

Mr. CALLAWAY. Well——

Mr. BALL. Tell us what happened.

Mr. CALLAWAY. We first went into the room. There was Jim Leavelle, the detective, Sam Guinyard, and then this busdriver and myself. We waited down there for probably 20 or 30 minutes. And Jim told us, "When I show you these guys, be sure, take your time, see if you can make a positive identification."

Mr. BALL. Had you known him before?

Mr. CALLAWAY. No. And he said, "We want to be sure, we want to try to wrap him up real tight on killing this officer. We think he is the same one that shot the President. But if we can wrap him up tight on killing this officer, we have got him." So they brought four men in.

I stepped to the back of the room, so I could kind of see him from the same distance which I had seen him before. And when he came out, I knew him.

Mr. BALL. You mean he looked like the same man?

Mr. CALLAWAY. Yes.

Mr. BALL. About what distance was he away from you—the closest that he ever was to you?

Mr. CALLAWAY. About 56 feet.

Mr. BALL. You measured that, did you?

Mr. CALLAWAY. Yes, sir.

Mr. BALL. Last Saturday morning?

Mr. CALLAWAY. Yes, sir.

Mr. BALL. Measured it with a tape measure?

Mr. CALLAWAY. Yes, sir.

Mr. BALL. Did he have the same clothes on in the lineup—did the man have the same clothes?

Mr. CALLAWAY. He had the same trousers and shirt, but he didn't have his jacket on. He had ditched his jacket.

Mr. BALL. What kind—when you talked to the police officers before you saw this man, did you give them a description of the clothing he had on?

Mr. CALLAWAY. Yes, sir.

Mr. BALL. What did you tell them you saw?

Mr. CALLAWAY. I told them he had some dark trousers and a light tannish gray windbreaker jacket, and I told him that he was fair complexion, dark hair.

Mr. BALL. Tell them the size?

Mr. CALLAWAY. Yes; I told them—I think I told them about 5'10''

Mr. DULLES. Did you see his front face at any time, or did you only have a side view of him?

Mr. CALLAWAY. He looked right at me, sir. When I called to him, he looked right at me.

Mr. DULLES. You saw front face?

Mr. CALLAWAY. Yes.

Mr. BALL. I have a jacket here—Commission's Exhibit No. 162. Does this look anything like the jacket that the man had on that you saw across the street with a gun?

Mr. GALLAWAY. Yes; it sure does. Yes, that is the same type jacket. Actually, I thought it had a little more tan to it.

Mr. BALL. Same type?

Mr. CALLAWAY. Yes.

Mr. BALL. I show you a shirt, 150. Does it look anything like the shirt he had on under the jacket?

Mr. CALLAWAY. Sir, when I saw him he didn't have—I couldn't see this shirt. I saw—he had it open. That shirt was open, and I could see his white T-shirt underneath.

Mr. BALL. He had a white T-shirt underneath?

Mr. CALLAWAY. Yes. That is the shirt he had on in the lineup that night.

Mr. BALL. Was he fat or thin?

Mr. CALLAWAY. He was just——

Mr. BALL. I mean the man you saw across the street?

Mr. CALLAWAY. Just a nice athletic type size boy, I mean. Neither fat nor thin.

Mr. BALL. What did you estimate his weight when you talked to the officer before the lineup?

Mr. CALLAWAY. I told him it looked to me like around 160 pounds.

Mr. DULLES. How fast was he going when you hailed him?

Mr. CALLAWAY. Just a good steady trot, not real fast.

Mr. DULLES. He was not walking and not running—it was a trot?

Mr. CALLAWAY. A trot; yes, sir.

Mr. DULLES. He stopped?

Mr. CALLAWAY. Almost. He slowed down, like a guy is trotting along, and he almost stopped, and kept going.

Mr. DULLES. And he looked at you?

Mr. CALLAWAY. Yes, sir.

Mr. DULLES. Did he say anything?

Mr. CALLAWAY. Yes, sir; he said something, but I could not understand it.

Mr. DULLES. You could not understand what he said?

Mr. CALLAWAY. That is right; yes, sir.

Mr. DULLES. And then did he resume his progress at a trot?

Mr. CALLAWAY. Yes, sir.

Mr. BALL. Did you ever ask Searcy if he followed him?

Mr. CALLAWAY. He didn't follow him.

He said something about "Follow him, hell. That man will kill you. He has a gun."

So instead of following him, he went back over and got behind the office building.

Mr. DULLES. Did he see him at any time?

Mr. CALLAWAY. Yes; he saw him the same time I did; yes, sir. I never could figure out why he didn't just follow that man. You could follow 50 yards behind him and keep a guy in sight. Chances are you wouldn't get killed 50 yards away.

Mr. DULLES. Had you had previous military service?

Mr. CALLAWAY. Yes, sir; I was in the Marine Corps 6 years, World War II, and during Korea.

Mr. DULLES. Did you ever tangle with the law in any way?

Mr. CALLAWAY. No, sir.

Mr. DULLES. What years were you in the Marine Corps?

Mr. CALLAWAY. 1942 through '45, and then '51 through '54.

Mr. DULLES. Were you in Korea?

Mr. CALLAWAY. No, sir; I didn't go to Korea. I was at Camp Pendleton as a troop trainer.

Mr. DULLES. Off the record.

(Discussion off the record.)

Mr. DULLES. Back on the record.

Mr. BALL. I would like to offer to Exhibit 539, inclusive.

Mr. DULLES. Can you tell me what the numbers are?

Mr. BALL. 537, 538, and 539.

Mr. DULLES. Exhibits 537, 538, and 539 previously identified will now be admitted in evidence.

(The documents heretofore marked for identification as Commission Exhibits Nos. 537 through 539 were received in evidence.)

Mr. DULLES. Thank you very much. We appreciate your coming.

(Whereupon, at 12:40 p.m., the President's Commission recessed.)

Monday, March 30, 1964

TESTIMONY OF DR. CHARLES JAMES CARRICO AND DR. MALCOLM OLIVER PERRY

The President's Commission met at 9:10 a.m. on March 30, 1964, at 200 Maryland Avenue NE., Washington, D.C.

Present were Chief Justice Earl Warren, Chairman; Representative Hale Boggs, Representative Gerald R. Ford, John J. McCloy, and Allen W. Dulles, members.

Also present were Arlen Specter, assistant counsel; Charles Murray, observer; and Dean Robert G. Storey, special counsel to the attorney general of Texas.

TESTIMONY OF DR. CHARLES JAMES CARRICO

The CHAIRMAN. All right, Dr. Carrico, you know the reason why we are here, what we are investigating.

If you will raise your right hand, please, and be sworn, sir.

You solemnly swear the testimony you give before this Commission shall be the truth, the whole truth and nothing but the truth, so help you God?

Dr. CARRICO. I do.

The CHAIRMAN. Mr. Specter will conduct the examination.

Mr. SPECTER. Dr. Carrico, will you state your full name for the record please?

Dr. CARRICO. Charles James Carrico.

Mr. SPECTER. And what is your address, Dr. Carrico?

Dr. CARRICO. Home address?

Mr. SPECTER. Please.

Dr. CARRICO. It is 2605 Ridgwood in Irving.

Mr. SPECTER. What is your professional address?

Dr. CARRICO. Parkland Memorial Hospital in Dallas, Tex.

Mr. SPECTER. How old are you, sir?

Dr. CARRICO. 28.

Mr. SPECTER. Will you outline briefly your educational background?

Dr. CARRICO. I attended grade school and high school in Denton, Tex.; received a Bachelor of Science in Chemistry from North Texas State University in 1947; received my M.D. from the University of Texas Southwestern Medical School in 1961; served an internship at Parkland Memorial Hospital from 1961 to 1962; and then did a year of fellowship at the surgery department at Southwestern Medical School, followed by my surgery residency at Parkland Hospital.

Mr. SPECTER. Are you duly licensed to practice medicine in the State of Texas, Dr. Carrico?

Dr. CARRICO. Yes; I am.

Mr. SPECTER. Are you board certified at the present time or are you working toward the board certification in surgery?

Dr. CARRICO. I am engaged in surgery residency which will qualify me for board certification.

Mr. SPECTER. What experience have you had, if any, with gunshot wounds?

Dr. CARRICO. In the emergency room at Parkland, during my residence school and internship and residency, we have seen a fair number of gunshot wounds.

Mr. SPECTER. Could you approximate the number of gunshot wounds you have treated in the course of those duties?

Dr. CARRICO. In all probably 150, 200, something in that range.

Mr. SPECTER. What were your duties at Parkland Memorial Hospital on November 22, 1963?

Dr. CARRICO. At that time I was assigned to the elective surgery service, which is the general surgery service treating the usual surgical cases. I was in the emergency room evaluating some patient for admission.

Mr. SPECTER. What were you doing specifically in the neighborhood of 12:30 p.m. on that day?

Dr. CARRICO. At that time I had been called to the emergency room to evaluate a patient for admission to the hospital.

Mr. SPECTER. Were you notified that an emergency case involving President Kennedy was en route to the hospital?

Dr. CARRICO. Yes, sir.

Mr. SPECTER. What is your best estimate as to the time that you were notified that President Kennedy was en route to the hospital?

Dr. CARRICO. Shortly after 12:30 is the best I can do.

Mr. SPECTER. How long thereafter was it that he actually did arrive at Parkland, to the best of your recollection?

Dr. CARRICO. Within 2 minutes approximately.

Mr. SPECTER. And precisely where were you at Parkland when you first observed him?

Dr. CARRICO. When I first observed him I was in the emergency room, seeing—actually Governor Connally had been brought in first, as you know, Dr. Dulany and I had gone to care for Governor Connally and when the President was brought in I left Governor Connally and went to care for the President.

Mr. SPECTER. Will you describe briefly the physical layout of Parkland with respect to the point where emergency cases are brought up to the building and the general layout of the building into the emergency room.

Dr. CARRICO. The emergency entrance is at the back of the building. There is an ambulance ramp. Then immediately adjacent to the ambulance ramp are, of course, double doors, swinging doors and a corridor which is approximately 30 feet long and empties directly into the emergency room.

Then inside the emergency room are several areas, the surgical area consists of about eight booths for treating, examination and treatment of patients, and four large emergency operating rooms.

Two of these are specifically set aside for acutely ill, severely ill, patients and these are referred to as trauma rooms.

Mr. SPECTOR. And were these trauma rooms used in connection with the treatment of President Kennedy and Governor Connally?

Dr. CARRICO. Yes, sir.

Mr. SPECTER. What precisely was the point where you met at his arrival?

Dr. CARRICO. The President was being wheeled into trauma room one when I saw him.

Mr. SPECTER. Who else, if anyone, was present at that time?

Dr. CARRICO. At that time, Dr. Don Curtis, Martin White.

The CHAIRMAN. Was he a doctor, too?

Dr. CARRICO. Yes, sir; Miss Bowron.

Mr. SPECTER. Who is Miss Bowron?

Dr. CARRICO. She is one of the nurses on duty at the emergency room.

Mr. SPECTER. Who was the first doctor to actually see the President?

Dr. CARRICO. I was.

Mr. SPECTER. Now, what did you observe as to the condition of President Kennedy when you first saw him?

Dr. CARRICO. He was on an ambulance cart, emergency cart, rather. His color was blue white, ashen. He had slow agonal respiration, spasmodic respirations without any coordination. He was making no voluntary movements. His eyes were open, pupils were seen to be dilated and later were seen not to react to light. This was the initial impression.

Mr. SPECTER. What was the status of his pulse at the time of arrival?

Dr. CARRICO. He had no palpable pulse.

Mr. SPECTER. And was he making any movements at the time of arrival?

Dr. CARRICO. No voluntary movements, only the spasmodic respirations.

Mr. SPECTER. Was any heartbeat noted at his arrival?

Dr. CARRICO. After these initial observations we opened his shirt, coat, listened very briefly to his chest, heard a few sounds which we felt to be heartbeats and then proceeded with the remainder of the examination.

Mr. SPECTER. In your opinion was President Kennedy alive or dead on his arrival at Parkland.

Dr. CARRICO. From a medical standpoint I suppose he was still alive in that he did still have a heartbeat?

Mr. SPECTER. What action, if any, was taken with respect to the removal of President Kennedy's clothing?

Dr. CARRICO. As I said after I had opened his shirt and coat, I proceeded with the examination and the nurses removed his clothing as is the usual procedure.

Mr. SPECTER. Was President Kennedy wearing a back brace?

Dr. CARRICO. Yes; he was.

Mr. SPECTER. Would you describe as precisely as you can that back brace?

Dr. CARRICO. As I recall, this was a white cotton or some sort of fiber standard brace with stays and corset, in a corset-type arrangement and buckles.

Mr. SPECTER. How far up on his body did it come?

Dr. CARRICO. Just below his umbilicus, as I recall.

Mr. SPECTER. How far down on his body did it go?

Dr. CARRICO. I did not examine below his belt at that time.

Mr. SPECTER. Did you at any time examine below his belt?

Dr. CARRICO. I did not; no, sir.

Mr. SPECTER. Do you know if anyone else did?

Dr. CARRICO. Not in a formal manner.

Mr. SPECTER. What action did you take by way of treating President Kennedy on his arrival?

Dr. CARRICO. After what we have described we completed an initial emergency examination, which consisted of, as we have already said, his color, his pulse, we felt his back, determined there were no large wounds which would be an immediate threat to life there. Looked very briefly at the head wound and then because of his inadequate respirations inserted an endotracheal tube to attempt to support these respirations.

Mr. SPECTER. Specifically what did you do with respect to the back, Dr. Carrico?

Dr. CARRICO. This is a routine examination of critically ill patients where you haven't got time to examine him fully. I just placed my hands just above the belt, but in this case just above the brace, and ran my hands up his back.

Mr. SPETER. To what point on his body?

Dr. CARRICO. All the way up to his neck very briefly.

Mr. SPECTER. What did you feel by that?

359

Dr. CARRICO. I felt nothing other than the blood and debris. There was no large wound there.

Mr. SPECTER. What source did you attribute the blood to at that time?

Dr. CARRICO. As it could have come from the head wound, and it certainly could have been a back wound, but there was no way to tell whether this blood would have come from a back wound and not from his head.

Mr. SPECTER. What action did you next take then?

Dr. CARRICO. At that time the endotracheal tube was inserted, using a curved laryngoscopic blade, inserting an endotracheal tube, it was seen there were some contusions, hematoma to the right of the larynx, with a minimal deviation of the larynx to the left, and ragged tissue below indicating tracheal injury.

The tube was inserted past this injury, and the cuff inflater was connected to a Bennett machine which is a respiratory assistor using positive pressure.

Mr. SPECTER. Will you describe briefly what you mean in lay terms by a cuffed endotracheal tube?

Dr. CARRICO. This is a plastic tube which is inserted into the trachea, into the windpipe, to allow an adequate airway, adequate breathing. The cuff is a small latex cuff which should prevent leakage of air around the tube, thus insuring an adequate airway.

Mr. SPECTER. Will you continue, then, to describe what efforts you made to revive the President.

Dr. CARRICO. After the endotracheal tube was inserted and connected, I listened briefly to his chest, respirations were better but still inadequate.

Dr. Perry arrived, and because of the inadequate respirations the presence of a tracheal injury, advised that the chest tube was to be inserted, this was done by some of the other physicians in the room.

At the same time we had been getting the airway inserted Dr. Curtis and Dr. White were doing a cutdown, venous section using polyethylene catheters through which fluid, medicine and blood could be administered.

Mr. SPECTER. Will you describe in lay language what you mean by a cutdown in relationship to what they did in this case?

Dr. CARRICO. This was a small incision over his ankle and a tube was inserted into one of his veins through which blood could be given, fluid.

Mr. SPECTER. Is the general purpose of that to maintain a circulatory system?

Dr. CARRICO. Right.

Mr. SPECTER. In wounded parties?

Dr. CARRICO. Yes.

(At this point, Representative Ford entered the hearing room.)

Mr. SPECTER. Would you now proceed again to describe what else was done for the President in an effort to save his life?

Dr. CARRICO. Sure. Dr. Perry then took over supervision and treatment, and the chest tubes were inserted, another cutdown was done by Dr. Jones on the President's arm.

Fluid, as I said, was given, blood was given, hydrocortisone was given. Dr. Clark, the chief neurosurgeon, Dr. Bashour, cardiologist, was there or arrived, and a cardiac monitor was attached and although I never saw any electro-activity, Dr. Clark said there was some electrical activity of the heart which means he was still trying to——

Mr. SPECTER. What is Dr. Clark's position in the hospital?

Dr. CARRICO. He is chief of the neurosurgery department and professor of the neurosurgery.

Mr. SPECTER. Dr. Carrico, will you continue to tell us then what treatment you rendered the President?

Dr. CARRICO. When this electrocardiac activity ceased, close cardiac massage was begun. Using this, and fluids and airway we were able to maintain fairly good color, apparently fairly good peripheral circulation as monitored by carotid and radial pulses for a period of time. These efforts were abandoned when it was determined by Dr. Clark that there was no continued cardiac response. There was no cerebral response, that is the pupils remained dilated and fixed; there was evidence of anoxia.

Mr. SPECTER. Will you describe in lay language what anoxia means?

Dr. CARRICO. No oxygen.

Mr. SPECTER. Was cardiac massage applied in this situation?

Dr. CARRICO. Yes, sir; it was, excellent cardiac massage.

Mr. SPECTER. Were bloods administered to the President?

Dr. CARRICO. Yes, sir.

(At this point, Mr. Dulles entered the hearing room.)

Mr. SPECTER. Dr. Carrico, was any action taken with respect to the adrenalin insufficiency of President Kennedy?

Dr. CARRICO. Yes, sir; he was given 300 milligrams of hydrocortisone which is an adrenal hormone.

Mr. SPECTER. And what was the reason for the administration of that drug?

Dr. CARRICO. It was recalled that the President had been said to have adrenal insufficiency.

Mr. SPECTER. Now, at what time was the death of the President pronounced, Doctor?

Dr. CARRICO. At 1 o'clock.

Mr. SPECTER. Who pronounced the death of the President?

Dr. CARRICO. Dr. Clark, I believe.

Mr. SPECTER. Was that a precise time fixed or a general time fixed for the point of death?

Dr. CARRICO. This was a general time, sir.

Mr. SPECTER. What, in your opinion, was the cause of death?

Dr. CARRICO. The head wound, the head injury.

Mr. SPECTER. Will you describe as specifically as you can the head wound which you have already mentioned briefly?

Dr. CARRICO. Sure.

This was a 5- by 71-cm defect in the posterior skull, the occipital region. There was an absence of the calvarium or skull in this area, with shredded tissue, brain tissue present and initially considerable slow oozing. Then after we established some circulation there was more profuse bleeding from this wound.

Mr. SPECTER. Was any other wound observed on the head in addition to this large opening where the skull was absent?

Dr. CARRICO. No other wound on the head.

Mr. SPECTER. Did you have any opportunity specifically to look for a small wound which was below the large opening of the skull on the right side of the head?

Dr. CARRICO. No, sir; at least initially there was no time to examine the patient completely for all small wounds. As we said before, this was an acutely ill patient and all we had time to do was to determine what things were life-threatening right then and attempt to resuscitate him and after which a more complete examination would be carried out and we didn't have time to examine for other wounds.

Mr. SPECTER. Was such a more complete examination ever carried out by the doctors in Parkland?

Dr. CARRICO. No, sir; not in my presence.

Mr. SPECTER. Why not?

Dr. CARRICO. As we said initially this was an acute emergency situation and there was not time initially and when the cardiac massage was done this prevented any further examination during this time this was being done. After the President was pronounced dead his wife was there, he was the President, and we felt certainly that complete examination would be carried out and no one had the heart, I believe, to examine him then.

Mr. SPECTER. Will you describe, as specifically as you can then, the neck wounds which you have heretofore mentioned briefly?

Dr. CARRICO. There was a small wound, 5- to 8-mm. in size, located in the lower third of the neck, below the thyroid cartilage, the Adams apple.

Mr. DULLES. Will you show us about where it was?

Dr. CARRICO. Just about where your tie would be.

Mr. DULLES. Where did it enter?

Dr. CARRICO. It entered?

Mr. DULLES. Yes.

Dr. CARRICO. At the time we did not know——

361

Mr. DULLES. I see.

Dr. CARRICO. The entrance. All we knew this was a small wound here.

Mr. DULLES. I see. And you put your hand right above where your tie is?

Dr. CARRICO. Yes, sir; just where the tie——

Mr. DULLES. A little bit to the left.

Dr. CARRICO. To the right.

Mr. DULLES. Yes; to the right.

Dr. CARRICO. Yes. And this wound was fairly round, had no jagged edges, no evidence of powder burns, and so forth.

Representative FORD. No evidence of powder burns?

Dr. CARRICO. So far as I know.

Representative FORD. In the front?

Dr. CARRICO. Yes.

Mr. SPECTER. Have you now described that wound as specifically as you can based upon your observations at the time?

Dr. CARRICO. I believe so.

Mr. SPECTER. And your recollection at the time of those observations?

Dr. CARRICO. Yes; an even round wound.,

Mr. DULLES. You felt this wound in the neck was not a fatal wound?

Dr. CARRICO. That is right.

Mr. SPECTER. That is, absent the head wound, would the President have survived the wound which was present on his neck?

Dr. CARRICO. I think very likely he would have.

Mr. SPECTER. Based on your observations on the neck wound alone did you have a sufficient basis to form an opinion as to whether it was an entrance or an exit wound?

Dr. CARRICO. No, sir; we did not. Not having completely evaluated all the wounds, traced out the course of the bullets, this wound would have been compatible with either entrance or exit wound depending upon the size, the velocity, the tissue structure and so forth.

Mr. SPECTER. Permit me to add some facts which I shall ask you to assume as being true for purposes of having you express an opinion.

First of all, assume that the President was struck by a 6.5 mm. copper-jacketed bullet from a rifle having a muzzle velocity of approximately 2,000 feet per second at a time when the President was approximately 160 to 250 feet from the weapon, with the President being struck from the rear at a downward angle of approximately 45 degrees, being struck on the upper right posterior thorax just above the upper border of the scapula 14 centimeters from the tip of the right acromion process and 14 centimeters below the tip of the right mastoid process.

Assume further that the missile passed through the body of the President striking no bones, traversing the neck and sliding between the large muscles in the posterior aspect of the President's body through a fascia channel without violating the pleural cavity, but bruising only the apex of the right pleural cavity and bruising the most apical portion of the right lung, then causing a hematoma to the right of the larynx which you have described, and creating a jagged wound in the trachea, then exiting precisely at the point where you observe the puncture wound to exist.

Now based on those facts was the appearance of the wound in your opinion consistent with being an exit wound?

Dr. CARRICO. It certainly was. It could have been under the circumstances.

Mr. SPECTER. And assuming that all the facts which I have given you to be true, do you have an opinion with a reasonable degree of medical certainty as to whether, in fact, the wound was an entrance wound or an exit wound?

Dr. CARRICO. With those facts and the fact as I understand it no other bullet was found this would be, this was, I believe, was an exit wound.

Mr. SPECTER. Were any bullets found in the President's body by the doctors at Parkland?

Dr. CARRICO. No, sir.

Mr. SPECTER. Was the President's clothing ever examined by you, Dr. Carrico?

Dr. CARRICO. No, sir; it was not.

Mr. SPECTER. What was the reason for no examination of the clothing?

Dr. CARRICO. Again in the emergency situation the nurses removed the clothing after we had initially unbuttoned enough to get a look at him, at his chest, and as the routine is set up, the nurses remove the clothing and we just don't take time to look at it.

Mr. SPECTER. Was the President's body then ever turned over at any point by you or any of the other doctors at Parkland?

Dr. CARRICO. No, sir.

Mr. SPECTER. Was President Kennedy lying on the emergency stretcher from the time he was brought into trauma room one until the treatment at Parkland Hospital was concluded?

Dr. CARRICO. Yes; he was.

Mr. SPECTER. At what time was that treatment concluded, to the best of your recollection?

Dr. CARRICO. At about 1 o'clock.

Mr. SPECTER. At approximately what time did you leave the trauma room where the President was brought?

Dr. CARRICO. I left right at one when we decided that he was dead.

Mr. SPECTER. And did the other doctors leave at the same time or did any remain in the trauma room?

Dr. CARRICO. I left before some of the other doctors, I do not remember specifically who was there. I believe Dr. Baxter was, Dr. Jenkins was still there, I believe. And I think Dr. Perry was.

Mr. SPECTER. You have described a number of doctors in the course of your testimony up to this point. Would you state what other doctors were present during the time the President was treated, to the best of your recollection?

Dr. CARRICO. Well, I have already mentioned Dr. Don Curtis, the surgery resident; Martin White, an interne; Dr. Perry was there, Dr. Baxter, Dr. McClelland, a member of the surgery staff; Dr. Ronald Jones, chief surgery resident; Dr. Jenkins, chief of anesthesia; several other physicians whose names I can't remember at the present. Admiral Burkley, I believe was his name, the President's physician, was there as soon as he got to the hospital.

Mr. SPECTER. What is your view, Dr. Carrico, as to how many bullets struck the President?

Dr. CARRICO. At the time of the initial examination I really had no view. In view of what we have been told by you, and the Commission, two bullets would be my opinion.

Mr. SPECTER. Based on the additional facts which I have asked you to assume——

Dr. CARRICO. Yes, sir.

Mr. SPECTER. And also based on the autopsy report from Bethesda——

Dr. CARRICO. Right.

Mr. SPECTER. Which was made available to you by me.

Dr. CARRICO. Right.

Mr. SPECTER. Now, who, if any one, has talked to you representing the Federal Government in connection with the treatment which you assisted in rendering President Kennedy at Parkland on November 22?

Dr. CARRICO. We have talked to some representatives of the Secret Service, whose names I do not remember.

Mr. SPECTER. On how many occasions, if there was more than one?

Dr. CARRICO. Two occasions, a fairly long interview shortly after the President's death, and then approximately a month or so afterwards a very short interview.

Representative FORD. When you say shortly after the President's death, you mean that day?

Dr. CARRICO. No, sir. Within a week maybe.

Mr. SPECTER. And what was the substance of the first interview with the Secret Service which you have described as occurring within 1 week?

Dr. CARRICO. This was a meeting in Dr. Shires' office, Dr. Shires, Dr. Perry, Dr. McClelland and myself, and two representatives of the Secret Service in which we went over the treatment.

They discussed the autopsy findings as I recall it, with Dr. Shires, and reviewed the treatment with him, essentially.

Mr. SPECTER. And what questions were you asked specifically at that time, if any?

Dr. CARRICO. I don't recall any specific questions I was asked. In general, I was asked some questions pertaining to his treatment, to the wounds, what I thought they were, and et cetera.

Mr. SPECTER. What opinions did you express at that time?

Dr. CARRICO. Again, I said that on the basis of our initial examination, this wound in his neck could have been either an entrance or exit wound, which was what they were most concerned about, and assuming there was a wound in the back, somewhere similar to what you have described that this certainly would be compatible with an exit wound.

Mr. SPECTER. Were your statements at that time different in any respect with the testimony which you have given here this morning?

Dr. CARRICO. Not that I recall.

Mr. SPECTER. Were your views at that time consistent with the findings in the autopsy report, or did they vary in any way from the findings in that report?

Dr. CARRICO. As I recall, the autopsy report is exactly as I remember it.

Mr. SPECTER. Were your opinions at that time consistent with the findings of the autopsy report?

Dr. CARRICO. Yes.

Mr. SPECTER. Will you identify Dr. Shires for the record, please?

Dr. CARRICO. Dr. Shires is chief of the surgery service at Parkland, and chairman of the Department of Surgery at Southwestern Medical School.

Mr. SPECTER. Now, approximately when, to the best of your recollection, did the second interview occur with the Secret Service?

Dr. CARRICO. This was some time in February, probably about the middle of February, and the interview consisted of the agent asking me if I had any further information.

I said I did not.

Mr. SPECTER. Was that the total context of the interview?

Dr. CARRICO. Yes, sir.

Mr. SPECTER. Now, did I interview you and take your deposition in Dallas, Tex., last Wednesday?

Dr. CARRICO. Yes, sir.

Mr. SPECTER. And has that deposition transcript been made available to you this morning?

Dr. CARRICO. It has.

Mr. SPECTER. And were the views you expressed to me in our conversation before the deposition and on the record during the course of the deposition different in any way with the testimony which you have provided here this morning?

Dr. CARRICO. No, sir; they were not.

Mr. SPECTER. Dr. Carrico, have you changed your opinion in any way concerning your observations or conclusions about the situation with respect to President Kennedy at any time since November 22, 1963?

Dr. CARRICO. No.

Mr. SPECTER. Do you have any notes or writings of any sort in your possession concerning your participation in the treatment of President Kennedy?

Dr. CARRICO. None other than the letter to my children I mentioned to you.

Mr. SPECTER. Will you state briefly the general nature of that for the Commission here today, please.

Dr. CARRICO. This is just a letter written to my children to be read by them later, saying what happened, how I felt about it. And maybe why it happened, and maybe it would do them some good later.

Mr. SPECTER. Did you also make a written report which was made a part of the records of Parkland Hospital which you have identified for the record during the deposition proceeding?

Dr. CARRICO. Yes; I did.

Mr. SPECTER. Do those constitute the total of the writings which you made concerning your participation in the treatment of the President?

Dr. CARRICO. Right.

Mr. DULLES. You spoke of a letter to your children. I don't want to invade your privacy in this respect in any way, but is there anything in that letter that you think would bear on our considerations here by this Commission?

Dr. CARRICO. No; I don't believe so. This thing doesn't mention the treatment other than to say probably by the time they read the letter it will be archaic.

Mr. DULLES. You spoke about the causes of it all, I don't know whether——

Dr. CARRICO. Just a little homespun philosophy. I just said that there was a lot of extremism both in Dallas and in the Nation as a whole, and in an attitude of extremism a warped mind can flourish much better than in a more stable atmosphere.

Mr. DULLES. Thank you.

Mr. SPECTER. Dr. Carrico, was the nature of the treatment affected, in your opinion, in any way by the fact that you were working on the President of the United States?

Dr. CARRICO. I don't believe so, sir. We have seen a large number of acutely injured people, and acutely ill people, and the treatment has been carried out enough that this is almost reflex, if you will. Certainly everyone was emotionally affected. I think, if anything, the emotional aspect made us think faster, work faster and better.

Mr. SPECTER. Do you have anything to add which you think would be helpful to the Commission in its inquiry on the assassination of President Kennedy?

Dr. CARRICO. No, sir.

Mr. SPECTER. Those conclude my questions, Mr. Chief Justice.

The CHAIRMAN. Mr. Dulles, have you any questions to ask of the Doctor?

Mr. DULLES. Looking back on it, do you think it was probable that death followed almost immediately after this shot in the head?

Dr. CARRICO. Yes, sir; as I said——

Mr. DULLES. I was absent, I am sorry, at that time.

Dr. CARRICO. Yes, sir. Medically, I suppose you would have to say he was alive when he came to Parkland. From a practical standpoint, I think he was dead then.

The CHAIRMAN. Congressman Ford?

Representative FORD. When did you say that he arrived, when you first started working on the President?

Dr. CARRICO. It would only be a guess. Probably about 12:35. It was about 12:30 when I got in the emergency room, and I was there 2 or 3 minutes when we were called, and he was there within 2 or 3 minutes.

Representative FORD. So approximately from 12:35 until 1 the President was examined and treatment was given by you and others?

Dr. CARRICO. Yes.

Representative FORD. Have you read and analyzed the autopsy performed by the authorities at Bethesda?

Dr. CARRICO. I have not read it carefully. I have seen it. Mr. Specter showed me parts of it, and I had seen a copy of it earlier, briefly.

Representative FORD. Is there anything in it that you have read that would be in conflict with your observation?

Dr. CARRICO. Nothing at all in conflict. It certainly adds to the observations that we made.

Representative FORD. Have you been interviewed by the press and, if so, when?

Dr. CARRICO. I think I have talked to the press twice.

Mr. Burrus, a reporter for the Dallas Times Herald, talked to me about 5 minutes, probably 3 or 4 days after the President's death, and then a reporter from Time called about 3 or 4 weeks after the President's death, and I talked to him for a very few minutes.

Representative FORD. Did you make any statements in either of these interviews that are different from the observations you have made here this morning?

Dr. CARRICO. Not that I recall.

Representative FORD. That is all.

Mr. DULLES. Mr. Chief Justice, could I—off the record.

(Discussion off the record.)

The CHAIRMAN. Well, Doctor, thank you very much. We appreciate your help.

Dr. CARRICO. Certainly. Glad to be here.

TESTIMONY OF DR. MALCOLM PERRY

The CHAIRMAN. Dr. Perry, will you be sworn now, please?

Would you raise your right hand and be sworn, please?

Do you solemnly swear the testimony you are about to give before the Commission will be the truth, the whole truth, and nothing but the truth, so help you God?

Dr. PERRY. I do.

The CHAIRMAN. Will you be seated, please?

Mr. Specter will conduct the examination.

Mr. SPECTER. Will you state your full name for the record, please?

Dr. PERRY. Malcolm Oliver Perry.

Mr. SPECTER. What is your residence address?

Dr. PERRY. 4115 Parkland, Dallas, Tex.

Mr. SPECTER. Your professional address?

Dr. PERRY. 5323 Harley Hines Boulevard.

Mr. SPECTER. Is that the address of Parkland Memorial Hospital?

Dr. PERRY. That is the address of the University of Texas Southwestern Medical School.

Mr. SPECTER. Is that situated immediately adjacent to Parkland Memorial Hospital?

Dr. PERRY. That is correct.

Mr. SPECTER. Would you state your age, sir?

Dr. PERRY. 34.

Mr. SPECTER. What is your profession?

Dr. PERRY. I am a physician and surgeon.

Mr. SPECTER. Were you duly licensed to practice medicine by the State of Texas?

Dr. PERRY. Yes.

Mr. SPECTER. Would you outline briefly your educational background, please?

Dr. PERRY. After graduation from Plano High School in 1947, I attended the University of Texas and was duly graduated there in January of 1951 with a degree of Bachelor of Arts.

I subsequently graduated from the University of Texas Southwestern Medical School in 1955 with a degree of Doctor of Medicine. I served an internship of 12 months at Letterman Hospital in San Francisco, and after 2 more years in the Air Force I returned to Parkland for a 4-year residency in general surgery.

I completed that in——

Mr. DULLES. Where did you serve in the Air Force, by the way?

Dr. PERRY. I was in Spokane, Wash., Geiger Field.

At the completion of my surgery residency in June of 1962, I was appointed an instructor in surgery at the Southwestern Medical School.

But in September 1962, I returned to the University of California at San Francisco to spend a year in vascular surgery. During that time, I took and passed my boards for the certification for the American Board of Surgery.

I returned to Parkland Hospital and Southwestern in September of 1963, was appointed an assistant professor of surgery, attending surgeon and vascular consultant for Parkland Hospital and John Smith Hospital in Fort Worth.

Mr. SPECTER. What experience have you had, Dr. Perry, if any, in gunshot wounds?

Dr. PERRY. During my period in medical school and my residency, I have seen a large number, from 150 to 200.

Mr. SPECTER. What were your duties at Parkland Memorial Hospital, if any, on November 22d, 1963?

Dr. PERRY. On that day I had come over from the medical school for the usual 1 o'clock rounds with the residents, and Dr. Ronald Jones and I, he being chief surgical resident, were having dinner in the main dining room there in the hospital.

Mr. SPECTER. Will you describe how you happened to be called in to render assistance to President Kennedy?

Dr. PERRY. Somewhere around 12:30, and I cannot give you the time accurately since I did not look at my watch in that particular instant, an emergency page was put in for Dr. Tom Shires, who is chief of the emergency surgical service in Parkland. I knew he was in Galveston attending a meeting and giving a paper, and I asked Dr. Jones to pick up the page to see if he or I could be of assistance.

The CHAIRMAN. Doctor, at this time I must leave for a session at the Supreme Court, and the hearing will continue. Congressman Ford, I am going to ask you if you will preside in my absence. If you are obliged to go to the Congress, Commissioner Dulles will preside, and I will be available as soon as the Court session is over to be here with you.

(At this point, Mr. Warren withdrew from the hearing room.)

Representative FORD. Will you proceed, please?

Mr. SPECTER. What action did you take after learning of the emergency call, Dr. Perry?

Dr. PERRY. The emergency room is one flight of stairs down from the main dining cafeteria, so Dr. Jones and I went immediately to the emergency room to render what assistance we could.

Representative FORD. May I ask this: In the confirmation of the page call, was it told to you that the President was the patient involved?

Dr. PERRY. It was told to Dr. Jones, who picked up the page, that President Kennedy had been shot and was being brought to Parkland. We went down immediately to the emergency room to await his arrival. However, he was there when we reached it.

Mr. SPECTER. Who else was present at the time you arrived on the scene with the President?

Dr. PERRY. When Dr. Jones and I entered the emergency room, the place was filled with people, most of them officers and, apparently, attendants to the Presidential procession. Dr. Carrico was in attendance with the President in trauma room No. 1 when I walked in. There were several other people there. Mrs. Kennedy was there with some gentleman whom I didn't know. I have the impression there was another physician in the room, but I cannot recall at this time who it was. There were several nurses there.

Mr. SPECTER. Were any other doctors present besides Dr. Carrico?

Dr. PERRY. I think there was another doctor present, but I don't know who it was, I don't recall.

Mr. DULLES. Can I ask a question here, Mr. Specter?

Mr. SPECTER. Certainly.

Mr. DULLES. What is the procedure for somebody taking command in a situation of this kind? Who takes over and who says who should do what? I realize it is an emergency situation. Maybe that is an improper question.

Dr. PERRY. No, sir.

Mr. DULLES. But it would be very helpful to me——

Dr. PERRY. No, sir; it is perfectly proper.

Mr. DULLES. In reviewing the situation to see how you acted.

In a military situation, you have somebody who takes command.

Dr. PERRY. We do, too. And it essentially is based on the same kind of thing.

Mr. DULLES. I would like to hear about that.

If it doesn't fit in here——

Mr. SPECTER. It is fine.

Dr. PERRY. It is based on rank and experience, essentially. For example, Dr. Carrico being the senior surgical resident in the area, at the time President Kennedy was brought in to the emergency suite, would have done what he felt was necessary and would have assumed control of the situation being as there were interns and probably medical students around the area, but being senior would take it. This, of course, catapulted me into this because I was the senior attending staff man when I arrived and at that time Dr. Carrico has noted I took over direction of the care since I was senior of all the people there and being as we are surgeons, the department of surgery operates that portion of the emergency room and directs the care of the patients.

Mr. DULLES. Did you try to clear the room of unnecessary people?

Dr. PERRY. This was done, not by me, but by the nurse supervisor, I assume, but several of the people were asked to leave the room. Generally, this is not necessary. In an instance such as this, it is a little more difficult, as you can understand.

Mr. DULLES. Yes.

Dr. PERRY. But this care of an acutely injured and acutely injured patients goes on quite rapidly. Over 90,000 a year go through that emergency room, and, as a result, people are well trained in the performance of their duties. There is generally no problem in asking anyone to leave the room because everyone is quite busy and they know what they have to do and are proceeding to do it.

Mr. DULLES. Thank you very much.

Mr. SPECTER. Upon your arrival in the room, where President Kennedy was situated, what did you observe as to his condition?

Dr. PERRY. At the time I entered the door, Dr. Carrico was attending him. He was attaching the Bennett apparatus to an endotracheal tube in place to assist his respiration.

The President was lying supine on the carriage, underneath the overhead lamp. His shirt, coat, had been removed. There was a sheet over his lower extremities and the lower portion of his trunk. He was unresponsive. There was no evidence of voluntary motion. His eyes were open, deviated up and outward, and the pupils were dilated and fixed.

I did not detect a heart beat and was told there was no blood pressure obtainable.

He was, however, having ineffective spasmodic respiratory efforts.

There was blood on the carriage.

Mr. DULLES. What does that mean to the amateur, to the unprofessional?

Dr. PERRY. Short, rather jerky contractions of his chest and diaphragm, pulling for air.

Mr. DULLES. I see.

Mr. SPECTER. Were those respiratory efforts on his part alone or was he being aided in his breathing at that time?

Dr. PERRY. He had just attached the machine and at this point it was not turned on. He was attempting to breathe.

Mr. SPECTER. So that those efforts were being made at that juncture at least without mechanical aid?

Dr. PERRY. Those were spontaneous efforts on the part of the President.

Mr. SPECTER. Will you continue, then, Dr. Perry, as to what you observed of his condition?

Dr. PERRY. Yes, there was blood noted on the carriage and a large avulsive wound on the right posterior cranium.

I cannot state the size, I did not examine it at all. I just noted the presence of lacerated brain tissue. In the lower part of the neck below the Adams apple was a small, roughly circular wound of perhaps 5 mm. in diameter from which blood was exuding slowly.

I did not see any other wounds.

I examined the chest briefly, and from the anterior portion did not see anything.

I pushed up the brace on the left side very briefly to feel for his femoral pulse, but did not obtain any.

I did no further examination because it was obvious that if any treatment were to be carried out with any success a secure effective airway must be obtained immediately.

I asked Dr. Carrico if the wound on the neck was actually a wound or had he begun a tracheotomy and he replied in the negative, that it was a wound, and at that point——

Mr. DULLES. I am a little confused, I thought Dr. Carrico was absent. That was an earlier period.

Dr. PERRY. No, sir; he was present.

Mr. DULLES. He was present?

Dr. PERRY. Yes; he was present when I walked in the room and, at that point, I asked someone to secure a tracheotomy tray but there was one already there. Apparently Dr. Carrico had already asked them to set up the tray.

Mr. SPECTER. Dr. Perry, backtracking just a bit from the context of the answer which you have just given, would you describe the quantity of blood which you observed on the carriage when you first came into the room where the President was located?

Dr. PERRY. Mr. Specter, this is an extremely difficult thing. The estimation of blood when it is either on the floor or on drapes or bandages is grossly inaccurate in almost every instance.

As you know, many hospitals have studied this extensively to try to determine whether they were able to do it with any accuracy but they cannot. I can just tell you there was considerable blood present on the carriage and some on his head and some on the floor but how much, I would hesitate to estimate. Several hundred CC's would be the closest I could get but it could be from 200 to 1,500 and I know by experience you cannot estimate it more accurately.

Mr. SPECTER. Would you characterize it as a very substantial or minor blood loss?

Dr. PERRY. A substantial blood loss.

Mr. SPECTER. Now, you mentioned the President's brace. Could you describe that as specifically as possible?

Dr. PERRY. No, sir; I did not examine it. I noted its presence only in an effort to reach the femoral pulse and I pushed it up just slightly so that I might palpate for the femoral pulse, I did no more examination.

Mr. SPECTER. In the course of seeking the femoral pulse, did you observe or note an Ace bandage?

Dr. PERRY. Yes, sir.

Mr. SPECTER. In the brace area?

Dr. PERRY. Yes, sir. It was my impression, I saw a portion of an Ace Bandage, an elastic supporting bandage on the right thigh. I did not examine it at all but I just noted its presence.

Mr. SPECTER. Did the Ace Bandage cover any portion of the President's body that you were able to observe in addition to the right thigh?

Dr. PERRY. No, sir; I did not go any further. I just noted its presence right there at the junction at the hip. It could have been on the lower trunk or the upper thigh, I don't know. I didn't care any further.

Mr. SPECTER. Would you continue to describe the resuscitative efforts that were undertaken at that time?

Dr. PERRY. At the beginning I had removed my coat and watch as I entered the room and dropped it off in the corner, and as I was talking to Dr. Carrico in regard to the neck wound, I glanced cursorily at the head wound and noted its severe character, and then proceeded with the tracheotomy after donning a pair of gloves. I asked that someone call Dr. Kemp Clark, of neurosurgery, Dr. Robert McClelland, Dr. Charles Baxter, assistant professors of surgery, to come and assist. There were several other people in the room by this time, none of which I can identify. I then began the tracheotomy making a transverse incision right through the wound in the neck.

Mr. SPECTER. Why did you elect to make the tracheotomy incision through the wound in the neck, Dr. Perry?

Dr. PERRY. The area of the wound, as pointed out to you in the lower third of the neck anteriorly is customarily the spot one would electively perform the tracheotomy.

This is one of the safest and easiest spots to reach the trachea. In addition the presence of the wound indicated to me there was possibly an underlaying wound to the neck muscles in the neck, the carotid artery or the jugular vein. If you are going to control these it is necessary that the incision be as low, that is toward the heart or lungs as the wound if you are going to obtain adequate control.

Therefore, for expediency's sake I went directly to that level to obtain control of the airway.

Mr. SPECTER. Would you describe, in a general way and in lay terms, the purpose for the tracheotomy at that time?

Dr. PERRY. Dr. Carrico had very judicially placed an endotracheal tube but unfortunately due to the injury to the trachea, the cuff which is an inflatable balloon on the endotracheal tube was not below the tracheal injury and thus he could not secure the adequate airway that you would require to maintain respiration.

(At this point, Mr. McCloy entered the hearing room.)

Mr. SPECTER. Dr. Perry, you mentioned an injury to the trachea.

Will you describe that as precisely as you can, please?

Dr. PERRY. Yes. Once the transverse incision through the skin and subcutaneous tissues was made, it was necessary to separate the strap muscles covering the anterior muscles of the windpipe and thyroid. At that point the trachea was noted to be deviated slightly to the left and I found it necessary to sever the exterior strap muscles on the other side to reach the trachea.

I noticed a small ragged laceration of the trachea on the anterior lateral right side. I could see the endotracheal tube which had been placed by Dr. Carrico in the wound, but there was evidence of air and blood around the tube because I noted the cuff was just above the injury to the trachea.

Mr. SPECTER. Will you now proceed to describe what efforts you made to save the President's life?

Dr. PERRY. At this point, I had entered the neck, and Dr. Baxter and Dr. McClelland arrived shortly thereafter. I cannot describe with accuracy their exact arrival. I only know I looked up and saw Dr. Baxter as I began the tracheotomy and he took a pair of gloves to assist me.

Dr. McClelland's presence was known to me at the time he picked up an instrument and said, "Here, I will hand it to you."

At that point I was down in the trachea. Once the trachea had been exposed I took the knife and incised the windpipe at the point of the bullet injury. And asked that the endotracheal tube previously placed by Dr. Carrico be withdrawn slightly so I could insert a tracheotomy tube at this level. This was effected and attached to an anesthesia machine which had been brought down by Dr. Jenkins and Dr. Giesecke for better control of circulation.

I noticed there was free air and blood in the right mediastinum and although I could not see any evidence, myself any evidence, of it in the pleura of the lung the presence of this blood in this area could be indicative of the underlying condition.

I asked someone to put in a chest tube to allow sealed drainage of any blood or air which might be accumulated in the right hemothorax.

This occurred while I was doing the tracheotomy. I did not know at the time when I inserted the tube but I was informed subsequently that Dr. Paul Peters, assistant professor of urology, and Dr. Charles Baxter, previously noted in this record, inserted the chest tube and attached it to underwater seal or drainage of the right pneumothorax.

Mr. DULLES. How long did this tracheotomy take, approximately?

Dr. PERRY. I don't know that for sure, Mr. Dulles. However, I have—a matter of 3 to 5 minutes, perhaps even less. This was very—I didn't look at the watch, I have done them at those speeds and faster when I have had to. So I would estimate that.

At this point also Dr. Carrico, having previously attached and assisting with the attaching of the anesthesia machine was doing another cut down on the right leg; Dr. Ronald Jones was doing an additional cut down, venous section on the left arm for the insertion of plastic cannula into veins so one may rapidly and effectively infuse blood and fluids. These were being done.

It is to Dr. Carrico's credit, I think he ordered the hydrocortisone for the President having known he suffered from adrenal insufficiency and in this particular instance being quite busy he had the presence of mind to recall this and order what could have been a lifesaving measure, I think.

Mr. SPECTER. Would you identify who Dr. Baxter is?

Dr. PERRY. Yes. Dr. Charles Baxter is, when I noted when I asked for the call, is an assistant professor of surgery also and Dr. McClelland.

Mr. SPECTER. And is Dr. McClelland occupying a similar position at Parkland Memorial Hospital as Dr. Baxter?

Dr. PERRY. That is correct.

Mr. SPECTER. Would you identify Dr. Jenkins?

Dr. PERRY. Dr. M. T. Jenkins is professor and chairman of the department of anesthesiology and chief of the anesthesia service, and Dr. Giesecke is assistant professor of anesthesiology at Parkland.

Mr. SPECTER. Have you now identified all of the medical personnel whom you can recollect who were present at the time the aid was being rendered to the President?

Dr. PERRY. No, sir; several other people entered the room. I recall seeing Dr. Bashour who is an associate professor of medicine and chief of the cardiology section at Parkland.

Dr. Don W. Seldin, who is professor and chairman of the department of medicine, and I previously mentioned Dr. Paul Peters, assistant professor of urology, and I believe that Dr. Jackie Hunt of the department of anesthesiology was also there, and there were other people, I cannot identify them, several nurses and several others.

Mr. SPECTER. Dr. William Kemp Clark arrived at about that time?

Dr. PERRY. Dr. Clark's arrival was first noted to me after the completion of the tracheotomy, and at this point, the cardiotachyscope had been attached to Mr. Kennedy to detect any electrical activity and although I did not note any, being occupied, it was related to me there was initially evidence of a spontaneous electrical activity in the President's heart.

However, at the completion of the tracheotomy and the institution of the sealed tube drainage of the chest, Dr. Clark and I began external cardiac massage. This was monitored by Dr. Jenkins and Dr. Giesecke who informed us we were obtaining a satisfactory carotid pulse in the neck, and someone whose name I do not know at this time, said they could also feel a femoral pulse in the leg. We continued external cardiac massage, I continued it as Dr. Clark examined the head wound and observed the cardiotachyscope. The exact time interval that this took I cannot tell you. I continued it until Dr. Jenkins and Dr. Clark informed me there was no activity at all, in the cardiotachyscope and that there had been no neurological or muscular response to our resuscitative effort at all and that the wound which the President sustained of his head was a mortal wound, and at that point we determined that he had expired and we abandoned efforts of resuscitation.

Mr. SPECTER. Would you identify Dr. Clark's specialty for the record, please?

Dr. PERRY. Dr. Clark is professor and chairman of the department of neurosurgery at the University of Texas Southwestern Medical School, and chief of the neurosurgical services at Parkland Hospital.

Mr. SPECTER. Now, you described a condition in the right mediastinum. Would you elaborate on what your views were of the condition at the time you were rendering this treatment?

Dr. PERRY. The condition of this area?

Mr. SPECTER. Yes, sir.

Dr. PERRY. There was both blood, free blood and air in the right superior mediastinum. That is the space that is located between the lungs and the heart at that level.

As I noted, I did not see any underlying injury of the pleura, the coverings of the lungs or of the lungs themselves. But in the presence of this large amount of blood in this area, one would be unable to detect small injuries to the underlying structures. The air was indicated by the fact that there was some frothing of this blood present, bubbling which could have been due to the tracheal injury or an underlying injury to the lung.

Since the morbidity attendant upon insertion of an anterior chest tube for sealed drainage is negligible and the morbidity which attends a pneumothorax is considerable, I elected to have the chest tube put in place because we were giving him positive pressure oxygen and the possibility of inducing a tension on pneumothorax would be quite high in such instances.

Mr. SPECTER. What is pneumothorax?

Dr. PERRY. Hemothorax would be blood in the free chest cavity and pneumothorax would be air in the free chest cavity underlying collapse of the lungs.

Mr. SPECTER. Would that have been caused by the injury which you noted to the President's trachea?

Dr. PERRY. There was no evidence of a hemothorax or a pneumothorax through my examination; only it is sufficient this could have been observed because of the free blood in the mediastinum.

Mr. SPECTER. Were the symptoms which excited your suspicion causable by the injury to the trachea?

Dr. PERRY. They were.

Mr. SPECTER. At what time was the pronouncement of death made?

Dr. PERRY. Approximately 1 o'clock.

Mr. SPECTER. By whom was death announced?

Dr. PERRY. Dr. Kemp Clark.

Mr. SPECTER. Was there any special reason why it was Dr. Kemp Clark who pronounced the President had died?

Dr. PERRY. It was the opinion of those of us who had attended the President that the ultimate cause of his demise was a severe injury to his brain with subsequent loss of neurologic function and subsequent massive loss of blood, and thus Dr. Clark, being a neurosurgeon, signed the death certificate.

Mr. SPECTER. In your opinion, would the President have survived the injury which he sustained to the neck which you have described?

Dr. PERRY. Barring the advent of complications this wound was tolerable, and I think he would have survived it.

Mr. SPECTER. Have you now described all of the treatment which was rendered to the President by the medical team in attendance at Parkland Memorial Hospital.

Dr. PERRY. In essence I have, Mr. Specter. I do not know the exact quantities of balance salt solutions or blood that was given. I mentioned the 300 mg. of hydrocortisone Dr. Carrico ordered and, of course, he was given oxygen under pressure which has been previously recorded. The quantities of substances or any other drugs I have no knowledge of.

Mr. SPECTER. In general you have recounted the treatment?

Dr. PERRY. That is correct.

Mr. SPECTER. Have you now stated for the record all of the individuals who were in attendance in treating the President that you can recollect at this time?

Dr. PERRY. Yes, sir; I have.

Mr. SPECTER. Will you now describe as specifically as you can, the injury which you noted in the President's head?

Dr. PERRY. As I mentioned previously in the record, I made only a cursory examination of the President's head. I noted a large avulsive wound of the right parietal occipital area, in which both scalp and portions of skull were absent, and there was severe laceration of underlying brain tissue. My examination did not go any further than that.

Mr. SPECTER. Did you, to be specific, observe a smaller wound below the large avulsed area which you have described?

Dr. PERRY. I did not.

Mr. SPECTER. Was there blood in that area of the President's head?

Dr. PERRY. There was.

Mr. SPECTER. Which might have obscured such a wound?

Dr. PERRY. There was a considerable amount of blood at the head of the cartilage.

Mr. SPECTER. Would you now describe as particularly as possible the neck wound you observed?

Dr. PERRY. This was situated in the lower anterior one-third of the neck, approximately 5 mm. in diameter.

It was exuding blood slowly which partially obscured it. Its edges were neither ragged nor were they punched out, but rather clean.

Mr. SPECTER. Have you now described the neck wound as specifically as you can?

Dr. PERRY. I have.

Mr. SPECTER. Based on your observations of the neck wound alone, do you have a sufficient basis to form an opinion as to whether it was an entrance wound or an exit wound,

Dr. PERRY. No, sir. I was unable to determine that since I did not ascertain the exact trajectory of the missile. The operative procedure which I performed was restricted to securing an adequate airway and insuring there was no injury to the carotid artery or jugular vein at that level and at that point I made the procedure.

Mr. SPECTER. Based on the appearance of the neck wound alone, could it have been either an entrance or an exit wound?

Dr. PERRY. It could have been either.

Mr. SPECTER. Permit me to supply some additional facts, Dr. Perry, which I shall ask you to assume as being true for purposes of having you express an opinion.

Assume first of all that the President was struck by a 6.5-mm. copper-jacketed bullet fired from a gun having a muzzle velocity of approximately 2,000 feet per second, with the weapon being approximately 160 to 250 feet from the President, with the bullet striking him at an angle of declination of approximately 45 degrees, striking the President on the upper right posterior thorax just above the upper border of the scapula, being 14 cm. from the tip of the right acromion process and 14 cm. below the tip of the right mastoid process, passing through the President's body striking no bones, traversing the neck and sliding between the large muscles in the posterior portion of the President's body through a fascia channel without violating the pleural cavity but bruising the apex of the right pleural cavity, and bruising the most apical portion of the right lung inflicting a hematoma to the right side of the larynx, which you have just described, and striking the trachea causing the injury which you described, and then exiting from the hole that you have described in the midline of the neck.

Now, assuming those facts to be true, would the hole which you observed in the neck of the President be consistent with an exit wound under those circumstances?

Dr. PERRY. Certainly would be consistent with an exit wound.

Mr. SPECTER. Now, assuming one additional fact that there was no bullet found in the body of the President, and assuming the facts which I have just set forth to be true, do you have an opinion as to whether the wound which you observed in the President's neck was an entrance or an exit wound?

Dr. PERRY. A full jacketed bullet without deformation passing through skin would leave a similar wound for an exit and entrance wound and with the facts which you have made available and with these assumptions, I believe that it was an exit wound.

Mr. SPECTER. Do you have sufficient facts available to you to render an opinion as to the cause of the injury which you observed in the President's head?

Dr. PERRY. No, sir.

Mr. SPECTER. Have you had an opportunity to examine the autopsy report?

Dr. PERRY. I have.

Mr. SPECTER. And are the facts set forth in the autopsy report consistent with your observations and views or are they inconsistent in any way with your findings and opinions?

Dr. PERRY. They are quite consistent and I noted initially that they explained very nicely the circumstances as we observed them at the time.

Mr. SPECTER. Could you elaborate on that last answer, Dr. Perry?

Dr. PERRY. Yes. There was some considerable speculation, as you will recall, as to whether there were one or two bullets and as to from whence they came. Dr. Clark and I were queried extensively in respect to this and in addition Dr. Carrico could not determine whether there were one or two bullets from our initial examination.

I say that because we did what was necessary in the emergency procedure, and abandoned any efforts of examination at the termination. I did not ascertain the trajectory of any of the missiles. As a result I did not know whether there was evidence for 1 or 2 or even 3 bullets entering and at the particular time it was of no importance.

Mr. SPECTER. But based on the additional factors provided in the autopsy report, do you have an opinion at this time as to the number of bullets there were?

Dr. PERRY. The wounds as described from the autopsy report and coupled with the wounds I have observed it would appear there were two missiles that struck the President.

Mr. SPECTER. And based on the additional factors which I have provided to you by way of hypothetical assumption, and the factors present in the autopsy report from your examination of that report, what does the source of the bullets seem to have been to you?

Dr. PERRY. That I could not say. I can only determine their pathway, on the basis of these reports within the President's body.

As to their ultimate source not knowing any of the circumstances surrounding it, I would not have any speculation.

Mr. SPECTER. From what direction would the bullets have come based on all of those factors?

Dr. PERRY. The bullets would have come from behind the President based on these factors.

Mr. SPECTER. And from the level, from below or above the President?

Dr. PERRY. Not having examined any of the wounds with the exception of the anterior neck wounds, I could not say. This wound, as I noted was about 5 mm., and roughly circular in shape. There is no way for me to determine.

Mr. SPECTER. Based upon a point of entrance in the body of the President which I described to you as being 14 cm. from the right acromion process and 14 cm. below the tip of the right mastoid process and coupling that with your observation of the neck wound, would that provide a sufficient basis for you to form an opinion as to the path of the bullet, as to whether it was level, up or down?

Dr. PERRY. Yes, it would.

In view of the fact there was an injury to the right lateral portion of the trachea and a wound in the neck if one were to extend a line roughly between these two, it would be going slightly superiorly, that is cephalad toward the head, from anterior to posterior, which would indicate that the missile entered from slightly above and behind.

Mr. SPECTER. Dr. Perry, have you been a part of or participated in any press conferences?

Dr. PERRY. Yes, sir; I have

Mr. SPECTER. And by whom, if anyone, were the press conferences arranged?

Dr. PERRY. The initial press conference, to the best of my knowledge, was arranged by Mr. Hawkes who was identified to me as being of the White House Press, and Mr. Steve Landregan of the hospital administration there at Parkland, and Dr. Kemp Clark.

They called me, I was in the operating suite at the time to assist with the care of the Governor, and they called and asked me if it would be possible for me to come down to a press conference.

Mr. SPECTER. At about what time did that call come to you, Doctor?

Dr. PERRY. I am not real sure about that but probably around 2 o'clock.

Mr. SPECTER. What action, if any, did you take in response to that call?

Dr. PERRY. I put in a page for Dr. Baxter and Dr. McClelland since they were also involved, and went down to the emergency room where I met Mr. Hawkes and Dr. Clark. And from there we went up to classrooms one and two which had been combined into a large press room, and was packed with gentlemen and ladies of the press.

Mr. SPECTER. In what building was that located?

Dr. PERRY. This was in Parkland Hospital, in the classroom section.

Mr. SPECTER. Are you able to identify which news media were present at that time?

Dr. PERRY. No, sir; there were numerous people in the room. I would estimate maybe a hundred.

Mr. SPECTER. What doctors spoke at that press conference?

Dr. PERRY. Dr. Clark and I answered the questions.

Mr. SPECTER. Who spoke first as between you and Dr. Clark?

Dr. PERRY. I did.

Mr. SPECTER. Would you state as specifically as you can the questions which were asked of you at that time and the answers which you gave?

Dr. PERRY. Mr. Specter, I would preface this by saying that, as you know, I have been interviewed on numerous occasions subsequent to that time, and I cannot recall with accuracy the questions that were asked. They, in general, were similar to the questions that were asked here. The press were given essentially the same, but in no detail such as have been given here. I was asked, for example, what I felt caused the President's death, the nature of the wound, from whence they came, what measures were taken for resuscitation, who were the people in attendance, at what time was it determined that he was beyond our help.

Mr. SPECTER. What responses did you give to questions relating to the source of the bullets, if such questions were asked?

Dr. PERRY. I could not. I pointed out that both Dr. Clark and I had no way of knowing from whence the bullets came.

Mr. SPECTER. Were you asked how many bullets there were?

Dr. PERRY. We were, and our reply was it was impossible with the knowledge we had at hand to ascertain if there were 1 or 2 bullets, or more. We were given, similarly to the discussion here today, hypothetical situations. "Is it possible that such could have been the case, or such and such?" If it was possible that there was one bullet. To this, I replied in the affirmative, it was possible and conceivable that it was only one bullet, but I did not know.

Mr. SPECTER. What would the trajectory, or conceivable course of one bullet have been, Dr. Perry, to account for the injuries which you observed in the President, as you stated it?

Dr. PERRY. Since I observed only two wounds in my cursory examination, it would have necessitated the missile striking probably a bony structure and being deviated in its course in order to account for these two wounds.

Mr. SPECTER. What bony structure was it conceivably?

Dr. PERRY. It required striking the spine.

Mr. SPECTER. Did you express a professional opinion that that did, in fact, happen or it was a matter of speculation that it could have happened?

Dr. PERRY. I expressed it as a matter of speculation that this was conceivable. But, again, Dr. Clark and I emphasized that we had no way of knowing.

Mr. SPECTER. Have you now recounted as specifically as you can recollect what occurred at that first press conference or is it practical for you to give any further detail to the contents of that press conference?

Dr. PERRY. I do not recall any specific details any further than that.

Representative FORD. Mr. Specter—was there ever a recording kept of the questions and answers at that interview, Dr. Perry?

Dr. PERRY. This was one of the things I was mad about, Mr. Ford. There were microphones, and cameras, and the whole bit, as you know, and during the course of it a lot of these hypothetical situations and questions that were asked to us would often be asked by someone on this side and recorded by someone on this, and I don't know who was recorded and whether they were broadcasting it directly. There were tape recorders there and there were television cameras with their microphones. I know there were recordings made but who made them I don't know and, of course, portions of it would be given to this group and questions answered here and, as a result, considerable questions were not answered in their entirety and even some of them that were asked, I am sure were misunderstood. It was bedlam.

Representative FORD. I was thinking, was there an official recording either made by the hospital officials or by the White House people or by any government agency?

Dr. PERRY. Not to my knowledge.

Representative FORD. A true recording of everything that was said, the questions asked, and the answers given?

Dr. PERRY. Not to my knowledge.

Mr. DULLES. Was there any reasonably good account in any of the press of this interview?

Dr. PERRY. No, sir.

Representative FORD. May I ask——

Dr. PERRY. I have failed to see one that was asked.

Representative FORD. In other words, you subsequently read or heard what was allegedly said by you and by Dr. Clark and Dr. Carrico. Were those reportings by the news media accurate or inaccurate as to what you and others said?

Dr. PERRY. In general, they were inaccurate. There were some that were fairly close, but I, as you will probably surmise, was pretty full after both Friday and Sunday, and after the interviews again, following the operation of which I was a member on Sunday, I left town, and I did not read a lot of 'them, but of those which I saw I found none that portrayed it exactly as it happened. Nor did I find any that reported our statements exactly as they were given. They were frequently taken out of context. They were frequently mixed up as to who said what or identification as to which person was who.

Representative FORD. This interview took place on Sunday, the 24th, did you say?

Dr. PERRY. No, there were several interviews, Mr. Ford. We had one in the afternoon, Friday afternoon, and then I spent almost the entire day Saturday in the administrative suite at the hospital answering questions to people of the press, and some medical people of the American Medical Association. And then, of course, Sunday, following the operation on Oswald, I again attended the press conference since I was the first in attendance with him. And, subsequently, there was another conference on Monday conducted by the American Medical Association, and a couple of more interviews with some people whom I don't even recall.

Representative FORD. Would you say that these errors that were reported were because of a lack of technical knowledge as to what you as a physician were saying, or others were saying?

Dr. PERRY. Certainly that could be it in part, but it was not all. Certainly a part of it was lack of attention. A question would be asked and you would incompletely answer it and another question would be asked and they had gotten what they wanted without really understanding, and they would go on and it would go out of context. For example, on the speculation on the ultimate source of bullets, I obviously knew less about it than most people because I was in the hospital at the time and didn't know the circumstances surrounding it until it was over. I was much too busy and yet I was quoted as saying that the bullet, there was probably one bullet, which struck and deviated upward which came from the front, and what I had replied was to a question, was it conceivable that this could have happened, and I said yes, it is conceivable.

I have subsequently learned that to use a straight affirmative word like "yes" is not good relations; that one should say it is conceivable and not give a straight yes or no answer.

"It is conceivable" was dropped and the "yes" was used, and this was happening over and over again. Of course, Dr. Shires, for example, who was the professor and chairman of the department was identified in one press release as chief resident.

Mr. DULLES. As what? I didn't get it.

Dr. PERRY. As chief resident. And myself, as his being my superior, whereas Dr. Ronald Jones was chief resident of course, nothing could be further from the truth in identifying Dr. Shires as chief resident. I was identified as a resident surgeon in the Dallas paper. And I am not impressed with the accuracy of the press reports.

Mr. McCLOY. I don't know whether you have covered this very well. Let me ask you about the wound, the wound that you examined in the President's neck.

You said that it would have been tolerable. Would his speech have been impaired?

Dr. PERRY. No, sir; I don't think so. The injury was below the larynx, and certainly barring the advent of any complication would have healed without any difficulty.

Mr. McCloy. He would have had a relatively normal life?

Dr. Perry. Yes, sir.

Mr. McCloy. Did you, any other time, or other than the press conference or any other period, say that you thought this was an exit wound?

Dr. Perry. No, sir; I did not.

Mr. McCloy. When the President was brought, when you first saw the President, was he fully clothed, or did you cut the clothing away?

Dr. Perry. Not at the time I saw him. Dr. Carrico and the nurses were all in attendance, they had removed his coat and his shirt, which is standard procedure, while we were proceeding about the examination, for them to do so.

Mr. McCloy. But you didn't actually remove his shirt?

Dr. Perry. No, sir; I did not.

Mr. McCloy. Did you get the doctor's experience with regard to gunshot wounds?

Mr. Specter. Yes, sir; I did.

Mr. McCloy. You said something to the effect that, of knowing the President had an adrenalin insufficiency, is that something you could observe?

Dr. Perry. This is common medical knowledge, sir, that he had had in the past necessarily taken adrenalin steroids to support this insufficiency. Dr. Carrico, at this moment of great stress, recalled this, and requested this be given to him at that time, this is extremely important because people who have adrenalin insufficiency are unable to mobilize this hormone at the time of any great stress and it may be fatal without support from exogeneous drugs.

Mr. McCloy. In other words, you had a general medical history of the President before he was—common knowledge.

Dr. Perry. No more so than anyone else, sir, except this would have stuck with us, sir, since they were already in that line.

Mr. McCloy. Did you discuss with any of the other doctors present, and you named quite a number of them, as to whether this was an exit wound or an entrance wound?

Dr. Perry. Yes, sir; we did at the time. But our discussion was necessarily limited by the fact that none of us knew, someone asked me now—you must remember that actually the only people who saw this wound for sure were Dr. Carrico and myself, and some of the other doctors were quoted as saying something about the wound which actually they never said at all because they never saw it, because on their arrival I had already made the incision through the wound, and despite what the press releases may have said neither Dr. Carrico nor myself could say whether it was an entrance or an exit wound from the nature of the wound itself and Dr. McClelland was quoted, for example, as saying he thought it was an exit wound, but that was not what he said at all because he didn't even see it.

Mr. McCloy. And it is a fact, is it not, that you did not see what we now are supposed to believe was the entrance wound?

Dr. Perry. No, sir; we did not examine him. At that time, we attended to the matters of expediency that were life-saving and the securing of an adequate airway and the stanching of massive hemorrhage are really the two medical emergencies; most everything else can wait, but those must be attended to in a matter of minutes and consequently to termination of treatment I had no morbid curiosity, my work was done, and actually I was rather anxious to leave.

Mr. McCloy. That is all.

Mr. Specter. Yes.

(Discussion off the record.)

Mr. Dulles. I suggest, Mr. Specter, if you feel it is feasible, you send to the doctor the accounts of his press conference or conferences.

And possibly, if you are willing, sir, you could send us a letter, send to the Commission a letter, pointing out the various points in these press conferences where you are inaccurately quoted, so we can have that as a matter of record.

Is that feasible?

Dr. Perry. That is, sir.

Would you prefer that each clipping be edited individually or a general statement?

Mr. DULLES. Well, I think it would be better to have each clipping dealt with separately. Obviously, if you have answered one point in one clipping it won't be necessary to answer that point if it is repeated in another clipping.

Dr. PERRY. Yes, sir.

Mr. DULLES. Just deal with the new points.

Dr. PERRY. I can and will do this.

Representative FORD. This would be where Dr. Perry is quoted himself, or Dr. Carrico, or anyone else, they would only pass judgment on the quotes concerning themselves.

Mr. DULLES. That would be correct.

Dr. PERRY. Yes, because some of the other circumstances in some of the press releases which have come to my attention have not been entirely accurate either, regarding sequence of events, and although I would not have knowledge about those you would not want those added necessarily, just any statement alluded to have been made by me.

Mr. DULLES. I think that would be better.

Don't you think so, Mr. Chairman?

Representative FORD. I think it would be the proper procedure.

Is this a monumental job, Mr. Specter?

Mr. SPECTER. No, I think it is one which can be managed, Congressman Ford. I might say we have done that with some of the clippings.

There was an article, as the deposition records will show when you have an opportunity to review them, they have not been transcribed, as to an article which appeared in La Expres, statements were attributed to Dr. McClelland——

Mr. DULLES. Which paper?

Mr. SPECTER. A French paper, La Expres. And I questioned the doctors quoted therein and developed for the record what was true and what was false on the statements attributed to them, so we have undertaken that in some circles but not as extensively as you suggest as to Dr. Perry, because we have been trying diligently to get the tape records of the television interviews, and we were unsuccessful. I discussed this with Dr. Perry in Dallas last Wednesday, and he expressed an interest in seeing them, and I told him we would make them available to him prior to his appearance, before deposition or before the Commission, except our efforts at CBS and NBC, ABC and everywhere including New York, Dallas and other cities were to no avail.

The problem is they have not yet cataloged all of the footage which they have, and I have been advised by the Secret Service, by Agent John Howlett, that they have an excess of 200 hours of transcripts among all of the events and they just have not cataloged them and could not make them available.

Mr. DULLES. Do you intend to catalog them?

Mr. SPECTER. Yes, they do, Mr. Dulles. They intend to do that eventually in their normal process, and the Secret Service is trying to expedite the news media to give us those, and it was our thought as to the film clips, which would be the most direct or the recordings which would be the most direct, to make comparisons between the reports in the news media and what Dr. Perry said at that time, and the facts which we have from the doctors through our depositions and transcript today.

Representative FORD. Can you give us any time estimate when this catalog and comparison might be made?

Mr. SPECTER. Only that they are working on it right now, have been for some time, but it may be a matter of a couple of weeks until they can turn it over.

(Discussion off the record.)

Mr. McCLOY. Mr. Chairman, I have some doubt as to the present propriety of making, of having the doctor make, comments in respect to a particular group of newspaper articles. There have been comments, as we all know, around the world, of great variety and great extent, and it would be practically impossible, I suppose, to check all of the accounts and in failing to check one would not wish to have it suggested that others, the accuracy of others was being endorsed.

I would suggest that the staff make an examination of the files that we have of the comments, together with such tape recordings as may have been taken of the actual press conferences, and after that examination is made we can then determine, perhaps a little more effectively, what might be done to clarify this

ituation so that it would conform to the actual statements that the doctor
was made.

Mr. DULLES. Well, Mr. McCloy, it is quite satisfactory with me and I agree with
you we cannot run down all of the rumors in all of the press and it is quite
satisfactory with me to wait and see whether we have adequate information to
deal with this situation when we get in the complete tapes of the various television, radio and other appearances, so that we have a pretty complete record
of what these two witnesses and others have said on the points we have been
discussing here today.

So I quite agree we will await this presentation to the doctors until we have
had a further chance to review this situation.

What I wanted to be sure was that when we are through with this we do have
in our files and records adequate information to deal with a great many of the
false rumors that have been spread on the basis of false interpretation of these
appearances before television, radio, and so forth and so on.

Representative FORD. Is that all, Mr. Dulles, and Mr. McCloy?

Mr. DULLES. Yes.

Mr. McCLOY. May I ask at this point, did you examine Governor Connally,
too?

Dr. PERRY. I was in the operating room briefly to see about his leg.

Mr. McCLOY. You haven't come to that point in your interrogation.

Mr. SPECTER. I did not.

Mr. McCLOY. I understood you to say you did examine Oswald.

Dr. PERRY. Yes, sir; I operated on Oswald.

Mr. SPECTER. Have you now described in general the press conferences in
which you participated immediately after the treatment which you rendered
to President Kennedy and following the treatment which you assisted in rendering to Mr. Oswald?

Dr. PERRY. To the best of my knowledge.

Mr. SPECTER. And did you make an effort to leave the area of Dallas immediately following the Monday after the weekend of the assassination and the
killing of Oswald in an effort to get away from the press conferences?

Dr. PERRY. I left Monday afternoon approximately 3 o'clock.

Mr. SPECTER. Where did you go?

Dr. PERRY. I went to McAllen, Tex., to the home of my mother-in-law.

Mr. SPECTER. And how far is that from Dallas?

Dr. PERRY. About 560 miles.

Mr. SPECTER. Did you leave instructions as to revealing the destination that
you set upon?

Dr. PERRY. No, only with Dr. Shires and my secretary.

Mr. SPECTER. And were you contacted by the press in McAllen?

Dr. PERRY. The following day.

Mr. SPECTER. And were your whereabouts given either by Dr. Shires or your
secretary?

Dr. PERRY. No, it was not.

Mr. SPECTER. Will you relate briefly the sequence that followed in McAllen,
Tex.

Dr. PERRY. The gentleman from UPI came out and knocked on the door,
and I was quite surprised, not having told anyone where I was going, and I
asked him if he would mind telling me how he found out how I was there, and
looking back at it I was kind of naive, I went to a relative and told no one else.
He had a wire in his hands which he showed me indicating it had come from the
Dallas office, naming the place where I was, and the exact address, and who I
was staying with.

Mr. SPECTER. Did he ask to take pictures of you?

Dr. PERRY. He did.

Mr. SPECTER. What was your response?

Dr. PERRY. This was denied.

Mr. SPECTER. And did he ask you questions?

Dr. PERRY. He did, essentially the same questions which I have reiterated as
to the emergency treatment that was undertaken. He did not press the point
as to the number of bullets or anything of that, and I told him I had no knowl-

edge of that. He only asked about the emergency measures I had taken and I related them to him as I have to you.

Mr. SPECTER. Subsequently, did an article appear about you in the Saturday Evening Post?

Dr. PERRY. It did.

Mr. SPECTER. Would you outline briefly the circumstances surrounding the appearance of that article as you felt them to be?

Dr. PERRY. We were contacted, not I directly but Dr. Shires, by the medical editor of the Saturday Evening Post, this was all related to me by Dr. Shires, in regard to a possible story. This was declined, since Dr. Shires and those of us in the department felt that the news value was gone and this was commercialism, and they told Dr. Shires, I am told, that they would not print anything.

However, an article appearing under a New York Herald Tribune uncopyrighted by-line apparently was subsequently acquired by them and published.

Mr. SPECTER. And was that article accurate, inaccurate, or what was the level of accuracy of the contents thereof?

Dr. PERRY. The level of accuracy was not very good at all. It was overly dramatic, garish and in poor taste, and ethically damaging to me.

Mr. SPECTER. In what way was it ethically damaging to you, Dr. Perry?

Dr. PERRY. As you know, it is our policy that the physician's name in the treatment of any patient be essentially kept quiet. There are unusual circumstances surrounding this one, of course, and our names were made public. But this mentions my name freely, published a photograph that apparently was taken of me at the press conference and had previously appeared in a newspaper, and a picture of the emergency room, trauma room No. 1, and although most of the people in the medical profession, I have subsequently been assured by the Society of Surgeons and AMA, that they realize I had no part in it, which is obvious to them because of the gross inaccuracies. Nonetheless it is harmful to me as a member of the faculty of the medical school to have such an article in print.

Mr. SPECTER. Dr. Perry, did you have occasion to discuss your observations with Comdr. James J. Humes of the Bethesda Naval Hospital?

Dr. PERRY. Yes, sir; I did.

Mr. SPECTER. When did that conversation occur?

Dr. PERRY. My knowledge as to the exact accuracy of it is obviously in doubt. I was under the initial impression that I talked to him on Friday, but I understand it was on Saturday. I didn't recall exactly when.

Mr. SPECTER. Do you have an independent recollection at this moment as to whether it was on Friday or Saturday?

Dr. PERRY. No, sir; I have thought about it again and the events surrounding that weekend were very kaleidoscopic, and I talked with Dr. Humes on two occasions, separated by a very short interval of, I think it was, 30 minutes or an hour or so, it could have been a little longer.

Mr. SPECTER. What was the medium of your conversation?

Dr. PERRY. Over the telephone.

Mr. SPECTER. Did he identify himself to you as Dr. Humes of Bethesda?

Dr. PERRY. He did.

Mr. SPECTER. Would you state as specifically as you can recollect the conversation that you first had with him?

Dr. PERRY. He advised me that he could not discuss with me the findings of necropsy, that he had a few questions he would like to clarify. The initial phone call was in relation to my doing a tracheotomy. Since I had made the incision directly through the wound in the neck, it made it difficult for them to ascertain the exact nature of this wound. Of course, that did not occur to me at the time. I did what appeared to me to be medically expedient. And when I informed him that there was a wound there and I suspected an underlying wound of the trachea and even perhaps of the great vessels he advised me that he thought this action was correct and he said he could not relate to me any of the other findings.

Mr. SPECTER. Would you relate to me in lay language what necropsy is?

Dr. PERRY. Autopsy, postmortem examination.

Mr. SPECTER. What was the content of the second conversation which you had with Comdr. Humes, please?

Dr. PERRY. The second conversation was in regard to the placement of the chest tubes for drainage of the chest cavity. And I related to him, as I have to you, the indications that prompted me to advise that this be done at that time.

Mr. SPECTER. Dr. Perry, did you observe any bruising of the neck muscles of President Kennedy when you were engaged in your operative procedure that you have described?

Dr. PERRY. This bruising, as you describe, would have been obscured by the fact that there was a large amount of blood, hematoma, present in the neck and the mediastinum and hence all the blood tissues were covered by this blood.

Mr. SPECTER. A few moments ago in response to a question by Mr. McCloy I believe you commented that, as you recollect it, very few of the doctors would have had an opportunity to observe the hole in the President's neck and I think you said that only you and Dr. Carrico would have had such an opportunity. Can you state, with absolute certainty, at which point the various doctors arrived in the room? And bear in mind on this that while you have not had the opportunity to review the depositions, some of the other doctors have expressed the view that they have had an opportunity to see the wound. Specifically, Dr. M. T. Jenkins said in a deposition that he did see the wound, and I have not had an opportunity to ask you that question before, because you made the comment during the course of the testimony today.

But I would like your comment on, in your opinion, whether the other doctors would have had an opportunity, perhaps, to observe the neck wound prior to the tracheotomy?

Dr. PERRY. Since I don't know with accuracy the exact times of their arrival, it is conceivable that others could have seen it. And Dr. Jenkins was apparently one of the early arrivals in the room.

However, at the time that I arrived, as I related, Dr. Carrico was present and Dr. Jones and I. Dr. Jones immediately directed himself toward obtaining another intravenous infusion, and I immediately went to the neck wound. At the time of arrival of the other surgeons which assisted me in the operation, I had already made the incision.

Dr. Jenkins could have arrived at the time that I was preparing to make the incision and seen the wound. It is possible, I don't know when he came in the room. I know he did not examine the wound per se.

Mr. SPECTER. And similarly Dr. Jones has commented in the course of his deposition about the situation with respect to the wound in the neck.

Based on your observations, would it be consistent with what you know to be fact that he had an opportunity to examine the neck wound?

Dr. PERRY. I know he might have seen it because he and I entered the room simultaneously, we came down together. To my knowledge, he did not examine the wound although he might have noted the wound present as I went to work.

Mr. SPECTER. Specifically what did he do then as you went to work?

Dr. PERRY. He was standing immediately on my left at that point, doing a venesection, a cut down in the left arm for the administration of fluids so he was able to observe the performance of the tracheotomy.

Mr. SPECTER. In your opinion, Dr. Perry, was President Kennedy alive or dead on arrival at Parkland?

Dr. PERRY. The President was alive in that spontaneous ineffective respiratory motions were observed by me, and although I never detected a pulse or a heartbeat, I was told there was also electrical activity on the cardiotachyscope when it was initially attached indicating there was spontaneous activity of the heart.

He was, therefore alive for medical purposes.

Mr. SPECTER. Who told you about the electrical activity on the cardiotachyscope?

Dr. PERRY. Dr. Clark.

Mr. SPECTER. Was any bullet found by you or by any other doctor at Parkland in the President's body?

Dr. PERRY. I found none. To the best of my knowledge neither did anyone else.

Mr. SPECTER. Was the President ever turned over at any time?

Dr. PERRY. Not by me nor did I see it done.

Mr. SPECTER. Were you present as long as any other doctor was present in the emergency room?

Dr. PERRY. No, sir; I think that at the time that I left trauma room number one, I went outside, and washed my hands, and I opened the door briefly to retrieve my coat which I had left there on the floor and the nurse handed me my coat.

At that time as I recall Doctor Jenkins was still in the room and there were several other people there including Mrs. Kennedy and the priest, and some gentlemen whom I did not know.

Mr. SPECTER. Now, did you make any effort to examine the clothing of President Kennedy?

Dr. PERRY. I did not.

(At this point, Representative Boggs entered the hearing room.)

Mr. SPECTER. Why was it, Dr. Perry, that there was no effort made to examine the clothing of President Kennedy and no effort to turn him over and examine the back of the President?

Dr. PERRY. At the termination of the procedure and after we had determined that Mr. Kennedy had expired, I cannot speak for the others but as for myself, my work was done. I fought a losing battle, and I actually obviously, having seen a lot of wounds, had no morbid curiosity, and actually was rather anxious to leave the room. I had nothing further to offer.

Mr. SPECTER. With the President having been declared dead, did you consider it was your function to make any further exploration of the President's body?

Dr. PERRY. This is not my function or my prerogative. This would be undertaken by suitable authorities at the time of postmortem, people with experience superior to mine in determining things of this sort.

Mr. SPECTER. Where was Mrs. Kennedy, if you know, during the course of the treatment which you have described that you performed?

Dr. PERRY. I had the initial impression she was in the room most of the time although I have been corrected on this. When I entered the room she was standing by the door, rather kneeling by the door, and someone was standing there beside her. I saw her several times during the course of the resuscitative measures, when I would look up from the operative field to secure an instrument from the nearby tray.

Mr. DULLES. Under your procedure who had the responsibility for declaring that the President was dead?

Dr. PERRY. This was a combination of factors, Mr. Dulles, undertaken by those of us all in attendance, by Dr. Clark and Dr. Jenkins and myself particularly since we were the senior people there.

I was informed subsequently that Mrs. Kennedy left the room several times to just outside the door but returned although as I say, I saw her several times in the room. I did not speak to her nor she to me so I do not have any knowledge as to exactly what she was doing.

Mr. SPECTER. Did you observe any wound in the President's chest?

Dr. PERRY. I did not.

Mr. SPECTER. Did you observe any wound on the left side of the President's head?

Dr. PERRY. No, sir.

Mr. SPECTER. Have you heretofore during the course of your testimony today described all of the wounds in the President which you have observed?

Dr. PERRY. I have.

Mr. SPECTER. Were you and the other doctors affected, in your opinion, in your treatment of the President by virtue of the fact that he was the President of the United States?

Dr. PERRY. Yes, sir; I am sure that is true. At the time that I was going down the stairs to the emergency room I was, of course, quite concerned, not knowing any of the circumstances surrounding the incident nor in what condition I would find him, and at the time that I entered the room, and it was my initial impression that he had a mortal wound.

At that point I directed myself to doing that which I could do and, of course, the time then became quite compressed during the course of the procedures and it was really not until afterwards that the full impact of what had happened began to hit me.

Mr. SPECTER. Did you have any occasion to render any treatment to Governor Connally at Parkland Hospital?

Dr. PERRY. I saw the Governor in regard to the consultation in regard to the injury to his leg. As I related earlier I am consultant in vascular surgery to the hospital, and the estimated course of the missile in his leg presupposed that he might have an injury to his femoral artery or vein and Dr. Shires asked me if I would put on a scrub suit and come to the operating room to assist in case it was necessary to do some arterial surgery.

It was not, however, so I did not operate.

Mr. SPECTER. At what time approximately did you arrive at the operating room where Governor Connally was being cared for?

Dr. PERRY. I don't know, sir.

Mr. SPECTER. Was it during the course of the operation performed by Dr. Shires?

Dr. PERRY. Yes, At that time I was there during the time Dr. Shires was there and Dr. Gregory was also operating on the arm at that point. Dr. Shaw had completed his portion of the procedure.

Mr. SPECTER. That would have been after the press conference had been completed?

Dr. PERRY. Yes, sir.

Mr. SPECTER. Did you have occasion to render medical aid to Lee Harvey Oswald on November 24?

Dr. PERRY. I did.

Mr. McCLOY. Before you get to that may I get clear, Dr. Shires and Dr. Gregory were in attendance?

Mr. SPECTER. Dr. Shaw in addition.

Dr. PERRY. Yes, and Shaw.

Mr. McCLOY. Shaw, Shires and Gregory?

Doctor PERRY. S-h-i-r-e-s.

Representative BOGGS. Before you get to Oswald may I ask one question? I am sure the doctor covered it. You said the minute you saw the President you felt he had suffered a mortal wound?

Dr. PERRY. Yes, sir.

Representative BOGGS. You saw the wound immediately then?

Dr. PERRY. Well, I saw his condition immediately, and as you are aware, I have attended a lot of people with severe injuries.

Representative BOGGS. Surely.

Dr. PERRY. And he obviously was in extremis when I walked in the room. And then I noted very cursorily the wound in the head and it was obvious that this was an extremely serious wound.

Representative BOGGS. Was he still alive when you saw him?

Dr. PERRY. He was.

Representative BOGGS. That is all.

Representative FORD. May I ask, Mr. Specter, during the total time that you were examining and treating the President, how much of his exposed body did you see?

Dr. PERRY. The upper trunk predominantly, Congressman Ford. His chest, and, of course, his arms were bare, neck and head. I did not examine any other portions of his body nor did I see any other portions except briefly when I felt for the femoral pulse on the left side.

Representative FORD. From the waist on up the front?

Dr. PERRY. Yes, sir.

Mr. SPECTER. Would you describe the treatment rendered to Mr. Oswald at Parkland Memorial Hospital by yourself and by others as you observed it?

Dr. PERRY. At the time I saw—starting with when I was called?

Mr. SPECTER. Yes.

Dr. PERRY. Well, I went immediately to the emergency room again, Dr. Jones and I who also was in the hospital again, and told me that I was the only attending surgeon present, and that they were bringing Mr. Oswald out, and I was in the surgery suite and I went directly to the emergency room just as he was being brought indoors.

Mr. SPECTER. At approximately what time was that?

Dr. PERRY. I really don't know, sir. It was about 11:15 or so when I was up in surgery. I had been seeing a baby in regard to an operation we had scheduled at 1 o'clock and then Dr. Jones came after me.

Mr. SPECTER. How long did it take you approximately to travel from the point where you received the notice that he was en route until your arrival at the emergency room?

Dr. PERRY. No more than 2 or 3 minutes.

Mr. SPECTER. And you say you arrived there simultaneously with Mr. Oswald?

Dr. PERRY. Just as he came in.

Mr. SPECTER. Precisely where in the hospital was it where you met Mr. Oswald?

Dr. PERRY. He was brought into the emergency room, trauma room number two, and as they wheeled him in I came around the corner.

Mr. SPECTER. What action did you take with respect to Mr. Oswald?

Dr. PERRY. Well, there were numerous people in attendance, more so than on the previous incident on Friday. He also obviously was quite seriously injured. He was cyanotic, very blue and although he also was attempting respirations, they were not effective, and an endotracheal tube was placed in him by one of the anesthesiologists, I think Dr. Jenkins, and I examined his chest and noted the entrance point of the bullet wound on the left side and I could feel the bullet just under the skin on the right side, right rear margin, indicating the bullet had passed entirely through his body and come to rest under the skin.

Mr. SPECTER. Where through his body?

Dr. PERRY. I beg your pardon sir, the bullet entered approximately the midaxillary line at about the 9th or 10th interspace on the left side of the chest cage, and came to rest just under the rib margin on the right side under the skin.

Mr. SPECTER. Could you supply in lay language what cyanotic means?

Dr. PERRY. Blue from lack of oxygen.

Mr. SPECTER. Could you explain in lay language the midaxillary line?

Dr. PERRY. It is about the mid portion of the fold extending down from the armpit on the left. This is just rough because I glanced at that briefly and determined the nature of the path of the bullet and from looking at him it was obvious that this had traversed major structures in his body in order to reach that particular place, so while a cutdown was being done again to administer fluid, I asked someone to put in a left chest tube on him because it appeared it went in and I recalled surgery until they were bringing him directly up.

Dr. Tom Shires, Chief of the Surgical Services, came into the door at a point and Dr. McClelland, and we left and went to surgery to change clothes and they brought him from there immediately to surgery and we proceeded with the operation.

Mr. SPECTER. Who was present, if anyone, with Mr. Oswald at the time you arrived there?

Dr. PERRY. In the emergency room?

Mr. SPECTER. Yes.

Dr. PERRY. Dr. Jenkins was there, Dr. M. T. Jenkins, Chief of Anesthesiology. I think Dr. Giesecke was also there again, although I am not sure of that. I saw Dr. Risk who is a resident in urology and I saw Dr. Dulany who is a resident in surgery. Dr. Boland, I believe who is a resident in thoracic surgery and, of course, Dr. Jones and myself, and there were several other people, the nurses, I don't recall.

Mr. SPECTER. Will you describe briefly the physical layout utilized in taking

Mr. Oswald from trauma room number two which you have already described up to the operating room?

Dr. PERRY. We have an express elevator that connects delivery room, operating room, emergency room and it is approximately 20 yards from trauma room two, I would estimate, just around the corner, in an even corridor and although I was not there as they took him up, I was in the operating room preparing and scrubbing, he was wheeled directly there to the express elevator and taken to the second floor where the operating suites are.

Mr. SPECTER. Approximately how long does it take to get a patient from the trauma room up to the operating room?

Dr. PERRY. It depends on a lot of factors. One is if the elevator is there or not or if it happens to be in surgery or in the delivery room. But I have on occasion where it was necessary that you must go with all dispatch to the operating room, have done it in a matter of a few minutes.

They brought him right in the door, placed him on the elevator with a finger controlling the hemorrhage where you could take him directly to the operating room. I have done that in a matter, I am sure, of less than 3 or 4 minutes if I had to.

Mr. SPECTER. Approximately how long did it take to get Oswald from trauma room two to the operating room?

Dr. PERRY. I don't know, I was told subsequently it was 12 minutes from the time we had him up. And——

Representative BOGGS. How long was it from the time he was shot until he reached the hospital?

Dr. PERRY. I have no knowledge of that, sir.

Representative BOGGS. Do you know?

Mr. SPECTER. No; I don't know.

Mr. DULLES. Was he conscious at any time so far as you know?

Dr. PERRY. No, sir; he did not say a word.

Mr. DULLES. He was not conscious?

Dr. PERRY. No, sir; and even had he been, of course, once we had the endotracheal tube in he could not have spoken.

Mr. SPECTER. Who was in charge of the operation performed on Mr. Oswald?

Dr. PERRY. Dr. Tom Shires.

Mr. SPECTER. Who was in assistance with Dr. Shires?

Dr. PERRY. I first assisted Dr. Shires and then Ronald Jones and Dr. McClelland were also at the operation.

Mr. SPECTER. Will you describe the operative procedures employed on Mr. Oswald please?

Dr. PERRY. Yes. From the nature of the trajectory of the wound and the nature of the path of the bullet on the other side it was obvious that it had traversed major vessels, the aorta and vena cava. The aorta and vena cava, the heart area, and then a midline incision was made. A rapid prep with iodine was done, the patient was draped. An incision was carried rapidly into the abdominal cavity at which time we noticed approximately 3 litres of free blood which is an excess of three quarts. This was removed by suction, lap packs and by just moving it out in the form of clots with the hands. It was noted there was considerable bleeding appearing in both the right upper and left upper quadrants of the body. There was a large hematoma retroperitoneally in the midline also, causing the bowels to be pushed forward rather strikingly.

We immediately dissected over the portal vein on the right since it was apparently injured, and placed a vascular occlusive clamp of the Sittinsky type in this area to control the bleeding. Noted an injury to the right kidney and to the lobe of the liver. We also noted there was an injury to the stomach, the pancreas, the spleen. At that point it became apparent that he had indeed struck major vessels, and appeared to be the aorta, so the left colon was reflected very rapidly in order to allow us to enter the space behind the intestines, the retroperitoneal space, and at that point I controlled the bleeding from the aorta by finger pressure below and above this area.

The bullet had knocked the superior mesenteric artery completely off the aorta exposing a large area.

After I had controlled the bleeding Dr. Shires was able to dissect around the area sufficient to allow us to gain control of the aorta, superior mesenteric artery and the vena cava and the placement of vascular clamps across these vessels in order to stop the hemmorhage.

At this point, he was being given blood and, of course, the suitable anesthesia measures which were oxygen under pressure. He did not require an anesthetic agent, I am told.

Mr. SPECTER. Who told you that, Dr. Perry?

Dr. PERRY. I think one of the residents did, one of the anesthesia residents. We at that point had restored his blood pressure. I don't know the exact recordings, but I was told subsequently it had returned to near normal levels since we had the bleeding controlled.

Mr. SPECTER. What was the situation with respect to his respiration at that time?

Dr. PERRY. It was being assisted and controlled, of course, by anesthesiology. This was no problem. We had a tube in place and was breathing for him so he had no problem with respiration. This was completely under control of anesthesia. The blood pressure was controlled and we stopped for a moment to determine how we would best go about repairing the structures and which would have priority, all the bleeding had stopped but, as I recall, the clamping of the aorta at the level of the superior mesenteric artery means, of course, that you must prevent blood from entering the kidneys, and this in itself can be hazardous if extended, and therefore we decided this must be repaired immediately in order to restore blood into the kidneys and the lower portion of the body.

Then Dr. Jenkins informed me and Dr. Shires that his cardiac action was becoming weak, and I don't remember all the details surrounding the medications and the things that were done at this particular time, but he developed a backward cardiac failure, his heart slowed abruptly and the blood pressure fell again and it was apparent the tremendous blood loss he had had set the stage for irreversible shock and lack of pumping action from the heart although he was being given massive transfusions, I don't know the exact number, probably he had 10 or 12 units. I believe it is in the record.

At this point when they told me a cardiac arrest had occurred as a result of the hemorrhage and blood loss I took a knife and opened the left chest in the fourth interspace and reached in to massage his heart, and the heart was flabby, and dilated, and apparently contained very little blood.

I began to massage the heart, to maintain it as we infused the blood and was able to obtain a palpable pulse in the carotid vessels going to the neck and into the head. We were unable to get the heart to go, and it began to fibrillate which is an uncoordinated motion of the muscles of the heart itself and the successive electrical shocks were applied with the defibrillator and to stimulate heart action, and we failed in this and the cardiac pacemaker was sewn in place, and it was handed to me by the thoracic surgery resident, and I sewed it into the heart to artificially induce heart action, this also was without benefit.

We were never able to restore effective heart action and then Dr. Jenkins informed us neurologically he was not responding, that his reflexes were gone, and he felt that he had expired.

Mr. SPECTER. At approximately what time did that occur?

Dr. PERRY. I don't know, Mr. Specter, I would have to look at the record.

Mr. SPECTER. At approximately how long after he arrived at the hospital did that occur?

Dr. PERRY. I don't know that, either.

Mr. SPECTER. Can you approximate the length of time of the operation itself?

Dr. PERRY. 45 minutes or so, I would say.

Mr. SPECTER. Is there any question but that he was alive during the course of your operative procedures?

Dr. PERRY. Oh, no, no question. The fact is we were very close, I think, to winning the battle. We have seen injuries of this magnitude, they rarely survive, this is a very serious injury and to the best of my knowledge I have not seen anyone with this particular set of injuries survive. But at one point once we controlled the hemorrhage and once I had control of the aorta and was ble to stop the bleeding of that area I actually felt we had a very good chance ince everything had proceeded with expediency.

Mr. SPECTER. Have you been interviewed by any representative of the Federal iovernment in connection with your treatment of President Kennedy, Dr. 'erry?

Dr. PERRY. Yes, I have.

Mr. SPECTER. By whom were you interviewed?

Dr. PERRY. I regret that I do not recall their names. I was interviewed 'y two gentlemen from the Secret Service approximately the following week, .s I recall, and again about a month ago.

Mr. SPECTER. And what questions were asked of you on the first interview 'y the Secret Service?

Dr. PERRY. Essentially in regard to the treatment and once again specu- ation as to where the bullets might have originated and what the nature of he wounds were and I was unable to supply them with any adequate in- ormation.

Mr. SPECTER. Were the responses given by you to the Secret Service on that irst interview essentially the same as you have given today?

Dr. PERRY. With minor variations in wording, they are essentially the same.

Mr. SPECTER. Approximately when did the second interview occur with he Secret Service?

Dr. PERRY. I think approximately a month ago, although I am not sure of that.

Mr. SPECTER. What was the content of that interview?

Dr. PERRY. A gentleman identified himself as being connected with the War- 'en Commission and Secret Service. I asked for his credentials which he duly supplied and he asked me in regard to any further information I might have 'ertaining to the events of that weekend, and we reiterated some of these statements which I made previously, and since I had nothing more to add, why t was terminated.

Mr. SPECTER. Did you supply any information which was in any way different 'rom that which you have testified to here today?

Dr. PERRY. In essence; no, sir.

Mr. SPECTER. On the second interview, did the man identify himself to you .s a Secret Service agent who was conducting a further inquiry at the request •f the President's Commission?

Dr. PERRY. Yes, sir; he said he was with the Warren Commission.

Mr. SPECTER. Did I discuss the facts within your knowledge or take your de- •osition in Dallas on Wednesday, March 25, 1964?

Dr. PERRY. Yes.

Mr. SPECTER. And was the information which you provided at that time in .dvance of the deposition and during the course of the deposition itself the same as the information which you provided here today concerning the treat- ment of President Kennedy, your observations and opinions on President Kennedy?

Dr. PERRY. It is.

Mr. SPECTER. Have I made that transcript available to you this morning •efore we started this testimony?

Dr. PERRY. Yes.

Mr. SPECTER. Have you at any time changed any opinion which you held :oncerning any matter relating to President Kennedy?

Dr. PERRY. No, sir.

Mr. SPECTER. Did you prepare a handwritten report on your care of Presi- lent Kennedy which became part of the record of Parkland Hospital?

Dr. PERRY. I did.

Mr. SPECTER. Which you identified during the course of the deposition pro- :eeding as being your report?

Dr. PERRY. Yes, that is correct.

Mr. SPECTER. Do you have any other notes of your own relating to any of the matters which you testified here today?

Dr. PERRY. None.

Mr. McCLOY. What was the condition of, general physical condition, apart from the wounds, of Oswald, as you observed him? Was his body healthy?

Dr. PERRY. I made only a very cursory examination, Mr. McCloy. He appeared rather thin to me.

Mr. McCLOY. Not, you wouldn't call him a muscular type?

Dr. PERRY. No, he would be what we would describe as a thinnish individual, that is very thin; was wiry rather than bulky muscles.

Mr. McCLOY. Were there any signs that you observed cursorily, symptoms of any prior disease?

Dr. PERRY. No, I did not look for those.

Mr. DULLES. No distinguishing marks on the body that you saw, prior operations?

Dr. PERRY. No, sir; I did not look. There was no evidence of previous surgical operation on his abdomen, and I didn't examine anything else.

Of course, this also can be missed unless you are looking for it. We went through the midline and unless one went looking for it we did not have time and we would not see it.

Mr. SPECTER. Dr. Perry, was the chest tube inserted in the President's chest abandoned or was that operation or operative procedure completed?

Dr. PERRY. The chest tube, to be placed there, was supposedly placed into the pleural cavity. However, I have knowledge that it was not.

Mr. SPECTER. And what was the reason for its not being placed into the plueral cavity?

Dr. PERRY. I did not speak with certainty but at that point I think that we were at the end of the procedure and they just did not continue with it.

Mr. SPECTER. Had it become apparent at that time that the President expired?

Dr. PERRY. That, I think, is probably true, but I did not state that with certainty because I cannot state the exact sequence. I was employed myself at the time, and I think if it had been determined that this was not in, it would have been completed, if there was still time, but I am not sure of that. That is speculation.

Mr. SPECTER. With respect to the condition of the neck wounds, was it ragged or pushed out in any manner?

Dr. PERRY. No, it was not. As I originally described it, the edges were neither cleancut, that is punched out, nor were they very ragged. I realize that is not a very specific description but it is in between those two areas.

Mr. SPECTER. Was there blood in that area which tended to obscure your view?

Dr. PERRY. It was exuding blood during that procedure and thus I did not examine it very closely. In retrospect, I think it would have been of much more value had I looked at these things more carefully but I had directed my attention to other things.

Mr. SPECTER. Those complete my questions.

Representative FORD. Mr. McCloy?

Mr. Dulles?

Have you examined the autopsy report made by the officials in Bethesda?

Dr. PERRY. Yes, sir, I have.

Representative FORD. Does your testimony conform to the facts stated in that report?

Dr. PERRY. I think so. At the time the testimony which I have given here of my knowledge without the—was given the same as it was without the basis of that report. But now having had access to that report, I think it ties in very nicely. I see no discrepancies at all. For example, had I known that he had these other two wounds, it would have been much easier at the time to state a little more categorically about the trajectory of the missiles, but not knowing about those I could only speculate.

Representative FORD. There is no basic conflict between what you have testified to or what you have said previously, and the autopsy report?

Dr. PERRY. None at all.

Representative BOGGS. Just one question. I presume this question has been asked.

This neck wound, was there any indication that that wound had come from the front?

Dr. PERRY. There is no way to tell, sir, for sure. As you may recall, passage of a high velocity missile, the damage it does, is dependent on two factors, actually, one being deformation of the missile, increase in its relative caliber, and the other the expending of the energy of that missile in the object it strikes.

For example, the energy used to carry the missile beyond the object that it struck is obviously not going to cause much of an injury. If there is a missile of relatively high velocity, although I consider this a medium velocity weapon, that the missile for entrance or exit had the bullet not been deformed would not be substantially different, had it not been deformed nor particularly slowed in its velocity.

Representative BOGGS. By that, you mean it would be difficult to determine the point of exit and the point of entrance under those circumstances?

Dr. PERRY. Yes, sir; unless one were able to ascertain the trajectory. If you could, for example, make check points between what the missile might have struck, then you could ascertain trajectory. But with a relatively high velocity missile, this also is difficult due to the amount of blast injury which occurs in enclosed tissues, similar to those I am sure you have seen to those discussed, so blast injury can be an area remote from the exact passage of the missile itself.

Representative BOGGS. Of course, your main concern was to try to save the President's life and not——

Dr. PERRY. Yes, sir; it actually never occurred to me until all the questions began to come, and I was ill-prepared to meet them, but it never occurred to me that, to investigate, because I was busy, and I have done these types of things many times.

It just never occurred to me to look into it until afterwards.

Representative FORD. Any questions, Dean Storey?

Mr. STOREY. No, thank you, sir.

Representative FORD. Mr. Murray?

Mr. MURRAY. No.

Mr. DULLES. I have one more question I would like to ask.

Did you know anything about the spent bullet that was found on, I don't know what you call it—the litter?

Dr. PERRY. On the carriage?

Mr. DULLES. On the carriage.

Dr. PERRY. My first knowledge of that was one of the newspaper publications had said there was a bullet found there. I don't know now whether it was or was not. I didn't find it.

Mr. SPECTER. May I say, Mr. Dulles, on that subject, I took several depositions on that subject in the Dallas Hospital and I think we have a reasonably conclusive answer on that question; and, in fact, it came from the stretcher of Governor Connally.

Dr. PERRY. They were quoted as having removed a bullet from Governor Connally's leg, the press quoted that, but a bullet was not removed from Governor Connally's leg.

Mr. SPECTER. There was no bullet removed from Governor Connally's leg, but there was a wound there, but there was a very small fragment embedded in the femur, as the deposition of Drs. Shaw, Shires, and Gregory will show. But the bullet was found on a stretcher and the question arose as to whose stretcher it was, and we have traced the two stretchers in a way so as to exclude the possibility of its being the stretcher on which President Kennedy was carried, and we have traced the path of Governor Connally's stretcher and have narrowed it to two stretchers. And the bullet came off of one of the two stretchers, so that, through the circumstances of the facts, it is reasonably conclusive that it came from the stretcher of Governor Connally.

Representative FORD. How long did it take you to go from where you were when the page came to get down to trauma room No. 1?

Dr. PERRY. A matter of no more than a minute or so, Congressman Ford. It is down one flight of stairs and the door is almost immediately adjacent to the dining room where we would go and we did not wait on the elevator. We went down the stairs.

Representative FORD. How long after the President was brought in before you went to trauma room No. 1?

Dr. PERRY. That I don't know either. My last recollection in regard to time was approximately 12:30 when I was having lunch prior to rounds, and Dr. Jones picked up the page and as we went downstairs I took off my watch and dropped it in my coat pocket, rather expecting to do some kind of procedure, and I took off my coat and I never looked at the clock until afterwards.

Mr. McCLOY. One more question, I want to get clear.

The extent to which you examined Governor Connally's wounds, as I gather, you were asked to stand by.

Dr. PERRY. That is right, sir.

Mr. McCLOY. Rather than to be involved in a close examination of the wounds.

Dr. PERRY. That is right, sir.

Mr. McCLOY. So you are not generally familiar?

Dr. PERRY. No, sir; all I did was come into the operating room, put on a scrub suit, cap and mask, and looked at the thigh wound before Dr. Shires started the operation. That was the extent of the episode into the wound, and I stayed there while he carried it down to the lower portion of the wound and indicated there was no serious injury, and I left the operating room at that point.

Mr. McCLOY. And you didn't see the other two wounds?

Dr. PERRY. I didn't see the other wounds at all, sir.

Representative FORD. Thank you very much, Dr. Perry.

Your testimony has been most helpful.

(Whereupon, at 11:45 a.m., the President's Commission recessed.)

Tuesday, March 31, 1964

TESTIMONY OF ROBERT A. FRAZIER AND RONALD SIMMONS

The President's Commission met at 9 a.m. on March 31, 1964, at 200 Maryland Avenue NE., Washington, D.C.

Present were Chief Justice Earl Warren, Chairman; Representative Hale Boggs and John J. McCloy, members.

Also present were J. Lee Rankin, general counsel; Melvin Aron Eisenberg, assistant counsel; Norman Redlich, assistant counsel; Charles Murray and Lewis Powell, observers; and Leon Jaworski, special counsel to the attorney general of Texas.

TESTIMONY OF ROBERT A. FRAZIER

The CHAIRMAN. Mr. Frazier, the purpose of today's hearing is to take the testimony of yourself and Mr. Ronald Simmons.

You are, we understand, a firearms expert with the FBI, and Mr. Simmons is a firearms expert with the Weapons System Division at Fort Meade, Md.

You are asked to provide technical information to assist the Commission in this work.

Would you raise your right hand and be sworn, please?

You solemnly swear the testimony you are about to give before this Commission will be the truth, the whole truth, and nothing but the truth, so help you God?

Mr. FRAZIER. I do.

The CHAIRMAN. You may be seated, please.

Mr. EISENBERG. Mr. Frazier, will you give your name and position?

Mr. FRAZIER. Robert A. Frazier, Special Agent, Federal Bureau of Investigation, assigned to the FBI Laboratory, Washington, D.C.

Mr. Eisenberg. And your education?

Mr. Frazier. I have a science degree which I received from the University of Idaho.

Mr. Eisenberg. Could you briefly state your training and experience in the fields of firearms, firearms identification, and ballistics?

Mr. Frazier. Beginning in 1937, I was on the University of Idaho Rifle Team, and the following year, 1938. In 1939 I enlisted in the National Guard and for 2 years was on the National Guard Rifle Team firing both small bore, or .22 caliber weapons, and the large bore, .30 caliber weapons, both being of the bolt-action type weapons.

In 1939 and 1940 I instructed in firearms in the Army of the United States, and acquired additional experience in firing of weapons, training in firing at moving targets, additional training in firing the .45 caliber automatic and machineguns. And to further my firearms, practical firearms training, I received in 1942 a training course offered by the Federal Bureau of Investigation after entering on duty with that organization in—on June 9, 1941. That firearms training course consisted of a basic training in handguns—that is, revolvers and automatic pistols, training in autoloading rifles, training in submachineguns, shotguns, and various other types of firearms.

One year later, approximately 1943, I received a specialized administrative firearms course which qualified me for training other agents in the field of law-enforcement type firearms.

Over the past 23 years, I have received the regular FBI firearms training, which is a monthly retraining in firearms, and a periodic, or every 4 years, detailed retraining in the basic FBI firearms—the firearms training with the rifle, submachinegun, shotgun, revolver.

In the FBI, training includes firing both at stationary targets and moving targets with both revolver and rifle and shotgun, and includes firing at slow-fire targets—that is aimed fire for accuracy and rapid fire to increase speed of firing.

Generally in the field of firearms identification, where I have been assigned for 23 years, I received specialized training given in the FBI Laboratory to train me for the position of firearms identification specialist. In that field, we make examinations of bullets and cartridge cases, firearms of various types, for the purpose of identifying weapons as to their caliber, what they are, their manufacturer, their physical characteristics, and determining the type of ammunition which they shoot.

We examine ammunition of various types to identify it as to its caliber, its specific designation, and the type or types of weapons in which it can be fired, and we make comparisons of bullets to determine whether or not they were fired from a particular weapon and make comparisons of cartridge cases for the purpose of determining whether or not they were fired in a particular weapon, or for determining whether or not they had been loaded into or extracted from a particular weapon.

That training course lasted for approximately 1 year. However, of course, the experience in firearms is actually part of the training and continues for the entire time in which you are engaged in examining firearms.

Briefly, that is the summary of the firearms training I have had.

Mr. Eisenberg. Could you estimate the number of examinations you have made of firearms to identify the firearms?

Mr. Frazier. Thousands, I would say—firearms comparisons—I have made in the neighborhood of 50,000 to 60,000.

Mr. McCloy. Have you written any articles on this subject?

Mr. Frazier. Yes. I have prepared an article for the "FBI Law Enforcement Bulletin" on firearms identification, which is published as a reprint and provided to any organization or person interested in the general field of firearms identification.

Mr. McCloy. Have you read most of the literature on the subject?

Mr. Frazier. Yes, I have.

Mr. McCloy. Is there any classical book on this subject?

Mr. Frazier. There are a number of fairly good texts.

The basic one, originally published in 1936, is by Maj. Julian S. Hatcher, who later, as a general, rewrote his book "Firearms Investigation, Identification, and Evidence."

There are many other books published on the subject.

Mr. EISENBERG. May I ask that this person be accepted as a qualified witness on firearms?

The CHAIRMAN. Yes, indeed.

Mr. EISENBERG. Mr. Frazier, I now hand you a rifle marked Commission Exhibit 139.

Are you familiar with this weapon?

Mr. FRAZIER. Yes, I am.

Mr. EISENBERG. And do you recognize it by serial number or by your mark?

Mr. FRAZIER. By serial number on the barrel, and by my initials which appear on various parts of the weapon.

Mr. EISENBERG. For the record, this is the rifle which was found on the sixth floor of the Texas School Book Depository Building on November 22.

Can you describe this rifle by name and caliber?

Mr. FRAZIER. It is a caliber 6.5 Italian military rifle, commonly referred to in the United States as a 6.5-mm. Mannlicher-Carcano.

It is a bolt-action clip-fed military rifle.

Do you wish a general physical description of the weapon at this time?

Mr. EISENBERG. Well, no; not at this time.

Can you explain the American equivalent to the 6.5-mm. caliber?

Mr. FRAZIER. That is the same as .25 caliber. Such weapons in the United States as the .25–20 Winchester, .25–35, the .250 Savage, and the .257 Roberts, are all of the same barrel diameter, or approximately the same barrel diameter. So a decimal figure of .257 inch is the equivalent of 6.5 mm.

Mr. EISENBERG. And can you explain what the caliber is a measure of?

Mr. FRAZIER. The caliber is the measure of the distance across the raised portions or the lands in the barrel. The groove diameter, or the spirals cut in the barrel to form the rifling, will be slightly larger—in this case between 7/1000ths and 8/1000ths of an inch larger than the actual bore diameter.

The caliber is normally determined by the bore diameter.

Mr. EISENBERG. Can you explain how you made the identification of this rifle?

Mr. FRAZIER. I identified it pictorially by comparing it with pictures in reference books. And the actual identification was of the manufacturer's name appearing on the barrel and serial number, which indicated it was an Italian military rifle.

Mr. EISENBERG. Did you independently determine the caliber of the rifle?

Mr. FRAZIER. Yes, I did.

Mr. EISENBERG. Can you tell us how you did that?

Mr. FRAZIER. The caliber and the caliber type may be confusing here.

The caliber, being the diameter of the barrel, is determined in two ways—one, by comparing the barrel with 6.5-mm. Mannlicher-Carcano ammunition, which we also chambered in the weapon and determined that it actually fit the weapon. And, secondly, we measured the width of the barrel with a micrometer. And in that connection, I would like to point out that we made a sulphur cast of the muzzle of the weapon which permitted us to use a micrometer to determine the land width and the groove width in the barrel.

Mr. EISENBERG. Do you have that sulphur cast?

Mr. FRAZIER. Yes, I do.

Mr. EISENBERG. And that was made by you or under your supervision?

Mr. FRAZIER. Yes, it was made by me.

Mr. EISENBERG. Mr. Chairman, I ask that this be admitted as Commission Exhibit No. 540.

The CHAIRMAN. It will be admitted.

(The article referred to was marked Commission Exhibit No. 540, and received in evidence.)

Mr. EISENBERG. Is there any reason that you can think of why this Exhibit 139 might be thought to be a 7.35- or 7.65-caliber rifle?

Mr. FRAZIER. From outward appearances, it could be a 7.35-mm. rifle, because, basically, that is what it is. But its mechanism has been rebarreled with a

6.5-mm. barrel. Photographs of the weapons are similar, unless you make a very particular study of the photographs of the original model 38 Italian military rifle, which is 7.35 mm.

Early in the Second World War, however, the Italian Government barreled many of these rifles with a 6.5-mm. barrel, since they had a quantity of that ammunition on hand. I presume that would be the most logical way of confusing this weapon with one of a larger caliber.

Mr. EISENBERG. And is the 6.5-caliber weapon distinguished from the 7.35-caliber weapon by name?

Mr. FRAZIER. Yes, it is; it is by the model number. The model 91/38 designates the 6.5-mm. rifle, whereas the model 38 designates the 7.35.

Mr. EISENBERG. Have you taken photographs of the various markings on the rifle?

Mr. FRAZIER. Yes, I did.

Mr. EISENBERG. Do you have those with you?

Mr. FRAZIER. Actually, I think we forwarded those photographs to the Commission.

Mr. EISENBERG. Are these the photographs that you took, or had taken?

Mr. FRAZIER. Yes, sir.

Mr. EISENBERG. Has the Federal Bureau of Investigation been supplied with information concerning the meanings and significances of these various markings?

Mr. FRAZIER. Yes, sir; we have.

Mr. EISENBERG. Can you state the source of that information?

Mr. FRAZIER. This information came to us by mail as a result of an inquiry of the Italian Armed Forces Intelligence Service, abbreviated SIFAR, by letter dated March 26, 1964, through the FBI representative in Rome, Italy.

This information is classified as secret by the Italian Government, who have advised that the material may be released to the Commission. However, they desire the retention of the information in a secret category.

The CHAIRMAN. Is this essential to the proof?

If it is not, I think we would rather not have it, because the fewer things we have to keep in secret, the better the situation is for us.

Mr. EISENBERG. Off the record.

(Discussion off the record.)

Mr. EISENBERG. Back on the record.

Based on your experience with firearms, is the placement of a specific serial number on a weapon generally confined to one weapon of a given type?

Mr. FRAZIER. Yes, it is. Particularly—may I refer to foreign weapons particularly?

The serial number consists of a series of numbers which normally will be repeated. However, a prefix is placed before the number, which actually must be part of the serial number, consisting of a letter.

Mr. EISENBERG. Have you been able to confirm that the serial number on this weapon is the only such number on such a weapon?

Mr. FRAZIER. Yes, it is.

Mr. EISENBERG. All right.

Now, without reference to any classified information, could you briefly describe the markings shown on these photographs?

Mr. FRAZIER. The first photograph is an overall photograph of the rifle.

Mr. EISENBERG. Excuse me.

These photographs—when you say "first photograph"—these photographs are marked No. 1, No. 2, et cetera, on the back.

Mr. FRAZIER. Yes, they are.

Photograph No. 1 is an overall photograph of the rifle.

Photograph No. 2 is made of the top of the barrel, showing the serial number C2766.

Photograph No. 3 is also of the top of the rifle, showing a portion of the inscription on the telescopic sight, and the figures 1940, which is the manufacturer's date, the words "Made Italy" and a figure in the form of a crown, under that the letters "R–E," and then a portion of the word "Terni."

Mr. EISENBERG. Can you explain the significance of "Terni?"

Mr. FRAZIER. Terni is the location for an Italian ordnance plant in Italy where rifles are made, and it is apparent that this weapon was made in Terni, because it is stamped with that name.

Mr. EISENBERG. And the significance of that crown?

Mr. FRAZIER. I think that would be just an Italian identification mark or proof mark.

Mr. EISENBERG. And are the words "Made Italy" likely to have been put on the weapon at the time of manufacture or subsequently?

Mr. FRAZIER. No, sir; the words "Made Italy" would be stamped on the weapon by a purchaser or an individual desiring to send the weapon to another country, to establish actually its origin.

Photograph No. 4 is again of the top of the weapon showing the same information—1940, "Made Italy," the crown, the place it was made, and the inscription "Caliber 6.5" across the top of the rear sight.

Photograph No. 5 shows a small circle which appears on the forward end of the receiver, or that portion into which the barrel is screwed, with the words "TNI" in the circle, and over these letters is again a small crown. This could be a proof mark or an inspector's stamp.

Photograph No. 6 is of an inscription on the side of the rear sight which has the appearance of the letter "i," or the letter "l," followed by a capital letter "A," and the capital letter "G," with the numbers "47," and "2," stamped underneath them. I do not know what the significance of that is. It could be, again, an inspector's stamp or a proof mark of some type.

Photograph No. 7 is made of the cocking piece on the end of the bolt, which gives the word "Rocca." This apparently would be the name of the manufacturer of that part of the rifle.

Photograph No. 8 is an inscription "PG" on the top of the bolt of the weapon. This inscription—I do not know of my own knowledge what that is—but it could be the mark of a manufacturer or a proof mark or an inspector's mark made at the time the handle was made to be welded to the bolt.

Photograph No. 9 was taken of the bottom of the receiver of the weapon, with the stock removed. It shows the Number "40," which could refer again to the year of manufacture, 1940, on the receiver, and at the rear of the photograph a small lettered inscription referring again to an inspector stamp, a proof stamp, of some nature. The identity of this, I do not know.

Mr. EISENBERG. Mr. Chairman, I ask that these photographs be admitted as a group under the number 541.

The CHAIRMAN. You are going to put all of them in under one number?

Mr. EISENBERG. Yes. They have the subnumbers on the back, which will differentiate them.

The CHAIRMAN. They will be admitted.

(The documents referred to were marked Commission Exhibit No. 541, and received in evidence.)

Mr. EISENBERG. Can you explain why someone might call Exhibit 139 a German-made Mauser rifle or a Mauser bolt-action rifle?

Mr. FRAZIER. The Mauser was one of the earliest, if not the earliest, and the basic bolt-action rifle, from which many others were copied. And since this uses the same type of bolt system, it may have been referred to as a Mauser for that reason.

Mr. EISENBERG. Does this weapon show—how much use does this weapon show?

Mr. FRAZIER. The stock is worn, scratched. The bolt is relatively smooth, as if it had been operated several times. I cannot actually say how much use the weapon has had. The barrel is—was not, when we first got it, in excellent condition. It was, I would say, in fair condition. In other words, it showed the effects of wear and corrosion.

Mr. EISENBERG. Is this weapon——

The CHAIRMAN. I didn't get that last.

Mr. FRAZIER. It showed the effects of wear and corrosion.

Mr. EISENBERG. Is this weapon used when it is sold into the United States?

Mr. FRAZIER. Yes, it is a surplus type of weapon.

Mr. EISENBERG. So that it is impossible to attribute any given amount of wear to the last user?

Mr. FRAZIER. Yes, sir; it is impossible.

Mr. EISENBERG. Have you measured the dimensions of this rifle assembled, and disassembled?

Mr. FRAZIER. Yes, I have.

Mr. EISENBERG. Could you give us that information?

Mr. FRAZIER. The overall length is 40.2 inches. It weighs 8 pounds even.

Mr. McCLOY. With the scope?

Mr. FRAZIER. Yes, with the scope.

The CHAIRMAN. And the sling?

Mr. FRAZIER. That is with the sling, yes, sir. The sling weighs 4¾ ounces. The stock length is 34.8 inches, which is the wooden portion from end to end with the butt plate attached. The barrel and action from the muzzle to the rear of the tang, which is this portion at the rearmost portion of the metal, is 28.9 inches. The barrel only is 21.18 inches.

Mr. EISENBERG. When you say, "this portion," Mr. Frazier, I don't think that is coming down clear in the record. I wonder whether you could rephrase that so as to describe the part of the barrel or part of the stock to which you are pointing when you say "tang."

Mr. FRAZIER. The tang is the rear of the receiver of the weapon into which the rear mounting screw is screwed to hold the rearmost part of the metal action of the weapon into the wooden stock. From the end of that portion to the muzzle of the weapon is 28.9 inches.

Mr. EISENBERG. And the length of the longest component when the rifle is disassembled, Mr. Frazier?

Mr. FRAZIER. 34.8 inches, which is the length of the stock, the wooden portion.

Mr. EISENBERG. Can you describe to us the telescopic sight on the rifle in terms of——

Mr. McCLOY. Before you get to the sight, can I ask a question?

Mr. EISENBERG. Surely.

Mr. McCLOY. How soon after the assassination did you examine this rifle?

Mr. FRAZIER. We received the rifle the following morning.

Mr. McCLOY. Received it in Washington?

Mr. FRAZIER. Yes, sir.

Mr. McCLOY. And you immediately made your examination of it then?

Mr. FRAZIER. We made an examination of it at that time, and kept it temporarily in the laboratory.

It was then returned to the Dallas Police Department, returned again to the laboratory—the second time on November 27th, and has been either in the laboratory's possession or the Commission's possession since then.

Mr. McCLOY. When you examined the rifle the first time, you said that it showed signs of some corrosion and wear?

Mr. FRAZIER. Yes, sir.

Mr. McCLOY. Was it what you would call pitted, were the lands in good shape?

Mr. FRAZIER. No, sir; the lands and the grooves were worn, the corners were worn, and the interior of the surface was roughened from corrosion or wear.

Mr. McCLOY. Was there metal fouling in the barrel?

Mr. FRAZIER. I did not examine it for that.

Mr. McCLOY. Could you say roughly how many rounds you think had been fired since it left the factory, with the condition of the barrel as you found it?

Mr. FRAZIER. No, sir; I could not, because the number of rounds is not an indication of the condition of the barrel, since if a barrel is allowed to rust, one round will remove that rust and wear the barrel to the same extent as 10 or 15 or 50 rounds just fired through a clean barrel.

Mr. McCLOY. Thank you.

Mr. EISENBERG. Could you describe the telescopic sight on the rifle? Magnification, country of origin?

Mr. FRAZIER. It is a four-power telescopic sight employing crosshairs in it as a sighting device, in the interior of the scope.

It is stamped "Optics Ordnance Incorporated, Hollywood California," and under that is the inscription "Made in Japan." It is a very inexpensive Japanese telescopic sight.

The mount attached to it was also made in Japan.

Mr. EISENBERG. Have you removed the mount?

Mr. FRAZIER. Yes, I have.

Mr. EISENBERG. How many holes did you find drilled into the receiver?

Mr. FRAZIER. There are two holes in the receiver.

Mr. EISENBERG. Could you form an opinion as to whether these were original holes or whether new holes—new and larger holes had been formed over the original holes?

Mr. FRAZIER. Normally, the receiver would have no holes at all, and would have to be drilled and tapped for the screws. In the sight itself there normally are three holes, two of which have been enlarged to accommodate the two mounting screws presently holding the mount to the rifle.

Mr. EISENBERG. Do you think, based on your experience with types of screws used in mounts, that these were the original screws and the original holes for the screws?

Mr. FRAZIER. I could not say—I could not answer that specifically. However, they appear to be the same type of screw as is present on the rest of the mount—although they are somewhat larger in size than the remaining hole which is present in the lower portion of the mount.

Mr. EISENBERG. Now, I now hand you a rifle which is marked C–250. Are you familiar with this rifle?

Mr. FRAZIER. Yes, sir.

Mr. EISENBERG. Can you describe it briefly?

Mr. FRAZIER. It is an identical rifle physically to the rifle Commission's Exhibit 139, in that it is the same caliber, 6.5-mm. Mannlicher-Carcano Italian Military rifle, Model 91/38.

Mr. EISENBERG. Did you attempt to determine by use of this rifle whether the scope was mounted on Exhibit 139 by the firm which is thought to have sold Exhibit 139?

Mr. FRAZIER. Would you repeat that, please?

Mr. EISENBERG. Yes.

Did you make an attempt to determine, by use of this C–250, whether the firm which had sold Exhibit 139 had mounted the scope on Exhibit 139?

Mr. FRAZIER. Yes, sir.

Mr. EISENBERG. Can you describe how you made that attempt?

Mr. FRAZIER. We contacted the firm, Klein's Sporting Goods in Chicago, and asked them concerning this matter to provide us with a similar rifle mounted in the way in which they normally mount scopes of this type on these rifles, and forward the rifle to us for examination.

In this connection, we did inform them that the scope should be in approximately this position on the frame of the weapon.

Mr. EISENBERG. Pardon me, Mr. Frazier. When you say "this position," so that the record is clear could you——

Mr. FRAZIER. Oh, yes; in the position in which it now is, approximately three-eighths of an inch to the rear of the receiver ring.

Mr. EISENBERG. On the——

Mr. FRAZIER. On the C–250 rifle.

When we received the rifle C–250, we examined the mount and found that two of the holes had been enlarged, and that screws had been placed through them and threaded into the receiver of the C–250 rifle.

The third hole in the mount had not been used.

We also found that an identical scope to the one on the Commission's rifle 139 was present on the C–250 rifle.

Mr. EISENBERG. Were the screws used in mounting the C–250 rifle—in mounting the scope on the C–250 rifle—type of screws as those used in mounting the scope on Exhibit 139?

Mr. FRAZIER. Yes, sir.

Mr. EISENBERG. And the holes were the same dimensions?

Mr. FRAZIER. Yes, they are. And the threads in the holes are the same.

Mr. EISENBERG. Mr. Chairman, I would like C-250 admitted into evidence as Commission Exhibit 542.

The CHAIRMAN. It may be admitted.

(The article referred to was marked Commission Exhibit No. 542, and received in evidence.)

The CHAIRMAN. At this time I will interrupt to say I must now leave to attend a session of the Supreme Court, and I will return at the conclusion of the session.

In the meantime, Mr. McCloy will preside at the Commission hearing, and in the event he should be required to leave, Mr. McCloy, whatever Commissioner is here will conduct the examination in his absence.

(At this point, Chairman Warren withdrew from the hearing room.)

Mr. EISENBERG. Have you examined the sling on Commission Exhibit 139?

Mr. FRAZIER. Yes, I did.

Mr. EISENBERG. Do you feel that this is—that this sling was originally manufactured as a rifle sling?

Mr. FRAZIER. No, sir; it is not in any way similar to a normal sling for a rifle. It appears to be a sling from some carrying case, camera bag, musical-instrument strap, or something of that nature.

We have made attempts to identify it, with no success.

Mr. EISENBERG. Apart from the addition of this sling and mounting of the telescopic sight, have any modifications been made in the C–139 rifle—in the Commission Exhibit 139 rifle?

Mr. FRAZIER. No, sir.

Mr. McCLOY. You would suggest, I gather, Mr. Frazier, that this is a home-made sling?

Mr. FRAZIER. Yes, sir; it appears to have been cut to length by inserting this strap, or this sling, on the rifle, and then trimming off the excess ends of the two straps to fit.

Mr. McCLOY. How would that broad patch on the sling—how would that be used, in your judgment, in firing the rifle? Would it be wrapped around the base of your——

Mr. FRAZIER. I find it very difficult to use the rifle with a sling at all. The sling is too short, actually, to do more than put your arm through it.

Mr. McCLOY. You get quite a leverage with that?

Mr. FRAZIER. Yes, sir, you do, in one direction. But it is rather awkward to wrap the forward hand into the sling in the normal fashion.

Mr. McCLOY. This gives a pretty tight——

Mr. FRAZIER. It can be used. But I don't feel that actually the position of this broad piece is of too much significance as far as use of the sling goes.

Mr. McCLOY. But certainly the sling would tend to steady the aim, even in this crude form?

Mr. FRAZIER. Oh, yes.

Mr. McCLOY. It would make more easy an offhand shot than if you didn't have a sling? It would make it more accurate?

Mr. FRAZIER. It would assist more in offhand than any other type of shooting, yes.

Mr. EISENBERG. Returning to the scope for a moment, on the basis of the experiment, so to speak, which you had Klein's conduct, would you form an opinion as to whether the telescopic sight was mounted on Exhibit 139—was likely to have been mounted—by Klein's, or likely to have been mounted subsequently?

Mr. FRAZIER. Well, I could not deduce from that—from the way the scope is mounted—who mounted it. I can only say that the two are mounted in identical fashion. And it is possible that the same person or persons mounted the two scopes.

Mr. EISENBERG. Could you briefly explain the operation of this rifle, the bolt action and the clip-feed mechanism?

Mr. FRAZIER. Yes, sir; the weapon is loaded by turning up the bolt handle, drawing the bolt to the rear, and inserting the clip from the top of the weapon, after the clip has been loaded with the number of rounds you desire to load.

The maximum number of rounds the clip holds is six. However, the weapon can be loaded with a clip holding 5, 4, 3, 2, or 1 round.

This is done by inserting the clip in the rear portion of the ejection port, and pushing it downwards until it clears the bottom of the bolt. The weapon then is loaded by moving the bolt forward. It picks up one cartridge out of the clip, carries it into the chamber of the weapon, and the bolt is then locked by turning down.

To fire the weapon, it is merely necessary to pull the trigger, since the closing of the bolt has cocked the cocking piece on the weapon.

Mr. EISENBERG. Can you proceed to show the extraction and ejection mechanism?

Mr. FRAZIER. Yes, sir. The extraction is merely by raising the bolt and drawing it to the rear. When the cartridge is first loaded, the rim on the base of the cartridge is caught under the extractor in the face of the bolt, so that drawing the bolt to the rear draws the fired cartridge or a loaded cartridge if it has not been fired, out of the chamber to the rear, where the opposite side of the cartridge strikes a projection in the ejection port called the ejector. The ejector strikes on the opposite side of the case from the extractor, causing the shell to be thrown out of the weapon on the right-hand side.

Mr. EISENBERG. Now, to fire the next shot, is any further action necessary, apart from closing the bolt and pulling the trigger, if remaining cartridges are in the clip?

Mr. FRAZIER. No, sir.

Mr. EISENBERG. Could you pull out the clip and explain any markings you find on it?

Mr. FRAZIER. The only markings are the manufacturer's markings, "SMI," on the base of the clip, and a number, 952. The significance of that number I am not aware of. It could be a part number or a manufacturer's code number.

Mr. EISENBERG. Is there any reason that you can think of why someone might call that a five-shot clip?

Mr. FRAZIER. No, sir, unless they were unfamiliar with it. There is an area of confusion in that a different type of rifle shooting larger ammunition, such as a .30–06 or a German Mauser rifle, uses five-shot clips, and the five-shot clip is the common style or size of clip, whereas this one actually holds six.

Mr. EISENBERG. Have you had occasion to purchase ammunition for this rifle?

Mr. FRAZIER. Yes, sir.

Mr. EISENBERG. Does the ammunition come in the clip?

Mr. FRAZIER. Normally it does not. The ammunition that we have purchased for this rifle comes in 20-shot boxes. It is possible—and I say this as a result of reading advertisements—to buy ammunition for this rifle, and to receive a clip or clips at the same time, but not necessarily part of the same shipment.

Mr. EISENBERG. When you ordered C–250, which is now Commission Exhibit 542, did you receive a clip with that rifle?

Mr. FRAZIER. No, sir.

Mr. EISENBERG. Would you deduce, therefore, that the clip—that someone wishing to shoot that rifle and use a clip in the rifle would have purchased the clip later?

Mr. FRAZIER. They would have to acquire it from some source, yes.

Mr. EISENBERG. Is it commonly available?

Mr. FRAZIER. Yes, sir.

Mr. McCLOY. Can you use that rifle without the clip?

Mr. FRAZIER. Yes; you can.

Mr. McCLOY. What is the advantage of the clip?

Mr. FRAZIER. It permits repeated firing of the weapon without manually loading one shot at a time.

Mr. McCLOY. The only other way you can fire it is by way of manual load?

Mr. FRAZIER. Yes, sir; one shot at a time.

Mr. McCLOY. When you say a six-cartridge clip, could that gun have been fired with the clip fully loaded and another one in the chamber?

Mr. FRAZIER. Yes, sir.

Mr. McCLOY. The same as the .30–06?

Mr. FRAZIER. Yes, sir; the weapon will hold a maximum of seven.

Mr. EISENBERG. I now hand you a cartridge in an envelope, marked Commission Exhibit 141. Are you familiar with this cartridge?

Mr. FRAZIER. Yes; I am. I received this cartridge for examination in the FBI laboratory, submitted to me as a cartridge removed from the rifle at the time it was recovered.

Mr. EISENBERG. Can you describe that cartridge in terms of name, manufacturer, and country of origin?

Mr. FRAZIER. It is a 6.5 mm. Mannlicher-Carcano cartridge, manufactured by the Western Cartridge Co., at East Alton, Ill.

It is loaded with a full metal-jacketed bullet of the military type. Cartridges of this type which I have examined, having this type of bullet, have bullets weighing 160 to 161 grains.

Mr. McCLOY. When you mentioned that cartridge as being a Mannlicher-Carcano cartridge, could that be fired, for example, in a Mannlicher 6.5 Schoenauer?

Mr. FRAZIER. I am not familiar with that.

Mr. McCLOY. That is the normal sporting rifle—that Mannlicher Schoenauer is the normal 6.5 Austrian sporting rifle that you buy. I just wondered if it was the same cartridge.

Mr. FRAZIER. I am sorry. I don't know whether there is a distinction between these two or not.

Mr. McCLOY. I happen to have one of those. And I was just wondering if it is the same cartridge.

Mr. EISENBERG. Mr. Frazier, I now hand you a series of three cartridge cases. I ask you whether you are familiar with these cartridge cases.

Mr. FRAZIER. Yes; I am. I received these cartridge cases on two different occasions for examination in the laboratory, and comparison with the rifle.

Mr. EISENBERG. Do these cases have your mark on them?

Mr. FRAZIER. Yes; they do. Each is marked with my initials and the inscription for identification purposes.

Mr. EISENBERG. Mr. Chairman, I would like to introduce these cartridge cases into evidence as Commission Exhibits 543, 544 and 545.

Mr. McCLOY. They may be admitted.

(The articles referred to were marked Commission Exhibits Nos. 543, 544, and 545 and received in evidence.)

Mr. McCLOY. Will you introduce evidence to show where they came from?

Mr. EISENBERG. Well, sir, the record will show at the conclusion of the hearings where they came from. This witness is able to identify them only as to his examination.

Mr. McCLOY. I understand that. I understand that witness cannot identify them. But I simply asked for the record whether you have evidence to show where they did come from.

Mr. EISENBERG. Yes; for the record, these cartridges were found on the sixth floor of the School Book Depository Building. They were found near the southeast corner window—that is, the easternmost window on the southern face of the sixth floor of that building.

Mr. Frazier, are these cartridge cases which have just been admitted into evidence the same type of cartridge—from the same type of cartridge—as you just examined, Commission Exhibit No. 141?

Mr. FRAZIER. Yes; they are.

Mr. EISENBERG. That is, 6.5 mm. Mannlicher-Carcano, manufactured by the Western Cartridge Co.?

Mr. FRAZIER. Yes, sir.

Mr. EISENBERG. You gave the weight of the bullet which is found in this type of cartridge. Could you give us a description of the contour of the bullet, and its length?

Mr. FRAZIER. The bullet has parallel sides, with a round nose, is fully jacketed with a copper-alloy coating or metal jacket on the outside of a lead core. Its diameter is 6.65 millimeters. The length—possibly it would be better to put it in inches rather than millimeters. The diameter is .267 inches, and a length of 1.185, or approximately 1.2 inches.

Mr. McCLOY. You say that the diameter is 6.65. Did you mean 6.65 or 6.5 millimeters?

Mr. FRAZIER. I was looking for that figure on that. It is about 6.6—6.65 millimeters.

The bullet, of course, will be a larger diameter than the bore of the weapon to accommodate the depths of the grooves in the barrel.

On the base of the bullet is a crimp ring, or a cannelure, which is located two-tenths of an inch from the base up the bullet and which is 6/100ths of an inch in width—that is, it is a band around the bullet 6/100ths of an inch wide.

I believe that is a description of the bullet.

Mr. EISENBERG. Have you tested Commission Exhibit 139 with the type of ammunition you have been looking at to determine the muzzle velocity of that type of ammunition in this weapon?

Mr. FRAZIER. Yes, sir. The tests were run to determine the muzzle velocity of this rifle, using this ammunition, at the Naval Research Laboratory in Washington, D.C., on December 2, 1963, using two different lots of ammunition—Lot No. 6,000 and Lot No. 6,003.

I might point out that there were four lots of ammunition manufactured by the Western Cartridge Co., only two of which are available.

Mr. EISENBERG. Can you give the results?

Mr. FRAZIER. Possibly I can give the results shot by shot, so the record will show each one, and then give an average for them.

Mr. EISENBERG. Fine.

Mr. FRAZIER. The first shot, Lot 6,000, the velocity was 2199.7 feet per second. Shot No. 2, Lot 6,000, velocity 2,180.3 feet per second.

The third shot, velocity—same lot—velocity 2,178.9 feet per second.

The third shot, velocity—and this is Lot No. 6,003—velocity was 2,184.8 feet per second.

The fourth shot, Lot No. 6,003, was 2,137.6 feet per second.

Fifth shot, Lot No. 6,000, 2,162.7 feet per second.

The sixth shot, Lot 6,003, 2,134.8 feet per second.

An average of all shots of 2,165 feet per second.

Mr. EISENBERG. How would you characterize the differences between the muzzle velocities of the various rounds in terms of whether that difference was a large or small difference?

Mr. FRAZIER. This is a difference well within the manufacturer's accepted standards of velocity variations. They permit in their standard ammunition manual, which is a guide to the entire industry in the United States, a 40-foot-per-second, plus or minus, variation shot to shot in the same ammunition.

Mr. EISENBERG. Have you calculated the muzzle energy of this 6.5 millimeter ammunition in this weapon?

Mr. FRAZIER. It was furnished by letter to the Commission. Yes, sir—the muzzle energy was calculated on the basis of the average velocity of 2,165 feet per second as 1,676 foot-pounds.

Mr. EISENBERG. This is a calculation rather than a measurement?

Mr. FRAZIER. Necessarily a calculation, because it is merely a term used to compare one bullet against another rather than for any practical purposes because—because of the bullet's extremely light weight.

The bullet's velocity and weight, and gravity enter into the determination of its energy in foot-pounds.

Mr. EISENBERG. Is the 6.5 millimeter Mannlicher-Carcano with which we are dealing an accurate type of ammunition as opposed to other types of military ammunition—as compared, I should say, with other types of military ammunition?

Mr. FRAZIER. I would say it is also accurate. As other types of ammunition the 6.5 millimeter cartridge or bullet is a very accurate bullet, and ammunition of this type as manufactured in the United States would give fairly reasonable accuracy. Other military cartridges may or may not give accurate results.

But the cartridge inherently is an accurate cartridge.

Mr. EISENBERG. Is this type of cartridge readily available for purchase?

Mr. FRAZIER. Yes; it is. Information we have indicates that 2 million rounds of this ammunition was reimported into this country and placed on sale.

Mr. EISENBERG. Commission Exhibit No. 141, the cartridge found in the chamber—I should say, was found in the chamber. Do you draw any inference from the fact that the cartridge was found in the chamber? In your experience, does one automatically reload whether or not one intends to fire, or is there a special significance in the fact that the cartridge had been chambered?

Mr. FRAZIER. I would say no, there would be no inference which I could draw based on human behavior as to why someone would or would not reload a cartridge. Normally, if you were—in my experience—shooting at some object, and it was no longer necessary to shoot, you would not reload.

You may or may not reload. It would be a normal thing to automatically reload. But not necessarily in every instance.

Mr. McCLOY. Do you have any information of your own knowledge as to whether this cartridge was in the chamber or not at the time the rifle was found?

Mr. FRAZIER. Only as furnished to me—it was submitted as having been removed from the rifle by the Dallas Police Department.

Mr. McCLOY. As having been removed from the chamber?

Mr. FRAZIER. From the chamber of the rifle.

Mr. McCLOY. But you did not remove it yourself?

Mr. FRAZIER. No, sir.

Mr. EISENBERG. Did you make a test to determine the pattern of the cartridge-case ejection of Commission Exhibit 139?

Mr. FRAZIER. Yes, sir; I made two studies in connection with the ejection pattern—one to determine distance and one to determine the angle at which the cartridge cases leave the ejection port.

Mr. EISENBERG. And did you summarize your examination by diagrams?

Mr. FRAZIER. Yes; I did.

Mr. EISENBERG. Could you show us those diagrams?

Mr. FRAZIER. In this diagram——

Mr. EISENBERG. Excuse me just a second, Mr. Frazier.

Were these diagrams prepared by you?

Mr. FRAZIER. Yes; they were—not the actual physical diagrams, but the figures on the diagrams were furnished by me to the draftsman.

Mr. EISENBERG. Mr. Chairman, may I introduce these diagrams as Commission Exhibits Nos. 546 and 547?

Mr. McCLOY. They may be admitted.

(The documents referred to were marked Commission Exhibits Nos. 546 and 547, and were received in evidence.)

Mr. EISENBERG. Could you give us the results of your tests by using these diagrams, Mr. Frazier?

Mr. FRAZIER. Yes, sir.

In this test, Commission Exhibit 546, the diagram illustrates the positions on the floor at which cartridge cases landed after being extracted and ejected from the rifle, Commission's Exhibit 139. In the top portion of Exhibit 546, the barrel was held depressed at a 45-degree angle, and in the lower half of the exhibit it shows the pattern with the barrel held in a horizontal position. Each spot marked with a figure on the diagram shows where one cartridge case landed in both instances, and each one is marked with the distance and the angle to which the cartridge case was ejected.

With the barrel held in the depressed condition, all of the cartridge cases landed within an 85-inch circle located 80 degrees to the right front of the rifle. That may be confusing. It was 80 degrees to the right from the line of sight of the rifle and at a distance of 86 inches from the ejection port.

Now, this circle will not necessarily encompass all cartridge cases ejected from the rifle, since the ejection is determined, not only by the angle of the weapon, but more by the force with which the bolt is operated. A very light force on the bolt can cause the cartridge case to tip gently out and fall at your feet. However, under normal conditions of reloading in a fairly rapid manner, we found the cartridge cases to land in this circle.

The same situation is true of the test made with the muzzle in the horizontal condition.

All of the cartridge cases landed within a 47-inch circle, which was located at right angles to the ejection port, or 90 degrees from the line of sight, and at a distance 80 inches from the ejection port.

In both of these tests, the ejection port of the weapon was held 32 inches above the floor.

In the second test performed, Commission Exhibit 547, the test was made to ascertain how high above the ejection port a cartridge case would fly as it was being ejected.

After ejecting numerous cartridge cases from the weapon with the barrel held in a depressed condition, it was found that the cartridge cases did not exceed two inches above the level of the ejection port. And with the muzzle held horizontally, it did not exceed 12 inches above the level of the ejection port.

Mr. EISENBERG. In making these tests, was the bolt pulled with a normal degree of rifle pull?

Mr. FRAZIER. It was pulled with various pulls, to determine what the effect would be with different speeds of the bolt.

Mr. EISENBERG. How did you select the distance above the floor at which the rifle was fired?

Mr. FRAZIER. We selected a distance which we thought might be typical of a condition which would give an overall picture of the ejection pattern, and not from any basis of previous information as to possibly how the weapon had been fired previously. Thirty-two inches happened to be approximately table height, so that we could control the height of the weapon readily.

Mr. EISENBERG. I now hand you three Commission Exhibits, 510, 511, and 512, which are photographs which have been identified as giving the location of the cartridges—cartridge cases—Nos. 543, 544, and 545, on the sixth floor of the School Book Depository Building. I ask you to examine these pictures, and to determine whether if the rifle had been fired from the window shown in these pictures, the location of the cartridge cases is consistent with the results of the tests you ran to determine the ejection patterns.

Mr. FRAZIER. I would say yes; it is consistent—although the cartridge cases are—two of them—against the wall. There is a stack of boxes fairly near the wall, and the position of the cartridge cases could very well have been affected by the boxes. That is, they could strike the box and bounce for several feet, and they could have bounced back and forth in this small area here and come to rest in the areas shown in the photographs.

Mr. EISENBERG. In making your tests, did you notice much ricochet?

Mr. FRAZIER. Yes; considerable. Each time a cartridge case hit the floor, it would bounce anywhere from 8 inches to 10 to 15 feet.

Mr. MCLOY. Make a lot of noise?

Mr. FRAZIER. Yes; a clatter.

Mr. EISENBERG. Have you tested Commission Exhibit 139 to determine its accuracy under rapid-fire conditions?

Mr. FRAZIER. Yes; I have.

Mr. EISENBERG. Can you describe these tests?

Mr. FRAZIER. A series of three tests were made. When we first received the rifle, there was not an opportunity to test it at long range, so we tested it at short range. After we had obtained sample bullets and cartridge cases from it, we fired accuracy and speed tests with it. Three examiners did the firing, all three being present at the same time.

The first tests were made at 15 yards, and shooting at a silhouette target.

Mr. EISENBERG. A silhouette of a man?

Mr. FRAZIER. A paper silhouette target of a man; yes.

Possibly you may wish to mark these, to refer to them.

Mr. EISENBERG. These targets were made by you or in your presence?

Mr. FRAZIER. These are actually copies of the actual targets. I have the actual targets here, if you would rather use those. However, the markings show better on the copies than they do on the actual targets.

Mr. EISENBERG. Mr. Chairman, I request permission to introduce the copies for the reasons given, as Commission Exhibits 548 and 549.

Mr. McCLOY. You have made these copies, Mr. Frazier?

Mr. FRAZIER. Well, I had them made. They are actual xerox copies of the original targets, which are black, and do not show the markings placed around the holes.

Mr. EISENBERG. Off the record.

(Discussion off the record.)

Mr. McCLOY. Back on the record.

Mr. Frazier, you have the original targets that were used in this experiment.

Mr. FRAZIER. Yes, sir.

Mr. McCLOY. Were you one of the three that fired?

Mr. FRAZIER. Yes, sir.

Mr. McCLOY. Can you identify your target as distinguished from the other two?

Mr. FRAZIER. Yes, sir.

Mr. McCLOY. Do you have the target that you fired?

Mr. FRAZIER. I fired—yes, I do. However, another examiner also fired at this same target.

Mr. McCLOY. Have you made a copy of that—or did you cause a copy of that target to be made?

Mr. FRAZIER. Yes, sir.

Mr. McCLOY. And you have that with you?

Mr. FRAZIER. Yes; I do.

Mr. McCLOY. Have you marked it yet?

Mr. EISENBERG. No. That would be 548.

Mr. McCLOY. Suppose you identify that copy.

Mr. EISENBERG. This copy that you are presenting to us has initials at the bottom "CC-R-CK"?

Mr. FRAZIER. Yes, sir.

Mr. EISENBERG. And the numbers and letters D-2 on the right-hand margin?

Mr. FRAZIER. Yes, sir.

Mr. EISENBERG. And that has been copied under your supervision?

Mr. FRAZIER. Yes, sir.

Mr. EISENBERG. Mr. Chairman?

Mr. McCLOY. That can be admitted as Commission Exhibit 548.

(The document referred to was marked Commission Exhibit No. 548, and received in evidence.)

Mr. McCLOY. Now, is Commission Exhibit 548 an accurate copy of the target which you have—that you fired, and which you presented?

Mr. FRAZIER. Yes; it is.

Mr. EISENBERG. Now, you also have a copy here which has the name on it Killion, and similar initials, letters, and numbers to the other target. Is this an accurate copy which you had prepared?

Mr. FRAZIER. Yes, sir. That was the target fired by Charles Killion in my presence.

Mr. EISENBERG. May I have this admitted as 549?

Mr. McCLOY. It may be admitted.

(The document referred to was marked Commission Exhibit No. 549, and received in evidence.)

Mr. EISENBERG. This test was performed at 15 yards, did you say, Mr. Frazier?

Mr. FRAZIER. Yes, sir. And this series of shots we fired to determine actually the speed at which the rifle could be fired, not being overly familiar with this particular firearm, and also to determine the accuracy of the weapon under those conditions.

Mr. EISENBERG. And could you give us the names of the three agents who participated?

Mr. FRAZIER. Yes, sir. Charles Killion, Cortlandt Cunningham, and myself.

Mr. EISENBERG. And the date?

Mr. FRAZIER. November 27, 1963.

Mr. EISENBERG. How many shots did each agent fire?

Mr. FRAZIER. Killion fired three, Cunningham fired three, and I fired three.

Mr. EISENBERG. And do you have the times within which each agent fired the three shots?

Mr. FRAZIER. Yes, sir. Killion fired his three shots in nine seconds, and they are shown—the three shots are interlocking, shown on Commission Exhibit No. 549.

Cunningham fired three shots—I know the approximate number of seconds was seven.

Cunningham's time was approximately seven seconds.

Mr. EISENBERG. Can you at a later date confirm the exact time?

Mr. FRAZIER. Yes, sir.

Mr. EISENBERG. And you will do that by letter to the Commission, or if you happen to come back by oral testimony?

Mr. FRAZIER. Yes, sir.

Mr. EISENBERG. And your time, Mr. Frazier?

Mr. FRAZIER. For this series, was six seconds, for my three shots, which also were on the target at which Mr. Cunningham fired, which is Exhibit 548.

Mr. EISENBERG. Could you characterize the dispersion of the shots on the two targets which you have been showing us, 548 and 549?

Mr. FRAZIER. The bullets landed approximately—in Killion's target, No. 549, approximately 2½ inches high, and 1 inch to the right, in the area about the size of a dime, interlocking in the paper, all three shots.

On Commission Exhibit 548, Cunningham fired three shots. These shots were interlocking, or within an eighth of an inch of each other, and were located approximately 4 inches high and 1 inch to the right of the aiming point. The three shots which I fired were—landed in a three-quarter inch circle, two of them interlocking with Cunningham's shots, 4 inches high, and approximately 1 inch to the right of the aiming point.

Mr. EISENBERG. Can you describe the second series of tests?

Mr. FRAZIER. The second test which was performed was two series of three shots at 25 yards, instead of 15 yards. I fired both of these tests, firing them at a cardboard target, in an effort to determine how fast the weapon could be fired primarily, with secondary purpose accuracy.

We did not attempt—I did not attempt to maintain in that test an accurate rate of fire.

This is the actual target which I fired.

Mr. EISENBERG. And that target has all six holes in it?

Mr. FRAZIER. Yes, sir—two series of three holes, the first three holes being marked with the No. 1, and the second series being marked No. 2.

Mr. EISENBERG. Mr. Chairman, I would like this introduced as 550.

Mr. McCLOY. That will be admitted.

(The document referred to was marked Commission Exhibit No. 550, and received in evidence.)

Mr. EISENBERG. Could you describe for the record the dispersion on the two series?

Mr. FRAZIER. Yes, sir. The first series of three shots were approximately— from 4 to 5 inches high and from 1 to 2 inches to the right of the aiming point, and landed within a 2-inch circle. These three shots were fired in 4.8 seconds. The second series of shots landed—one was about 1 inch high, and the other two about 4 or 5 inches high, and the maximum spread was 5 inches.

That series was fired in 4.6 seconds.

Mr. EISENBERG. And do you have the date?

Mr. FRAZIER. That also was on the 27th of November.

Mr. EISENBERG. Same date as the first tests?

Mr. FRAZIER. Yes, sir.

Mr. EISENBERG. And you performed one more test, I believe?

Mr. FRAZIER. Yes, sir. We fired additional targets at 100 yards on the range at Quantico, Va., firing groups of three shots. And I have the four targets we fired here.

Mr. EISENBERG. Mr. Chairman, I would like these admitted as 551, 552, 553, and 554.

Mr. McCLOY. They may be admitted.

(The documents referred to were marked Commission Exhibits Nos. 551 through 554, and received in evidence.)

Mr. EISENBERG. Who fired these shots, Mr. Frazier?

Mr. FRAZIER. I fired them.

Mr. EISENBERG. Can you characterize the dispersion on each of the four targets?

Mr. FRAZIER. Yes, sir.

On Commission Exhibit 551 the three shots landed approximately 5 inches high and within a 3½-inch circle, almost on a line horizontally across the target. This target and the other targets were fired on March 16, 1964 at Quantico, Va. These three shots were fired in 5.9 seconds.

The second target fired is Commission Exhibit 552, consisting of three shots fired in 6.2 seconds, which landed in approximately a 4½ to 5-inch circle located 4 inches high and 3 or 4 inches to the right of the aiming point.

Commission Exhibit No. 553 is the third target fired, consisting of three shots which landed in a 3-inch circle located about 2½ inches high and 2 inches to the right of the aiming point.

These three shots were fired in 5.6 seconds.

And Commission Exhibit No. 554, consisting of three shots fired in 6.5 seconds, which landed approximately 5 inches high and 5 inches to the right of the aiming point, all within a 3½-inch circle.

Mr. McCLOY. The first one is not exactly 5 inches to the right, is it?

Mr. FRAZIER. No, sir. The center of the circle in which they all landed would be about 5 inches high and 5 inches to the right.

Mr. EISENBERG. Mr. Frazier, could you tell us why, in your opinion, all the shots, virtually all the shots, are grouped high and to the right of the aiming point?

Mr. FRAZIER. Yes, sir. When we attempted to sight in this rifle at Quantico, we found that the elevation adjustment in the telescopic sight was not sufficient to bring the point of impact to the aiming point. In attempting to adjust and sight-in the rifle, every time we changed the adjusting screws to move the crosshairs in the telescopic sight in one direction it also affected the movement of the impact or the point of impact in the other direction. That is, if we moved the crosshairs in the telescope to the left it would also affect the elevation setting of the telescope. And when we had sighted-in the rifle approximately, we fired several shots and found that the shots were not all landing in the same place, but were gradually moving away from the point of impact. This was apparently due to the construction of the telescope, which apparently did not stabilize itself—that is, the spring mounting in the crosshair ring did not stabilize until we had fired five or six shots.

Mr. EISENBERG. Pardon me, Mr. Frazier. Have you prepared a diagram of the telescopic sight?

Mr. FRAZIER. Yes, sir.

Mr. EISENBERG. I wonder whether you could show us that now to help illustrate the point you are making.

Let me mark that.

This diagram was prepared by you?

Mr. FRAZIER. Yes; it was.

Mr. EISENBERG. And illustrates——

Mr. FRAZIER. Excuse me. The actual diagram was copied by me from a textbook, showing a diagrammatic view of how a telescopic crosshair ring is mounted in a telescope.

Mr. EISENBERG. This is a generalized diagram, rather than a diagram of the specific scope on Exhibit 139?

Mr. FRAZIER. Yes; it is. However, I have checked the scope on Exhibit 139 and found it to be substantially the same as this diagram.

Mr. EISENBERG. Mr. Chairman, may I have this admitted as 555?

Mr. McCLOY. It may be admitted.

(The document referred to was marked Commission Exhibit No. 555, and received in evidence.)

Mr. FRAZIER. Commission Exhibit No. 555 is a diagrammatic drawing of the manner in which the crosshair ring is mounted in Exhibit 139, showing on the right-hand side of the diagram a circular drawing indicating the outer part of the tube, with an inner circle with a crossed line in it representing the crosshairs in the telescope.

There is an elevation-adjusting screw at the top, which pushes the crosshair ring down against a spring located in the lower left-hand portion of the circle, or which allows the crosshair ring to come up, being pushed by the spring on the opposite side of the ring. There is a windage screw on the right-hand side of the scope tube circle which adjusts the crosshair ring laterally for windage adjustments.

The diagram at the left side of Commission's Exhibit 555 shows diagrammatically the blade spring mounted in the telescope tube which causes the ring to be pressed against the adjusting screws.

We found in this telescopic sight on this rifle that this ring was shifting in the telescope tube so that the gun could not be sighted-in merely by changing the screws. It was necessary to adjust it, and then fire several shots to stabilize the crosshair ring by causing this spring to press tightly against the screws, to the point that we decided it would not be feasible to completely sight the weapon inasfar as windage goes, and in addition found that the elevation screw could not be adjusted sufficiently to bring the point of impact on the targets down to the sighting point.

And, therefore, we left the rifle as soon as it became stabilized and fired all of our shots with the point of impact actually high and to the right.

Mr. EISENBERG. As I understand it, the construction of the scope is such that after the elevation or windage screw has been moved, the scope does not—is not—automatically pushed up by the blade spring as it should be, until you have fired several shots?

Mr. FRAZIER. Yes; that is true—when the crosshairs are largely out of the center of the tube. And in this case it is necessary to move the crosshairs completely up into the upper portion of the tube, which causes this spring to bear in a position out of the ordinary, and for this windage screw to strike the side or the sloping surface of the ring rather than at 90 degrees, as it shows in Exhibit 555. With this screw being off center, both in windage and elevation, the spring is not strong enough to center the crosshair ring by itself, and it is necessary to jar it several times, which we did by firing, to bring it to bear tightly so as to maintain the same position then for the next shots.

Mr. EISENBERG. And because of the difficulty you had stabilizing the crosshair, you did not wish to pursue it to a further refinement, is that correct?

Mr. FRAZIER. We sighted the scope in relatively close, fired it, and decided rather than fire more ammunition through the weapon, we would use these targets which we had fired.

Mr. EISENBERG. Now, once the crosshairs had been stabilized, did you find that they stayed, remained stabilized?

Mr. FRAZIER. Yes; they did.

Mr. EISENBERG. How long do you think the crosshairs would remain stabilized in Exhibit 139, assuming no violent jar?

Mr. FRAZIER. They should remain stabilized continuously.

Mr. EISENBERG. Do you know when the defect in this scope, which causes you not to be able to adjust the elevation crosshair in the manner it should be—do you know when this defect was introduced into the scope?

Mr. FRAZIER. No; I do not. However, on the back end of the scope tube there is a rather severe scrape which was on this weapon when we received it in the laboratory, in which some of the metal has been removed, and the scope tube could have been bent or damaged.

Mr. EISENBERG. Did you first test the weapon for accuracy on November 27th?

Mr. FRAZIER. Yes, sir.

Mr. EISENBERG. Have you any way of determining whether the defect preexisted November 27th?

Mr. FRAZIER. When we fired on November 27th, the shots were landing high and slightly to the right. However, the scope was apparently fairly well stabilized at that time, because three shots would land in an area the size of a dime under rapid-fire conditions, which would not have occurred if the interior mechanism of the scope was shifting.

Mr. EISENBERG. But you are unable to say whether—or are you able to say whether—the defect existed before November 27th? That is, precisely when it was introduced?

Mr. FRAZIER. As far as to be unable to adjust the scope, actually, I could not say when it had been introduced. I don't know actually what the cause is. It may be that the mount has been bent or the crosshair ring shifted.

Mr. EISENBERG. Mr. Frazier, when you were running, let's say, the last test, could you have compensated for this defect?

Mr. FRAZIER. Yes; you could take an aiming point low and to the left and have the shots strike a predetermined point. But it would be no different from taking these targets and putting an aiming point in the center of the bullet-impact area. Here that would be the situation you would have—an aiming point off to the side and an impact area at the high right corner.

Mr. EISENBERG. If you had been shooting to score bulls-eyes, in a bulls-eye pattern, what would you have—what action, if any, would you have taken, to improve your score?

Mr. FRAZIER. I would have aimed low and to the left—after finding how high the bullets were landing; you would compensate by aiming low left, or adjusting the mount of the scope in a manner which would cause the hairlines to coincide with the point of impact.

Mr. EISENBERG. How much practice had you had with the rifle before the last series of four targets were shot by you?

Mr. FRAZIER. I had fired it possibly 20 rounds, 15 to 20 rounds, and in addition had operated the bolt repeatedly.

Mr. EISENBERG. Does practice with this weapon—or would practice with this weapon—materially shorten the time in which three shots could be accurately fired?

Mr. FRAZIER. Yes, sir; very definitely.

Mr. EISENBERG. Would practice without actually firing the weapon be helpful—that is, a dry-run practice?

Mr. FRAZIER. That would be most helpful, particularly in a bolt-action weapon, where it is necessary to shift your hand from the trigger area to the bolt, operate the bolt, and go back to the trigger after closing the bolt.

Mr. EISENBERG. Based on your experience with the weapon, do you think three shots could be fired accurately within 5½ seconds if no rest was utilized?

Mr. FRAZIER. That would depend on the accuracy which was necessary or needed or which you desired. I think you could fire the shots in that length of time, but whether you could place them, say, in a 3- or 4-inch circle without either resting or possibly using the sling as a support—I doubt that you could accomplish that.

Mr. EISENBERG. How—these targets at which you fired stationary at 100 yards—how do you think your time would have been affected by use of a moving target?

Mr. FRAZIER. It would have slowed down the shooting. It would have lengthened the time to the extent of allowing the crosshairs to pass over the moving target.

Mr. EISENBERG. Could you give an amount?

Mr. FRAZIER. Approximately 1 second. It would depend on how fast the target was moving, and whether it was moving away from you or towards you or at right angles.

Mr. EISENBERG. Do you think you could shorten your time with further practice with the weapon?

Mr. FRAZIER. Oh, yes.

Mr. EISENBERG. Could you give us an estimate on that?

Mr. FRAZIER. I fired three shots in 4.6 seconds at 25 yards with approximately a 3-inch spread, which is the equivalent of a 12-inch spread at a hundred yards. And I feel that a 12-inch relative circle could be reduced to 6 inches or even less with considerable practice with the weapon.

Mr. EISENBERG. That is in the 4.6-second time?

Mr. FRAZIER. Yes. I would say from 4.8 to 5 seconds, in that area—4.6 is firing this weapon as fast as the bolt can be operated, I think.

Mr. EISENBERG. I am now going to ask you several hypothetical questions concerning the factors which might have affected the aim of the assassin on November 22d, and I would like you to make the following assumptions in answering these questions: First, that the assassin fired his shots from the window near which the cartridges were found—that is, the easternmost window on the south face of the sixth floor of the School Book Depository Building, which is 60 feet above the ground, and several more feet above the position at which the car was apparently located when the shots were fired.

Second, that the length of the trajectory of the first shot was 175 feet, and that the length of the trajectory of the third shot was 265 feet.

And third, that the elapsed time between the firing of the first and third shots was 5½ seconds.

Based on those assumptions, Mr. Frazier, approximately what lead would the assassin have had to give his target to compensate for its movement—and here I would disregard any possible defect in the scope.

Mr. FRAZIER. I would say he would have to lead approximately 2 feet under both such situations. The lead would, of course, be dependent upon the direction in which the object was moving, primarily. If it is moving away from you, then, of course, the actual lead of, say, 2 feet which he would have to lead would be interpreted as a considerably less lead in elevation above the target, because the target will move the 2 feet in a direction away from the shooter, and the apparent lead then would be cut to one foot or 12 inches or 8 inches or something of that nature, due to the movement of the individual.

Mr. EISENBERG. Have you made calculations to achieve the figures you gave?

Mr. FRAZIER. I made the calculations, but I don't have them with me.

Mr. EISENBERG. Could you supply these to us, either in further testimony or by letter, Mr. Frazier?

Mr. FRAZIER. I have one object here, a diagram which will illustrate that lead, if you would like to use that. This is drawn to scale from those figures which you quoted as building height, and distances of 175 feet and 265 feet.

Mr. EISENBERG. For the record, these figures are approximations of the figures believed to be involved in the assassination.

Will you supply the data at a later date?

Mr. FRAZIER. Yes; I can furnish that.

Mr. EISENBERG. May I have permission to introduce this as 556?

Mr. McCLOY. That will be admitted.

(The document referred to was marked Commission Exhibit No. 556, and received in evidence.)

Mr. EISENBERG. Could you show the lead in that diagram, Mr. Frazier?

Mr. FRAZIER. In Commission Exhibit 556, it shows a triangular diagram with the vertical line on the left-hand side illustrating the height of the building. The figures of a 60-foot building height plus——

Mr. EISENBERG. That is height of the muzzle above the ground?

Mr. FRAZIER. No—window sill—60-foot window sill height above the ground, with an assumed 2-foot height in addition to accommodate the height of the rifle above the possible—the possible height of the rifle above the window sill.

The horizontal line extends outward from the building to a small rectangular block, and then a sloping line illustrates a 5-foot slope from the 175-foot point to the 265-foot point.

(At this point, Representative Boggs entered the hearing room.)

Mr. FRAZIER. The time of flight of the bullet of approximately 8/100ths of a second and, again, it was necessary to assume—the time of flight of the bullet from the window to this first location of 175 feet is approximately 8/100ths of a second, which means a 2-foot lead on the target. That is, the target would move 2 feet in that interval of time, thereby necessitating shooting slightly ahead of the target to hit your aiming point. That has been diagrammatically illustrated by a 2-foot distance laid off on this rectangular block here, and two lines, very fine lines, drawn back towards the window area.

The right-hand side of Commission's 556 shows the same rectangular block, again with two lines drawn to it, one illustrating the point of aim and the other the amount of lead which would be necessary to strike an object aimed at which was moving, according to the time of flight of the projectile.

Mr. EISENBERG. And you calculated the speed of the car by translating the figures on total time elapsed between first and third shots?

Mr. FRAZIER. Yes, sir. The time—the speed of the moving object was calculated on the basis of an assumed 5.5-second interval for a distance of 90 feet, which figures out mathematically to be 11.3 miles per hour.

Mr. EISENBERG. Now, you said before that in order to give this 2-foot lead, you would have to aim 2 inches—for a target going away from you, you would have to aim 2 inches above the target, or in front of the target.

Mr. FRAZIER. 2 feet in front of the target, which would interpolate into a much lower actual elevation change.

Mr. EISENBERG. The elevation change would be 2 inches, is that it?

Mr. FRAZIER. Well, no. It would be on the order of 6 to 8 inches.

Mr. EISENBERG. 6 to 8 inches?

Mr. FRAZIER. Yes.

Mr. EISENBERG. What was your 2-inch figure?

Mr. FRAZIER. I don't recall.

Mr. EISENBERG. But it is 6 to 8 inches in elevation?

Representative BOGGS. May I ask a question?

Using that telescopic lens, how would you aim that rifle to achieve that distinction?

Mr. FRAZIER. Well, it would be necessary to hold the crosshairs an estimated distance off the target, of say, 6 inches over the intended target, so what when the shot was fired the crosshairs should be located about 6 inches over your target, and in the length of time that the bullet was in the air and the length of time the object was moving, the object would move into actually, the path of the bullet in approximately 1/10th to 13/100ths of a second.

Mr. EISENBERG. So that if the target of the assassin was the center of the President's head, and he wanted to give a correct lead, where would he have aimed, if we eliminate the possibility of errors introduced by other factors?

Mr. FRAZIER. He would aim from 4 to 6 inches—approximately 2 inches, I would say, above the President's head, which would be actually 6 inches above his aiming point at the center of the head.

Mr. EISENBERG. How difficult is it to give this—a lead of this size—to this type of target?

Mr. FRAZIER. It would not be difficult at all with a telescopic sight, because your target is enlarged four times, and you can estimate very quickly in a telescopic sight, inches or feet or lead of any desired amount.

Mr. EISENBERG. Would it be substantially easier than it would be with an open or peep sight?

Mr. FRAZIER. Yes. It would be much more difficult to do with the open iron sights, the notched rear sight and the blade front sight, which is on Exhibit 139.

Mr. EISENBERG. Now, you have been able to calculate the precise amount of lead which should be given, because you have been given figures. If you had been in the assassin's position, and were attempting to give a correct lead, what lead do you think you would have estimated as being the necessary lead?

Mr. FRAZIER. It would have been a very small amount, in the neighborhood of a 3-inch lead.

Mr. EISENBERG. As opposed to the 6 or 8 inches?

Mr. FRAZIER. As opposed to about 6 inches, yes.

Mr. EISENBERG. What would the consequence of the mistake in assumption as to lead be—that is, if you gave a 3-inch lead rather than the correct lead?

Mr. FRAZIER. It would be a difference of a 3-inch variation in the point of impact on the target.

Mr. EISENBERG. Now, if you had aimed at the center of the President's head, and given a 3-inch lead, again eliminating other errors, where would you have hit, if you hit accurately?

Mr. FRAZIER. It would be 3 inches below the center of his head—from the top—it would be not the actual center from the back, but the center would be located high. The bullet would strike at possibly the base of the skull.

Mr. EISENBERG. Now, suppose you had given no lead at all and aimed at that target and aimed accurately. Where would the bullet have hit?

Mr. FRAZIER. It would hit the base of the neck—approximately 6 inches below the center of the head.

Mr. EISENBERG. Mr. Frazier, would you have tried to give a lead at all, if you had been in that position?

Mr. FRAZIER. At that range, at that distance, 175 to 265 feet, with this rifle

409

and that telescopic sight, I would not have allowed any lead—I would not have made any correction for lead merely to hit a target of that size.

Mr. McCLOY. May I ask a question?

In your experimentation, in your firing of those shots that you have testified to a little while back, when you fired the first shot, was the shot in the chamber, or did you have to push it into the chamber by use of the bolt?

Mr. FRAZIER. This was fired with a loaded chamber, and timed from the time of this first shot until the last shot.

Mr. McCLOY. Did you shoot offhand or did you shoot with a rest?

Mr. FRAZIER. We shot with a rest, both the other individuals and myself, on each occasion, with one arm resting on a bench or a table.

Mr. McCLOY. Were you prone, or were you standing up?

Mr. FRAZIER. Well, we were sitting, actually, sitting or kneeling, in order to bring the arm down to the rest we were using.

Mr. McCLOY. One other question.

You keep referring to, and the questions kept referring to, "lead." By "lead," in this instance, you would mean height above the aiming point rather than——

Mr. FRAZIER. Yes, sir.

Mr. McCLOY. To the right, let's say, of the aiming point?

Mr. FRAZIER. Yes, sir; that is correct.

Mr. McCLOY. Because it was a going away shot?

Mr. FRAZIER. Yes, sir.

Mr. McCLOY. That is all.

Representative BOGGS. May I ask a question?

Where did you conduct these tests?

Mr. FRAZIER. The targets were fired both on the indoor range in the FBI range here in Washington and the 100-yard tests were fired at the Quantico, Va., FBI ranges.

Representative BOGGS. Have any tests—have there been any simulated tests in the building in Texas?

Mr. FRAZIER. I don't know, sir.

Representative BOGGS. But the FBI has not conducted any?

Mr. FRAZIER. Not to my knowledge. There may have been measurements and things of that nature taken, but I don't know.

Representative BOGGS. Now, in these tests, was there any difficulty about firing this rifle three times within the space or period of time that has been given to the Commission—5 seconds, I think.

Mr. FRAZIER. Well, let me say this. I fired the rifle three times, in accordance with that system of timing it from the first shot with the chamber loaded until the last shot occurred—three times in 4.6 seconds, 4.8 seconds, 5.6 seconds, 5.8, 5.9, and another one a little over 6, or in that neighborhood. The tenth of a second variation could very easily be as a result of the timing procedure used. A reflex of just not stopping the stopwatch in a tenth of a second.

Representative BOGGS. You were firing at a simulated target?

Mr. FRAZIER. These targets previously introduced, or copies of the targets, are those which we actually fired.

Representative BOGGS. My questions are really a followup of the Chairman's question.

These practices—were you just practicing for time, or were you practicing under conditions similar to those existing in Dallas at the time of the assassination?

Mr. FRAZIER. The tests we ran were for the purposes of determining whether we could fire this gun accurately in a limited amount of time, and specifically to determine whether it could be fired accurately in 6 seconds.

Now, we assumed the 6 seconds empirically—that is, we had not been furnished with any particular time interval. Later we were furnished with a time interval of 5.5 seconds. However, I have no independent knowledge—had no independent knowledge of the time interval or the accuracy. But we merely fired it to demonstrate the results from rapidly firing the weapon, reloading the gun and so on, in a limited time.

Representative Boggs. Were there other tests conducted to determine the accuracy of the weapon and so on?

Mr. Frazier. No, sir—only the rapid-fire accuracy tests were fired by the FBI.

Representative Boggs. There is no reason to believe that this weapon is not accurate, is there?

Mr. Frazier. It is a very accurate weapon. The targets we fired show that.

Representative Boggs. That was the point I was trying to establish.

Mr. Frazier. This Exhibit 549 is a target fired, showing that the weapon will, even under rapid-fire conditions, group closely—that is, one shot with the next.

Representative Boggs. How many shots in the weapon? Five?

Mr. McCloy. The clip takes six itself. You can put a seventh in the chamber. It could hold seven, in other words. But the clip is only a six-shot clip.

Representative Boggs. Was the weapon fully loaded at the time of the assassination?

Mr. McCloy. I don't know how many shells—three shells were picked up.

Mr. Eisenberg. Off the record.

(Discussion off the record.)

Mr. McCloy. Back on the record.

Mr. Eisenberg. Mr. Frazier, turning back to the scope, if the elevation crosshair was defective at the time of the assassination, in the same manner it is now, and no compensation was made for this defect, how would this have interacted with the amount of lead which needed to be given to the target?

Mr. Frazier. Well, may I say this first. I do not consider the crosshair as being defective, but only the adjusting mechanism does not have enough tolerance to bring the crosshair to the point of impact of the bullet. As to how that would affect the lead—the gun, when we first received it in the laboratory and fired these first targets, shot high and slightly to the right.

If you were shooting at a moving target from a high elevation, relatively high elevation, moving away from you, it would be necessary for you to shoot over that object in order for the bullet to strike your intended target, because the object during the flight of the bullet would move a certain distance.

The fact that the crosshairs are set high would actually compensate for any lead which had to be taken. So that if you aimed with this weapon as it actually was received at the laboratory, it would be necessary to take no lead whatsoever in order to hit the intended object. The scope would accomplish the lead for you.

I might also say that it also shot slightly to the right, which would tend to cause you to miss your target slightly to the right.

Mr. Eisenberg. Now, on that last question, did you attempt to center the windage crosshair, to sight-in the windage crosshair?

Mr. Frazier. We attempted to, and found that it was changing—the elevation was changing the windage. So we merely left the windage as it was.

Mr. Eisenberg. Can you say conclusively that the windage crosshair could not be centered in, sighted-in?

Mr. Frazier. No, sir. I would say that the windage could have been centered in the telescope to bring the windage to the aiming line.

Mr. Eisenberg. So that—and if that had been done, then you would not have this problem of dispersion to the right?

Mr. Frazier. That's true.

Mr. Eisenberg. Now, turning to——

Representative Boggs. Excuse me just a moment. Do you have any opinion on whether or not the sight was deliberately set that way?

Mr. Frazier. No, sir; I do not. And I think I must say here that this mount was loose on the rifle when we received it. And apparently the scope had even been taken off of the rifle, in searching for fingerprints on the rifle. So that actually the way it was sighted-in when we got it does not necessarily mean it was sighted-in that way when it was abandoned.

Mr. Eisenberg. Carrying this question a little bit further on the deliberateness of the sighting-in, the problem with the elevation crosshair is built into the mounting of the scope, is that correct?

Mr. Frazier. Yes. The mount is not screwed to the rifle in such a fashion that it points the scope at the target closely enough to permit adjusting the crosshair to accurately sight-in the rifle.

Representative Boggs. One other question, then.

It is possible, is it not, to so adjust the telescopic sight to compensate for that change in the target?

Mr. Frazier. Oh, yes. You can accomplish that merely by putting shims under the front of the scope and over the back of the scope to tip the scope in the mount itself, to bring it into alinement.

Representative Boggs. So an accomplished person, accustomed to using that weapon, anticipating a shot of that type, might very well have made such an adjustment prior to using the rifle; isn't that so?

Mr. Frazier. If it were necessary; yes. There were no shims in the weapon, either under the mount, where it screws to the weapon, or in the two mounting rings, when we received it in the laboratory.

Mr. Eisenberg. Do you have any shims with you, Mr. Frazier?

Mr. Frazier. Yes. When we received the weapon yesterday, there were shims mounted in the rifle. The one under the front end of the mount is in this envelope.

Representative Boggs. But they were not there when you received it originally?

Mr. Frazier. No, sir. These were placed there by some other individual.

Mr. Eisenberg. For the record, these were placed by the ballistics laboratory of the Army, a representative of which will testify later.

Now, turning to another possible source of error in aim, Mr. Frazier, if a rifle such as Exhibit 139 is sighted-in with the use of a target at a given distance, and it is aimed at a target which is further away or closer than the target which was used for sighting-in purposes, will any error be introduced by reason of the fact that the target is further or closer away than the sighting-in target?

Mr. Frazier. Yes, it will, because the bullet in leaving the muzzle follows a curved path rather than a straight path, and in order to hit a specific target at a specific range, it is necessary for the bullet to travel up and drop down to the target, rather than have the bore pointed right at the target at the time of discharge.

Mr. Eisenberg. Can you calculate the amount of error which would be introduced by a specific projectile?

Mr. Frazier. Yes.

Mr. Eisenberg. Have you made such calculations?

Mr. Frazier. I have taken calculations for similar weight and velocity bullets from ballistics tables, which bullets approximate the velocity of the 6.5 mm. bullet and the weight of that bullet as fired from 139.

Mr. Eisenberg. Are these results affected by the rifle which is employed, or do they depend upon the missile?

Mr. Frazier. They depend upon the weight and shape of the missile and the velocity, but not upon the weapon.

Mr. Eisenberg. Could you give us the results of these calculations?

Mr. Frazier. Yes, sir; if you, for instance, take this rifle with a telescopic sight and sight it in for 300 feet—that is, the bullet will strike where you are looking when you are shooting at 300 feet—at 200 feet the bullet will be above the line of sight approximately one-quarter of an inch, and at 100 feet it will be approximately one-quarter of an inch below the line of sight. That is accomplished because the bullet is still coming up at 100 feet, it crosses the line of sight, and does not descend again to it until you come to the sighting-in distance of 300 feet.

If you sighted-in to strike at 450 feet, the bullet at 100 feet would be just at the line of sight—that is, on its way up would just cross the line of sight at about 100 feet. It would be one inch high at 200 feet, and approximately one and one-eighth inches high at 300 feet.

It would, of course, drop back down to the point of aim at 450 feet. If you sighted-in at 600 feet, then at 100 feet it would be approximately one-half inch high. At 200 feet it would be 2 inches high, and at 300 feet it would be approximately 3 inches high.

Representative Boggs. Is this a stationary target?

Mr. Frazier. Yes, this is shooting from a rest at a stationary target.

Representative Boggs. This is just a normal——

Mr. Frazier. This is just the trajectory of the bullet.

Representative Boggs. I understand.

Mr. Frazier. As calculated——

Mr. McCloy. Putting it another way, what would be the drop of the bullet at a hundred yards if you aim point-blank straight at that target?

Mr. Frazier. Assuming no sighting or anything, the bullet would drop about 1.2 inches from the line of the bore at 100 yards.

Representative Boggs. 1.2 inches?

Mr. Frazier. Yes, sir.

Representative Boggs. But now the telescopic sight at a hundred yards would correct that?

Mr. Frazier. Yes, sir. Actually, you would sight so that the muzzle is tipped up slightly with reference to the sight.

Mr. Eisenberg. The error would be introduced if you shot at a target which is closer or further away than the sighting-in target; is that correct?

Mr. Frazier. Yes, that's right.

Mr. Eisenberg. Would you characterize these errors as material?

Mr. Frazier. No, sir; I would not—unless you began shooting at distances well beyond your sighting-in point—then the amount of variation increases very rapidly.

Mr. Eisenberg. What would be the usual minimum distance you use for sighting-in a weapon such as Exhibit 139?

Mr. Frazier. It would vary from place to place depending upon shooting conditions, and I would say it would seldom be sighted-in for less than 150 or 200 yards.

Mr. Eisenberg. So that if the shots involved in the assassination were fired at 175 feet and 265 feet respectively, they would be shorter than the sighting-in distance and therefore not materially affected by the trajectory characteristics, is that correct?

Mr. Frazier. That is correct, yes.

Mr. Eisenberg. Now, based upon the characteristics of Exhibit 139, and the ammunition it employs, and based upon your experience with the weapon, would you consider it to have been a good choice for the commission of a crime such as the assassination?

Mr. Frazier. Yes, sir; I would.

Mr. Eisenberg. Can you explain that?

Mr. Frazier. Yes. Any rifle, regardless of its caliber, would be a good choice if it would shoot accurately.

Mr. Eisenberg. And did you find this shot accurately?

Mr. Frazier. Yes, sir.

Representative Boggs. Would you consider the shots difficult shots—talking about the shots from the sixth-floor window to the head of the President and to Governor Connally?

Mr. Frazier. No, sir; I would not under the circumstances—a relatively slow-moving target, and very short distance, and a telescopic sight.

Representative Boggs. You are not answering that as an expert.

Mr. Frazier. From my own experience in shooting over the years, when you shoot at 175 feet or 260 feet, which is less than a hundred yards, with a telescopic sight, you should not have any difficulty in hitting your target.

Representative Boggs. Putting my question another way, you would not have to be an expert marksman to accomplish this objective?

Mr. Frazier. I would say no, you certainly would not.

Representative Boggs. And a man is a relatively large target, is he not?

Mr. Frazier. Yes, sir; I would say you would have to be very familiar with the weapon to fire it rapidly, and do this—hit this target at those ranges. But the marksmanship is accomplished by the telescopic sight. I mean it requires no training at all to shoot a weapon with a telescopic sight once you know that you must put the crosshairs on the target and that is all that is necessary.

Mr. EISENBERG. How does the recoil of this weapon compare with the recoil of the average military rifle?

Mr. FRAZIER. Considerably less. The recoil is nominal with this weapon, because it has a very low velocity and pressure, and just an average-size bullet weight.

Mr. EISENBERG. Would that trend to improve the shooter's marksmanship?

Mr. FRAZIER. Under rapid-fire conditions, yes.

Mr. EISENBERG. Would that make it a better choice than a more powerfully recoiling weapon for the type of crime which was committed?

Mr. FRAZIER. For shooting rapidly, this would be a much better choice, because the recoil does not throw the muzzle nearly so far off the target, it does not jar the shooter nearly so much, as a higher-powered rifle, such as a .30/06 or a .270 Winchester, or a German 8 mm. Mauser, for instance, or one of the other military-type weapons available.

Mr. EISENBERG. Is the killing power of the bullets essentially similar to the killing power at these ranges—the killing power of the rifles you have named?

Mr. FRAZIER. No, sir.

Mr. EISENBERG. How much difference is there?

Mr. FRAZIER. The higher velocity bullets of approximately the same weight would have more killing power. This has a low velocity, but has very adequate killing power with reference to humans, because it is a military—it is an established military weapon.

Representative BOGGS. This is a military weapon, is it not?

Mr. FRAZIER. Yes, sir.

Mr. McCLOY. That is designed to kill a human being.

Representative BOGGS. Exactly.

Mr. EISENBERG. Unless there are further questions on the weapon, I am going to move into the area of the identification of the cartridge cases and the bullets.

Mr. McCLOY. I may say I have to leave at twelve o'clock for a twelve-fifteen appointment. I will be back this afternoon.

Mr. EISENBERG. Mr. Frazier, returning to the cartridge cases which were marked earlier into evidence as Commission Exhibits 543, 544, and 545, and which, as I stated earlier for the record, had been found next to the window of the sixth floor of the Texas School Book Depository, can you tell us when you received those cartridge cases?

Mr. FRAZIER. Yes, sir; I received the first of the exhibits, 543 and 544, on November 23, 1963. They were delivered to me by Special Agent Vincent Drain of the Dallas FBI Office.

And the other one I received on November 27, 1963, which was delivered by Special Agents Vincent Drain and Warren De Brueys of the Dallas Office.

Mr. EISENBERG. After receiving these cartridge cases, did you clean them up or in any way prepare them for examination?

Mr. FRAZIER. Yes. The bases were cleaned of a paint which was placed on them by the manufacturer. In spots this red lacquer on the base of the case was overlapping the head of the case where some of the microscopic marks were located, and some of that color was taken off.

Mr. EISENBERG. Why is that lacquer put on the cartridge cases?

Mr. FRAZIER. It seals the primer area against moisture.

Mr. EISENBERG. Were there any other changes made in the preparation of the cartridge cases?

Mr. FRAZIER. No, sir.

Mr. EISENBERG. You have examined the cartridge cases previously. Are they in the same condition now that they were when you received them in the laboratory except for the cleaning of the lacquer?

Mr. FRAZIER. Yes, sir; they are.

Mr. EISENBERG. After receiving the cartridge cases, did you examine them to determine whether they had been fired in Commission Exhibit 139?

Mr. FRAZIER. Yes, sir.

Mr. EISENBERG. When did you make the examinations?

Mr. FRAZIER. On the dates I mentioned, that is, November 23, 1963, and November 27, 1963.

Mr. EISENBERG. And what were your conclusions, Mr. Frazier?

Mr. FRAZIER. I found all three of the cartridge cases had been fired in this particular weapon.

Mr. EISENBERG. Can you describe the examination which you conducted to reach these conclusions?

Mr. FRAZIER. The first step was to fire test cartridge cases in this rifle to pick up the microscopic marks which are left on all cartridge cases fired in this weapon by the face of the bolt. Then those test cartridge cases were mounted on a comparison microscope, on the right-hand side, and on the left-hand side of the comparison microscope was mounted one of the three submitted cartridge cases, so that you could magnify the surfaces of the test and the evidence and compare the marks left on the cartridge cases by the bolt face and the firing pin of the rifle.

(At this point, Mr. McCloy left the hearing room.)

Mr. EISENBERG. I now hand you two cartridge cases, and ask you whether you can identify these cartridge cases?

Mr. FRAZIER. Yes, sir; these are the two cartridge cases we fired for test purposes in Exhibit 139.

Mr. EISENBERG. Do they have your mark on them?

Mr. FRAZIER. Yes, they do.

Mr. EISENBERG. Commissioner Boggs, may I introduce these as 557?

Representative BOGGS. They may be admitted.

(The items referred to were marked Commission Exhibit No. 557 for identification and received in evidence.)

Mr. EISENBERG. These were the only two cartridge cases fired as tests in Exhibit 139—as tests for the purpose of identification of the cartridge cases which you examined before, 543, 544, and 545?

Mr. FRAZIER. Yes, sir; these two were used in those tests. There were many other cartridge cases fired, but not for that purpose.

Mr. EISENBERG. Can you explain how you are able to come to a conclusion that a cartridge case was fired in a particular weapon to the exclusion of all other weapons?

Mr. FRAZIER. Yes, sir; during the manufacture of a weapon, there are certain things done to the mechanism of it, which are by machine or by filing, by grinding, which form the parts of the weapon into their final shape. These machining and grinding and filing operations will mark the metal with very fine scratches or turning marks and grinding marks in such a way that there will be developed on the surface of the metal a characteristic pattern. This pattern, because it is made by these accidental machine-type operations, will be characteristic of that particular weapon, and will not be reproduced on separate weapons. It may be a combination of marks that—the face of the bolt may be milled, then it may be in part filed to smooth off the corners, and then, as a final operation, it may be polished, or otherwise adjusted during the hand fitting operation, so that it does have its particular pattern of microscopic marks.

The bolt face of the 139 rifle I have photographed and enlarged in this photograph to show the types of marks I was referring to.

Mr. EISENBERG. You took this photograph yourself, and it is a photograph of the bolt face of the 139 rifle?

Mr. FRAZIER. Yes, sir.

Mr. EISENBERG. May I have this introduced as 558?

Representative BOGGS. It may be admitted.

(The photograph referred to was marked Commission Exhibit No. 558, and received in evidence.)

Mr. EISENBERG. What is the magnification of this bolt-face photograph?

Mr. FRAZIER. Approximately 11 diameters.

Mr. EISENBERG. Could you slip out the bolt of the rifle so we could see how it compares, and show us the part of the bolt which is photographed?

Mr. FRAZIER. Orienting the photograph with the writing at the bottom, orients the bolt also, as it comes out of the rifle—with the slot shown as a groove on the bottom of the bolt. Then the extractor on the bolt, is the area shown at the left side of the photograph, as you view it—the actual bolt face itself is inset into the bolt below the surface of the extractor, and a supporting shoulder around it, and in the center, of course, is the firing-pin hole and the firing pin.

The marks produced during manufacture are the marks seen on the bolt face; filing marks, machining marks of the various types, even forging marks or casting marks if the bolt happens to be forged or cast. And then variations which occur in these marks during the life of the weapon are very important in identification, because many of the machining marks can be flattened out, can be changed, by merely a grain of sand between the face of the cartridge case and the bolt at the time a shot is fired, which will itself scratch and dent the bolt face. So the bolt face will pick up a characteristic pattern of marks which are peculiar to it.

The same is true of extractors and ejectors. They are in turn machined and will have a pattern of marks or scratches on their surfaces which will mark cartridge cases in the same manner each time.

The comparison we made was of the marks appearing in this photograph, 558, in fairly close proximity to the firing pin hole, since that is the area that the primer in the head of the cartridge case comes in contact with.

The primer in a cartridge case normally takes marks more readily than the surrounding brass portion of the cartridge case, which is a considerably harder metal and is not impressed with these marks as readily.

The three cartridge cases, 553, 554, and 555, were compared——

Mr. Eisenberg. Is that 543, 544, and 545?

Mr. Frazier. I am sorry—yes, 543, 544, and 545. These three cartridge cases were placed one at a time on the comparison microscope, and the surfaces having the breech-face marks or the bolt marks were compared with those on the test cartridge cases, Exhibit 557. As a result of comparing the pattern of microscopic markings on the test cartridge cases and those marks on Exhibits 543, 544, and 545, both of the face of the bolt and the firing pin, I concluded that these three had been fired in this particular weapon.

Representative Boggs. Who manufactured these cartridges?

Mr. Frazier. Western Cartridge Co., East Alton, Ill.

Representative Boggs. They manufacture cartridges and bullets for all manner of rifles?

Mr. Frazier. Yes, they do.

Representative Boggs. This is not—this rifle is not common in the United States, is it?

Mr. Frazier. It is fairly common now, but at the time it was manufactured or used primarily it was not. It was imported into this country as surplus military equipment, and has been advertised quite widely.

Representative Boggs. These three cartridges—these three shells that you had were the same as the live ones that were found there, were they not?

Mr. Frazier. There was one live cartridge found. They are identical.

Representative Boggs. And the live one was manufactured also by——

Mr. Frazier. Yes, the Western Cartridge Co. It bears the head stamp "WCC" and "6.5. mm."

Representative Boggs. These are not difficult to obtain? You can buy them anywhere?

Mr. Frazier. Well, you can buy them from mail-order houses primarily, or a few gun shops that have accumulated a supply by ordering them. The information we have is that two million rounds were imported into the United States in one lot, one shipment—and they have been transmitted over the country and are for sale by several different surplus gun shops—used guns—mail-order houses and places of that nature—and gunsmiths, and firearms shops sell this ammunition.

Representative Boggs. Go ahead.

Mr. Eisenberg. Mr. Frazier, what is the basis of the statement you made earlier that no two bolt faces would be the same?

Mr. FRAZIER. Because the marks which are placed on any bolt face are accidental in nature. That is, they are not placed there intentionally in the first place. They are residual to some machining operation, such as a milling machine, in which each cutter of the milling tool cuts away a portion of the metal; then the next tooth comes along and cuts away a little more, and so on, until the final surface bears the combination of the various teeth of the milling cutter. In following that operation, then, the surface is additionally scratched—until you have numerous—we call them microscopic characteristics, a characteristic being a mark which is peculiar to a certain place on the bolt face, and of a certain shape, it is of a certain size, it has a certain contour, it may be just a little dimple in the metal, or a spot of rust at one time on the face of the bolt, or have occurred from some accidental means such as dropping the bolt, or repeated use having flattened or smoothed off the surface of the metal.

Mr. EISENBERG. Why doesn't a series of the same machines, or repeated use of the same machines, cause the same results, apart from future accidental markings?

Mr. FRAZIER. In some instances a certain type of cutter will duplicate a certain pattern of marks. In general you will find for a milling cutter a circular mark. And you may find the same pattern of circles. But that milling cutter does not actually cut the steel; it tears it out, it chips it out, and the surface of the metal then is rough—even though the circle is there, the circle is not a smooth circle, but it is a result of tearing out the metal, and you will have a very rough surface. When magnified sufficiently, you can detect the difference even between two similarly milled surfaces because of the minor variations in the cutting operation.

Mr. EISENBERG. Have you had occasion to examine such similarly-milled surfaces?

Mr. FRAZIER. Oh, yes; many times.

Mr. EISENBERG. Would you go into detail on that?

Mr. FRAZIER. Well, part of my work in the laboratory is dealing with tool-marks of all types, from drills, mills, files, cutting instruments, and so on. And when you are dealing with filing marks or milling marks and so on, it is sometimes possible to identify a particular mill as having made a certain mark on the basis of the grinding marks on that particular mill. But such as a case like this, where the cutting marks have now been altered through use of the weapon and corrosion, or in wear or in filing, some of the original marks are removed, and other marks are in their place, until eventually you reach a condition where that bolt face will be entirely different from any other bolt face. It is a matter actually—when you get down to the basis of it, it is a matter of a mathematical impossibility in the realm of human experience for any two things to ever be exactly alike.

Mr. EISENBERG. That is because the original markings will not be exactly like, and then you have added accidental markings on top of the original ones?

Mr. FRAZIER. That is right; yes, sir.

Mr. EISENBERG. Returning for a moment to the original markings, as I understand it, you have worked with the tools themselves and the impressions the tools themselves leave, as opposed to a tooled surface, such as this.

Mr. FRAZIER. I have worked with both. In other words, in comparing tool-marks, you examine not only the tool, but the marks they produce.

Mr. EISENBERG. And in working with these tools, as I understand your testimony, you have found that the markings which a tool leaves, which the same tool leaves, will be distinctive.

Mr. FRAZIER. That is true, yes. When it is a scrape or an impression from its surface, or something of that nature, it can be very readily identified. But if it is a drill or something of that nature, where you have a tearing operation, then it is not readily identified, but it occasionally can be identified.

Mr. EISENBERG. Well, how many such examinations do you think you have made?

Mr. FRAZIER. Thousands of them.

Mr. EISENBERG. Have you noticed whether the marks left by a given tool—that you have examined—change over the course of the use of the tool?

Mr. FRAZIER. Yes, they change very rapidly when a tool is used to cut a hard object.

Mr. EISENBERG. Could you elaborate on what you mean by "very rapidly"?

Mr. FRAZIER. Well, for instance, when using a pry bar, for example, one insertion of a pry bar into the hard insulation of a safe, with pressure applied to it can change the entire blade of the tool to the extent that you could not identify a succession of marks, because of the abrasion by the insulation. But that same tool, used to mark a soft steel or brass or copper, could make mark after mark without changing, or only a small portion of it may change with each impression. Or it may gradually change over a period of time.

Mr. EISENBERG. Now, is the metal in the bolt face a hard metal or a soft metal?

Mr. FRAZIER. I would say it was hard metal——

Mr. EISENBERG. Well——

Mr. FRAZIER. With reference to copper or other softer metals—it is a steel. I could not say how hard it actually is.

Mr. EISENBERG. What will the effect of the metal used in the bolt face be upon the tool which is used to finish it off, cut it and finish it off?

Mr. FRAZIER. The tool will gradually wear out.

Mr. EISENBERG. Well, will the tool leave different marks on the end of the bolt face from one bolt to the very next bolt face?

Mr. FRAZIER. Oh, yes; that very often happens. The tool is worn out or the small cuttings get underneath the edge, between the tool, and nick the edge of the tool, so that the tool will gradually change over a period of time. The cutting edge—the amount of change depends upon the amount of wear, the heat involved, and the hardness of the metal—the relative hardness of the metal.

Mr. EISENBERG. Will that particular change be noticed invariably in two consecutive bolt faces?

Mr. FRAZIER. No, sir.

Mr. EISENBERG. So what is the genesis of the difference in the two consecutive bolt faces as they come from the manufacturer?

Mr. FRAZIER. The change, as I said, depends on the bolt you are using. It does not always take place, because some bolts are made of a very soft metal, and they will not necessarily change a machining tool to that extent.

Mr. EISENBERG. But the markings, you said, would be different on two consecutive bolt faces?

Mr. FRAZIER. Oh, yes.

Mr. EISENBERG. And if the tool is not changed, what is the origin of the difference between the markings?

Mr. FRAZIER. There are other accidental markings placed there during the machining operation.

Mr. EISENBERG. Could you describe that?

Mr. FRAZIER. For instance, as the blade of a milling machine travels around a surface, it takes off actually a dust—it is not actually a piece of metal— it scrapes a little steel off in the form of a dust—or a very fine powder or chip—that tooth leaves a certain pattern of marks—that edge. That milling cutter may have a dozen of these edges on its surface, and each one takes a little more. Gradually you wear the metal down, you tear it out actually until you are at the proper depth. Those little pieces of metal, as they are traveling around, can also scratch the face of the bolt—unless they are washed away. So that you may have accidental marks from that source, just in the machining operation.

Now, there are two types of marks produced in a cutting operation. One, from the nicks along the cutting edge of the tool, which are produced by a circular operating tool—which produce very fine scratches in a circular pattern. Each time the tool goes around, it erases those marks that were there before. And when the tool is finally lifted out, you have a series of marks which go around the surface which has been machined, and you will find that that pattern of marks, as this tool goes around, will change. In one area, it will be one set of marks—and as you visually examine the surface of the metal, these very fine marks will extend for a short distance, then disappear, and a new mark of a new type will begin and extend for a short distance. The entire surface, then, will have a—be composed of a series of circles, but the individual marks seen in the microscope will not be circular, will not form complete circles around the face of the bolt.

Mr. EISENBERG. Have you had occasion to examine two consecutive bolt faces from a factory?

Mr. FRAZIER. Oh, yes.

Mr. EISENBERG. And what did you find on that examination?

Mr. FRAZIER. There would be no similarity in the individual microscopic characteristics between the two bolt faces.

Mr. EISENBERG. There actually was none?

Mr. FRAZIER. No, there was none.

Mr. EISENBERG. In the bolt face with which we are dealing, Exhibit 139, can you say from inspection whether the markings on that bolt face are predominantly the accidental markings introduced subsequent to manufacture, or the markings of the manufacture?

Mr. FRAZIER. I would say that these were filing marks for the most part which were made during manufacture, some of which have been obliterated and changed through use—possibly corrosion.

Mr. EISENBERG. Mr. Frazier, taking Exhibit 543, did you prepare a photograph of this exhibit——

Mr. FRAZIER. Yes, sir.

Mr. EISENBERG. Compared with the test cartridge case?

Mr. FRAZIER. Yes, sir; this is the photograph, showing the test cartridge case from Exhibit 557 on the right and the cartridge case 543 on the left.

Mr. EISENBERG. This was prepared by you or under your supervision?

Mr. FRAZIER. Yes, sir.

Mr. EISENBERG. Mr. Chairman?

Representative BOGGS. It may be admitted.

(The item referred to was marked Commission Exhibit No. 559 and received in evidence.)

Mr. EISENBERG. Now, that is marked on the left C–14, and on the right, C–6.

Mr. FRAZIER. Yes, sir.

Mr. EISENBERG. And the left-hand photograph is a photograph of what?

Mr. FRAZIER. Of the cartridge case 543.

Mr. EISENBERG. That is the actual fired case?

Mr. FRAZIER. Yes, sir; it shows just a portion of the primer, and a very small portion of the firing-pin impression.

Mr. EISENBERG. And the right-hand side of that photograph, marked C–6?

Mr. FRAZIER. It is a test cartridge case, fired in the rifle Exhibit 139.

Mr. EISENBERG. What is the magnification, Mr. Frazier?

Mr. FRAZIER. Approximately 100 diameters.

Mr. EISENBERG. And is that magnification equal on both sides of the picture?

Mr. FRAZIER. Yes, sir.

Mr. EISENBERG. Did you make your identification of Exhibit 543, that is the identification of that exhibit as having been fired in the rifle 139, on the basis of your examination under the microscope, or on the basis of the photograph?

Mr. FRAZIER. Under the microscope. The photograph has no relationship whatsoever to the examination.

Mr. EISENBERG. Can you explain that?

Mr. FRAZIER. The examination is made microscopically through the use of your eyes, and your eyes will record depths and shapes to a much greater extent than can be shown in a photograph. So that the examination and comparison is made of these irregular surfaces mentally, rather than mechanically by any means. The photograph is taken primarily to illustrate the types of marks found and their location, relatively, on the specimen.

Representative BOGGS. We will have to adjourn and come back at 2.

(Whereupon, at 12:15 p.m., the President's Commission recessed.)

TESTIMONY OF ROBERT A. FRAZIER RESUMED

The President's Commission reconvened at 2:10 p.m.

Mr. McCloy. You are still under oath, you know.

Mr. Frazier. Yes, sir.

Mr. Eisenberg. I would like to begin by clearing up a few items which have been covered or left open during the morning session.

First, you were going to supply us with certain figures concerning the times which were taken by two of the Agents to fire three shots in the first series of tests which were made for determining the accuracy of the firing under rapid-fire conditions.

Mr. Frazier. Yes, sir; that was at two targets. The first one I gave you—Killion fired in 9 seconds. The other was a target marked Cunningham and Frazier. Cunningham fired his three shots in 8 seconds and I fired my three shots in 5.9 seconds.

Mr. Eisenberg. Now also you had made certain calculations concerning what we have been calling the lead that had to be given to a target, assuming various factors which were supplied to you. Do you have those calculations now?

Mr. Frazier. Yes, sir; the lead would amount to shooting over the target at 175 feet, a distance of 6.7 inches, and the decimal on that figure is not an accurate decimal because this figure relates to an average velocity of ammunition of this type, and is concerned with a speed of a vehicle which is also estimated, and a distance which may or may not be exactly accurate.

But at a ground speed of 11 miles an hour, it would be necessary to shoot over or lead a target 6.7 inches for the bullet to hit the intended spot on the target. At 265 feet the lead would be .51 feet, or 6.1 inches.

I might say that the variation, that of less lead at the longer distance, is in great part due to the fact that the target is farther away and that the shot is more nearly in line with the direction in which the target is moving, which would account for much of the drop in the amount of lead.

And, in addition, I calculated this on the basis of the fact that there was a slight slope between the 175-foot and the 265-foot location downwards away from the shooter, which would also tend to more nearly cause the target to be moving in the same path as the bullet.

Mr. Eisenberg. And did you convert those lead distances into the amount of inches which the shooter would have to sight above the head, above the point of the target?

Mr. Frazier. Those figures I gave were the elevations or the sighting distances above the target. The 6.7 inches vertical lead or sighting over the target is the equivalent of leading on the ground of 1.4 feet.

Mr. Eisenberg. And that table also shows leads at other car speeds?

Mr. Frazier. This table—I could calculate them—it only shows miles per hour translated into feet per second.

Mr. Eisenberg. I mean, does it show various miles per hour?

Mr. Frazier. Yes; it shows miles per hour in feet per second.

Mr. Eisenberg. Without going into detail at this time, may I have permission to introduce this table into evidence?

Mr. McCloy. It may be admitted.

Mr. Eisenberg. This will be Commission Exhibit 560.

(The item identified as Commission Exhibit No. 560 was received in evidence.)

Mr. Eisenberg. Now, Mr. Frazier, in the construction of this table and also in your last tests for rapid fire for this rifle, you used a five-and-a-half second figure as a factor in your calculations, and in your attempt at rapid fire accuracy placements. Can you give us the source of that figure?

Mr. Frazier. Yes, sir. You were the source of it, based on examination, as I understood it, of a movie taken at the scene, and measurements taken at the scene. However, I have no knowledge of the actual time.

Mr. Eisenberg. For the record, I just wanted to establish that this is a source that was supplied by the Commission and which is tentative, and it is not to imply any final conclusion on the part of the FBI; is that correct?

Mr. FRAZIER. I hope it is taken that way, because we don't know what the time actually was.

Mr. EISENBERG. Another point then, which should have been covered this morning, Mr. Frazier, in your qualifications: have you testified before in court?

Mr. FRAZIER. Yes; I have.

Mr. EISENBERG. Can you estimate the number of times?

Mr. FRAZIER. Approximately 400 times.

Mr. EISENBERG. Finally, we had discussed briefly your examination of consecutively manufactured bolt faces to see whether any two such consecutively manufactured bolt faces were identical in their microscopic characteristics. How many such examinations have you performed?

Mr. FRAZIER. I would say about four examinations of pairs of bolt faces which have been consecutively manufactured.

Mr. EISENBERG. And in each case the result was what?

Mr. FRAZIER. The marks on one bolt face in no way resembled the marks on the other bolt face.

Mr. EISENBERG. Mr. Frazier, we were just beginning to discuss, before the recess, Commission Exhibit 559, which is a picture, as you described it, of Exhibit No. 543 and a test cartridge under a microscope, and that is also known as C–6 and C–14, is that right?

Mr. FRAZIER. Yes, sir.

Mr. EISENBERG. Could you discuss, by using that picture, some of the markings which you have seen under the microscope and on the basis of which you made your identification?

Mr. FRAZIER. Yes, sir. In the photograph I have drawn some small circles and numbered them, those circles, correspondingly on each side of the photograph. The purpose of the circles is not to point out all the similarities, but to call attention to some of them and to help orient in locating a mark on one with a mark on the opposite side of the photograph. In general the area shown is immediately outside of the firing pin in the bolt of the 139 rifle, on the left side of the photograph, and Commission Exhibit 543 on the right side.

The circles have been drawn around the dents or irregularly shaped ridges, small bumps, and depressions on the surface of the metal in six places on each side of the photograph. It is an examination of these marks, and all of the marks on the face of the breech, microscopically which permits a conclusion to be reached. The photograph itself actually is a substitute to show only the type of marks found rather than their nature, that is, their height, their width, or their relationship to each other, which is actually a mental, visual, comparison on the two specimens themselves.

Mr. EISENBERG. Referring for a second to this mental, visual, comparison, Mr. Frazier, would a person without firearms training—firearms-identification training—be able to look under a microscope and make a determination for himself concerning whether a given cartridge case had been fired in a given weapon?

Mr. FRAZIER. In that connection that person could look through the microscope. He may or may not see these individual characteristics which are present, because he does not know what to look for in the first place, and, secondly, they are of such a nature that you have to mentally sort them out in your mind going back and forth between one area and the other until you form a mental picture of them in a comparison such as this.

If it was a different type of comparison, of parallel marks or something of that nature, then he could see the marks, but in either instance, without having compared hundreds and hundreds of specimens, he would not be able to make any statement as to whether or not they were fired from the same rifle.

Mr. EISENBERG. Would you say that this is, then, a matter of expert interpretation rather than a point-for-point comparison which a layman could make?

Mr. FRAZIER. I would say so; yes. I don't think a layman would recognize some of the things on these cartridge cases and some shown in the photographs as actually being significant or not significant, because there will be things present which have nothing whatsoever to do with the firing of the cartridge case in the gun.

There may be a depression in the primer to begin with, and there are no marks registered at that point as a result of the firing. Unless these things are known to occur, someone may actually arrive at a different conclusion, because of the absence of similar marks.

Mr. EISENBERG. Now having reference to the specific exhibit before you, which is 559——

Mr. FRAZIER. Yes.

Mr. EISENBERG. Are all the marks shown in both photographs identical?

Mr. FRAZIER. No.

Mr. EISENBERG. And could you go into detail on a mark which is not identical to explain why you would get such a result?

Mr. FRAZIER. Well, for instance, between what I have drawn here as circle 4 and circle 5, there is a slanting line from the upper left to the lower right on C–6. This line shows as a white line in the photograph.

On the other side there is a rough, very rough ridge which runs through there, having an entirely different appearance from the relatively sharp line on C–6. The significant part of that mark is the groove in between, rather than the sharp edge of the mark, because the sharp corner could be affected by the hardness of the metal or the irregular surface of the primer and the amount of pressure exerted against it, pressing it back against the face of the bolt, at the time the cartridges were fired. So that you would never expect all the marks on one cartridge case to be identical with all the marks on the other cartridge case.

In fact, you would expect many differences. But the comparison is made on the overall pattern, contour, and nature of the marks that are present.

Mr. EISENBERG. Off the record.

(Discussion off the record.)

Mr. EISENBERG. Back on the record.

Mr. Frazier, could you discuss or characterize those points which you have circled on Commission Exhibit 559, starting from the top?

Mr. FRAZIER. Number 1 circle is drawn around a depression in the metal of irregular shape. I might say that number 1 shows on the right side of the photograph, and only half of it shows on the left side because of the relative position of the two cartridge cases in the photograph.

Number 2 is a circle drawn around a long line which extends obliquely across each cartridge case from the upper left to the lower right. The long line itself is a means of orienting the cartridge cases one with the other, but the circle is drawn around a break in that line in the form of a very small hump or an absence of metal which shows up as an actual break in the long line.

Number 3 again is a depression between two grooves, which is rather similar in shape. I cannot tell you how deep it is because the photograph only shows two dimensions. But on the cartridge cases it has a very characteristic depth to it, which is readily apparent.

It is formed by two parallel lines extending from the upper left to the lower, towards the lower right, with the depression in between, and again one side of the depression is formed by a small raised area in the primer metal which is seen in each photograph as a conical, almost a conical-shaped bump or raised area.

Number 4 is another raised portion on the photograph. In connection with 4, I would like to point out that a portion of this bump has been erased from the test cartridge case on the left-hand side of the photograph, the erasure caused by the turning of the bolt of the weapon while being pressed against the primer, which has smoothed off some of the protruding rough areas on the primer.

Number 5 is a horizontal ridge which has two depressions, one on the top and one on the bottom, shown on both sides of the photograph, and number 6 is a wishbone type of ridge, a wide ridge which divides into two smaller ridges on the left-hand edge, and in the middle of the dividing lines, the forked lines, is a small dent or raised portion. Those six which I have marked are only portions of those shown in the photograph, and of course the photograph does not show the entire surface of the primer.

Mr. EISENBERG. Were you able to find identifying marks on the brass as well as the primer on this cartridge case?

Mr. FRAZIER. No; I did not notice any marks on the brass portions outside of the primer.

Mr. EISENBERG. Is that typical of cartridge-case identification?

Mr. FRAZIER. Generally that is true, unless there is a great pressure, unless the brass of the cartridge case is soft, or unless the marks are very sharp on the breech face; then they will be impressed into the brass.

Mr. EISENBERG. This picture represents only a portion of the primer. You examined the entire primer to make your identification?

Mr. FRAZIER. Yes, sir.

Mr. EISENBERG. And found?

Mr. FRAZIER. It would not have been necessary to examine the entire primer necessarily, but of course we do examine the entire primer, pick out all of the marks on the left and the right, and rotate the cartridge cases and look at them from various angles, before arriving at a conclusion.

Mr. EISENBERG. Can you amplify the meaning of the statement that it would not be necessary to examine the entire primer?

Mr. FRAZIER. There are sufficient marks shown in this photograph upon which to base an identification. In other words, it would not be necessary to have the rest of the primer if it had been mutilated or destroyed or something of that nature.

Mr. EISENBERG. Did you also examine the firing-pin impression in the cartridge?

Mr. FRAZIER. Yes, sir.

Mr. EISENBERG. Did you take a picture of that examination?

Mr. FRAZIER. Yes. Here is the photograph of the firing-pin impression, again on the left the rifle, and on the right the cartridge case, Commission's 543.

Mr. EISENBERG. That bears the number C–14 and C–6, corresponding to the numbers on Commission Exhibit 559?

Mr. FRAZIER. Yes; it does.

Mr. EISENBERG. Did you take this photograph or have it taken under your supervision?

Mr. FRAZIER. Yes, sir.

Mr. EISENBERG. What is the magnification of this photograph?

Mr. FRAZIER. 90 diameters.

Mr. EISENBERG. Is it equal on both sides?

Mr. FRAZIER. Yes.

Mr. EISENBERG. Mr. Chairman, may I have this admitted?

Mr. McCLOY. It may be admitted.

Mr. EISENBERG. That will be 561.

(The item identified as Commission Exhibit No. 561 was received in evidence.)

Mr. EISENBERG. Could you proceed with the discussion of the circled marks on this photograph, number 561?

Mr. FRAZIER. In the case of firing-pin impressions which are shown on Exhibit 561, the marks result from two related sources; excuse me, not sources, but from two related causes, one being the force given to the firing pin driving it into the primer to set off the cartridge, and the second being the force of the powder charge inside the cartridge being driven back—driving the primer back against the firing pin at the same time, so that the metal of the primer is caused to flow or be stamped by the firing pin and pressed against by the gases, so that any irregularities in the firing pin will be impressed into the primer of the cartridge case.

Number 1 consists of a double horizontal line, one a fairly wide coarse line at the top. Immediately under that approximately one-eighth of an inch is a fairly fine horizontal line.

Circled and marked number 2 is a very coarse, wide ridge, very short in length, approximately one-half an inch, and an eighth to a quarter of an inch

423

in height. This ridge is formed by two grooves, a straight groove across the top, and a curved or crescent-shaped groove across the bottom.

Number 3 is a circle drawn around two small raised areas in the primer metal separated by a depression.

Number 4 is a section from a large ridge across the metal of the primer, which has a break in its surface in the lower portion of the circle, and immediately above the break is a groove, and immediately above that again is another ridge which is at a little steeper angle upwards to the left.

Number 5 is a depression, is a portion of a depression appearing at the bottom of the circle with a very short ridge running horizontally across the circle.

Mr. EISENBERG. Again there are dissimilar marks on these two pictures, Mr. Frazier?

Mr. FRAZIER. Yes; there are, for the same reason, that metal does not flow the same in every instance, and it will not be impressed to the same depth and to the same amount, depending on the type of metal, the blow that is struck, and the pressures involved.

Mr. EISENBERG. Is your identification made therefore on the basis of the presence of similarities, as opposed to the absence of dissimilarities?

Mr. FRAZIER. No, that is not exactly right. The identification is made on the presence of sufficient individual microscopic characteristics so that a very definite pattern is formed and visualized on the two surfaces.

Dissimilarities may or may not be present, depending on whether there have been changes to the firing pin through use or wear, whether the metal flows are the same, and whether the pressures are the same or not.

So I don't think we can say that it is an absence of dissimilarities, but rather the presence of similarities.

Mr. EISENBERG. Any further questions on this cartridge case?

Mr. McCLOY. No.

Mr. EISENBERG. Mr. Frazier, you have testified also that you identified the cartridge case which is Exhibit 544 as having been fired from this rifle, in this rifle, to the exclusion of all others. Did you take a photograph of the comparison that you made under the microscope of number 544?

Mr. FRAZIER. Yes. I again took two photographs, one of the breech-face or bolt-face marks, and one of the firing-pin marks.

Mr. EISENBERG. This exhibit which I am holding is a picture of the breech-face marks?

Mr. FRAZIER. Yes, sir.

Mr. EISENBERG. And was that taken by you or under your supervision?

Mr. FRAZIER. Yes, sir; it was.

Mr. EISENBERG. And the magnification here is what?

Mr. FRAZIER. 90 diameters.

Mr. EISENBERG. May I have this admitted, Mr. Chairman?

Mr. McCLOY. It may be admitted.

Mr. EISENBERG. That will be number 562, Mr. Reporter.

(The item described as Commission Exhibit No. 562 was received in evidence.)

Mr. EISENBERG. Could you discuss the markings on this picture, Mr. Frazier?

Mr. FRAZIER. Yes, sir. In Commission Exhibit 562, there is again the vertical dividing line which is the top of the prism in the microscope which divides your view. On the left hand side is a portion of the primer and a portion of the head of the test cartridge case from Exhibit 139. On the right side of the photograph is a portion of the surface of the primer and a portion of the firing-pin impression of the cartridge case, Commission Exhibit 544.

To assist in pointing out on the photograph some of the areas where individual microscopic characteristics are present, I have had circles drawn, circling at the top, number 1, an oval-shaped depression in the metal, having an irregularly shaped or wavy ridge across the bottom of the circle. Immediately below that is another ridge which has a flat top, and is more or less of a diamond shape.

Number 3 circle is over a very coarse, wide ridge separated by two fairly deep grooves on each side.

Number 4 circle is over a conical-shaped raised portion on the primer which represents a dent in the metal of the bolt face, and number 5 again is a raised area on the primer which is a portion of a ridge. In this instance this is more or less of a compound ridge which runs horizontally with a small break in it pointing down toward the lower left.

Mr. McCLOY. Is that same break apparent in the left hand photograph?

Mr. FRAZIER. Yes, sir; it is. Looking very closely and right at the hairline, you can see the break in the ridge where it forms more or less of a Y. The actual connecting point is not present, but you can see the portion of the ridge as it heads towards the horizontal ridge. The hairline has separated that portion of it.

Mr. EISENBERG. Would you call these marks strongly characteristic marks, Mr. Frazier?

Mr. FRAZIER. Oh, yes; very characteristic. They are primarily characteristic because of their irregular shape. If they had been regular in shape, it wouldn't have meant nearly as much as it does to have the irregular rough surfaces and contours of the marks.

Mr. EISENBERG. I think you have identified the next picture I am holding as having been taken by you?

Mr. FRAZIER. Yes, sir; it was. That is a 70-diameter magnification photograph of Exhibit 544 on the right, and the test from the rifle on the left.

Mr. EISENBERG. And this bears the numbers C–14 and C–7, and is a firing-pin photograph?

Mr. FRAZIER. Yes, sir.

Mr. EISENBERG. May this firing-pin mark photograph be admitted, Mr. Chairman?

Mr. McCLOY. It may be admitted.

Mr. EISENBERG. That is 563.

(The item was numbered 563, and was received in evidence.)

Mr. EISENBERG. Could you review that photograph, Mr. Frazier?

Mr. FRAZIER. Yes, sir. In Exhibit 563 the test cartridge case representing the rifle is on the left side of the photograph, and shows most of the firing-pin impression in that cartridge case. Five circles have been drawn over towards the right-hand edge of the firing-pin impression, and five similarly located circles have been drawn over the area at the right-hand edge of the firing-pin impression of Exhibit 544.

Mr. EISENBERG. Which is actually the left-hand side of the right-hand part of the picture?

Mr. FRAZIER. It would be—that is right; at the dividing line, the circles on 544 are drawn close to the dividing line, which shows only a very small portion of the firing pin of that cartridge case.

Beginning with number 1, it has a gently sloping ridge running from upper left toward lower right in each instance, with a break in the ridge contour at the middle in the form of an extension upwards toward the top of the photograph.

In number 2 there is a circle drawn around the end of a very long line in the left-hand side of the photograph. The circle is drawn to show a Y-shaped break in this line located on both cartridge cases.

Number 3 is a photograph of an irregular-shaped raised portion on the firing-pin impression, which is very difficult to describe in words.

Number 4 is a groove extending from upper right to lower left which has a break in its lower side to allow a horizontal groove to come in towards the main groove. The lower portion of that groove coming in from the lower side is in the form of a crescent-shaped ridge, which starts horizontally from the left and then falls off towards the lower right-hand side of the photograph.

The circle, number 5, is again a Y-shaped or wishbone-shaped ridge, with a horizontal bar on the right, and then extending ridges upward toward the left and downward to the left.

Mr. EISENBERG. Again, are these firing-pin marks what you would call strongly characteristic?

Mr. FRAZIER. Yes; I would say so.

Mr. EISENBERG. Does the firing pin give any evidence of having been altered subsequent to the original manufacture?

Mr. FRAZIER. No, sir; only in an accidental sort of way, that is, very fine scratches which may have been caused by firing or dirt on a cartridge or something which may have scratched the firing pin.

Mr. EISENBERG. Are firing-pin marks usually as characteristic of a given cartridge case as the primer marks?

Mr. FRAZIER. Yes, sir; I would say they are as characteristic. However, they may not always be as evident, they may not be seen as readily. However, they are just as characteristic.

Mr. McCLOY. Just to repeat again, what is this side of this picture? What does this represent?

Mr. FRAZIER. That represents the rifle cartridge.

Mr. McCLOY. The rifle cartridge itself?

Mr. FRAZIER. Yes, sir.

Mr. McCLOY. And this on the right?

Mr. FRAZIER. This is one of the three cartridge cases recovered from the building, Exhibit 544.

Mr. EISENBERG. Mr. Frazier, you fired two test cartridges in the rifle, is that correct?

Mr. FRAZIER. We fired several test cartridge cases. These two are the ones that were used in the comparisons.

Mr. EISENBERG. Did you fire several for possible comparison purposes, or only two for possible comparison purposes?

Mr. FRAZIER. Those we fired were in the time-fire test and we retained some of those for possible use in comparing, but it was not necessary to use them, actually.

Mr. EISENBERG. Did you use both of these test cartridge cases in the photographs, or only one of them?

Mr. FRAZIER. I could not tell by these photographs. We did not make any distinction when we were comparing tests with the evidence as to which test cartridge case we were using.

Mr. EISENBERG. When you made your selection among cartridge cases to select the items which would be used as test cases for comparison purposes, were the items you rejected much different from those you selected?

Mr. FRAZIER. No. The marks were generally the same on all of them. Those we used in this comparison were two tests which we fired on November 23d and used them in our tests—made our examination, our identification.

Later on we fired accuracy tests and speed tests and retained some of those cartridge cases, but they were not necessarily retained for test purposes, for identification of the weapon, but merely as a result of the other tests that were made.

Mr. EISENBERG. Could you just as easily have used other of the items from your original November twenty——

Mr. FRAZIER. Oh, yes; yes.

Mr. EISENBERG. Getting to the last cartridge case, Exhibit 545, did you take a photograph of the exhibit together with the test case under the microscope after making your identification?

Mr. FRAZIER. Yes; I did. This photograph shows that cartridge case 545 on the right, and the test cartridge case from the rifle, 139, on the left.

Mr. EISENBERG. This is marked on the right C–38 and on the left C–14?

Mr. FRAZIER. Yes, sir.

Mr. EISENBERG. Again this is a photograph taken by you or under your supervision?

Mr. FRAZIER. Yes, sir.

Mr. EISENBERG. And that is of the primer?

Mr. FRAZIER. Yes; it is.

Mr. EISENBERG. And you have a second photograph here also, marked C–14 and C–38, also taken by you or under your supervision?

Mr. FRAZIER. Yes, sir.

Mr. EISENBERG. And this is of the markings of the firing pin?

Mr. FRAZIER. Yes; it is.

Mr. EISENBERG. Can you give us the magnification first of the primer-markings photograph?

Mr. FRAZIER. That is 100 diameters enlargement on the primer, and on the firing-pin it is 80 diameters.

Mr. EISENBERG. Now in all the cases of the photographs you have given us, the magnifications are equal on both sides, are they?

Mr. FRAZIER. Yes; they are.

Mr. EISENBERG. Mr. Chairman, may I have these admitted into evidence?

Mr. McCLOY. They may be admitted.

Mr. EISENBERG. They will be 564 and 565.

(The items, identified as Commission Exhibits Nos. 564 and 565, were received in evidence.)

Mr. EISENBERG. Could you discuss the photograph, Exhibit 564 please, Mr. Frazier?

Mr. FRAZIER. Exhibit 564 is again, a portion of the primer of the cartridge case fired by me in the rifle number 139 appearing on the left side of the vertical dividing line through the center of the photograph, and on the right side a portion of the surface of the cartridge case, Exhibit 545, showing its primer and the marks on it.

In the photograph four circles, or portions of circles, have been drawn, circling some of the areas where individual microscopic characteristics are found which permitted identifying the two cartridge cases as having been fired in the same weapon.

In the upper circle are again two ridges separated by a groove, the lower right-hand end of which is blocked by a raised portion in the metal of the primer.

Circle number 2 is again a depression bounded on the top by a long sloping groove, sloping from the upper left subsequently to the lower right.

In circle number 3 there is a series of ridges running horizontally across the photograph. The lowest of these three ridges is a rather wide round-topped ridge.

Circle number 4 shows the left-hand side of a figure which you could roughly call a Z in the primer, which consists of a horizontal or nearly horizontal line running from left to right which meets a second line running from right down to the left, which again meets a third line which runs from the left to the right. This is shown in both photographs as the three lines which form the shape of a Z on the primer.

Mr. EISENBERG. Mr. Frazier, on this photograph there is shown a mark at approximately 3 o'clock on the left-hand side of the picture, and 9 o'clock on the right-hand side, and the marks seem to be different in the two pictures, being broader on the left-hand, C–14, than on the right, C–38. Could you explain the genesis of the difference? It seems to extend further down.

Mr. FRAZIER. Approximately in the center of the photograph where the two images meet, there is a scraped area which is the result of the surface of the metal of the bolt scraping the surface of the primer as the bolt was turned in opening the bolt to extract the cartridge.

On the test cartridge case, this area is much broader and coarser because the bolt was pressing more tightly against the primer when it was turned. On the evidence cartridge case, the marks are relatively fine, separated, and even show portions of the surface of the primer in between the circular marks left by the rotating bolt. The reason is that this primer was not being pressed as tightly against the bolt at the time it was turned.

Mr. EISENBERG. Would that be due to differences in the construction of the cartridge—the two cartridges?

Mr. FRAZIER. It could be differences in the cartridge, but primarily it would be a difference in the amount of setback of the cartridge against the bolt at the time it was fired.

If a cartridge is slightly away from the bolt when it is fired, the primer is blown back out of the cartridge. As the pressure builds up, the cartridge then moves back and reseats the primer in the primer pocket. The manner in which that movement of the primer out and back in is accomplished determines how tightly the primer will bear against the face of the breach after the cartridge has been fired.

It could be that, and it could be just a slight difference in the hardness of the metal of the primer which caused this one to flow back more and be marked more.

Mr. EISENBERG. Could you discuss Exhibit No. 565?

Mr. FRAZIER. Yes, sir; in Commission Exhibit No. 565 is shown the firing-pin impressions of the test cartridge case from the 139 rifle on the left and the cartridge case, 545, on the right, with a dividing line through the middle separating the primer of one cartridge case from the primer of the other.

No circles have been drawn around this photograph because the marks shown are marks of an abraded area on the firing pin, and are more or less parallel and formed parallel patterns, so that the eye can follow from one line across to the opposite side of the photograph.

In this area shown of the firing pin of the weapon, there was a small scraped area which left these microscopic ridges and grooves shown on the left photograph, and also reproduced in the 545 primer or firing-pin impression on the right side of the photograph.

Mr. McCLOY. State for me again what is on the left side? What is this C–14?

Mr. FRAZIER. This is the rifle cartridge case, the test cartridge case.

Mr. McCLOY. The test rifle?

Mr. FRAZIER. Yes; the cartridge case which I fired in 139.

Mr. McCLOY. In 139. And the one on the right?

Mr. FRAZIER. This the cartridge case from the building, Exhibit 545.

Mr. McCLOY. Which was found in the building?

Mr. FRAZIER. Found in the building.

Mr. McCLOY. On all of these on the left is it always the same——

Mr. FRAZIER. Yes, sir; on all of the photographs we have discussed so far.

Mr. McCLOY. I just wanted to make that clear.

Mr. EISENBERG. Mr. Frazier, it appears to the eye that only a portion of this is in focus. Is that correct?

Mr. FRAZIER. Only a portion of the entire photograph is in focus, yes, and that is the area where these individual marks appear, occur.

Mr. EISENBERG. Can you explain?

Mr. FRAZIER. Yes, sir; the reason being the outer area, the area up to the edge of the firing-pin impression is considerably higher, and the microscope does not have the depth of focus to focus on a very deep groove or depression such as the firing pin at the botton of it and still maintain the top in focus.

The firing pin is circular, I should say, hemispherical in shape, so that it leaves a cup-shaped impression of it—only one portion of it can be in focus at the same time; the other part being either higher or lower will be out of focus.

Mr. EISENBERG. Mr. Frazier, I now hand you Commission Exhibit 399, which, for the record, is a bullet, and also for the record, it is a bullet which was found in the Parkland Hospital following the assassination. Are you familiar with this exhibit?

Mr. FRAZIER. Yes, sir. This is a bullet which was delivered to me in the FBI laboratory on November 22, 1963 by Special Agent Elmer Todd of the FBI Washington Field Office.

Mr. EISENBERG. Does that have your mark on it?

Mr. FRAZIER. Yes, it does.

Mr. EISENBERG. The bullet is in the same condition as it was when you received it?

Mr. FRAZIER. Yes, sir; except for the marking of my initials and the other examiners. There is a discoloration at the nose caused apparently by mounting this bullet in some material which stained it, which was not present when received, and one more thing on the nose is a small dent or scraped area. At this area the spectographic examiner removed a small quantity of metal for analysis.

Mr. EISENBERG. Did you prepare the bullet in any way for examination? That is, did you clean it or in any way alter it?

Mr. FRAZIER. No, sir; it was not necessary. The bullet was clean and it was not necessary to change it in any way.

Mr. EISENBERG. There was no blood or similar material on the bullet when you received it?

Mr. FRAZIER. Not any which would interfere with the examination, no, sir. Now there may have been slight traces which could have been removed just in ordinary handling, but it wasn't necessary to actually clean blood or tissue off of the bullet.

Mr. EISENBERG. Did you examine this exhibit to determine whether it had been fired in Exhibit 139?

Mr. FRAZIER. Yes, sir.

Mr. EISENBERG. And what was your conclusion?

Mr. FRAZIER. It was. Exhibit 399 was fired in the rifle 139.

Mr. EISENBERG. That is to the exclusion of all other rifles?

Mr. FRAZIER. Yes, sir.

Mr. EISENBERG. Can you describe the types of markings which are generated onto a bullet, as opposed to those which are generated onto a cartridge case?

Mr. FRAZIER. A bullet when it is fired picks up the marks of the barrel of the weapon. These marks consist of rifling marks of the lands and the grooves, the spiral grooves in the barrel, and, in addition, the abrasion marks or rubbing marks which the bullet picks up due to the friction between the barrel and the surface of the copper jacket on the bullet, or if it is a lead bullet, with the lead.

Mr. McCLOY. You said the marks of the groove. You mean the marks of the groove or the marks of the lands?

Mr. FRAZIER. Both, sir; both are present. In this barrel there are four lands and four grooves. Each of the raised portions in the barrel will be impressed into the surface of the bullet causing four—we call them land impressions—on the bullet, and, in between, four groove impressions.

Mr. EISENBERG. How are you able to conclude that a given bullet was fired in a given weapon to the exclusion of all other weapons, Mr. Frazier?

Mr. FRAZIER. That is based again upon the microscopic marks left on the fired bullets and those marks in turn are based upon the barrel from which the bullets are fired.

The marks in the barrel originate during manufacture. They originate through use of the gun, through accidental marks resulting from cleaning, excessive cleaning, of the weapon, or faulty cleaning.

They result from corrosion in the barrel due to the hot gases and possibly corrosive primer mixtures in the cartridges used, and primarily again they result from wear, that is an eroding of the barrel through friction due to the firing of cartridges, bullets through it.

In this particular barrel the manufacturer's marks are caused by the drill which drills out the barrel, leaving certain marks from the drilling tool. Then portions of these marks are erased by a rifling tool which cuts the four spiral grooves in the barrel and, in turn, leaves marks themselves, and in connection with those marks of course, the drilling marks, being circular in shape, there is a tearing away of the surface of the metal, so that a microscopically rough surface is left.

Then removing part of those marks with a separate tool causes that barrel to assume an individual characteristic, a character all of its own.

In other words, at that time you could identify a bullet fired from that barrel as having been fired from the barrel to the exclusion of all other barrels, because there is no system whatever to the drilling of the barrel. The only system is in the rifling or in the cutting of the grooves, and in this case of rifle barrels, even the cutters wear down as the barrels are made, eventually of course having to be discarded or re-sharpened.

Mr. EISENBERG. Have you examined consecutively manufactured barrels to determine whether their microscopic characteristics are identical?

Mr. FRAZIER. Yes, sir; I have three different sets of, you might say, paired barrels, which have been manufactured on the same machine, one after the other, under controlled conditions to make them as nearly alike as possible, and in each case fired bullets from those barrels could not be identified with each other; in fact, they looked nothing at all alike as far as individual microscopic characteristics are concerned. Their rifling impressions of course would be identical, but the individual marks there would be entirely different.

Mr. EISENBERG. Mr. Frazier, did you determine the weight of the exhibit—that is, 399?

Mr. FRAZIER. Yes, sir. Exhibit 399 weighs 158.6 grains.

Mr. EISENBERG. How much weight loss does that show from the original bullet weight?

Mr. FRAZIER. We measured several standard bullets, and their weights varied, which is a normal situation, a portion of a grain, or two grains, from 161 grains—that is, they were all in the vicinity of 161 grains. One weighed—160.85, 161.5, 161.1 grains.

Mr. EISENBERG. In your opinion, was there any weight loss?

Mr. FRAZIER. There did not necessarily have to be any weight loss to the bullet. There may be a slight amount of lead missing from the base of the bullet, since it is exposed at the base, and the bullet is slightly flattened; there could be a slight weight loss from the end of the bullet, but it would not amount to more than 4 grains, because 158.6 is only a grain and a half less than the normal weight, and at least a 2 grain variation would be allowed. So it would be approximately 3 or 4 grains.

Mr. EISENBERG. Were the markings on the bullet at all defaced?

Mr. FRAZIER. Yes; they were, in that the bullet is distorted by having been slightly flattened or twisted.

Mr. EISENBERG. How material would you call that defacement?

Mr. FRAZIER. It is hardly visible unless you look at the base of the bullet and notice it is not round.

Mr. EISENBERG. How far does it affect your examination for purposes of identification?

Mr. FRAZIER. It had no effect on it at all.

Mr. EISENBERG. Can you explain why?

Mr. FRAZIER. Because it did not mutilate or distort the original microscopic marks beyond the point where you could recognize the pattern and find the same pattern of marks on one bullet as were present on the other.

Mr. EISENBERG. Did you take a photograph of your comparison of Exhibit 399 with a test bullet?

Mr. FRAZIER. Yes, sir.

Mr. EISENBERG. This photograph was prepared by you or under your supervision?

Mr. FRAZIER. Yes, sir.

Mr. EISENBERG. Can you tell us the magnification?

Mr. FRAZIER. 70 diameters.

Mr. EISENBERG. And this reads C-14 on the left and C-1 on the right?

Mr. FRAZIER. Yes; it does.

Mr. EISENBERG. Mr. Chairman, may I have that admitted?

Mr. McCLOY. The one on the right is the cartridge that you just——

Mr. FRAZIER. Yes. 399, yes, sir.

Mr. McCLOY. 399?

Mr. FRAZIER. And the one on the left is the test bullet.

Mr. McCLOY. The test. It may be admitted.

Mr. EISENBERG. That will be 566, Mr. Reporter.

(The item so described was identified as Commission Exhibit No. 566 and received in evidence.)

Mr. EISENBERG. Mr. Frazier, could you discuss photograph 566?

Mr. FRAZIER. This exhibit shows on the left side of a dividing vertical line representing the top of the prism in the microscope which was used for the comparison, a portion of the surface from the test bullet from the rifle, 139, and on the right side of the photograph a portion of the surface of the bullet, 399.

The marks shown in the photograph are on an area representing approximately one-half of one groove impression in the barrel of the weapon, which extends from approximately 2 inches up from the bottom of the photograph, being the edge of one land impression, and the beginning of a groove impression up to the top of the photograph, that area being approximately one-half or possibly two-thirds of a groove impression.

The microscopic marks which were used in the identification, after being observed through the microscope and making the comparison and the identification, were photographed, and this photograph shows a portion of the surface of that bullet, showing parallel lines extending from the left side of the photograph coming up to the hairline and continuing across on the right side of the photograph, these microscopic marks being very fine grooves and ridges on the surface of the bullet, very coarse ridges on the surface of the bullet, and inbetween size scratches left on the bullet by the barrel of the weapon.

There will be some marks which will not show up on one bullet which show up on the other bullet, and similarly some marks on the other bullet, in this case Exhibit 399, will not be present on the test bullet, that situation being due to a number of causes.

One, the bullets could have originally been slightly different in diameter, the larger bullet, of course, picking up more marks during its passage through the barrel.

Secondly, the two bullets may not have expanded exactly the same, due to the pressure of the powder behind them as they passed through the barrel.

Third, with each bullet fired through the barrel, there are certain changes that occur due to the wearing away of the surface of the metal of the barrel, so that after a series of shots through a particular barrel, it would be expected that the pattern of microscopic marks produced by it would change.

The identification is based on areas such as this on the bullet and the comparison of the microscopic marks around the entire surface of the bullet which bears individual characteristics.

Mr. EISENBERG. Mr. Frazier, running through the middle of the exhibit there seem to be finer lines on the right-hand side than on the left. Could you explain that, the reason why the lines come out with more detail or that there are more lines on the right side than on the left?

Mr. FRAZIER. Those marks could be the result of the bullet striking some object after it was fired, or they could be the result of changes having taken place in the barrel.

For instance, even a piece of coarse cloth, leather or some other object could have polished the surface of the metal slightly and left infinitesimal scratches which, when enlarged sufficiently, actually look like marks on the bullet.

Mr. EISENBERG. In making your examination of the bullet, what was the relative attention you gave to the broader lines we see in this picture and the finer lines such as those we have just been referring to?

Mr. FRAZIER. The broader lines would be more characteristic or they are looked for most, because they change less rapidly than the fine lines. For instance, firing two or three bullets through a barrel could completely erase microscopic marks which would appear as fine lines in a certain area, whereas the coarser lines and grooves on the bullet would be maintained over a series of fired bullets.

Mr. EISENBERG. In evaluating these lines, do you examine the lines individually, or are you interested in their relationship with one another in addition?

Mr. FRAZIER. It is a combination. You actually examine each mark and each line individually, but it is a mental process rather than a matter of adding one line to another. It is a process of looking at a series of lines and you actually notice that they are composed of round-topped ridges, V-topped ridges, flat-topped ridges, and it is a mental process of looking at the whole pattern rather than the individual marks.

Mr. EISENBERG. All these lines that we are looking at lie within a groove, within one groove, did you say?

Mr. FRAZIER. Yes; except for the lower portion of the photograph, there is a portion of a land impression showing one rather deep groove running across the bottom of the picture, and a series of grooves shown next to the edge of the land impression.

Mr. EISENBERG. Will you identify the circular-looking mark on the right-hand side of the picture?

Mr. FRAZIER. That could be either a flaw in the bullet, the metal itself, before it was fired, or could be the result of the bullet having struck some object after it was fired and before it stopped, or as it stopped, or could be the result of having been dropped or roughly handled.

This particular mark there would be invisible practically speaking to the naked eye when looking at the bullet.

Mr. McCLOY. The mark to which you refer is the one on the right-hand side of the exhibit toward the top, about an inch and a half from the center line?

Mr. FRAZIER. Yes, sir.

Mr. EISENBERG. Is that about 11 o'clock?

Mr. FRAZIER. Yes, sir.

Mr. EISENBERG. Do you have another photograph, Mr. Frazier, of this?

Mr. FRAZIER. No, sir.

Mr. EISENBERG. I now hand you a bullet fragment, what appears to be a bullet fragment, in a pill box which is labeled Jacket and Lead Q-2, and it has certain initials on it. For the record, this was found—this bullet fragment was found—in the front portion of the car in which the President was riding. I ask you whether you are familiar with this object.

Mr. FRAZIER. Yes; I am.

Mr. EISENBERG. Is your mark on it?

Mr. FRAZIER. Yes, sir.

Mr. EISENBERG. Did you examine this? Is this a bullet fragment, Mr. Frazier?

Mr. FRAZIER. Yes, sir. This consists of a piece of the jacket portion of a bullet from the nose area and a piece of the lead core from under the jacket.

Mr. EISENBERG. How were you able to conclude it is part of the nose area?

Mr. FRAZIER. Because of the rifling marks which extend part way up the side, and then have the characteristic leading edge impressions and no longer continue along the bullet, and by the fact that the bullet has a rounded contour to it which has not been mutilated.

Mr. EISENBERG. Did you examine this bullet to determine whether it had been fired from Exhibit 139 to the exclusion of all other weapons?

Mr. FRAZIER. Yes, sir.

Mr. EISENBERG. What was your conclusion?

Mr. FRAZIER. This bullet fragment was fired in this rifle, 139.

Mr. EISENBERG. Mr. Frazier, did you weigh this fragment?

Mr. FRAZIER. Yes; I did. It weighs 44.6 grains.

Mr. EISENBERG. Did you take a photograph of the fragment as compared with a test bullet?

Mr. FRAZIER. Yes, sir.

Mr. EISENBERG. This photograph is labeled C-14 on the left and C-2 on the right, and it is a photograph taken by you or under your supervision?

Mr. FRAZIER. Yes, sir.

Mr. EISENBERG. C-14 being the test bullet?

Mr. FRAZIER. The test bullet from 139.

Mr. EISENBERG. And what is the magnification of this photograph?

Mr. FRAZIER. It would be 70 diameters.

Mr. EISENBERG. Mr. Chairman, may that be admitted?

Mr. McCLOY. C-2 is the actual fragment?

Mr. EISENBERG. Yes.

Mr. McCLOY. It may be admitted.

Mr. EISENBERG. Can we go back a second? I don't think I asked for admission of the bullet fragment which Mr. Frazier identified. May I have that admitted?

Mr. McCLOY. It may be admitted.

Mr. EISENBERG. The bullet fragment will be 567 and the photograph just identified by Mr. Frazier will be 568.

Mr. McCLOY. It may be admitted.

(The items described, identified as Commission Exhibits Nos. 567 and 568, were received in evidence.)

Mr. EISENBERG. Mr. Frazier, could you discuss this photograph with us?

Mr. FRAZIER. In Commission Exhibit 568 is again the vertical dividing line through the center of the photograph, with the test bullet from the rifle 139 on the left, and the bullet, Exhibit 567, on the right. Am I right in that the bullet jacket fragment is 567?

Mr. EISENBERG. I think I put it down here. That is right, 567.

Mr. FRAZIER. Approximately two-thirds of a groove impression from each of the two bullets is shown, with a very small portion at the bottom of the photograph of a land impression. The individual microscopic characteristics which were used in the comparison, and on which the identification was made, were photographed and are as shown in this photograph. However, this photograph did not enter into the actual conclusion reached. The microscopic characteristics appear as parallel horizontal lines extending from the test bullet on the left to the bullet Exhibit 567 on the right.

The marks used in the identification are grooves, paired lines, a series of ridges up and down the hairline on one bullet, and they also appear on the opposite side of the photograph.

In one particular instance it will be seen that at the edge of the land impression at the lower left portion of the photograph is a very definite paired ridge which appears on the right side of the photograph but in a slightly different area.

The reason for the difference in the location of this paired line on the exhibit, Exhibit 567, can be explained by the fact that this is a jacket fragment, that it was torn from the rest of the bullet, and is greatly mutilated, distorted, and bears only a very few areas suitable for identification purposes because of that fact.

The distortion has foreshortened the area of the jacket fragment, 567, to the extent that over this approximately one-tenth-of-an-inch surface represented in this photograph, these lines do not coincide exactly on the lower part of the photograph when they are lined up on the upper part of the photograph.

Mr. EISENBERG. When you say they don't correspond exactly, do you mean at all, or do you mean they aren't——

Mr. FRAZIER. I mean that the marks are present, but they do not line up at the hairline.

Mr. EISENBERG. But in your opinion the marks on the left are the same as the marks on the right?

Mr. FRAZIER. The marks on the left are the same marks as those on the right. In the examination this is easily determined by rotating the two bullets. As you rotate them, you can see these characteristic patterns line up.

Then you will notice these do not line up. But as you rotate one bullet, you can follow the individual marks mentally and see that the same pattern is present and you can line them up in your mind, even though they are not actually physically lined up in the microscope.

Mr. McCLOY. They are not lined up in the microscope because there is mutilation on the fragment?

Mr. EISENBERG. Yes, sir.

Mr. McCLOY. And there is no mutilation on the test cartridge?

Mr. FRAZIER. Yes, sir.

Mr. EISENBERG. Mr. Frazier, in the lower portion of each side of that photograph, which I take it is the groove of the bullet, or the land impression of the rifle—is that correct?

Mr. FRAZIER. The land on the rifle leaves this groove on the bullet.

Mr. EISENBERG. Yes; the right-hand side seems to be slightly striated while the left-hand side does not seem to be striated. Can you explain that?

Mr. FRAZIER. Well, the striae in this side are not apparent in this photograph. I don't know whether they actually exist on the bullet or not. You can't tell from the photograph, because they are so fine as to possibly not show at all.

A close examination right at the hairline shows a whole series of very fine scratches which do not appear further away from the hairline, and that could be very easily due to differences in the metal, as the bullet passed down the barrel, being pressed less forcibly against the barrel, or could also be due to the fact that at the edges of the lands it is very often evident that hot gases from the burning powder had passed the bullet through these cracks and actually will melt or erode away the surface of the bullet.

433

As to why they may or may not be present is difficult to say from an examination of the photograph.

Mr. EISENBERG. What portion of the bullet fragment provided enough markings for purposes of identification, approximately?

Mr. FRAZIER. I would say that one-fourth, in this instance, one-fourth of 567's surface was available. One-fifth to one-sixth would have been sufficient for identification, based on the character of the marks present.

Mr. EISENBERG. Now this portion of the fragment was an even smaller portion of the bullet, the entire bullet, is that correct?

Mr. FRAZIER. Yes; it was.

Mr. EISENBERG. So when you say one-fifth and one-sixth, are you referring now to the proportion of marks on the fragment, as opposed to the proportion of marks you would want from an entire bullet?

Mr. FRAZIER. No; I am referring to the proportion of marks on the fragment which were used in the examination as compared to the total bullet circumference which would have existed on an unmutilated bullet.

Mr. EISENBERG. Mr. Frazier, do you feel that the amount of markings here were sufficient to make positive identification?

Mr. FRAZIER. Yes, sir.

Mr. EISENBERG. Have you made identifications in the past with as few or less markings as are present on this bullet fragment?

Mr. FRAZIER. Oh, yes; and on less, much less of an area. The character of the marks is more important than the number of the marks.

Mr. EISENBERG. Mr. Frazier, here you were of course unable to see all of the lines which were present on the bullet before mutilation. Have you ever had an occasion where you examined a bullet and saw one portion of it which was an apparent match and then found out that the balance of the bullet was not an apparent match?

Mr. FRAZIER. No, sir; and if I understand your words "apparent match," there is no such thing as an apparent match. It either is an identification or it isn't, and until you have made up your mind, you don't have an apparent match. We don't actually use that term in the FBI. Unless you have sufficient marks for an identification, you cannot say one way or the other as to whether or not two bullets were fired from a particular barrel.

In other words, you cannot nonidentify on the absence of similarities any more than you can identify when you have no similarities present.

Mr. EISENBERG. In other words, you won't make an identification unless you feel enough marks are present to constitute a basis for a positive identification?

Mr. FRAZIER. That is right, and I would not report any type of similarities unless they were sufficient for an identification, because unless you can say one bullet was fired from the same barrel as a second bullet, then there is room for error, and in this field of firearms identification, we try to avoid any possible chance of error creeping in.

Mr. EISENBERG. Do you avoid the category of "probable" identification?

Mr. FRAZIER. Oh, yes; we never use it, never.

Mr. EISENBERG. And why is that?

Mr. FRAZIER. There is no such thing as a probable identification. It either is or isn't as far as we are concerned.

Mr. EISENBERG. And in this case it is?

Mr. FRAZIER. It is, yes.

Mr. EISENBERG. Any further questions on this bullet fragment, Mr. Chairman?

Mr. McCLOY. Do we have any proof in the record thus far as to where the fragment referred to a moment ago came from?

Mr. EISENBERG. Honestly, I am not sure. I know it will be in the record eventually, but I have not taken that up as part of this testimony.

Mr. McCLOY. That will be subject to further proof.

Mr. EISENBERG. Yes.

Mr. McCLOY. If it is not in the record. As a result of all these comparisons, you would say that the evidence is indisputable that the three shells that were identified by you were fired from that rifle?

Mr. FRAZIER. Yes, sir.

Mr. McCLOY. And you would say the same thing of Commission Exhibit 399, the bullet 399 was fired from that rifle?

Mr. FRAZIER. Yes, sir.

Mr. McCLOY. And the fragment 567——

Mr. FRAZIER. 567, the one we have just finished.

Mr. McCLOY. Was likewise a portion of a bullet fired from that rifle?

Mr. FRAZIER. Yes, sir.

Mr. McCLOY. You have no doubt about any of those?

Mr. FRAZIER. None whatsoever.

Mr. EISENBERG. Now finally in the category of bullets and bullet fragments, I hand you what is apparently a bullet fragment, which is in a pill box marked Q–3, and which, I state for the record, was also found in the front portion of the President's car, and I ask you whether you are familiar with this item, marked Q–3?

Mr. FRAZIER. Yes, sir; this was submitted to me as having been found beside the front seat of the automobile.

Mr. EISENBERG. Your mark is on that fragment?

Mr. FRAZIER. Yes, it is.

Mr. EISENBERG. When did you receive that fragment, Mr. Frazier?

Mr. FRAZIER. At 11:50 p.m., November 22, 1963, from Special Agent Orrin Bartlett, our liaison agent with the Secret Service, in the FBI laboratory.

Mr. EISENBERG. And the last bullet fragment you examined, Exhibit 567, when did you receive that?

Mr. FRAZIER. It was received at the same time from Special Agent Bartlett.

Mr. EISENBERG. Did you examine both at that time, Mr. Frazier?

Mr. FRAZIER. Yes, sir; beginning the following morning, November 23.

Mr. EISENBERG. Mr. Chairman, may I have this bullet fragment marked Q–3 admitted as Commission 569?

Mr. McCLOY. It may be admitted.

(The item, identified as Commission Exhibit No. 569, was received in evidence.)

Mr. EISENBERG. Mr. Frazier, did you examine this bullet fragment with a view to determining whether it had been fired from the rifle, Exhibit 139?

Mr. FRAZIER. Yes, sir.

Mr. EISENBERG. What was your conclusion?

Mr. FRAZIER. This bullet fragment, Exhibit 569, was fired from this particular rifle, 139.

Mr. EISENBERG. Again to the exclusion of all other rifles?

Mr. FRAZIER. Yes, sir.

Mr. EISENBERG. Did you weigh this fragment, Mr. Frazier?

Mr. FRAZIER. Yes, I did. It weighs 21.0 grains.

Mr. EISENBERG. Can you describe the fragment?

Mr. FRAZIER. Yes. It consists of the base or most rearward portion of the jacket of a metal-jacketed bullet, from which the lead core is missing.

Mr. EISENBERG. How can you tell that it is the most rearward portion?

Mr. FRAZIER. It has the shape which bases of bullets have. It has the cannelure which is located at the rear, on the portion of bullets of this type.

Mr. EISENBERG. Can you determine whether this bullet fragment, 567, and 569 are portions of the originally same bullet?

Mr. FRAZIER. No, sir.

Mr. EISENBERG. You cannot?

Mr. FRAZIER. There is not enough of the two fragments in unmutilated condition to determine whether or not the fragments actually fit together.

However, it was determined that there is no area on one fragment, such as 567, which would overlap a corresponding area on the base section of 569, so that they could be parts of one bullet, and then, of course, they could be parts of separate bullets.

Mr. EISENBERG. Now 569 is without the core; is that correct?

Mr. FRAZIER. Yes, sir.

Mr. EISENBERG. Could you estimate how much weight you would add if you had the core?

Mr. FRAZIER. No, I cannot.

Mr. EISENBERG. Not at all?

Mr. FRAZIER. No. I do not have the figure on the core weight.

Mr. EISENBERG. In your opinion, is it possible that if you did make such an estimate, the weight, the projected weight of 569 plus the actual weight of 567 would exceed the bullet weight of the 6.5 mm. bullet?

Mr. FRAZIER. Oh, no; it would not.

Mr. EISENBERG. It would not?

Mr. FRAZIER. It would not come even close to it, because the amount of core is only—one-quarter inch of the bullet is all that remains at the base, and that much core would not weigh more than 40 grains at the most.

Mr. EISENBERG. No cannelure shows on 567, is that correct?

Mr. FRAZIER. That is correct.

Mr. EISENBERG. Mr. Frazier, did you make a comparison photograph of 569 with a test bullet?

Mr. FRAZIER. Yes, sir.

Mr. EISENBERG. This photograph is marked C–14 on the left and C–3 on the right; is that correct?

Mr. FRAZIER. Yes, it is.

Mr. EISENBERG. C–14 being the test?

Mr. FRAZIER. Yes, from the rifle 139, and C–3 is Exhibit 569.

Mr. EISENBERG. And the magnification on this photograph is what, Mr. Frazier?

Mr. FRAZIER. 70 diameters.

Mr. EISENBERG. And this was taken by you or under your supervision?

Mr. FRAZIER. Yes, sir.

Mr. EISENBERG. Mr. Chairman, may I have this admitted?

Mr. McCLOY. It may be admitted.

Mr. EISENBERG. 570.

(The item was identified as Commission Exhibit No. 570 and was received in evidence.)

Mr. EISENBERG. Can you discuss this picture?

Mr. FRAZIER. Commission Exhibit 570 shows a portion of the test bullet from Exhibit 139 on the left side of the photograph, and a portion of the bullet 569 on the right side, divided by a hairline.

The photograph was taken of the microscopic marks, examined through the comparison microscope, consisting of very fine and very coarse grooves, or scratches, or ridges, on the surface of each of the bullets as compared with those on the other bullet.

The photograph did not, of course, enter into the conclusion reached in the examination, but was merely taken to demonstrate, to illustrate the types of marks present insofar as a photograph can show them.

Mr. EISENBERG. Mr. Frazier, what portion of the Exhibit 569 was unmutilated enough to allow you to make a comparison of its markings?

Mr. FRAZIER. Approximately one-third. Actually, the entire base section of the bullet was present, but approximately one-half of that base was mutilated. On the mutilated area, either marks were destroyed completely by striking some object, or being compressed or stretched, or they were thrown out of relationship with each other by stretching or compressing to the extent that they were of no value.

So I would estimate approximately one-third of the area was present.

Mr. EISENBERG. Now, when you say one-third, is this total area or circumference?

Mr. FRAZIER. Circumference—one-third of the circumference.

Mr. EISENBERG. Do you have any further pictures of any of the bullets, Mr. Frazier?

Mr. FRAZIER. No, I do not.

Mr. EISENBERG. Mr. Frazier, I hand you two bullets and ask whether you are familiar with them.

436

Mr. FRAZIER. Yes, I am. These are the two test bullets which I fired from his rifle, Exhibit 139.

Mr. EISENBERG. Do they have your mark on them?

Mr. FRAZIER. Yes, they do.

Mr. EISENBERG. Mr. Chairman, may I have these admitted as Exhibit 572?

Mr. McCLOY. They may be admitted.

(The document referred to was marked Commission Exhibit No. 572, and received in evidence.)

Mr. EISENBERG. Getting back to the two bullet fragments mentioned, Mr. Frazier, did you alter them in any way after they had been received in the laboratory, by way of cleaning or otherwise?

Mr. FRAZIER. No, sir; there was a very slight residue of blood or some other material adhering, but it did not interfere with the examination. It was wiped off to clean up the bullet for examination, but it actually would not have been necessary.

Mr. EISENBERG. Is that true on both fragments?

Mr. FRAZIER. Yes, sir.

Mr. EISENBERG. You also mentioned there was blood or some other substance on the bullet marked 399. Is this an off-hand determination, or was there a test to determine what the substance was?

Mr. FRAZIER. No, there was no test made of the materials.

Mr. EISENBERG. As you examined the bullet and the two bullet fragments, are they in the same condition now as they were when they entered your hands?

Mr. FRAZIER. Yes, sir.

Mr. EISENBERG. One other question on the cartridge cases.

Did you examine the cartridge cases for chambering marks, extraction marks, or ejection marks?

Mr. FRAZIER. Yes, I did, but I did not make any comparisons of either extractor or ejector marks or chambering marks, since the purpose of my examination was primarily to determine whether they were fired in this rifle, and such marks would not have assisted in that determination. They were not necessary because they would have indicated only that it may have been loaded into and extracted from the weapon, whereas the marks which I found served to identify it as having been fired in the weapon, actually.

Mr. EISENBERG. Mr. Chairman, unless you have further questions on the cartridge cases or bullets, I would like to move on to another subject.

Mr. McCLOY. From your examination of the actual bullets that you have been told were fired on the day of the assassination from this rifle, and from your—how many separate bullets do you identify?

Mr. FRAZIER. Two, at the maximum—possibly three, if these two jacket fragments came from different bullets. If they came from one bullet, then there would be a maximum of the whole bullet 399 and this bullet in two parts.

Mr. McCLOY. And you cannot tell whether these two particles came from one bullet or two separate ones?

Mr. FRAZIER. No, sir.

Mr. EISENBERG. When you say "two at the maximum," do you mean two at the minimum?

Mr. FRAZIER. I meant at least two bullets.

Mr. McCLOY. There were at least two different bullets?

Mr. FRAZIER. At least two, yes.

Mr. EISENBERG. Mr. Frazier, can you give an estimate of the total number of bullets fired in the various tests made with this rifle?

Mr. FRAZIER. Approximately 60 rounds.

Mr. EISENBERG. And were all of these rounds 6.5 mm. Western Mannlicher-Carcano ammunition?

Mr. FRAZIER. Yes, sir.

Mr. EISENBERG. Did you have any misfires?

Mr. FRAZIER. No, sir.

Mr. EISENBERG. Did you find the ammunition dependable?

Mr. FRAZIER. Very dependable.

Mr. EISENBERG. Can you think of any reason why someone might think this is an undependable type of ammunition?

437

Mr. Frazier. No, sir; The Western Cartridge Co. has always manufactured, in my experience, very dependable ammunition. There is other ammunition on the market available for this particular rifle in this caliber, which in my opinion is undependable or would be a very poor quality of ammunition. It may have been a confusion between that other ammunition of the same caliber and this Western ammunition.

Mr. Eisenberg. Can you elaborate as to what that other ammunition consists of?

Mr. Frazier. Certain companies have imported into the United States cartridges of foreign manufacture. Those I have seen for this rifle were of Italian manufacture. They have pulled the military bullets from those cartridges and reloading hunting type or soft-point bullets into the cartridges. In doing that, they did not, apparently, take any great pains in loading them. Occasionally, the mouth of the case would be bent over and the bullet driven in right on top of the bent case.

I have seen split cartridge cases, even before they were fired, badly corroded cartridge cases. All in all, the ammunition is of generally poor overall appearance, and it has been reported to me that it was of poor firing quality.

I have not fired any of it, personally.

Mr. Eisenberg. Have you heard anything about the dependability of the Italian-made ammunition, unreloaded?

Mr. Frazier. No, sir; not as such.

However, I have experienced the examination of Italian ammunition of various years of manufacture and, of course, various makes. And I think it is rather poor quality in this particular caliber, primarily due to the very short seating depth to which bullets of this type are seated in the cartridge, which causes the bullets to loosen very readily in the cartridge case even before they are loaded into a clip or fired.

Mr. Eisenberg. Did you notice, Mr. Frazier, in your examination of targets and so forth, whether there was any marked degree of yaw or tumbling by the bullets?

Mr. Frazier. No evidence at all of tumbling or yaw.

Mr. Eisenberg. In your opinion, would the firing of 60 shots materially affect the microscopic charactertistics of Exhibit 139?

Mr. Frazier. It would change them, if not completely, practically completely.

Mr. Eisenberg. Mr. Frazier, some witnesses to the assassination have stated that they heard more than three shots. Can you think of any reason why they might have come to that conclusion—in terms of acoustical properties of high-velocity bullets?

Mr. Frazier. They could very readily have heard other sounds which could be confused with shots. It is apparent—it is obvious with any weapon in which the bullet travels faster than the speed of sound, which is 1,127, approximately, feet per second, the bullet itself will cause a shock wave or a sound wave, and a person standing in front of that weapon will hear the report of the bullet passing and then subsequently the sound will reach them of the cartridge explosion, which could very easily be confused with two shots. There will be the crack of the bullet going by, overhead or in the vicinity, and then the sound of the shot.

So that you would hear for three shots actually six reports, which could have caused some confusion.

Mr. Eisenberg. Mr. Frazier, I now hand you a bullet in a pill box which is marked Q-188. I ask you whether you are familiar with this bullet.

I would like to state for the record that this bullet was found in the Walker residence after the attempted assassination of General Walker.

Mr. McCloy. As far as you know, we have no proof of that yet?

Mr. Eisenberg. That is right.

Mr. Frazier. Yes, I am familiar with it. I have made an examination of that bullet.

With reference to this bullet, I could furnish everything except the weight of it.

Mr. EISENBERG. All right. Just taking one thing at a time. You are familiar with it. Does it have your marking on it?

Mr. FRAZIER. Yes, it does.

Mr. EISENBERG. Mr. Chairman, may I have this admitted as 573?

Mr. McCLOY. It may be admitted.

(The article referred to was marked Commission Exhibit 573, and received in evidence.)

Mr. EISENBERG. When did you receive this bullet, do you recall, Mr. Frazier?

Mr. FRAZIER. I would need to refer to my notes for that.

Mr. EISENBERG. Could you supply that for us at a subsequent time?

Mr. FRAZIER. Yes, sir.

Mr. EISENBERG. And the weight.

Is this bullet in the same condition as it was when you received it in the laboratory, Mr. Frazier?

Mr. FRAZIER. Yes, it is.

Mr. EISENBERG. Did you clean it up or in any way alter it when you received it?

Mr. FRAZIER. No, sir.

Mr. EISENBERG. Mr. Frazier, did you examine this bullet to determine whether it was or might have been fired in Exhibit 139?

Mr. FRAZIER. Yes, I did.

Mr. EISENBERG. And what was your conclusion?

Mr. FRAZIER. I was unable to reach a conclusion as to whether or not it had been fired from this rifle. The conclusion went slightly further than that, in that we determined that the general rifling characteristics of the rifle 139 are of the same type as those found on the bullet, Exhibit 573, and, further, on this basis, that the bullet could have been fired from the rifle on the basis of its land and groove impressions. And, second, that all of the remaining physical characteristics of this bullet, 573, are the same as Western 6.5-mm. Mannlicher-Carcano bullets of the type normally loaded in ammunition made for this rifle, 139. However, the mutilation of the nose of the bullet has eliminated the length characteristics, and it cannot be definitely stated that Exhibit 573 is in fact a Western Cartridge Co. product, but all of the remaining characteristics of base shape, distance from the base to the cannelure, the width of the cannelure, and the overall appearance, coloration, and so forth, are similar to Western ammunition.

Mr. EISENBERG. Is this a jacketed bullet?

Mr. FRAZIER. Yes, it is a copper-alloy jacketed bullet having a lead core.

Mr. EISENBERG. Can you think of any reason why someone might have called this a steel-jacketed bullet?

Mr. FRAZIER. No, sir; except that some individuals commonly refer to rifle bullets as steel-jacketed bullets, when they actually in fact just have a copper-alloy jacket.

Mr. EISENBERG. Can you describe the general rifling characteristics which you referred to?

Mr. FRAZIER. Yes. They consist of impressions from four lands and grooves. The bullet is mutilated on a portion of its surface. However, it can be determined that there were four land impressions and four groove impressions originally on this bullet.

The width of the land impression is 7/100ths of an inch, that is 0.07 inch—whereas the width of the groove impression is 0.13 inch, or 13/100ths of an inch.

The bullet is flattened so that it was not possible to measure its diameter. However, by adding the land width to the groove width, and multiplying by the number of lands and grooves, you can determine the circumference of the bullet and mathematically determine its diameter, which in this case corresponds to 6.5 mm. ammunition, or approximately .267 inch.

Mr. EISENBERG. What was the direction of the twist?

Mr. FRAZIER. To the right.

Mr. EISENBERG. Could you estimate how many types of rifle would produce, on a 6.5 mm. bullet, four lands and four grooves, right twist, with the width of lands and grooves which you established as being those on this bullet?

Mr. FRAZIER. Only from experience, I could say that it would be relatively few which would agree with all of those characteristics. I have, of course, not seen or measured all of the foreign rifles, and therefore I could not estimate the number that there might be.

Mr. EISENBERG. Did you find any miscroscopic characteristics or other evidence which would indicate that the bullet was not fired from 139?

Mr. FRAZIER. No, sir.

Mr. EISENBERG. Were you able to determine the depth of the grooves of the bullet?

Mr. FRAZIER. The bullet, 573, had what appeared to be normal-depth grooves. However, this bullet is completely flattened due to hitting a plaster or cement or other hard material on one side, and the opposite side, as a result of the flattening—has assumed a concave appearance, which has stretched the surface in various places and changes its overall appearance—that is the basis for actually having to state that there were not enough unmutilated marks for identification purposes on it.

Mr. EISENBERG. But you do conclude that this was fired from a Mannlicher-Carcano 91/38, or a rifle with similar barrel characteristics?

Mr. FRAZIER. Yes, sir.

Mr. EISENBERG. Mr. Chairman, do you have any further questions on this?

Mr. McCLOY. When you say you were able to determine it was fired from this type of rifle or one similar to it, that would include a number of different kinds of rifles besides the Mannlicher-Carcano?

Mr. FRAZIER. Yes, sir; it could include a variety of weapons with which I am not familiar in the foreign field.

Mr. McCLOY. But it is definitely, according to your best judgment, a 6.5 mm. bullet?

Mr. FRAZIER. Yes, sir.

Mr. McCLOY. And the bullet, such as we find it, has now characteristics similar to the type of bullet which was our Exhibit No. 399?

Mr. FRAZIER. Yes, it does. Placing them side by side, the cannelure, which is really the only physical characteristic apparent, comes to exactly the same place on both 399 and 573, indicating that this bullet was loaded to exactly the same depth in the cartridge—the two bullets, both 399 and 573.

Mr. McCLOY. I think I have no further questions.

Mr. EISENBERG. Mr. Frazier, did any other firearms experts in the FBI laboratory examine the three cartridge cases, the bullet, and the two bullet fragments which you have testified as to today?

Mr. FRAZIER. Yes, all of the actual firearms comparisons were also made by Charles Killion and Cortlandt Cunningham. These examinations were made separately, that is, they made their examination individually and separately from mine, and there was no association between their examination and mine until both were finished.

Mr. EISENBERG. Did the three of you come to the conclusions which you have given us today as your own conclusions?

Mr. FRAZIER. Yes, sir.

Mr. EISENBERG. Did anyone in the FBI laboratory who examined the evidence come to a different conclusion as to any of the evidence you have discussed today?

Mr. FRAZIER. No, sir.

Mr. EISENBERG. Is there anything you would like to add to your testimony, Mr. Frazier?

Mr. FRAZIER. Not with reference to this material, no.

Mr. EISENBERG. Are you thinking of——

Mr. FRAZIER. I am thinking of other examinations which I made, but which probably will come up at another time.

Mr. EISENBERG. You are referring to examinations such as the clothing, holes in the clothing, and the fracture in the automobile windshield?

Mr. FRAZIER. Yes, sir.

Mr. EISENBERG. Yes. There will be testimony elicited at another time on those examinations, Mr. Frazier.

Mr. McCLOY. Mr. Frazier will be a witness in those, too?

Mr. EISENBERG. Yes, sir.

Mr. Specter will probably elicit that testimony.

Mr. Chairman, or gentlemen, are there any other questions?

Thank you very much, Mr. Frazier.

Mr. FRAZIER. Excuse me. I have one photograph here that might be useful in this regard, and that is of a clip showing the six cartridges loaded into it.

Mr. McCLOY. I think that might be a good idea. You might identify that, to show what we mean by clips.

Mr. EISENBERG. You have shown us photographs of a clip—the clip from the Exhibit 139 rifle?

Mr. FRAZIER. Yes, sir.

Mr. EISENBERG. One photograph loaded, and one unloaded?

Mr. FRAZIER. Yes. In one instance I put six cartridges in the clip and photographed it.

Mr. EISENBERG. Did you take those photographs?

Mr. FRAZIER. Yes, sir.

Mr. McCLOY. Mr. Frazier, you testified that if you didn't use the clip you would only be able to shoot one shell at a time, is that right?

Mr. FRAZIER. Yes, sir; this weapon does not have the box magazine commonly found in most military weapons which holds the cartridges and can be reloaded one at a time, but they must remain in the clip, or they will malfunction. The follower in the weapon will throw the cartridges right back out of the gun.

Mr. McCLOY. That explains it to my mind, because I know I have fired rifles with clips and fired them without clips. But they were much more convenient in loading.

Mr. FRAZIER. Yes, sir; this one is designed——

Mr. McCLOY. For example, the Springfield you could load with clip or load without a clip.

Mr. FRAZIER. Yes, sir.

Mr. McCLOY. But this one has to have a clip in order not to malfunction?

Mr. FRAZIER. Yes, it does.

Mr. EISENBERG. Those will be 574 and 575.

Mr. McCLOY. They may be admitted.

(The photographs referred to were marked Commission Exhibits Nos. 574 and 575, and received in evidence.)

Mr. McCLOY. Thank you very much, Mr. Frazier. You have been very helpful.

TESTIMONY OF RONALD SIMMONS

Mr. EISENBERG. Our next witness will be Mr. Simmons.

Mr. McCLOY. Would you hold up your right hand?

Do you solemnly swear that the testimony you will give in this hearing will be the truth, the whole truth, and nothing but the truth, so help you God?

Mr. SIMMONS. I do.

Mr. McCLOY. Please be seated.

This, as you know—the constitution of the Commission and its purpose—we want to ask you something about the firearm aspect of our hearings, and certain characteristics of this rifle that we would like to hear from you about, and if there is anything else you have that can throw light on our problems.

If you can state for the record, first, your name, and where you live.

Mr. SIMMONS. My name is Ronald Simmons. I live near Havre de Grace, Md.

Mr. McCLOY. Mr. Eisenberg?

Mr. EISENBERG. Can you give us your position, Mr. Simmons?

Mr. SIMMONS. I am the Chief of the Infantry Weapons Evaluation Branch of the Ballistics Research Laboratory of the Department of the Army.

Mr. EISENBERG. And how long have you held this position?

Mr. SIMMONS. This position, about four years, and previous employment has been in these laboratories.

Mr. EISENBERG. How long have you been working, Mr. Simmons, in the area of evaluation of weapons?

Mr. SIMMONS. Since 1951, in various classes of weapons.

Since 1957, however, I have had the responsibility for the laboratories on small arms.

Mr. EISENBERG. Has part of it—of these—have part of these evaluations been conducted with military rifles, Mr. Simmons?

Mr. SIMMONS. Most of our evaluations have been associated with military rifles.

Mr. EISENBERG. How long altogether have you spent in this area?

Mr. SIMMONS. In the area of rifles?

Mr. EISENBERG. Yes.

Mr. SIMMONS. Some experience beginning from about 1953. I have been continuously concerned with this since 1957.

Mr. EISENBERG. Can you give a rough estimate of how many weapons you have evaluated as to accuracy?

Mr. SIMMONS. No. We have been concerned with almost all of the weapons which the Army has tested, either in preliminary stages or as developmental weapons.

Mr. EISENBERG. But your specialty is the evaluation of weapons systems, including military rifles, and you have been engaged in this for 13 years, as to all weapons systems, and since 1953 as to——

Mr. SIMMONS. Yes, that is correct.

Mr. McCLOY. In the course of that you have examined hundreds of rifles, though, have you not?

Mr. SIMMONS. Well, our examination of rifles is not the detailed engineering, design experiment which a gunsmith or a rifle expert as such would concern himself with. We are more concerned with establishing a framework by which we can put numbers to the performance of military rifles in tactical employment. And this means that for a specific—specific classes of weapons, we have had to establish, for example, round-to-round dispersion, the accuracy with which they can be employed, and the wounding power of the projectiles.

Mr. McCLOY. In the course of this you have fired a great many rifles yourself?

Mr. SIMMONS. No, sir; I don't fire them.

Mr. McCLOY. Somebody else fires them?

Mr. SIMMONS. Yes.

Mr. McCLOY. But you make the studies in relation to the accuracy of the weapons?

Mr. SIMMONS. Yes, that is correct. The firing is accomplished by employees of the development and proof services, which is the weapons testing facility at the Aberdeen Proving Ground.

Mr. McCLOY. Your task is primarily evaluation——

Mr. SIMMONS. Yes, sir.

Mr. McCLOY. Of the characteristics of the rifle, particularly in terms of its accuracy and its wounding power, killing power?

Mr. SIMMONS. Yes, sir.

Mr. EISENBERG. Mr. Chairman, may this witness be admitted as an expert to testify in this area?

Mr. McCLOY. Yes.

Mr. EISENBERG. Mr. Simmons, did you conduct a test from a machine rest, a test of round-to-round dispersion of this weapon, or have such tests conducted?

Mr. SIMMONS. May I check the serial number?

Mr. EISENBERG. I should ask first if you are familiar with this weapon.

I have handed the witness Commission Exhibit 139.

Mr. SIMMONS. Yes. We fired this weapon from a machine rest for round-to-round dispersion. We fired exactly 20 rounds in this test, and the dispersion which we measured is of conventional magnitude, about the same that we get with our present military rifles, and the standard deviation of dispersion is .29 mil.

Mr. EISENBERG. That is a fraction of a degree?

Mr. SIMMONS. A mil is an angular measurement. There are 17.7 mils to a degree.

Mr. EISENBERG. Do I understand your testimony to be that this rifle is as accurate as the current American military rifles?

Mr. SIMMONS. Yes. As far as we can determine from bench-rest firing.

Mr. EISENBERG. Would you consider that to be a high degree of accuracy?

Mr. SIMMONS. Yes, the weapon is quite accurate. For most small arms, we discover that the round-to-round dispersion is of the order of three-tenths of a mil. We have run into some unusual ones, however, which give us higher values, but very few which give us smaller values, except in selected lots of ammunition.

Mr. McCLOY. You are talking about the present military rifle—will you designate it?

Mr. SIMMONS. The M-14.

Mr. McCLOY. Is it as accurate as the Springfield 1906 ammunition?

Mr. SIMMONS. I am not familiar with the difference between the M-14 in its accuracy and the 1906 Springfield. These are very similar in their dispersion.

Mr. McCLOY. At a hundred yards, what does that amount to? What is the dispersion?

Mr. SIMMONS. Well, at a hundred yards, one mil is 3.6 inches, and 0.3 of that is a little more than an inch.

Mr. EISENBERG. You tested this with what type of ammunition, Mr. Simmons?

Mr. SIMMONS. The ammunition was labeled Type Ball, and it was made by the Western Cartridge Co., Division of Olin Industries.

Mr. EISENBERG. Was that a 6.5 mm.?

Mr. SIMMONS. 6.5-mm. Mannlicher-Carcano.

Mr. EISENBERG. In the course of this test from a machine rest, Mr. Simmons, did you also attempt to determine the muzzle velocity?

Mr. SIMMONS. Yes; we also measured muzzle velocities for approximately 10 rounds of the ammunition. We gather from these measurements that the nominal velocity, the nominal muzzle velocity is of the order of 2,200 feet per second, and the velocity at about 200 feet from the muzzle is approximately 2,000 feet per second. And there is some variation in velocity from round to round as there is with all small-arms ammunition. But the variation is relatively small, and within the same order of magnitude as for conventional ammunition.

Mr. EISENBERG. Did you test the bullets for yaw?

Mr. SIMMONS. Yes; we measured yaw also, and all measurements of yaw were also small. We had no values in excess of 2 degrees, and many values were less than 1 degree in yaw, indicating that the round is quite stable.

Mr. EISENBERG. How did you test for yaw?

Mr. SIMMONS. We took spark shadowgraph pictures at various stations down range from the muzzle, so that we actually have pictures of the position of the bullet relative to the top and bottom of our range.

Mr. EISENBERG. Did you bring those pictures with you?

Mr. SIMMONS. No ; I do not have them with me.

Mr. EISENBERG. Could you furnish those to the Commission at a later date?

Mr. SIMMONS. They could be made available later. I would like to point out these are not pictures, however. They are on large pieces of glass, and they are not photos.

Mr. EISENBERG. Can they be read by a layman?

Mr. SIMMONS. That I do not know. I do not read them.

Mr. EISENBERG. Well, I wonder whether you can send them up, and we could take a look at them.

Mr. SIMMONS. Yes; we can have them forwarded.

Mr. EISENBERG. Was it reported to you by the persons who ran the machine-rest tests whether they had any difficulties with sighting the weapon in?

Mr. SIMMONS. Well, they could not sight the weapon in using the telescope, and no attempt was made to sight it in using the iron sight. We did adjust the telescopic sight by the addition of two shims, one which tended to adjust the azimuth, and one which adjusted an elevation. The azimuth correction could have been made without the addition of the shim, but it would have meant that we would have used all of the adjustment possible, and the shim was a more convenient means—not more convenient, but a more permanent means of correction.

Mr. EISENBERG. By azimuth, do you refer to the crosshair which is sometimes referred to as the windage crosshair?

Mr. SIMMONS. Yes.

Mr. EISENBERG. Would you recognize these shims that I display to you, Mr. Simmons, as being the shims that were placed in the weapon?

Mr. SIMMONS. I saw the shims only when they were in the weapon, but those look very much like what was evident from the external view, after they were in place.

Mr. EISENBERG. For the record, Mr. Chairman, these shims were given to me by the FBI who told me that they had removed them from the weapon after they had been placed there by Mr. Simmons' laboratory.

May I have these introduced as evidence?

Mr. McCLOY. Yes.

Mr. EISENBERG. Mr. Simmons, I find there are three shims here. You mentioned two. Would three be consistent with what you were told?

Mr. SIMMONS. I was told two. These were put in by a gunsmith in one of our machine shops—rather a machinist in one of our machine shops.

Mr. EISENBERG. Mr. Simmons, I wonder whether you could take these shims back after I have marked them to find out whether the three had been placed?

Mr. SIMMONS. Yes.

Mr. EISENBERG. I am marking these 576, 577, and 578. They consist of three shims in three small envelopes.

(The items referred to were marked Commission Exhibits Nos. 576, 577, and 578, and received in evidence.)

Mr. EISENBERG. Mr. Simmons, did you have a test run to determine the possibility of scoring hits with this weapon, Exhibit 139, on a given target at a given distance under rapid-fire conditions?

Mr. SIMMONS. Yes; we did. We placed three targets, which were head and shoulder silhouettes, at distances of 175 feet, 240 feet, and 265 feet, and these distances are slant ranges from the window ledge of a tower which is about 30 feet high. We used three firers in an attempt to obtain hits on all three targets within as short a time interval as possible.

I should make one comment here relative to the angular displacement of the targets. We did not reproduce these angles exactly from the map which we had been given because the conditions in the field were a little awkward for this. But the distance—the angular distance from the first target to the second was greater than from the second to the third, which would tend to correspond to a longer interval of time between the first and second impact than between the second and the third. The movement of the rifle was greater from the first to the second target than from the second to the third.

Mr. EISENBERG. Mr. Simmons, were your marksmen instructed to aim at the three targets in consecutive order?

Mr. SIMMONS. The marksmen were instructed to take as much time as they desired at the first target, and then to fire—at the first target, being at 175 feet—to then fire at the target emplaced at 240 feet, and then at the one at 265 feet.

Mr. EISENBERG. Can you state where you derived these distances?

Mr. SIMMONS. These distances were the values given on the survey map which were given to us.

Mr. EISENBERG. Are you sure they were not the values I gave to you myself?

Mr. SIMMONS. I stand corrected. These are values—we were informed that the numbers on the survey map were possibly in error. The distances are very close, however.

Mr. EISENBERG. For the record, the figures which I gave Mr. Simmons are approximations and are not to be taken as the Commission's conclusive determination of what those distances are.

Mr. SIMMONS. For our experiment, I do not see how a difference of a few feet would make any difference.

Mr. EISENBERG. Now, Mr. Simmons, did you take pictures or have pictures taken showing what that range looked like?

Mr. SIMMONS. Yes; I have copies of these pictures here. I show you three pictures—the first showing the window from which the weapon was fired in our experiments; the second showing the view of the three targets from the window; and the third showing a rifleman in position.

Mr. EISENBERG. Mr. Simmons, did you take these pictures yourself?

Mr. SIMMONS. No; these pictures were taken by one of the cameramen from the development and proof services.

Mr. EISENBERG. Did you see the scenes represented in these pictures?

Mr. SIMMONS. Yes.

Mr. EISENBERG. Are these pictures accurate reproductions of these scenes?

Mr. SIMMON. Yes, sir.

Mr. EISENBERG. Mr. Chairman, I would like to have the first, second, and third pictures described by Mr. Simmons admitted as exhibits. That will be 579 for the first, 580 for the second, and 581 for the third.

Mr. McCLOY. They may be admitted.

(The photographs referred to were marked Commission Exhibits Nos. 579, 580, and 581 and received in evidence.)

Mr. EISENBERG. Mr. Simmons, the targets were—well, can you describe the targets for us?

Mr. SIMMONS. The targets are standard head-and-shoulders silhouettes, and they consist of approximately 2 square feet in area.

Mr. EISENBERG. How many marksmen were involved?

Mr. SIMMONS. We used three riflemen.

Mr. EISENBERG. And can you tell us what their background was?

Mr. SIMMONS. Yes. All three riflemen are rated as Master by the National Rifle Association. Two of them are civilian gunners in the Small Arms Division of our Development and Proof Services, and the third is presently in the Army, and he has considerable background as a rifleman, and also has a Master rating.

Mr. EISENBERG. Each fired one or more series of three rounds?

Mr. SIMMONS. Each fired two series of three rounds, using the telescopic sight. Then one of the firers repeated the exercise using the iron sight—because we had no indication whether the telescope had been used.

Mr. EISENBERG. So the total number of rounds fired was what?

Mr. SIMMONS. 21.

Mr. EISENBERG. Did you bring with you targets or copies of the targets?

Mr. SIMMON. I brought photos of the targets.

Mr. EISENBERG. Did you take these photographs, Mr. Simmons, or have them taken under your supervision?

Mr. SIMMONS. These photographs were taken by the photographic laboratory in our Ballistic Measurements Laboratory, which is one of the complex of laboratories within the Ballistic Research Laboratory.

Mr. EISENBERG. Can you verify these photographs as being accurate reproductions of the targets?

Mr. SIMMONS. Yes, sir.

Mr. EISENBERG. Mr. Chairman, may I have these admitted as 582, 583 and 584?

Mr. McCLOY. They may be admitted.

(The photographs referred to were marked Commission Exhibits Nos. 582, 583, and 584 for identification and received in evidence.)

Mr. EISENBERG. Mr. Simmons, could you discuss the results of the tests you ran, by using these photographs?

Mr. SIMMONS. Exhibit 582 is the target which was emplaced at 175 feet. All firers hit the first target, and this was to be expected, because they had as much time as they desired to aim at the first target.

As you can see from the picture, the accuracy of the weapon is quite good.

Mr. McCLOY. That first target is what distance?

Mr. SIMMONS. 175 feet. And we had to make an assumption here about the point of aim. It is quite likely that in fact each man was aiming at a different portion of the target—there were no markings on the target visible to the firer.

Mr. EISENBERG. Did I understand you just told the firers to aim at the target without referring to——

Mr. SIMMONS. Yes.

Mr. EISENBERG. There is an apparent crossline running darkly through that photograph.

Mr. SIMMONS. These lines were drawn in afterwards, in order for us to make some measurements from the actual impact point.

The target which was emplaced at 240 feet, as shown in Exhibit 583—we had rather an unusual coincidence with respect to this target. This involved the displacement of the weapon to a sufficient angle that the basic firing position of the man had to be changed. And because they knew time was very important, they made the movement very quickly. And for the first four attempts, the firers missed the second target. Of course, we made a rather, I guess, disadvantageous error in the test by pointing out that they had missed on the second target, and there was a conscious effort made on the additional rounds to hit the second target.

On the third target, the angle through which the weapon had to be moved to get to the third target from the second was relatively small, and there were only two rounds which did not hit the target at 270 feet. One of these rounds, by the way, was used in the sequence where the iron sight was employed.

Mr. EISENBERG. Mr. Simmons, when you said that the firers had to make a large shift relatively in their firing position, and were in a hurry, is this your interpretation or is this based on discussions with them subsequently?

Mr. SIMMONS. This is based on discussions with the firers after the experiment.

Mr. EISENBERG. After these tests were finished, did you make a determination of the amount of error—average amount of error in the aim of these riflemen?

Mr. SIMMONS. Yes. By assuming that all riflemen had aimed at the intersection of the lines that we have drawn on these pictures, we calculated the total aiming—the aiming error associated with the three riflemen—this is one number to describe the accuracy of all three riflemen. And against the first target the accuracy observed was about .7 mils, in standard deviation. Against the second target, the accuracy was 1.4 mils. And against the third target, it was 1.2 mils.

Mr. EISENBERG. Again, could you convert those at a hundred yards to inches?

Mr. SIMMONS. 0.7 of a mil at 100 yards is approximately 2 inches. 1.4 mils is approximately 4 inches. And 1.2 mils is approximately 3½ inches.

Mr. EISENBERG. In arriving at these figures, had you discounted the round-to-round dispersion as determined in the bench rest test?

Mr. SIMMONS. Yes. We have subtracted out the round-to-round dispersion.

Mr. EISENBERG. But the actual accuracy of the riflemen would have to include the round-to-round dispersion, would it not?

Mrs. SIMMONS. Yes; it would.

Mr. EISENBERG. Why did you then substract the round-to-round dispersion figure, or discount it?

Mr. SIMMONS. We wanted to determine what the aiming error itself was associated with the rifle.

Mr. EISENBERG. Can you give us the times in which the various riflemen used to fire the three shots in each sequence?

Mr. SIMMONS Yes. And the numbers which I will give you will be the average of two readings on stop watches.

Mr. EISENBERG. For each rifleman?

Mr. SIMMONS. For each exercise.

Mr. Hendrix fired twice. The time for the first exercise was 8.25 seconds; the time for the second exercise was 7.0 seconds.

Mr. Staley, on the first exercise, fired in 6¾ seconds; the second attempt he used 6.45 seconds.

Specialist Miller used 4.6 seconds on his first attempt, 5.15 seconds in his second attempt, and 4.45 seconds in his exercise using the iron sight.

Mr. EISENBERG. What was the accuracy of Specialist Miller?

Mr. SIMMONS. I do not have his accuracy separated from the group.

Mr. EISENBERG. Is it possible to separate the accuracy out?

Mr. SIMMONS. Yes; it is, by an additional calculation.

Mr. Miller succeeded in hitting the third target on both attempts with the telescope. He missed the second target on both attempts with the telescope, but he hit the second target with the iron sight. And he emplaced all three rounds on the target, the first target.

Mr. EISENBERG. How did he do with the iron sight on the third target?

Mr. SIMMONS. On the third target he missed the boards completely. And we have not checked this out. It appears that for the firing posture which Mr. Miller—Specialist Miller uses, the iron sight is not zeroed for him, since his impacts on the first and second targets were quite high, and against the third target we would assume that the projectile went over the top of the target, which extended only a few inches over the top of the silhouette.

Mr. EISENBERG. What position did the rifleman fire from, Mr. Simmons?

Mr. SIMMONS. The firers braced an elbow on the window sill and used pretty much a standard sitting position, using a stool.

Mr. EISENBERG. How much practice had they had with the weapon, Exhibit 139, before they began firing?

Mr. SIMMONS. They had each attempted the exercise without the use of ammunition, and had worked the bolt as they tried the exercise. They had not pulled the trigger during the exercise, however, because we were a little concerned about breaking the firing pin.

Mr. EISENBERG. Could you give us an estimate of how much time they used in this dry-run practice, each?

Mr. SIMMONS. They used no more than 2 or 3 minutes each.

Mr. EISENBERG. Did they make any comments concerning the weapon?

Mr. SIMMONS. Yes; there were several comments made—particularly with respect to the amount of effort required to open the bolt. As a matter of fact, Mr. Staley had difficulty in opening the bolt in his first firing exercise. He thought it was completely up and it was not, and he had to retrace his steps as he attempted to open the bolt after the first round.

There was also comment made about the trigger pull, which is different as far as these firers are concerned. It is in effect a two-stage operation where the first—in the first stage the trigger is relatively free, and it suddenly required a greater pull to actually fire the weapon.

Mr. EISENBERG. Mr. Simmons, did you prepare a table showing the probability of hit at a given target at given ranges by riflemen with given degrees of accuracy?

Mr. SIMMONS. Well, we prepared a table which showed what the probability of a hit would be on specific sizes of target as a function of aiming error, and using the appropriate round-to-round dispersion also in these calculations.

Mr. EISENBERG. What were the targets that you used in your calculations?

Mr. SIMMONS. We used two circular targets, one of 4 inches in radius and one of 9 inches in radius, to approximate the area of the head and the area of the shoulders, or the thorax, actually. And a significant point to these calculations to us is that against the larger target, if you fire with the 0.7 mil aiming error which was observed against the first target, the probability of hitting that target is 1, and it is 1 at all three ranges, out to 270 feet.

Mr. EISENBERG. Can you explain the meaning of the probability being 1?

Mr. SIMMONS. Well, the probability is effectively one. Actually the number is 0.99 and several more digits afterwards. It is rounded off to 1. Simply implying that the probability of a hit is very high with the small aiming errors and short range.

Mr. EISENBERG. Now of course this aiming error is derived from the three riflemen who you employed in the tests, is that correct?

Mr. SIMMONS. Yes.

Mr. EISENBERG. Could you proceed to the other two?

Mr. SIMMONS. Using the 1.2 mil aiming error, again at the larger targets, the probability of hitting the target at 175 feet is 1; at 240 feet it is 0.96; and at 270 feet it is 0.92.

Mr. EISENBERG. How would you characterize the second two figures in terms of probability?

Mr. SIMMONS. These also are very high values.

Mr. EISENBERG. The mil figure was 1.2, was it?

Mr. SIMMONS. Yes.

Mr. EISENBERG. Does that include, did you say, both aiming error and round-to-round dispersion?

Mr. SIMMONS. The 1.2 is the aiming error. When we include the round-to-round dispersion, it becomes only 1.24 mils.

Mr. EISENBERG. Does the probability reflect the 1.2 or the 1.24 figure?

Mr. SIMMONS. It reflects the total error, which is 1.24.

Mr. EISENBERG. And the same on the first series of calculations you gave us?

Mr. SIMMONS. Yes.

Mr. EISENBERG. Would you go on to the third?

Mr. SIMMONS. Using the 1.4 mil aiming error, and the round-to-round dispersion, giving a total error of 1.43 mils, the probability of hit at the 175 foot target is 0.99; at 240 feet it is 0.91; at 270 feet it is 0.85.

Mr. EISENBERG. Could you give us the figures for the smaller target?

Mr. SIMMONS. Using the 0.7 mil aiming error, the probability of a hit at 175 feet is 0.96; at 240 feet, 0.81; at 270 feet, 0.73.

For the 1.2 mil aiming error, the probability is 0.69 at 175 feet; 0.74 at 240 feet; 0.39 at 270 feet.

Using the——

Mr. EISENBERG. Can you characterize those, or explain them in lay terms?

Mr. SIMMONS. Well, against a shorter target, the probability is still almost 0.7, which is a relatively high value. The effective-range increase is beginning to show, however, because at 270 feet the value of 0.4 tends to be small.

Mr. EISENBERG. Does 0.4 mean you have 4 chances in 10 of hitting?

Mr. SIMMONS. Yes.

Now, our assumption throughout all of this is that the actual target was probably not either a small—the small area, but tending to be a larger area, as indicated by the crosshairs in these targets which we placed at this point.

Mr. EISENBERG. Now, you have given us probabilities of hit with three variations of aiming error. You have selected these three variations in what manner, Mr. Simmons?

Mr. SIMMONS. These were actually the three values which were demonstrated in the experiment.

Mr. EISENBERG. But each of those values is associated with one target?

Mr. SIMMONS. Yes.

Mr. EISENBERG. However, you have applied them to all three targets?

Mr. SIMMONS. Yes.

Mr. EISENBERG. Did you have a special reason for doing that?

Mr. SIMMONS. No. We are victims of habit, and we tend to provide such information in parametric form.

Mr. EISENBERG. Now, Mr. Simmons, of course the assassin's aiming error must be unknown. But do you have any opinion concerning the probable aiming error of an assassin using this weapon against the aiming error displayed by the three riflemen you employed?

Mr. SIMMONS. Well, it looks like to achieve hits as indicated, the accuracy, overall accuracy of the three rounds would have to be of the order of 1.2 mils. And this is really not a small number as far as marksmanship goes. There have been many exercises in which we have been involved where the aiming error turns out to be much smaller, smaller than this. And in match competition, of course, the numbers actually turn out to be—the total aiming error turns out to be about equal to the round-to-round dispersion.

Mr. EISENBERG. When you make the reference to many exercises, are you referring to exercises solely with skilled riflemen?

Mr. SIMMONS. If we have skilled riflemen, the values for aiming error tend to be of the order of 1 mil. As a matter of fact, to qualify as expert on Army rifle courses, about a 1 mil aiming error is required—a standard deviation of 1 mil.

Mr. EISENBERG. Is that with a rest or without a rest?

Mr. SIMMONS. This would be without a rest. This would be the actual aiming error from the fixed position, firing range.

Mr. EISENBERG. And is this with open or telescopic sights?

Mr. SIMMONS. This would be with the peepsight on the conventional rifle.

Mr. EISENBERG. Have you exercises which you feel would be applicable to the assassination—that is, exercises conducted with—under noncombat conditions, with a telescopic sight and a rest?

Mr. SIMMONS. The only experience that we have with the telescopic sight with which I am familiar is the exercise using this weapon. There have been experiments made using telescopic sights, but these are of limited interest militarily.

Mr. EISENBERG. In your opinion, what effect does the introduction of a rest and telescopic sight have on probable aiming error?

Mr. SIMMONS. From a position where the movement of the weapon is not great, and where the target is slowly moving, the fixed position on the telescope should enhance the probability of a hit.

Mr. EISENBERG. Do you think a marksman who is less than a highly skilled marksman under those conditions would be able to shoot in the range of 1.2-mil aiming error?

Mr. SIMMONS. Obviously considerable experience would have to be in one's background to do so. And with this weapon, I think also considerable experience with this weapon, because of the amount of effort required to work the bolt.

Mr. EISENBERG. Would do what? You mean would improve the accuracy?

Mr. SIMMONS. Yes. In our experiments, the pressure to open the bolt was so great that we tended to move the rifle off the target, whereas with greater proficiency this might not have occurred.

Mr. EISENBERG. Could this experience in operating the bolt be achieved in dry practice, Mr. Simmons?

Mr. SIMMONS. Yes: it could be, if sufficient practice were used. There is some indication of the magnitude of change with one of our shooters who in his second attempt fired three-tenths of a second less time than he did in the first.

Mr. EISENBERG. Mr. Simmons, has data been compiled showing the effect of the time taken between shots on the accuracy of the shots?

Mr. SIMMONS. There have been experiments run where aiming error has been measured as a function of the time one has to aim.

Mr. EISENBERG. Do those experiments show that aiming error is directly proportionate to the length of time one has to aim?

Mr. SIMMONS. Not directly proportionate, but aiming error decreases as time increases. But once you get to the area of about 4 seconds in time, then there is very small decrease in aiming error for increase in time.

Mr. EISENBERG. Translating that to this weapon, does that mean that taking more than 8 seconds between three shots should not appreciably affect the degree of accuracy?

Mr. SIMMONS. The 8 seconds I was referring to is between shots.

Mr. EISENBERG. You said 4 seconds, I thought.

Mr. SIMMONS. I beg your pardon.

Mr. EISENBERG. And I was saying, if you took 4 seconds between the first and second, and 4 seconds between the second and third, for a total of 8 seconds, on the basis of this data would that mean after 8 seconds you would not be substantially increasing your accuracy by taking more time?

Mr. SIMMONS. That is correct.

Mr. EISENBERG. Approximately how many bullets did you fire in the course of your tests?

Mr. SIMMONS. We fired 47 bullets.

Mr. EISENBERG. Did you have any misfires?

Mr. SIMMONS. None.

Mr. EISENBERG. Were you aware when you performed your tests of the conclusions of any other body concerning the accuracy of this weapon?

Mr. SIMMONS. No; we were not.

Mr. EISENBERG. Are you aware of such conclusions at this point?

Mr. SIMMONS. No; I am not.

Mr. EISENBERG. Mr. Chairman?

Mr. McCLOY. You said that these riflemen, or one or two of them at least, had the rank of master. What is that?

Mr. SIMMONS. I again fall back on my comment earlier that I am not a shooter myself. A master is one of the ratings given to highly qualified riflemen by the National Rifle Association. These men have all participated in national match competitions in the National Rifle Association.

Mr. McCLOY. Is that a higher grade than sharpshooter in the Army?

Mr. SIMMONS. There is really no comparison between the rating of master in the NRA and the rating of sharpshooter in the Army.

Mr. EISENBERG. I am not sure whether or not you answered this question, but do you feel that if the target was moving, rather than having the rifleman move, there would have been a difference in aiming error, increased or decreased aiming error—if the target was moving 5 to 10 miles an hour?

Mr. SIMMONS. I think the movement of the target in this case would have practically no effect on the accuracy of fire, because from the map we are led to believe that the movement was primarily away from the firer, so that the back of the President was fully exposed to the rifleman at all times.

Mr. EISENBERG. Could you explain your reference to a map? You have made several references to that.

Mr. SIMMONS. I refer to the survey plat which is dated December 5, 1963.

Mr. EISENBERG. And how were you supplied with that?

Mr. SIMMONS. To the best of my knowledge, you gave it to one of the employees in my office.

Mr. EISENBERG. Mr. Chairman, this is a plat made by a licensed surveyor of the area immediately adjoining the Texas School Book Depository. I would like to introduce it into evidence solely to show the basis which Mr. Simmons was using in his test, and not for the truth of the measurements which are shown in here.

Mr. McCLOY. It may be received.

Mr. EISENBERG. That would be Commission 585.

(The document referred to was marked Commission Exhibit No. 585 and received in evidence.)

Mr. EISENBERG. I have no further questions.

Mr. McCLOY. I have no further questions.

Mr. EISENBERG. Is there anything you would like to add to your testimony?

Mr. SIMMONS. I think not.

Mr. EISENBERG. I wonder whether we could have a copy of your table?

Mr. SIMMONS. Yes.

Mr. McCLOY. From your experience, Mr. Simmons, do you feel that with a man who had been in the Marine Corps, with the rifle instruction he had there, using this rifle, and what you know of the shots that killed the President— do you think he was an extraordinarily good shot, do you think he was just shooting in accordance with what might be taken to be the skill that service in the Marine Corps would give him?

Mr. SIMMONS. Well, in order to achieve three hits, it would not be required that a man be an exceptional shot. A proficient man with this weapon, yes. But I think with the opportunity to use the weapon and to get familiar with it, we could probably have the results reproduced by more than one firer.

Mr. McCLOY. I think that is all.

Mr. EISENBERG. One thing, Mr. Chairman. May I have this admitted as 586, this table which Mr. Simmons prepared, from which he was giving testimony earlier? This is "Table I, Hit Probability as a Function of Range and Aiming Error."

Mr. McCLOY. It may be admitted.

(The table referred to was marked Commission Exhibit No. 586 and received in evidence.)

Mr. EISENBERG. When you say proficiency with this weapon, Mr. Simmons, could you go into detail as to what you mean—do you mean accuracy with this weapon, or familiarity with the weapon?

Mr. SIMMONS. I mean familiarity basically with two things. One is the action of the bolt itself, and the force required to open it; and two, the action of the trigger, which is a two-stage trigger.

Mr. EISENBERG. Can familiarity with the trigger and with the bolt be acquired in dry practice?

Mr. SIMMONS. Familiarity with the bolt can, probably as well as during live firing. But familiarity with the trigger would best be achieved with some firing.

Mr. Eisenberg. Why is there this difference between familiarity with the bolt and familiarity with the trigger in dry firing?

Mr. Simmons. There tends to be a reaction between the firer and the weapon at the time the weapon is fired, due to the recoil impulse. And I do not believe the action of the bolt going home would sufficiently simulate the action of the recoil of the weapon.

Mr. Eisenberg. One further question.

Looking at the figures for aiming error, as discounted by round-to-round dispersion, how would you characterize the actual performance of men with this rifle—that is, not the accuracy of the weapon, but the accuracy of man and weapon.

Mr. Simmons. I am not sure I understand your question.

Mr. Eisenberg. Do you feel on the basis of the aiming error, discounted for round-to-round dispersion or including it, that this weapon is an easy one with which to be accurate, or a difficult one?

Mr. Simmons. It appears to be relatively conventional in that regard, I assume. The telescope helps in the accuracy against a target which is well displayed, as was the case here. And the weapon is reasonably conventional. So that I think it would not be significantly different from any other weapon.

Mr. McCloy. If you were having a dry run with this, you could certainly make yourself used to the drag in the trigger without discharging the rifle, could you not?

Mr. Simmons. Yes. But there are two stages to the trigger. Our riflemen were all used to a trigger with a constant pull. When the slack was taken up, then they expected the round to fire. But actually when the slack is taken up, you tend to have a hair trigger here, which requires a bit of getting used to.

Mr. McCloy. This does not have a hair trigger after the slack is taken up?

Mr. Simmons. This tends to have the hair trigger as soon as you move it after the slack is taken up. You achieve or you feel greater resistance to the movement of the trigger, and then ordinarily you would expect the weapon to have fired, and in this case then as you move it to overcome that, it fires immediately. And our firers were moving the shoulder into the weapon.

Mr. McCloy. I have no further questions.

Mr. Eisenberg. That is all.

Mr. McCloy. Thank you very much. You have been very helpful.

We shall recess now until 9 o'clock tomorrow morning.

(Whereupon, at 5:25 p.m., the President's Commission recessed.)

Wednesday, April 1, 1964

TESTIMONY OF CORTLANDT CUNNINGHAM AND JOSEPH D. NICOL

The President's Commission met at 9 a.m. on April 1, 1964, at 200 Maryland Avenue NE., Washington, D.C.

Present were Chief Justice Earl Warren, Chairman; Representative Hale Boggs, Representative Gerald R. Ford, and Mr. Allen W. Dulles, members.

Also present were Melvin Aron Eisenberg, assistant counsel; Norman Redlich, assistant counsel; Samuel A. Stern, assistant counsel; Charles Murray and Charles Rhyne, observers.

TESTIMONY OF CORTLANDT CUNNINGHAM

The Chairman. The Commission will be in order.

Mr. Cunningham, the purpose of today's hearing is to take the testimony of yourself and Mr. Joseph Nicol. We understand that you are a firearms expert with the FBI, and Mr. Nicol is a firearms expert with the Bureau of Criminal

Identification and Investigation of the Department of Public Safety of the State of Illinois.

You have both been asked to provide technical information to assist the Commission in its work.

Would you raise your right hand and be sworn, please?

Do you solemnly swear that the testimony you shall give will be the truth, the whole truth, and nothing but the truth, so help you God?

Mr. CUNNINGHAM. I do.

The CHAIRMAN. Will you be seated, please.

You may proceed with the examination.

Mr. EISENBERG. Mr. Cunningham, would you state your name and position?

Mr. CUNNINGHAM. Cortlandt Cunningham. I am a Special Agent of the FBI.

Mr. EISENBERG. And in what branch of the FBI do you work?

Mr. CUNNINGHAM. I am assigned to the Firearms Identification Unit of the FBI Laboratory, here in Washington, D.C.

Mr. EISENBERG. What is your education?

Mr. CUNNINGHAM. I have a Bachelor of Science degree from Northwestern University, and a Bachelor of Laws degree from the University of Miami.

Mr. EISENBERG. Could you briefly state your qualifications in the field of firearms identification?

Mr. CUNNINGHAM. Upon entering the FBI Laboratory, I underwent an extensive training course under the supervision of experienced examiners in the field of firearms identification, which consisted of making thousands of examinations and comparisons of bullets, cartridge cases, and weapons.

I have also done some reading in the subject. I have done some research and conducted many experiments in the field. And, of course, I have made thousands of examinations on my own and testified numerous times in State and Federal courts.

Mr. EISENBERG. How many years have you been in the Laboratory, Mr. Cunningham?

Mr. CUNNINGHAM. Over 5 years, and I have been in the Bureau over 10 years.

The CHAIRMAN. The witness is qualified.

Mr. EISENBERG. To begin with, Mr. Cunningham, we had some testimony yesterday on the bullet which is thought to have been fired at General Walker. That is Commission Exhibit No. 573. Are you familiar with this bullet, Mr. Cunningham?

Mr. CUNNINGHAM. I am.

Mr. EISENBERG. Can you supply the weight of that bullet, which was going to be supplied to us?

Mr. CUNNINGHAM. I can. This bullet weighed 148.25 grains.

Mr. EISENBERG. Does that show some weight loss, if the bullet was from a 6.5 mm. Mannlicher-Carcano cartridge?

Mr. CUNNINGHAM. It does. Those bullets weigh 161 grains, but there is a great deal of mutilation on this bullet.

Mr. EISENBERG. And could you tell us when you received this bullet in your laboratory, Mr. Cunningham?

Mr. CUNNINGHAM. Yes. It was received from the Dallas office of the FBI on December 4, 1963.

Mr. EISENBERG. And when was it examined?

Mr. CUNNINGHAM. It was examined that date.

Mr. EISENBERG. Mr. Cunningham, I now hand you Commission Exhibit No. 143, and I ask you whether you are familiar with this exhibit, which, for the record, is a revolver.

Mr. CUNNINGHAM. If you will excuse me, I won't open the cylinder. I have checked the cylinder, and there are expended or fired cartridge cases in the cylinder.

Mr. EISENBERG. Which you have placed in it for a special demonstration?

Mr. CUNNINGHAM. I fired it, yes, prior to my testimony here today. I have seen this weapon before.

Mr. EISENBERG. Again for the record, this is the weapon which is believed to have been used in the murder of Officer Tippit. Can you describe this weapon in terms of name, caliber and so forth?

Mr. CUNNINGHAM. Do you want me to describe it as it is today?

Mr. EISENBERG. As it is today.

Mr. CUNNINGHAM. As it is today, it is a .38 Special Smith and Wesson, Victory Model revolver.

Mr. EISENBERG. And was it always a .38 Special?

Mr. CUNNINGHAM. No, it was not. Originally this weapon was known as a 38-200 British Service revolver. In this country the weapon would be known as a .38 caliber Smith and Wesson revolver, Victory Model. However, the British gave the designation .38-200 to it.

Mr. EISENBERG. Was this revolver made in the United States?

Mr. CUNNINGHAM. It was.

Mr. EISENBERG. And has it been in England subsequent to that?

Mr. CUNNINGHAM. Yes.

Mr. EISENBERG. And how can you tell that, Mr. Cunningham?

Mr. CUNNINGHAM. Well, first of all, all weapons going into England have to be proofed. They are proofed at, usually, the Birmingham proofhouse.

Representative FORD. What does that mean?

Mr. CUNNINGHAM. They are tested for whether they will withstand a certain charge. They place in the cylinders overloaded cartridges, and they are fired, in the cylinder, as this one has been. It has been proofed to 3½ tons. Each chamber in the cylinder has been proofed.

You can tell that, because each chamber has been stamped with the Birmingham proofmark, indicating that each chamber in the cylinder has been proofed.

Mr. EISENBERG. Mr. Cunningham, could you explain to us the difference between a .38 S&W and a .38 Special?

Mr. CUNNINGHAM. They are completely different cartridges. One cartridge is a .38 Special, and the other cartridge is a .38 S&W, or actually written out it would be Smith and Wesson. It was developed for their weapons, and it is quite an old cartridge, and it is known—usually as appears on a box of ammunition—as merely a .38 S&W. However, there are many differences in the cartridges.

Mr. EISENBERG. Have you brought two—an example of each type of cartridge with you?

Mr. CUNNINGHAM. I have. First of all, this is actually a Western .38 S&W cartridge. You will see the head stamping on the base of this cartridge signifies it to be a .38 S&W.

Mr. EISENBERG. Before you go any further—Mr. Chairman, may I have this marked as an exhibit—this specimen?

I am holding a cartridge marked Western .38 S&W, and it is submitted as Commission Exhibit 587.

The CHAIRMAN. It may be admitted.

(The article referred to was marked Commission Exhibit No. 587, and received in evidence.)

Mr. CUNNINGHAM. If you would care to see one broken down, I have one with me. That is the same cartridge where the bullet has been pulled and the powder has been dumped out.

Mr. EISENBERG. That is also a .38 S&W cartridge, but it has been disassembled into a bullet and a cartridge case?

Mr. CUNNINGHAM. That is correct. The bullet has been pulled out of the cartridge case and the powder removed.

Mr. EISENBERG. Mr. Chairman, may I have this admitted as an exhibit?

The CHAIRMAN. It may be. What is the number?

Mr. EISENBERG. That will be 588.

The CHAIRMAN. It will be admitted as Commission Exhibit 588.

(The article referred to was marked Commission Exhibit No. 588, and received in evidence.)

Mr. CUNNINGHAM. This particular cartridge, which is one complete cartridge, is a Remington-Peters .38 S&W. These two components actually are of the same cartridge. All I have done is pull the bullet, and it is also a Remington-Peters .38 S&W.

Mr. EISENBERG. That is the same cartridge as Exhibits 588 and 587?

Mr. CUNNINGHAM. That is correct. The only difference is that they are different brands. They were made by two different manufacturers.

Mr. EISENBERG. Could you show that to the Chairman for his examination?

The CHAIRMAN. These appear to be lead bullets.

Mr. CUNNINGHAM. They are, sir.

The CHAIRMAN. The others appeared to be jacketed.

Mr. CUNNINGHAM. They are not, sir. It is known as gilding metal. They are copper-coated lead bullets. Actually, it is an alloy—it is not pure copper. They have been flash coated, for sales appeal, more than anything else.

Mr. EISENBERG. Does that coating serve to prevent distortion to any measurable extent when the bullet has penetrated a body?

Mr. CUNNINGHAM. No, it would not, to any appreciable amount. It is such a thin coat, as you can see. Later on I will show you the ones that have been fired, and also the bullets removed from Officer Tippit's body. You can see the coating comes off—it flakes off—it is very thin.

Mr. EISENBERG. So that Exhibits 587 and 588 are substantially similar to the R-P cartridge you have just been discussing?

Mr. CUNNINGHAM. Yes. They are both loaded to the same specifications, even though there are two manufacturers. All commercially made ammunition in this country is loaded to a specific muzzle velocity.

Mr. EISENBERG. Mr. Chairman, may I have this R-P cartridge which Mr. Cunningham has been discussing admitted into evidence as Commission Exhibit 589?

The CHAIRMAN. It may be admitted.

(The article referred to was marked Commission Exhibit No. 589, and received in evidence.)

Mr. EISENBERG. You have been showing us a .38 S&W, Mr. Cunningham?

Mr. CUNNINGHAM. Yes, sir.

Mr. EISENBERG. Do you have an example of a .38 Special?

Mr. CUNNINGHAM. I do. The first one is a Western .38 Special copper-coated lead bullet of Western manufacture, a .38 Special. The other components I have here are components of the same cartridge from which the bullet has been pulled.

Mr. EISENBERG. May I have the cartridge case, bullet, and cartridge admitted into evidence as 590?

The CHAIRMAN. It may be admitted.

(The article referred to was marked Commission Exhibit No. 590, and received in evidence.)

Mr. EISENBERG. Now, Mr. Cunningham, could you describe to us briefly the difference——

Mr. CUNNINGHAM. Do you want the Remington-Peters?

Mr. EISENBERG. You are holding in your hand a Remington-Peters disassembled and assembled .38 Special?

Mr. CUNNINGHAM. Yes, sir.

Mr. EISENBERG. Would you hand that to the Chief Justice? May this be admitted into evidence as Exhibit 591?

The CHAIRMAN. It may be admitted.

(The article referred to was marked Commission Exhibit No. 591, and received in evidence.)

Mr. EISENBERG. This consists of an assembled R-P .38 Special and a disassembled R-P .38 Special.

Again, I notice, Mr. Cunningham, that the R-P bullet has a lead-colored look, whereas Exhibit 590 had a copper-colored look.

Mr. CUNNINGHAM. Yes, sir. The Western coating is known by the trade name "Lubaloy." It is a trade name of the Western Cartridge Co., and it is nothing more than a gilding metal—actually, it is just a flash coating on the outside of the bullet. There is some advantage, a very small advantage, as to leading. But it is mostly for sales appeal, because with Winchester bullets, some do and some don't have the coating. Most of Winchesters which is the same bullet, have not been copper coated—that they are selling today.

Mr. EISENBERG. Now, can you explain the difference in terms of dimensions and contour, weight, and so forth, between the .38 Special bullets which you have just shown us and the .38 S&W bullets which you have shown to us?

Mr. CUNNINGHAM. Yes, sir. The complete .38 Special cartridges, both brands, they are approximately the same—they are made to specifications, and they are within—just 1/1000th difference between the two of them. They are very close. In some cases, there is a slight difference, but generally they are the same size.

The .38 Special cartridges are a little over 1½ inches in length. The .38 S&W cartridges are approximately 1.2 inches in length. In other words, there is about 4/10ths of an inch difference in their length.

The bullets of the .38 Special weigh 158 grains—both brands. The bullets in the .38 S&W cartridges—there is one grain difference—Western Lubaloy bullets weigh 145 grains, and Remington's bullets weigh 146 grains, which is very close, when you figure there are 7,000 grains to the pound.

The length of the bullets themselves—the .38 Special bullets are approximately .72 plus inch. The .38 S&W bullets are approximately .6 plus inch. The lengths of the cartridge cases are also different. A .38 Special is approximately 1.15 inches for both brands. The .38 S&W cartridge cases are approximately .77 inch. And there you have approximately a quarter of an inch difference between the lengths of the cartridge cases.

The diameters of the bullets—the .38 Special bullets, at the portion of the bullet where the case is crimped into the bullet are approximately .357".

Mr. EISENBERG. That is the groove around the base of the bullet, also known as the cannelure?

Mr. CUNNINGHAM. No, it is just above the two grooves, which are known as cannelures, where the bullet is crimped. It is known as the crimp ring. It is nothing more than where the case has been crimped in.

Mr. EISENBERG. I have pulled out the bullet from Exhibit 591, and there is a little groove running above the second groove from the top—from the bottom, the base, of the bullet.

Mr. CUNNINGHAM. That would be your crimping groove. Up at approximately that area, both .38 Specials are approximately .357". However, the bases of the .38 Specials, both brands, are about .350".

In other words, there is about 7/1000ths difference between the base and where they are crimped, and both brands of .38 Specials seem to run—slightly undersized at the base.

On the .38 Special the diameter of the bullets where they are crimped is .357". The .38 S&W Remington-Peters bullets run about .360", or just slightly less, which is about 3/1000ths larger. Their bases, both brands, run about .356". In other words, they run about 6/1000ths larger at the base—even though the bullets are shorter overall in the .38 S&W.

Mr. EISENBERG. To summarize that, in terms of the diameter, do I understand that the .38 Special and the .38 S&W have a similar diameter as you approach the nose of the bullet, but that the .38 has a somewhat larger diameter at the base than the .38 Special?

Mr. CUNNINGHAM. .38 S&W.

Mr. EISENBERG. Now, why would the gun be rechambered from the original chamber, which was designed for the .38 S&W, to the chamber as it stands now, which you tell us is designed for the .38 Special?

Mr. CUNNINGHAM. In this country, the .38 S&W is not a popular cartridge at the present time. In years gone by, many, many, many weapons have been made for that particular cartridge. But they are usually the top-break, the cheaper type of weapon. The .38 Special cartridge is a better cartridge. There is a higher velocity and everything about the cartridge is better than the .38 S&W, ballistically.

The .38 Special has become popular in this country for revolvers. And the reason it was chambered in .38 S&W originally is because in England and on the Continent it is a popular cartridge. The .38 S&W in England is the .38–200. They loaded a 200-grain bullet into the same cartridge case, and it was the standard British Army load for this particular weapon and others. Why they took that particular cartridge, I do not know.

Mr. EISENBERG. Was the gun rebarreled as well as rechambered?

Mr. CUNNINGHAM. No, it was not. The barrel of this weapon has been cut off approximately 2¾ inches. The original barrel was 5 inches for this model.

Mr. EISENBERG. Would the failure to rebarrel affect the accuracy of the weapon?

Mr. CUNNINGHAM. It should slightly, if you are firing .38 Special bullets, because they are slightly undersized in a .38 S&W barrel. On the average, .38 S&W barrels are approximately 4/1000ths larger than the normal .38 Special barrel. In this particular weapon, that holds true.

Mr. EISENBERG. Would it affect accuracy at close range?

Mr. CUNNINGHAM. None whatsoever. And there, again, the shortening of the barrel would affect the accuracy more than the use of .38 Special, due to the fact that your sight radius has been cut down.

Mr. EISENBERG. That is to say, when you shorten the barrel, the length between the front and the back sights is shorter, therefore giving more room for error?

Mr. CUNNINGHAM. Yes, sir. In other words, the movement of the front sight will cause more of a discrepancy at the target at longer ranges, due to the shorter sight radius.

Mr. EISENBERG. Is there any functional reason for cutting the barrel down to its present short size?

Mr. CUNNINGHAM. Sales appeal, I would say, is the main reason. Also, concealment.

Mr. EISENBERG. In your experience, is a short barrel, cut-down barrel weapon like this usually purchased for legitimate purposes by other than police officers?

Mr. CUNNINGHAM. Possibly a collector. Among target shooters, it is not a popular weapon, due to the short sight radius. Revolvers with 6-inch barrels are very accurate weapons. A target shooter would not use a weapon of the short barrel type. Therefore, it is not a very popular weapon for sportsmen.

Mr. EISENBERG. Does the cutting off of the barrel increase the possibility of concealment?

Mr. CUNNINGHAM. It does, because it makes it handier. I carried, when I was in the field 5 years—I carried my personally owned firearm, which had a 2-inch barrel, due to the fact that for concealment you could not see it when I wore a suit, and it was more discreet in the type of work I was doing.

The CHAIRMAN. Can both kinds of cartridges be used interchangeably in this gun?

Mr. CUNNINGHAM. In this particular gun, yes sir. It makes no difference.

The CHAIRMAN. Either an S&W or S&W Special?

Mr. CUNNINGHAM. Yes, sir; the chambers of this particular cylinder have been bored out, it appears from the very rough marks, to accommodate the forward portion of a .38 Special cartridge. Also, when this barrel was made—or the cylinder was made—the chambers had a shoulder or lip that the .38 S&W cartridge case would fit up against. The bullet would go forward farther, but the cartridge case would fit up against this shoulder at the neck.

And in order to chamber a .38 Special, that forward portion had to be bored out slightly, several thousandths to accommodate the longer cartridge, which, by the way, is a very common thing on these surplus weapons. Practically all of them are being rechambered, due to the popularity of the .38 Special cartridge.

The CHAIRMAN. I see.

Mr. EISENBERG. Mr. Cunningham, this weapon—was this weapon sold into the United States after it had been used in England?

Mr. CUNNINGHAM. Yes, sir.

Mr. EISENBERG. How much sign of use does it show?

Mr. CUNNINGHAM. It has definitely been used, there is no doubt. However, the cylinder is quite tight, and I would say that this weapon is in good operating condition.

Mr. EISENBERG. Now, since it was sold used, are you unable to attribute any amount of use to the last user?

Mr. CUNNINGHAM. That is right, you would not be able to tell.

Mr. EISENBERG. Mr. Cunningham, could you explain briefly the manner in which this revolver is operated, paying particular attention to extraction and loading and reloading?

Mr. CUNNINGHAM. Yes, sir. First of all, the weapon has a frame into which a barrel has been screwed and a cylinder which is hinged on a crane is also fitted into the frame. There is a cylinder release on the left-hand side of this weapon which enables one to push the cylinder to the left.

The cylinder has six chambers—in other words, it is a six-shot weapon. There is an extractor rod and an extractor in the rear portion of the cylinder. When you press on the extractor rod, either loaded cartridges or fired cartridge cases may be extracted from the cylinder so that it may be reloaded again.

Mr. EISENBERG. Now, Mr. Cunningham, in the operation of this weapon, the cylinder takes six bullets—is that correct?

Mr. CUNNINGHAM. That is correct.

Mr. EISENBERG. In the operation of this weapon, when six bullets have been loaded into the cylinder, is any action needed for firing except six consecutive trigger pulls?

Mr. CUNNINGHAM. That is correct. You can fire this weapon either single or double action.

Mr. EISENBERG. Now, can you explain the meaning of that?

Mr. CUNNINGHAM. Yes. Double action is accomplished by pulling the trigger. In other words, you just pull the trigger each time and you can fire this weapon six times before reloading. This weapon can also be cocked, which puts the sear on the step of the hammer and reduces the trigger pull, and may be fired that way. This is known as single action.

Mr. EISENBERG. Now, if a person using the gun and having it fully loaded with six bullets fired less than six bullets, can he use this ejector-extraction mechanism without losing his unfired bullets as well as the empty cartridge cases?

Mr. CUNNINGHAM. Yes, sir—by merely tipping the weapon. The unfired cartridge is heavier, and will fall out of the cylinder into his hand. Then he can extract the cartridge cases and load in more.

Mr. EISENBERG. Could you demonstrate that?

Mr. CUNNINGHAM. If I may have a cartridge, please.

Mr. EISENBERG. Do you have any fired cartridges in the cylinder?

Mr. CUNNINGHAM. Yes, sir; I do. Prior to my appearance here today, this morning, I fired five cartridges in this weapon, and they are still in the cylinder.

Mr. EISENBERG. You are now placing an unfired——

Mr. CUNNINGHAM. An unfired cartridge in the sixth chamber of the cylinder. Now, in a normal way, you would hit the cylinder release, push in your hand like this, and tip it up. The unfired cartridge will fall right out into your hand, due to the fact that the chambers of the cylinder are naturally larger than the cartridge you are loading in there—for ease of putting them in. When you fire a cartridge in a revolver, the case expands as wide as the cylinder. In other words, when the firing pin hits the primer, there is an explosion in the primer, the powder is ignited in the cartridge, and the terrific pressure will expand the cartridge case to tightly fit the chamber.

Mr. EISENBERG. I would like the record to show that when Mr. Cunningham tipped the revolver, the unfired bullet tipped out, but the five expended shells remained in.

The CHAIRMAN. Very well.

Mr. EISENBERG. Now, Mr. Cunningham, would you show how you would eject the five expended shells?

Mr. CUNNINGHAM. Yes. These are very difficult, by the way, to extract, due to the fact that the chamber has been rechambered. And as you can see, you get on your cartridge cases a little ballooning with these smaller diameter cases in the .38 Special.

Mr. EISENBERG. I would like the record to show that Mr. Cunningham extracted the five expended cartridge cases merely by one push of the ejector rod.

Mr. CUNNINGHAM. You won't be able to see it again, but when you eject a cartridge case—later on for the powder pattern test, I will show that you can have residues of unburned powder. That is what would happen if you ejected

457

these cartridge cases in your hand. You would pick up unburned powder, residues, and partially burned powder.

Mr. EISENBERG. Mr. Cunningham had ejected five cartridge cases from the revolver into his hand, and his right hand is now filled with small black particles, whose composition I am unable to determine.

Representative FORD. That would happen any time that you did it?

Mr. CUNNINGHAM. Yes, sir; every time you eject them, these particles will come out from the cylinder into your hand—unburned powder, partially burned powder, and gunpowder residues.

Representative FORD. Had you fired this morning these particular bullets?

Mr. CUNNINGHAM. Yes, sir; at 8:15.

Mr. EISENBERG. Mr. Cunningham, these cartridge cases which you ejected were .38 Special cartridge cases?

Mr. CUNNINGHAM. They were.

Mr. EISENBERG. What time did you fire those bullets, those .38 Special bullets in this revolver?

Mr. CUNNINGHAM. At approximately 8:15 this morning.

Mr. EISENBERG. Let the record show that it is now 9:45. Now, Mr. Cunningham, could this revolver be loaded on the run, or while walking?

Mr. CUNNINGHAM. It could.

Mr. EISENBERG. Have you personally loaded a revolver like this while walking?

Mr. CUNNINGHAM. Yes. And running.

Mr. EISENBERG. Does this revolver have a serial number on it?

Mr. CUNNINGHAM. It does.

Mr. EISENBERG. Could you read that number to us, please?

Mr. CUNNINGHAM. V–510210.

Mr. EISENBERG. Is this serial number unique to this particular type of weapon?

Mr. CUNNINGHAM. Yes. Smith and Wesson does not duplicate numbers. You may have a similar number, but not with the prefix "V."

Mr. EISENBERG. So this is the only such weapon with this serial number that is in existence?

Mr. CUNNINGHAM. That is correct. As far as I know. I have never found one in my experience, and Smith and Wesson does not duplicate serial numbers in a particular series of weapons.

Mr. EISENBERG. Smith and Wesson claims not to duplicate?

Mr. CUNNINGHAM. That is correct.

Mr. EISENBERG. Mr. Cunningham, how fast could one get off shots from this weapon, shooting rapid fire, and without sighting?

Mr. CUNNINGHAM. In a combat stance, that is crouched, with a gun at belt level, and your wrist locked, you would have no trouble at all getting off five shots in from 3 to 4 seconds.

Mr. EISENBERG. With what degree of accuracy at close range?

Mr. CUNNINGHAM. Excellent. All FBI agents, for instance, practice at 7 yards, which is 21 feet, and we are hitting in the "kill zone" without any problem.

Mr. EISENBERG. How much training would one have to have with this weapon to get four hits in four or five shots at close range into a human body?

Mr. CUNNINGHAM. None whatsoever—if you can pull the trigger and point directly at a person, at 8 feet you would not likely miss—with one exception. If you did not lock your wrist, there is a possibility you could shoot too low, or you could pull to the side. Anyone with a little bit of knowledge and with—and really grabbing hold of the weapon, would have little difficulty at all at that distance.

Mr. EISENBERG. When you say "lock your wrist," do you mean just pointing the wrist so that it is in a straight line with your lower forearm?

Mr. CUNNINGHAM. Yes. In other words, to tighten it, and not be in a relaxed position. By merely tightening the wrist, you would have no trouble at all hitting a person, approximately the same distance as Mr. Eisenberg and myself.

The CHAIRMAN. I suppose a person who had the normal small-arms training that he gets in the Marine Corps would have the ability to do what you have just spoken of?

Mr. CUNNINGHAM. Definitely, sir. As a matter of fact, with any training at all with a revolver, I would say that he would hit 90 percent of the time.

Representative FORD. Is there a recoil action at all from this kind of weapon?

Mr. CUNNINGHAM. Yes, sir; you get recoil. But if you have had any training with a weapon of this sort, the recoil is not even noticed. The first time you ever fired this weapon the recoil or the noise, might bother you. But if you have ever fired a handgun, you don't even think about recoil. You automatically adjust.

Mr. EISENBERG. Mr. Cunningham, you mentioned distance between you and me earlier, a few sentences ago. Could you estimate that distance?

Mr. CUNNINGHAM. Approximately 8 feet.

Mr. EISENBERG. If there are no further questions on the revolver, I propose to move on to identification of bullets and cartridge cases associated with the Tippit murder.

The CHAIRMAN. I have none.

Mr. EISENBERG. Mr. Cunningham, I hand you Commission Exhibits Nos. 145 and 518, which, for the record, consist of bullets, unfired bullets which were found in the revolver and the pocket of Lee Harvey Oswald following his arrest on November 22. I ask you whether you are familiar with the bullets in these exhibits.

You are now looking at which exhibit, Mr. Cunningham?

Mr. CUNNINGHAM. Commission Exhibit 518.

I have seen them before.

Mr. EISENBERG. Can you describe these bullets very briefly?

Mr. CUNNINGHAM. Yes, sir. They are cartridges. There are four cartridges. Two are Western .38 Special with copper-coated lead bullets loaded into these cartridges. The other two are Remington-Peters .38 Special cartridges, which are loaded with lead bullets.

Mr. EISENBERG. Could you describe the bullets in the other exhibit?

Mr. CUNNINGHAM. Commission Exhibit 145 consists of one Western .38 Special cartridge, which is also loaded with a copper-coated lead bullet, and the other cartridge is a Remington-Peters .38 Special cartridge, which is loaded with a lead bullet.

Mr. EISENBERG. I now hand you another group of bullets, marked Q–82 through Q–86.

The CHAIRMAN. Mr. Eisenberg, would you state for the record at this time what those two bullets are? They are introduced another time.

Mr. EISENBERG. Yes; all the bullets which Mr. Cunningham examined were found either in the pocket or the—pocket of Lee Harvey Oswald—or the cylinder of his revolver at the time of his arrest on November 22.

I now hand you another group of bullets marked Q–82 through Q–86, and with certain other markings on them.

Are you familiar with these bullets? And may I state for the record that the bullets I have just handed Mr. Cunningham derive from the same source.

Mr. CUNNINGHAM. I am familiar with these bullets.

Mr. EISENBERG. Could you describe these briefly?

Before I do that—Mr. Chairman, may I have these bullets admitted into evidence as a group, as Exhibit 592?

The CHAIRMAN. They may be admitted.

(The articles referred to were marked Commission Exhibit No. 592, and received in evidence.)

The CHAIRMAN. At this time, I shall have to leave to attend a session of the Supreme Court.

Commissioner Ford, would you preside?

And, during the morning, Commissioner Dulles will be here, I am told, and if you leave, leave him in charge, will you, please?

Representative FORD. Yes, sir.

The CHAIRMAN. Thank you very much.

Mr. Cunningham, thank you for your assistance. Glad to have seen you. (At this point, Mr. Warren withdrew from the hearing room.)

Mr. EISENBERG. Could you describe the bullets in Exhibit 592, Mr. Cunningham?

Mr. CUNNINGHAM. Yes, sir; all five of them are Western .38 Special cartridges, which are loaded with copper-coated lead bullets.

Mr. EISENBERG. So that of a total of—you have examined a total of 11 bullets, and three are Remington-Peter—well, at any rate, of the 11 they are divided 3 and 8 into Remington-Peter and Western .38 Special bullets?

Mr. CUNNINGHAM. Yes, sir.

Mr. EISENBERG. Now, Mr. Cunningham, I hand you four cartridge cases in an envelope marked Q–74, Q–75, Q–76, and Q–77. And I ask you whether you are familiar with these cartridge cases.

Mr. Cunningham, before going on to the cartridge cases I just handed you, could you explain when you received the bullets which are comprised in the last three exhibits, and who you received them from, and how they were presented to you?

Mr. CUNNINGHAM. Yes, sir. Commission Exhibit 145 consists of the two cartridges that we received—the FBI received from the U.S. Secret Service. We received them on December 3, 1963.

That is correct. They were personally delivered to the laboratory by Special Agent Orrin Bartlett of the FBI, who is a liaison agent with the Secret Service. And he delivered them to us on December 3, 1963.

Mr. EISENBERG. And did he identify them in any way to you when he delivered them? Did he describe their origin to you?

Mr. CUNNINGHAM. No, sir; he did not describe them to us.

Mr. EISENBERG. All right. Could you go on to the next group of five cartridges?

Mr. CUNNINGHAM. Yes. I don't know the exhibit number.

Mr. EISENBERG. That is Exhibit 592.

Mr. CUNNINGHAM. Commission Exhibit 592 was received in the FBI Laboratory from the Dallas office of the FBI on November 30, 1963.

Mr. EISENBERG. Can you tell us who you received them from?

Mr. CUNNINGHAM. The Dallas office of the FBI. I have no first-hand knowledge. I know that they were received from the Dallas Police Department—but that was due to what I have read in an FBI investigative report. The laboratory received them from the Dallas office on November 30.

Mr. EISENBERG. Can you go on to the last group of four bullets?

Mr. CUNNINGHAM. Commission Exhibit 518 was also received from the Dallas office of the FBI on November 30, 1963.

Mr. EISENBERG. Now, for the record, I would like to state that to the best of my knowledge the group of two and the group of four bullets, which together total six, were taken by the Dallas Police from the chamber of the revolver which is Exhibit 143, after the apprehension of Lee Harvey Oswald. They were then split into two groups of two and four as we have them now, two bullets being given to the Secret Service and eventually, as Mr. Cunningham relates, to the FBI, and four bullets going to the Dallas office of the FBI.

The group of five bullets was taken from a pocket of Lee Harvey Oswald, following his apprehension on November 22 and was kept separated from the remaining bullets, I believe, merely because they had been taken from a different source—that is, the pocket rather than the chamber of the revolver.

Mr. Cunningham, returning to Exhibit 145, do either of the two cartridges in Exhibit 145 bear any signs of having suffered an impact from the firing pin in the revolver, Exhibit 143?

Mr. CUNNINGHAM. An examination of these two cartridges, the primers of these two cartridges, reveals no marks that could be associated with the firing pin in Commission Exhibit 143, or any other weapon.

Mr. EISENBERG. Are there any nicks on either of those cartridges?

Mr. CUNNINGHAM. Yes. There is a small nick, an indentation, up near the edge of the primer in the Remington-Peters .38 Special cartridge.

Mr. EISENBERG. Could this nick have been caused by the firing pin?

Mr. CUNNINGHAM. There was no indication, from an examination, that that nick had been so caused by a firing pin.

First of all, it is in the wrong position, it is not in the center of the primer. And, also, a microscopic examination of that nick gave no indication that it was made by a firing pin.

Mr. EISENBERG. Did you microscopically examine the bases of both cartridge cases?

Mr. CUNNINGHAM. Yes, sir.

Mr. EISENBERG. Now, turning to Exhibit 518, consisting of four bullets, which, as I mentioned earlier, were, like the two bullets in Exhibit 145, taken from the chamber of the revolver, did you find any nicks in any of these bullets, the bases of any of these bullets?

Mr. CUNNINGHAM. Just by handling, there are bound to be small microscopic scratches of one kind or other. But there was no indication that any of the primers in these four cartridges had been struck by a firing pin.

Mr. EISENBERG. Were these also examined microscopically?

Mr. CUNNINGHAM. They were, individually.

Mr. EISENBERG. When you say there was no indication that they were struck by a firing pin, in your opinion, based on the construction of this weapon, if the firing pin had been drawn back to any extent and then released, would it have left a mark on one of the cartridges?

Mr. CUNNINGHAM. That is—yes and no. It depends on how far it is drawn back. As soon as the hammer internally clears the rebound block, the hammer is then able to go forward and it probably would have fired. But up to that point, the hammer is held back from striking, it cannot—under normal conditions—be made to fire a cartridge.

However, it has been found with this particular weapon, a drop of approximately 3 feet on the hammer would fire a cartridge in the chamber.

Representative FORD. How far back does the hammer have to be drawn in order to fire?

Mr. CUNNINGHAM. That can be shown very easily by holding the cylinder. By holding the cylinder, that distance can be seen, which is approximately ⅜ to ½ inch.

Mr. EISENBERG. The witness is demonstrating.

The hammer, as he says, is going back about ⅜ of an inch.

Mr. CUNNINGHAM. Once you allow the cylinder to rotate, then the rebound block is pushed out of the way, as you can see. Then you can cock the weapon.

Mr. EISENBERG. Could you demonstrate for us the sound which would be heard if you held the cylinder, pulled back, and then released the trigger?

Mr. CUNNINGHAM. Yes. A snapping sound can definitely be heard.

Mr. EISENBERG. There is a very audible snapping sound. Would that snap— that amount of snap—leave a mark on the base of the cartridge case against which the firing pin——

Mr. CUNNINGHAM. Under these conditions it could not leave a mark, because the rebound block is in the way.

Mr. EISENBERG. When you say rebound block, this is a block between the firing pin and the base of the cartridge case?

Mr. CUNNINGHAM. No, sir; it is the block that is forcing the trigger to go forward after it is pulled back. You see, your trigger will snap back. It is done by a spring in the block.

Mr. EISENBERG. To put it differently, this block would prevent the firing pin from emerging from its hole?

Mr. CUNNINGHAM. That is correct. That is exactly it.

Mr. EISENBERG. Now, could the firing pin emerge from its hole without having traveled a considerable distance back? That is, to say, at what point does the rebound block release the hammer?

Mr. CUNNINGHAM. At approximately—well, right there you can hear it. That is a good half inch.

Mr. EISENBERG. Could you pull it back and then release that half an inch to disengage the rebound block?

(The witness did so.)

Mr. EISENBERG. If the firing pin hit the cartridge with that amount of force, do you believe the cartridge would be fired?

Mr. CUNNINGHAM. Yes, sir; I do.

Mr. EISENBERG. Is there any possibility it would not be fired? Any substantial possibility?

Mr. CUNNINGHAM. It would still make a mark.

Mr. EISENBERG. It would make a mark, at any rate?

Mr. CUNNINGHAM. Let me clarify it. It still will not fire because the block will go forward.

Mr. EISENBERG. What will go forward?

Mr. CUNNINGHAM. In other words, the trigger has to be pulled through the whole cycle in a Smith——

Mr. EISENBERG. In order to disengage——

Mr. CUNNINGHAM. Either that, or cocked before the block will be out of the way. When you pull the trigger and you don't release it or if it is in the cocked position and the trigger is pulled and not released, the hammer will stay forward. The firing pin will stay forward, so you can see it out through the breech face, as long as the trigger is pulled. Then when you release the trigger, the rebound block throws your trigger forward, so the weapon can be fired again.

Mr. EISENBERG. You are modifying what you had said previously?

Mr. CUNNINGHAM. Yes.

Mr. EISENBERG. And you do that upon closer examination of the weapon?

Mr. CUNNINGHAM. No; it is on the basis of trying to describe an internal part without seeing it. If you would care to, I can show you what it looks like. I have a photograph of the National Rifle Association breakdown. It would be easier to explain if I could show you what I am referring to.

Mr. EISENBERG. Could you, please?

Mr. CUNNINGHAM. Yes.

Mr. EISENBERG. Before you refer to this diagram, could I take a look at it? Congressman Ford, could I have that diagram admitted into evidence?

Representative FORD. It will be admitted.

Mr. EISENBERG. That will be 593.

(The document referred to was marked Commission Exhibit No. 593, and received in evidence.)

Representative FORD. Mr. Eisenberg, do you want the whole article?

Mr. EISENBERG. I think we might as well put the whole article in, yes.

(To Mr. Cunningham.) Perhaps it would be easiest if you came around here, since the diagram is a small one.

Now, the diagram which you are referring to is on page 61, the second page of this Exhibit 593?

Mr. CUNNINGHAM. Right.

As you can see, it is a diagram with the sideplate removed, which is this portion right here. It is the right-hand side of the weapon. (Witness pointing to revolver.) We are looking down on it with the sideplate on. These four screws hold on the sideplate.

When you pull the trigger of——

Mr. EISENBERG. The sideplate is marked 20 over here?

Mr. CUNNINGHAM. Yes—No. 20 is the sideplate.

Mr. EISENBERG. That is in the diagram.

Mr. CUNNINGHAM. No. 42 in the diagram is the trigger. There is a sear arrangement on the trigger, attached to the trigger. If you cock it, the sear arrangement will go up into a notch on the hammer right there, and hold it back—right in here.

Mr. EISENBERG. That is number——

Mr. CUNNINGHAM. You see, this is the sear.

Mr. EISENBERG. Mr. Cunningham, could you use numbers?

Mr. CUNNINGHAM. Yes. No. 39 is the sear, and the sear is attached to the trigger, which is No. 42 in the diagram.

Mr. EISENBERG. Now, we are referring to the first page of the exhibit.

Mr. CUNNINGHAM. When the trigger is pulled on this particular weapon, or if the hammer is drawn back, there is a notch on the hammer which is engaged by the sear. When the hammer is back you have to pull the trigger to disengage the sear mechanism from the hammer. When you pull back and it is in the notch, that is known as single-action firing.

Also, No. 30 in the diagram is known as the rebound slide or block, and this rebound slide is positioned right behind the trigger on an internal part of the weapon. When the trigger is pulled, the recoil slide runs in a horizontal direction. As you can see by the larger drawing right here—it is a small camming action. It comes up, and is being pushed back.

Mr. EISENBERG. That is in the middle of the second page of the exhibit.

Mr. CUNNINGHAM. Now, do you see the rounded portion of the hammer right here, right in front of the notch?

Mr. EISENBERG. That is No.——

Mr. CUNNINGHAM. Number—on No. 42, the hammer, on the bottom, right next to the notch that the sear engages, is a rounded portion. That is—in actuality, this rebound slide acts as an internal safety, so the hammer cannot go forward unless the trigger is pulled or it is cocked, because it is in the way. It cannot go all the way forward, due to the fact that—right there you can see it very plainly in the schematic numbered drawing on page 2.

Mr. EISENBERG. The number you are pointing to is what?

Mr. CUNNINGHAM. It is on the trigger, number——

Mr. EISENBERG. Forty-two?

Mr. CUNNINGHAM. Not trigger—the hammer, No. 34.

By the way, on the prior 42 I meant 34. I got the wrong number. I was referring to the right piece, but the wrong number.

But you can see this little—it is like a curved portion. It prevents the hammer from going any further forward. The firing pin will not come out of the hole in the breech face.

Now, as soon as you pull the hammer back, the rebound slide, No. 30, is out of the way.

Also, when you pull the weapon through double action, that slide pushes back, and your sear doesn't even touch the groove in the hammer, but it just keeps on going right on through. In other words, you are pulling the trigger strictly against the mainspring all the way. When it is on the notch, it is being held, and the only pressure needed, is to take off the sear.

Mr. EISENBERG. Now, Mr. Cunningham, to focus this line of questioning, Officer McDonald, who has reported that he was in a struggle with Lee Harvey Oswald on November 22d, while Oswald was in possession of this revolver, has stated that—I am reading now from an affidavit, from a letter from Officer McDonald to Mr. J. E. Curry, chief of police of the Dallas Police Force, dated December 3, 1963.

He states in this letter that as he came in contact with Oswald, "I managed to get my right hand on the pistol over the suspect's hand. I could feel his hand on the trigger. I then got a secure grip on the butt of the pistol. I jerked the pistol and as it was clearing the suspect's clothing and grip, I heard the snap of the hammer, and the pistol crossed over my left cheek. I marked the pistol and six rounds at central station. The primer of one round was dented on misfire at the time of the struggle with the suspect."

Now, in light of your examination of this weapon, and your discussion, could you comment on this statement?

Mr. CUNNINGHAM. I personally have fired this weapon numerous times, as well as Special Agents Robert Frazier and Charles Killion. At no time did we ever attempt to fire this weapon that it misfired. It operated excellently and every time we have tried to fire it, it has fired.

It is very possible when he says that he reached across, and he grabbed it, that he locked the cylinder, which I think any trained police officer would do. You want to stop this cylinder from rotating. As soon as you do that, you have actually stopped the hammer falling on a live round, because if the hammer is allowed to go forward again, and it hasn't gotten into the cocked position, the rebound slide, as I was stating before, would block the firing pin from striking the primer of the cartridge.

Mr. EISENBERG. As I understand it, the cylinder is so interconnected with the trigger, that the trigger cannot be pulled all the way back when the cylinder has been firmly grasped?

Mr. CUNNINGHAM. That is correct.

Mr. EISENBERG. And if the hammer has not been pulled all the way back, the rebound slide will not allow the firing pin to strike the cartridge?

Mr. CUNNINGHAM. That is correct.

Mr. EISENBERG. Now, Officer McDonald's statement that the primer of one round was dented on misfire: as far as you can tell, could this statement be confirmed?

Mr. CUNNINGHAM. No, sir; we found nothing to indicate that this weapon's firing pin had struck the primer of any of these cartridges.

Mr. EISENBERG. Now, if the firing pin had struck the primer, it could only have been after the trigger was pulled all the way back, under the discussion you have just given us, is that correct?

Mr. CUNNINGHAM. Or after cocking.

Mr. EISENBERG. Or after it had been cocked and pulled?

Mr. CUNNINGHAM. Yes; if it is in the cocked position, grabbing the cylinder will do you no good; due to the fact that in the very operation of cocking this weapon, the cylinder is rotated, and it is ready to be fired.

Mr. EISENBERG. Now, in either event, the hammer would have traveled almost to the outermost extremity to which it can go. That is, the hammer would have traveled back all the way, whether it was cocked or fired in a double-action manner. If that had happened, what would the likelihood be that upon returning to the cartridge case, it would not fire the cartridge case—that upon returning to the cartridge, the cartridge would not be fired?

Mr. CUNNINGHAM. You mean actually the hammer had gone all the way through its cycle?

Mr. EISENBERG. Yes.

Mr. CUNNINGHAM. I can only say that from my examination internally, as well as having fired this weapon—I found no reason why you would get a misfire with this weapon.

Mr. EISENBERG. Now, if a man had put his hand between the hammer and the point at which the hammer enters, with the firing pin, into the breech face, would that stop the weapon from firing?

Mr. CUNNINGHAM. Yes and no. It is very possible that you can do it. And it hurts, by the way, because the mainspring in this one—you can see the indentation in my thumb—is a very strong mainspring. It would be possible. You could put something in there.

Now, the question is when you pull that object out, would there be enough distance and enough force to set off the primer?

That is quite a moot point, because you could grab the hammer and recock it.

Mr. EISENBERG. Apart from that question, would the man's finger or whatever object he stuck in there be firmly fixed for a second or two, between the hammer and the breech face?

Mr. CUNNINGHAM. It could be.

Mr. EISENBERG. Would he feel the impact?

Mr. CUNNINGHAM. He would definitely feel the impact—if he had a piece of tissue of his hand in between. Now, if a piece of material, of course, went between it which I don't know how it could happen—if you were struggling over the gun, and he said he grabbed the gun—I don't know how he could have anything except a portion of his hand, and I am sure he would feel it if the trigger was pulled.

Mr. EISENBERG. Finally, if he had just grasped the cylinder, and Oswald had pulled back on the trigger, could you demonstrate the sound which might have been heard?

Mr. CUNNINGHAM. Yes; you can hold it, and you get a snapping sound—if the gun is grabbed away forcefully, and he would be really grabbing hard. So there could have been an attempt to shoot and a snap would be heard. Yes, sir.

Mr. EISENBERG. The only thing which is unlikely is that the primer would be dented on the misfire?

Mr. CUNNINGHAM. You would not get any denting if the cylinder was held and the gun was jerked forcibly out of Oswald's hands. You would hear the snap, but you would get no mark on the primer whatsoever.

The same thing he could hear if he jerked it out of his hands and he accidentally, somehow, hit the hammer—you would still get a noise, a snapping sound. But the firing pin would not come in contact with the primer of the cartridge.

Representative FORD. Because of the discussion we had a few minutes ago?

Mr. CUNNINGHAM. Yes, sir.

Representative FORD. Using the diagram that was inserted as Exhibit 593.

Mr. EISENBERG. One final question. Officer McDonald says in this letter, "I then got a secure grip on the butt of the pistol."

Now, would that grip in itself in any way interfere with the action of the pistol—the revolver?

Mr. CUNNINGHAM. I don't know what he means by that.

Mr. EISENBERG. If he means what he says, that is, if he got a secure grip on the butt——

Mr. CUNNINGHAM. If he got a secure grip on the butt, that would take him away.

Mr. EISENBERG. Take him away from what?

Mr. CUNNINGHAM. That would take him away from the cylinder. If you are fighting over a weapon, the first thing is to get it off of you and then get hold of the cylinder. And then you can get both hands on the gun to jerk it away. That is what I would do.

As I say, it is the way we are taught. You want to get the gun off of you first, so you are not in direct line, and then go in and attempt to get it away from the person.

Mr. EISENBERG. Now, suppose the gun was pulled away from Oswald as Oswald had his grip on the trigger, so that he could not get the trigger through the complete cycle. Would there be a snapping noise made?

Mr. CUNNINGHAM. Definitely. If you locked the cylinder and jerked it away, you would get a snapping noise.

Mr. EISENBERG. Suppose you did not lock the cylinder, but for some reason or other the full trigger cycle was not gone through?

Mr. CUNNINGHAM. Then you would also get it. It would be difficult, but you could get it.

Mr. EISENBERG. How hard do you have to pull on that trigger in order to fire the weapon?

Mr. CUNNINGHAM. For double action—that is, without cocking, it is approximately 11 to 12 pounds, which is normal for this type of weapon.

Mr. EISENBERG. Now, I handed you earlier four cartridge cases in a plastic envelope marked Q-74, Q-75, Q-76, and Q-77, also marked C47-C50. Are you familiar with these cartridge cases?

Mr. CUNNINGHAM. I am. I have previously looked at them.

Mr. EISENBERG. Do they have your mark on them?

Mr. CUNNINGHAM. They do. Right on the side of each one, right there.

Mr. EISENBERG. When did you receive these cartridge cases?

Mr. CUNNINGHAM. These cartridge cases were received from the Dallas office of the FBI on November 30, 1963.

Mr. EISENBERG. For the record, I would like to state that these cartridge cases were found in the immediate proximity of the site at which Officer Tippit was killed. They were found on the ground near the street where Officer Tippit was killed on November 22.

Representative FORD. These are the ones that were found in the street near the automobile?

Mr. EISENBERG. Well, either in the street or in a lawn in front of a private residence, or semiapartment house.

Representative FORD. I see. In other words, they were possibly some of those that were on the lawn in the front of 400?

Mr. EISENBERG. Yes, sir; again, for the record only, since this witness is unable to testify as to where they were picked up. The mechanism of this revolver is such that the shells are not ejected until the user decides to eject them—unlike a bolt-action rifle where the cartridge must be ejected where you shoot from.

Mr. Chairman, I would like to have these four cartridge cases introduced into evidence as 594.

Representative FORD. They may be admitted.

(The articles referred to were marked Commission Exhibit No. 594, and received in evidence.)

Mr. EISENBERG. Now, Mr. Cunningham, could you describe the make of these cartridge cases?

Mr. CUNNINGHAM. Two of these cartridge cases are Remington-Peters .38 Special cartridge cases. The other two cartridge cases are Western .38 Special cartridge cases.

Mr. EISENBERG. Now, you examined earlier six bullets which I told you had been—six cartridges which I told you had been taken from the chamber of the revolver which we have been looking at.

Those cartridges were divided into three Remington-Peters and three Western, were they not?

(At this point, Representative Boggs entered the hearing room.)

Mr. CUNNINGHAM. Yes, sir.

Mr. EISENBERG. So that—or 50-50. So that the division is the same, the division of the cartridge cases is the same, as between Remington-Peters and Western, as the division of the cartridges found—which I told you were found in the chamber?

Mr. CUNNINGHAM. Yes, sir.

Mr. EISENBERG. Did you examine the cartridge cases in Exhibit 594 in an attempt to determine whether they had been fired in Exhibit 143, the revolver, to the exclusion of all other revolvers?

Mr. CUNNINGHAM. I did.

Mr. EISENBERG. Can you tell us your conclusion?

Mr. CUNNINGHAM. As a result of my examination, it is my opinion that those four cartridge cases, Commission Exhibit 594, were fired in the revolver, Commission Exhibit 143, to the exclusion of all other weapons.

Mr. EISENBERG. When did you perform this examination, Mr. Cunningham?

Mr. CUNNINGHAM. On November 30, 1963.

Mr. EISENBERG. And how did you make the examination?

Mr. CUNNINGHAM. I first marked these cartridge cases upon receiving them. There were four. I would like to state, first of all that Special Agents Frazier and Killion also independently examined these four cartridge cases, and made the same comparisons that I am going to state. I am telling you what I found—although they independently arrived at the same conclusion.

The cartridge cases were first marked and examined for the presence of any individual characteristic marks on these cartridge cases whereby it would be possible to identify them as having been fired in a weapon. I then test-fired Commission Exhibit 143, using similar ammunition, and microscopically compared the four cartridge cases—one at a time—that is Commission Exhibit 594—with the tests obtained from the revolver, Commission Exhibit 143.

Mr. EISENBERG. I hand you here two cartridge cases, and ask you whether you are familiar with these cartridge cases?

Mr. CUNNINGHAM. I am.

Mr. EISENBERG. And can you describe these cartridge cases to us?

Mr. CUNNINGHAM. Yes. One is a Western .38 Special cartridge case. The other is a Winchester .38 Special cartridge case.

Mr. EISENBERG. And how did you get possession of these cartridge cases?

Mr. CUNNINGHAM. These were test-fired in Commission Exhibit No. 143, by myself.

Mr. EISENBERG. So these are the test cartridges you were referring to?

Mr. CUNNINGHAM. That was a portion of them; yes.

Mr. EISENBERG. Mr. Chairman, may I have these admitted as Commission Exhibit 595?

Representative FORD. They will be admitted.

(The articles referred to were marked Commission Exhibit No. 595, and received in evidence.)

Mr. CUNNINGHAM. I also would like to state that we were test firing Remington-Peters, also.

Mr. EISENBERG. How many test cartridges were fired, Mr. Cunningham?

Mr. CUNNINGHAM. To begin with, three. And we have since fired the weapon many times.

Representative BOGGS. How many cartridges were fired by Oswald?

Mr. EISENBERG. We are going to get into that. This is a difficult question which you are going to have to make a decision on. So I would rather develop that slowly.

I notice that one of the cartridge cases in Exhibit 595 is split on the side, Mr. Cunningham.

Mr. CUNNINGHAM. Yes, sir.

Mr. Eisenberg. Why is that?

Mr. Cunningham. That is due to the oversized chambers of this revolver. As I previously testified, the weapon was originally chambered for the .38 S&W, which is a wider cartridge than .38 Special. And when a .38 Special is fired in this particular weapon, the case form fits to the shape of each chamber. And in one of those cartridges, the metal just let go. Normally it does not; however this one particular case split slightly.

Representative Ford. Does that have any impact on the rest of the operation?

Mr. Cunningham. No, sir. As a matter of fact, I test-fired the weapon originally, and I didn't even know it had split until I tried to eject it.

Mr. Eisenberg. You mentioned before, by the way, that there had been no misfires with this weapon. Approximately how many times was the weapon fired altogether?

Mr. Cunningham. I would have no way of knowing exactly, but I imagine we are approaching close to a hundred times by now.

Mr. Eisenberg. And no misfires?

Mr. Cunningham. And no misfires.

Mr. Eisenberg. Now, Mr. Cunningham, did you take photographs of the cartridge cases which you have just identified as having been fired from 143, and the cartridge cases which are Commission Exhibit No. 595?

Mr. Cunningham. I did.

Mr. Eisenberg. Did you make your identification on the basis of the photographs or on the basis of your examination under the microscope?

Mr. Cunningham. My conclusions were arrived at strictly on the basis of my examinations. These photographs in no way entered into the identification and are strictly for demonstrative purposes.

Mr. Eisenberg. Could you show us those photographs, Mr. Cunningham?

Mr. Cunningham. Yes, sir.

Mr. Eisenberg. Let's take them one at a time, and let's introduce them as exhibits, one at a time. I have here—you have given me five photographs.. Did you take each of these photographs?

Mr. Cunningham. As a matter of fact; I did. I personally took these.

Mr. Eisenberg. And these are photographs of what?

Mr. Cunningham. They are photographs of the individual characteristic marks on the base and in the firing-pin impression on test cartridge cases obtained from Oswald's revolver, and also the marks on the base and in the firing-pin impression on the cartridge cases, Commission Exhibit No. 594.

Mr. Eisenberg. Mr. Chairman, I would like these admitted, if you would, as 596, 597, 598, 599, and 600.

Representative Ford. They may be admitted.

(The documents referred to were marked Commission Exhibits Nos. 596 through 600, and received in evidence.)

Representative Ford. Will the witness explain to the Commission what they mean?

Mr. Eisenberg. Yes; he will. Did you also make a photograph of the breech face of the weapon, Mr. Cunningham?

Mr. Cunningham. I did. I didn't take this photograph. I was present when it was taken. I have compared the negative with the actual breech face of Commission Exhibit 143, and I found it to be a true and accurate reproduction.

Mr. Eisenberg. Could you show us that photograph? May I have that admitted as 601, Mr. Chairman?

Representative Ford. It may be admitted.

(The document referred to was marked Commission Exhibit No. 601, and received in evidence.)

Mr. Eisenberg. Could you show us the area of the revolver which corresponds to the area shown in the photograph, Exhibit 601?

Mr. Cunningham. Yes, sir. The cylinder was first removed to facilitate the photograph. That is very easily done by removing the forward sideplate screw, which is just above the trigger, which allows the crane to slide right out, and the cylinder removed.

The photograph was taken from the right side, looking in toward the firing-pin hole.

467

Representative Boggs. Just the way you are holding the revolver now?

Mr. Cunningham. Yes, sir ; just the way I am holding it now.

Representative Boggs. With the cylinder removed?

Mr. Cunningham. With the cylinder removed.

Mr. Eisenberg. Now, there is a cylindrical-shaped object in the center of that picture, Mr. Cunningham. Could you describe what that is—right in the center of the picture?

Mr. Cunningham. That is known by two different names. It is known as a hammer-nose bushing, or a recoil block. It is—Smith and Wesson presses this particular block in. It forms the hole through which the firing pin comes out of the breech face.

Mr. Eisenberg. That is, the firing pin strikes the center of the cartridge, or the primer, as it is called?

Mr. Cunningham. Yes.

Mr. Eisenberg. Which causes the cartridge to fire. Now, what is the magnification of the photograph of the breech face?

Mr. Cunningham. Of the breech face, it is approximately 17 times.

Mr. Eisenberg. There are a number of markings or lines on this breech face. Are these the microscopic characteristics which reproduce on the cartridge cases?

Mr. Cunningham. That is correct.

Mr. Eisenberg. And are the microscopic characteristics of this breech face individual to this weapon, to the exclusion of all other weapons?

Mr. Cunningham. They are.

Mr. Eisenberg. This is your method of determining that a given cartridge case has been fired from a given weapon?

Mr. Cunningham. The breech face marks, as well as the individual imperfections in the firing pin.

Representative Boggs. Let me ask a very elementary question, the answer to which I used to know years ago, but I have forgotten. Just exactly what does the firing pin do? What happens after that strikes?

Mr. Cunningham. Well, it is easier to start with the cartridge itself. The components of a cartridge are a bullet, a cartridge case, a primer in the base of the cartridge case, and powder.

Now, the primer is made out of a very soft metal that can be dented. These primers at manufacture are filled with, basically, an explosive. For instance, Remington-Peters cartridges have PETN, which is one of Du Pont's explosives. RDX is used as one of the components of Western cartridge cases, as well as lead styphnate, lead azides, and other explosive materials.

When the firing pin strikes, there is a small explosion. Fire is given off——

Representative Boggs. How does that bring about the explosion?

Mr. Cunningham. It is sensitive to detonation by a sharp blow.

Mr. Eisenberg. That is, the primer is sensitive?

Mr. Cunningham. Yes ; it is an explosive. To differentiate from the powder, which is not explosive. Powder burns.

Mr. Eisenberg. Now, I have taken Commission Exhibit No. 591, which consists of an unfired cartridge, and there is a round circle in the middle of the base of that cartridge. Is that the primer?

Mr. Cunningham. Yes. That is actually a separate entity that has been pressed into a hole in the base of the cartridge case.

Mr. Eisenberg. And that is more sensitive to shock than the powder in the cartridge case itself?

Mr. Cunningham. Yes. Powder is relatively insensitive. You don't set off powder by a blow.

Mr. Eisenberg. But the primer is quite sensitive?

Mr. Cunningham. That is normally. I am talking about a normal blow. The primer is very sensitive. I just named a few of the components, but there are many other compounds in priming mixtures, which are considered secret by each company. But I know that they are explosive mixtures. And the actual striking of the firing pin—with enough force—causes a small detonation to occur. The fire given off, goes through holes in the base, and into where the powder is, and starts the powder burning. It is the gases that are given off when powder urns, which actually cause the bullet to move forward—the pressure builds up ehind it, and the bullet goes forward.

Representative Boggs. That is a very good explanation. Thank you.

Mr. Eisenberg. Mr. Cunningham, I wonder whether you could review the ictures with us, and discuss some of the markings which you found in those ictures that led you to decide that the cartridge cases shown therein have een fired in the revolver we have been discussing.

Mr. Cunningham. Yes. The first photograph is a photograph of the breech-ace marks, the individual characteristic marks remaining on test cartridge cases btained from the revolver, and on the C–50 cartridge case that was recovered rom the scene. C–50 is on the left. C–15 is on the right. And the hairline, he magnified hairline down the center separates the two cartridge cases.

Mr. Eisenberg. Now, is the invariable procedure to put the test cartridge n the right and the suspect cartridge on the left? Or at least is that your tandard procedure?

Mr. Cunningham. I usually put the suspect on the left.

Mr. Eisenberg. Well, in the photographs at any rate, in all the photographs e are going to see, the test cartridge is on the right, and the suspect cartridge s on the left?

Mr. Cunningham. Usually.

Mr. Eisenberg. And what is the magnification of this photograph?

Mr. Cunningham. It is approximately 91 times.

Mr. Eisenberg. Could you go on, please?

Mr. Cunningham. Yes. On the left you will see the stamping, "SP", which s in the cartridge case itself. And over here next to the hairline you will see he individual characteristic marks. And you will see similar marks con-inuing on the other side of the hairline.

On the C–15, the revolver side, you will see a dark portion running vertically own through. That is the space that the Congressman was asking about—ow it fits the primer. That is the small space at the top where the primer ts into the base of the cartridge. And over here to the right of that dark 1ark you will see a lighter colored object with more individual characteristic 1arks, that is actually the primer, the individual characteristic marks on the rimer of the test cartridge case.

Mr. Eisenberg. Now, as I understand it, in effect this picture can be viewed s a composite cartridge? That is, the picture on the left begins where the icture on the right ends, in terms of position on the cartridge case?

Mr. Cunningham. In essence; yes.

Mr. Eisenberg. And the point of the picture is to show that when you make his composite, the lines on each case show up as if there were no composite t all, but as if they were simply one case, because they are so close together n microscopic markings?

Mr. Cunningham. Yes; in proximity. And they are brought together.

Representative Boggs. And so similar?

Mr. Cunningham. Yes.

Representative Boggs. What is the magnification again?

Mr. Cunningham. That is approximately 91 times.

Mr. Eisenberg. Are there any dissimilarities on the two—on the test and he suspect cartridge cases, Mr. Cunningham?

Mr. Cunningham. Yes, sir; there are always dissimilarities. However, the imilarities so outweigh the dissimilarities that it is an identification. If there re no dissimilarities, I would be suspicious that it would be faked—using the ame photograph and just cut and put together.

There are always dissimilarities.

Mr. Eisenberg. Can you explain why there are always dissimilarities when he two cartridge cases are fired in the very same weapon?

Mr. Cunningham. The metal is different; one cartridge case is slightly 1arder than another; for some reason the cartridge case wasn't driven back, 1pon firing, into the breech face exactly the same way. In other words, these 1arks are reproducing, but you don't get exactly the same hit. It would not 2e possible to get exactly the same hit time after time with different cartridge 2ases.

469

Representative FORD. What ratio of similarities and dissimilarities do you have to have?

Mr. CUNNINGHAM. There is no ratio. Based upon the examiner's training and experience, he comes to the conclusion that a particular cartridge case or bullet has been fired from a particular weapon. As in this photograph, you can see the dissimilarity is very slight. These are excellent marks.

Representative FORD. There was never any doubt in your mind, then?

Mr. CUNNINGHAM. None whatsoever.

Mr. EISENBERG. You say these are particularly strong marks?

Mr. CUNNINGHAM. These are very, very, good marks.

Mr. EISENBERG. Now, these marks are on the brass, so to speak, of the cartridge case, rather than in the primer?

Mr. CUNNINGHAM. Yes; that is correct. Actually, it is brass, it is nickelplated brass.

Mr. EISENBERG. Is that unusual, to be able to pick up such strong marks in the brass as opposed to the primer of the cartridge case?

Mr. CUNNINGHAM. It is not really unusual; no. It depends upon the particular weapon.

Mr. EISENBERG. Did you also examine the microscopic markings on the primer?

Mr. CUNNINGHAM. I did.

Mr. EISENBERG. And you found what?

Mr. CUNNINGHAM. I could identify the weapon on the basis of the imperfections, individual characteristic marks, in the firing-pin impression.

Mr. EISENBERG. The firing-pin impression. And what about the area of the primer around the firing-pin impression?

Mr. CUNNINGHAM. Yes, sir.

Mr. EISENBERG. In other words, each of these three areas—the brass, the primer, and the firing-pin impression—carries individually characteristic microscopic marks which would be the basis of identification?

Mr. CUNNINGHAM. Yes, you cannot make a flat statement.

Mr. EISENBERG. No; in this case.

Mr. CUNNINGHAM. In this particular case, I knew at the time I was examining it, all of the firing-pin impressions were excellent, and some portions of the breechface marks were. But you cannot say they will mark in exactly the same place, due to the fact that these cases will mark in different areas, they are different cartridges, they have been fired at a different time. You will get good areas, and then in another area your marks will not be sufficient. In other words, it is just the way the cartridge case was driven back at the time of the explosion in the primer, and the bullet is fired.

They can hit slightly different, hit deeper on one side, be lighter on the other. When a primer is set in a little bit deeper, it will not pick up these marks on the primer part, whereas the firing-pin impression can be excellent—one portion of the case will be excellent. But each one is a different examination. And many times they will mark in different places.

Mr. EISENBERG. Could you show us the next photograph?

Mr. CUNNINGHAM. Yes, sir. This is Commission document No. 597. This is a photograph, photomicrograph, rather, of the breech face marks on two cartridge cases. The one on the left is C–49, which is our number C–49, and the one on the right of the hairline is a test cartridge case from this revolver.

Mr. EISENBERG. What is the magnification?

Mr. CUNNINGHAM. This one was approximately 120 times.

Mr. EISENBERG. Is the magnification equal on both sides?

Mr. CUNNINGHAM. It is.

Mr. EISENBERG. Is that true of all the pictures you are showing us today?

Mr. CUNNINGHAM. Yes, sir. The negative is taken at exactly the same time. You are photographing through a single eyepiece, with a focusable hairline down the middle, whatever is on both stages of your comparison microscope.

Mr. EISENBERG. Could you turn that picture around again?

Mr. CUNNINGHAM. Yes.

Mr. EISENBERG. These marking are also on the brass, or outside of the primer?

Mr. CUNNINGHAM. That is correct.

Mr. EISENBERG. And again it is a sort of a composite photograph?

Mr. CUNNINGHAM. That is correct.

Mr. EISENBERG. Now, these markings seem a little less distinct than the others.

Mr. CUNNINGHAM. It is in a different area. On this particular case, the marks are excellent. You can see down in here some nice fine marks, and then the heavier marks coming across there. They are good marks.

Representative FORD. Could you point out, as you look at the photograph, what you consider good similarities, which would help you in the identification?

Mr. CUNNINGHAM. Yes, sir. Now, this is not the only point of similarity. These strictly demonstrate the type of marks. There are many more marks on these cartridge cases, all over the base of the cartridge cases, as well as in the firing-pin impressions. But Mr. Eisenberg asked that we have a photograph to demonstrate the type of marks on each particular cartridge case.

Representative FORD. This is only illustrative, then?

Mr. CUNNINGHAM. That is correct. My identification was not based on this picture. It was based on my complete microscopic examination and comparison of test cartridge cases from the revolver with this particular cartridge case.

Representative FORD. Could you show me the similarities?

Mr. CUNNINGHAM. Yes. You see, you have your large—it is slightly out of focus up towards this end——

Mr. EISENBERG. Excuse me, as you demonstrate this, could you mark with circles and with a number what you are talking about, so when the record is looked at it is clear what you are talking about?

Mr. CUNNINGHAM. All right—up here, near the top, you will find a very deep ridge, which I will mark "1." As you are coming down, you will find another real deep ridge, which I will mark "2."

When you consider this is 120 times, this is actually quite close together, except it has been magnified—you have a set of marks resembling "railroad tracks," which I will mark "3."

You will find over here—you go down to your next step. There are similarities in between there. The next big set of "railroad tracks" I will mark "4."

Then you move down, and you will find another similarity, four nice marks down near the bottom. This whole area is similar. You are going out of focus, but you can see these "railroad tracks." They are running along very nicely, and that is being marked "No. 5."

The next photograph is a photograph—on the left of the hairline——

Mr. EISENBERG. What Commission exhibit is that?

Mr. CUNNINGHAM. No. 598.

On the left of the hairline is our number C–47, the cartridge case. On the right is a test from the C–15 revolver, which is Commission Exhibit 143. These also are breech-face marks in the base of the cartridge cases.

On the right you can see the space between the primer and the base of the cartridge case, and also the individual characteristic marks in the primer.

Mr. EISENBERG. What is the magnification?

Mr. CUNNINGHAM. This is approximately 123½ times.

Mr. EISENBERG. Congressman Ford, would you care for a discussion of this?

Representative FORD. No. The one previously gave the basis.

Mr. CUNNINGHAM. Actually, this seems to be a slightly larger area. You have again the same "railroad tracks," all up and down, going across the two cartridge cases.

Representative FORD. To the layman that seems even more——

Mr. CUNNINGHAM. Demonstrative, yes. I don't know if you saw the photographs of the cartridge cases in the rifle, the assassination rifle. Those marks are just as distinctive as the more demonstrative marks in this particular breech face. But to a trained examiner, they stand out. They are harder to see than those on these particular photographs. And even in these photographs, the photograph you were asking me, they were not quite as vivid as they are on this photograph.

But there, again, it goes back to what I told you—each cartridge case will strike the breech face in a slightly different way, and you don't get complete similarity.

Mr. EISENBERG. To illustrate your point, Mr. Cunningham, I hand you Commission Exhibit 565, which is a photograph, which was explained yesterday, of the cartridge case fired in the rifle, and a test cartridge.

Mr. CUNNINGHAM. Yes, this demonstrates it very well.

This is the very rough surface on the bolt of the assassination rifle.

Mr. EISENBERG. The bolt face?

Mr. CUNNINGHAM. Yes; the bolt face, and it is just as distinctive as these striae on my photographs of the breech-face marks of the revolver.

Mr. EISENBERG. By "striae" you mean lines?

Mr. CUNNINGHAM. Yes; just lines. But it is more difficult to see, due to the character of these marks—even though one type of mark is just as characteristic as the other type.

Mr. EISENBERG. As I understand your testimony, to the trained observer the photograph shown—the cartridges shown in the photographs on 565 can be as easily identified with each other as the cartridges shown on, let's say, 598?

Mr. CUNNINGHAM. That is correct.

Mr. EISENBERG. But to the layman it is easier to see the similarities on 598, with its striae, than 565 with its grosser imperfections?

Mr. CUNNINGHAM. Yes, sir; due to the type of marks on each of the cartridge cases, one is easier for the layman to see.

The next photograph is Commission document No. 599. On the left of the hairline is our number C-48, the cartridge case. On the right is the test cartridge case from Oswald's revolver.

Now, here you asked about what happens—somebody asked what happens on the other side. Here you have the other side. In this particular cartridge case——

Mr. EISENBERG. That is the other half of the cartridge case?

Mr. CUNNINGHAM. Yes, sir. In other words, you are seeing the primer, the space between the primer and the brass on the cartridge case itself—on the questioned cartridge case this time—and the base of the cartridge case of the test is on the right. It looks like it is one. It is just the opposite side of the cartridge case from the other photographs.

In other words, you take the photograph of the most demonstrative marks—which look real good, naturally. The examination is of all the marks. That is the big difference. And this time you will see—it is very demonstrative—on each side of the hairline, a great deal of similarity between these marks.

Mr. EISENBERG. And the magnification here?

Mr. CUNNINGHAM. It is approximately 96 times.

Mr. RHYNE. Why do you vary the magnification?

Mr. CUNNINGHAM. The magnification of every photograph you take, sir, depends on the length of the bellows of the camera. The microscope will have a set magnification. But each time that you focus the length of the bellows can change, which will increase or decrease the magnification. Also with some photographs you mask off areas which are out of focus. You certainly would not want to print a whole negative where you have distortion. You bring into focus one small portion of the surface of that bullet.

If, say, one surface of the bullet is slightly flattened and the other surface is rounded—the rounded surface will be going out of focus much faster than the flattened side, and it would be very confusing. That is the type of thing. You mask differently.

Then when you have the negatives enlarged, you can enlarge one negative more than you do the other. So it can be based either on the length of the bellows, or on the amount you have enlarged it.

Mr. EISENBERG. Is that all the photographs?

Mr. CUNNINGHAM. No, there is one more.

This photograph is a photograph of the firing-pin impression of the C-49 cartridge case, and the firing-pin impression on the test from Oswald's revolver, and this is Commission document 600.

Mr. EISENBERG. And the magnification?

Mr. CUNNINGHAM. 120 times, approximately.

Now, here you have very distinctive marks, but it is much more difficult for a layman to pick them out. That is the reason I have circled these marks and

472

numbered them, 1, 2, 3, 4, 5, 6, on each side of the hairline. On the left is C–49, and on the right is the cartridge case obtained from C–143.

You have this very large, very distinctive imperfection.

Mr. EISENBERG. You are pointing to circle number 1?

Mr. CUNNINGHAM. In number 1. Also, in number 2, it looks like a little set of railroad tracks, and this one with the same shape coming down through. You can see this little piece and this little piece. Over here you have a real small "railroad track."

Mr. EISENBERG. That is number 3?

Mr. CUNNINGHAM. That is number 3. And it looks like a little hump or bump, and that is very distinctive.

There is a slight overlapping here, but you can see it is sort of a V shape—in number 4, very distinctive. Down here you have a Z line with a line through it, number 6. I only brought those out to show six of the similarities. If you go through you can pick out places in the firing-pin impressions, that are similar, by yourself.

Mr. EISENBERG. On the top of each of these photos, C–49 and C–15, there is a large comma-shaped indentation, or comma-shaped mark. What is that caused by, Mr. Cunningham?

Mr. CUNNINGHAM. That is caused by a very large imperfection—a very distinctive imperfection in the firing pin itself. And here it is.

Here I am looking at Commission document 601, the breech face and firing pin. If you will look at the firing pin in this photograph, you will see over on this side, this very large imperfection. It is like a facet—it is a flattened side. It shows up in the photograph of the firing pin.

It is indented—since it is missing from the firing pin, it will show as a flattened area in the firing-pin impression. In other words, what is concave on the firing pin itself, will be convex in the firing-pin impression.

Mr. EISENBERG. If there are no further questions on the cartridge cases, I will move on to the bullets.

Representative FORD. Mr. Boggs?

Representative BOGGS. Just one question. What you are saying is that there is no doubt about the fact that the cartridges that you examined came from this revolver?

Mr. CUNNINGHAM. That is correct.

Representative BOGGS. And, of course, there is no question about the fact that this was Mr. Oswald's revolver. Is that so?

Mr. EISENBERG. That will be proved, I hope, before the end of the hearings. This witness cannot himself testify.

Representative BOGGS. I understand that. I am asking you.

Mr. EISENBERG. There is no question, I don't think, about that. That will be the subject of testimony.

Representative BOGGS. I know—we are not following the exact rules of evidence around here.

Mr. EISENBERG. We will connect it up.

Representative BOGGS. In that connection—how many bullets were recovered?

Mr. EISENBERG. Four were recovered from the body of the officer. But as you will see from the testimony which we will get into right now, that doesn't mean four shots were fired, because there is a slight problem here. I would rather have the witness develop it.

Representative BOGGS. You are being very mysterious now, but it is all right.

Mr. EISENBERG. Mr. Cunningham, I hand you four bullets in plastic cases marked C–251, C–252, Q–13, and C–253, which have also certain other markings on them, and I ask you if you are familiar with these bullets.

Mr. CUNNINGHAM. I am.

Mr. EISENBERG. Are your marks on these bullets?

Mr. CUNNINGHAM. Yes, they are.

Mr. EISENBERG. For the record, I would like to state these four bullets were recovered from the body of Officer Tippit.

When did you receive these bullets, Mr. Cunningham?

Mr. CUNNINGHAM. The Q–13 bullet was delivered to the Laboratory the first

473

time on the morning of November 23d, and it was delivered to the Laboratory by Special Agent Vincent Drain of the Dallas office of the FBI.

Mr. EISENBERG. And the remaining bullets?

Mr. CUNNINGHAM. By the way, it was returned to Dallas, and then it was returned to the Laboratory, delivered again by Special Agent Vincent Drain, of the Dallas office, also, Special Agent Warren De Brueys. They delivered our Q–13 a second time on November 27th.

Representative FORD. When you say "our," what do you mean by "our"?

Mr. CUNNINGHAM. In other words, to facilitate reporting in the Laboratory, we usually give these items a Q or a K number. A Q number is a questioned item, like a bullet from a body, and a known is a gun, the K is a known, like a weapon.

That is for reporting purposes. But since this case began, we have so much evidence, and we have received so much evidence, it was considered practical to reassign a C number by us—like Mr. Eisenberg said, they are C–253, C–252, and C–251. They also have a Q number. Q–13 is C–13. That is the reason why I said "our" Q–13.

Mr. EISENBERG. When did you examine Q–13, Mr. Cunningham?

Mr. CUNNINGHAM. November 23d, the first time. That was when I made my examination. It was returned on the other date. But it was examined on 11–23.

Mr. EISENBERG. Now, Q–13 has in it a brass colored object, as well as a bullet—that is, the box containing Q–13, your Q–13.

Mr. CUNNINGHAM. Yes. That was identified as the button—the button—from the coat of Officer Tippit. The bullet struck that button and when the bullet was removed from the body, the button was also removed.

Representative BOGGS. Went right in?

Mr. CUNNINGHAM. Yes, sir. I have no first-hand knowledge. But that is what it was identified as.

Mr. EISENBERG. Mr. Chairman, I would like these four bullets admitted as 602, 603, 604, and 605.

Representative FORD. They will be admitted.

(The articles referred to were marked Commission Exhibits Nos. 602 through 605, and received in evidence.)

Mr. EISENBERG. When did you receive what are now marked 603, 604, and 605, Mr. Cunningham?

Mr. CUNNINGHAM. They were received in the FBI Laboratory on March 16th of this year, and they were submitted to the Laboratory by the Dallas office of the FBI.

Mr. EISENBERG. When were they examined?

Mr. CUNNINGHAM. They were examined on March 17, 1964.

Mr. EISENBERG. Can you explain the great time difference between the receipt and examination of the first bullet and the receipt and examination of the last three bullets?

Mr. CUNNINGHAM. At your request, you asked us to postpone the examination of these three bullets in order to facilitate other examinations you wished more expedited than the examinations of these bullets.

Mr. EISENBERG. Now you are explaining the time between the receipt and the examination?

Mr. CUNNINGHAM. Yes.

Mr. EISENBERG. Now, can you explain why these three bullets——

Mr. CUNNINGHAM. Oh, between the first submission and the second?

Mr. EISENBERG. Yes; between the submission of the first bullet, and the submission to you of the second three bullets.

Mr. CUNNINGHAM. Well, it is my understanding the first bullet was turned over to the FBI office in Dallas by the Dallas Police Department. They reportedly said this was the only bullet that was recovered, or that they had. Later at the request of this Commission, we went back to the Dallas Police Department and found in their files that they actually had three other bullets.

Mr. EISENBERG. Now, did you examine these four bullets to determine whether they had been fired in the revolver, Exhibit No. 143, to the exclusion of all other weapons?

Mr. Cunningham. I am sorry.

Mr. Eisenberg. Did you examine the four bullets which have just been marked into evidence to determine whether those four bullets had been fired in the revolver, No. 143?

Mr. Cunningham. I did.

Mr. Eisenberg. And can you give us your results, your conclusions?

Mr. Cunningham. Yes, sir.

First of all, Commission Exhibit 602, which is our Q-13 bullet, I found to be a .38 Special, copper-coated lead bullet of Western-Winchester manufacture which had been fired from a barrel having five lands and grooves, right twist. I also found the other three bullets——

Mr. Eisenberg. 603——

Mr. Cunningham. 603, 604, and 605, Commission Exhibits, which are C-253, C-252, and C-251, respectively. I found that 251 and C-253——

Mr. Eisenberg. Could you give us the Commission numbers?

Mr. Cunningham. Commission Exhibits 605, 603, they, too, were .38 Special copper-coated lead bullets of Winchester-Western manufacture, which had been fired from a barrel having five lands and grooves, right twist.

The grooves in the barrel ran in a right-hand direction, a right twist.

Mr. Eisenberg. That accounts for three bullets.

Mr. Cunningham. Yes.

And Commission Exhibit 604, which is C-252, is a .38 Special Remington-Peters lead bullet, which has been fired from a barrel having five lands and grooves, right twist.

Mr. Eisenberg. Winchester-Western, you say?

Mr. Cunningham. No, sir; that is Remington——

Mr. Eisenberg. Let's go over that.

We have 603——

Mr. Cunningham. 602, 603, and 605 are your copper-coated lead bullets of Winchester-Western manufacture.

Mr. Eisenberg. And 604?

Mr. Cunningham. And 604 is a Remington-Peters lead bullet.

Mr. Eisenberg. Now, were you able to determine whether those bullets have been fired in this weapon?

Mr. Cunningham. No; I was not.

Mr. Eisenberg. Can you explain why?

Mr. Cunningham. Yes, sir.

First of all, Commission Exhibit No. 602 was too mutilated. There were not sufficient microscopic marks remaining on the surface of this bullet, due to the mutilation, to determine whether or not it had been fired from this weapon.

However, Commission Exhibits 603, 604, and 605 do bear microscopic marks for comparison purposes, but it was not possible from an examination and comparison of these bullets to determine whether or not they had been fired—these bullets themselves—had been fired from one weapon, or whether or not they had been fired from Oswald's revolver.

Further, it was not possible, using .38 Special ammunition, to determine whether or not consecutive test bullets obtained from this revolver had been fired in this weapon.

Mr. Eisenberg. Do you have an opinion as to why it was impossible to make either type of determination?

Mr. Cunningham. Yes, sir; this weapon, using .38 Special bullets, was not producing marks consistent with each other. Each time it was fired, the bullet would seem to pass down the barrel in a different way, which could be due to the slightly undersized bullets in the oversized .38 S&W barrel. It would cause an erratic passage down the barrel, and thereby, cause inconsistent individual characteristic marks to be impressed or scratched into the surface of the bullets.

Representative Ford. When you say this weapon, will you identify what you mean by "this weapon"?

Mr. Cunningham. This particular revolver, Commission Exhibit 143.

Mr. Eisenberg. So this brings us back to your earlier testimony, that the

475

gun had been rechambered for a .38 Special, which is slightly smaller in one respect than the .38 S&W, but it had not been rebarreled for the .38 Special?

Mr. CUNNINGHAM. That is correct.

The original .38 Smith and Wesson barrel is still on the weapon.

Mr. EISENBERG. So that the .38 Special, when fired in that gun, might wobble slightly as it passes through the barrel?

Mr. CUNNINGHAM. I don't know if wobble is the correct word. But as the bullet is passing down this shortened .38 barrel, we are probably getting an erratic passage, so the marks won't reproduce.

Mr. EISENBERG. Is it possible to say that the bullets were not fired from this weapon, No. 143?

Mr. CUNNINGHAM. No, it is not; since the rifling characteristics of Commission Exhibit 143—this revolver—are the same as those present on the four bullets.

Mr. EISENBERG. Now, you said that there were three bullets of Winchester-Western manufacture, those are 602, 603, and 605, and one bullet of R.-P. manufacture.

Mr. CUNNINGHAM. That is correct.

Mr. EISENBERG. However, as to the cartridge cases, Exhibit 594, you told us there were two R.-P. cartridge cases and two Western cartridge cases.

Mr. CUNNINGHAM. That is correct.

Mr. EISENBERG. So that the recovered cartridge cases, there is one more recovered R.-P. cartridge case than there was recovered bullet?

Mr. CUNNINGHAM. Yes.

Mr. EISENBERG. And as to the bullets, there is one more recovered Winchester-Western bullet than there is Winchester-Western cartridges?

Mr. CUNNINGHAM. That is correct.

Representative BOGGS. How would you account for that?

Mr. CUNNINGHAM. The possibility exists that one bullet is missing. Also, they may not have found one of the cartridge cases.

Representative BOGGS. Are you able to match the bullet with the cartridge case?

Mr. CUNNINGHAM. It is not possible.

Representative BOGGS. So that while you can establish the fact that the cartridge case, the four that we have, were fired in that gun——

Mr. CUNNINGHAM. Yes, sir.

Representative BOGGS. You cannot establish the fact that the bullets were fired in that gun?

Mr. CUNNINGHAM. That is correct.

Representative BOGGS. And you cannot—having the cartridge case and the bullet—you cannot match them up?

Mr. CUNNINGHAM. No, you cannot.

Representative BOGGS. There is no way to do it?

Mr. CUNNINGHAM. No; other than what I have said. In other words, you can tell manufacture. But there is no way of—that I know of—of connecting or identifying a particular bullet having been loaded into a particular cartridge case.

Representative BOGGS. But there is no doubt about the fact that the four cartridge cases came from firing in that weapon?

Mr. CUNNINGHAM. They were fired in that weapon to the exclusion of all other weapons.

Mr. EISENBERG. Now, when you said before that you would be missing a bullet—under the explanation you gave—would you be missing both a bullet and a cartridge case?

Representative BOGGS. Excuse me, before you answer that question. What testimony have we developed with reference to this delay in the transmission of these bullets to either the FBI or to the Commission?

Mr. EISENBERG. Just what you have heard. Would you like to have it developed further?

Representative BOGGS. Well, is this within his competence?

Mr. EISENBERG. I do not think so. I can state for the record myself that about 2 weeks ago I requested—I made a request of Mr. Conrad, who is the

Assistant Director in charge of the FBI Laboratory—that the three Tippit bullets which had not theretofore been examined, be examined. At that point they had not yet been sent from the Dallas Police to the FBI, and no request had apparently been made for them.

Representative Boggs. Well, the FBI obtained one almost immediately.

Mr. Eisenberg. Yes.

Representative Boggs. And then there was how long a delay before the other three?

Mr. Eisenberg. You have the dates there, Mr. Cunningham?

Mr. Cunningham. The date was—we obtained the first one on November 23, 1963, and then——

Representative Boggs. The day after the killing of Officer Tippit?

Mr. Cunningham. Yes; it was delivered at the same time as all the other material. And then it was returned November 17, 1963.

As far as the FBI is concerned, sir, we have no jurisdiction in that case. We were doing the lab work for the Dallas Police Department, but in the investigation of the death of Officer Tippit we do not have jurisdiction.

Representative Boggs. How did the Commission ascertain that these additional bullets were there?

Mr. Eisenberg. Well, upon review of the underlying materials, it developed that while one bullet had been taken out of Officer Tippit as soon as he got to the hospital, which was apparently the first bullet, the one examined November 23, three further bullets were taken out at the autopsy. And since we knew that only one bullet had been examined by the FBI, and since we knew at that point that three further bullets had been taken out, we asked that those three further bullets be examined.

Representative Boggs. What proof do you have though that these are the bullets?

Mr. Eisenberg. Well, again, we will have to connect it up at a subsequent time. They were turned over to the FBI Dallas Office, were they, Mr. Cunningham?

Mr. Cunningham. That is correct.

Representative Boggs. I am talking about the three bullets now, not the first bullet.

Mr. Eisenberg. Yes; turned over to the FBI Dallas Office by the Dallas Police. Now, we will have to connect up by deposition or testimony before the Commission on the origin of those bullets, and proof is not in the record now, as it is not in the case of many of these items, as to origin. However, I have no doubt that we will be able to connect it up and put it all in the record.

Representative Boggs. Has there been any inquiry made as to why there was this delay in removing the other three bullets to the FBI?

Mr. Eisenberg. Well, as Mr. Cunningham stated, I was told since this was not within the jurisdiction of the FBI, they would only examine evidence which was given to them.. And since it had not been given to them, they had not examined it.

When I asked for it, there was a formal request made for them, and they made their examination at that point.

Is that your understanding, Mr. Cunningham? ˙

Mr. Cunningham. That is correct, sir. In other words, we will do laboratory examinations for any duly constituted law-enforcement agency upon request. And we did it in this case. We offer our facilities but do not go out and ask for work. Since we have no jurisdiction in the killing of Officer Tippit, we would make no investigation and therefore, we would have no reason to go and ask for additional bullets, until of course this Commission asked us to, and then we did on behalf of the Commission.

Representative Boggs. Do you have any theory, and this is just a theory, you understand, as to this discrepancy in these results as compared to the cartridge cases?

Mr. Cunningham. Inasmuch as there are three Western bullets, you would be missing one Western cartridge case, and one Remington bullet. You are missing one of each. He could have missed one of the shots. I do not know how many times he actually fired the weapon. But he could have missed once. It is very

477

possible that he could have. And depending on the angle, it would be very difficult to find that bullet unless it struck some close intervening object. Also I have no first-hand information, again, but I believe that some neighbor turned in these cartridge cases to the Dallas Police Department.

Mr. EISENBERG. I believe that is correct.

Mr. CUNNINGHAM. You have received a letter from the Dallas office of the FBI just recently, I believe, setting forth that information.

Representative BOGGS. That would account for one. There would still be another one, would there not?

Mr. CUNNINGHAM. There would be just one cartridge case missing.

Mr. EISENBERG. Is there any other logical theory which could explain the results?

Mr. CUNNINGHAM. Of course, he could have had an empty cartridge case remaining in the weapon at the time he fired it. Then he would only have fired four shots, and then a bullet is still unaccounted for. That would explain it also.

Mr. EISENBERG. In other words, if he had an unejected R–P cartridge case?

Mr. CUNNINGHAM. No—a Western.

Mr. EISENBERG. You mean an unejected Western cartridge case?

Mr. CUNNINGHAM. Yes.

Mr. EISENBERG. And he fired two Winchester and two R–P bullets—now in that case—and, if he then ejected he would get three Winchester and two R–P bullets, would he not—that is, cartridge cases—if he had an extra cartridge case?

Mr. CUNNINGHAM. If he had an extra cartridge case——

Mr. EISENBERG. He would get five cartridge cases?

Mr. CUNNINGHAM. In other words, if he had an extra cartridge case, say a Remington——

Mr. EISENBERG. I was right the first time. Suppose he has an extra Remington?

Mr. CUNNINGHAM. Well, then you would have lost a Western. If he fires four times?

Mr. EISENBERG. Yes?

Mr. CUNNINGHAM. And he has the fifth one in. You would still have to have three Western cartridges loaded in and one Remington cartridge.

Mr. EISENBERG. But then——

Mr. CUNNINGHAM. Which is four.

Mr. EISENBERG. But then you only have to lose one cartridge case. You do not have to lose a bullet and a cartridge case.

Mr. CUNNINGHAM. That is right. You do have to lose one case.

Mr. EISENBERG. And the case you lose would be a Western case?

Mr. CUNNINGHAM. That is correct. Western.

Representative FORD. Is it unusual to have a mixture of this kind in a pistol?

Mr. CUNNINGHAM. Yes, sir. Usually they are all the same brand. Although if you have two boxes—.38 Special cartridges come in boxes of 50. And you will see hand-loaders once in a while. By the way, we found no indication that they had been hand loaded.

Representative BOGGS. Is this a police weapon as well?

Mr. CUNNINGHAM. Yes; and a very good one. Not in that particular caliber. In other words, the caliber——

Representative BOGGS. That is what I meant.

Mr. CUNNINGHAM. .38 S&W is not a popular cartridge in this country. The .38 Special is.

Representative BOGGS. .38 Special is?

Mr. CUNNINGHAM. Yes, sir. That cartridge.

Representative BOGGS. With police forces?

Mr. CUNNINGHAM. We use it. Most of your larger police forces use the .38 Special. It is a better cartridge.

Mr. EISENBERG. Getting back to the example we were using before as a second possible theory—the cartridge case that would be lost would be a Western case, I believe actually?

Mr. CUNNINGHAM. Yes, it would be a Western case.

Mr. EISENBERG. Now, also getting back to a subject we were discussing, I will quote in part from a letter from Mr. Hoover to Mr. Rankin dated March 31, 1964.

"On March 30, 1964, Mr. Eisenberg requested that the Dallas Police Department be contacted to determine whether any additional cartridge cases had been recovered." And I say parenthetically I mean in addition to the four which we have seen here.

"On March 30, 1964, Lieutenant Carl Day, Dallas Police Department, advised the Dallas office of this Bureau that all of the cartridge cases and bullets recovered had been previously submitted to the FBI."

You mentioned or discussed the question of hand loading. Can you describe what you mean by hand loading?

Mr. CUNNINGHAM. Hand loading is nothing more than taking components and by means of a press you make your own cartridges. You put them together.

Mr. EISENBERG. In this process, would you be able to take a bullet of one manufacturer and a cartridge case of another?

Mr. CUNNINGHAM. Yes.

Mr. EISENBERG. You said that you found no evidence that that had been done in this case?

Mr. CUNNINGHAM. We found no sizing marks on the cartridge cases, which after the first time it has been fired, you many times have to resize it, due to the fact that one chamber can be too large. They always full-length resize, for in a police department many officers will be using this ammunition. You might not resize if one were only firing them in one gun. In other words, you are limiting the chambers of your cylinder that they will fit into. But normally they are full-length resized, and from this you get these sizing marks. Actually they are scrape marks from the sizing die.

Mr. EISENBERG. In a hand-loading operation, is the equipment needed bulky or small?

Mr. CUNNINGHAM. It is quite bulky.

Mr. EISENBERG. If Oswald had hand-loading equipment, would it have been likely to have been turned up among his personal effects? Could it be easily missed?

Mr. CUNNINGHAM. You could not miss it; no, sir.

Representative FORD. When you say bulky——

Mr. CUNNINGHAM. A "C" press or an "O" press will stand anywhere from 10 to 12 inches high with a 2-foot handle. Your turret-type would run almost a foot and a half high above the table. And they are all made very heavy because of your full-length resizing—not only on your small revolver cartridges, but for all your hunting cartridges—that takes great pressure. They are heavy duty. And you need quite a bit of equipment. Most of the time there will be a case trimmer, your complete press—there is a primer press, and then you have to have dies for the cartridge you are loading—your sizing dies and your bullet dies that you use to press the bullet into the cartridge case. Then there are all sorts of sundry equipment that go along with hand loading—your powder measurer, which is usually quite large if it is one that will do it volumetrically. True, you can have a balance and weigh out a particular amount for each one, but it takes an awful lot of time. Normally they are volumetric powder measures. You tip it and it puts a certain amount of powder into the cartridge case.

Representative FORD. Is it expensive equipment to buy?

Mr. CUNNINGHAM. Originally, yes. Comparatively so. A good press, I think you can buy one anywhere from $29 to over $100. You will have to invest, I would say, $150 to have a fairly good outfit. But over the years it is a cheap investment. Instead of paying $2.80 a box, or $2.85 a box, you are turning out cartridges, once you have your brass, for—even rifle, hunting cartridges—for about 7 cents, and lead bullet cartridges down to around 3 cents apiece.

Representative FORD. $2.80 a box?

Mr. CUNNINGHAM. I have the component list here from Western. I do not have the cost per box of ammunition, but it can run anywhere from $2.25 all the way up to $6 to $8 for some of your larger hunting rifle cartridges—boxes of 20 in hunting ammunition, boxes of 50 in your revolver and pistol ammunition.

Even buying components, it is comparatively cheap. If you buy them by the hundred, and they will run, for instance the .38 Special, 158 grain lead bullets per hundred, only $2.80, and that is for original components. If you have the brass, your powder cost is negligible—probably a penny a cartridge, half a cent a cartridge for a .38 Special. So it saves you so much money if you are a target shooter, for instance, it is advantageous to do it if you like to shoot.

Mr. EISENBERG. Is that a skilled operation, hand loading?

Mr. CUNNINGHAM. Basically, no. Once you have the basic—if you do any reading on it, and you take your time, and are very careful, it is not a difficult operation at all.

Mr. EISENBERG. Now, would a——

Representative BOGGS. How are these cartridges loaded mechanically—not like this hand loading.

Mr. CUNNINGHAM. It is all done on large machines. They buy their lead, for instance, in rods. They ask for a lead alloy of a certain hardness. Then these machines—they feed in the rods in the bullet-making machines, and they cut them off to length. They have different diameter rods. For a .38 the rod diameter would be approximately .357″ or .358″. Then this machine comes down in a swaging operation.

Another machine puts the knurling around—forming the lubricating grooves, and another groove. They tumble out as fast as the machine can run.

Then you have your case formation. They buy their cases—they look like little cups of copper. Actually it is a copper alloy. And then you go through a drawing process, and then an annealing, and a drawing and annealing, and a drawing and annealing of these brass cases. And then once you get them to approximate length, you full-size them and form the cases. The machine keeps tumbling them out.

And a small lathe—as these cases are going around—turns the case and puts in the extraction groove—all automatically. Another machine comes up from the bottom and puts the head stamp in. Another one is a drilling operation, and it puts in the holes for the primer and also the flash holes into the case. All done automatically. And they tumble into a big box.

Then they take those components and they put them on the line. The primers are all done by hand, except for shotgun primers at Western.

There are girls sitting at these presses who do 50 or 100 at a time. They put guide plates into the machine in which the girls put the primers. They are automatically loaded. All the primers are put in by hand, in essence.

Mr. EISENBERG. Mr. Cunningham, what is the advantage of hand loading in terms of cost, if you do not have your own shells to start with?

Mr. CUNNINGHAM. There again your initial cost is fairly expensive. For instance, for the .38 Special, unprimed cases, the list price per hundred last year, was $4.60 a hundred. The primed cost $5. The primers cost 20 cents——

Mr. EISENBERG. So there is a saving even if you do not provide your own shells?

Mr. CUNNINGHAM. Oh, yes—and the bullets would cost——

Mr. EISENBERG. How many primers?

Mr. CUNNINGHAM. One hundred. And 158 grain lead, .38 Special bullets are $2.80. So $7.80 plus $2.00 worth of powder and you are in business.

Mr. EISENBERG. For $9.80?

Mr. CUNNINGHAM. Yes.

Mr. EISENBERG. And how much would the bullets cost you if you bought them commercially already prepared?

Mr. CUNNINGHAM. I think it is $2.50 per 50.

Mr. EISENBERG. Well, that is more. $2.25 per 50, did you say?

Mr. CUNNINGHAM. $2.85? I never buy any ammunition of that type. I do not know.

Mr. EISENBERG. So for a hundred that would be $5.90.

Mr. CUNNINGHAM. I would say it is closer to $8 per hundred for .38 Special.

Mr. EISENBERG. So it is cheaper to buy them that way than to buy the components?

Mr. CUNNINGHAM. It is cheaper to buy your components when you do not have to buy the cartridge cases.

Mr. EISENBERG. Well, now, is it possible that a gunsmith would buy the components, including new cases, and reload together a case from Western-Winchester and a bullet from Remington-Peters?

Mr. CUNNINGHAM. I don't think that a gunsmith would buy the new cases. That is what I was saying. For instance, used .30–.06 brass, right here in town—you can buy it locally. You can buy National Match Cases, which are excellent brass. I think they are a nickel a piece ; $5 a hundred.

Mr. EISENBERG. Are they as good as the new cases?

Mr. CUNNINGHAM. They are once-fired cases. They are excellent.

Mr. EISENBERG. So in your opinion does the possibility that this discrepancy in bullets and cartridge cases can be explained in terms of reloading make much sense? Does it have a high degree of probability or a low degree of probability, would you think?

Mr. CUNNINGHAM. I am sorry.

Mr. EISENBERG. Would you think it probable or improbable, in light of all your testimony, that the discrepancy between the number of recovered bullets and the number of recovered cartridge cases can be explained in terms of a reloading operation of some kind, or hand loading?

Mr. CUNNINGHAM. No, sir; I do not. It is improbable, because we found no indication of any reloading operation. And in an examination of all the cartridges that we had examined, there was no indication of a reloading operation on those. They looked like factory bullets and factory cases.

Mr. EISENBERG. And if you were going to reload, you would use used cartridges rather than new ones?

Mr. CUNNINGHAM. You would use used brass, because you usually can pick it up at ranges and places like that. You would not even have to buy it.

Representative BOGGS. By that you mean you would use these? (Referring to Commission Exhibit No. 595.)

Mr. CUNNINGHAM. Yes, sir; well—these would be very difficult—in other Mr. CUNNINGHAM. Yes, sir ; well—these would be very difficult on account of the case. They would be hard to resize on account of the fact the case is pushed out due to the rechambering. But they could be used ; yes, sir.

Mr. EISENBERG. When you say there is no indication, would there be an indication if they were resized?

Mr. CUNNINGHAM. Yes; usually—unless the sizing die was extremely clean—usually you will get your resizing marks from the resizing die.

Mr. EISENBERG. And in particular you say the cartridge cases from this particular weapon show a substantial amount of bulge?

Mr. CUNNINGHAM. They do. As you brought to my attention, there is a crack in the one case. I would not care to use this type of brass if I were hand loading. I would find brass that had been fired in a .38 Special.

Mr. EISENBERG. Now, by the way, the various cartridge cases, the four cartridge cases and four bullets that you have identified, and that you obtained from your Dallas Office and other sources, that is, Exhibits 594 and 602, 603, 604, and 605, are these now in the same condition as they were when you originally got them?

Mr. CUNNINGHAM. Substantially. A small sample was taken off the noise which was run spectrographically. But the major portions of all these bullets are the same as when they were received in the laboratory.

Mr. EISENBERG. Did you clean them in any way or alter them?

Mr. CUNNINGHAM. Yes; we had to clean them. They were removed from the body and were bloody. You could not see the surfaces. We had to put them in haemo-sol, which is nothing more than a material that will take out the blood.

Mr. EISENBERG. Is that true of all four bullets? That is true of the last three bullets as well as the original bullet?

Mr. CUNNINGHAM. Q–13 was cleaned of blood tissue in haemo-sol. I do not think I have anything in the notes that the last three were cleaned at all.

Mr. EISENBERG. Would that indicate they were not cleaned?

Mr. CUNNINGHAM. I would say so, because I would have put it down.

Mr. EISENBERG. Was the substance removed from the first bullet tested to see whether it was blood, or did you just assume it was blood?

Mr. CUNNINGHAM. No examination was made of it.

Mr. EISENBERG. Was there any dirt on the cartridge case?

Mr. CUNNINGHAM. I don't remember any.

Mr. EISENBERG. Would your notes show if you had cleaned it up?

Mr. CUNNINGHAM. Yes.

Mr. EISENBERG. And they do not show any cleaning up?

Mr. CUNNINGHAM. No.

Mr. EISENBERG. You said these revolver bullets were sold in boxes of how many?

Mr. CUNNINGHAM. Fifty.

Mr. EISENBERG. Will a storekeeper, a gun man who sells bullets, sell less than 50 usually, in your experience?

Mr. CUNNINGHAM. Maybe some small outfit would. But I just don't know of any around here that will.

Mr. EISENBERG. Now, Oswald was found with two types of ammunition, two makes of .38 Special cartridges. Would you infer than that——

Representative BOGGS. What two types?

Mr. EISENBERG. R.–P., or Remington-Peters, and Western-Winchester.

Mr. CUNNINGHAM. They were Westerns.

Mr. EISENBERG. Would you infer on the basis of your previous statement that he had probably bought a larger quantity?

Mr. CUNNINGHAM. The inference would be that he had at least two boxes.

Mr. EISENBERG. At some point?

Mr. CUNNINGHAM. Yes; either that or he had obtained them from another individual.

Mr. EISENBERG. How about the rifle ammunition, this 6.5 Mannlicher-Carcano rifle ammunition—how is that commonly sold—the Western brand?

Mr. CUNNINGHAM. That would depend on the surplus house, how it is sold.

Mr. EISENBERG. You think that might be sold in less than fixed minimum quantities?

Mr. CUNNINGHAM. Many times that type of ammunition, surplus ammunition, is sold in any amount. They will give a single price, single cartridge price—or they will take off some if you buy them by the thousand or the hundred. That is a lot different than commercially made ammunition for sale in this country.

Mr. EISENBERG. Mr. Chairman, I would like to examine this witness now on the paraffin test, if there are no further questions on the areas we have been covering up to now.

Representative FORD. Any questions, Mr. Boggs?

Representative BOGGS. I don't think so.

Representative FORD. Mr. Rhyne?

Mr. RHYNE. Yes; you said that you were positive that these cartridge cases that were found near where Officer Tippit was killed, and which are over in front of Representative Boggs now, were fired in this gun.

Mr. CUNNINGHAM. As I stated the first time, in my opinion those cartridge cases were fired in that particular weapon to the exclusion of all other weapons.

Mr. RHYNE. And with respect to the bullets that were found in the body of Officer Tippit, you testified that you could not be positive that they were fired by this weapon, Exhibit 143.

Mr. CUNNINGHAM. I could not identify those bullets as having been fired from that gun. However, the rifling characteristics on the bullets are the same as produced by that weapon. Also, I could not identify consecutive tests obtained from that revolver, using .38 Special ammunition, and I could not identify, even though there are microscopic marks on three of these bullets for comparison purposes—I could not identify them with each other.

Mr. RHYNE. Now, based on your many, many years of experience, is this usual or unusual, that you are unable to identify bullets from such a gun under these circumstances?

Mr. CUNNINGHAM. It is not unusual in this particular case. I have had other cases with these rechambered .38 S&W revolvers, that are rechambered to a .38 Special; it is not unusual to not be able to identify them. And especially when the barrel has been cut off 2¾ inches, it even cuts down the possibility a little bit more.

Mr. RHYNE. I was under the impression that you people down at the FBI could identify almost any bullet as coming from almost any gun. That is not strictly true, then?

Mr. CUNNINGHAM. Thank you, but it is not.

Representative BOGGS. How much has this barrel been cut off?

Mr. CUNNINGHAM. About 2¾ inches. You measure the length of the barrel from—you see the cylinder——

Representative BOGGS. Yes.

Mr. CUNNINGHAM. And the portion coming out from the frame, that is a portion of the barrel. And the barrel is measured from there to the muzzle. And the barrel now is 2¼ inches long. The original barrel was 5 inches long—or at least it is similar to the model that would have a 5-inch barrel.

Representative BOGGS. What is the advantage of reducing the length of the barrel?

Mr. CUNNINGHAM. Two things—sales appeal and concealment.

Representative BOGGS. Does it affect the firing quality of the weapon?

Mr. CUNNINGHAM. It affects your accuracy inasmuch as it cuts down on your sight radius. Your longer barrel will be more accurate than a shorter barrel, due to the longer sight radius. The reason that rifles are inherently more accurate than a hand weapon is due, in part, to the longer sight radius. That is the reason the farther you can get away from the sight when you are firing a revolver, the more accurate. Lengthening your sight radius will increase the accuracy.

Mr. RHYNE. Based on your experience in your study of these bullets, do you have an opinion as to whether or not they were fired by this gun?

Mr. CUNNINGHAM. No, sir; I cannot determine that.

Mr. RHYNE. You have no opinion at all?

Mr. CUNNINGHAM. The only thing I can testify to, is they could have, on the basis of the rifling characteristics—they could have been. However, no conclusion could be reached from an actual comparison of these bullets with test bullets obtained from that gun.

Mr. RHYNE. Even though there are a lot of similar markings.

Mr. CUNNINGHAM. There are not; no, sir. There are not a lot of similar markings. They are similar. The rifling characteristics, are the same, or similar. But, in the individual characteristic marks, there are not a lot of similarities. There are not sufficient similarities to effect an identification.

Representative BOGGS. Stating Mr. Rhyne's question negatively, these bullets could have been fired by another weapon?

Mr. CUNNINGHAM. That is correct. Either this weapon or another weapon which has the same rifling characteristics.

Representative FORD. You are limiting that to the bullets now?

Mr. CUNNINGHAM. The bullets.

Mr. RHYNE. Yes; my question related just to the bullets.

Mr. CUNNINGHAM. I identified the cartridge cases.

Mr. RHYNE. He was positive about the cartridge cases, but not about the bullets.

Representative BOGGS. Now, would it be likely to find these cartridge cases, which you can positively identify as having been fired from this weapon—would it be likely that these bullets which you cannot identify as having been fired from this weapon—would it be likely that they would be fired from another weapon under those circumstances?

Mr. CUNNINGHAM. Well, that, sir, depends on other extraneous facts other than my comparisons and examinations. In other words, I can only testify to what I actually found from an examination and comparison of those bullets with these test bullets from that gun. And as to anything else, I cannot testify. I mean—that would be based upon other facts.

Mr. EISENBERG. Carrying some of these questions a little bit further, Mr. Cunningham, you say that this bullet could have been fired from this gun, and was fired from a gun with these rifling characteristics?

Mr. CUNNINGHAM. Yes.

Mr. EISENBERG. Which you said were five lands, five grooves, right twist?

Mr. CUNNINGHAM. Yes.

Mr. EISENBERG. What about the widths of the lands and grooves? Did you measure those?

Mr. CUNNINGHAM. Yes; they were also the same. In other words, when I say it has similar rifling characteristics—the widths of the lands and the grooves is taken into account the rifling characteristics. It has the same width and number of lands and grooves and a right twist.

Mr. EISENBERG. Now, how many other—well, before I ask that, you have also established that the bullets were .38 Specials?

Mr. CUNNINGHAM. That is correct.

Mr. EISENBERG. And the manufacturer of each bullet?

Mr. CUNNINGHAM. That is correct.

Mr. EISENBERG. Would you say they had been fired therefore from a gun chambered for a .38 Special?

Mr. CUNNINGHAM. Yes; there was no indication that they were fired in a weapon other than .38 caliber.

Mr. EISENBERG. So that the weapon was a .38 Special weapon with five lands, five grooves, right twist, and with the same dimensions for each land and each groove.

Mr. CUNNINGHAM. Yes, sir.

Mr. EISENBERG. Now, would the entire production run of this model conform to that description?

Mr. CUNNINGHAM. Yes. And also there are other models.

Mr. EISENBERG. Other models also produced by Smith and Wesson?

Mr. CUNNINGHAM. Yes; in .38 Special.

Mr. EISENBERG. Could you estimate the number of those guns?

Mr. CUNNINGHAM. May I have the NRA reprint? My estimate comes from the figures that are set forth in Commission Exhibit 593, which states that by 1942 there were a million "Military and Police" revolvers, which is the prior model to the Victory model, which they produced.

Representative BOGGS. That is this model?

Mr. CUNNINGHAM. No, sir. But the model has similar rifling characteristics. You could not distinguish between them. In other words, one is a commercially made gun—this is strictly a wartime gun. Also production of the "S" series continued until 1948, when the "C" series was started, including over one million "M&P" models, including the Victory model, which was this model, were manufactured between 1942 through March of 1948; and since that date, Smith and Wesson has produced over 500,000 "M&P" revolvers in the "C" series, which, when you add them up—there are over two and a half million.

Mr. EISENBERG. Two and a half million?

Mr. CUNNINGHAM. Over 2½ million.

Mr. EISENBERG. Now, apart from specially handmade or equivalent weapons, how many other types of weapons have you encountered which have these rifling characteristics?

Mr. CUNNINGHAM. Other than possibly a Spanish-made copy of the Smith—the Smith is the only one in .38 Special now that will have similar rifling characteristics.

Mr. EISENBERG. Now, when you say Spanish-made, you are referring to the basement type of operation?

Mr. CUNNINGHAM. Yes.

Mr. EISENBERG. Now, this weapon did not produce, and does not produce—that is, the weapon 143—does not produce identical microscopic characteristics from bullet to bullet, you have testified. And you have told us that the reason might be that the weapon was rechambered but not rebarrelled, so that the .38 Special is slightly undersized for the barrel?

Mr. CUNNINGHAM. It has not been rebarrelled.

Mr. EISENBERG. That's right. So when you fire a .38 Special, it is slightly undersized, and this might affect the barrel characteristics? Wasn't that your testimony? That the .38 Special is slightly undersized?

Mr. CUNNINGHAM. Yes; approximately four-thousandths of an inch.

Mr. EISENBERG. Now, could you therefore limit the number of possible weapons from which the bullets might have been fired, not only to the 2½ million

S&W's which you discussed, plus the possibility of Spanish homemade weapons, but also to those weapons, that subcategory of weapons within those 2½ million, which does not produce microscopic characteristics such that you can identify bullets fired from them?

Mr. CUNNINGHAM. No, sir; you cannot, due to the fact that there was also the possibility that the inability to identify consecutive tests from that weapon could be caused from an accumulation of lead or from barrel wear—the barrel was actually physically changing.

Mr. EISENBERG. That is not quite what I meant. Out of every ten S&W 38 Specials, on the basis of your experience, how many do you think would produce rifling characteristics such that you could identify bullets fired from them?

Mr. CUNNINGHAM. Well, you could tell if the rifling characteristics are similar. But as far as the individual characteristic marks, that would be on an individual basis. Much depends on the imperfections in the barrel. Now, if you have some real deep imperfections in a barrel, it would be possible to pick them up each time. Even though you would have a lot of dissimilarities, the similarities would be so distinctive that there is always a possibility you could identify them. But not this weapon.

Mr. EISENBERG. Mr. Rhyne asked before whether it was usual or unusual to get this type of weapon not producing microscopic characteristics such that you could identify the bullet to the gun. You said it was not unusual.

Mr. CUNNINGHAM. It is not unusual.

Mr. EISENBERG. Now, I say out of every 10 such weapons, how many would you expect to be in this condition—that is, in a condition such that you cannot make an identification?

Mr. CUNNINGHAM. I would have no way of knowing that.

Mr. EISENBERG. On the basis of your experience, the experience that led you to say it is not unusual to have this condition?

Mr. CUNNINGHAM. I can only say that you find them, that you cannot identify them, so it is not unusual. But as to numbers, I could not say. When you go back and you take all the hundreds and hundreds of examinations I have made, it is not unusual. But I also will not say that it is usual. I will go to the negative, I will say it is not unusual.

Mr. EISENBERG. Would you agree that out of the 2½ million possible weapons it could only have been fired from a gun which will not produce microscopic characteristics such that you can identify the bullet to the weapon?

Mr. CUNNINGHAM. There is a good indication of that; yes. However, there is mutilation on all four of the bullets. But the three we are talking about, the ones that had marks for comparison purposes, now, even though the possibility is remote, it is still possible that there is mutilation in different areas of each bullet, so you would not be able to identify them. Even if the bullets—even if they had not been mutilated, you maybe still could not identify them. In other words, your mutilation on different parts of each bullet would preclude the possibility of identifying them with each other. So I cannot answer your question positively.

Mr. EISENBERG. Well, Mr. Chairman, I have one subject remaining with this witness. Mr. Cunningham, are you familiar with the paraffin test?

Mr. CUNNINGHAM. I am.

Mr. EISENBERG. Have you administered this test?

Mr. CUNNINGHAM. I have.

Mr. EISENBERG. Can you give us the approximate number of times you have administered it?

Mr. CUNNINGHAM. I don't know the exact number, but I must have performed this test at least 100 times, and probably more.

Mr. EISENBERG. Now, I will state for the record—I know you do not know of this of your own knowledge, Mr. Cunningham—but a paraffin test was performed on Lee Harvey Oswald by the Dallas Police. Three paraffin casts were made, one of the right cheek, one of the right hand, and one of the left hand. There was no reaction on the paraffin test of the right cheek. There was a reaction on the paraffin test of each of the right and left hands.

485

I will now hand you a sketch which was made by a participant in those tests, which shows the distribution of the blue or violet dots which constitute a positive reaction to this test on the left and right hands of Lee Harvey Oswald.

Representative Boggs. Before you do that, Mr. Cunningham, will you describe briefly the procedure on a paraffin test? I want to understand exactly what it is.

Mr. Cunningham. The so-called paraffin test is the making of reinforced paraffin casts, of a person's hands, and then treating either with either one of two reagents. One is diphenylamine, and the other is diphenylbenzidine.

Representative Boggs. Is that when the cast is on?

Mr. Cunningham. That is definitely after it is removed.

Representative Ford. You actually make a cast of the individual's hand?

Mr. Cunningham. Oh, yes.

Representative Boggs. You make the casts. Then you take the casts off.

Mr. Cunningham. You slit it.

Mr. Eisenberg. Can you describe how the cast is made?

Mr. Cunningham. Yes. You first take warm paraffin. Each paraffin melts at a slightly different temperature. What we were using in our tests melts at about 130°. And this hot paraffin is placed on the hands. It is spread on with a brush, or it can be poured over. If you are sure that your brush is absolutely clean and will not react—and we checked all of our equipment so that we were not getting a reaction from the diphenylbenzidine—we let it pour on from the brush. Once you get a coating, you can just brush it on, because then you won't be disturbing any materials on the hands. And after you get a coat on, you take gauze bandages and lay them on top and put more paraffin on them. The gauze does nothing more than to give it reinforcement so it won't fall apart or crumble when it gets real cool. Then you cut them off the hands after they cool. Then they are chemically processed with either diphenylamine or diphenylbenzidine.

Representative Boggs. The cast?

Mr. Cunningham. Yes; the portion of the cast next to the hand.

Representative Boggs. Right. I understand now.

Mr. Eisenberg. Can you explain why paraffin is used? What is the action of the paraffin?

Mr. Cunningham. Well, the warm paraffin has the effect of opening up the pores of the skin and many times material that you cannot get off from washing will be picked up in the sticky paraffin. As it is cooling, the dirt and the foreign material on the hands will become embedded in the paraffin.

Mr. Eisenberg. So the paraffin acts as a base to pick up——

Mr. Cunningham. It acts as a medium in which the foreign material is picked up from the hands.

Mr. Eisenberg. When you add the reagent, what is considered to be a positive reaction?

Mr. Cunningham. It turns a blue color.

Mr. Eisenberg. That is the cast? When you say "it," it is the cast?

Mr. Cunningham. Well, specks on the cast.

Mr. Eisenberg. Dots?

Mr. Cunningham. Yes, or an area of the cast. The theory of the test is that it is a test for gunpowder residues. Now, that is the theory, and it is fallacious, inasmuch as the reagents used in these two tests are not specific for gunpowder residues. Now, it is true that the nitrates and nitrites in gunpowder residues will react positively with diphenylamine and diphenylbenzidine, but they are not specific. They will react—these two reagents will react with most oxidizing agents.

Mr. Eisenberg. Can you give us a few examples?

Mr. Cunningham. Yes. Urine, tobacco, cosmetics, pharmaceuticals, soil, fertilizer—I have a list here of the different families or classes of compounds that will react.

In addition to nitrates and nitrites, substances such as dichromates, permanganates, hypochlorites, periodates, some oxides, such as selenium dioxide and so forth. Also, ferric chloride and chromates and chlorates. The list of oxidizing agents is so large—that will react—that you cannot specifically say it was a gunpowder residue.

Mr. CUNNINGHAM. Supposedly it is to determine whether or not a person has fired a weapon. In actuality, in chemistry it is a good indication that an oxidizing agent is present. The reagents have a valid use in a chemistry laboratory.

Representative Boggs. Let me put the question this way. Given a dozen ordinary people in the ordinary walk of life, what would be the chance of a positive reaction on any one of these 12 people?

Mr. CUNNINGHAM. Excellent, sir.

Mr. EISENBERG. Has the FBI performed an experiment to determine this?

Mr. CUNNINGHAM. Yes; we have. The early sets of tests we ran with diphenylamine. And 17 men were involved in this test. Each man fired five shots from a .38 caliber revolver. Both the firing hand and the hand that was not involved in the firing were treated with parffin casts, and then those casts treated with diphenylamine. A total of eight men showed negative or essentially negative results on both hands. A total of three men showed positive results on the idle hand, but negative on the firing hand. Two men showed positive results on their firing hand and negative results on their idle hands. And four men showed positive on both hands, after having fired only with their right hands. That was the first test we ran.

The second test—we used people who had not washed their hands in any way. They were going about their duties during the day. Their hands were soiled. Nine people fired weapons out of 20—20 people just had the casts made.

The first person fired a revolver. Both right hand and left hand were positive. The second person fired a revolver. Both hands positive. A person fired an automatic pistol, where you would not expect to find residue. Both hands positive. Shooting with the right hand only, again one with a revolver and three people firing automatics, all positive. Shooting with the left hand only, one person with a revolver, one with an automatic, both hands positive.

Now, of the 20 people that had not come in contact with a gun—they definitely had just gone about their business—every one of them showed positive tests on either or both hands. A heavy smoker, for instance, would come up positive in the area of the hand where you expect to find residues from firing a gun.

Representative FORD. That is the hand that you use for smoking?

Mr. CUNNINGHAM. That's correct. And I noticed you with your pipe. You are also sure to react because you touch the tobacco in your pipe. You do it unconsciously. During another test we performed recently I did not know that the diphenylbenzidine was on the corner of the cast I was trying to pick up to wash off. I just touched it, and both my fingers which had touched my cigar turned a blue color. That is how sensitive it is.

Now, of these 20 people—true there were some that had one hand that did not get a reaction, but they all got a reaction, one hand or another, or both.

Now, recently in connection with the assassination we made casts—the three of us, Special Agents Frazier, Killion, and myself, for neutron-activation. However, two of the casts we treated with diphenylbenzidine. We obtained a cast of the left hand after firing this particular revolver four times and reloading. We obtained a cast of the right hand after firing that revolver four times, and reloading. We treated both casts, fronts and backs with diphenylbenzidine. This particular one was run on me. I washed my hands thoroughly with green soap—and the green soap, by the way, did not react because we checked it—the gauze used and the parffin were all checked, to see if they would react, and they did not. We found numerous, numerous reactions on the casts of both hand. And I did not fire a weapon with my left hand. However, as I previously showed you, when I demonstrated how you ejected cartridge cases, all of those residues showed up, as well as, I am sure, other foreign material that the parffin removed from my hands. And there were reactions on both hands, fronts and backs.

Now, theoretically, you should not find them on the backs over here, because I had my left hand behind me, and you would find it on the palm. We found reactions everywhere on the casts.

Representative FORD. It is 12:30 now. We will recess until 2 o'clock this afternoon.

(Whereupon, at 12:30 p.m., the President's Commission recessed.)

Afternoon Session

TESTIMONY OF CORTLANDT CUNNINGHAM RESUMED

The President's Commission reconvened at 2 p.m.

Mr. DULLES. You are still under oath, Mr. Cunningham, so we won't swear you again. Will you proceed?

Mr. EISENBERG. Mr. Cunningham, I would like to take up a few things relating to this morning's testimony and then we will go back to paraffin test.

First, I hand you two bullets and I ask you whether you are familiar with these bullets?

Mr. CUNNINGHAM. I am.

Mr. EISENBERG. Is your mark on those bullets?

Mr. CUNNINGHAM. On the nose; yes.

Mr. EISENBERG. Can you identify them to us?

Mr. CUNNINGHAM. These are two of the tests that I fired from Commission Exhibit 143, Oswald's revolver.

Mr. EISENBERG. One is a——

Mr. CUNNINGHAM. One of them is a copper-coated lead bullet. In this case, I know that it is Western, because that was the cartridge I used, and the other one is a Winchester .38 Special lead bullet.

Mr. EISENBERG. Mr. Chairman, may I have these admitted in evidence as Commission Exhibit 606?

Mr. DULLES. They may be admitted as 606.

(The bullets referred to were marked Commission Exhibit No. 606, and received in evidence.)

Mr. EISENBERG. Now, using these bullets as demonstrations, could you tell us how you determined that the bullets that were recovered from the body of Officer Tippit, which you looked at this morning, and those were Exhibits 602 through 604, were respectively a Western-Winchester .38 Special and a Remington-Peters .38 Special?

Mr. CUNNINGHAM. Yes, sir; however, I couldn't do it with these two bullets.

Mr. EISENBERG. Sure, use 602 to——

Mr. CUNNINGHAM. The copper-coated lead bullet. I could use and I did use it—I made a photograph.

Mr. EISENBERG. Before we discuss that further, let's see if we can mark that for identification. Can you describe what is in this photograph?

Mr. CUNNINGHAM. Yes. It is a photograph of four bullets. The first bullet starting from the left is Commission Exhibit No. 604. As you can see right on the label, it is Q-501, which would be Commission Exhibit 604. The next bullet to it is a test bullet that I fired from Commission Exhibit 143, which is a known 158-grain lead bullet of Remington-Peters manufacture.

The third bullet in the photograph is our number C-253, which is Commission Exhibit No. 603. And the fourth bullet in the photograph is this particular bullet which you have given Commission Exhibit 606. It is a copper-coated lead bullet of Western manufacture.

Mr. EISENBERG. Did you take this photograph?

Mr. CUNNINGHAM. I was present when it was taken. I compared the bullets with the negative, and I can testify that this photograph is a true representation—an accurate representation of the four bullets that were photographed.

Mr. DULLES. And this photograph is Commission Exhibit No.——

Mr. EISENBERG. If you will admit it into evidence, it will be 607.

Mr. DULLES. It may be admitted.

(The photograph referred to was marked Commission Exhibit No. 607 and was received in evidence.)

(At this point Representative Ford entered the hearing room.)

Mr. DULLES. All right.

Mr. EISENBERG. Mr. Cunningham, we have introduced a photograph, which is Commission Exhibit No. 607, which shows four bullets labeled "C-252," "R-P," "C-253," and "Western."

Are two of those bullets the bullets which you just identified as Exhibit 606?

Mr. CUNNINGHAM. No; Commission Exhibit 606, the copper-coated Western bullet, is the same bullet that was in this photograph, labeled the Western bullet.

Mr. EISENBERG. Could you hold that up?

Mr. CUNNINGHAM. Yes, sir; that is the bullet.

Mr. EISENBERG. The copper-coated or copper-colored bullet in 606 corresponds with the far right-hand side bullet labeled "Western" in 607?

Mr. CUNNINGHAM. That is right.

Mr. EISENBERG. What about the lead-colored bullet in 606?

Mr. CUNNINGHAM. That is a Remington-Peters 158-grain lead bullet. I do not have that one with me.

Mr. EISENBERG. This would be similar in appearance though to the bullet which was photographed as the "R-P" bullet?

Mr. CUNNINGHAM. No, it isn't.

Mr. EISENBERG. Why is that?

Mr. CUNNINGHAM. Because this is a Winchester.

Mr. EISENBERG. Why isn't it copper coated?

Mr. CUNNINGHAM. The Western Cartridge Division of Olin Mathieson Corp. loads both lead- and copper-coated bullets into their .38 Specials.

As of today, Winchester is only loading—under that brand—uncoated bullets. That is what their latest catalog says.

Only Western is loading copper-coated bullets. They are both made in the same factory—they are both made by the Western Cartridge Division of Olin Mathieson Chemical Corp. in East Alton, Ili.

Mr. EISENBERG. So you didn't give us an R-P test bullet?

Mr. CUNNINGHAM. I did not.

Mr. EISENBERG. I see. Did you use an R-P test bullet in attempting to make your identification?

Mr. CUNNINGHAM. Yes; you asked for our first two tests.

Mr. EISENBERG. I see. Okay. Can you show by use of that photograph, Exhibit 607, how you were able to determine that certain of the bullets found in Officer Tippit were of R-P manufacture, .38 Special, and certain were Winchester-Western?

Mr. CUNNINGHAM. Yes.

First of all, in the manufacture of these bullets, each manufacturer has his own specifications for how they are to look. By that I mean generally that both manufacturers' bullets are similar. They are similar in weight. They are generally similar in size and diameter as well as length. However, the number and the spacing between the grooves—these grooves, the cannelures, are not similar. It is actually a knurling process, you can see the knurling marks.

Mr. DULLES. What is the purpose of those?

Mr. CUNNINGHAM. Lubrication grooves. .38 Specials being lead bullets—in order to keep down excessive leading they put in a lubricant—Remington-Peters—they use a very dark heavy lubricant. Western-Winchester, they use a very light-colored waxy type of lubricant.

Mr. DULLES. Thank you.

Mr. CUNNINGHAM. Up above you will see a small groove. It is nothing more than just a slight groove. That can be caused when the case is crimped, the bullet is crimped into the case.

Representative FORD. That is in the R-P?

Mr. CUNNINGHAM. On both of them, sir.

Representative FORD. That is on both?

Mr. CUNNINGHAM. Yes; you see one here, that has actually been put in. They load up to that certain place and they crimp into that groove, which is known as a crimping groove.

Mr. EISENBERG. When you say crimping groove, do you mean the cartridge is tightened around the case?

Mr. CUNNINGHAM. The neck of the case is tightened around—is crimped into the bullet. The distance between the base to the first cannelure, and the width of the cannelure, the portion of the bullet between the two cannelures, and the width of the next cannelure, is individual with Remington-Peters bullets.

In other words, Western-Winchester bullets are not made with the same width cannelures and the same distances between the two of them. Each manufacturer prefers to have a certain distance between cannelures and a certain width of cannelure, and it is strictly individual to each company. By these specifications—and also another very important thing is the base shape—you can determine whether or not a bullet is of one manufacture or another.

If you will take these two, one of the tests in Commission Exhibit No. 606, you will see that the number, the width and everything about the copper-coated Western and the uncoated Winchester are the same. In other words, they put a flash coat of the gilding metal on the bullet and as I testified previously its chief value is for sales appeal, and, a secondary value to prevent leading.

(Discussion off the record.)

Mr. DULLES. Back on the record again. Continue please.

Mr. EISENBERG. Mr. Cunningham, as of November 22, 1963, how many major manufacturers were there in the United States who were manufacturing .38 Special bullets?

Mr. CUNNINGHAM. Three.

Mr. EISENBERG. Who were they?

Mr. CUNNINGHAM. First, is the Western Cartridge Division of Olin Mathieson Chemical Corp., East Alton, Ill., which manufactures ammunition under the trade names "Western" as well as "Winchester."

The next major manufacturer is Du Pont, and they manufacture in their Remington Cartridge Division ammunition under the trade names "Remington" and "Peters," and the third manufacturer is Federal Cartridge Co. in Minneapolis.

Mr. EISENBERG. How many manufacturers of .38 Special ammunition are there outside the United States, approximately?

Mr. CUNNINGHAM. I would have no way of knowing all of them. I know it is manufactured in Canada by Dominion, and Norma also manufactures it.

Mr. DULLES. What was that name?

Mr. CUNNINGHAM. Norma.

Mr. DULLES. N-o-r-m-a?

Mr. CUNNINGHAM. Yes, sir.

Representative FORD. In Canada too?

Mr. CUNNINGHAM. No, sir; it is in Sweden.

DWM in Germany must manufacture it, I am just recalling these larger manufacturers that should manufacture it. Also, some English manufacturers.

Mr. EISENBERG. How are you certain that one of the bullets found in Officer Tippit was not manufactured by one of the foreign manufacturers, either one you are acquainted with or one you are not?

Mr. CUNNINGHAM. We maintain a Test Specimen and a Standard Ammunition File, and we have foreign ammunition in them, although I don't think we have all of the foreign. But we have never come across a foreign-made bullet with the same physical characteristics as the bullets represented by those removed from the body of Office Tippit.

Mr. EISENBERG. Do you attempt to get a complete file of .38 Special ammunition?

Mr. CUNNINGHAM. We definitely maintain an up-to-date file in our Standard Ammunition File in the laboratory of all domestic manufactured ammunition as well as some foreign, for instance, Norma and Dominion, and we have specimens from other foreign manufacturers.

Mr. EISENBERG. And you say that of the specimens you do have which you feel are as complete as possible you have never come across two types which are similar at least to these .38 Specials?

Mr. CUNNINGHAM. That is correct.

Mr. EISENBERG. Now Mr. Frazier yesterday said that the Walker bullet seemed to be a 6.5 millimeter bullet or may have been fired from the 6.5 millimeter Mannlicher-Carcano rifle, had the same general rifling characteristics as was found on that rifle which is in evidence as Commission Exhibit——

Mr. CUNNINGHAM. 139.

Mr. EISENBERG. Yes; 139.

Now do you have a complete file of 6.5 or a large file of 6.5 millimeter ammunition?

Mr. CUNNINGHAM. We have some.

Mr. EISENBERG. Do you feel it is as complete as your .38 Special file?

Mr. CUNNINGHAM. No; I do not. However, we have never found any foreign manufacturer manufacturing 6.5 Mannlicher-Carcano ammuntion that was similar to this.

From its general appearance, it has all the similarities of a western-world-manufactured bullet——

Mr. EISENBERG. Now this is Commission——

Mr. CUNNINGHAM. In other words, the knurling is typical—the physical characteristics were similar to those of the bullets manufactured by the Western Cartridge Co.

Mr. EISENBERG. This is Commission Exhibit 573, which is the—as to which Mr. Frazier has testified, and which is believed to be the bullet found in the Walker residence.

Are you familiar with it?

Mr. CUNNINGHAM. Yes, sir.

Mr. EISENBERG. And you have examined it as well as Mr. Frazier?

Mr. CUNNINGHAM. I have.

Mr. EISENBERG. Would you say that this bullet was a 6.5-mm. Western copper-jacketed Mannlicher-Carcano bullet?

Mr. CUNNINGHAM. I would.

Mr. EISENBERG. As definitely as you say the bullets which we have just been looking at are respectively Remington-Peters and Western-Winchester .38 Special bullets?

Mr. CUNNINGHAM. Yes, sir.

Mr. DULLES. Could I see that just a moment?

What did that hit, the brick wall of the house?

Mr. CUNNINGHAM. I have no idea, sir.

Mr. DULLES. You don't know?

Mr. CUNNINGHAM. I don't know. I have no first-hand knowledge of it. It is in essentially the same condition as when we received it in the laboratory, and all I know would be what has already been furnished your Commission by report.

Mr. DULLES. Thank you.

Mr. EISENBERG. Now given the fact that that was a 6.5-millimeter Mannlicher-Carcano cartridge, could that have been fired in any other 6.5-millimeter rifle?

Mr. CUNNINGHAM. No, sir; it has to be a rifle that is chambered specifically for this particular cartridge. In other words, there are other 6.5-millimeter cartridges.

Mr. EISENBERG. Now, as I understand it, your conclusion and Mr. Frazier's was only that this cartridge, that this bullet, could have been fired from Exhibit 139 or a rifle with similar——

Mr. CUNNINGHAM. On the basis of the rifling characteristics it could have been fired from 139. However, there are insufficient marks remaining to determine whether or not it had actually been so fired.

Mr. EISENBERG. Now the testimony yesterday as I recall it was that it was fired either from Exhibit 139 or from a rifle with similar, or from a weapon with similar rifling characteristics?

Mr. CUNNINGHAM. That is correct.

Mr. EISENBERG. But according to your testimony it would have to be similar to a 6.5-millimeter Mannlicher-Carcano rifle?

Mr. CUNNINGHAM. No; I did not so testify. You asked if you could fire another 6.5-mm. cartridge other than the cartridge——

Mr. EISENBERG. I asked if that cartridge, if a Western manufacture 6.5-mm. Mannlicher-Carcano cartridge could be fired in a gun other than the 6.5-mm. Mannlicher-Carcano. And you said, as I recall it, "It could only be fired from a gun chambered for that cartridge."

Mr. CUNNINGHAM. That is correct. That 6.5-mm. Mannlicher-Carcano cartridge could only be fired in a weapon that is chambered for that particular cartridge. Further we have never found another cartridge that this particular type bullet has been loaded into.

Mr. EISENBERG. Have you any reason to believe there is another 6.5-millimeter rifle manufactured that is chambered for that cartridge?

Mr. CUNNINGHAM. None that I know of. Maybe I misunderstood you. You mean, if the weapon is chambered for a 6.5-millimeter Mannlicher-Carcano, then that is commonly known as its caliber?

Mr. EISENBERG. Yes.

Mr. CUNNINGHAM. But you can rechamber weapons for another cartridge, as they do all the time with the military surplus Springfield rifles. You can have them rebarreled and rechambered.

Mr. EISENBERG. Apart from rechambering, talking just about original manufacture, do I understand that the only weapon which you have encountered, the only 6.5 millimeter weapon you have encountered which would fire the particular type of cartridge which is Exhibit 573 is the Mannlicher-Carcano rifle?

Mr. CUNNINGHAM. Yes, sir; the various models of it.

Mr. EISENBERG. Okay.

Before the luncheon—are there any further questions along this line?

Before the luncheon recess we were talking about the paraffin test and we were discussing the significance of a positive result, and you had given testimony concerning two experiments which the FBI had run which indicated that positive results might be obtained even by a person who had not recently fired a weapon?

Mr. CUNNINGHAM. That is correct.

Mr. EISENBERG. A paraffin test was also run of Oswald's cheek and it produced a negative result.

Mr. CUNNINGHAM. Yes.

Mr. EISENBERG. Do your tests, or do the tests which you ran, or your experience with revolvers and rifles, cast any light on the significance of a negative result being obtained on the right cheek?

Mr. CUNNINGHAM. No, sir; I personally wouldn't expect to find any residues on a person's right cheek after firing a rifle due to the fact that by the very principles and the manufacture and the action, the cartridge itself is sealed into the chamber by the bolt being closed behind it, and upon firing the case, the cartridge case expands into the chamber filling it up and sealing it off from the gases, so none will come back in your face, and so by its very nature, I would not expect to find residue on the right cheek of a shooter.

Mr. EISENBERG. Would you expect to find residues on a person who has fired a revolver such as Commission Exhibit 143?

Mr. CUNNINGHAM. There again, by its design, you would expect to find something, although there are cases where you won't find it.

Mr. EISENBERG. Why do you expect to find a residue in the case of the revolver as opposed to the rifle?

Mr. CUNNINGHAM. A revolver has a revolving cylinder. There is a space between the barrel and the front portion of the cylinder.

Mr. EISENBERG. I wonder whether you could show that by use of Exhibit 143?

Mr. CUNNINGHAM. You can see when you close the cylinder, and each chamber lines up, there is a few thousandths space between. When the bullet is fired, the bullet jumps across this space and enters the ramp and then into the rifling.

The gases always escape through this small space. The loss is negligible, but the gases are escaping on every shot. After you fire this revolver, you can see residues, smoke deposits and other residues around the entrance to the rear portion of the barrel which is next to the cylinder, as well as on the cylinder itself.

So you would expect to find gunpowder residues on a person's hands after he fired a revolver.

Mr. EISENBERG. Do I understand your testimony to be that there is no equivalent gap in the manufacture of a rifle?

Mr. CUNNINGHAM. That is correct.

Mr. EISENBERG. Did you run any kind of a test with this revolver which would indicate whether it did in fact leave residues?

Mr. CUNNINGHAM. Yes; I did, or we did, three of us, Mr. Frazier, Mr. Killion, and myself. The tests were run on me. I was the one who washed my hands thoroughly. I did not use a brush, I just washed them with green soap and rinsed them in distilled water.

Mr. EISENBERG. The purpose of this washing was what?

Mr. CUNNINGHAM. To remove possible dirt from my hands. I washed my hands. The gun was then wiped off with dilute HCl to get rid of any deposits already on the gun, and I fired it in our bullet-recovery room, four times—and then after firing I opened it up and ejected the cartridge cases into my hand, as I showed you earlier today. The amount of residue that you pick up on your hands from ejection of the cartridge cases was in my hand at the time.

I then, under ideal conditions naturally, went back and had paraffin casts made of my hands and these were treated with a solution of diphenylbenzidine.

The results of this examination were that we got a positive result on both casts, front and back. Many reactions in this area where I had ejected the cartridge cases in my hand were noted.

Mr. EISENBERG. By the way, you testified this morning that many common substances will produce a positive reaction to the nitrate test, so-called paraffin test.

Will the handling of an unclean weapon also produce a positive reaction?

Mr. CUNNINGHAM. Just as much as firing it will. That is what makes this test so unreliable. Handling a recently fired weapon, that is covered with residues—you would get just as many oxidizing agents in the form of nitrates and nitrites on your hands as you would from firing it and in some cases more—especially up here and around here you would.

Mr. DULLES. Does the time between the tests, between the firing and the test, make very much difference, within a few hours?

Mr. CUNNINGHAM. If the residues are on the skin they will react. In other words, if the material has been washed off completely, then you are all through, but if it remains on the skin or is imbedded in the pores of the skin it would still react, but so will so many other things.

Mr. EISENBERG. Just to review for a second your testimony this morning, in the experiments that the FBI ran, a revolver or automatic pistol were used as opposed to rifles, as I recall it?

Mr. CUNNINGHAM. Yes.

Mr. EISENBERG. Were there any negative results following the shooting of the revolver or automatic pistol?

Mr. CUNNINGHAM. None of those were negative results, but they were not run under the same conditions. By the way, with an automatic pistol you shouldn't expect to find any residues, for the same reason as with a rifle—the cartridge is chamber, and the boltface comes in right behind.

Mr. EISENBERG. Could you look at your notes for your first experiment, because as I recall there were some negative results on that.

Mr. CUNNINGHAM. The only negative results were on the 20 people who were run as a control and who had never fired a gun, and even for those people they all got positive reactions at least on one hand.

Mr. EISENBERG. I am talking about the first experiment now, not the second one.

Mr. CUNNINGHAM. The first experiment—yes; that was true. This test was a little bit different.

In other words, they were not just taking people from their work. These people had washed their hands.

Mr. EISENBERG. In other words, their hands were cleaned before they fired the weapon?

Mr. CUNNINGHAM. Yes.

Mr. EISENBERG. But then some of them fired a revolver and still didn't get a residue, as I remember your testimony?

Mr. CUNNINGHAM. That is correct.

Mr. EISENBERG. Did you make a test with the exhibit, with the rifle, 139, to determine whether that left a powder residue on the right cheek?

Mr. CUNNINGHAM. We did.

Mr. EISENBERG. Will you describe that test?

Mr. CUNNINGHAM. Yes; this time we ran a control. We were interested in running a control to find out just what the possibility was of getting a positive reaction after a person has thoroughly washed their hands. Mr. Killion used green soap and washed his hands, and we ran a control, both of the right cheek and of both hands.

We got many reactions on both the right hand and the left hand, and he had not fired a gun that day.

Mr. EISENBERG. This was before firing the rifle?

Mr. CUNNINGHAM. Yes, sir. That was before firing the rifle. We got no reaction on the cheek.

Mr. EISENBERG. Also before firing the rifle?

Mr. CUNNINGHAM. Yes.

We fired the rifle. Mr. Killion fired it three times rapidly, using similar ammunition to that used in the assassination. We reran the tests both on the cheek and both hands. This time we got a negative reaction on all casts.

Mr. EISENBERG. So to recapitulate, after firing the rifle rapid-fire no residues of any nitrate were picked off Mr. Killion's cheek?

Mr. CUNNINGHAM. That is correct, and there were none on the hands. We cleaned off the rifle again with dilute HCl. I loaded it for him. He held it in one of the cleaned areas and I pushed the clip in so he would not have to get his hands near the chamber—in other words, so he wouldn't pick up residues, from it, or from the action, or from the receiver. When we ran the casts, we got no reaction on either hand or on his cheek. On the controls, when he hadn't fired a gun all day, we got numerous reactions.

Mr. EISENBERG. Are there any further questions on the paraffin test?

Representative FORD. Based on your testimony this morning, and what you have told us in the last few minutes, why are paraffin tests conducted and how extensively are they?

Mr. CUNNINGHAM. Many local law-enforcement agencies do conduct these tests, and at their request the FBI will process them. They take the cast and we will process them.

However, in reporting, we give them qualified results, since we frequently will get some reaction. Numerous reactions or a few reactions will be found on the casts. However, in no way does this indicate that a person has recently fired a weapon. Then we list a few of the oxidizing agents, the common ones, such as in urine and tobacco and cosmetics and a few other things that one may come in contact with. Even Clorox would give you a positive reaction.

Representative FORD. Is this a test that has been conducted by law-enforcement agencies for some time. Is it a new test?

Mr. CUNNINGHAM. No, sir; the first test that I reported on here were conducted in 1935.

There may be some law-enforcement agencies which use the test for psychological reasons.

Mr. DULLES. Explain that.

Mr. CUNNINGHAM. Yes, sir; what they do is they ask, say, "We are going to run a paraffin test on you, you might as well confess now," and they will—it is—

Mr. DULLES. I get your point.

Mr. EISENBERG. Following up Congressman Ford's question, does the FBI run paraffin tests except on request from other law-enforcement agencies?

Mr. CUNNINGHAM. We don't, no. Basically, the paraffin test is the preparing of the cast. We don't do that. We will run the chemical processing of these casts at the request of the local law-enforcement agency.

Mr. EISENBERG. To rephrase it, if the FBI is having an investigation by itself in a matter it has primary jurisdiction over, will it use the paraffin test?

Mr. CUNNINGHAM. No; not the paraffin-chemical test.

Representative FORD. Is that because of the feeling that it is not as reliable as it should be?

Mr. CUNNINGHAM. It is the feeling that it is definitely not reliable as to determining whether or not a person has fired a weapon. It is positive, and diphenlybenzidine solution is very positive and very sensitive, as to whether or not an oxidizing agent is present and it is used in chemistry.

Mr. DULLES. You and I with our pipes would be in trouble here, wouldn't we?

Mr. CUNNINGHAM. Yes, sir; I mentioned that this morning.

Representative FORD. He brought it out this morning.

Mr. CUNNINGHAM. I would be willing to state right now if we processed both of your hands you would come up positive, because invariably pipe smokers stick their finger in the bowl and you would get a positive reaction.

I am a cigar smoker, I also would come up positive.

Mr. EISENBERG. I don't have any further questions, Mr. Chairman.

Mr. DULLES. Do you have any further questions?

Representative FORD. I have no questions.

Mr. RHYNE. I take it in sum and substance that these paraffin tests are practically worthless?

Mr. CUNNINGHAM. For the determination of whether or not a person has fired a weapon.

Mr. RHYNE. A gun?

Mr. CUNNINGHAM. Yes.

Now the test is not worthless in chemistry.

Mr. DULLES. What use are they then except possibly from this psychological angle that you have mentioned?

Mr. CUNNINGHAM. We don't——

Mr. DULLES. Are they useful in other ways than but for the psychological reasons you mentioned?

Mr. CUNNINGHAM. As far as whether or not a person has fired a gun?

Mr. DULLES. Yes.

Mr. CUNNINGHAM. No. Even with the mere handling of this weapon I could pick up residues. One could not testify that a person has fired a weapon because he had residues on his hands, which I showed you this morning, for example.

There is a spot right there on my hand, and all I have done is empty the weapon.

Representative FORD. Did the FBI conduct a paraffin test on Oswald?

Mr. CUNNINGHAM. No, sir; the Dallas Police Department did.

Representative FORD. The FBI did not?

Mr. CUNNINGHAM. We did not, sir.

Representative FORD. You didn't analyze it?

Mr. CUNNINGHAM. We did not. We obtained the paraffin casts and another agent in the spectographic unit took them to Oak Ridge and had them subjected to neutron activation, with which I am not familiar. But we did not do the original examination and the reporting. I don't know definitely as to what the Dallas Police Department did.

Mr. EISENBERG. It was under the supervision of the Dallas Police Department. I think a doctor performed the test, I am not sure whether it was a police doctor or not.

By the way, after the paraffin test is run, does the positive reaction stay evident on the paraffin cast?

Mr. CUNNINGHAM. No, it does not, due to the fact you have to wash it off. The solution of diphenylbenzidine is 70 percent sulphuric acid. The solution we were using in these tests was .25 grams of diphenylbenzidine to 100 ml. of 70 percent sulphuric acid, and sulphuric acid is corrosive. In other words, the majority of the solution is 70 percent sulphuric acid.

495

Mr. EISENBERG. So the casts as they are now don't show anything except white paraffin?

Mr. CUNNINGHAM. That is correct.

Mr. DULLES You have no further questions?

Mr. MURRAY. No, thank you, sir.

Mr. DULLES. Thank you very much. Mr. Cunningham. Thank you very much, sir.

TESTIMONY OF JOSEPH D. NICOL

Mr. DULLES. Mr. Nicol, I am presiding at the request of the Chief Justice.

Will you kindly raise your right hand. Do you swear the testimony you will give before this Commission is the truth, the whole truth, and nothing but the truth, so help you God?

Mr. NICOL. I do.

Mr. EISENBERG. Mr. Nicol, would you state your name and position?

Mr. NICOL. Joseph D. Nicol, Superintendent of the Bureau of Criminal Identification and Investigation for the State of Illinois.

Mr. EISENBERG. Could you briefly describe your qualifications in the field of firearms investigation?

Mr. NICOL. I began studying this field in 1941 in the Chicago Police Crime Laboratory under Charles Wilson, remained there as a firearms technician for approximately 9 years, and then moved to Pittsburgh, where I directed and set up the Pittsburgh and Allegheny County Crime Laboratory, also working in the field of ballistics.

Then I went to Miami, Fla., and set up the Dade County Crime Laboratory and worked there for 5 years. I went to Michigan State and taught for 4 and now I am back in Illinois, in Springfield, as Superintendent of the Bureau.

Mr. EISENBERG. Could you tell us approximately how many bullets and cartridge cases you have examined to identify them or attempt to identify them to suspect weapons?

Mr. NICOL. This would number in the thousands, I do not have an exact figure, but our caseload in Chicago is approximately 4,000 guns annually, of which we would make approximately between 10 and a dozen comparisons, so the comparisons that would be conducted by myself or those under my direct supervision would be approximately 50,000 a year. Now this is just a rough figure.

Mr. EISENBERG. Do you have any publications or lectures?

Mr. NICOL. I have one minor publication in the field of firearms. Most of my publication work has been with the "Journal of Criminology" in the area of the technical note and abstract section.

I do not have any major publications in the firearms field.

Mr. EISENBERG. What is your association with that Journal?

Mr. NICOL. I am associate editor of the "Journal of Criminal Law and Criminology."

Mr. EISENBERG. Do you lecture on any regular basis?

Mr. NICOL. At the present time I am lecturing with the University of Illinois in criminal investigation, at the Chicago campus, and prior to that I had been on the staff at Michigan State University for approximately 4 years.

Mr. EISENBERG. What was your education before you went into this field?

Mr. NICOL. I have a Bachelor of Science degree in Chemistry from Northwestern, and during the period that I was with the Chicago Crime Laboratory I got a Master's in Physics also from Northwestern.

Mr. EISENBERG. Mr. Chairman, I would like permission to take Mr. Nicol's testimony as an expert witness in the field of firearms identification.

Mr. DULLES. You may proceed.

Mr. EISENBERG. Now, Mr. Nicol, I will hand you 3 exhibits, 3 items, Commission Exhibits 399, 567, and 569, which I will describe for the record as being a bullet and 2 bullet fragments, and I ask you whether you are familiar with those 3 Commission Exhibits?

Mr. NICOL. May I examine them?

Mr. EISENBERG. Yes, you may.

Mr. NICOL. Yes, this was the exhibit that was given to me as Q–1 in the original transmission.

Mr. EISENBERG. This being which Commission exhibit?

Mr. NICOL. This being 399.

Exhibit 567, this was referred to as Q–2, and also accompanied the other exhibit.

Commission Exhibit 569, this is Q–3.

Mr. EISENBERG. Are your marks on those exhibits?

Mr. NICOL. Yes, I have marked my initials on an unrifled portion of each one of these exhibits. There were also other marks on it at the time I received the specimens.

Mr. EISENBERG. I don't know whether you gentlemen have seen these. These are rifle bullets and bullet fragments.

Mr. DULLES. Is this the one that was found on the stretcher?

Mr. EISENBERG. Exhibit 399 is the bullet that was found on the stretcher. Exhibits 567 and 569 were found in the front portion of the President's car.

Mr. DULLES. These are pretty badly mutilated, aren't they?

Mr. NICOL. Apparently they are separated so that one can't tell whether they come from a single bullet or from two separate projectiles. One is a nose portion and the other is a base.

Mr. DULLES. Is this the one that is the nose portion?

Mr. EISENBERG. You are handing, Mr. Dulles is handing Mr. Nicol Commission Exhibit 569.

Mr. NICOL. No, that would be the base portion.

Mr. DULLES. That is what I thought. Are those different parts of the same bullet possibly?

Mr. NICOL. That is possible, because there appears to be an interval of approximately an eighth of an inch that is not present, so that the area where one begins is not even with the other, so it is not possible to tell, at least I couldn't to express an opinion.

Mr. EISENBERG. That is, they might be two separate bullets or two parts of the same bullet?

Mr. NICOL. Two parts of the same or separate bullets, that is right.

Mr. EISENBERG. I hand you Commission Exhibit 572, which for the record consists of two bullets, and ask you whether you are familiar with those bullets?

Mr. NICOL. These are the two projectiles which were given to me as K–1, and were used by me as standards or tests.

Mr. EISENBERG. Now, when you say "standards or tests," could you amplify that?

Mr. NICOL. On the basis of information on the cartridge, or on the envelope, rather, it was my understanding that these had been fired from a weapon. I have not any personal knowledge of the weapon from which they were fired, but they were used as comparison standards to be compared against rifling impressions on the other three exhibits.

Mr. EISENBERG. Can you tell us how you obtained these four exhibits which you have just looked at?

Mr. NICOL. All these exhibits were obtained from Mr. Eisenberg on March 24, here in this office.

Mr. EISENBERG. And for the record, I obtained these items from the Federal Bureau of Investigation, and transmitted them directly to Mr. Nicol for his examination.

Now, Mr. Nicol, you therefore did not fire the two test bullets which you used in your comparison?

Mr. NICOL. No, sir; I did not.

Mr. EISENBERG. And can you go into that at any length as to—do you have any reason for that?

Mr. NICOL. Well, probably two very basic reasons. One, the matter of time, and secondly the fact that I did not have facilities in the area where I was working for the collection of such tests from a high-powered weapon.

There is the other problem, as developed later, it was apparent that the weapon, even in the firing of this small sequence, was undergoing some changes, and it was my understanding that several shots had been fired since these tests were fired and there might be some likelihood of transitory changes which would make these the best specimens rather than those I might fire now after this series.

Mr. EISENBERG. Again for the record, I had been informed by the FBI that some 50 or more bullets had been fired from the rifle, and that the firing of this many bullets from a high-velocity weapon would seriously alter the characteristics of the barrel.

Representative FORD. Would that be your conclusion, too?

Mr. NICOL. Yes, it would be. It has been my experience that there is a rapid erosion with the high pressures and high temperatures that are involved in a weapon of that velocity.

Mr. EISENBERG. Now, Mr. Nicol, did you examine the three exhibits which were given to you as Q–1, Q–2, and Q–3, and which are now, I believe 567, 569, and 399——

Mr. NICOL. Yes sir; I did.

Mr. EISENBERG. To determine whether or not they had come from the identical barrel as that in which the two—the bullets in Exhibit 572 had been fired?

Mr. NICOL. Yes, I did.

Mr. EISENBERG. Can you give us your conclusions?

Mr. NICOL. Yes. It is my opinion that the same weapon that fired Commission's Exhibit 572 also fired the projectiles in Commission's Exhibits 569, 567, and 399.

Mr. EISENBERG. That would be to the exclusion of all other weapons?

Mr. NICOL. Correct.

Mr. EISENBERG. Did you take photographs of the test and suspect items?

Mr. NICOL. Yes; I did.

Mr. EISENBERG. Under the comparison microscope?

Mr. NICOL. Yes, sir.

Mr. EISENBERG. And have you brought those photographs with you?

Mr. NICOL. Yes, sir; I have.

I might say in passing that this was done in Philadelphia with equipment that I was not thoroughly conversant with, that is, a type that I have used, but each piece has some idiosyncrasy, and considering the time element I do not offer these as the best quality that could be produced under the circumstances.

Representative FORD. Does that make any difference in your judgment or opinion?

Mr. NICOL. No, sir; it doesn't, because my opinion is based upon a visual examination. That is, photography is not an integral part of arriving at the conclusion, except in one facet which I will discuss later.

Mr. EISENBERG. On that subject, have you testified in court on firearms identification?

Mr. NICOL. Yes, sir; many times.

Mr. EISENBERG. Do you usually use photographs when you testify?

Mr. NICOL. No. As a matter of fact, I can't recall an instance in which I have.

Mr. EISENBERG. And why were these prepared?

Mr. NICOL. These were prepared at your request so that there would be documentary evidence of what I was observing. However—and this one, for example, will serve to illustrate the type of photography that is involved.

Mr. EISENBERG. Excuse me a second.

You are holding up a photograph labeled Q–1, K–1. Did you take that photograph, Mr. Nicol?

Mr. NICOL. Yes, this was taken under a comparison microscope.

Mr. EISENBERG. And Q–1 is one of the bullets which I have called the suspect bullets, and K–1 is the test bullet?

Mr. NICOL. Yes, Q–1 would be 399, and K–1 would be one of the projectiles in 572.

Mr. EISENBERG. Mr. Chairman, may I have this photograph admitted as Commission Exhibit No. 608?

Mr. DULLES. It may be admitted.

(The photograph referred to was marked Commission Exhibit No. 608 and received in evidence.)

Mr. EISENBERG. Using this photograph, Mr. Nicol, could you explain some of the markings which led you to the conclusion that Q-1 or Exhibit 399 had been fired from the same barrel through which K-1 was fired?

Mr. DULLES. Before you do that, just for an amateur, would you explain what this is a photograph of, the inside of the barrel?

Mr. NICOL. No, this is a photograph of two projectiles.

Mr. DULLES. Projectiles?

Mr. NICOL. This is the dividing line of the comparison bridge actually. You see a portion of one, of K-1 on one side and Q-1 on the other.

Mr. DULLES. Yes.

Mr. EISENBERG. Is that groove on the right a cannelure?

Mr. NICOL. There is a cannelure, that would be the position at which the projectile is crimped and held in the cartridge case.

Representative FORD. Why wouldn't that show on Q-1?

Mr. NICOL. It would be over here on the other side. You see you only see this much of Q-1, and it may show on Q-1, but it will be over underneath, and you only see this much of it—in half the field.

Representative FORD. This is an overlay in effect?

Mr. NICOL. In a sense, yes, and you are actually masking off half of each one that is represented over here, and masking off half of the K-1 over here.

(Discussion off the record.)

Mr. EISENBERG. What is the magnification of these photographs, by the way?

Mr. NICOL. These were taken on five by seven, I would estimate about 30 diameter.

Mr. EISENBERG. And is the magnification of Q-1 the same as the magnification of K-1?

Mr. NICOL. Yes, sir; the optics are carefully matched in order that they magnify identically.

Mr. EISENBERG. Will that statement be true of all the comparison photographs that will be shown?

Mr. NICOL. Yes, sir. They may not be at the same magnification because I took some of the subsequent ones on a different unit which had different optics.

Mr. EISENBERG. But the left and right side of the pictures would be at the same magnification as each other?

Mr. NICOL. They will be at matched magnification, correct.

Mr. EISENBERG. Why don't you continue.

Mr. NICOL. Starting up at the top you will notice a white patch which represents a land impression on the two projectiles. Immediately below that a large patch with a similarity of the contours of the edges.

Mr. EISENBERG. Mr. Nicol, do you think you could circle that and mark it "1" so that people looking at the record in the future will know what you are referring to? Circle it or make an arrow?

Mr. NICOL. All right.

Below that in approximately this position you will see a line on Q-1 that is found over in the comparable position on K-1.

Below that at a point representing an imperfection on Q-1, slight damage to the projectile, you will notice a line which continues across.

Below that a pair of lines, and then a larger line, below that a pair of fairly deep impressions, and below that another pair of single broad grooves, and then another pair, one of the lines is not in the same size, and then as one gets further down the match is—the bullets are no longer in a match relationship, simply because Q-1 is somewhat distorted as a result of having struck some hard object at the base portion, so that it is oval.

In the case here we are comparing two surfaces of different radii so that they do not—looking at them as a projection they do not match up.

But in this particular region, from approximately this fill-in in the cannelure, there is a sufficient number of points of identification to lead me to the conclusion they were both fired in the same weapon.

499

Mr. EISENBERG. Could you mark that, that you mention as "2"?

Mr. DULLES. This again, at least the "Q" part of this, is the bullet that was found in the stretcher?

Mr. NICOL. Yes, sir; this specimen here.

Mr. DULLES. That is on the left-hand side, is it?

Mr. NICOL. Yes, sir.

Mr. EISENBERG. "Q," as Mr. Cunningham stated, is the FBI mark for "questioned," whereas "K" is the FBI mark for "known."

Mr. NICOL. I retained the same nomenclature so I would not add any unnecessary marks.

Mr. EISENBERG. Now do you have another photograph?

Mr. NICOL. Yes. I took three different positions of Q–1 and K–1. This would be now with the same projectiles under the comparison microscope but rotated to a new position. Each one of these positions shows a similar rotation.

Do you want to mark these?

Mr. EISENBERG. This photograph was also taken by you, Mr. Nicol?

Mr. NICOL. Yes, sir.

Mr. EISENBERG. May I have this admitted as 609?

Mr. DULLES. It shall be admitted.

(The photograph referred to was marked Commission Exhibit No. 609, and was received in evidence.)

Mr. EISENBERG. This is also marked Q–1 and K–1.

That will be Commission Exhibit 609.

Would you discuss that photograph briefly, Mr. Nicol?

Mr. NICOL. This represents a new position of Q–1 and K–1 in a match relationship. Both have been rotated simultaneously through the same angle, and looking at the bottom this time, the large broad area represents a land impression.

Then coming up to a point approximately a half inch above the land edge there is a deep groove paired up with several other deep indentations. These are worth noting because these represented very prominent index marks on both Q–1, Q–2, and Q–3. This was used as, you might say, a point of departure in lining up the projectiles. And again this shows what I would consider evidence of similarity between the rifling impressions on both projectiles.

Mr. DULLES. You wouldn't go further than that—"evidence of similarity"?

Mr. NICOL. Well, I would go so far as to say that based upon the individual characteristics that I observed, these, plus those shown on the other photograph, would lead me to the opinion that they were fired in the same gun.

When I refer to similarities, these would be individual characteristics which would be in the same category as the individual points of identification on a fingerprint. This would be tantamount to the fingerprint of that particular weapon.

Mr. EISENBERG. This is the third photograph?

Mr. NICOL. This is a third photograph of another very prominent mark on both projectiles.

Mr. EISENBERG. Taken by you, Mr. Nicol?

Mr. NICOL. Right.

Mr. EISENBERG. May I have this admitted as Commission Exhibit 610?

Mr. DULLES. It will be admitted.

(The photograph referred to was marked Commission Exhibit No. 610 and was received in evidence.)

Representative FORD (addressing Mr. Eisenberg). Now both Q–1 and K–1 were fired from the Commission Exhibit 139?

Mr. EISENBERG. 139, yes. The FBI fired K–1 from Exhibit 139.

Mr. Nicol has now identified Q–1 as having been fired from the same source as K–1, and, therefore, from Exhibit 139.

Representative FORD. Yes.

Mr. NICOL. This represents a third position of Q–1 and K–1, and in this third position, of course, the first two positions still are in match relationship, that is to say in a relative sense; because of mutilation of Q–1 they would not be precise, there would be some mild adjustments.

What I am illustrating here is a very prominent groove. In this particular case, Q-1 has displaced slightly in the mechanics of photography so that the lower broad shoulder that you see here of this heavy line does not match up. This should come up just slightly above.

The photographer in printing chose this negative rather than another one which would have been superior, and I apologize for this particular photograph.

But this groove, along with the other pattern shown on 609, also appear prominently on Q-2 and Q-3 as prominent index marks.

Mr. DULLES. I don't quite understand 610. This is the last one we have just admitted.

Are these ridges the same? This wouldn't be very clear for the record—this is 609 that I have here.

Mr. NICOL. No, this is not the same view.

Mr. DULLES. That is not the same view at all. It is a different part of the bullet.

Mr. NICOL. This is rotated, both of them rotated simultaneously the same amount to bring those into position here.

Mr. DULLES. Now on 610, I don't see anything comparable on the Q-1 bullet, a ridge comparable on the Q-1 bullet to the one I find on the K-1 bullet.

Mr. NICOL. The dividing line is right through here.

Mr. DULLES. Yes.

Mr. NICOL. And it is this big groove gouged through there.

Mr. DULLES. It stops there at that point?

Mr. NICOL. It stops right here. This is the base of the bullet. The lead is protruding, that is what you see down here.

Mr. DULLES. I see.

Mr. EISENBERG. Could you circle the mark you are discussing now?

Mr. NICOL. That comprises the three positions of the comparison of Q-1 and K-1.

Mr. EISENBERG. Did you also take photographs of Q-2, which is our Commission number 567?

Mr. NICOL. Yes, sir; this particular position is a comparison of Q-2 and Q-1.

Mr. EISENBERG. You took this photograph, Mr. Nicol?

Mr. NICOL. Right.

Mr. EISENBERG. May I have this admitted as 611?

Mr. DULLES. Yes.

(The photograph referred to was marked Commission Exhibit No. 611 for identification and received in evidence.)

Mr. NICOL. Due to the extent of mutilation of these two projectiles, I found it more advantageous to compare Q-1 and Q-2 rather than comparing Q-2 and K-1.

Mr. EISENBERG. In other words, you took Q-1, which you had already identified as having been fired through—from the same rifle as K-1, and compared it with Q-2 in the photograph?

Mr. NICOL. Right.

Mr. EISENBERG. Now, in determining whether Q-2 had been fired from the same rifle as K-1, that is, in determining whether the suspect bullet had been fired from the same rifle as the test bullet, did you match up Q-2 against the test bullet or against Q-1?

Mr. NICOL. I did both. But photographically, I could get a better illustration between Q-1 and Q-2 rather than K-1, because what was apparent was that the heavy groove here, which would be a projection in the barrel, and, of course, being outstanding, would be subject to rapid wear, had changed somewhat between the Q specimens and the K specimens. And so in order to get closer to the actual time of the original firing, it was advantageous to make a comparison of Q-1 and Q-2.

Mr. EISENBERG. But you arrived at a conclusion independently also on the basis of K-1?

Mr. NICOL. Yes, also on the basis of other striations which are not as easily illustrated photographically, the reason being the mutilation of the projectile. And here we are comparing a curved surface with a flat surface, or a curved surface that is flattened out, and the geometry is no longer the same.

501

Mr. Eisenberg. But you did compare Q-2 to K-1 under the microscope?

Mr. Nicol. Yes.

Mr. Eisenberg. And did you arrive at a positive conclusion?

Mr. Nicol. Yes, I did. It is my conclusion that the same weapon that fired K-1 fired Q-2.

Mr. Eisenberg. So the photograph that compares Q-1 and Q-2 is only for illustrative purposes?

Mr. Nicol. Yes, sir.

Mr. Dulles. For clarification purposes, am I correct that Q-2 is the mutilated fractured bullet that was found in the car?

Mr. Nicol. Yes, sir.

Mr. Dulles. And was Q-3 in such a situation that it furnished any useful test or not?

Mr. Nicol. Yes; I could use it for comparison.

Mr. Dulles. That was the other part, or separate part found in the President's car?

Mr. Nicol. Q-2 is the nose.

Mr. Dulles. Yes, I remember that. I looked at that.

Mr. Nicol. You see, what I have to work with is this flat back portion there, as against the round part, and of course the geometry is just not the same.

Mr. Eisenberg. You were pointing just now to——

Mr. Nicol. Q-2.

Mr. Dulles. Q-2 is the nose and Q-3 is the base?

Mr. Nicol. Base portion, correct.

Mr. Dulles. Of the fractured bullet.

Mr. Nicol. Or bullets.

Mr. Dulles. Or bullets.

Mr. Eisenberg. Now, you had just begun to show us photograph 611.

Mr. Nicol. 611 represents, for purposes of illustration—it represents Q-1 on the right and Q-2 on the left, and the major mark that I referred to on the comparison of K-1 and Q-1 is represented by this deep gouge across the field here. There are also other smaller striations that are in the match, above it.

Mr. Eisenberg. You now show me a photograph of Q-1 and Q-3?

Mr. Nicol. Right.

Mr. Eisenberg. Did you take this photograph?

Mr. Nicol. I did.

Mr. Dulles. It will be admitted as Commission Exhibit 612.

(The photograph referred to was marked Commission Exhibit No. 612 and received in evidence.)

Mr. Eisenberg. Again I ask, Mr. Nicol, whether in arriving at your conclusion you made a comparison of Q-3 directly against K-1?

Mr. Nicol. Yes, sir; I did. And the purpose here, as expressed before, is that the illustration seemed to be better between Q-1 and Q-3, as far as the photographic presentation was concerned.

We have here Q-1 on the right and Q-3 on the left. Just down at the base portion of Q-1, just the small portion visible here, there is a group of very prominent marks that are in a match relationship there. These are the same group referred to in——

Mr. Dulles. That is Q-1 and Q-3 that Mr. Rhyne is looking at?

Mr. Rhyne. Yes.

Mr. Nicol. It would be the same area as referred to in 609.

Mr. Eisenberg. Now, does that complete your photographs of the three bullets in Exhibits 399, 567, and 569?

Mr. Nicol. That's right—against Commission Exhibit 572.

Mr. Eisenberg. Now, Mr. Nicol, I hand you Commission Exhibit 573 and I ask you whether you are familiar with this item, which I state for the record is a bullet found inside the Walker residence after the attempted assassination of General Walker.

Mr. Nicol. Yes, sir; I have seen this.

Mr. Eisenberg. Is your mark on that?

Mr. NICOL. Correct.

Mr. EISENBERG. Mr. Nicol, did you make an examination of Commission Exhibit 573 to determine whether it was fired from the same rifle as Commission Exhibit 572, which we have—one of which we have also been calling K–1?

Mr. NICOL. Yes, sir; I did.

Mr. EISENBERG. And what was your conclusion?

Mr. NICOL. I found that within the limits that Commission Exhibit 573 is badly mutilated as a result of having struck some hard object on the side—that the class characteristics generally correspond, that is to say it would be fired from a weapon of comparable rifling to Commission Exhibit 572. Then looking at an area which I can best describe on 609 as being a burr that develops along the edge of the rifling, I found both on the upper surface, which would be the groove impression, and along on the shoulder, quite a few points, individual characteristics, which matched up in each of the positions which were visible.

Because of the mutilation I was not able to put these in the kind of a match relationship that would suggest a positive identification. However, I did not find anything on Commission Exhibit 573 that was incompatible with Commission Exhibit 572, so without going to the degree of saying that there is a positive identification, I would express it this way—that there is a fair probability that Commission Exhibit 573 was fired from the same weapon that fired 572.

Mr. EISENBERG. Now, Mr. Nicol, we had testimony from a Mr. Frazier yesterday of the FBI Firearms Section, and he testified that the FBI does not make probable identifications, but merely positive or negative identifications.

Mr. NICOL. I am aware of their position. This is not, I am sure, arrived at without careful consideration. However, to say that because one does not find sufficient marks for identification that it is a negative, I think is going overboard in the other direction. And for purposes of probative value, for whatever it might be worth, in the absence of very definite negative evidence, I think it is permissible to say that in an exhibit such as 573 there is enough on it to say that it could have come, and even perhaps a little stronger, to say that it probably came from this, without going so far as to say to the exclusion of all other guns. This I could not do.

Mr. DULLES (addressing Mr. Eisenberg). Would you refresh my memory as to this other exhibit—I don't remember—is 573 the actual bullet that was fired and mutilated in the Walker attempt?

Mr. EISENBERG. Yes.

Mr. DULLES. And 572 is what?

Mr. EISENBERG. Those are the test bullets fired by the FBI.

Mr. DULLES. I was a little puzzled by the order.

Mr. EISENBERG. Yes. That is just the order in which they were introduced in evidence.

Mr. DULLES. And really 573 came before 572 in terms of time.

Mr. EISENBERG. Yes.

Mr. DULLES. That clears it up for me.

Mr. NICOL. This is the condition of the bullet.

Mr. DULLES. I have seen the bullet, yes.

Mr. NICOL. It is in sad shape, to say the least.

Mr. EISENBERG. As I understand your testimony, therefore, you feel that there are sufficient identical microscopic characteristics on 572 and 573 to say that they were probably fired from the same weapon, but not enough to say that they were definitely fired from the same weapon.

Mr. NICOL. Yes. My opinion would be based upon the finding of families of lines that would be of the order of two to four fine striations on the burr that I referred to. For a stronger identification, I would want a larger group, I would want perhaps five or six in a given area, all matching in terms of contour as well as position. But this I did not find. And so for that reason, I would not want to express this as a positive finding. However, I would not want to be misunderstood or suggest that this could not have come from that particular gun.

Mr. EISENBERG. Now, you say burr. This is a burr in the barrel of the rifle which produced——

Mr. NICOL. No, I believe it is the result of a displacement of metal as the land impresses into the jacket material, and actually machines up a burr along here on the driving edge.

Mr. EISENBERG. So is there an extrusion on—on the rifle barrel which would produce that?

Mr. NICOL. It may have been true at one time. It appeared at some point in the passage through the barrel, this portion of the jacket curled up and subsequently before it left the barrel was touched by the rifling, so that it is now flat and even. When I refer to it as a burr, it is not raised up. It is even with the rest of this surface. But you can see the definite outline of that burr at the land edge.

(At this point the Chairman entered the hearing room.)

Mr. EISENBERG. Now, would this be caused by an extrusion in the barrel or a concavity in the barrel?

Mr. NICOL. It is probably the result of erosion back at the chamber, back at the rear of the barrel, along the land edge here, and then as the bullet gets to the end of the barrel, pressures decrease, so erosion also decreases, and therefore there is still rifling enough left to press this down and make some impression on the projectile itself.

Mr. EISENBERG. And does this lie within a land impression, or the edge of a land impression?

Mr. NICOL. It would be actually in the groove impression.

Mr. EISENBERG. In the groove impression of the bullet?

Mr. NICOL. Of the bullet.

Mr. EISENBERG. Now, you found this same mark on the Walker bullet as you found on the bullets that were——

Mr. NICOL. All the Q specimens and the K specimens had this characteristic burr. Now, I could not honestly say that this would not be found, the burr would not be found on other weapons of similar construction, similar velocity. However, the fine lines that you can see visible in this photograph, by which an identification could be made, would be the same individual characteristics as any other fine lines on the rifling impression.

Mr. EISENBERG. Now, Mr. Nicol, was this burr in the same position in its relation to the edge of the groove on what we have been calling the Walker bullet as it was in the other bullets?

Mr. NICOL. Yes, sir. And, as a matter of fact, repeated in about the same extent in those land positions and groove positions which are still visible on that projectile.

Mr. EISENBERG. So that you not only have the existence of the burr, but you have it at a characteristic distance from the edge of a groove impression?

Mr. NICOL. Correct. And while the contour matched, this is not as significant, because any two guns manufactured with the same rifling cutter, as perhaps a production weapon like this would be, would have the same contour characteristics. So this would not necessarily be definitive. But the presence of those individual characteristics which are referred to, although not sufficient for a positive, certainly would indicate that there is a possibility that this is fired from that particular gun.

Mr. EISENBERG. Were you able to secure photographs of this Walker bullet under the microscope?

Mr. NICOL. No; I could not, because what I would be comparing would be a curved surface that is flattened out with the test bullets, which would be still in curved geometry. So that while I might get one point in match, the others, you see, would be spread out. So that—actually, an identification of that kind is made in a dynamic fashion. That is to say, one bullet is slid and the other bullet is rotated. So that it is in a sense unfolding the curved bullet so that it resembles in a progressive way the flattened out projectile.

Mr. EISENBERG. Mr. Nicol, I now hand you Commission Exhibit—well, before I go into that, is there any further testimony you wish to give on the subject of the rifle bullets?

Mr. Nicol. No. The only other work I did on it was with respect to an examination of the nose of Q-1 to ascertain whether there was any evidence of ricochet or perhaps contact with fabric and so on.

However, although there were some fine striations on there, there was nothing of such a nature that it would suggest a pattern, like a weave pattern or anything of that nature. So that except for the nick, which I understand has been explained as a site where spectrographic tests were conducted, no further tests were run on either of those projectiles.

Mr. Eisenberg. Yes.

For the record, the nick which Mr. Nicol refers to was in the nose of what was given to you as Q-1—and which I have been informed was a bit of metal that was taken out by the FBI to make a spectrographic test on the chemical composition of the bullet, and therefore was not produced in the process of firing the bullet.

Now, Mr. Nicol, I hand you Commission Exhibits 545, 543, and 544, which for the record consist of three shells, three rifle cartridge cases, which were found on the sixth floor of the TSBD building at the easternmost corner of the south face. I ask you whether you are familiar with those shells?

Mr. Dulles. They bear your mark?

Mr. Nicol. Yes, sir; there is a little JDN inscribed very lightly under the Q position.

Mr. Eisenberg. You are familiar with these shells?

Mr. Nicol. Yes, sir. And these were given to me by you on the same day I received the projectiles.

Mr. Eisenberg. I hand you Commission Exhibit 557, which also consists of—which consists of two expended shells, and I ask you whether you are familiar with them.

Mr. Nicol. Yes, sir. These are the specimens, the two shells which I used as standards or tests to compare against the other three fired cartridge cases.

Mr. Eisenberg. And you obtained those from what source?

Mr. Nicol. I obtained these from Mr. Eisenberg on the 24th of March here in this office.

Mr. Eisenberg. Again for the record, I obtained these shells from the FBI and turned them over directly to Mr. Nicol, and they have been identified earlier as having been fired by the FBI from Exhibit 139, the rifle found on the sixth floor of the TSBD building.

Now, Mr. Nicol, did you examine the shells in Exhibits 543, 544, and 545 to determine whether they had been fired from the same rifle as fired the shells in Exhibit 557?

Mr. Nicol. Yes; I did.

Mr. Eisenberg. And what was your conclusion?

Mr. Nicol. Based upon the similarity of the firing-pin impressions and the breech-block markings, as well as ejector and extractor marks, it is my opinion that all three of the exhibits, 545, 543, and 544, were fired in the same weapon as fired Exhibit 557.

Mr. Eisenberg. Mr. Nicol, did you take photographs of the various shells under the microscope?

Mr. Nicol. I took photographs of the specimen which I referred to, or was referred to, as Q-48, which would be this.

Mr. Eisenberg. Yes. That is Commission Exhibit 545.

Mr. Nicol. These were also taken under the comparison microscope in the same fashion as the other specimens.

Mr. Eisenberg. And these were taken by you?

Mr. Nicol. These were taken by me.

Mr. Eisenberg. Mr. Chairman, I ask permission to introduce this as Exhibit 613.

Mr. Dulles. It may be received.

(The photograph referred to was marked Commission Exhibit No. 613 and received in evidence.)

Mr. Eisenberg. Now, you have extra copies of this photograph?

Mr. Nicol. Yes; I do.

Mr. EISENBERG. By use of this photograph, could you explain some of the markings on Q–48, which is illustrated on the left-hand side and which is Commission Exhibit 545, and K–1, which is on the right-hand side, which is the test cartridge, which led you to the conclusion that both shells were fired from the same rifle?

Mr. DULLES. 545 is one of the shells found on the sixth floor?

Mr. EISENBERG. That's correct.

Mr. NICOL. This was the lone one that was found, I understand.

Mr. EISENBERG. L-o-n-e?

Mr. NICOL. Right.

Mr. EISENBERG. Again, for the record, what Mr. Nicol is referring to is that for some reason the shells were grouped into a group of two and a group of one shells by the Dallas police, apparently on the basis that two shells were very close together, and the third shell was a little further away. But they were actually all within a quite small area. And this is just an arbitrary grouping.

Mr. NICOL. Now, although this compares—is a comparison of Q–48 and K–1, Commission Exhibits 545 and 572—I'm sorry. 557—the same would apply to comparable regions on Exhibits 543 and 544.

I have placed arrows just for fiduciary marks so we can be looking at the same area.

Taking the top arrow, the area running across there is rather broad, an eroded or corroded band, a valley. Below it is a fairly distinct mark. The two small marks appear below it. And then on the projectile, at the middle arrow, there is a broad flat plane. This plane has an irregular contour, and what I have attempted to do is match a projection at the lower portion of this—you also see that the contour at the top is equivalent, insofar as the spacial area.

Below, there are at the lower arrow some additional marks. These begin to come to the edge of the primer. What we are looking at here is actually the primer of the cartridge case, and the marks are the breech-block markings as the result of the pressure of the set-back of the shell.

I have a sequence of these where the division moves across. Do you want to introduce all of them?

Mr. EISENBERG. Yes; I think we should mark them in evidence.

Mr. NICOL. All right.

This would be the dividing line of the comparison bridge moved over a small portion. You see the entire flat area here, but the match has now shifted over slightly.

Mr. EISENBERG. I am holding two photographs, both marked Q–48 and K–1. You took both photographs?

Mr. NICOL. Yes, sir.

Mr. DULLES. I wonder if, for clarification, we could take one of those shells and see from what angle the photograph is taken and what is covered in the photograph. I am a little confused. It doesn't make any difference which one.

Mr. NICOL. All right, sir.

The area shown between this dark ring would represent the area between these two grooves right here. Actually, it is the entire primer. This is the firing-pin impression you are looking at right here.

Mr. DULLES. Thank you.

Mr. EISENBERG. Mr. Chairman, may I have these admitted, these last photographs, as 614 and 615?

Mr. DULLES. 614 and 615, exhibits as described, will be admitted.

(The photographs referred to were marked Commission Exhibits Nos. 614 and 615 and received in evidence.)

Mr. NICOL. Now, this again illustrates Q–48 and K–1 with the position now such that the division of the field is moved over approximately a sixteenth of an inch from the position we looked at previously. And again at the points indicated by the arrow, there are individual characteristics running across the dividing line of the comparison in both the top and bottom region.

Mr. EISENBERG. Now, from the position of the firing-pin hole on Q–48, on this last exhibit, it appears that it is not perfectly aligned with the position of the firing-pin hole on K–1, Mr. Nicol. I am looking at the mark on the right-hand side of Q–48.

Mr. NICOL. Yes. And the purpose for the mis-alignment was in order to show these smaller marks that appear right at the edge of the firing-pin impression.

Mr. EISENBERG. So that at the top the markings on Q–48 and K–1 will not run into each other, as well as on the bottom?

Mr. NICOL. If they are divergent, of course, they will not. If they are parallel, it makes no difference where the position is.

Now, this is another setting, going to the opposite side of the firing-pin impression, just translating the two cartridge cases the same distance, so that we are now looking at a division at the other side, and a comparison of the breech-block markings on the other side of the two shells.

Mr. EISENBERG. Again marked Q–48 and K–1. You took this photograph?

Mr. NICOL. I did.

Mr. EISENBERG. May I have permission to mark this 615?

Mr. DULLES. It shall be admitted.

(The photograph referred to was marked Commission Exhibit No. 615 and received in evidence.)

Mr. NICOL. Looking at the position of the upper arrow, there is a pair of diagonal marks, a small mark immediately below it going down to the lower part of the breech-block markings. There are a series of parallel lines at approximately a 45-degree angle to the division of the bridge. These were duplicated on both—all of the cartridge cases submitted.

Mr. DULLES. I am not entirely clear in my mind what this demonstrates.

Mr. NICOL. This is the basis upon which I arrived at the conclusion that the two cartridge cases, K–1 and Q–48, were fired in the same weapon. Actually, we could take a good match, such as shown here, or even this one, and this would be sufficient. All I have done here is repeat this by moving the two bullets, or the two cartridge cases together the same translated distance, and then taking a series of photographs at each particular position. So they represent actually the same thing in each one.

Mr. DULLES. As the hammer comes down on the cartridge, it makes a distinctive mark, is that the idea?

Mr. NICOL. No. I have not compared the firing-pin impression. What this is is the setback of the shell against the breech face, against the rear of the chamber.

Mr. DULLES. The breech face makes an impression on the shell, and that is a distinctive impression?

Mr. NICOL. Very definitely, just as individual as a fingerprint.

Mr. EISENBERG. These are two further photographs that you took, Mr. Nicol?

Mr. NICOL. Yes.

Mr. EISENBERG. And they both illustrate the same cartridge case, the same two cartridge cases, the one questioned and the one known?

Mr. NICOL. Right.

Mr. EISENBERG. And you have moved the hairline somewhat over to the right?

Mr. NICHOL. Right.

Mr. EISENBERG. Mr. Chairman, may I introduce these as 616 and 617?

Mr. DULLES. They shall be admitted.

(The photographs described were marked Commission Exhibits Nos. 616 and 617 and were received in evidence.)

Mr. EISENBERG. Mr. Chairman, I suggest that in the interest of time, since these two photographs are merely continuations of the first series, we go on to the next.

Mr. Nicol, you have further photographs now. These are marked Q–48 and K–1, and these are separate photographs?

Mr. NICOL. Same photographs.

Mr. EISENBERG. That is submitted as 618, Mr. Chairman.

Mr. DULLES. It shall be admitted.

(The photograph referred to was marked Commission Exhibit No. 618 and received in evidence.)

Mr. Eisenberg. Now, was this photograph taken to show the same point as the previous photographs?

Mr. Nicol. Not exactly. This shows the rim of the two cartridge cases. K-1 is just barely visible. Q-48 represents the other half of the picture. And what we are looking at here in the match relationship, at the point of the arrow, is a patch which represents the extractor riding around the rim of the shell at the time that the cartridge was introduced into the chamber. I might qualify that by saying this: in order to be certain of the exact factor which produced this, I would have had to examine the weapon and conducted some tests to ascertain whether this was the extractor or the bolt pushing the cartridge into the chamber when the mechanism was operated.

In any case, the same tool, whether it be the extractor or the bolt, produced this pattern of lines on both the known and the unknown cartridge cases.

Mr. Eisenberg. Now, did you find that mark repeated on the cartridge case in other places?

Mr. Nicol. This was repeated on Q-6 and 7. However, what you may be referring to is another series which was only found on Q-6.

Mr. Eisenberg. Now, could you get to that photograph you just mentioned, Q-6?

Mr. Nicol. I photographed the Q-6 in three different positions, which I designated as 1, 2, and 3.

Mr. Dulles. Have we identified Q-6 before on the record?

Mr. Eisenberg. Yes. Q-6, I think it is stated on the record, is the equivalent of our Commission Exhibit 543.

Mr. Dulles. What is 543?

Mr. Eisenberg. 543 is a shell found in the TSBD building.

Mr. Nicol. This is a photograph I took of the head—a portion of the head of Q-6, or Commission Exhibit 543.

Mr. Eisenberg. May I have this admitted as 619, Mr. Chairman?

Mr. Dulles. It shall be admitted as 619.

(The photograph described was marked Commission Exhibit No. 619 and received in evidence.)

Mr. Nicol. It might be well to introduce these, too. These are the same as the ones·which are mounted, except that I have cut them for the purpose of matching them.

Mr. Eisenberg. I would like to introduce these two photographs—also taken by you, Mr. Nicol?

Mr. Nicol. Right.

Mr. Eisenberg. Which are similar, or taken from this photograph. That will be 620 and 621, Mr. Reporter.

Mr. Dulles. Exhibits 620 and 621 as described will be admitted.

(The photographs described were marked Commission Exhibits Nos. 620 and 621 and were received in evidence.)

Mr. Nicol. Perhaps in order to illustrate this we ought to get all the three in, or at least another set, so I can show the match relationship photographically—so that this represents another position of Q-6, or 543.

Mr. Eisenberg. And this is a photograph which has not been admitted yet?

Mr. Nicol. No.

Mr. Eisenberg. Mr. Chairman, may I have this admitted as 622, please?

Mr. Dulles. 622 and 623.

(The items referred to were marked Commission Exhibits Nos. 622 and 623, and received in evidence.)

Mr. Dulles. Would you just briefly describe these?

Mr. Nicol. This represents another position of the cartridge case, the head of the case—you are looking at the rim, and this is the portion of the head stamp representing millimeter. This was a 6.5 millimeter. You see just a portion of the "5." And what I will be talking about is the marks down against the rim in all of these exhibits.

Now, this is the same cartridge as represented by these other two photographs, with a slight rotation.

Now, we have only one which we might have to pass around. But if the photograph 621 is placed in a position corresponding to the arrows, a match of the fine striations, the pairs of broad lines as well as the fine lines, can be seen.

The reason that this could not be taken under the comparison miscroscope is that because of course we cannot divide the cartridge case, so that this had to be done photographically rather than being done on a comparison basis.

Now, this illustrates the fact that the same operation occurred twice on this particular cartridge case.

Do you want to introduce the third at this time?

Mr. EISENBERG. Yes.

This is a photograph taken by you?

Mr. NICOL. Yes, sir.

Mr. EISENBERG. Of the same cartridge case?

Mr. NICOL. Same cartridge case in a different position, rotated in a different position.

Mr. EISENBERG. May I have permission to introduce this as 624, Mr. Chairman?

Mr. DULLES. It may be admitted.

(The photograph described was marked Commission Exhibit No. 624 and was received in evidence.)

Mr. NICOL. If we compare 624 and 621 in the same general fashion, again we we have a match of the individual characteristics. So that again the same mechanical operation occurred on this cartridge case, 543, three different times, and in a rather random fashion. They are not the angular relationship between each of these sets of patterns—it is not divisible by any particular number. It is just a random occurrence.

Associated with this is another mark that occurs on all three of the positions, however not in any particular relationship to the group of lines, and perhaps not as definitive. And it was on the basis of the match of these patterns that I would conclude that this cartridge had been introduced into a chamber at least three times prior to its final firing. So that this would represent, you might say, a practice or dry-run loading the gun and unloading it for purpose of either determining its—how it functions, or whether it was in proper function, or just for practice.

Mr. EISENBERG. Just to review this testimony, Mr. Nicol, this is a mark which occurs on the base of the cartridge case, is that correct?

Mr. NICOL. That is correct.

Mr. EISENBERG. And are you able to say definitely whether it is an extractor or an ejection mark or a chambering mark?

Mr. NICOL. It appears to me to be an extractor mark, although I was not able to identify this as similar to any extractor mark or any other marks on either Q–7 or 544 or any of the tests, 557.

Mr. EISENBERG. Did extractor marks appear on those other cartridge cases?

Mr. NICOL. Yes, sir.

Mr. EISENBERG. And when you say you were not able to identify them, do you mean that they were not identical to or——

Mr. NICOL. They were absent.

Mr. EISENBERG. They were absent?

Mr. NICOL. Absent in all the other cases.

Mr. EISENBERG. So that extractor marks did not appear in the other cases?

Mr. NICOL. Extractor marks appeared, but these marks did not appear.

Mr. EISENBERG. Well, two sets of extractor marks have been put on——

Mr. NICOL. This would be possible—perhaps the violence with which the weapon was activated in this particular incident—or it might be the result of something not associated with the internal mechanism of the weapon, but might be the result of the charger or the cartridge carrier that is introduced into—the way the cartridges are introduced into the magazine.

Mr. EISENBERG. Now, what led you to the conclusion that this was an extractor mark?

Mr. NICOL. Only that it appears at the location of the cartridge case where an extractor mark would normally be found. That is to say, this would be the mark where the extractor strikes the edge of the case, and then springs around as the cartridge is driven into the chamber.

Mr. EISENBERG. But you could not definitely say whether it is an extractor mark produced by the rifle through which the test bullets you were given were fired?

Mr. NICOL. No, sir; I could not.

Mr. EISENBERG. Now, I am not quite clear as to why another set of marks should have appeared on the other cases, which you also think are extractor marks.

Mr. NICOL. I cannot say that this could not have been produced by another gun.

Mr. EISENBERG. That might have been produced by another gun?

Mr. NICOL. Yes.

Mr. EISENBERG. But it was produced by the same source, whether it was this gun or another gun, three different times?

Mr. NICOL. Correct.

Mr. EISENBERG. Somebody had done one operation, in your opinion, with this cartridge at three different times?

Mr. NICOL. Right.

Mr. EISENBERG. Now, just to set this in context, I have taken the bolt from Commission Exhibit 139, the rifle found on the sixth floor, and could you show the Commission what the extractor is on this bolt?

Mr. NICOL. The extractor is this semicircular piece extending back in the bolt, and its purpose is to withdraw the cartridge from the chamber at the time that the bolt is drawn back. It rides in the extractor groove, which is machined in the head of the cartridge case. At the time that the weapon is loaded, oftentimes this springs around, it first contacts the rim of the cartridge case, and then springs around the rim of the cartridge and produces marks such as these, or marks such as I have illustrated on the three sets.

Mr. EISENBERG. Now, is it possible that the reason the marks were present on this cartridge but not on the other cartridge case—on this cartridge case but not on the other cartridge cases you examined—is because these marks were produced by dry firing as opposed to actual firing?

Mr. NICOL. This is possible. The weight of the empty shell would be different of course from one which had a projectile in it, so that its dynamics might be different, and it might produce a different mark—although in the absence of accessibility of the weapon, or the absence of these marks on the tests, I really am unable to say what is the precise origin of those marks, except to speculate that they are probably from the extractor, and that the second mark that appears here, which I have indicated with a similar number, is probably an ejector mark.

Now, this, I might add, is a different type of ejector mark than the mark found on the rim from the normal firing of these tests and the evidence cartridges.

Mr. EISENBERG. Now, you stated that another mark appeared in all three—associated in juxtaposition with the three marks you have been describing?

Mr. NICOL. Yes; and in the same angular relationship to a radii through the center of the head.

Mr. EISENBERG. Now, again, if it is an ejector mark, might the difference have been caused by the fact that it may have been associated with a dry firing rather than an actual firing?

Mr. NICOL. That might be possible.

Mr. EISENBERG. Do you think a person would apply a different bolt pressure in a dry firing as opposed to an actual firing?

Mr. NICOL. Well, since this is a manually operated weapon, it is quite possible that no two operations are done with exactly the same force. However, with reasonable reproduceability, all these marks appear to the same depth and to the same extent, so that it would appear that whatever produced them operated in identically the same fashion.

Mr. EISENBERG. Do you have anything you would like to add to your testimony on the rifle bullets or the rifle cartridge cases, Mr. Nicol?

Mr. NICOL. No, sir; I don't think so.

Mr. EISENBERG. If there are no further questions on that particular subject, I will proceed to the Tippit bullets and cartridge cases.

Mr. DULLES. Off the record.

(Discussion off the record.)

Mr. DULLES. Back on the record.

Mr. EISENBERG. I hand you, Mr. Nicol, a group of four cartridge cases marked Commission Exhibit 594, which, for the record, are cartridge cases found in the area of the Tippit crime scene, and ask you whether you are familiar with those cartridge cases?

Mr. NICOL. Yes, sir; these are cartridge cases which were given to me on March 26th by Mr. Eisenberg.

Mr. EISENBERG. They have your mark on them?

Mr. NICOL. No; I made notes of the FBI designations, and these are the same—they have the JH and the CK and RF and the Q designations that were placed on there by the FBI.

Mr. EISENBERG. Those initials are initials apparently of examining agents?

Mr. NICOL. I presume so.

Mr. EISENBERG. I hand you Commission Exhibit 595 and ask you whether you are familiar with the cartridge cases contained in that exhibit?

Mr. NICOL. Yes; these are two fired cartridge cases designated K-3 by the FBI and marked with their identification marks—CK, JH, and RF.

Mr. EISENBERG. Now, for the record, these cartridge cases were earlier identified as having been fired by the FBI in Commission Exhibit No. 143, the revolver believed to have been used to kill Officer Tippit.

Also for the record, I obtained these cartridge cases, both Exhibit 595, which are test cases, and Exhibit 594, which are cases from the murder scene, from the FBI, and transmitted them directly to Mr. Nicol for his examination.

Mr. Nicol, did you examine the cartridge cases in Exhibit 594 to determine whether they had been fired from the weapon in which the cartridge cases in Exhibit 595 had been fired?

Mr. NICOL. Yes, sir; I did.

Mr. EISENBERG. And can you give us your conclusions?

Mr. NICOL. It is my opinion, based upon the similarity of class and individual characteristics, that the four cartridge cases in 594 were fired in the same weapon as produced the cartridge cases in 595.

Mr. EISENBERG. Mr. Nicol, did you take photographs of the comparisons?

Mr. NICOL. No, sir; I did not.

Mr. EISENBERG. However, you are certain in your own mind of the identification?

Mr. NICOL. Yes; the marks on the firing pin particularly were very definitive. Apparently this firing pin had been subjected to some rather severe abuse, and there were numerous small and large striations which could be matched up very easily.

Mr. DULLES. What do you mean by severe abuse?

Mr. NICOL. It appeared as though it had either been touched up with a file, or in the initial manufacture the finishing operation was rather crude. It was not what I would consider a well-finished firing pin.

Mr. EISENBERG. Mr. Nicol, just to review your earlier testimony, as I recall you stated that you do not use photographs to make your identification, and usually do not testify with photographs?

Mr. NICOL. That's correct.

Mr. EISENBERG. But that the other photographs were made as an accommodation to us, at my request, so that the Commission could see them?

Mr. NICOL. The material I am just talking about could well have been illustrated. However, I ran out of time.

Mr. EISENBERG. Mr. Nicol, finally I hand you a group of four bullets marked Commission Exhibits 602, 603, 604, and 605, which I state for the record were recovered from the body of Officer Tippit, and a group of two bullets marked Commission Exhibit 606, which I state for the record were fired by the FBI through the revolver, Commission Exhibit 143.

I ask you whether you are familiar with this group of exhibits.

Mr. NICOL. These two are fired lead projectiles that were designated by the FBI as K-3, companions to the tests in 595.

Mr. EISENBERG. When you say companions, you mean they were given to you——

Mr. NICOL. They were given to me simultaneously in an envelope, at that time wrapped in cotton.

Mr. EISENBERG. And the other Exhibits?

Mr. NICOL. This was the projectile designated by the FBI, I believe, as Q–13. This is a .38 Special projectile designated Q–502. That would correspond to Commission Exhibit 603.

Mr. EISENBERG. And the item you just identified?

Mr. NICOL. Q–13 would correspond with 602.

This is Q–501, corresponding to Exhibit 604.

This is Q–500, corresponding to Exhibit 605.

Mr. EISENBERG. Are you familiar with all of those?

Mr. NICOL. Yes; I have seen and examined all of these.

Mr. EISENBERG. Did you examine Exhibits 602 through 605 to determine whether they have been fired from the same weapon as fired 606?

Mr. NICOL. Yes; I did.

Mr. EISENBERG. What was your conclusion?

Mr. NICOL. Due to mutilation, I was not able to determine whether 605, 604, and 602 were fired in the same weapon. There were similarity of class characteristics—that is to say, there is nothing evident that would exclude the weapon. However, due to multilation and apparent variance between the size of the barrel and the size of the projectile, the reproduction of individual characteristics was not good, and therefore I was unable to arrive at a conclusion beyond that of saying that the few lines that were found would indicate a modest possibility. But I would not by any means say that I could be positive.

However, on specimen 602—I'm sorry—603, which I have designated as Q–502, I found sufficient individual characteristics to lead me to the conclusion that that projectile was fired in the same weapon that fired the projectiles in 606.

Mr. EISENBERG. That is to the exclusion of all other weapons?

Mr. NICOL. Yes, sir.

Mr. EISENBERG. By the way, on the cartridge cases, that was also to the exclusion of all other weapons?

Mr. NICOL. Correct.

Mr. EISENBERG. Did you take a photograph of this identified missile?

Mr. NICOL. I took a photograph of one position, and that is shown here as a comparison of K–3 and what I designated as Q–502.

Mr. EISENBERG. Mr. Chairman, may I have this admitted? That would be 625.

(The item described was marked Commission Exhibit No. 625 and received in evidence.)

Mr. EISENBERG. These arrows, Mr. Nicol, can you explain why they are different?

Mr. NICOL. This was one I made up originally and then decided that the illustration would be ample with one arrow in that one position.

Mr. DULLES. The one that is being admitted is the one-arrow photograph.

Mr. EISENBERG. The arrows are placed on mechanically after the photograph is developed?

Mr. NICOL. That is correct.

Mr. EISENBERG. And therefore it can vary?

Mr. NICOL. Yes. This is not a part of the photographic process.

Mr. EISENBERG. What is the magnification here, Mr. Nicol?

Mr. NICOL. It would be pretty close to 25 to 30 diameters. I cannot measure exactly the magnification.

Mr. NICOL. This illustrates some of the lines, not all of them, that I saw on a comparison of 502 and K–3. At the position of the arrow, you are looking at the top of the groove; adjacent to it in the lower portion is a land impression. And on that shoulder there are approximately five or six matching lines. They are very fine striations. These would be indicative of the fact that the same portion of the barrel had ridden on both projectiles.

Mr. EISENBERG. Well, now, there seems to be significantly less markings here than on the bullets which were seen earlier, which had come from the rifle. Does that same condition pertain when the bullet is viewed under the microscope?

Mr. NICOL. Yes. Of course, we are dealing with two different types of ammunition. One is a lead projectile, and the other is a metal-case projectile. And the ability of the metal-case projectile to pick up and retain fine striations, even in spite of distortion and mutilation, far exceeds what the lead projectile will do.

Furthermore, the lead being a soft and low-melting-point material is more subject to erosion of hot gases. So that there are many more variables in the reproduction in terms of a lead projectile as over against a metal-case projectile.

Mr. EISENBERG. You found enough similarities to satisfy yourself that there is an identification here?

Mr. NICOL. I am satisfied that the two projectiles came from the same weapon.

Mr. EISENBERG. Now, we have received testimony that the weapon which is marked Commission Exhibit 143 was rechambered but not rebarreled, so that a .38 Special bullet fired through the barrel would be slightly undersized.

Mr. NICOL. Of course I have not had a chance to examine the weapon. But on the information that you gave me, this was originally manufactured for English ammunition, and has been rechambered for American domestic ammunition, is that correct?

Mr. EISENBERG. Yes.

Mr. NICOL. The undersized bullet going through an oversized barrel of course presents some serious identification problems, because it does not go through with the same conformity as a projectile going through the proper-sized barrel, so that it is apt to, you might say, skip and bear more on one surface than on another in subsequent firings, so that the identification is made more complex and it is expected that more dissimilarities occur under those circumstances.

However, at the points where it did reproduce at the land edges, as shown in this photograph, I found sufficient lines of identification to lead me to the conclusion that they had both been fired in the same weapon.

Mr. EISENBERG. Is it consistent with the markings you found on this bullet that it had been fired in a slightly oversized barrel?

Mr. NICOL. Slight. However, due to the malleability of lead, it does accommodate itself more than a metal-case projectile, and therefore the evidence of being fired in an oversized barrel is not as pronounced as it would be if it were fired, let's say, a .32-20 fired in a .38 Special, which would be possible, and would give very distinct evidence of the difference in the size of the bullet and the barrel. However, in neither case is an identification completely precluded. What is necessary is that tests are available which have borne on the same surface. If this is true, and if the marks have not been mutilated, then an identification is still possible.

Mr. EISENBERG. When you say the bullet will accommodate itself, you mean it will expand to fill out all or part of the lands and grooves?

Mr. NICOL. Yes. Actually, with the pressure on the base and the inertia of the bullet, it is in a sense shorter and expanded in diameter to accommodate for the larger-sized barrel.

Mr. EISENBERG. Now, I was not clear whether you drew any conclusion on the other three bullets—that is, did you definitely—find yourself definitely unable to identify those bullets, or did you reach a "probable" conclusion?

Mr. NICOL. I would say there was nothing, no major marks to preclude it. However, I was unable to find what would satisfy me to say that it positively came from that particular weapon. So that I would place it in the category of bullets which could have come from this particular weapon, but not to the exclusion of all others.

Mr. EISENBERG. Is this short of the "probable" category in which you placed the Walker bullets, or is it in the same category?

Mr. NICOL. This is in a gray area between black and white, and it is somewhat nebulous to pin it down to a precise percentage dimension.

Mr. EISENBERG. Mr. Nicol, were you able to identify the type of bullet which is involved in each of these four exhibits—that is, the manufacturer of 603, 602, 604, and 605?

Mr. NICOL. No; I did not attempt this, because I did not have an adequate reference collection against which to make the comparison.

Mr. EISENBERG. I do not have any further questions, Mr. Chairman.

The CHAIRMAN. I have no questions.

Mr. RHYNE. No questions.

Mr. EISENBERG. Mr. Nicol, do you have anything you would like to add before we conclude?

Mr. NICOL. No; I think I have covered everything.

Mr. DULLES. We want to thank you very much.

Mr. EISENBERG. There is one further question I have.

When you made your examination, were you aware of the conclusions which any other examining agent or body had come to?

Mr. NICOL. No. I of course was aware of the fact that tests were conducted. However, I was not aware either through the press or any other media as to the conclusions. This represents my own personal conclusions without benefit of any other knowledge.

Mr. EISENBERG. And do you know at this point what any other body has come to in the way of conclusions?

Mr. NICOL. No, sir.

Mr. DULLES. I wonder if you would be willing to give us your views as to the effectiveness of paraffin tests?

Mr. NICOL. I have used the paraffin test both in case work and in experiments, as an investigative aid. However, I have a very low level of confidence in it—either as a positive or negative, as far as that's concerned.

Experimentally, as the literature well demonstrates, it is possible to fire a gun and get nothing on the hands. It is also possible to take people at random off the street and test them with the reagent which is not specific for powder and find all kinds of reactions. And while there are some "experts" who—and I say that with quotes—who allege that they can differentiate one product from another, actually the end product of the oxidation of diphenylamine is a definite quinoid structure, which has only one blue color, and I am not sure how they make this differentiation. I cannot do it.

I have used it as an investigative aid with positive results if and when I find in the cast a particle of powder that I can definitely identify as powder—not just simply the reaction, but something I can take out, put it under the microscope and I can say this is a particle of powder. Then I will say that this hand has been in the presence of the discharge of a weapon.

Mr. DULLES. You do not need a paraffin test for that, do you?

Mr. NICOL. I don't think so. I think if you actually examine the subject's hands, you probably can find that. Although as a rule in the laboratory we do not see the subject, and so this is the medium by which we get a look at the surface of the hand.

Sometime ago in Los Angeles a series of experiments was conducted whereby—and this was on shooting victims, including only those where they could be certain by other investigative means as to the exact status of the case. One of the technicians placed the paraffin on the hand. This was presented to the other technician who had no knowledge of the case whatsoever. And that I guess must have included both the controls of non-shooting victims as well as shooting victims. And the net result was if this fellow almost flipped a coin he could be in the ball park as far as whether or not this person had actually fired a weapon.

It just is not particularly accurate.

I might go further to say that there have been several cases in which I would say a fair amount of injustice was done to the defendant or the suspect in the case simply because people have gone overboard on the application of the paraffin test.

It is one of these areas in which everyone would like a nice test. It would certainly be beneficial. But it is not one in which a competent technician places much confidence.

Mr. DULLES. I understand that pipe smokers are quite likely to get caught on these, on these tests.

Mr. NICOL. Or someone who strikes a kitchen match, or in the spring, a man fertilizing his lawn. A man working in the meatpacking industry, where they preserve meats with nitrates, might also have difficulties. Certain of the common things, such as urine, I think can be discounted, because the diffused pattern can be easily determined. But as far as pinpoints of striking a match, I could not differentiate one from the other.

Mr. DULLES. Thank you very much.

Mr. NICOL. I realize this doesn't help.

The CHAIRMAN. Mr. Nicol, thank you very much, sir, for helping us. You have been very helpful.

Mr. NICOL. Thank you, sir.

Mr. DULLES. We will recess at this time until 9 o'clock tomorrow morning.

(Whereupon, at 5:10 p.m., the President's Commission recessed.)